Handbook of
# The Psychology of Aging

# The Handbooks of Aging
## Consisting of Three Volumes

Critical comprehensive reviews of
research knowledge, theories, concepts, and issues

### Editor-in-Chief
### James E. Birren

### Handbook of the Biology of Aging
Edited by Edward L. Schneider and John W. Rowe

### Handbook of the Psychology of Aging
Edited by James E. Birren and K. Warner Schaie

### Handbook of Aging and the Social Sciences
Edited by Robert H. Binstock and Linda K. George

# Handbook of
# The Psychology of Aging
## Fourth Edition

Editors
## James E. Birren
## K. Warner Schaie

Volume Associate Editors
Ronald P. Abeles, Margaret Gatz,
and Timothy A. Salthouse

Academic Press

San Diego   New York   Boston   London   Sydney   Tokyo   Toronto

Copyright © 1996, 1990, 1985, 1977 by ACADEMIC PRESS, INC.

Academic Press, Inc.
A Division of Harcourt Brace & Company
525 B Street, Suite 1900, San Diego, California 92101-4495

*United Kingdom Edition published by*
Academic Press Limited
24-28 Oval Road, London NW1 7DX

Library of Congress Cataloging-in-Publication Data

Handbook of the psychology of aging / edited by James E. Birren, K.
    Warner Schaie ; volume associate editors, Ronald P. Abeles, margaret
    Gatz, Timothy J. Salthouse. -- 4th ed.
            p.        cm. -- (The handbooks on aging)
    Includes bibliographical references and index.
    ISBN 0-12-101260-3 (case : alk. paper). -- ISBN 0-12-101261-1
(paper : alk. paper)
    1. Aging--Psychological aspects.  I. Birren, James E.
II. Schaie, K. Warner (Klaus Warner), date.  III. Series.
BF724.55.A35H36   1995
155.67--dc20                                              95-19905
                                                         CIP

PRINTED IN THE UNITED STATES OF AMERICA
96   97   98   99   00   01   QW   9   8   7   6   5   4   3   2   1

# Contents

## Part One
## Concepts, Theory, and Methods in the Psychology of Aging

# Part Two
# Biological and Social Influences on Behavior

## 4. Gerontological Behavior Genetics
*Nancy L. Pedersen*

## 5. Brain and Life Span in Primates
*Atiya Hakeem, Gisela Rodriguez Sandoval, Marvin Jones, and John Allman*

## 6. Structural and Functional Changes in the Aging Brain
*Arnold B. Scheibel*

## 7. Health, Behavior, and Aging
*Dorly J. H. Deeg, Jan W. P. F. Kardaun, and James L. Fozard*

# Part Three
## Behavioral Processes

# Contributors

Numbers in parentheses indicate the pages on which the authors' contributions begin.

Ronald P. Abeles (149) Behavioral and Social Research, National Institute on Aging, Bethesda, Maryland 20892

Lise Abrams (251) Department of Psychology, University of California at Los Angeles, Los Angeles, California 90095

John Allman (77) Division of Biology, California Institute of Technology, Pasadena, California 91125

Stig Berg (323) Institute of Gerontology, University College of Health Sciences, S-551 11 Jönköping, Sweden

James E. Birren (3) Center on Aging, University of California at Los Angeles, Los Angeles, California 90024

Fredda Blanchard-Fields (149) School of Psychology, Georgia Institute of Technology, Atlanta, Georgia 30332

Peter Coleman (308) Geriatric Medicine, Faculty of Medicine, University of Southampton, Southampton SO16 6YD, United Kingdom

Linda M. Collins (37) Department of Human Development and Family Studies and the Methodology Center, Pennsylvania State University, University Park, Pennsylvania 16802

Dorly J. H. Deeg (129) Department of Psychiatry and Department of Sociology and Social Gerontology, Vrije Universiteit, 1075 AZ Amsterdam, The Netherlands

Sigrun-Heide Filipp (217) Department of Psychology, University of Trier, D-54286 Trier, Germany

James L. Fozard (129) National Institute on Aging, Gerontology Research Center, Longitudinal Studies Branch, Baltimore, Maryland 21224

Margaret Gatz (365) Department of Psychology, University of Southern California, Los Angeles, California 90089

Atiya Hakeem (77) Bekesy Laboratory of Neurobiology, University of Hawaii, Honolulu, Hawaii 96822

Christopher Hertzog (23) School of Psychology, Georgia Institute of Technology, Atlanta, Georgia 30332

Marvin Jones (77) Zoological Society of San Diego, San Diego, California 92101

Jan W. P. F. Kardaun (129) Advice Research Computing on Health and Aging, B.V. Rotterdam, The Netherlands

Michele J. Karel (365) Psychology Service, 116B, Brockton/West Roxbury VA Medical Center, Brockton, Massachusetts 02401

Julia E. Kasl-Godley (365) Department of Psychology, University of Southern California, Los Angeles, California 90089

Donald W. Kline (181) Department of Psychology, University of Calgary, Calgary, Alberta, Canada T2N 1N4

Albert Kozma (338) Department of Psychology, Memorial University of Newfoundland, St. John's, Newfoundland, Canada A1B 3X9

Herschel W. Leibowitz (203) Department of Psychology, The Pennsylvania State University, University Park, Pennsylvania 16802

Donald G. MacKay (251) Department of Psychology, University of California at Los Angeles, Los Angeles, California 90095

Todd J. Maurer (353) School of Psychology, Georgia Institute of Technology, Atlanta, Georgia 30332

Susan H. McFadden (161) Department of Psychology, University of Wisconsin Oshkosh, Oshkosh, Wisconsin 54901

Nancy L. Pedersen (59) Institute of Environmental Medicine, The Karolinska Institute, S-171 77 Stockholm, Sweden

Gisela Rodriguez Sandoval (77) Division of Biology, California Institute of Technology, Pasadena, California 91125

Jan-Erik Ruth (308) Kuntokallio Center for Gerontological Training and Research, 01100 Östersundom, Finland

Timothy A. Salthouse (353) School of Psychology, Georgia Institute of Technology, Atlanta, Georgia 30332

K. Warner Schaie (265) Department of Human Development and Family Studies, The Pennsylvania State University, University Park, Pennsylvania 16802

Arnold B. Scheibel (105) Departments of Neurobiology and Psychiatry and Biobehavioral Sciences, and Brain Research Institute, University of California Center for the Health Sciences, Los Angeles, California 90024

Johannes J. F. Schroots (3) ERGO/European Research Institute on Health and Aging, University of Amsterdam, 1018 WB Amsterdam, The Netherlands

Charles T. Scialfa (181) Department of Psychology, University of Calgary, Calgary, Alberta, Canada T2N 1N4

Guy G. Simoneau (203) Program in Physical Therapy, Marquette University, Milwaukee, Wisconsin 53233

Anderson D. Smith (235) School of Psychology, Georgia Institute of Technology, Atlanta, Georgia 30332

Michael J. Stones (338) Department of Health Studies and Gerontology, University of Waterloo, Waterloo, Ontario, Canada N2L 3G1 and University Institute of Social Gerontology of Quebec, Canada

Sherry L. Willis (287) Department of Human Development and Family Studies, The Pennsylvania State University, University Park, Pennsylvania 16802

# Foreword

This volume is one of three handbooks on aging now in their fourth editions: *Handbook of the Biology of Aging; Handbook of the Psychology of Aging;* and *Handbook of Aging and Social Sciences.* Their publication reflects a dramatic expansion of research on aging with an accompanying acceleration in the publication rate of information.

The handbooks are being used by research personnel, graduate students, and professionals for efficient access to contemporary research literature on aging. It is gratifying to see the subject matter of aging becoming a mainstream topic in the scientific disciplines and professions. The editors are pleased to provide these volumes that reflect advances in research findings, theory, and concepts that will guide further research as well as efforts to improve the well-being of older persons.

Stimulation of research on aging by government and private foundation sponsorship is a major factor in the growth of publications. There has also been an expansion of teaching in the universities and colleges of related subject matter. Furthermore, the growth of professional services to older persons has brought about an increasing interest in the knowledge base for organizing services in the health professions, social welfare, and design of institutions serving the elderly.

Aging is one of the most complex topics to challenge modern science and it is difficult to put all of the relevant information in one volume. For this reason, we have focused on three sources of influence on aging: the biological, the psychological, and the social. Human aging is an ecological phenomenon reflecting the influences of genetics, physical and social environments, and the organization of individual behavior. In the early 20th century, infectious diseases contributed highly to mortality and left residual effects expressed as later-life disabilities. Given the ecological character of aging, it is expected that there will continue to be drifts in the amount of variance contributed from different sources.

These volumes can be used to trace pathways through a large volume of scientific information about particular aspects of aging. Not all of the topics covered in early editions appear in the present volumes. It is suggested that readers also consult earlier volumes, not only for historical background, but for information on topics that developed earlier in methods and findings.

I thank the editors of the individual volumes for their cooperation and efforts: Robert H. Binstock, Linda K. George, John W. Rowe, K. Warner Schaie, Edward L. Schneider. I also thank the associate editors: Ronald Abeles, Margaret Gatz, Nikki Holbrook, Thomas Johnson, Victor W. Marshall, John H. Morrison, George C. Myers, Timothy A. Salthouse, and James H. Schulz.

I express my appreciation to Nikki Fine, the editor at Academic Press whose cooperation facilitated the publication of the handbooks.

James E. Birren

# Preface

This new edition of the handbook continues to provide an authoritative review for the scientific and professional literature on the psychology of adult development and aging. It is designed to offer a definitive reference source for researchers, graduate students, and professionals in the behavioral sciences. The major emphasis is on basic behavioral processes in order to describe and provide explanatory models for changes in behavioral expression and capacity that occur with advancing age.

A wide range of factors is required to give an authoritative account. These include biological influences and disease, as well as social influences such as generational (cohort) differences and historical events. As in previous editions, we asked the contributors to provide comprehensive reviews, but not to provide an exhaustive set of references to all publications on their subject matter. In contrast to annual review articles, these chapters are designed to give a systematic organization of information of the field as well as to provide conceptualizations and theoretical formulations that will stimulate future research.

The origin of the present fourth edition can be traced back to the *Handbook of Aging and the Individual*, published in 1959. The pace of research on behavioral aging has exploded since that time. Substantial financial support for research on aging and behavior provided by public agencies and private foundations in the United States, Europe, and Japan have encouraged growth of an area of knowledge that in 1959 was pioneering. Research on the psychology of aging continues to expand, and the academic setting has also changed. During its early phases, the psychology of aging was often considered to be a marginal topic and was not commonly found among the standard offerings in teaching or in research in departments of psychology. Now, there are departments of psychology and departments of human development that have several members with expertise in research on aging. In applied psychology, the aging of the workforce, the abandonment of mandatory retirement, and the recognition of dementia as a major societal problem have led to increased research efforts and professional careers. Although this volume is devoted primarily to the understanding of behavioral aging, we do hope that these chapters will also stimulate work that leads to improvement in the condition and quality of human life.

The intense collegial cooperation that resulted in this handbook was accom-

panied by prime motivation, high cooperation, and high academic standards that
bode well for the prosperity of our field. In
addition to a heavy emphasis on theoretically driven research, there has also been an
increasing preoccupation with the important role of individual differences in occurrence and rate of change of aging phenomena. This emphasis has been supported by an
increasing number of well-designed longitudinal studies, as well as a marked increase in cross-national and cross-cultural
comparative studies. The chasm between
the experimental and correlational emphases in the study of aging seems on the verge
of being bridged by a new generation of
methodologically sophisticated investigators.

Although the first (1977) edition of this
handbook attempted to be comprehensive
in nature, the demand for space and increasing publication costs have required increasing selectivity. Consequently, there
are topics represented in the first three editions that are not represented in the present
one because we decided that there had not
been sufficient progress since the previous
handbook edition to warrant a new presentation. The reader is therefore encouraged
to consult previous editions, which contain definitive treatments of particular topics that remain pertinent to current research.

We continue to follow an editorial policy
of enlisting new authors to review topics
previously covered, both to provide a turnover in perspectives and to provide a forum
over time for all major researchers in our
field. The interested reader should therefore consult previous editions to obtain alternative perspectives on material updated
or newly conceptualized in the present volume. Likewise, the reader will note chapters by previous contributors who review
new topics rather than revising their earlier
chapters. The third edition contained some
"half chapters" for new topics that seemed
important but in which, in the judgment of
the editors, only relatively little progress

had yet occurred. During the editorial process of that edition we found that some of
the half chapters simply did not allow
enough room for well-developed presentations, and we therefore decided not to repeat this "experiment." Instead, we reduced the number of topics to keep the
volume at an affordable length and yet provide more space for the chapters.

We wish to emphasize that our selection
of topics in no way represents a judgment as
to the overall importance of a particular
topic. Because of the 1992 publication of a
revision of the *Handbook of Mental Health
and Aging*, this edition has given somewhat less emphasis to topics involving the
clinical psychology of aging.

The editors wish to express their thanks
to the associate editors, Ronald Abeles,
Margaret Gatz, and Timothy Salthouse, for
their assistance in planning the book, selecting topics and authors, and spending
many hours in reviewing the draft chapters.
Each chapter was read by one of the editors
and one of the associate editors, and all
chapters were revised substantially by the
authors before attaining their final form.
We also wish to thank the authors for their
commitment to scholarship and for producing their original manuscripts and the
final drafts in a timely manner. Once again
we are proud of the fact that the handbook
was assembled and produced close to the
original schedule.

The editors are much indebted to the editorial coordinator, Pauline Robinson, for
her professional handling of the book and
author relationships and assembling its
complex content throughout the editorial
process. We also thank Anna Shuey for her
patience and her skill in assuring that
manuscripts, telephone messages, and correspondence did not go astray.

The psychology of aging is a vigorous
field in which researchers and professionals contribute much to advances in knowledge as well as to applications for enhancing the quality of life for the ever-growing
population of mature persons and the well-

being of our society. Both the editors and the contributors are hopeful that the present edition will continue the tradition of the previous ones in advancing research and teaching of the subject of adult development and aging, as well as providing a solid scientific foundation for professionals seeking improvement in the area of human services.

James E. Birren
K. Warner Schaie

# About the Editors

## James E. Birren

is currently Associate Director of the Center on Aging at the University of California, Los Angeles, and serves as an adjunct professor in medicine, psychiatry, and biobehavioral sciences. He is also professor emeritus of gerontology and psychology at the University of Southern California. Dr. Birren's previous positions include serving as Chief of the section on aging of the National Institute of Mental Health, founding Executive Director and Dean of the Ethel Percy Andrus Gerontology Center of USC, founding Director of the Anna and Harry Borun Center for Gerontological Research at UCLA, and President of the Gerontological Society of America, the Western Gerontological Society, and the Division on Adult Development and Aging of the American Psychological Association. Dr. Birren's many awards include the Brookdale Foundation Award for Gerontological Research, the Sandoz prize for Gerontological Research, and the award for outstanding contribution to gerontology by the Canadian Association of Gerontology. Author of over 250 scholarly publications, Dr. Birren has research interests including how speed of behavior changes with age, the causes and consequences of slowed information processing in the older nervous system, the effect of age on decision-making processes, and the role of expertise in skilled occupations. He has served as a delegate to several White House Conferences on Aging and continues to have a strong interest in developing national priorities for research and education related to issues of aging.

## K. Warner Schaie

is the Evan Pugh Professor of Human Development and Psychology and Director of the Gerontology Center at the Pennsylvania State University. He also holds an appointment as Affiliate Professor of Psychiatry and Behavioral Science at the University of Washington. A fellow of the Gerontological Society and the American Psychological Association, Professor Schaie has served as president of the APA Division of Adult Development and Aging and as editor of the *Journal of Gerontology: Psychological Sciences.* Author of over 250 scholarly publications on the psychology of aging, Dr. Schaie has interests including the life course of adult intelligence, its antecedents and modifiability, and methodological issues in the developmental sciences. Dr. Schaie has received the Kleemeier Award for Distinguished Research Contributions from the Gerontological Society of America and the Distinguished Scientific Contributions award from the American Psychological Association.

## Ronald P. Abeles

is currently Associate Director for Behavioral and Social Research at the National Institute on Aging. His past positions include serving as Deputy Associate Director and Acting Associate Director of BSR/NIA, Vice Chair and Chair of the NIH Health and Behavior Coordinating Committee, as well as many elected offices in the aging sections of the American Sociological Association and the American Psychological Association. Dr. Abeles is a fellow of the APA and editor of the newsletter of the ASA section on the Sociology of Aging. He is the recipient of the NIH Director's Award and the NIH Award of Merit for "leadership and contributions to the advancement of behavioral and social research on aging." His areas of interest include the sense of control, and the interface between social structure and behavior, and he continues to publish scholarly works and organize symposia on the many aspects of the life course and aging research.

## Margaret Gatz

is a professor of psychology at the University of Southern California and Senior Research Associate at USC's Ethel Percy An-drus Gerontology Center. Dr. Gatz is a fellow of the Gerontological Society of America, the American Psychological Association, the American Psychological Society, and the American Association of Applied and Preventive Psychology. She currently serves as associate editor of *Psychology and Aging*. Best known for fostering awareness among clinical psychologists of the need for training in work with older adults, Dr. Gatz was honored as Outstanding Mentor by USC's Graduate Association of Students in Psychology and was invited to be the keynote speaker for the Vermont Conference on Primary Prevention of Psychopathology in 1993. Author of over 70 articles and chapters and editor of one book, she currently studies the areas of genetic and environmental influences on course and etiology of dementia, depressive symptoms and depression in older adults, effects of the loss of a spouse on mortality and well-being, and family ties and how a sense of personal control influences the impact of and preparedness for earthquakes.

## Timothy A. Salthouse

is a professor of psychology at the Georgia Institute of Technology. He is a fellow in Divisions 3 and 20 of the American Psychological Association, and a fellow in the American Psychological Society. Current editor of the journal, *Psychology and Aging*, he has written four books, co-edited one book, and written approximately 100 chapters and articles on the topic of aging and cognition. He has received research funds from the National Institute of Aging since 1978, including a Research Career Development Award and a MERIT Award.

# Part One

# Concepts, Theory, and Methods in the Psychology of Aging

One

# History, Concepts, and Theory in the Psychology of Aging

James E. Birren and Johannes J. F. Schroots

The psychology of aging is in a growth phase, with a large volume of scientific literature and specialized publications. In this chapter we examine the psychology of aging from a historical perspective, tracing its roots in the development of nineteenth-century European science, and discuss the growth of concepts and theories.

## I. History of the Psychology of Aging

At the same time that the psychology of aging is a modern subject it is also an ancient one. Speculation about aging can be traced to Greek mythology and even earlier. The history of ideas about aging prior to the scientific era suggests that many myths have been generated to relieve anxieties about growing old and contemplation of death (Gruman, 1966). For many persons, aging remains an uneasy topic for discussion, perhaps because protective beliefs are slow to be replaced by knowledge provided by research.

Despite the long prescientific concern with explaining aging, the scientific history of the psychology of aging is quite brief (Birren, 1961a, 1961b). Why it took so long for research in the subject matter to emerge is itself a question, although today's psychologists appear increasingly willing to look directly at how we develop, mature, and die in modern society.

### A. Intellectual Roots

The roots of modern research on the psychology of aging clearly lie in the intellectual soil of nineteenth-century European science. With the advance of the scientific method and its usefulness in discarding improbable explanations of events, the conviction spread in the early nineteenth century that all matters could be examined by research and reduced to lawful generalizations, including the subject matter of aging.

Gompertz published in 1825 a paper that pointed out a lawful relationship between death rates and age. He described an inexorable acceleration of the death rate with age from about age 10 to the end of the usual life span. This acceleration in observed death rates with age, called the *force of mortality*, remains a focal point for research on aging with a view to identifying contributing forces (see Manton, Stallard, Woodbury, & Dowd, 1990).

*Handbook of the Psychology of Aging, Fourth Edition*

In 1835 the Belgian scientist Quetelet published a book that included information about differences in mortality rates and about physical and behavioral characteristics of people according to age. His commitment to studying the lawfulness of behavior over the life span is seen in his statement: "It will first be necessary to determine the period at which memory, imagination, and judgment commence, and the stages through which they necessarily pass in their progress to maturity: thus having established the maximum point, we may extend our inquiries to the law of their decline" (Quetelet, 1968/1835, p. 74).

The intellectual explorers of the nineteenth century tended to be persons of high social status with the economic means to support their intellectual interests. Such a person was the Englishman, Francis Galton, who sponsored the London Exposition in 1884, which extended over 6 years and gathered data on over ten thousand persons of all ages. The data included the first findings on age differences in speed of reaction time.

Toward the end of the nineteenth century, departments of psychology began to be created, following the pattern of the department of psychology at Leipzig, Germany, founded by Wilhelm Wundt in 1879. A major figure of his time, Wundt did not encourage students to do research on development or aging. In the nineteenth-century tradition he was interested in discovering the natural laws of human behavior. He pursued his goal with a kind of structuralism or elementalism borrowed from the successes of the physical sciences. Although laws of learning and memory were pursued, for the most part they were pursued in organisms of constant age, and little of the dynamics of development or aging was studied. No mention is made in the histories of early psychology of comparisons of the behavior of young and old subjects, although histories of psychology occasionally make passing mention of

child psychology as a topic. Histories of psychology tend to characterize child psychology as applied in its goals and therefore of somewhat lower scientific status than the experimental psychology promulgated by leaders of psychology from about 1875 to 1900. The need to educate prospective teachers was apparently one factor that prompted the study of the development of children, although not necessarily on a large scale.

An article published in the *American Journal of Psychology* in 1896 by Collin Scott was directed at the psychology of aging and death. He was a student of G. S. Hall at Clark University and apparently he was encouraged by Hall to pursue the topic. But there is little evidence in other publications of the period that departments of psychology or individual psychologists in America were concerned with adult development and aging.

Some early interest was shown in age differences in rat behavior with the appearance of four publications (Hubbert, 1915; Slonaker, 1907, 1912; Yerkes, 1909). Hubbert appears to be the first woman and perhaps the first psychologist in America who did a doctoral dissertation on aging. She studied age differences in rat maze learning and observed a slower maze running time in older rats.

At the turn of the century, psychometrics and test development became important topics in psychology. An early leader in the exploration of intelligence was Spearman, although he regarded the changes in intellectual functioning with age an "irrelevancy" (1904, p. 223). Applications of intelligence tests were primarily directed at children, although some involved adults of different ages, as in the estimations of abilities of military recruits in World War I. The scope of the psychometric trend is shown by the fact that by 1914–1915 a two-volume compendium was published describing the content and age norms for a wide range of tests (Whipple, 1914, 1915). The emergence of intelligence test scores in relation to age produced a large body of literature with many distinguished investigators (see Jones, 1959).

In 1922 G. S. Hall published his book *Senescence: The Second Half of Life*. It can be looked upon as marking the beginning of the psychology of aging. Earlier, Hall had studied children and adolescents and had been active as a pioneer contributor to developmental psychology. His book reveals his curiosity about the second half of life and reflects his growing interest in the whole course of life. *Senescence* was a broadly conceived book, and Hall reviewed the evidence about aging from all contemporary sciences at the time, for example, physiology, medicine, anatomy, philosophy, and something of the humanistic content about the psychology of the aging adult.

## B. Early Systematic Efforts

One of the first applied efforts in working with older adults was that of Lillian Martin. In 1929 she founded a guidance center for older adults in San Francisco after she retired as professor of psychology at Stanford University (Martin & de Gruchy, 1930). She continued her work in San Francisco into the 1930s when she was over 90 years old. It is quite likely that she was encouraged to work with older adults at Stanford University by Lewis Terman, the translator of the Binet-Simon test of intelligence. He was a child developmental psychologist, who in his late career became interested in the adult outcomes of high childhood intelligence. This intimates that he may have encouraged not only the work of Lillian Martin but also the subsequent experimental work by Walter Miles at Stanford (see Miles, 1933).

The first laboratory of psychology in America devoted to the study of aging appears to have been at Stanford between the years 1927 and 1932. The five doctoral dissertations and one postdoctoral research study carried out during that period are impressive in their quality and scope. After completing their studies the individual graduate students apparently did not find faculty positions related to the psychology of aging, and no subsequent identification of their names with the study of aging appears in the literature. In 1933 Walter Miles left Stanford to take another position at Yale University. His move appears to have broken the course of aging studies at Stanford, although there were subsequent reports of the follow-up of the "Terman gifted children" into adulthood (but not in Miles's experimental tradition; Miles, 1967).

During the late 1930s infectious diseases were diminishing as major health threats and chronic diseases were moving up in the list of major causes of death. This prompted a broader look at the aging individual, which included the contributions from psychology. In the 1939 volume by E. V. Cowdry, there was a definite attempt to examine aging from biological, behavioral, and social points of view; this volume set the stage for the modern period of the study of aging. A growth of interest occurred at this time in aging and mental health in which psychology was also to play an active research role. In 1941 a conference on mental health in later maturity was organized by the U.S. Public Health Service (1943) with active participation by psychologists.

## C. Post–World War II Initiatives

After the disruptions of World War II there was a resumption of interest in research on aging. The U.S. Public Health Service had founded its research program on aging in Baltimore in 1941 under the direction of Nathan Shock, but because of the war its efforts were diverted until 1945, when physiological investigations of human aging were started. In 1947 a broad range of psychological research was initiated by

James Birren and Jack Botwinick (see Birren, 1961a,b).

At the University of Cambridge the Nuffield Unit for Research into Problems of Ageing was established in 1946. It was attached to the Psychological Laboratory until it was discontinued in 1956 as a result of the appointment of a new Chair of the Department of Psychology. The research of the unit was oriented toward the experimental analysis of the relationships between age and skill. Welford has reported on the many findings of that group (Welford, 1951; see also Welford, 1958).

In 1955 there was enough promise in the growth of the subject matter that the American Psychological Association (APA) held a research conference on the psychology of aging, supported by funding from the National Institute of Mental Health (Anderson, 1956). By 1959 sufficient information had been gathered for a handbook summarizing research progress on aging and behavior to be published, and in 1964 the first textbook on the psychology of aging was published (Birren, 1959, 1964).

The Division on Adult Development and Aging of the APA was founded in 1947. It is worth noting that this division now has a larger membership than its parent division, Developmental Psychology, which primarily focuses on children. In the allied field of psychiatry, Cohen (1992) noted that "until 1978 . . . in the history of the United States, there had been only one department of psychiatry offering specialized training in geriatric psychiatry" (p. 894). By 1991 the American Board of Psychiatry and Neurology established a subspecialization in geriatric psychiatry. The recency of these actions reflect a tardiness of specialized professional training to understand and meet the needs of older adults. Conjecture about the slow emergence of professional training may have to take into account many elements, for example: latent fears about aging, cultural emphases on children and youth, and perhaps the lack of economic incentives for specialized careers in aging.

This brief excursion into the history of the psychology of aging provides some evidence that, despite its long intellectual roots, the subject was slow to emerge as a major field of psychological study. The recent growth of specialized journals, the creation of the National Institute on Aging in 1975, and the rate of research publications suggest an exponential growth of the subject (Riegel, 1977). The slowness of psychology to embrace the study of adult development and aging can be attributed partly to the early atomistic "bottom-up" approach in which psychology was emulating the successes of chemistry and physics, but also to the unease about the complexity of the issues of aging and about the association of the topic of death with advancing age.

## II. Concepts of Aging

Since the publication of Sacher's (1980) critical review of theories in gerontology, there has been a growing interest within the field of aging in contributions of a theoretical nature. Birren and Birren (1990) have discussed the profusion of research findings and the lack of integrative theory in the psychology of aging. Their discussion may be summarized as follows: First, due to the exponential growth of research and publications, there has not been time to integrate concepts and findings. Second, professional services tend to be organized around the age of the population served, for example, preschool children, adolescents, or the elderly. This may contribute to the relatively low interest in theory and integration of knowledge across age levels. Third, the emergence of theory has been slow, perhaps because of the inherent complexity of the subject matter. A result is that the psychology of aging is currently data rich but theory poor.

For the future development of research we should recall the advice of Lewin (1951) that there is nothing so practical as a good theory. Unfortunately, attempts to develop formal (i.e., rigorous, precise, and at least potentially quantitative) theories in the psychology of aging have not been very successful. Almost imperceptibly, the attention of researchers was turned to the development of models, which—generally speaking—are regarded as more simple and quantifiable than theories (Salthouse, 1988), but also as more focused on limited aspects of aging.

Logical, mathematical, or statistical formalization does not lead automatically to useful theory—or to models, for that matter. In fact, it may be said that the proposition or equation by itself is not the model or theory (Hutten, 1954). For example, Schaie's equation $A = P - C$ is not Schaie's (1965) general developmental model. The equation for three time parameters—Age, Period, and Cohort—is a model only, because the equation represents sources of behavioral change in reference to maturation and to past and present environments. Once interpretation and context are added, the logical, mathematical, or statistical lose their separate identity, and the scientist finds him- or herself again in the process of theory development.

## A. The Psychology of the Aged

Research in the psychology of aging has been guided by a somewhat diverse collection of theories, models, and metaphors of early structuralism. Historically, there are three foci: the aged, age, and aging (Schroots, 1995c). The first, the psychology of the aged, focuses on older people and later life. Grounded in a stages-of-life perspective, most studies of the aged demonstrate a thematic, descriptive approach and little coherence. For example, the new journal, *Abstracts in Social Gerontology*, has selected rather arbitrarily more than 70 different themes, varying from Alzheimer's disease, life satisfaction, widowhood, and retirement to cognition, death, and dying. Most research findings, as reported in the abstracts, consist essentially of descriptive statements about the orga-

nization of behavior in the aged and their social and medical problems. Given the wide variety of themes and findings, the psychology of the aged may be broadly defined as the study of the problematic and nonproblematic elderly.

Traditionally, some psychologists have adopted an ordered-change orientation to childhood and a stability orientation to adulthood. Freud and Piaget are the classic examples of this. Their stages of psychosexual and cognitive development are largely descriptive of childhood and adolescence.

Estes and Binney (1989) have shown clearly that the psychological study of the aged is heavily infested with biomedical conceptions of aging as a disease or a result of some deteriorative process. For instance, cognitive processes at older age are often described in terms of failure, loss, insufficiency, inadequacy, impoverishment, decrement, inefficiency, or impaired performance. These biomedical conceptions reflect the dominant metaphor that aging is a biological or medical problem, and that the elderly make up a problem group in society. The implications of this metaphor are, among others, ageism (defined as the systematic stereotyping and discrimination against people because they are old) and the denial of the virtual existence of nonproblematic elderly (cf. Kenyon, Birren, & Schroots, 1991). Most older people, however, live independently and have the vitality and resilience to function at a high level (Gilford, 1988). Future psychological studies of the aged should take into account the nonproblematic aspects of aging as well as functional decline and disease, which may require professional help.

## B. The Psychology of Age

The second approach in psychogerontology falls within *the psychology of age, which focuses on age differences*. Most research in this approach has been crosssectional, describing and comparing groups of people of different ages measured at the same time. The central research question concerns the relation between age as the primary independent variable and some other factor of interest as the primary dependent variable, for example, mortality, morbidity, autonomy, quality of life, mental abilities, or productivity. The research questions often concern the extent to which intervening variables, such as sociodemographic, environmental, psychosocial, biophysiologic, or lifestyle factors, are related to the observed differences with age.

Age differences found in cross-sectional studies are frequently misinterpreted in terms of age changes, aging, or changes in behavior over time. Over the last two decades, however, researchers have realized gradually that age differences do not equal age changes, or—to put it differently— that chronological age used as the independent variable does not help much to explain the aging process. The question arises: What is the theoretical status of the age variable?

Schaie (1965) was one of the first to realize that cohort and period may have more interesting explanatory properties than age, and—accordingly—he designed the age–period–cohort (APC) general developmental model (see earlier part of Section II). However, due to the dependency of these three time parameters on calendar time (both dependent and independent variables are expressed in terms of the same calendar time), there is always the problem of time confounds, regardless of how data are collected or statistically analyzed (for a full discussion, see Schroots & Birren, 1988). A radical solution to the problem of time confounds is to get rid of time itself. Recently, Schaie (1992) made an attempt to solve the APC problem by reconceptualizing the two time parameters.

A second point of view regarding the age variable is based on Wohlwill's (1973) conception of age as a dummy or index variable that needs further explanation in terms of developmental (or aging) pro-

cesses. Most researchers use chronological age implicitly as a dummy variable that stands not for a single underlying aging process, but for a host of processes. These may operate independently and in combination to bring about the changes we call *aging*. This means that fruitful research will have to focus on identifying the causes and consequences of the processes responsible for age-related differences. It is particularly in the field of cognitive aging that this type of cross-sectional experiment can be found, although longitudinal information is needed to reach more definitive conclusions about the hypothesized aging processes (cf. Salthouse, 1991). From a differential perspective, however, the index of chronological age needs to be supplemented by other independent variables that are sensitive to individual variations with age at various levels of the organism, for example, at the biological, psychological, and social levels of individual functioning (cf. Schroots, 1992; see also Birren & Fisher, 1992). Birren's observation should be remembered: Chronological age or the elapsed time in days, months, and years since birth is "one of the most useful single items of information about an individual if not the most useful" (1959, p. 8). Nevertheless it should be kept in mind that although useful as an index, *age* itself does not explain much.

## C. The Psychology of Aging

The third approach in psychogerontology is the psychology of aging, which studies —briefly summarized—the regular changes in behavior after young adulthood (cf. Birren & Birren, 1990; Birren & Cunningham, 1985; Birren & Renner, 1977). In order to study changes in individuals, it is necessary to carry out longitudinal research, which essentially means that the performance of a group of subjects from a single cohort is compared with that group's own performance at other periods. In this context, the term *aging* is often used both as a label for an independent variable to explain other phenomena (e.g., mortality, productivity, health, competence) and as a dependent variable that is explained by other processes (see Schroots, 1993a, for a comprehensive overview of the status and future of longitudinal studies of aging).

Here, it is important to discuss the implications of the phrase *after young adulthood* in the above definition. So defined, the psychology of aging is grounded in a two-stages-of-life perspective; the two stages, development and aging, are usually thought of as two successive processes of change in time, with the transition point or apex at maturity. The classic metaphor for the two stages of age-related change in life is the hill metaphor, based on biological conceptions of growth and decline, particularly, the so-called mortality curve: Mortality rates are high for infants, regularly decline to a minimum at about age 10, and then rise progressively throughout the remainder of the life span. Psychological processes of change, however, do not necessarily parallel the mortality curve. For example, fluid mental abilities, like speed of information processing, reflect more influence of genetic-biological determinants and tend to decline in middle age. Crystallized abilities, on the other hand, reflect cultural-social influences (e.g., general world knowledge) and may display some growth with age (Birren & Fisher, 1993; Horn, 1989). This cognitive phenomenon raises the question of the extent to which processes of development and aging are different from each other, because both processes refer to age-related changes.

In 1987 Baltes introduced the so-called gain/loss view of development:

According to this view, development at all points of the life course is a joint expression of features of growth (gain) and decline (loss). It is assumed that any developmental progression displays at the same time new adaptive capacity and the loss of previously existing capacity. No developmental change during the life course is pure gain. (p. 616)

A suitable metaphor for Baltes's view of development, which implicitly recognizes a process of aging, would be the profit-and-loss account. In extended form this metaphor corresponds with Labouvie-Vief's (1982) hierarchical life span model, which suggests a view of life span development as a succession of single-peaked functions of different modes, each of which undergoes a period of growth and decline as it is superseded by a new mode.

The joint occurrence of gain (growth) and loss (decline) throughout the life course corresponds also with Birren and Schroots's (1984) earlier conceptualization of development and aging as two parallel but related processes of change, which might be conceived as two sides of the same coin of life. For example, the most rapid loss of neurons in the brain occurs in infancy; a much slower loss occurs in adult life. This illustrates the point that loss of cells may parallel functional gains due perhaps to increased dendritic growth during the loss of cells (see Scheibel, Ch. 6, this volume).

At the start of ontogenesis (conception), the developmental process is most visible or manifest, while at the same time the signs of aging are still obscure or latent, and vice versa at the end of ontogenesis (death). Following Birren's (1960) counterpart theory, the metaphor of counterpart has been introduced to define aging as both the diachronic and synchronic counterpart of development (Schroots, 1991).

Birren and Schroots placed their conceptions of development and aging in the metatheoretical perspective of general systems theory. The dominant metaphor in this theory is the human organism, hierarchically organized from many subsystems, such as cells, tissues, organs, and so on (Miller, 1978). The growth and development of living systems (organisms, individuals) are explained in terms of absorbing information and the free and continuous exchange of information at each level of the hierarchical organization.

Senescence and aging, on the other hand, are explained in terms of increasing entropy or disorganization with age (second law of thermodynamics). The concepts have different backgrounds and have to be studied in more detail to permit integration.

As it has turned out, both general systems theory and Baltes's gain–loss conceptions partially fail to describe and explain the complex phenomena of development and aging. This is because there is no essential difference between the terms *development*, *gain*, and *information*, on the one hand, and the terms *aging*, *loss*, and *entropy*, on the other hand, except that they are opposite terms, which differ only by a minus sign. The concept of information, for example, might be described in terms of negative entropy (negentropy). Both processes can be conceived as age-related changes during the life course. But this answer, on second thought, does not elaborate our understanding of the nature of aging, or the *regular* changes in behavior, as the psychology of aging has been characterized before. In this context, the adjective *regular* refers to the orderly or typical changes in behavior, as found in longitudinal research on aging (Schroots & Birren, 1993). It is to the nature of these so-called *patterns of change* that the next question should be addressed.

## III. Patterns of Change

*Pattern* refers to identifiable clusters of changes associated with aging. Aging at the population level has been traditionally defined in terms of a mortality pattern showing progressive increase in age-specific mortality. Emphasis has been on death or the probability of dying with age, and not on the aspects of aging as reflected in the great variety of patterns of functions, with different aging rates, onset, range, and outcome. In this respect Shock et al. (1984) have listed six general patterns of change with age: normal aging; stability; patho-

logical aging; terminal decline; compensatory aging; and cultural or cohort effects.

A major unresolved issue is what changes are typical or normal processes of change in the organism, and what changes are atypical, abnormal, or pathological patterns. The boundaries between these phenomena are often indistinct. For example, progressive decline in bone density seems to occur in all persons after age 50, but certain pathological states, such as osteoporosis, are almost indistinguishable qualitatively from the typical or normal processes in older individuals. To clarify this issue, Busse (1969) made a conceptual distinction between *primary* and *secondary* aging. Primary aging refers to changes intrinsic to the aging process that are ultimately irreversible. Secondary aging refers to changes caused by illnesses that are correlated with age but may be reversible or preventable. Later, a third distinction was added, *tertiary* aging, which refers to changes that occur precipitously in old age (Birren & Cunningham, 1985, p. 22).

One of the general conclusions that can be drawn from longitudinal studies of aging is that aging is at least in part an individualized process that differs among individuals and among functions (Shock, 1985). Recent conceptions in the psychology of aging emphasize variability along with average functioning (see also Dannefer, 1988; Morse, 1993). It seems that a differential psychology of aging, or perhaps an ecological psychology of aging, is slowly developing. Under the subtitles of primary, secondary, tertiary, and differential aging, respectively, a discussion of some major patterns of change follows.

### A. Primary Aging

Busse's distinction between primary and secondary aging became clouded when the concept of primary aging was substituted for terms such as *normal* (Shock et al., 1984), *healthy* (Butler, 1983), or *usual* (Rowe & Kahn, 1987) aging, while secondary aging was replaced, accordingly, with *pathological* aging. In particular, the term *normal aging* proved to be confusing because this term is defined more or less tautologically as "a normal concomitant of the passage of time that takes place in everyone; disease occurs in only a part of the population" (Shock et al., 1984, p. 1). In practice, normally aging persons are defined as those without a specific diagnosis (Siegler & Costa, 1985).

Increasing slowness is one of the most reliable features of behavior associated with advancing age. It may prove to be one of the more useful markers of primary aging by virtue of its dependence on brain integrity on the one hand and its consequences for cognitive functioning on the other (Birren & Fisher, 1992, 1995).

Patterns of primary aging in psychology have been studied in two other domains: cognition and personality. In the cognitive domain, a general pattern of average declines with advancing age has been reliably established (Schaie, 1983). Within this pattern, another classic pattern of cognitive aging can be distinguished (i.e., the relative increase of verbal information with age compared with decline in spatial-perceptual performance) (Botwinick, 1973). Age-comparative studies have consistently found a marked age decline in measures of fluid intelligence and almost no or little decline in measures of crystallized intelligence (Horn, 1989).

One of the most extensive studies of cognitive aging, the Seattle Longitudinal Study (SLS), was carried out by Schaie (1994). Throughout the study, with an elegant sequential design, subjects were assessed on five cognitive measures from Thurstone's battery of tests of primary mental abilities. Briefly summarized, Schaie's data lend support to this conclusion:

Although decline in cognitive functioning occurs for many individuals as the sixties are reached, such decline is differential in nature. Virtually none of the individuals contained in our data set showed univer-

sal decline on all abilities monitored, even by the eighties. (Schaie, 1990, p. 114)

Plausible determinants of different patterns of maintenance and decline are cardiovascular disease, education, and occupational level. In the longitudinal Gothenburg Study, it has been found that subjects with cardiovascular disease had greater decline in intelligence test scores between the ages of 70 and 75 than subjects without such disease (Steen & Djurfeldt, 1993).

A special pattern of aging concerns the ancient topic of *wisdom*, which traditionally includes formal knowledge, as well as moral behavior and being aware of what one does not know (Clayton & Birren, 1980; Sternberg, 1990b). Most people believe that wisdom is most likely to be found among the old. Recent research on wisdom-related tasks by Baltes and his colleagues (Baltes, Smith, & Staudinger, 1992) confirms this belief and shows that older adults are among the top performers. However, whether wisdom actually appears depends on a person's life experience, motivation, and personal resources. Thus, not only expanded knowledge is involved in wisdom, but also personality, the second domain in primary aging (see Birren & Dieckmann, 1991, for an account of the different approaches to the study of wisdom).

Research on patterns of personality with age has been concerned mainly with the degree to which personality changes or remains stable across adulthood (Bengtson, Reedy, & Gordon, 1985; Kogan, 1990). Generally speaking, sequential studies of personality traits have consistently found a marked pattern of stability in both mean levels and individual differences; that is, about half of the variance is attributed to individual differences independent of age (Costa & McCrae, 1993).

Field (1991) drew attention to the argument that the stability of personality patterns might be explained by the use of self-report measures in most longitudinal studies, for example, the Bonn (Lehr & Thomae, 1987), Duke (Siegler, George, & Okun, 1979), Baltimore (McCrae & Costa, 1987), and Normative Aging (Costa & McCrae, 1977–1978) studies. It is suggested that self-report measures reflect one's ideas about oneself, which may rigidify over the life course, in contrast to other personality attributes.

Although the evidence points decidedly to stability, it has been suggested that there may be changes for subsets of individuals. Because personality is a composite of cognitive, affective, and motivational elements, it may yet be found to change with age despite component stability (see also Ruth & Coleman, Ch. 17, this volume).

### B. Secondary Aging

Recently, Heikkinen et al. (1993) stated that definitions of "healthy" aging and "normal" aging are like good Swiss cheese, full of holes. Not surprisingly, the same is true of "pathological" aging, as there is an ongoing debate in gerontology with regard to the relationship between aging and disease. The higher prevalence of chronic disease with age makes it understandable that conceptions of primary aging are strongly associated with aspects of illness, deficit, and decline. Nevertheless, the conceptual distinction between primary and secondary aging is far from simple. Evans (1988), for example, argued that there is

no reason to suppose that what occurs normally in the sense of frequently is necessarily normal in the sense of being optimal for health, and even less reason to suppose that whatever is normal will be distributed normally, in the sense of a Gaussian function around the population mean. In fact, to draw a distinction between disease and normal ageing is to attempt to separate the *undefined from the indefinable* [italics added]. (p. 40)

Generally speaking, three points of view can be distinguished in this ongoing debate: (a) aging is a disease; (b) aging and disease are separate processes; and (c) the

relationship between aging and disease forms a continuum.

Early in the field of gerontology, aging was considered to be an expression of disease or general senescent decline that made the organism increasingly vulnerable to disease. Even recently some scientists have argued that age-associated disorders like senile dementia of the Alzheimer's type should be regarded as an aging process (cf. Goodwin, 1991). Essentially, their argument is based on epidemiological data with regard to the similarity or synchronicity of patterns of aging and disease, in that mortality and morbidity patterns show a similar, almost exponential form with age (Forbes & Hirdes, 1993). However, not all age-associated diseases follow this pattern. Brody and Schneider (1986), for instance, suggested a more detailed distinction in age-dependent versus age-related diseases. The latter are defined as those that have specific temporal patterns for their occurrence and, therefore, are not necessarily related to primary aging processes. An example is multiple sclerosis, where the disorder can occur occasionally at older ages, but where vulnerability is essentially limited to the third and fourth decades of life. Age-dependent diseases (e.g., cerebro- and cardiovascular diseases), on the other hand, show a mortality pattern with remarkable resemblance in exponential form to age-specific mortality rates for all causes of death (i.e., primary aging). This distinction has met some criticism from Evans (1988), who noticed that not all age-dependent diseases (e.g., stroke) follow an exponential function of incidence, but rather some follow a power-law function. Age-dependent diseases, however, come closest to what is generally understood as pathological or secondary aging.

Most scientists appear to subscribe to Shock's (1961) traditional view that aging is not necessarily associated with deterioration and disease. This view is based on the proposition that primary or normal aging is defined by such criteria as intrinsicality, progressiveness, and universality, whereas disease is caused by extrinsic agents (Blumenthal, 1993). An example of secondary aging is the age-dependent chronic disease of arteriosclerosis, characterized by decreased function with age as well as by increased prevalence of its various related symptoms within numerous populations. In Japan, however, the symptoms are relatively infrequent: The related symptoms do not occur in all older persons (a failure to meet the criterion of universality). Therefore, arteriosclerosis is conceived as a form of secondary aging.

As Rowe (1985) suggested, the relationship between normal aging and disease can be conceptualized along a continuum. At one end, aging can be separated clearly from disease, whereas at the other end of the continuum the two shade into each other. In the middle, physiology and pathology interact in complex ways. At the former end, we find physiological functions that hardly change with age (e.g., volume of red blood cells, resting heart rate), as well as age-related physiological changes that do not result in disease (e.g., graying of hair). At the opposite end of the continuum, there are age-dependent physiological changes that, beyond a certain point, can hardly be distinguished from disease (e.g., cataract formation, arteriosclerosis).

Summarizing, it may be stated that attempts to make a conceptual distinction between patterns of primary and secondary aging have not been very successful. Given the complex, yet hardly understood interactions between aging and disease, future research should address their relationships and patterns as they change over the life span. One of the goals, for instance, would be to identify the degree to which nonpathological age changes influence our vulnerability to disease. In this respect, Steen and Djurfeldt (1993, p. 167) reported from the Gothenburg Study that factors that may increase the risk of mental disorders (like loneliness, bereavement, loss of earlier status in society, physical diseases, as well as perceptual and neurobiological changes) increase with age, especially after the age of 80. A similar goal, according to Fozard, Metter, Brant, Pearson, and Baker (1993), would be to study the role of age in epidemiological studies of risk factors for disease. In the Framingham Study, age was found to be a significant risk factor for coronary heart disease in men aged 40–49, but the association was weaker in men aged 50–62, and was not significant in men aged 20–39 (Halperin, Blackwelder, & Verter, 1971). Recently, similar findings from the Gothenburg Study have been reported by Mellström (1993, p. 139), who concluded explicitly that predictive risk factors for mortality and morbidity might change and even show an inverse effect after the age of 70 (e.g., body weight and blood pressure).

## C. Tertiary Aging

In 1962 Kleemeier concluded on the basis of longitudinal changes in intelligence of individuals aged 60–90 that "factors related to the death of the individual cause a decline in intellectual performance, and that the onset of this decline may be detected in some instances several years prior to the death of the person" (p. 293). This conclusion is known in the literature as the *terminal drop hypothesis* (i.e., when the average rate of decline in performance per year is calculated, those who die have a faster rate or more precipitous decline than those who survive) (Siegler, 1987; see also Berg, Ch. 18, this volume).

The pattern of terminal decline or tertiary aging has been supported by various results since that hypothesis was formulated. For instance, in the Gothenburg longitudinal study of aging, intelligence test results have been analyzed in relation to death or survival. The analysis showed a terminal decline pattern, pervasive for cognitive abilities, in which survivors had performed at a superior level at preceding measurement occasions, and the decline in performance among nonsurvivors emerged several years prior to death. The analysis also revealed a gender effect in the sense that women performed better than men late in life, a finding that is consistent with their differential survival (Johansson & Berg, 1989). Whether terminal decline is a universal process has yet to be established, although clearly for many persons nearness to death is accompanied by abrupt changes in a number of mental abilities and other functional capacities.

Hagberg, Samuelsson, Lindberg, and Dehlin (1991) analyzed the personality test results on the Rod-and-Frame Test of field dependence–independence in another Swedish longitudinal study of aging. As might be expected, a pattern of strong stability was found in this personality dimension, because the majority (80%) of the participants did not change during the 6 years between the ages of 67 and 73 when they were tested. Surprisingly, however, stability of the field independence–dependence dimension between ages 67 and 73 predicted survival to age 83. If the participants did change in field dependence or field independence, this change was associated with death within 10 years. In other words, a pattern of terminal decline is found in the personality domain.

Birren and Cunningham (1985) presented a picture of the general pattern of tertiary aging expected to be found in future longitudinal studies:

Some individuals may go through a period of behavioral change that may be larger and/or qualitatively different from normal age changes in behavior. This period of time may range from months to years but is characterized by cognitive and social "slipping"— that is, a deterioration of previous levels of performance that brings about not only greater losses than expected in age-sensitive variables, but losses in variables that are usually regarded as age-insensitive. (p. 21)

Hagberg and colleagues (1991) explained their findings in terms of destabilization and increased vulnerability of the complex personality organization with age, due to primary and secondary aging processes. Indeed, it would seem that the three patterns of aging interact, producing what has been called the *cascade metaphor of aging* (Birren & Cunningham, 1985, p. 23): Primary aging is believed to result in a slowing of the speed with which information is processed; secondary aging, particularly cardiovascular and chronic disease, is hypothesized to incur increased losses with age; and tertiary aging is viewed as being pervasive, with causal links to all processes. Thus, the general pattern of aging may be conceived as a trickling away of functioning that gains momentum until it cascades and forces the individual over the brink of life.

## D. Differential Aging

Findings from the above-mentioned longitudinal studies of aging lend strong support to Shock's classic dictum that aging is a highly individualized process (1985, p. 738). With increasing age, there is an increase of interindividual differences in the onset, rate, and direction of most functions and processes, resulting in a pattern of differential aging. Paraphrasing George Orwell, one might say that all people are different, but older people may be more different than the young.

The general pattern of differential aging, which embraces primary and secondary as well as tertiary aging processes, has been supported by Nelson and Dannefer (1992, p. 22) in a comprehensive review of gerontological studies examining age-related changes or differences. Overall, a majority of the studies presenting dispersion data report increases in variability with age. Moreover, the dominance of the pattern of increasing variability does not appear to be domain specific; the same general finding emerged across physical, personality, and cognitive domains. As some authors alternately refer to variability as heterogeneity, individual differences, variation, variance, or diversity, adherence to a broad definition of variability is suggested—as the scattering of the values of a frequency distribution around their average. Regardless of the definition of variability, however, Nelson and Dannefer's results emphasize that studies of aging, which focus on trends in average functioning with age, should be complemented with dispersion measures for the variability of functioning.

The question to be raised now is, What are the determinants of the empirical pattern of differential aging? Part of the observed increasing variability with age can be explained by secondary aging processes or the increased prevalence of illnesses with age. As discussed before, aging processes can be modulated by different patterns of pathologies, but this phenomenon does not explain the observed variability due to primary and tertiary aging processes, even when all health factors are considered (Fozard et al., 1993). However, new developments provide the field with tentative solutions.

## IV. New Developments

The advancement of theory in the psychology of aging may benefit from a more constructivist view of science. This view holds that science characteristically employs metaphors, and that the processes of concept formation and theory formation are in an essential way metaphorical (Leatherdale, 1974). For example, as noted before (Section II.C), a well-known metaphor in the field of cognitive aging is the so-called hill metaphor, which expresses that sooner or later one will pass the apex of his or her abilities (Hall, 1922). On the basis of this metaphor, models and theories have been constructed that view cognitive development and aging as a single-peaked function that parallels biological growth and decline, respectively (cf. Craik & Salthouse, 1992). For a few decades, however, the notion has been growing that

psychological processes of change do not necessarily parallel biological changes along the life span. The psychological attribute of wisdom, for instance, represents an integrated view of behavior in middle and late adulthood (Birren & Fisher, 1990; Sternberg, 1990b). As such, wisdom does not reflect the traditional hill metaphor of cognitive rise and decline and, consequently, new metaphors of cognitive aging have been introduced in the field. Baltes et al. (1992) have developed a model or metaphor of wisdom as expertise in the fundamental pragmatics of life. Sternberg's book on wisdom (1990b) appears to have opened a new era in research and theory on this complex view of the mature mind, blending cognition, affect, and conation.

In this respect, it should be noted that the concept of metaphor is used in a broad sense to include not only similes and analogies, but also what is ordinarily called a *model*. Sternberg (1990a), for example, did not make a distinction between metaphors and models of intelligence when he stated that "the root source of many of the questions asked about intelligence appears to be the model, or metaphor, that drives the theory and research" (p. 3). From the above perspective it may now be stated that the metaphor, either explicit or implicit, drives the theory in the psychology of aging, and that the model functions as a more general, extended, or systematic kind of metaphor, which connects theory with empirical research (Schroots, 1991). As such, a constructivist view of aging helps to understand, develop, and direct theory and research more effectively than a positivist view.

### A. Gerodynamics

In the past it was expected that general psychology would provide the scientific structure of thought around which the psychology of aging would be organized. Now there is greater recognition that general psychology is largely nondynamic, because it studies aspects of behavior in organisms of the same age, often undergraduate students. Questions are increasingly raised about the conditions of change for development and aging. The dynamic principles are beginning to be fed back into general psychology, and newer introductory textbooks often have concluding chapters about development and aging. It is conceivable that the introductory psychology books of the future will be organized around principles of development and aging into which will be fitted the elements of perception, learning, memory, and personality. It is even possible that in the next century general psychology will become organized around the principles of development and aging. This prediction is not without precedent.

Philip Handler, past president of the National Academy of Sciences and professor of biochemistry at Duke University, in the 1960s said that biochemistry until then had been studying the building blocks of metabolism (personal communication, 1964). He predicted that the biochemistry of the future was going to be the biochemistry of differentiation and aging. If the study of the dynamics of growth and aging is important in the future of biochemistry it seems no less important for psychology.

Pressure for knowledge about processes of aging arises not only because of the practical needs of an aging society but also because science is coming to realize that there is a need for deeper insights into the principles of the dynamics of development and aging. For ethical reasons psychology is precluded from manipulating many variables thought to be important in behavioral development and aging. However, psychology can gain insights into the dynamic processes by inference from "natural experiments" in the form of cross-sectional and longitudinal studies of individuals of different genetic backgrounds, exposed to different environmental conditions (Schaie, 1992; see also Pedersen, Ch. 4, this volume).

The hierarchical organization of behavior is important in this future view because changes in behavior can derive from "bottom-up" influences (e.g., energy) or "top-down" (e.g., information). One of the legacies of general psychology has been its lack of success in building a picture of the hierarchical organization of behavior. The result is that psychological research findings about aging cannot be readily interpreted in terms of their primacy or significance for complex behavior.

Presumably, one should find distinct clusters of variables surrounding fluid and crystallized intelligence interacting with demographic variables and morbidity and mortality. Questions may be raised about which second- and third-order factors (Carroll, 1993) are most significant for features of adult life, such as survival, adaptation to social demands, quality of life, and mental health.

Because fluid intelligence appears to be a dynamic variable, possibly energy related, and crystallized intelligence is a store of information, it seems productive to pursue the question of which differences in behavior with age are primarily due to changes in energy or to changes in stored information.

Sacher (1980) said that most studies of aging have been "aspect studies." This is particularly true for psychology: Many aspects of behavior have been studied, but it is very difficult to attach significance to research findings with regard to the broader functioning and well-being of the organism and also to predict the consequences for other functions. Schroots and Birren (1988) use the term *gerodynamics* for a comprehensive theory of aging that embraces the biological, behavioral, and social processes of aging (see also Yates & Benton, 1995). Gerodynamics is based on general systems theory, particularly the second law of thermodynamics, and modern chaos theory. The second law of thermodynamics refers to an increase of disorder with time in energetic systems. Chaos theory postulates that under far-from-equilibrium conditions, order can arise out of disorder through a process of self-organization. Aging of living systems can be defined as the self-organizing process of increasing entropy with age, from which more disorder than order emerges, and which results in the system's death. Self-organization, in this context, denotes a process by which a structure or pattern of change emerges with time (i.e., a finite series of bifurcations toward increasingly disorderly and orderly structures of increasing uniqueness). Gerodynamics provides the basis for a new aspect theory, the so-called branching theory of aging, which hypothesizes typical patterns of stability and change in the form of a branching tree at the biological, behavioral, and social levels of the aging system (Schroots, 1995b, 1995c).

Psychology could well employ the concept of gerodynamics, and examine the changes in behavior using information and energy concepts. Sorely needed at this point are concepts that will lead to the replacement of chronological age as the sole criterion to analyze changes in the adult organism. That is, the parameters of behavioral gerodynamics should correlate with chronological age but they should also correlate with the criteria of behavioral integrity and effectiveness (Schroots, 1995b).

## B. Criteria of Aging beyond Chronological Age

Chronological age is an initially appealing false lover who tells you everything and nothing. The common point of departure for research on aging has been the extent to which human characteristics are associated with chronological age. However, age is only an index to processes. It is a useful and first step toward the analysis of change, but it is not an effective variable in pointing to the dynamic forces leading to change.

Birren and Fisher (1992) proposed adding other criteria to chronological age and the passage of time for separating and gaining clues about the organization of adult change. These criteria were originally proposed to judge the significance of slowness of behavior as a behavioral marker of aging, and are suggested here for general use in analysis of clusters or single variable changes. In addition to its correlation with chronological age the variable should (a) be related to length of life, (b) be observed in adjacent species, (c) show different patterns in males and females because females live significantly longer than males, (d) be related to physiological and anatomical markers of aging, (e) show relationships with other behavioral processes that relate to age, (f) be modulated but not eliminated by manipulation (by practice) and by optimum health behaviors, and (g) be exacerbated by age-associated disease but not eliminated by absence of particular diseases.

Other criteria can also be proposed for differentiating patterns of adult change, such as increments in knowledge, strategies, and wisdom, together with both concurrent variables representing environmental influences and also biological senescence. Presumably there will be identified clusters of behavioral variables associated with social and environmental influences along with heritable biological processes (see Pedersen, Ch. 4, this volume).

The psychology of aging appears poised for a metamorphosis into a more complex and sophisticated subject matter, and perhaps a more useful one. Research on aging continues to expand at all levels of analysis. Neuroscience studies of brain chemistry and imaging methods are beginning to link circumscribed functions of the nervous system with behavior (see Scheibel, Ch. 6, this volume). With the growth of neuropsychology and the assessment of function in persons with suspected disease or brain damage, new knowledge is being developed to distinguish forms of pathology from "normal aging." This advance in turn is leading to quasi-hypothesis-driven studies of behavior patterns in diagnostic groups in comparison with healthy adults. Thus contrasting patient behavior in samples of subjects with Parkinson's disease, schizophrenia, stroke, depression, and other diagnoses is expected to lead to the identification of suspected weaknesses in brain neurotransmitters and localized structural damage. At the microlevel of behavioral processes, deficit states associated with age are being identified. At the macrolevel, complex behavioral processes such as wisdom are being explored (Sternberg, 1990b). The scope of data embraced by the psychology of aging is expanding at both the micro- and macrolevels to answer the most fundamental question: How is individual behavior transformed over the course of life? A parallel question is: What pattern of age changes in behavior is typical of humans as a species?

Longitudinal research on adults has been a great stimulus to improved understanding of patterns of change over the adult years (Schroots, 1993b). There has also been renewed interest in the very old (e.g., through longitudinal studies of centenarians). Rather than long-term linear progressions, change in the organism may be eruptive and discontinuous.

Methodological advances in statistics make it possible to characterize the pathways over time of individual functioning. The use of structural equation methods is enabling investigators to understand the relative strength of interactions with time, leading to hypotheses about presumed causality of outcomes (Collins & Horn, 1991). Characterization of individual pathways over time is also subject to detailed analysis leading to the identification of bifurcation points or threshold phenomena.

The term *ecology of aging* is used to refer to the fact that organisms not only express their genome but the expression is done in interaction with particular physical and social environments. In human studies it is not possible to expose subjects to widely varying environments for the purpose of studying experimentally the range of environmental influences. However, sequential longitudinal studies can reveal cohort differences that arise from nongenetic sources. The psychology of aging may increasingly adopt an ecological point of view toward human aging that will embrace major modifications of our behavioral characteristics as we change our environments and styles of life.

Narrative material is increasingly being used to explore varieties of personal experiences of growing up and growing old. The expansion of what has been called *qualitative* research on aging has identified many topics of psychological importance not only for quantitative research (Schroots, 1995a) but also for the care of older adults (Burnside & Schmidt, 1994). Diaries, autobiographies, and letters are being used for a wide range of research studies of the way aging or old age is experienced as well as for characterizing historical epochs (Birren, Kenyon, Ruth, Schroots, & Svensson, 1995). Future research may well undertake the task of linking the experiences of growing old and being old with health, social class, and other behavioral variables.

## V. Summary

This chapter traced the roots of the psychology of aging to the development of nineteenth-century European science. Although the psychology of aging was slow to develop, it is now in a phase of rapid expansion with a large volume of published research and many specialized journals and books. Early psychologists tended to favor the study of elements of behavior in a style patterned after the successes of chemistry and physics. This focus gave little encouragement to either the study of the dynamics of child development or the study of aging. Works of some of the early pioneers have been described and the growth of the field has been traced through its post-World War II expansion.

The psychology of aging is a complex subject and at present it is data rich but theory poor, with many of its theories adapted from other interest areas of psychology. Much research has been on "aspects of aging" with little evidence of the significance of findings for the broader functioning and well-being of the organism.

Dominating past research has been the study of cognitive capacities, although recent trends show an interest in broadening the scope of context variables, because the mere correlation of an ability with age does not provide insight into the dynamics of the processes of change.

There have been three approaches to the study of the subject matter: the aged, age, and aging. Studies of the aged examine the characteristics of the problematic and the nonproblematic elderly. Careful descriptions of aged persons are useful as a basis for meeting the needs of the elderly but do not of themselves provide insight into the origins of their needs.

The content of the psychology of age has largely derived from cross-sectional studies of persons of different age. Although age is a convenient broad index, it is a dummy variable in the sense that it does not stand for a single process but for many processes that may operate independently. Therefore, it does not explain much.

The psychology of aging is concerned with patterns of changes in individuals as they mature and grow old. An open question is what patterns of change are typical and which are atypical, abnormal, or pathological. Increasingly, the psychology of aging is depending on data from longitudinal studies to gain insights into the patterns and processes of change. Findings suggest that there is a wide range of individual differences in the rate and manner of aging.

The term *gerodynamics* has been discussed together with concepts that relate to the processes of change in living systems. The discussion is aimed at encouraging the development of theory and replacing chronological age as the sole criterion for judging the significance of observed changes for the functioning and well-being of the organism.

## References

Anderson, J. E. (Ed.). (1956). *Proceedings, research conference on the psychological aspects of aging*. Washington, DC: American Psychological Association.

Baltes, P. B. (1987). Theoretical propositions of life-span developmental psychology: On the dynamics between growth and decline. *Developmental Psychology, 23*, 611–626.

Baltes, P. B., Smith, J., & Staudinger, U. M. (1992). Wisdom and successful aging. In T. B. Sonderegger (Ed.), *Nebraska Symposium on Motivation*: Vol. 39. *Psychology and aging* (pp. 123–167). Lincoln: University of Nebraska Press.

Bengtson, V. L., Reedy, M. N., & Gordon, C. (1985). Aging and self-conceptions: Personality processes and social contexts. In J. E. Birren & K. W. Schaie (Eds.), *Handbook of the psychology of aging* (2nd ed., pp. 544–593). New York: Van Nostrand-Reinhold.

Birren, J. E. (1959). Principles of research on aging. In J. E. Birren (Ed.), *Handbook of aging and the individual* (pp. 3–42). Chicago: Chicago University Press.

Birren, J. E. (1960). Behavioral theories of aging. In N. W. Shock (Ed.), *Aging: Some social and biological aspects* (pp. 305–332). Washington, DC: American Association for the Advancement of Science.

Birren, J. E. (1961a). I. A brief history of the psychology of aging. *Gerontologist, 1*, 69–77.

Birren, J. E. (1961b). II. A brief history of the psychology of aging. *Gerontologist, 1*, 127–134.

Birren, J. E. (1964). *The psychology of aging*. Englewood Cliffs, NJ: Prentice-Hall.

Birren, J. E., & Birren, B. A. (1990). The concepts, models and history of the psychology of aging. In J. E. Birren & K. W. Schaie (Eds.), *Handbook of the psychology of aging* (3rd ed., pp. 3–20). San Diego, CA: Academic Press.

Birren, J. E., & Cunningham, W. R. (1985). Research on the psychology of aging: Principles, concepts and theory. In J. E. Birren & K. W. Schaie (Eds.), *Handbook of the psychology of aging* (2nd ed., pp. 3–34). New York: Van Nostrand-Reinhold.

Birren, J. E., & Dieckmann, L. (1991). Concepts and content of quality of life in the later years: An overview. In J. E. Birren, J. E. Lubben, J. C. Rowe, & D. E. Deutchman (Eds.), *The concept and measurement of quality of life in the frail elderly* (pp. 344–360). San Diego, CA: Academic Press.

Birren, J. E., & Fisher, L. M. (1990). The elements of wisdom: An overview and integration. In R. Sternberg (Ed.), *Wisdom: Its nature, origin, and development* (pp. 317–332). Cambridge, England: Cambridge University Press.

Birren, J. E., & Fisher, L. M. (1992). Speed of behavior and aging: Consequences for cognition and survival. In T. B. Sonderegger (Ed.), *Nebraska Symposium on Motivation*: Vol. 39. *Psychology and aging* (pp. 2–37). Lincoln: University of Nebraska Press.

Birren, J. E., & Fisher, L. M. (1993). Speed of behavior as a reflection of health and aging. In J. J. F. Schroots (Ed.), *Aging, health and competence: The next generation of longitudinal research* (pp. 161–182). Amsterdam: Elsevier.

Birren, J. E., & Fisher, L. M. (1995). Aging and speed of behavior: Possible consequences for psychological functioning. *Annual Review of Psychology, 46,* 329–353.

Birren, J. E., Kenyon, G., Ruth, J.-E., Schroots, J. J. F., & Svensson, T. (Eds.). (1995). *Biography and aging: Explorations in adult development.* New York: Springer.

Birren, J. E., & Renner, V. J. (1977). Research on the psychology of aging: Principles and experimentation. In J. E. Birren & K. W. Schaie (Eds.), *Handbook of the psychology of aging* (pp. 3–38). New York: Van Nostrand-Reinhold.

Birren, J. E., & Schroots, J. J. F. (1984). Steps to an ontogenetic psychology. *Academic Psychology Bulletin, 6,* 177–190.

Blumenthal, H. T. (1993). Editorial: The aging-disease dichotomy is alive, but is it well? *Journal of the American Geriatric Society, 41,* 1272–1273.

Botwinick, J. (1973). *Aging and behavior.* New York: Springer.

Brody, J. A., & Schneider, E. L. (1986). Diseases and disorders of aging: A hypothesis. *Journal of Chronic Diseases, 39,* 871–876.

Burnside, I., & Schmidt, M. G. (Eds.). (1994). *Working with older adults.* London: Jones & Bartlett.

Busse, E. W. (1969). Theories of aging. In E. W. Busse & E. Pfeiffer (Eds.), *Behavior and adaptation in late life* (pp. 11–32). Boston: Little, Brown.

Butler, R. N. (1983). An overview of research on aging and the status of gerontology today. *Health and Society; Milbank Memorial Fund Quarterly, 61,* 351–361.

Carroll, J. B. (1993). *Human cognitive abilities: A survey of factor-analytic studies.* New York: Cambridge University Press.

Clayton, V. P., & Birren, J. E. (1980). The development of wisdom across the life span: A reexamination of an ancient topic. In P. B. Baltes & O. G. Brim, Jr. (Eds.), *Life-span development and behavior* (Vol. 3, pp. 103–135). New York: Academic Press.

Cohen, G. D. (1992). The future of mental health and aging. In J. E. Birren, R. B. Sloane, & G. D. Cohen (Eds.), *Handbook of mental health and aging* (pp. 893–914). San Diego, CA: Academic Press.

Collins, L. M., & Horn, J. L. (Eds.). (1991). *Best methods for the analysis of change.* Washington, DC: American Psychological Association.

Costa, P. T., Jr., & McCrae, R. R. (1977–1978). Age differences in personality structure revisited: Studies in validity, stability, and change. *International Journal of Aging and Human Development, 8,* 261–275.

Costa, P. T., Jr., & McCrae, R. R. (1993). Psychological research in the Baltimore Longitudinal Study of Aging. *Zeitschrift für Gerontologie, 26,* 138–141.

Cowdry, E. V. (Ed.). (1939). *Problems of aging.* Baltimore: Williams & Wilkins.

Craik, F. I. M., & Salthouse, T. A. (Eds.). (1992). *Handbook of aging and cognition.* Hillsdale, NJ: Erlbaum.

Dannefer, D. (1988). Differential gerontology and the stratified life course: Conceptual and methodological issues. *Annual Review of Gerontology and Geriatrics, 8,* 3–36.

Estes, C. L., & Binney, E. A. (1989). The biomedicalization of aging: Dangers and dilemmas. *Gerontologist, 29,* 587–596.

Evans, J. G. (1988). Ageing and disease. *Ciba Foundation Symposium, 134,* 38–47.

Field, D. (1991). Continuity and change in personality in old age—Evidence from five longitudinal studies: Introduction to a special issue. *Journal of Gerontology: Psychological Sciences, 46,* P271–P274.

Forbes, W. F., & Hirdes, J. P. (1993). The relationship between aging and disease: Geriatric ideology and myths of senility. *Journal of the American Geriatric Society, 41,* 1267–1271.

Fozard, J. L., Metter, E. J., Brant, L. J., Pearson J. D., & Baker, G. T. (1993). Goals for the next generation of longitudinal studies. In J. J. F. Schroots (Ed.), *Aging, health and competence: The next generation of longitudinal research* (pp. 35–52). Amsterdam: Elsevier.

Gilford, D. M. (Ed.). (1988). *The aging population in the twenty-first century.* Washington, DC: National Academy Press.

Gompertz, S. (1825). On the expressive law of human mortality and a new mode of determining the value of life contingency. *Philosophical Transactions of the Royal Society of London, 115,* 513–585.

Goodwin, J. S. (1991). Geriatric ideology: The myth of the myth of senility. *Journal of the American Geriatric Society, 39,* 627–631.

Gruman, G. J. (1966). *A history of the ideas about the prolongation of life: The evolution of prolongevity hypotheses to 1800.* Philadelphia: American Philosophical Society.

Hagberg, B., Samuelsson, G., Lindberg, B., & Dehlin, O. (1991). Stability and change of personality in old age and its relation to survival. *Journal of Gerontology: Psychological Sciences, 46,* P285–P291.

Hall, G. S. (1922). *Senescence: The second half of life.* New York: Appleton.

Halperin, M., Blackwelder, W. C., & Verter, J. I. (1971). Estimation of the multivariate logistic risk function: A comparison of the discriminant function and maximum likelihood approaches. *Journal of Chronic Diseases, 24,* 125–158.

Heikkinen, E., Era, P., Jokela, J., Jylha, M., Lyyra, A.-L., & Pohjolainen, P. (1993). Socioeconomic and life-style factors as modulators of health and functional capacity with age. In J. J. F. Schroots (Ed.), *Aging, health and competence: The next generation of longitudinal research* (pp. 65–86). Amsterdam: Elsevier.

Horn, J. L. (1989). Models of intelligence. In R. Linn (Ed.), *Intelligence: Measurement,*

theory and public policy (pp. 29–73). Urbana: University of Illinois.

Hubbert, H. (1915). The effect of age on habit formation in the albino rat. *Behavior Monographs, 2* (No. 11).

Hutten, E. H. (1954). The role of models in physics. *British Journal for the Philosophy of Science, 4,* 284–301.

Johansson, B., & Berg, S. (1989). The robustness of the terminal decline phenomenon: Longitudinal data from the Digit-Span memory test. *Journal of Gerontology: Psychological Sciences, 44,* P184–P186.

Jones, H. E. (1959). Intelligence and problem solving. In J. E. Birren (Ed.), *Handbook of aging and the individual* (pp. 700–738). Chicago: University of Chicago Press.

Kenyon, G. M., Birren, J. E., & Schroots, J. J. F. (Eds.). (1991). *Metaphors of aging in science and the humanities.* New York: Springer.

Kleemeier, R. W. (1962). Intellectual changes in the senium. *Proceedings of the Social Statistics Section of the American Statistical Association, 1,* 290–295.

Kogan, N. (1990). Personality and aging. In J. E. Birren & K. W. Schaie (Eds.), *The handbook of the psychology of aging* (3rd ed., pp. 330–346). San Diego, CA: Academic Press.

Labouvie-Vief, G. (1982). Individual time, social time, and intellectual aging. In T. K. Hareven & K. J. Adams (Eds.), *Aging and life course transitions: An interdisciplinary perspective* (pp. 151–182). London: Tavistock.

Leatherdale, W. H. (1974). *The role of analogy, model and metaphor in science.* Amsterdam: North-Holland.

Lehr, U., & Thomae, H. (Eds.). (1987). *Formen seelischen Alterns: Ergebnisse der Bonner Gerontologischen Längsschnittstudie (BOLSA)* [Patterns of psychological aging: Results of the Bonn Longitudinal Study of Aging]. Stuttgart: Ferdinand Enke Verlag.

Lewin, K. (1951). *Field theory in social science.* New York: Harper.

Manton, K. G., Stallard, E., Woodbury, M. A., & Dowd, J. E. (1990). Time-varying covariates in models of human mortality and aging: Multidimensional generalizations of the Gompertz. *Journal of Gerontology, 49,* 169–208.

Martin, L., & de Gruchy, C. (1930). *Salvaging old age.* New York: Macmillan.

McCrae, R. R., & Costa, P. T., Jr. (1987). Validation of the five-factor model of personality across instruments and observers. *Journal of Personality and Social Psychology, 52*, 877–883.

Mellström, D. (1993). A longitudinal and cross-sectional gerontological population study in Gothenburg. In J. J. F. Schroots (Ed.), *Aging, health and competence: The next generation of longitudinal research* (pp. 127–141). Amsterdam: Elsevier.

Miles, W. R. (1933). Age and human ability. *Psychological Review, 40*, 99–123.

Miles, W. R. (1967). Walter R. Miles. In E. G. Boring & G. Lindzey, (Eds.) *A history of psychology in autobiography*. Vol. 5, pp. 221–252. New York: Appleton Century Crofts.

Miller, J. G. (1978). *Living systems*. New York: McGraw-Hill.

Morse, C. K. (1993). Does variability increase with age: An archival study of cognitive measures. *Psychology of Aging, 8*, 156–164.

Nelson, E. A., & Dannefer, D. (1992). Aged heterogeneity: Fact or faction? The fate of diversity in gerontological research. *Gerontologist, 32*, 17–23.

Quetelet, M. A. (1968). *A treatise on man*. New York: Burt Franklin. (Reprinted from *Sur l'homme et le développement de ses facultes*. 1835, Paris: Bachelier (translated into English in 1842).

Riegel, K. F. (1977). History of psychological gerontology. In J. E. Birren & K. W. Schaie (Eds.), *Handbook of the psychology of aging* (pp.70–102). New York: Van Nostrand-Reinhold.

Rowe, J. W. (1985). Interaction of aging and disease. In C. M. Gaitz & T. Samorajski (Eds.), *Aging 2000: Our health care destiny: Vol 1. Biomedical issues* (pp. 247–257). New York: Springer.

Rowe, J. W., & Kahn, R. L. (1987). Human aging: Usual and successful. *Science, 237*, 143–149.

Sacher, G. A. (1980). Theory in gerontology. Part I. *Annual Review of Gerontology and Geriatrics, 1*, 3–25.

Salthouse, T. A. (1988). Initiating the formalization of theories of cognitive aging. *Psychology and Aging, 3*, 3–16.

Salthouse, T. A. (1991). *Theoretical perspectives on cognitive aging*. Hillsdale, NJ: Erlbaum.

Schaie, K. W. (1965). A general model for the study of developmental problems. *Psychological Bulletin, 64*, 92–107.

Schaie, K. W. (Ed.). (1983). *Longitudinal studies of adult psychological development*. New York: Guilford.

Schaie, K. W. (1990). The optimization of cognitive functioning in old age: Predictions based on cohort-sequential and longitudinal data. In P. B. Baltes & M. M. Baltes (Eds.), *Successful aging: Perspectives from the behavioral sciences* (pp. 94–117). Cambridge, England: Cambridge University Press.

Schaie, K. W. (1992). The impact of methodological changes in gerontology. *International Journal of Aging and Human Development, 35*, 19–29.

Schaie, K. W. (1994). The course of adult intellectual development. *American Psychologist, 49*, 304–313.

Schroots, J. J. F. (1991). Metaphors of aging and complexity. In G. M. Kenyon, J. E. Birren, & J. J. F. Schroots (Eds.), *Metaphors of aging in science and the humanities* (pp. 219–243). New York: Springer.

Schroots, J. J. F. (1992). Aging as hypothetical construct. *European Journal of Gerontology, 1*, 457–479.

Schroots, J. J. F. (Ed.). (1993a). *Aging, health and competence: The next generation of longitudinal research*. Amsterdam: Elsevier.

Schroots, J. J. F. (1993b). Health and aging from a behavioral perspective. In J. J. F. Schroots (Ed.), *Aging, health and competence: The next generation of longitudinal research* (pp. 145–159). Amsterdam: Elsevier.

Schroots, J. J. F. (1995a). The fractal structure of lives: Continuity and discontinuity in autobiograhpy. In J. E. Birren, G. M. Kenyon, J.-E. Ruth, J. J. F. Schroots, & T. Svensson (Eds.), *Biography and aging: Explorations in adult development* (pp. 117–130). New York: Springer.

Schroots, J. J. F. (1995b). Gerodynamics: Toward a branching theory of aging. *Canadian Journal on Aging, 14*, 74–81.

Schroots, J. J. F. (1995c). Psychological models of aging. *Canadian Journal on Aging, 14*, 44–66.

Schroots, J. J. F., & Birren, J. E. (1988). The nature of time: Implications for research on aging. *Comprehensive Gerontology C, 2*, 1–29.

Schroots, J. J. F., & Birren, J. E. (1993). Theoretical issues and basic questions in the planning of longitudinal studies of health and aging. In J. J. F. Schroots (Ed.), *Aging, health and competence: The next generation of longitudinal studies* (pp. 4–34). Amsterdam: Elsevier.

Scott, C. (1896). Old age and death. *American Journal of Psychology, 8*, 67–122.

Shock, N. W. (1961). The role of research in solving the problems of the aged. *Gerontologist, 1*, 14–16.

Shock, N. W. (1985). Longitudinal studies of aging in humans. In C. E. Finch & E. L. Schneider (Eds.), *Handbook of the biology of aging* (2nd ed., pp. 721–743). New York: Van Nostrand-Reinhold.

Shock, N. W., Greulich, R. C., Andres, R., Arenberg, D., Costa, P. T., Jr., Lakatta, E. G., & Tobin, J. D. (1984). *Normal human aging: The Baltimore longitudinal study of aging* (NIH Publication No. 84–2450). Washington, DC: U.S. Government Printing Office.

Siegler, I. C. (1987). Terminal drop. In G. L. Maddox (Ed.), *The encyclopedia of aging* (pp. 664–665). New York: Springer.

Siegler, I. C., & Costa, P. T., Jr. (1985). Health behavior relationships. In J. E. Birren & K. W. Schaie (Eds.), *Handbook of the psychology of aging* (2nd ed., pp. 144–166). New York: Van Nostrand-Reinhold.

Siegler, I. C., George, L. K., & Okun, M. A. (1979). A cross-sequential analysis of adult personality. *Developmental Psychology, 15*, 350–351.

Slonaker, J. R. (1907). The normal activity of the white rat at different ages. *Journal of Comparative Neurology and Psychology, 17*, 342–359.

Slonaker, J. R. (1912). The normal activity of the albino rat from birth to natural death. *Journal of Animal Behavior, 2*, 20–42.

Spearman, C. (1904). "General intelligence" objectively determined and measured. *American Journal of Psychology, 8*, 201– 293.

Steen, B., & Djurfeldt, H. (1993). The gerontological and geriatric population studies in Gothenburg, Sweden. *Zeitschrift fuer Gerontologie, 26*, 163–169.

Sternberg, R. J. (1990a). *Metaphors of mind: Conceptions of the nature of intelligence.* Cambridge, England: Cambridge University Press.

Sternberg, R. J. (Ed.). (1990b). *Wisdom: Its nature, origins, and development.* Cambridge, England: Cambridge University Press.

U.S. Public Health Service. (1943). *Mental health in later maturity* (Suppl. 168). Washington, DC: U.S. Government Printing Office.

Welford, A. T. (1951). *Skill and age.* Oxford: Oxford University Press.

Welford, A. T. (1958). *Aging and human skill.* Oxford: Oxford University Press.

Whipple, G. M. (1914). *Manual of mental and physical tests: Part I. Simpler processes.* New York: Warwick & York.

Whipple, G. M. (1915). *Manual of mental and physical tests: Part II. Complex processes.* New York: Warwick & York.

Wohlwill, J. F. (1973). *The study of behavioral development.* New York: Academic Press.

Yates, F. E., & Benton, L. A. (in press). Biological aging: Loss of integration and stability. *Canadian Journal on Aging.*

Yerkes, R. M. (1909). Modifiability of behavior in its relation to the age and sex of the dancing mouse. *Journal of Comparative Neurology and Psychology, 19*, 237–271.

# Two

# Research Design in Studies of Aging and Cognition

Christopher Hertzog

## I. Introduction

The topic of general research design has been covered in previous editions of this *Handbook*, and several other *Handbook* chapters have directly addressed important methodological issues in aging research (e.g., Botwinick, 1977). The present chapter focuses on a limited set of issues involving inferences about aging, age-related changes, and age-related differences in the domain of cognitive psychology. Given both (a) the importance of the area of aging and cognition in the larger field of gerontology, and (b) the fact that the fundamental design and measurement issues in cognitive research generalize to other domains of gerontology, this choice appears justified.

The underlying rationale for this chapter is that there is a gap between, on the one hand, our declarative knowledge and understanding of design and measurement principles, as articulated in the literature on gerontology (and, especially, life span developmental methodology; e.g., Baltes, Reese, & Nesselroade, 1977) and, on the other hand, standard research practice in the area of aging and cognition. Procedures are often modeled after the behavior of other scientists, and the original rationale and caveats concerning the techniques can be forgotten or distorted. Design and measurement choices are often made automatically, as it were, without careful thought about possible limitations and rival interpretations. Most of the concerns discussed here have been articulated elsewhere. Nevertheless, the disparity between our knowledge and our behavior suggests some benefit from revisiting the issues.

## II. Design Validity in Research on Adult Cognition

### A. The Dominant Paradigm: Cognitive Aging

Design presupposes theory; one cannot make decisions about who, what, how, when, and why to measure without both (a) a metatheoretical perspective—with its derivative assumptions, paradigmatic lines of reasoning, and implicit values regarding the feasibility, viability, and importance of research questions, and (b) a specific theoretical framework that specifies empirical predictions of substantive hypotheses about aging and psychological phenomena (see Dixon & Hertzog, in press).

Research in the area of adult cognition requires a set of decisions regarding (a) the nature of aging and age effects, given the questions of interest; (b) the best method of operationally defining age-related phenomena of interest; (c) conceptualization of developmental changes (or stability) in cognitive structures and mechanisms; and (d) methods of measuring the cognitive constructs of interest. Many researchers investigating cognition and aging are trained primarily as experimental psychologists. As such, decisions about methods of measuring cognitive constructs benefit directly from—and in that sense are derivative from—the logic of experimental design, current theories, and experimental tasks in the general cognitive literature (Birren, 1970; Salthouse, 1991). The benefits of this training include greater sophistication of methods for measuring cognitive processes in gerontological research conducted in recent years, compared to the discipline's formative period.

One of the potential costs, however, is an implicit assumption that the principles of design and inference embodied in the experimental paradigm (Cronbach, 1957) generalize to the dimension of aging and age-related variation. Many scientists studying aging and cognition implicitly assume that treating chronological age as a between-subjects factor is tantamount to studying development—that the analysis of variance (ANOVA) design logic that appears to apply so cleanly and cogently to experimentally manipulated phenomena is inherently sufficient for the study of aging. To the contrary, aging is a characteristic of persons that cannot be experimentally manipulated. Hence it can be measured only as a characteristic of the persons who have been sampled. Research into adult cognitive development *must* merge the two scientific disciplines identified by Cronbach (1957)—the experimental and the differential. It must incorporate to a degree the logic and methods associated with studying naturally occurring individual differences. Implementation of the standard logic and practice of the experimental method in aging research, by itself, *does not necessarily lead to valid scientific inferences regarding cognitive development*. Much of this chapter will be devoted to discussing the methodological implications of a differential perspective on gerontological research.

The term *cognitive aging* has emerged as a common label for this area of specialization in gerontology. The implicit assumptions regarding operational definitions of aging prevalent in the cognitive aging research paradigm appear to be as follows: (a) aging is a primary, biological process that is fundamentally ontogenetic in origin; (b) aging phenomena are universal, even though they may differ in time of onset and rate of change; (c) chronological age is a useful proxy for indexing aging effects; (d) cross-sectional age differences, perhaps indexed by the correlation of chronological age with measures of cognition, are the best available measure of the effects of aging on cognition; and (e) research questions in aging and cognition should focus on identifying the conditions under which these correlations vary as a function of cognitive task, vary as a function of type of individual, and covary with age correlations in potential explanatory variables. Each of these assumptions can be challenged (e.g., Baltes & Willis, 1977; Labouvie-Vief, 1985; Rybash, Hoyer, & Roodin, 1986). Nevertheless, research in this domain often seems to adopt the cognitive aging paradigm without further critical evaluation of its standard practices.

## B. The Primacy and Recency of Cross-Sectional Designs

### 1. Pragmatics and Dogmatics

Despite the criticism of cross-sectional designs that characterized the life span development literature on methodology of the 1970s, a very high percentage of published research on age and cognition is conducted with some kind of cross-sectional design. The modal implementation is an *extreme-age-groups design*, in which a group of young adults (often college students) is contrasted with a group of older volunteers (often an accidental or purposive sample obtained through recruitment at senior centers or churches, or obtained through advertisements in newspapers or newsletters).

What accounts for the widespread use of this method, given its several limitations (see Schaie, 1977)? After all, one sees a diminishing frequency in the current literature of caveats in published *Discussion* sections regarding the distinction between age differences and age changes, the possible confound of cohort differences, and the problems of inferring aging effects from cross-sectional age differences. One can cite the vigorous counterattack by experimental gerontologists (e.g., Arenberg & Robertson-Tchabo, 1977; Botwinick, 1977; Kausler, 1982) against advocacy of longitudinal and sequential methods. These critics disputed the superiority of sequential designs and argued that cohort effects in cognition were either implausible or that the differences in results regarding age-related effects between the alternative methods were minor. Certainly it does appear to be true that cohort differences are less likely for certain kinds of cognitive tasks and psychometric tests (Schaie, 1994); nevertheless, it seems hazardous to assume that any measure of cognition is, ipso facto, immune to the problem of possible cohort effects.

In my view the principal explanation is that pragmatics overcame all other considerations. The chief advantage of the cross-sectional method is its efficiency (in terms of time), and the extreme-age-groups design is the sine qua non of efficiency. Indeed, given that cognitive psychology is a discipline in rapid flux in theory and measurement, and that much research on aging and cognition is derivative from that primary literature, there are major advantages of quickly assessing age differences in new tasks and conceptual domains.

One can argue that the best way for research on aging and cognition to proceed is through a sequence of studies: (a) begin with extreme-age-groups studies to establish possible age-related differences; (b) extend to full cross-sectional studies across the adult life span, first, to estimate full adult life span trajectories of age differences, and second, to establish effects with a better defined population and sampling frame; and (c) extend further to longitudinal/sequential designs to examine average age changes and, more importantly, individual differences in cognitive change that could be predicted by other variables. From a purely pragmatic point of view, the benefits of an initial, rapid production of experiments with differing design features, emphasizing different experimental manipulations, outweigh the risk of erroneous inferences due to cohort differences or other confounded variables. Nevertheless, one could also argue that these potential confounds needed to be addressed by more painstaking and time-consuming methods before more complete and subtle inferences regarding the course and extent of age-related effects could be fully justified.

## 2. *The Achilles Heel: Selection Effects*

Perhaps the largest single design problem in gerontological research is the extent to which the internal validity threat of selection represents a rival explanation for observed group differences (Nesselroade, 1988; Nesselroade & Labouvie, 1985). Given that aging is, by definition, an intraorganismic phenomenon, use of between-person comparisons to estimate average age effects requires the assumption that the persons being compared are equivalent on all aspects other than chronological age per se. Potential pitfalls include (a) mortality and morbidity effects, which affect population composition and sampling frame composition, respectively (e.g., Baltes et al., 1977); (b) creation of nonequivalent sampling frames for different age groups (e.g., comparison of young university students to old nursing home residents); and (c) differential sampling techniques across different age levels. Selection effects can create or mask cross-sectional age differences (and can create or mask cohort effects in sequential designs).

Psychologists interested in aging and cognition would profit from carefully thinking through the issues associated with population composition and sampling, especially regarding primary aging versus normative and nonnormative age-related influences (see, e.g., Baltes & Willis, 1977; Salthouse, 1991). Are psychologists interested in chronological age correlations, averaging over all possible age-related sources (as seemed to be implied by Horn and Hofer, 1992, when they argued that one should expect age effects because of cumulative impacts of a number of factors, including lifelong practices of alcohol consumption and other sources of trauma to the central nervous system)? Should samples of older adults include individuals with Alzheimer's disease, proportional to representation in the population? Probably not, if the average age curves are intended to reflect average developmental change. Are psychologists trying to separate effects of age-graded phenomena that may shift—due to socioculturally determined patterns of behavior and advances in medical progress—from ontogenetic change? Ideally, one would build a case for inclusion and exclusion criteria in any particular study based on the specific question of interest, as well as on a specific conceptualization of the nature of the age-related phenomena under study. Unthinking use of chronological age comparisons without attending to such issues creates a gerontological science of neither fish nor fowl.

Cognitive researchers have recognized issues of subject selection effects for some time (e.g., Camp, West, & Poon, 1989). Nevertheless, comparisons of university students with heterogeneous samples of older adults is a fairly common practice, owing no doubt to easy access to university student comparison groups by university professors. Clearly, obtained age differences could reflect, in whole or in part, selection artifacts.

Some curious practices have arisen as an attempt to justify comparisons of young and old samples in such extreme-age-group designs. For example, one typically observes cursory description of young and old samples in terms of variables like vocabulary, self-reported health, and education. Broad representativeness of one's age group is implicitly substituted for equivalence with respect to all phenomena other than aging. The choice of variables for comparison seems largely grounded in modeling the behavior of others, and the implicit claim that samples are comparable if they have similar levels of self-reported health, education, and so forth is rarely stated. This is probably a good idea, for it is by no means clear that comparability—let alone equivalence—is established by statistical tests of age differences on such measures. For instance, it is usually the case that older samples are superior to younger samples on measures of verbal ability. Obtaining a significant mean age difference, favoring older adults, shows at a crude level that the sample's attributes conform to expectations. It does not establish that the two samples are either representative of their respective birth cohorts or equivalent with respect to all other factors other than chronological age. If establishing representativeness is the goal, one should demonstrate it on background variables that are relevant for the particular construct under study, and one should establish equivalence with respect to norm-referenced evaluation of the subpopulations of interest (see Salthouse, Kausler, & Saults, 1988).

Such comparisons may not even be substantively meaningful. Consider statistical tests of differences in mean years of education in studies comparing university students with older samples. Discovering that one cannot reject the null hypothesis of group differences in mean years of education is virtually irrelevant to the issue of selection effects! If one's sample of college students has a mean of 13 years of education, it implies one has, on average, sampled sophomores. After the cohort of students graduates, this same sample will probably have a mean of 15.7 years of education (and a standard deviation of 0.3 years). On the other hand, a mean of 13 years of education in the older sample implies a mixture of levels of final educational attainment, and its usually larger standard deviation suggests greater diversity in final educational attainment. Although this pattern of attainment may be representative of the older population, it is still problematic for establishing sample equivalence. Mean age differences in cognitive task performance could be predominantly influenced by the lower quartile of older adults, which will include at least some individuals who are not high school graduates.

The belief in the need for a representative sample may actually be part of the problem. Provided that the inference one is interested in concerns the effects of aging, then population representativeness per se is not necessarily the most desirable characteristic of the sample. One can argue that the goal of obtaining representative samples of population birth cohorts (while highly desirable, in general) actually *detracts* from the internal validity of extreme-age-group designs by increasing the probability of unwanted selection effects. This argument seems strange to social scientists who are accustomed to addressing research questions about population composition, incidence and prevalence rates, and the like. Given their typical research questions, obtaining probability samples is absolutely crucial for valid inferences.

One can make the case that psychologists who wish to use extreme-age-group designs are asking a fundamentally different question: How does the aging process influence cognition? This question is not easily addressed by comparing representative samples of the current population, in part because of age-graded and cohort-specific influences on population composition. To address the aging-as-process question with cross-sectional designs, one should follow the model of structured observation as instantiated in principles of quasi-experimental design (Cook & Campbell, 1979). In this approach representativeness is primarily treated as a problem of generalization (external validity). Emphasis is placed on obtaining maximally comparable (perhaps homogeneous) subgroups that may not be fully representative of the entire population. One does not seek to represent the entire population with the age comparison. Instead one attempts to artificially construct a between-persons comparison that is an analog to within-person aging. Lachman, Lachman, and Taylor (1982) discussed the rationale and benefits of this approach, arguing for "occupational matching" and comparing samples of young and old educators.

Weaning researchers from the use of young college student comparison groups might be desirable. Use of an early-to-mid-twenties comparison sample might be preferable, but the pragmatic difficulties of obtaining such samples would introduce new selection effects, and will in any case probably continue to inhibit this practice. Hence the best design solution is probably to compare students with older university alumni.

Admittedly, this approach has several problems, including confounds of current educational status, quality of education at host institution, and so on. To the extent that the cognitive construct is knowledge- or information-saturated, and acculturation may strongly influence performance (e.g., comprehension of expository texts on current foreign affairs), then one should be aware that controlling for educational attainment does not control for subsequent effects of experience and acculturation. On the other hand, even if the cognitive construct under study is a purportedly "basic" mechanism, one cannot routinely ignore embedded educational differences between age groups. Educational attainment is affected by fluid intelligence, which arguably is related to the efficiency of a number of basic information-processing mechanisms (e.g., Marr & Sternberg, 1987). Age differences in educational levels of a sample could result in group differences in measures of basic cognitive mechanisms. Thus comparing homogeneous subgroups of highly educated adults, although not providing perfect control for such factors, would probably be superior to today's common research practices.

The counterargument that older alumni are not representative of their birth cohort is not troubling from a quasi-experimental perspective. Such a sampling process would work against finding age differences favoring young adults, so tests of age-decrement hypotheses, at least, load the dice against the hypothesis by forming such groups. This approach must acknowledge that age effects found in one subgroup in the population may not generalize to other subgroups (the external validity issue). Ultimately the field as a whole requires studies characterizing age differences across the entire population and attacking the problem of differential mortality, population composition effects, and the like. Such questions can and should be the topic of subsequent, more elaborate cross-sectional and longitudinal studies.

## C. Aging and Individual Differences in Cognition

### 1. Individual Differences in Cognitive Change

One important focus of research on aging and cognition involves measuring and explaining individual differences in pat-

terns, onset, and magnitude of age-related changes. Repeated observations on the same persons over time (as in, but not restricted to, longitudinal panel designs) generate optimal data for this purpose. Such data are required to provide direct estimates of change at the level of specific individuals (Baltes et al., 1977). Methods of measuring change have progressed rapidly over the last decade (see Collins, Ch. 3, this volume), and intraindividual research designs and methods hold great promise for research on aging and cognition (Hertzog & Dixon, in press).

Results from longitudinal panel studies of aging and psychometric intelligence indicate a high degree of stability of individual differences across time, even in the presence of age-related changes in mean levels of intellectual performance (e.g., Hertzog & Schaie, 1988). Such results could be construed as indicating that aging is accompanied by minimal individual differences in patterns of cognitive change (see Salthouse, 1991). The issue is important, because high stability, coupled with little systematic covariation in whatever changes were found, would represent patterns of age-related changes consistent with an ontogenetic view of cognitive aging. However, (a) the magnitude of stability is not perfect, indicating at least some individual differences in change; (b) such patterns may be specific to certain kinds of cognitive variables (e.g., speeded psychometric tests like the Primary Mental Abilities test used by Schaie, 1994); and (c) longitudinal panel studies may overestimate stability unless special efforts are made to measure individuals who might otherwise be lost through attrition due to substantial late-life decline. Thus, although the literature supports a view of adult cognitive development as displaying relative continuity and stability, future studies of individual differences in cognitive change may identify new and important patterns of cognitive change and variables associated with them.

One advantage of longitudinal designs is

that aging effects need not be indexed by chronological age per se. If one presumes that chronological age is an imperfect indicator of biological, psychological, and social aging processes, then it stands to reason that shared cognitive change due to aging will only partially covary with chronological age. Under these circumstances, effects that would otherwise be masked by stronger sources of between-persons differences—including some that would covary with chronological age for reasons having little to do with aging, per se— would have an opportunity to be observed and measured. Indeed, longitudinal studies have in some cases identified intriguing patterns of cognitive change and predictors of change that are not fully consistent with cross-sectional results (Hultsch, Hertzog, Dixon, & Small, 1995; Schaie, 1994).

## 2. Partitioning Age-Related Variance

Work by Horn, Donaldson, and Engström (1981), Salthouse (1991, 1992), and others has sought to examine relationships of measures of psychometric intelligence with chronological age and other cognitive variables (e.g., working memory, secondary memory, processing speed). The goal of such analyses is to characterize age differences for multiple cognitive tasks, and to determine the degree to which age differences in complex task performance are shared with or independent from variance in information-processing abilities and skills. Such studies use multiple regression or related techniques to evaluate these questions.

What are the general features of cross-sectional designs appropriate to address such questions? Such designs should be characterized by (a) sufficiently large sample size to permit statistically powerful tests of partial independence (i.e., significant increments to $R^2$); (b) use of multiple measures to reduce contamination of reliability and validity by systematic and random measurement errors; and (c) ap-

propriate sampling procedures to minimize the kinds of selection confounds referred to earlier (Section II.B.2; see Salthouse, 1991, 1992, for an extended discussion). Attention to the first point may, given limited resources, force a choice between (a) a wide age range with large sample size, or (b) a conceptually motivated restriction of age range to ensure adequate replications at each age level.

The basic logic of the statistical approach can be understood in terms of mediational hypotheses using the logic of structural equation models (Kliegl & Mayr, 1992; Salthouse, 1992). Age is conceptualized as influencing basic resource measures, which then in turn influence more complex task performance. If the basic resources fully and completely mediate the effects of aging on more complex task performance, then one would find no salient path from age to the complex abilities independent of the mediated influences. That is, the hypothesis of complete mediation would imply zero partial covariance of age and complex skills, controlling for resources such as working memory and perceptual speed. On the other hand, if aging influences processes other than working memory and perceptual speed, then there should be a residual, direct effect of age on complex performance even when the indirect route of influence mediated by the resource variables is taken into account.

Tests of the null hypothesis of full mediation (zero partial covariance of age and complex tasks) have most often been rejected in empirical studies, although the proportion of variance uniquely attributable to age, controlling for other variables, is usually reduced rather substantially. Commonality analysis can be used to estimate the proportion of shared prediction with chronological age (e.g., Hertzog, 1989). Salthouse (1994b) has recently proposed a variant on this method, a "quasi-partial correlation," as a method of indexing the shared variance of prediction by age and resource variables.

There are several limitations of using commonality analysis and related techniques, some of which have not been either explicitly acknowledged or fully delineated in the primary literature. First, violation of the implicit assumption of linear chronological age effects may bias estimates of unique and shared age-related variance. This hypothesis should be evaluated with polynomial regression techniques, because curvature in the age function, with steeper decline late in life, has been demonstrated in some studies (e.g., Hertzog, 1989; Hultsch et al., 1995). If significant curvature is detected, then the commonality analysis should examine linear *and* nonlinear components of age-related variance.

Second, the logic assumes additive linear effects, as opposed to more complicated interaction effects (moderated regression). Resource × Age interaction effects would invalidate the logic used to partition age-related variance, and one should instead proceed to characterize and decompose the interaction (Aiken & West, 1991). Mc-Clelland and Judd (1993) recently demonstrated that it is difficult to detect continuous variable interactions via moderated regression unless the sample has sufficient representation of cases whose joint observations are extreme in the space of the independent variable. Accepting the null hypothesis of no interaction is ill advised unless either sample size is large or unusual cases have been oversampled.

Third, the logic of partitioning variance using multiple regression techniques assumes no measurement error, and does not necessarily provide unbiased population estimates of independent components of age-related variance. The best way to avoid this problem is the use of structural equation models to estimate the regression relationships while correcting for measurement error (Kliegl & Mayr, 1992; Lindenberger, Mayr, & Kliegl, 1993).

However, the problems associated with application of statistical procedures per se may not be the most important issues associated with this approach. By far the most important issue is the theoretical assumption that the resource measures are cognitive primitives that can be treated as basic building blocks for more complex cognitive operations. Multiple regression techniques can reveal whether age-related variance in a sample is shared by different variables, but it is the cognitive theory alone that stipulates how the patterns of shared variance should be interpreted. For example, recent work by Lindenberger and Baltes (1994), showing a high degree of shared prediction by age and sensory functioning for intelligence test performance in an old-old sample, suggests that such outcomes may reflect aging as a common cause of both resource and cognitive tasks, as opposed to resource-as-processing-mediator. From a design perspective, more complicated cross-sectional designs that add attempts to measure directly the hypothesized mediating processes (e.g., Salthouse, 1994a) will enable more compelling tests of the resource mediation hypothesis.

## 3. The Need for Moderation

Interaction effects ought not to be seen merely as nuisance factors that complicate interpretations of linear models and commonality analyses. Important research questions involving both (a) qualitative age differences in cognition and (b) individual differences in age-related change can be indirectly assessed through cross-sectional methods (Hertzog, 1985).

For example, Rogers, Fisk, and Hertzog (1994) used structural equations models to test hypotheses about changes in relationships of intellectual abilities to reaction time (RT) in a visual search task as a function of extensive practice. Previous work had suggested age differences in the development of an automatic attention response in consistently mapped (CM) visual search task conditions. Younger adults show greater disruption of mean visual search RT when they are transferred from the training conditions to a reversal condition (trained targets become distractors; trained distractors become targets).

Rogers et al. (1994) added new evidence for qualitative age differences in acquisition of automaticity in skilled visual search by demonstrating age differences in relationships of individual differences in cognitive abilities to transfer condition RTs. The relevant models are shown in Figure 1. For both age groups, two different types of speeded abilities—semantic memory access speed and perceptual speed—predicted early (untrained) CM performance, and perceptual speed predicted late CM performance (and hence, change in CM RT as a function of practice). However, there were major age differences in the patterns of prediction of transfer performance, both for the reversal condition and a new CM condition (in which stimuli used in varied mapping training were used in new CM visual search trials during transfer). Older adults' transfer performance was highly related to individual differences in late CM (trained RT prior to transfer). In contrast, younger adults' performance was best predicted by the two ability factors that predicted initial (untrained) performance.

A model forcing age group equivalence in the regression of transfer RT on the ability measures was explicitly tested and rejected by Rogers et al. (1994). The structural equation models strongly suggest qualitative differences in the underlying learning in CM visual search between the two age groups. Individual differences in older adults' transfer performance was, in essence, a continuation and preservation of individual differences produced by training, whereas transfer performance in the younger adults reinstated prediction relationships from the two speeded abilities that had been observed before development of automaticity.

## D. Design Implications of a Learning Perspective

The study just described is part of a larger research effort, currently in progress, designed to examine aging and individual differences in learning and skill acquisition (Rogers et al., 1994; see also Fisk, Cooper, Hertzog, Anderson-Garlach, & Lee, 1995). Results from these studies suggest the importance of careful consideration of a major design issue in aging research, namely, the nature and amount of practice and instruction provided to participants before collecting data on the experimental task of interest.

There are perhaps two chief models for subjects in experimental tasks: the naive observer versus the expert observer. The first model is most likely to be invoked in studies of reasoning and learning skills. For example, in order to obtain valid estimates of inductive reasoning, psychometricians have long argued that too many practice trials risk invalidating test performance by "training the test" (e.g., Marr & Sternberg, 1987). This logic justifies the use of brief, standardized instructions for group administration of psychometric tests that include only a few example problems. The second model, that of the trained or expert observer, derives originally from psychophysical research (e.g., Swets & Pickett, 1982). The underlying rationale is that extensive training of an observer is required to reduce influences of unwanted, irrelevant sources of variability in judgments. The first model risks including such sources because of the assumption that task experience qualitatively alters the nature of the underlying cognitive processes under study. The second model assumes that the processes of interest endure despite practice and become a more salient influence on task performance.

The study by Fisk et al. (1995) of practice on memory search tasks provides illustrations of both kinds of effects. In the CM

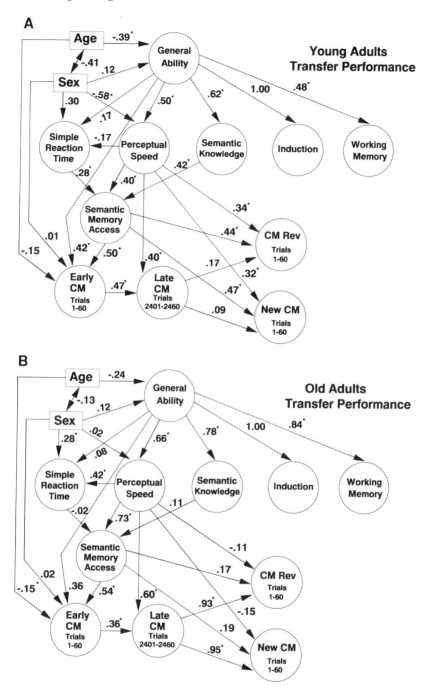

**Figure 1** Ability-transfer structural equation models for young adults (A) and old adults (B) from Rogers, Fisk, and Hertzog (1994). CM, consistent mapping; CM Rev, CM reversal at transfer. Asterisks denote regression coefficients that were significantly greater than zero. (Reproduced with permission from the American Psychological Association.)

conditions of their study, younger adults' memory search slopes (reflecting increasing decision times as a function of increases in the size of the memory set) rapidly diminish to zero (see Figure 2). Older adults' slopes also diminish to zero, although they require more practice to do so. Likewise, correlations of CM slopes with other abilities vary randomly around zero—no doubt because automaticity in memory search has eliminated individual differences in speed of memory search as function of increasing memory set size (see Figure 2). A very different pattern of results obtains for variably mapped (VM) memory search. Here, memory search slopes do not change appreciably as a function of extended practice, and practice does not eliminate correlations of VM memory search slopes with other abilities. Practice does result in some changes in overall RT (and in memory search intercepts), and it appears that the effects of

practice are larger for older adults than for younger adults.

The results of these studies suggest that in standard experimental tasks with varied mapping procedures (where stimulus–response mappings vary randomly from trial to trial), extended practice prior to experimental assessment can actually be beneficial. It appears to reduce unwanted variability early in practice and reduces the likelihood of producing artifactual age differences due to general task learning that is typically not the focus of the investigation (see Fisk et al., 1995). Such results are potentially important for procedures that require large numbers of experimental trials to generate estimates (such as new psychophysical procedures developed by Kliegl and colleagues; see Kliegl, 1995). Practice effects will occur for such tasks, but may act essentially as random error given that experimental conditions are randomly ordered and replicated. On

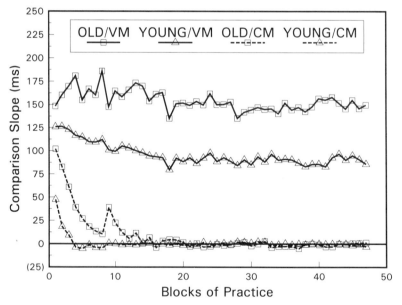

**Figure 2** Age-related patterns of improvement in mean reaction time slopes in milliseconds across memory set size as a function of practice on a semantic category memory search task. The graphs show slopes for young and old adults on consistently mapped (CM) or variably mapped (VM) stimulus conditions. (Data reported in Fisk et al., 1995.)

the other hand, the kind of rapid learning that occurs with the CM task would be highly problematic for procedures that rely on the expert observer paradigm, such as the Kliegl (1995) method or more traditional speed–accuracy designs (e.g., Hertzog, Vernon, & Rypma, 1993). The choice of an experimental method must attend to the type and extent of learning that can be expected as a function of practice.

What kind of task is a psychometric test of reasoning, and how should one view the issue of practice effects on these tasks? Older adults' reasoning test scores improve substantially as a function of simple test practice (e.g., Baltes, Sowarka, & Kliegl, 1989). Should extensive prior instruction and coaching be used to ensure that older adults fully understand task requirements before proceeding with group testing? Failure to ensure that older participants understand the task instructions could inflate estimates of mean age differences. A possibly more serious problem is that older subjects with low ability (perhaps due to aging) will be differentially less likely to understand task instructions under brief, standardized instructions. Such an outcome could create misleading performance-specific individual differences in older adults' test scores, and could produce artifactual increases in the relationship of a general intelligence factor to performance on standardized primary ability tests. This effect could, in principle, inflate the estimated contribution of general resources to age differences in complex task performance.

Careful consideration of the nature of the learning that is occurring in testing situations—on a task-by-task basis—might lead to fundamental changes in how older adults are tested. The common assumption that the naive subjects model ought to apply to all standardized testing may have unintended negative consequences for inferences regarding observed age differences.

## III. Conclusions

Experimental research in the area of aging and cognition is currently characterized by an unprecedented increase in the technological and methodological quality of those aspects of the research that are associated with experimental methods for assessing cognition. This chapter has argued that this area suffers in comparison in adequacy of methods for protecting the validity of inferences about the developmental research questions that are at the heart of gerontological research. Long-standing issues in the area of developmental research design such as measurement equivalence across age levels or methods of selection of adults in cross-sectional samples are generally recognized as potential problems, but are often ignored in practice. This chapter advocates a careful rethinking of some common practices, attempts to identify pragmatic constraints that have a legitimate role in shaping research design decisions, and provides in some cases discussion and recommendations regarding alternative procedures. There are no easy solutions to these difficult problems. A first step is a more complete awareness of the theoretical and methodological basis for the problem and the potential solutions. Hopefully, this chapter will serve to refocus attention of gerontologists to the relevant issues.

References

Aiken, L. S., & West, S. G. (1991). *Multiple regression: Testing and interpreting interactions*. Newbury Park, CA: Sage.
Arenberg, D., & Robertson-Tchabo, E. A. (1977). Learning and aging. In J. E. Birren & K. W. Schaie (Eds.), *Handbook of the psychology of aging* (pp. 421–449). New York: Van Nostrand-Reinhold.
Baltes, P. B., Reese, H. W., & Nesselroade, J. R. (1977). *Life-span developmental methodology: Introduction to research methods*. Monterey, CA: Brooks-Cole.

Baltes, P. B., Sowarka, D., & Kliegl, R. (1989). Cognitive training research on fluid intelligence in old age: What can older adults achieve by themselves? *Psychology and Aging, 4,* 217–221.

Baltes, P. B., & Willis, S. L. (1977). Toward psychological theories of aging and development. In J. E. Birren & K. W. Schaie (Eds.), *Handbook of the psychology of aging* (pp. 128–154). New York: Van Nostrand-Reinhold.

Birren, J. E. (1970). Toward an experimental psychology of aging. *American Psychologist, 25,* 124–135.

Botwinick, J. (1977). Intellectual abilities. In J. E. Birren & K. W. Schaie (Eds.), *Handbook of the psychology of aging* (pp. 580–605). New York: Van Nostrand-Reinhold.

Camp, C. J., West, R. L., & Poon, L. W. (1989). Recruitment practices for psychological research in gerontology. In M. P. Lawton & A. R. Herzog (Eds.), *Special research methods for gerontology* (pp. 163–189). Amityville, NY: Baywood.

Cook, T. D., & Campbell, D. T. (1979). *Quasi-experimentation: Design and analysis issues for field settings.* Chicago: Rand-McNally.

Cronbach, L. J. (1957). The two disciplines of scientific psychology. *American Psychologist, 12,* 671–684.

Dixon, R. A., & Hertzog, C. (in press). Theoretical issues in the study of aging and cognition. In F. Blanchard-Fields & T. M. Hess (Eds.), *Perspectives on cognitive changes in adulthood and aging.* New York: McGraw-Hill.

Fisk, A. D., Cooper, B. P., Hertzog, C., Anderson-Garlach, M. M., & Lee, M. D. (1995). Understanding performance and learning in consistent memory search: An age-related perspective. *Psychology and Aging, 10,* 255–268.

Hertzog, C. (1985). An individual differences perspective: Implications for cognitive research in gerontology. *Research on Aging, 7,* 7–45.

Hertzog, C. (1989). The influence of cognitive slowing on age differences in intelligence. *Developmental Psychology, 25,* 636–651.

Hertzog, C., & Dixon, R. A. (in press). Methodological issues in research on cognition and aging. In F. Blanchard-Fields & T. M. Hess (Eds.), *Perspectives on cognitive changes in adulthood and aging.* New York: McGraw-Hill.

Hertzog, C., & Schaie, K. W. (1988). Stability and change in adult intelligence: 2. Simultaneous analysis of longitudinal means and covariance structures. *Psychology and Aging, 3,* 122–130.

Hertzog, C., Vernon, M. C., & Rypma, B. (1993). Age differences in mental rotation task performance: The influence of speed/accuracy tradeoffs. *Journal of Gerontology: Psychological Sciences, 48,* P150–P156.

Horn, J. L., Donaldson, G., & Engström, R. (1981). Apprehension, memory, and fluid intelligence decline in adulthood. *Research on Aging, 3,* 33–84.

Horn, J. L., & Hofer, S. M. (1992). Major abilities and development during the adult period. In R. J. Sternberg & C. A. Berg (Eds.), *Intellectual development* (pp. 44–99). New York: Cambridge University Press.

Hultsch, D. F., Hertzog, C., Dixon, R. A., & Small, B. J. (1995). *Individual differences in aging and memory: The Victoria Longitudinal Study.* Manuscript in preparation.

Kausler, D. H. (1982). *Experimental psychology and human aging.* New York: Wiley.

Kliegl, R. (1995). From presentation time to processing time: A psychophysics approach to episodic memory. In W. Schneider & F. E. Weinert (Eds.), *Memory performance and competencies: Issues in growth and development* (pp. 89–110). Hillsdale, NJ: Erlbaum.

Kliegl, R., & Mayr, U. (1992). Commentary on Salthouse (1992), "Shifting levels of analysis in the investigation of cognitive aging." *Human Development, 35,* 343–349.

Labouvie-Vief, G. (1985). Intelligence and cognition. In J. E. Birren & K. W. Schaie (Eds.), *Handbook of the psychology of aging* (2nd ed., pp. 500–530). New York: Van Nostrand-Reinhold.

Lachman, R., Lachman, J. L., & Taylor, D. W. (1982). Reallocation of mental resources over the productive lifespan: Assumptions and task analyses. In F. I. M. Craik & S. Trehub (Eds.), *Aging and cognitive processes* (pp. 279–308). New York: Plenum.

Lindenberger, U., & Baltes, P. B. (1994). Sensory functioning and intelligence in old age: A strong connection. *Psychology and Aging, 9,* 339–355.

Lindenberger, U., Mayr, U., & Kliegl, R. (1993). Speed and intelligence in old age. *Psychology and Aging, 8,* 207– 220.

Marr, D. B., & Sternberg, R. J. (1987). The role of mental speed in intelligence: A triarchic perspective. In P. A. Vernon (Ed.), *Speed of information processing and intelligence* (pp. 271–294). Norwood, NJ: Ablex.

McClelland, G. H., & Judd, C. M. (1993). Statistical difficulties of detecting interactions and moderator effects. *Psychological Bulletin, 114,* 376–390.

Nesselroade, J. R. (1988). Sampling and generalizability: Adult development and aging research issues examined with the general methodological framework of selection. In K. W. Schaie, R. T. Campbell, W. Meredith, & S. C. Rawlings (Eds.), *Methodological issues in aging research* (pp. 13–42). New York: Springer.

Nesselroade, J. R., & Labouvie, E. W. (1985). Experimental design in research on aging. In J. E. Birren & K. W. Schaie (Eds.), *Handbook of the psychology of aging* (2nd ed., pp. 35–60). New York: Van Nostrand-Reinhold.

Rogers, W. A., Fisk, A. D., & Hertzog, C. (1994). Do ability-performance relationships differentiate age and practice effects in visual search? *Journal of Experimental Psychology: Learning, Memory, and Cognition, 20,* 710–738.

Rybash, J. M., Hoyer, W. J., & Roodin, P. A. (1986). *Adult cognition and aging.* New York: Pergamon.

Salthouse, T. A. (1991). *Theoretical perspectives on cognitive aging.* Hillsdale, NJ: Erlbaum.

Salthouse, T. A. (1992). *Mechanisms of age-cognition relations in adulthood.* Hillsdale, NJ: Erlbaum.

Salthouse, T. A. (1994a). Aging associations: Influence of speed on adult age differences in associative learning. *Journal of Experimental Psychology: Learning, Memory, and Cognition, 20,* 1486–1503.

Salthouse, T. A. (1994b). How many causes are there of aging-related decrements in cognitive functioning? *Developmental Review, 14,* 413–437.

Salthouse, T. A., Kausler, D., & Saults, J. S. (1988). Investigation of student status, background variables, and feasibility of standard tasks in cognitive aging research. *Psychology and Aging, 3,* 29–37.

Schaie, K. W. (1977). Quasi-experimental research designs in the psychology of aging. In J. E. Birren & K. W. Schaie (Eds.), *Handbook of the psychology of aging* (pp. 39–58). New York: Van Nostrand-Reinhold.

Schaie, K. W. (1994). The course of adult intellectual development. *American Psychologist, 49,* 304–313.

Swets, J. A., & Pickett, R. M. (1982). *Evaluation of diagnostic systems: Methods from signal detection theory.* New York: Academic Press.

# Three

# Measurement of Change in Research on Aging: Old and New Issues from an Individual Growth Perspective

Linda M. Collins

## I. Introduction

The change that accompanies the aging process is a fascinating topic for scientific inquiry. Many different kinds of questions can be asked. One may be interested simply in establishing the amount of change that has occurred. One may be interested in the determinants of change, that is, what causes change to happen, what causes more change in some people than in others, and whether an intervention can slow or stop change. One may be interested in the consequences of change, for example the behavioral effects of age-related physiological changes. One may be interested in the nature of change—is it continuous? Linear? Stage sequential? Change must be measured well in order to answer any such questions. This chapter focuses on exactly what is meant by "measured well" in the context of change, and on some ideas about how to achieve good measurement and representation of change in longitudinal research.

In this chapter, I take a particular point of view on the measurement of change that will color everything that is said here. Change over time produces differences within an individual across multiple observations taking place at different occasions. Heavily emphasized in this chapter is the idea that this change within the individual (i.e., intraindividual change) is the appropriate unit of analysis for the study of change, and that precise and valid measurement of intraindividual change is a logical prerequisite to assessment of *inter*individual differences in growth and decline. This runs counter to the philosophy behind most widely accepted traditional measurement strategies. Measurement and statistical theory for the behavioral sciences stemmed originally from mental testing research, where the interest lay in detecting interindividual differences and group differences. The procedures developed work well in that context, but they are ill equipped for detecting and modeling change in individuals over time.

For many years the behavioral sciences have focused on adapting existing measurement and data analysis procedures to the study of change, retaining a heavy emphasis on interindividual differences. Historically, measurement of change has consisted of measuring something reliably and validly at each point in time, according to the well-established guidelines of classical test theory, and then assessing change by examining the magnitude of the difference between adjacent times. Gradually, researchers have become uncomfortable with this approach. There is considerable evidence that change cannot be treated with the same methods used in other kinds of research (e.g., Collins & Horn, 1991; Rogosa, Brandt, & Zimowski, 1982; von Eye, 1990). The study of change requires its own set of new measurement and data analysis procedures. Reflected in many new procedures for studying change is an emphasis on tracing individual growth over time, and using individual growth as a starting point for analyses examining group differences in various aspects of growth. Along with the emphasis on individual growth is an emphasis on modeling growth explicitly, usually with time included in some form as a predictor variable. Examples are latent growth modeling (McArdle & Hamagami, 1991; Willett & Sayer, 1994) and hierarchical models (Bryk & Raudenbush, 1992). These are exciting new developments, because they allow the researcher to formulate and test questions about change in a much more conceptually appealing and direct way. However, these approaches are very demanding of the data, because some aspects of model fitting must be carried out essentially on data from individuals. If the new procedures are to fulfill their potential, highly precise measurement of growth will be very important.

This chapter discusses some old issues related to measurement of change, and also some relatively new methodologies. As a starting point, it is useful to draw a distinction between two types of latent variables: static and dynamic. By static latent variables, we mean latent variables that do not change in systematic ways over time, or where change is not of interest. By dynamic latent variables, we mean latent variables that do change in systematic ways over time, and where this change is of interest. Virtually all longitudinal studies involve dynamic latent variables;

if change is not of interest, there is no reason to undergo the expense of a longitudinal study.

## II. The Difference Score as a Measure of Change

The points made in this section have been made before in excellent articles by Rogosa and colleagues (e.g., Rogosa et al., 1982) and also in articles by the current author and colleagues (Collins, 1991; Collins & Cliff, 1990). But the message has not been received everywhere, so it is included again here: Assuming there are no ceiling or floor effects, there is nothing inherently unsound about difference scores.

It is true that subtracting a later observation from an earlier one is a less than optimal way to study growth, but the reason has little to do with difference scores per se. Instead, the reason is that any study limited to two waves of data can give at best a very narrow idea of the nature of growth, because the researcher is then limited to linear growth models. But of course many studies are limited to two waves, for financial, logistical, or even historical reasons. Although designs limited to a pretest and posttest are not ideal, much valuable information can be gained from them nevertheless. It is unfortunate that researchers who must live with the limitations of pre–post designs are so reluctant to use difference scores. Often difference scores are conceptually the simplest and most readily interpretable measure of growth in a two-wave design.

### A. Reliability of Difference Scores and Precision of Measurement

For many years researchers have been struggling with the issue of how to represent change when conducting data analyses, usually in the context of simple pretest–posttest designs. It has been a struggle for two reasons: (a) there has been a failure to take an intraindividual growth point of view, and (b) the (in)famous article by Cronbach and Furby (1970) left researchers very nervous about the most obvious, simple, and conceptually clear approach, the difference (or gain) score. There is a belief that something inherent in difference scores makes them unreliable, and by implication imprecise, measures of change. Today the contention that "difference scores are unreliable" has become almost a truism in behavioral research, leading journal editors to be sharply critical of their use and, perhaps as a consequence, many researchers to avoid difference scores all together. However, in reality there is no reason to be any more nervous about difference scores than about any other measure.

Although difference scores are often unreliable, it does not follow that they are necessarily imprecise measures of change. To see the logic behind this seemingly paradoxical statement, consider the traditional definition of reliability:

$$\rho_{xx} = \frac{\sigma_T^2}{\sigma_X^2} = \frac{\sigma_T^2}{\sigma_T^2 + \sigma_E^2} \tag{1}$$

where $\sigma_T^2$ represents interindividual true score variance at one time. It is apparent from Equation 1 that given a fixed amount of error variance, a measure with a large $\sigma_T^2$ has a larger reliability than a measure with a smaller $\sigma_T^2$. When (1) is used to define the reliability of difference scores, $\sigma_T^2$ represents interindividual variability (i.e., heterogeneity) in change. Given a fixed $\sigma_T^2$, difference scores are unreliable when there is little heterogeneity in the amount and direction of change. This is true even when there is a lot of change (i.e., large intraindividual variance) and even when difference scores are a highly precise (or perfect) measure of this change. Thus whether difference scores are reliable or unreliable, at least according to the traditional definition of reliability, says nothing about whether they are precise or imprecise measures of change.

In other words, the problem is less with difference scores than with the use of reliability, with its irrelevance to the measurement of intraindividual change, as a definition of measurement precision. Willett (1989) suggested a different approach to assessing the reliability of measures of growth, based on growth curve modeling. His approach has the great advantage of making use of information from more than two waves of data in the reliability computation. However, he argued that even this new approach does not solve the fundamental problem of measurement reliability's dependence on interindividual differences:

That growth-rate reliability can only be high if there exist inter-individual differences in true growth rate to be detected, regardless of the precision with which measurement has occurred, is very unfortunate. Reliability must, therefore, be perceived as an extremely misleading criterion for judging the measurement qualities of an instrument, as it *confounds* the unrelated influences of group heterogeneity in growth-rate and measurement precision. (p. 595)

The idea of the overriding importance of interindividual differences is inextricably bound with the idea of reliability as an operational definition of measurement precision. Later in this chapter (Section IV) an alternative approach to defining measurement precision, a model-based approach that does not make reference to interindividual differences, is discussed.

## B. Reliability of Difference Scores and the Time 1–Time 2 Correlation

It has been argued that difference scores cannot be simultaneously both reliable and valid. There are two parts to this argument. One part of the argument suggests that a small Time 1–Time 2 correlation means different constructs are being measured at each time and therefore the measure is invalid. For example, Pedhazur and Schmelkin (1991) stated that "obtaining gain scores when the correlation between the pretest and posttest is zero makes as much sense as the proverbial addition or subtraction of apples and oranges" (p. 293). But in fact, it is possible for a highly valid instrument to show a low, zero, or even negative correlation between Time 1 and Time 2, depending upon the heterogeneity of both rate and direction of growth in a sample. For example, suppose a study of intellectual development in the elderly is being conducted with a highly heterogeneous sample, involving participants of many different ages, ranging from young-old to old-old, and many different health statuses. In reality the younger or healthier members of the sample are holding steady or even increasing, whereas the older or less healthy are declining. A perfectly valid measure of intellectual development will reflect this fact and will produce a low Time 1–Time 2 correlation.

The other part of the argument notes the tendency for reliable difference scores to be associated with a small correlation between Time 1 and Time 2. There is an imperfect relationship between the reliability of the difference score and the Time 1–Time 2 correlation. If there is a small Time 1–Time 2 correlation, then there is a great deal of interindividual variability in change over time in the observed scores and, depending on the amount of error, reliability may be high for reasons discussed in Section II.A. If there is a large Time 1–Time 2 correlation, interindividual variability in change over time is limited to several forms that do not greatly disrupt the rank order of individuals over time. One possibility is that all individuals change approximately the same amount (including no change). An example of this is illustrated in Figure 1, where the correlation between Time 1 and Time 2 is 1.0 and all subjects change by approximately the same amount. This results in little interindividual variability in change and, hence, unreliable difference scores. Another possibility is that the Time 2 score is a multiplicative transformation of the Time 1 score; for example, Time 2 scores could be 110% of Time 1 scores. This results in the pattern of growth known as a *fan spread*. Under these conditions, there may be

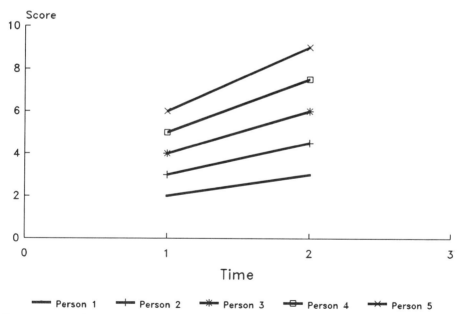

**Figure 1** Hypothetical data showing a perfect Time 1–Time 2 correlation and little interindividual variability in change over time.

quite a bit of interindividual variability; there may even be a mixture of growth and decline in the sample, as illustrated in Figure 2. This high degree of interindividual variability will tend to produce more reliable difference scores, all else being equal.

There are a couple of points worth emphasizing here. First, a large Time 1–Time 2 correlation does not preclude the possibility that significant change over time has occurred, as Figures 1 and 2 illustrate. Second, a large Time 1–Time 2 correlation may be associated with high or low reliability difference scores, depending on the amount of interindividual variability in growth. Although in practice a large Time 1–Time 2 correlation tends to be the result of relatively little interindividual variability, and thus has become associated with unreliable difference scores, it does not render reliable difference scores impossible.

## III. Validity

Validity is a concept that cuts across any and all measurement theories, and is the bottom line in all measurement. There are well-established procedures for assessing validity of measures of static latent variables. It is argued here that these procedures do not necessarily transfer over into the domain of dynamic latent variables, and that new approaches to establishing validity should be considered. The three major domains of validity are criterion validity, content validity, and construct validity.

### A. Criterion Validity

With criterion validity, another measure or variable is used as a standard or criterion. If the measure in question is valid, it will show a substantial relation with the criterion. Criterion validity can be assessed as concurrent or as predictive validity. With concurrent validity, the data on the criterion are collected at approximately the same time as the measure in question. With predictive validity, the measure is considered valid if it can successfully predict a criterion measured at a later time.

Questions about criterion validity

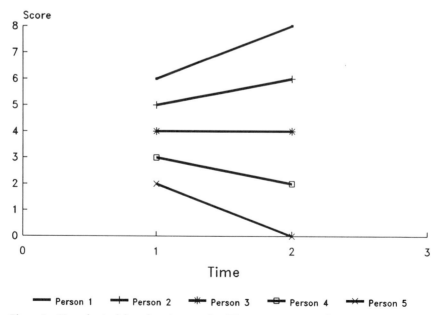

**Figure 2**  Hypothetical data showing a perfect Time 1–Time 2 correlation and a fan spread pattern, with interindividual variability in change over time.

should be phrased somewhat differently if the validity of a measure of a dynamic latent variable is being assessed. Here we are measuring a variable that changes over time, so the validity question should have to do with change. In order to assess concurrent validity, for example, we should investigate whether two variables track along together concurrently over time. This cannot be assessed by examining panel correlations over time, that is, by correlating the two variables at Time 1, then correlating them again at Time 2, and so on. In fact, this approach can be very misleading. This is illustrated in Figure 3, which plots hypothetical data on two dynamic variables for two persons at three points in time. Few would argue that the two dynamic variables track along together over time. Yet *at each time* the panel correlation of the two variables is 1.0. Dynamic concurrent validity must be assessed by examining change over time for each individual. For example, growth curve modeling can be used to model the growth trajectory on each variable for each individual, and to examine whether there is a relationship between the growth tra-

jectories. This approach would have made it immediately clear that Variable 1 can be represented by a linear model, whereas Variable 2 requires a quadratic model, suggesting different underlying growth processes and poor concurrent validity.

Dynamic predictive validity is the degree to which a measure of interest tracks along with the criterion, but after some time lag. Figure 4 shows hypothetical data on a dynamic predictor and a dynamic criterion variable. Although the two variables do not appear to track along together, in fact they are perfectly related: the criterion is exactly equal to the predictor one time unit earlier. In Figure 5, where the predictor variable is moved one time unit to the right, it is apparent that there is a perfect relationship between the two variables. A lagged relationship between two variables will be evident in ordinary panel correlations where the appropriate temporal lag is used (in the example, it would be the criterion one time unit later than the predictor).

It can be difficult, however, to establish dynamic predictive validity in designs where observations are taken infrequently,

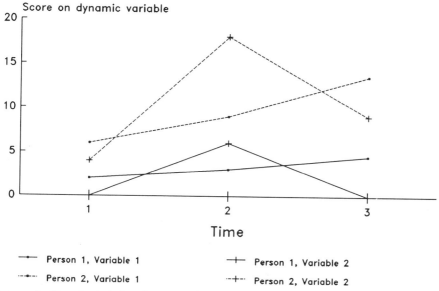

Figure 3 Hypothetical data from two dynamic latent variables that do not track along together over time, but are correlated 1.0 at each individual time.

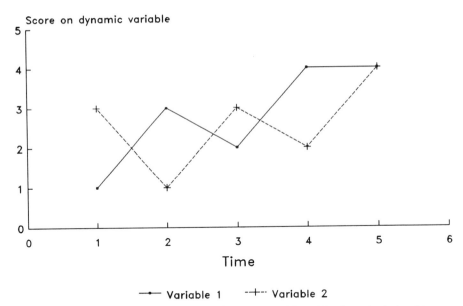

**Figure 4**   Hypothetical data from two dynamic variables with a lagged relationship.

because it may not be possible to correlate the variables using the appropriate temporal lag (Cohen, 1991; Collins & Graham, 1991). For example, suppose the validity of a measure of dietary intake is being assessed. It is hypothesized that intake of a certain category of foods affects levels of a particular blood chemical the next day. If food intake and the blood chemical can be measured a day apart, this relation will be revealed in plots like Figures 4 and 5. But if these variables are mea-

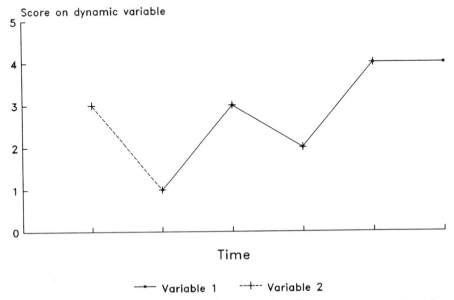

**Figure 5**   Variables in Figure 2, with predictor variable shifted one time unit to the right.

sured a week apart, the relation will probably not emerge. There are then no data on the relation between food intake and the blood chemical a day later; instead, the relation between food intake and the blood chemical a week later must be substituted, even though there may be no relation at all between them. In this situation it would be possible to conclude mistakenly that the food-intake measure has poor predictive validity, because the study design does not permit measurement to take place at the appropriate temporal lag.

## B. Content Validity

Content validity is the extent to which the items making up a measure cover the entire domain being measured. With dynamic latent variables, it is important to consider what constitutes the domain being measured. One aspect of this is the range of skills, abilities, attitudes, and so on being measured. This is what is ordinarily considered in measurement of static variables, and it is important in measurement of dynamic variables as well. But there is an additional aspect of the domain being measured that is important in dynamic variables. Because a dynamic variable is a process changing over time, different items will be relevant to different phases of the process. In other words, the instrument should include some items relevant in the early, middle, and late stages of the process. For example, an instrument to measure decline occurring as a result of Alzheimer's disease should include some items that are sensitive to the very beginnings of the disease ("Do you ever become momentarily confused finding your way home?"), items that come as close as possible to the end stages of the disease ("Can you name your children?"), and an array of items relevant to intermediate phases. Often items relevant to a single content area but covering a wide range of level of skill required or extremity of attitude will be sufficient to ensure content validity. Oth-

er times, depending on the dynamic latent variable being measured, items in different content domains will be needed to measure different phases of the process. For example, different kinds of tasks are used to measure different phases of Piagetian development.

It is important to keep content validity in mind when measuring dynamic latent variables, because traditional instrument development procedures often work against inclusion of items relevant to the early and late ends of the temporal continuum (Collins & Cliff, 1990). This is particularly true when the items are constants at one or more times of measurement in a longitudinal study. For example, an Alzheimer's study following a sample of newly diagnosed patients would probably find that at the beginning all subjects who are asked "Can you name your children?" can perform this task easily for the first several waves of data collection; therefore, this item is a constant for the first few occasions. Because a constant has no variance and, therefore, no correlation with other items or the total score, most instrument development procedures would lead to a decision to discard this item. However, this item is needed in order to measure the advanced phase of the disease. Furthermore, most individuals in the sample who pass the item early in the process will fail it later in the process, and the item is thus sensitive to intraindividual change.

## C. Construct Validity

Construct validity is the sine qua non of measurement. With static latent variables, construct validity is usually demonstrated by making a theoretical prediction and testing it using the instrument in question. For example, if a theory predicts that there are differences between age groups on a particular latent variable, then age differences should ideally emerge on the instrument in question. Theoretical predictions can be used as a way of

establishing construct validity of measures of dynamic latent variables in much
the same way, but here, the theoretical prediction is about change over time. For example, if a theory predicts change over
time, then a valid instrument will show
change. If a theory predicts that change occurs during a certain period and not during
other periods, or in a certain direction, or in
a subset of individuals only, then the instrument should reflect this. Construct validity can be assessed by plotting repeated
measurements on the instrument as a function of time for individuals.

The multitrait multimethod (MTMM)
matrix (Campbell & Fiske, 1959) is often
advocated as a way of assessing construct
validity. In this framework, several latent
variables are measured using several different techniques. Construct validity is
established by demonstrating high correlations between different techniques
measuring the same latent variable and
low correlations between instances of the
same technique measuring different latent
variables. This approach was developed for
static latent variables, and there are no
guidelines for using it to assess construct
validity for dynamic latent variables.
Clearly it is inadvisable to examine an
MTMM matrix at each wave of a longitudinal study, at least where the traits are
dynamic. As has been shown above, cross-
sectional correlations involving dynamic
latent variables can be very misleading. A
generalization of the MTMM matrix to dynamic latent variables is needed.

## IV. The Longitudinal Guttman Simplex and Related Measurement Models

In the preceding sections it has been
argued that alternatives to traditional definitions of measurement precision and validity are needed for dynamic latent variables. A general strategy is indicated by

Coombs's (1964) penetrating observation
that "all measurement theory is actually a
theory of behavior" (p. 5). This is particularly apropos when discussing measurement of human development, and suggests that a useful starting point for
measuring dynamic latent variables is a
theory of development. For example, usually when a traditional measurement theory is used to construct a measure of development, the focus is on a total score.
However, this leaves a great deal unspecified about the nature of the development being measured. For example, if a
theory of math skills development spe-
cifies that students learn various skills in a
certain order, then the theory also spe-
cifies the order in which students will pass
items requiring these skills as their level
of competence increases over time. In this
section a family of measurement models is
presented where a model of development
specifying the order in which items are
passed or failed over time is incorporated.

These measurement models are based
on the classic Guttman scale (1950). Recall that the Guttman scale is a *joint order*,
usually of persons and items. Table I,
which contains hypothetical data forming
a Guttman scale, can be used to show what
is meant by the term *joint order*. This table shows that, in a Guttman scale, the
persons' responses can be used to order the
items along a difficulty (or, in the case of
attitude measurement, extremity) continuum, and simultaneously the items can be
used to order the persons along a continuum reflecting what the scale measures,

**Table I**
Hypothetical Data Forming a Guttman Scale

|          | Item 1 | Item 2 | Item 3 | Item 4 |
|----------|--------|--------|--------|--------|
| Person 1 | fail   | fail   | fail   | fail   |
| Person 2 | pass   | fail   | fail   | fail   |
| Person 3 | pass   | pass   | fail   | fail   |
| Person 4 | pass   | pass   | pass   | fail   |
| Person 5 | pass   | pass   | pass   | pass   |

such as performance, extremity of attitude, and so on. It is evident that Item 4 is most difficult, followed by Item 3 and then Item 2, with Item 1 the least difficult. It is also evident, assuming for the moment that the scale measures ability, that Person 5 is most able, followed by Persons 4, 3, 2, and 1, in that order. An important feature of the Guttman scale is that the scale score contains a lot of information. For example, if an individual obtains a score of 3 on a Guttman scale, we know not only that the person passed (or endorsed) three items but also *which* three items.

Collins and colleagues (Collins & Cliff, 1990; Collins, Cliff, & Dent, 1988) have extended the Guttman scale to include a third set. These authors have described three different variations on the three-set Guttman scale, referred to as Case 1, Case 2, and Case 3. For the most common application where the three sets are items, times, and persons, the three-set Guttman scale models are definitions of human development.

A. Case 1

Case 1 is defined as a full three-set joint order, in other words, a joint order among persons, items, and times. This means that for each time, there is a joint order between persons and items, and the joint order is consistent across times; for each item, there is a joint order between persons and times, and the joint order is consistent across items; and for each person, there is a joint order between items and times, and the joint order is consistent across persons.

Suppose a researcher wishes to construct a scale that will measure change in ability to function in everyday life, similar to the Activities of Daily Living scale (Katz, Ford, Moskowitz, Jackson, & Jaffee, 1963) or the Instrumental Activities of Daily Living scale (Duke University Center for the Study of Aging and Human Development, 1978). Table II contains hypothetical data forming a Case 1 three-set Guttman simplex. In this illustrative example there are three items: needs help grocery shopping, needs help with light housework, and needs help dressing. There are two particularly salient features of this table. First, the order of the persons in terms of disability does not change over items or, perhaps more important conceptually, over times. This limits the amount of heterogeneity in developmental rate possible in this model. Second, the items-times joint order is consistent across persons. This represents a particular kind of development, where change in disability is monotonic in the same direction for all individuals, and where the rank order of persons in terms of disability does not change over time.

Figure 6 gives examples of development defined by Case 1 by plotting the total score (i.e., number of items passed or endorsed), at various times for three hypothetical individuals. Figure 6 shows that development is occurring in the same direction for all three individuals. There is some variability in the rate of development. Person 1 grows rapidly and then levels off; Person 2 grows at a constant rate; and Person 3 starts slowly but grows rapidly in later times. However, the rank order of individuals is not disturbed over the

**Table II**
Hypothetical Data Consistent
with a Case 1 Model

|  | Need help grocery shopping | Need help with light housework | Need help dressing |
|---|---|---|---|
| Person A |  |  |  |
| Time 1 | No | No | No |
| Time 2 | Yes | No | No |
| Time 3 | Yes | Yes | No |
| Person B |  |  |  |
| Time 1 | Yes | No | No |
| Time 2 | Yes | Yes | No |
| Time 3 | Yes | Yes | Yes |

48                                                                    Linda M. Collins

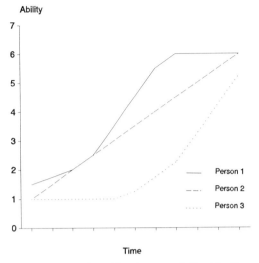

**Figure 6** Examples of development defined by Case 1 of the three-set Guttman simplex (Collins & Cliff, 1985).

time they are observed here, limiting the amount of heterogeneity that is allowed. Although in this example growth is increasing overall, it also would be consistent with the Case 1 model if growth were monotonically decreasing overall.

## B. Case 2, the Longitudinal Guttman Simplex

Case 2, which has been named the Longitudinal Guttman Simplex (LGS), is a slightly less restrictive version of Case 1. The LGS is an items-times joint order that is consistent across persons. In this model the persons order can vary across items and across times. However, there is an items-persons joint order for each time, although it may differ across times, and there is a times-persons joint order for each item, although it may differ across items. Table III uses the same scale items as appeared in Table II to show a hypothetical example of data perfectly represented by a Case 2 three-set Guttman scale. As in Case 1, disability is monotonically increasing for all individuals,

and the items-times joint order is consistent across times. In contrast to Case 1, it is consistent with the model for the disability order of individuals to change from one time of measurement to another. This allows unlimited heterogeneity in developmental rate. Table III shows that Person B is more disabled than Person A at the first and second occasion. However, between the second and third occasion Person B does not decline at all while Person A experiences a fast rate of decline. The result is that Person A is more disabled at the third occasion than is Person B.

Figure 7 plots the total score on a Case 2 three-set Guttman scale at various times for three individuals, giving several examples of development defined by Case 2. Figure 7 shows that, as in Figure 5, development is occurring in the same direction for all three individuals. However, here there is considerable variability in the rate of development, so much so that the persons order varies from one time to another. During the early times Person 3 shows the most ability, Person 2 is in the middle, and Person 1 shows the least ability. Later, Person 1 has the lead, followed by Person 2 and then Person 3. At the end of the study, yet another ability order has emerged: Person 2 has the most ability, with Person 3 in the middle and Person 1 last.

**Table III**
Hypothetical Data Consistent
with a Case 2 Model

|  | Need help grocery shopping | Need help with light housework | Need help dressing |
|---|---|---|---|
| Person A |  |  |  |
| Time 1 | No | No | No |
| Time 2 | Yes | No | No |
| Time 3 | Yes | Yes | Yes |
| Person B |  |  |  |
| Time 1 | Yes | No | No |
| Time 2 | Yes | Yes | No |
| Time 3 | Yes | Yes | No |

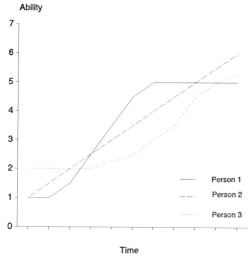

**Figure 7** Examples of development defined by Case 2 of the three-set Guttman simplex model, the Longitudinal Guttman Simplex (Collins & Cliff, 1985).

## C. Case 3

Case 3 is the least restrictive model of development of the three cases, because it allows both growth and decline. In Case 3, the order of the items is consistent across times and across persons. At each time there is a persons-items joint order, but these joint orders are not consistent across times. At each person there is an items-times joint order, but these joint orders are not consistent across persons. In Case 3 there is no persons-times joint order. Case 3 is a model where development may be highly heterogenous across persons, to the point where individual growth trajectories may differ greatly in speed and direction, and may even be nonmonotonic. However, all growth is cumulative, and change between times takes place in a particular way: Items are passed and failed in a consistent order. The term *cumulative* as used here does not mean that once an item is passed, it is retained forever. Rather, it means that an individual who passes an item, say Item X, passes all of the items that are easier than Item X as well, and an individual who fails an item, say Item Y, fails all of the items that are harder than

Item Y. If development were noncumulative according to this definition, as overall skill increased and the ability to pass more difficult items was gained, it would be possible to lose the ability to pass less difficult items. Coombs and Smith (1973) discussed this kind of development, which they have called a *parallelogram* model.

A Case 3 three-set Guttman scale is illustrated in Table IV using the same hypothetical scale measuring change in the ability to function in everyday life that was used in Tables II and III. Person A starts out only moderately disabled, increases rapidly to need help in all three areas at the second occasion, and then recovers somewhat by the third occasion. Person B starts out needing help in all three areas, recovers substantially by the second occasion, and then shows some additional disability by the third occasion. Note that the increases and decreases in disability are consistent with the underlying model of development, which provides an order among the items. For example, if it is known that Person A needs help in all three areas at Time 2, and it is known that Person A recovered one ability by Time 3, then it is known *which* ability Person A recovered. Under these circumstances only recovery of the ability to dress oneself is consistent with the cumulative nature of the model.

**Table IV**
Hypothetical Data Consistent
with a Case 3 Model

|  | Need help grocery shopping | Need help with light housework | Need help dressing |
|---|---|---|---|
| Person A |  |  |  |
| Time 1 | Yes | No | No |
| Time 2 | Yes | Yes | Yes |
| Time 3 | Yes | Yes | No |
| Person B |  |  |  |
| Time 1 | Yes | Yes | Yes |
| Time 2 | Yes | No | No |
| Time 3 | Yes | Yes | No |

Figure 8 illustrates development consistent with the responses given by five hypothetical respondents. As Figure 8 shows, a wide variety of developmental trajectories are consistent with the Case 3 model. Person 1 undergoes a series of increases and decreases; Person 2 shows initial rapid decline followed by a leveling off; Person 3 increases at a variable rate; Person 4 declines steadily; and Person 5 increases up to a peak and then decreases. It may be difficult to see what model of development underlies a set of widely different growth trajectories like those in Figure 8. However, there is more order there than perhaps meets the eye. It is still the case that development is cumulative, and that individuals are proceeding through the items in a specific order. Furthermore, an individual's scale score still reveals exactly which items the individual has passed and which he or she has failed. Thus, although in instruments developed by traditional means there is no embedded developmental model, here a model of

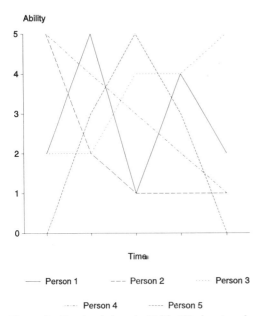

**Figure 8** Graph of data in Table IV showing developmental trajectories consistent with a Case 3 model.

cumulative development underlies the measure.

There is a software program available to assist researchers interested in developing measures fitting the LGS model. It is called LGSINDEX (Collins & Dent, 1986), and it computes a consistency index and index-if-item-deleted. The consistency index is intended to give the user an idea of how consistent a given set of data are with an LGS model. The index-if-item-deleted gives some indication of which items should be removed in order to produce a more consistent scale. As of this writing, the software is suitable only for Case 2 models.

## V. Representing Change over Time

### A. Continuous Variables

In analysis of continuous longitudinal data, the emphasis should be on modeling individual growth over time. A clear conceptual explanation of this appears in Willett and Sayer (1994; see also Rogosa & Willett, 1985). Willett and Sayer's latent growth modeling approach essentially fits two different levels of a model to longitudinal data. The first level is the individual growth curve. Using the time of each observation as a predictor, a general model is selected a priori—linear, quadratic, or whatever is felt to represent the overall shape of growth best. Usually the simplest reasonable model is chosen. This model is fitted to each individual subject's data to represent each subject's growth trajectory.

For example, in a linear model, each subject has a slope and intercept. A subject who starts low and grows a lot over the course of a study will have a small intercept and a large and positive slope. A subject who starts high and declines over the course of a study will have a large intercept and a negative slope. The second level uses the individually fitted growth parameters as dependent variables in further analyses. For example, suppose, in a study of cognitive decline in the elderly, an intervention involving cognitive exercises is given to a treatment group while a placebo intervention is given to a control group. In a latent growth modeling framework, if the intervention is successful it would be expected that the slopes for the treatment group will be less steeply negative than the slopes for the control group. Willett and Sayer (1994) demonstrated how to conduct latent growth modeling with commonly available covariance structure modeling software. A conceptually similar approach can be taken using hierarchical linear modeling with software such as HLM (Bryk & Raudenbush, 1992).

This general approach has many important benefits. One is the light it sheds on another old issue, the correlation between change and initial status. For years researchers have lamented the fact that the amount of change is often partly a function of initial status, so that, for example, individuals who start out high appear to gain the most from a program. Residualized change scores, where initial score is partialed out of a later score in an attempt to "control for" initial status, has been advocated as a way of dealing with the perceived problem. However, as Rogosa et al. (1982) argued, in most cases the residualized change score is difficult to interpret conceptually. When an individual growth modeling approach is taken, the correlation between the intercept and the slope can be estimated. Perhaps more importantly, the intercept itself can be predicted by other variables in order to model the relationship between change and initial status.

An individual growth modeling approach also helps to clarify another issue that arises in longitudinal research in aging and other areas: When is it appropriate to report group-level growth curves? It is very common in longitudinal research to represent group-level growth by simply graphing group means across time. Figure 9 shows such a group-level growth curve. When an individual growth perspective is taken, it becomes easy to see that this can be highly misleading. Figures 10 and 11 show two very different sets of individual growth trajectories that, when combined,

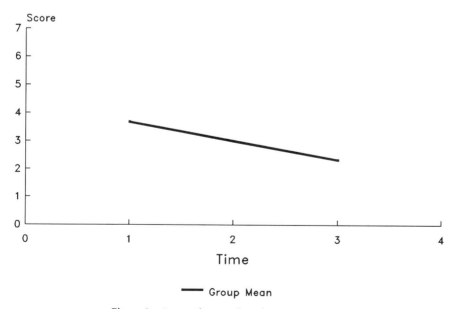

Figure 9   A growth curve based on group means.

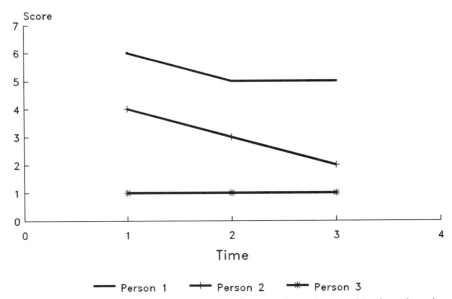

**Figure 10**  One possible set of individual growth curves that, when combined, produce the group growth curve in Figure 9.

yield the linear and decreasing group-level growth curve shown in Figure 9. Figure 9 is a reasonable representation of the growth curves in Figure 10. The curves are all more or less linear and there seems to be a prevailing downward trend. In contrast, the collection of growth curves depicted in Figure 11 is not represented well at all by Figure 9. One curve shows a downward trend, one goes down slightly and then

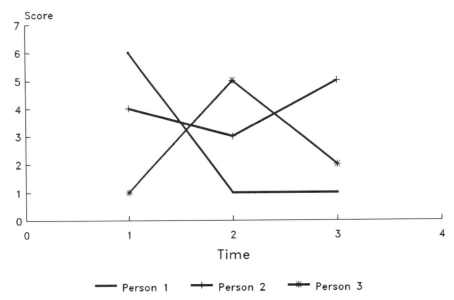

**Figure 11**  Another possible set of individual growth curves that, when combined, produce the group growth curve in Figure 9.

goes up, and one goes up steeply and then goes down steeply. Furthermore, all three of these growth curves suggest that the growth process is quadratic rather than linear, even though the aggregated growth curve is linear. Thus, group-level growth curves should not be interpreted as representative of an overall tendency in individual growth trajectories. In fact, there may be so much variability in the individual growth trajectories that the group-level growth curve is not very much like any of the individual growth curves.

## B. Categorical Latent Variables: Latent Transition Analysis

In some instances change over time is best represented as a sequence of categorical stages, either because of discontinuities in the process or because the change has some qualitative aspects. Latent Transition Analysis (LTA) (Collins & Wugalter, 1992; Graham, Collins, Wugalter, Chung, & Hansen, 1991) is a measurement model for stage-sequential dynamic latent variables. It is an extension of latent class theory to longitudinal data.

Comparing and contrasting LTA with structural equation modeling (SEM) may be helpful to the reader familiar with the latter technique. Both techniques involve latent variables, but they differ in the type of latent variable. SEM involves continuous latent variables, usually with continuous indicators. LTA involves discrete latent variables, with discrete indicators. In SEM a score on a latent variable places the individual along a continuum, whereas in LTA, the latent variable divides the sample up into mutually exclusive groups. Both approaches attempt to approximate data by fitting a model. In covariance structure models, the data are in the form of a correlation, covariance, or cross-products matrix. The user designs a model with a certain number of latent variables, fixes or constrains certain parameters and freely estimates others, and then assesses

how well the model reproduces the data. In LTA, the data are in the form of response pattern proportions or, in other words, cell proportions. The user designs a model involving a certain number of stages, fixes or constrains certain parameters and freely estimates others, and then assesses how well the model fits the data. In SEM, relations between latent variables are expressed in terms of correlations or regressions between latent variables, and relations between latent variables and indicator items are expressed in terms of factor loadings. In LTA, relations between stages are expressed in terms of transition probabilities, and relations between stages and indicator items are expressed in terms of the probability of item responses conditional on stage membership.

Table V shows some hypothetical data designed to illustrate a very simple LTA model. Suppose a researcher is interested in testing a model of cognitive decline and its prevention. According to the model, there are just two stages in the process: adequate functioning and inadequate functioning. Suppose a study is undertaken to test a cognitive enhancement program for the elderly. Subjects are randomly assigned to either a treatment condition, where they take a class involving cognitive exercises, or a control condition. Before and after the treatment program the subjects are given three cognitive tasks to perform. The outcome of each task is either a pass or a fail, and an individual who is functioning adequately can pass all three tasks. Table V illustrates some of the parameters that are estimated as part of the LTA model.

The procedure estimates the proportion of individuals in each stage at the first measurement. In our example, the treatment group and the control group each contain 70% adequately functioning individuals and 30% inadequately functioning individuals. The procedure also estimates transition probabilities. These are the probabilities of being in a particular stage

**Table V**
A Hypothetical Example of a Latent Transition Analysis Model

|  | Adequate functioning | Inadequate functioning |
|---|---|---|
| Treatment group | | |
| Proportion at Time 1 | .70 | .30 |
|  | Stage at Time 2 | |
| Stage at Time 1 | | |
| Adequate functioning | .95 | .05 |
| Inadequate functioning | .55 | .45 |
| Control group | | |
| Proportion at Time 1 | .70 | .30 |
|  | Stage at Time 2 | |
| Stage at Time 1 | | |
| Adequate functioning | .75 | .25 |
| Inadequate functioning | .35 | .65 |

at Time 2, conditional on Time 1 stage membership. These parameters represent the amount and rapidity of change over time. In the hypothetical example, differences between the treatment and control group are evident. In the treatment group, the probability is 95% that an individual who is adequately functioning at Time 1 will remain adequately functioning at Time 2, whereas in the control group this probability is only 75%. In the treatment group the probability is 55% that an inadequately functioning individual will return to adequate functioning, whereas the corresponding probability in the control group is only 35%. Note that because the rows of the transition probability matrix are conditional on initial status, it gives the researcher a straightforward way to examine the relationship between change and initial status.

The measurement parameters are an important part of the LTA model. Examples of measurement parameters for the hypothetical data appear in Table VI. The measurement parameters are conceptually similar to factor loadings, in the sense that they reflect the relationship between a manifest variable and a latent variable. However, they are scaled differ-

ently than factor loadings. Because the measurement parameters are probabilities, they range between 0 and 1. A value close to 0 or 1 reflects a strong relationship between the latent variable and the observed variable, whereas a value closer to the middle of the range reflects a weak relationship. For example, Table VI shows that the probability of passing Task 1 given that an individual is in the adequate stage is .9, indicating that there is a strong relationship between Task 1 and the adequate stage. In contrast, the probability of passing Task 3 is .55. Thus Task 3 contains little information about whether an individual is in the adequate stage beyond what would be obtained by tossing a coin.

**Table VI**
Measurement Parameters
for Hypothetical Model in Table IV

|  | Probability of passing, conditional on stage | | |
|---|---|---|---|
|  | Task 1 | Task 2 | Task 3 |
| Adequate functioning | .9 | .9 | .55 |
| Inadequate functioning | .05 | .05 | .35 |

There is software available for estimation and testing of LTA models. Collins, Wugalter, and Rousculp (1992) developed a program that estimates LTA models by means of the EM (Expectation Maximization) algorithm. Other software that can be used for similar analyses is PANMARK (van de Pol, Langeheine, & de Jong, 1989).

## VI. Summary

Starting from an individual growth perspective, this chapter has explored some ideas about how to measure and represent change over time in research on aging. The classic issue of difference scores was discussed, with a plea that perhaps difference scores are useful in some situations. Another classic issue, validity, was discussed, but with some new twists resulting from applying these ideas to dynamic latent variables. A measurement model for continuous dynamic variables, the three-set Guttman simplex, was presented. It was shown that taking an individual growth curve approach to representing continuous dynamic latent variables sheds light on how to handle the inevitable correlation between initial status and change, and also suggests that group growth curves are likely to be misleading if interpreted as representative of overall trends in individual growth. A way of estimating and testing models of stage-sequential development, LTA, was also discussed. This approach represents change in the form of a transition probability matrix, which conditions the probability of stage transitions on initial stage membership.

## Acknowledgments

The research presented in this chapter was partially supported by National Institute on Drug Abuse grant R01–DA04111. Some of the material in this chapter was originally presented at an invited address by the author at the annual meetings of the American Psychological Association, August 1994.

## References

Bryk, A. S., & Raudenbush, S. W. (1992). *Hierarchical linear models: Applications and data analysis methods.* Newbury Park, CA: Sage.

Campbell, D. T., & Fiske, D. W. (1959). Convergent and discriminant validation by the multitrait-multimethod matrix. *Psychological Bulletin, 56,* 81–105.

Cohen, P. (1991). A source of bias in longitudinal investigations of change: A problem posed to attenders at the "Best Methods for the Analysis of Change" conference. In L. M. Collins & J. L. Horn (Eds.), *Best methods for the analysis of change: Recent advances, unanswered questions, future directions* (pp. 18–25). Washington, DC: American Psychological Association.

Collins, L. M. (1991). Measurement in longitudinal research. In L. M. Collins & J. L. Horn (Eds.), *Best methods for the analysis of change: Recent advances, unanswered questions, future directions* (pp. 137–148). Washington, DC: American Psychological Association.

Collins, L. M., & Cliff, N. (1985). Axiomatic foundations of a three-set Guttman simplex model with applicability to longitudinal data. *Psychometrika, 50,* 147–148.

Collins, L. M., & Cliff, N. (1990). Using the Longitudinal Guttman Simplex as a basis for measuring growth. *Psychological Bulletin, 108,* 128–134.

Collins, L. M., Cliff, N., & Dent, C. W. (1988). The longitudinal Guttman simplex: A new methodology for measurement of dynamic constructs in longitudinal panel studies. *Applied Psychological Measurement, 12,* 217–230.

Collins, L. M., & Dent, C. W. (1986). *LGS-INDEX user's guide.* Los Angeles: University of Southern California.

Collins, L. M., & Graham, J. W. (1991). Comment on "A source of bias in longitudinal investigations of change: A problem posed to attenders at the 'Best Methods for the Analysis of Change' conference." In L. M. Collins & J. L. Horn (Eds.), *Best methods for the analysis of change: Recent advances, un-*

answered questions, future directions (pp. 137–148). Washington, DC: American Psychological Association.

Collins, L. M., & Horn, J. L. (Eds.). (1991). *Best methods for the analysis of change: Recent advances, unanswered questions, future directions.* Washington, DC: American Psychological Association.

Collins, L. M., & Wugalter, S. E. (1992). Latent class models for stage-sequential dynamic latent variables. *Multivariate Behavioral Research, 27,* 131–157.

Collins, L. M., Wugalter, S. E., & Rousculp, S. S. (1992). *Latent Transition Analysis (LTA) program manual (Version 1.0).* Los Angeles: University of Southern California.

Coombs, C. H. (1964). *A theory of data.* Ann Arbor, MI: Mathesis.

Coombs, C. H., & Smith, J. E. K. (1973). On the detection of structure in attitudes and developmental processes. *Psychological Review, 80,* 337–351.

Cronbach, L. J., & Furby, L. (1970). How should we measure change—or should we? *Psychological Bulletin, 74,* 68–80.

Duke University Center for the Study of Aging and Human Development. (1978). *Multidimensional functional assessment: The OARS methodology.* Durham, NC: Duke University Press.

Graham, J. W., Collins, L. M., Wugalter, S. E., Chung, N. K., & Hansen, W. B. (1991). Modeling transitions in latent stage-sequential processes: A substance use prevention example. *Journal of Consulting and Clinical Psychology, 59,* 48–57.

Guttman, L. (1950). The basis for scalogram analysis. In S. A. Stouffer, L. Guttman, E. A. Suchman, P. Lazarsfeld, S. A. Star, & J. A. Clausen (Eds.), *Measurement and prediction* (pp. 60–90). Princeton, NJ: Princeton University Press.

Katz, S., Ford, A. B., Moskowitz, R. W., Jackson, B. A., & Jaffee, M. W. (1963). Studies of illness in the aged—The index of ADL: A standardized measure of biological and psychosocial function. *JAMA, Journal of the American Medical Association, 185,* 94–101.

McArdle, J. J., & Hamagami, F. (1991). Modeling incomplete longitudinal and cross-sectional data using latent growth structural models. In L. M. Collins & J. L. Horn (Eds.), *Best methods for the analysis of change: Recent advances, unanswered questions, future directions* (pp. 276–304). Washington, DC: American Psychological Association.

Pedhazur, E. J., & Schmelkin, L. P. (1991). *Measurement, design, and analysis: An integrated approach.* Hillsdale: Erlbaum.

Rogosa, D., Brandt, D., & Zimowski, M. (1982). A growth curve approach to the measurement of change. *Psychological Bulletin, 92,* 726–748.

Rogosa, D., & Willett, J. B. (1985). Understanding correlates of change by modeling individual differences in growth. *Psychometrika, 50,* 203–228.

van de Pol, F., Langeheine, R., & de Jong, W. (1989). *PANMARK user manual: PANel analysis using MARKov chains.* Voorburg: Netherlands Central Bureau of Statistics.

von Eye, A. (Ed.). (1990). *Statistical methods in longitudinal research.* New York: Academic Press.

Willett, J. B. (1989). Some results on reliability for the longitudinal measurement of change: Implications for the design of studies of individual growth. *Educational and Psychological Measurement, 49,* 587–601.

Willett, J. B., & Sayer, A. G. (1994). Using covariance structure analysis to detect correlates and predictors of individual change over time. *Psychological Bulletin, 116,* 363–381.

# Part Two

# Biological and Social Influences on Behavior

Four

# Gerontological Behavior Genetics

Nancy L. Pedersen

## I. Introduction

The development of the behavioral genetic study of aging has gone through an extremely rapid evolution. The chapters on behavioral genetics in the first and second editions of the *Handbook of the Psychology of Aging* relied heavily on a description of what could be done, results from animal studies, and the pioneering New York State Psychiatric Institute Study of Aging by Kallmann, Jarvik, and colleagues (Jarvik & Bank, 1983; Kallmann & Sander, 1948). The chapter in the third edition by Plomin and McClearn (1990) reported some early results from the Swedish Adoption/Twin Study of Aging (SATSA) (Pedersen et al., 1991) but remained primarily a promissory note. There are now reports available from five twin studies of normal aging, genetically relevant data from several normative aging studies, and reports concerning dementia and cognitive impairment from yet another three twin studies.

Not only has there been an explosion in the number of studies concerned with behavioral genetic issues in aging, but there have been comparable methodological advances to take advantage of the wealth of multivariate, longitudinal data. Most spheres of gerontology are addressed— psychological, sociological, and biomedical —but the key approach is best described as multidimensional. In this chapter, current behavioral genetic studies of aging are described briefly, followed by a review of a number of current issues, with relevant examples from these studies.

## II. A Brief Introduction to Behavioral Genetic Methods and Issues

The primary objective of behavioral genetic analyses is to apportion the variation found in a population into genetic and environmental components. In a gerontological context, the question, Why do people age so differently? can be answered with such statements as, Forty percent of the differences seen in personality among the elderly are due to genetic differences among them, and, conversely, 60% of the variance is environmental in origin. In order to address questions concerning individual differences, behavioral geneticists examine similarities and differences among pairs of relatives with differing amounts of genetic and environmental relatedness, such as identical and fraternal twins (who share 100% and 50% of their segregating genes, respectively); siblings or parents and offspring (50% alike genetically); or twins reared apart (who have no rearing environment in common) and twins reared together (with the same rearing environment).

These techniques can be expanded to address issues concerning the associations within and among domains (are traits influenced by the same or different genes?), as well as issues pertinent to information gathered from longitudinal studies (how important are genetic and environmental factors for stability and change?). For a more detailed description of behavioral genetic methodologies see Plomin, DeFries, and McClearn (1990) and Neale and Cardon (1992).

## III. Current Behavioral Genetic Studies of Aging

### A. The Swedish Adoption/Twin Study of Aging

SATSA (Pedersen, Friberg, Floderus-Myrhed, McClearn, & Plomin, 1984; Pedersen et al., 1991) is a longitudinal study of all twin pairs in the Swedish Twin Registry who indicated that they had been separated before the age of 10 and reared apart, and a control sample of twins reared together. Both members of 351 pairs of twins reared apart and 407 matched control pairs of twins reared together, aged 26 to 87 (mean = 58.8, SD = 13.6), responded to a questionnaire in 1984. Participants in SATSA have thus far been assessed by four questionnaires at 3-year intervals between 1984 and 1993. The questionnaires have covered personality, health and health-related behaviors, social support, life events, and the family and work environments. A subsample of 303 pairs aged

50 years and older has been examined through three waves of in-person testing and health examinations (at 3-year rolling intervals) for cognitive and functional capabilities, personality, health, and exposure to potential risk factors for dementia.

### B. Minnesota Study of Adult Development and Aging

The Minnesota Study of Adult Development and Aging (MTSADA) (Finkel & McGue, 1993; McGue, Hirsch, & Lykken, 1993) is a cross-sectional study of 287 adult twin pairs aged 27 to 88 (as of January 1994; mean = 56.8, SD = 14.8). Cognitive, biographical, medical, life-events, and activities data were collected during two interview sessions within a 2-week interval. A self-report questionnaire concerning personality, social support, and self-rated ability (talent) was completed during the intersession interval.

### C. Kinki University Adult Twin Registry

Results have also been reported from a Japanese study of 97 twin pairs (aged 50–78) (Hayakawa, Shimizu, Ohba, & Tomioka, 1992). These pairs have been given a comprehensive medical examination and tests of cognitive abilities, but it is not clear whether the study will remain cross-sectional or become longitudinal.

### D. OCTO-Twin

The focus of OCTO-Twin (Berg et al., 1992) is all intact pairs of twins in Sweden aged 80 or older (i.e., born 1911 or earlier). During the first wave of OCTO-Twin, 351 pairs of like-sexed twins age 79.4–97.8 (mean = 83.6, SD = 3.2) were tested in an in-home procedure. All the domains of assessment included in SATSA are covered in OCTO-Twin as well as additional measures sensitive to cognitive decline in the very old. Up to two longitudinal waves of follow-up at 2-year intervals are planned, the first of which was started in 1994. Given the nature of the sample (i.e., that both members of the pair had to survive their 80th birthday) this may be considered a study of successful agers.

### E. Black Elderly Twin Study

All of the samples described above are made up almost exclusively of Caucasians (there are a few black pairs in MTSADA). In the Black Elderly Twin Study, a newly developed ascertainment mechanism based on the U.S. Social Security number is being employed to identify elderly black twin pairs for subsequent study of biomedical and biobehavioral endpoints (Miles, Furner, Goldberg, & Meyer, 1992). Although the testing has not yet started, 700 pairs are expected to be located and contacted by a telephone interview.

### F. Young Behavioral Genetic Samples Now Growing Older

Samples initially compiled for purposes other than the study of aging are currently being evaluated in a gerontological context. A registry of male twin veterans is maintained by the National Academy of Sciences–National Research Council (NAS-NRC). These men were born between 1917 and 1927 and were veterans of World War II, or the Korean conflict, or both. As part of a study of Alzheimer's disease (see Section III.H), a cognitive screening examination was administered to both members of 4302 twin pairs, at which time the average age was 66 (*SD* 3.1) (Brandt et al., 1993).

The National Heart, Lung, and Blood Institute (NHLBI) Twin Study was initially established to investigate psychological, demographic, metabolic, cardiorespiratory, anthropometric, and social aspects of proneness to coronary heart disease in a subset of twins from the NAS-NRC registry (Feinleib et al., 1977). From the original

cohort, a subset of 267 pairs participated in cognitive screening tests, and longitudinal data (5-year interval) are available for 44 pairs (Swan et al., 1990). The average age of the twins at first cognitive screening was 63.

### G. Behavioral Genetic Issues in Other Elderly Samples

Behavioral genetic methodologies may be applied to samples not initially compiled to address questions concerning genetic and environmental influences on individual differences as long as information is collected from genetically informative populations. The many generational studies of aging may be reanalyzed with this perspective if it is possible to link members within families, such as parents and offspring. For example, this has been done with the Longitudinal Study of Generations, which includes information on personality from 200 multigenerational families (Bengtson & Roberts, 1991).

Longitudinal data in normative studies of aging may be complemented with information from first-degree relatives of study participants, enabling not only standard behavioral genetic analyses, but also the opportunity to address complex issues concerning cohort and age differences. This has been done by Schaie and colleagues, who expanded the Seattle Longitudinal Study (SLS) to include the offspring and siblings of SLS participants (Schaie et al., 1993). Thus, data on cognitive abilities and perceptions of the family environment are available from 531 parent–offspring pairs and 309 sibling pairs.

### H. Twin Studies of Dementia

Three registry-based studies of dementia in twins are currently underway: Bergem, Engedal, and Kringlen (1992) in Norway, Breitner et al. (1990) in the United States, and Gatz and colleagues (Gatz, Pedersen, Reynolds, & Lowe, 1993) in Sweden.

Bergem matched records from geriatric services in old-age homes with the Norwegian twin registry. The study of Breitner and his colleagues, which is in progress, entails screening pairs from the NAS-NRC registry (see Section III.F). The Study of Dementia in Swedish Twins entailed screening the 2394 individuals in SATSA who were born before 1935. These three studies provide data pertinent to the importance of genetic and environmental variability in Alzheimer's disease and other dementias.

## IV. Analytical Approaches and Applications

### A. Univariate Analyses

#### 1. Heritability Estimates in the Elderly

The fundamental aim of behavioral genetic analyses is to describe the origins of individual differences. A first step is to determine the importance of genetic and environmental influences for variation in traits through univariate analysis. Indeed, most of the progress thus far in gerontological behavioral genetics has been in characterizing heritability (i.e., the relative importance of genetic variation for total variation in a population) for a wide range of behavioral and biomedical phenotypes.

a. *Personality and Psychological Well-Being.* Plomin and McClearn (1990) summarized univariate results concerning the relative importance of genetic and environmental influences on personality in the elderly. Three major findings were indicated:

1. Heritability for most personality traits was on average .29 (i.e., approximately 30% of the variance in personality reflects genetic variance). These findings are similar to those found in younger adult samples. For the Locus of Control subscale "Luck," no evidence of the importance of genetic influences could be found, and for three measures, Lack of Assertiveness, Hostility, and Agreeableness, alternative models indicate that heritability could be considered negligible. Thus, although personality traits are highly reliable and relatively stable, they are only moderately heritable. Contrary to some expectations (Costa & McCrae, 1992), characteristics need not be highly heritable in order to be considered stable traits.

2. Sharing the same rearing family environment did not contribute to any great extent to twin similarity in personality later in life. This may not be surprising given the age range of the sample, but is in contrast to predictions of environmentally oriented researchers (Hoffman, 1991).

3. By far the most important influence for individual difference in personality in adults is the nonshared environment (i.e., individual specific environmental effects that contribute to differences among family members).

b. *Cognitive Abilities.* Considerable previous behavioral genetic work has been directed toward estimating the relative importance of genetic effects (heritability) for individual differences in cognitive abilities early in the life span. The results from several of the studies cited in Section III have now provided heritability estimates for cognitive abilities among older adults. Eighty percent of the differences seen among older adults for general cognitive ability (IQ) are due to genetic differences (see Table I) (Finkel, Pedersen, McGue, & McClearn, 1995; Pedersen, Plomin, Nesselroade, & McClearn, 1992). This value is somewhat higher than those found in adolescence and early adulthood, but is consistent with reports from middle-aged adults (Bouchard, Lykken, McGue, Segal, & Tellegen, 1990; Tambs, Sundet, & Magnus, 1984).

**Table I**
Summary of Proportions of Variance for Cognitive Measures
Due to Genetic and Environmental Effects

| Cognitive measure | Study | Heritability | Shared environment | Nonshared environment |
|---|---|---|---|---|
| Information | SATSA[a] | 60[c] | 14[e] | 26 |
| | MTSADA[b] | 77 | 0 | 23 |
| Block design | SATSA | 58[c] | 11[e] | 30 |
| | MTSADA | 49 | 23 | 28 |
| | Kinki[d] | 60[c] | 0 | 40 |
| Digit symbol | SATSA | 64[c] | 0 | 36 |
| | MTSADA | 62 | 0 | 38 |
| | Kinki[d] | 22 | 33 | 45 |
| Digit span forward | SATSA | 37 | 0 | 63 |
| | MTSADA | 40 | 0 | 60 |
| | Kinki[d] | 0 | 35 | 65 |
| Digit span backward | SATSA | 44 | 0 | 56 |
| | MTSADA | 47 | 0 | 53 |
| General cognitive ability | SATSA | 81 | 0 | 19 |
| | MTSADA | 80 | 0 | 20 |

[a]Swedish Adoption/Twin Study of Aging (SATSA) results are from Pedersen et al., 1992.
[b]Minnesota Study of Adult Development and Aging (MTSADA) results are from Finkel et al., 1995.
[c]Genetic variance is nonadditive.
[d]Computed by author from published intraclass correlations in Hayakawa et al. (1992).
[e]Shared variance is from rearing environment.

Measures of specific cognitive abilities show more moderate heritabilities; 50–75% of the variance in crystallized abilities (such as Information) and fluid abilities (such as Block Design) reflects genetic variance. Heritabilities for measures of Perceptual Speed (such as Digit Symbol) are about .63, whereas heritability for memory measures tends to be lower (.40–.50). Thus, although fluid abilities are generally considered to be more biologically and genetically influenced and crystallized abilities to be more environmentally and culturally influenced (Baltes, 1993), there is little evidence for differential heritability dependent on domain of cognitive ability.

Findings from the Kinki Study, indicating substantial shared environmental effects for Digit Span and Digit Symbol (Hayakawa et al., 1992), are not similar to those of MTSADA or SATSA. The Japanese data are not corrected for age, which tends to increase spuriously the fraternal-twin correlations for variables correlated with age and hence mimic a shared environmental effect. Thus, it is not clear whether analytic, population, or sampling differences underlie the discrepant findings.

Parent–offspring and sibling correlations may also be used to indicate the importance of familial effects on cognitive abilities, although genetic effects are confounded with shared family environmental influences. In the SLS, the sibling correlations on tests of cognitive abilities based on the Thurstone framework are generally similar to the fraternal twin correlations for similar measures in SATSA and MTSADA (fraternal twins and other sibling pairs both share 50% of their genes in common). Parent–offspring correlations are similar to the sibling correlations, but familial estimates from both pairings are somewhat lower than results from twin studies. Nevertheless, the results support the hypothesis that genetic effects are important late in life.

Three of the twin studies have reported heritability for measures of cognitive performance typically used as screening devices for dementia (Table II). The relative importance of genetic influences for these measures is lower than that for general cognitive abilities, and more similar to measures in the memory domain. The lower heritability of these tests, which predominantly assess memory, may indicate either that these measures are more sensitive to environmentally induced decrements in performance or that there is a restricted range of variation resulting in less twin similarity and, hence, a lower heritability.

On the whole, these results suggest that genetic factors are of considerable importance for individual differences in cognitive abilities in the elderly. Genetic effects may have less influence on memory and on screening devices for dementia. Shared family influences, such as growing up in the same home, do not contribute consistently to familial similarity later in life.

## 2. Cross-Sectional Age Differences in Heritability

In general, most of the behavioral genetic studies of the elderly have reported heritabilities based on the entire sample. This is due in part to the need to maintain sufficient sample sizes for reasonable power.

On the other hand, this often results in samples with broad age ranges, spanning up to 35 years. There is no genetic reason why heritability must remain stable throughout the life span. Variance may increase (or decrease) across the life span as a result of an increase (or decrease) in genetic or environmental variance or both. Thus, a particularly pertinent topic for behavioral genetic studies of aging is the extent of age differences and age changes in heritability. (For a detailed discussion of cross-sectional and longitudinal applications and interpretations of behavioral genetic analyses, see Pedersen, 1991.)

In order to evaluate age differences, it is possible to partition samples into arbitrary cohorts and test whether there are significant cohort differences in estimates of heritability and environmental effects. In a comprehensive examination of age differences in heritability for health later in life, the SATSA sample was divided into four cohorts and total variance was depicted in terms of their genetic and environmental components (Harris, Pedersen, McClearn, Plomin, & Nesselroade, 1992). As can be seen in Figure 1, total variation increases linearly across the four age groups. For self-rated health, the increase in total variance is best explained by an increase in environmental variance. A similar pattern is found for a measure of chronic illnesses (sum of illnesses); the oldest age group,

**Table II**
Summary of Proportions of Variance (Genetic and Environmental) for Males
on Cognitive Performance Screening Instruments

| Screening instrument | Study | Heritability | Shared environment | Nonshared environment |
| --- | --- | --- | --- | --- |
| MMSE | SATSA[a] | .39 | | .61 |
| | NHLBI[b] | .38 | .13 | .62 |
| Iowa Screening | NHLBI[b] | .22 | | .88 |
| TICS | NAS[c] | .30 | | .70 |

[a]Swedish Adoption Twin Study on Aging (SATSA) from Pedersen, Reynolds, and Gatz (1994).
[b]National Heart, Lung, and Blood Institute (NHLBI) from Swan et al. (1990).
[c]National Academy of Science (NAS) from Brandt et al. (1993).

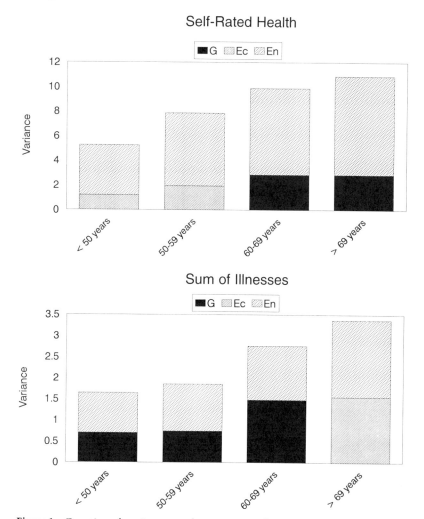

**Figure 1**  Genetic and environmental components of variance in two measures of self-reported health for four age groups. G, genetic variance, Ec, shared environmental variance, En, nonshared environmental variance. (Adapted from "Age Differences in the Etiology of the Relationship Between Life Satisfaction and Self-rated Health," by J. R. Harris, N. L. Pedersen, C. Stacey, G. E. McClearn, and J. R. Nesselroade, 1992, *Journal of Aging and Health, 4*, pp. 349–368. Copyright by the Gerontological Society of America. Adapted with permission).

however, does not conform to the pattern established in the younger groups, suggesting a cohort effect.

In other analyses of SATSA, the sample has arbitrarily been divided into two cohorts. Significant differences in heritabilities in younger twins (under 60 years of age) and older twins (60 years and older) were found for depressive symptoms as measured by the Center for Epidemiological Studies-Depression (CES-D) (Gatz, Pedersen, Plomin, Nesselroade, & McClearn, 1992). Heritabilities for the Psychomotor Retardation subscale were greater in the older than the younger cohort. Similarly, heritability for life satisfaction was greater in older (≥ 65) than younger (<65) twins (Harris, Pedersen, Stacey,

McClearn, & Nesselroade, 1992). Whereas genetic effects may become more important for well-being, accumulation of environmental insults appears to become more important for indicators of homeostasis and frailty. These results point to the need for formulating theories of aging that allow for domain-specific influences that may vary across the life span.

Although the initial reports of cognitive abilities from SATSA and MTSADA pooled the entire sample of twins, recent analyses have been concerned with comparisons across age groups and nationalities. A recent investigation of general cognitive abilities found some differences across age groups (Finkel, Pedersen et al., 1995). There were no significant differences between nationalities in the estimates of genetic and environmental influence on cognitive measures assessing verbal ability, spatial ability, perceptual speed, and memory for twins under 65 years of age. However, older Swedish twins (≥65 years) demonstrated a significantly lower heritability for general cognitive abilities (IQ), suggesting a possible inverted L-shaped function for the relationship between heritability and IQ later in the life span. If confirmed with longitudinal data and older samples such as OCTO-Twin, these results suggest that environmental influences become increasingly important for individual differences in reserve capacity late in life.

A number of tentative conclusions can be drawn from these cross-sectional results. For some phenotypes, genetic effects are at least as important if not more so for older adults than for adolescents and younger adults. For other traits, environmental influences are more important for individual differences in the elderly. In other words, the age differences in genetic effects are phenotype-specific. Needless to say, caution should be taken in drawing conclusions from cross-sectional analyses. The results may reflect cohort effects or special selection effects, such that only

pairs in which both members are alive are available for participation. Nevertheless, these analyses are an important first step in understanding group differences across the life span.

## 3. Longitudinal Issues and Findings

From a longitudinal perspective, there are several types of stability that may be considered. Most familiar to gerontologists is *phenotypic stability* (i.e., stability in the level of measures and stability as indicated by the correlation between the same measures on successive occasions). *Structural stability* is another concept of interest in developmental studies. Behavioral genetic analyses can contribute to the understanding of stability by elucidating the etiology of phenotypic or structural stability in terms of genetic and environmental components. Phenotypic stability is a result of the relative influence of genes and environments on two occasions (heritability) as well as the *stability of the genetic and environmental effects* between those occasions.

Genetic and environmental correlations describe the extent to which genetic and environmental effects, respectively, are stable. Loosely interpreted, the genetic correlation indicates the extent to which there is "overlap" in genetic effects operating on two or more occasions (for a more rigorous discussion, see Carey, 1988). Genetic effects may be highly stable, regardless of their relative importance at any two time points. Similarly, new or "innovative" genetic effects may come into play at selected developmental stages. Perhaps one of the most common misconceptions concerning the nature of genetic effects is that because we are born with a full complement of genes, their influence must be stable and invariant throughout the life span. Whether or not genetic influence is stable should be evaluated empirically for each phenotype of interest.

There have been relatively few behavioral genetic analyses of longitudinal data, and most of these have been applied to data collected on children or adolescents. Recently, measures of personality and cognition at two time points with a 3–year interval have been analyzed using behavioral genetic techniques in SATSA. Not only phenotypic but also genotypic and environmental stability were of interest. Phenotypic stability was relatively high for measures of both personality and cognitive abilities, on average .70 (Pedersen, 1993; Plomin, Pedersen, Lichtenstein, & McClearn, 1994).

In the second step, the extent of genetic and environmental stability was calculated. For two measures of personality (neuroticism and extroversion), genetic correlations (stabilities) were 1.00 and .88, respectively, whereas for specific cognitive abilities, genetic correlations were somewhat lower, ranging from .32 to .67 (average .52). Environmental stabilities were considerably lower in both domains.

In the next step, genetic and environmental components of the phenotypic stabilities were determined. As mentioned above, these components are a function of not only the respective stabilities of the genetic and environmental factors, but also the relative importance of the factors at the two time points. Heritability was very similar at the two time points for measures of both personality and cognitive abilities, but greater for cognitive abilities than personality at each time point. Nevertheless, because of the greater genetic stability for personality than cognitive ability, the net importance of genetic effects for phenotypic stability in cognitive abilities was somewhat less than that for personality: Genetic and environmental effects are equally important for phenotypic stability in personality across a 3-year period for adults over 50 years of age, but account on average for 40% (range 25–57%) of the phenotypic stability for specific cognitive abilities.

These results demonstrate that high heritability at two times does not necessarily imply substantial phenotypic stability nor does it imply that the genetic component of stability is substantial. If the genetic correlation is low, the genetic contribution to stability may be low despite high heritabilities. Although many developmentalists associate the adjectives *genetic* and *stable*, these results demonstrate the fallacy of this misconception.

Thus far, data from only two points of time have been available for analysis, and hence the results must be interpreted with caution. When data from more than two occasions are available, a number of interesting questions can be addressed. Among them are issues related to the nature of growth curves or terminal decline. Models are available for addressing issues concerning mean level stability or average growth curves (McArdle, 1986; Molenaar, Boomsma, & Dolan, 1991). Simultaneous modeling of means and covariances allows for hypothesis testing concerning whether means and covariances are influenced by common underlying processes.

Stability and change are not necessarily antonyms, at least from a quantitative genetic perspective. The etiology of change may be very different from the etiology of stability (Plomin & Nesselroade, 1990), because the heritability of change is a function not only of the heritability of the trait, but also the genetic correlation between occasions *and* the phenotypic stability. Although studies of change may be intuitively appealing, power is considerably lower in analysis of change scores, and the likelihood of finding significant genetic variance for change is reduced. In a 5-year follow-up of a small subsample of the NHLBI Twin Study, change in digit-symbol substitution scores was examined (Swan, LaRue, Carmelli, Reed, & Fabsitz, 1992). Identical twins were more concordant than fraternal twins (45% and 8%, respectively) for decline >1 SD, suggesting a possible role of genetic factors in change for this measure and sample.

Both stability (Plomin et al., 1994) and change (Swan et al., 1992) are thus in part influenced by genetic effects. Comparisons of decliners and their nondeclining co-twins in discordant pairs reveal that some cardiovascular risk factors (initial systolic blood pressure, serum cholesterol, and heart rate) differ at baseline in the decliners. Although the sample was small, the results indicate that for some measures there may be sufficient decline to be able to examine the etiology of individual differences in change.

Finally, stability in terms of structural invariance can be assessed by comparing factor structures at different measurement occasions within a quantitative genetic design. This approach has the advantage of providing information on the role of genetic and environmental factors for structural invariance or change. How stable is the genetic covariance structure? To what extent does phenotypic structural invariance reflect stability in the genetic or environmental structure? These questions may be addressed with information from genetically informative populations of the elderly.

Longitudinal analyses of health and behavior within a behavioral genetic perspective are in their infancy. Not before further measurement occasions become available in these twin studies will the potential of these methodologies be harnessed.

B. Associations among and within Domains

1. Associations among Domains

One of the most exciting developments in behavioral genetic methodology is the analysis of associations within and among different phenotypic domains. Rather than simply describing the extent of associations —for example, the importance of social networks for personality or health later in life—the nature of the associations can be

evaluated. Much the same as variance can be partitioned into genetic and environmental components, correlations or covariation can be partitioned into genetic and environmental components. The research question now becomes, To what extent is the association between social support and health due to genetic or environmental factors or both? Several recent reports from SATSA, MTSADA, and the NHLBI study have taken this approach. These analyses have focused on associations both within and among domains relevant to gerontological issues.

*a. Psychosocial Factors, Health, and Well-Being.* Although the ability to maintain an adequate social support network and mental health is well established (for a review, see Broadhead et al., 1983), little is known about the underlying mechanisms. Previous reports from SATSA have indicated that individual differences in both mental health (Gatz et al., 1992) and perceived quality of social support (Bergeman, Plomin, Pedersen, Mc-Clearn, & Nesselroade, 1990) reflect to some extent genetic differences. It is therefore possible that the associations between these measures also reflect genetic influences. A multivariate analysis of perceived social support, mental health, and life satisfaction indicates that *both* genetic and environmental factors influence the perceived support–well-being associations. In other words, the genetic influences that contribute to an individual's perception of the adequacy of the social support system also contribute to depressive symptoms and life satisfaction (Bergeman, Plomin, Pedersen, & McClearn, 1991). The process by which this relationship occurs is not known and requires longitudinal data for further explication, but similar findings based on younger samples suggest that the genetic and environmental effects that contribute to perceptions of social support (and not support itself) act as a buffer for psychological well-being

(Kessler, Kendler, Heath, Neale, & Eaves, 1992).

In a similar analysis, the relationship between life satisfaction and self-rated health has also been examined (Harris, Pedersen, Stacey et al., 1992). Just as there were age-group differences for the relative importance of genetic effects for life satisfaction and self-rated health, there were age-group differences for the mediation of the relationships between these two measures. The phenotypic correlation in twins 65 years and older ($r = .47$) was mediated approximately equally by genetic and environmental effects, whereas for those under 65 the correlation ($r = .38$) was exclusively due to environmental influences. Thus, in the younger adults, experiences (such as familial transitions and leisure activities) result in an association between life satisfaction and self-rated health. However, for the elderly both experiences and genetic effects are important for the association between these two indicators of well-being.

The complexity of the aging process is further illustrated by data concerning sex differences in the associations between self-reported health and social and psychosocial factors such as stressful life events, perceived social support, and loneliness. In SATSA, for example, correlations between self-rated health and these psychosocial factors ranged between .10 and .25 for women but ranged between 0 and .15 for men (Figure 2) (Lichtenstein & Pedersen, in press). Furthermore, the mediators of the associations were quite different in men and women. For women, the associations reflected both genetic and environmental mechanisms, whereas for men the associations were entirely attributable to environmental events and experiences. The involvement of nonshared environmental influences suggests that idiosyncratic events, such as the death of a spouse, are important for the relationship between psychosocial factors and health. Nonshared effects were not, however, the

most important mediator of the relationships. Genetic effects were considerably more important for the women, and shared environmental effects (of the sort that contribute to familial similarity) were more important for men. It is not clear whether the sex difference reflects sex differences in biological aging or whether the psychosocial factors assess different concepts in men and women.

*b. Cognitive and Physical Functioning.* Steuer and Jarvik hypothesized that "the brain may be seen as a monitor of the organism's general functioning" and further that "cognitive functioning may be regarded as a sensitive indicator system of the human organism's total functioning" (1981, p. 248). On the other hand, Baltes concluded that "how well the mind functions intellectually has little or no relationship with how persons characterize their subjective state of wellness" (in press, p. 14). Both points of view are supported by recent results from SATSA (Harris & Pedersen, 1994). Measures of cognitive abilities correlated significantly with measures of functional capacity (e.g., mobility, strength, gait, and balance) but not with self-rated health. In younger twins (under 65), associations of functional capacity with all specific cognitive abilities except memory are mediated by genetic influences. In the older twins, unique, nonshared environmental influences are also important mediators.

The greater association between measures in the older group seems to be attributable to unique experiences that begin to emerge after age 65. Onset of nongenetic diseases could be one type of unique environmental event. These findings suggest that, in accord with wear-and-tear hypotheses of aging, variability in vitality in old age reflects baseline genetic variation and an increasing accumulation of environmental stressors.

Using data from MTSADA, Finkel and colleagues (Finkel & McGue, 1993) have

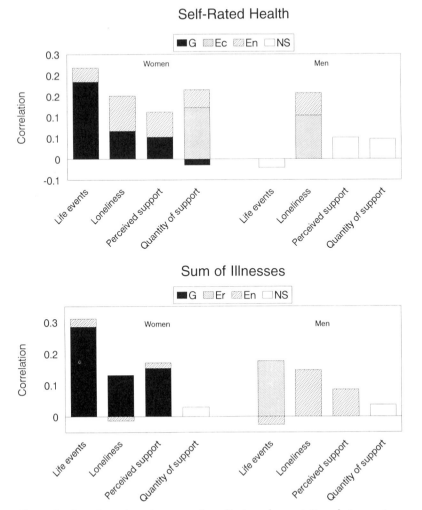

**Figure 2** Genetic and environmental mediation of associations between two measures of self-reported health and psychosocial factors. G, genetic variance, Ec, shared environmental variance, Er, rearing environmental variance, En, nonshared environmental variance, NS, nonsignificant phenotypic correlation. (Adapted from "Social relationships, stressful life events, and self-reported physical health: Genetic and environmental influences" by P. Lichtenstein and N. L. Pedersen, 1995, *Psychology and Health*. Copyright by Harwood Academic Publishers. Adapted with permission).

also found that environmental effects are important mediators of the associations between memory measures and lifestyle measures. They have applied a somewhat different approach to the study of the associations between cognitive and physiological domains (Finkel, Whitfield, & McGue, 1995). In a three-step process, stepwise multiple regressions were first run to find the set of cognitive and physiological variables that predicted chronological age. These 12 variables were then factor analyzed, resulting in three factors of "functional age": a cognitive factor, a speed factor, and a physiological factor.

In the third step, a genetic model was

applied to the factor scores to determine not only the importance of genetic and environmental effects for these three factors, but also the extent to which these factors were influenced by the same genetic or environmental effects, or both. Although heritability ($h^2$) was lower for the speed and physiological factors ($h^2 = .18$ and .20, respectively) than for the cognitive factor ($h^2 = .51$), there was complete overlap in the genetic influences for these components of functional age. There was also considerable overlap in the environmental influences on the three factors. The relatively lower heritabilities for the speed and physiological factors are interesting in light of the stronger associations found with age for speeded tasks.

Taken together, the cross-sectional suggestion of a decrease in heritability for general cognitive ability and health measures in advanced age and the increasing importance of environmental effects for associations between cognitive and physical indicators lead to the speculation that age-related phenomena such as critical loss, which involves both cognitive and physical aspects (see Berg, Ch. 18, this volume), will evidence considerable environmental variation. One could imagine that individual differences in baseline maintenance of homeostasis predominantly reflect genetic variance. A decline in reserve capacity or plasticity may result from the accumulation of environmental stressors, the timing of which is individual-specific. Furthermore, these findings underscore the need for multidimensional approaches to the study of aging (Baltes, in press).

*c. Risk Factors for Dementia.* Low educational attainment has been identified as a risk factor for both Alzheimer's disease and dementia in general (Mortimer & Graves, 1993), and there is a well-documented association between scores on the Mini-Mental State Examination (MMSE) and educational attainment (Magaziner, Bassett, & Hebel, 1987).

Three interpretations have been suggested: (a) low education is a proxy for a variety of putative risk factors over the life span, such as poorer nutrition early in life, greater use of alcohol, or occupations with greater exposure to neurotoxins, all of which in turn could lead to impaired cognitive performance (Mortimer & Graves, 1993); (b) higher education may reflect greater cerebral capacity and hence greater neuronal reserve (Katzman, 1993; Mortimer, 1994); and (c) individuals with higher education tend to seek intellectually stimulating tasks hence activating nerve cells and inhibiting neuronal degeneration, the result of which is better maintenance of cognitive level (Swaab, 1991).

The etiology of the association between MMSE scores and education has recently been addressed in the NHLBI Twin Study (Carmelli, Swan, & Cardon, 1995) and in SATSA (Pedersen, Reynolds, & Gatz, in press). Both studies demonstrated that for men the association is primarily due to a common genetic factor influencing both education and MMSE performance. Furthermore, the genetic influences on MMSE performance almost entirely reflect genetic influences on general cognitive abilities (i.e., intelligence). The results support the hypothesis that the association between education and MMSE performance predominantly reflects cerebral capacity rather than test bias or health-endangering lifestyles in less educated individuals.

## 2. Associations within Domains

Much can also be learned about the structure of a phenotype by applying behavioral genetic techniques. Conventional psychometric analyses characterize the phenotypic factor structure, but the structure may result from different underlying genetic and environmental factors. For example, there is increasing consensus for a five-factor theory of personality, although there are correlations among the factors, and genetic effects are of similar importance across the five factors. Behavioral genetic analyses could determine whether there is a general genetic factor affecting all aspects of personality, but distinct environmental factors of importance for the individual aspects. Similarly, issues concerning domains in cognitive aging may be addressed to find the genetic and environmental structure. Assumptions about the "biological-genetic" determination of fluid intelligence versus the "environmental-cultural" control of crystallized intelligence are best tested in genetically informative populations.

Multivariate behavioral genetic models have explored whether there are genetic effects for specific abilities that are independent of general cognitive ability (or $g$). Bivariate analyses of the associations of four memory measures with cognitive and lifestyle factors suggest that the relationship between memory and cognitive variables is predominantly genetic in nature, whereas environmental influences are also important for the associations with the lifestyle variables (Finkel & McGue, 1993). Although much genetic influence for separate tests can be explained by genetic effects on $g$, 12 of 13 tests showed significant genetic influence independent of genetic influence on general cognitive ability (Pedersen, Plomin, & McClearn, 1994). These findings are pertinent to issues concerning dedifferentiation of cognitive abilities with increasing age. One might predict that dedifferentiation reflects genetic influences akin to those important for $g$, and that differentiation is due more to environmental influences.

Measures of information processing in the elderly have also been subjected to behavioral genetic analyses (Whitfield, Cherny, Finkel, & McGue, 1994). Simple and choice reaction time loaded on a speed factor, whereas backward digit span and arithmetic loaded on a working memory factor. These two factors, especially the latter, represent to a substantial extent the

genetic influences on the four information-processing tasks. Furthermore, there is a significant correlation in the genetic effects influencing the two factors. The results further demonstrate the importance of genetic factors for individual differences in cognitive processing late in life.

## C. Heritability of Normal versus Extreme Behaviors

The results described in the previous sections were concerned with the influence of genetic and environmental influences on the normal range of behaviors in the elderly. Many of these behaviors have pathological counterparts, for example memory versus dementia, or depressive symptoms versus clinical depression. Until now, most studies of extreme behaviors have been performed in selected samples in which one or more family members have developed a disease. Evidence is accumulating that genetic factors are important for the manifestation of Alzheimer's disease later in life. Preliminary results from the three twin studies mentioned in Section III.H indicate that concordances for dementia in identical twin pairs are substantially higher than those in fraternal twin pairs (Breitner et al., 1993) and that heritability may be as high as .72 for late-age-of-onset dementias. On the other hand, heritability for memory in the normal range is considerably lower, .40 on average (see Section IV.A.1.b).

A similar pattern of lower heritability in normal range behavior is evident for depressive symptoms versus clinical depression. Whereas Gatz et al. (1992) found low or nonsignificant influences of genetic variance on individual differences for depressive symptoms, Kendler and colleagues (Kendler, Pedersen, Johnson, Neale, & Mathé, 1993) reported heritabilities of .64 for affective disorders. Is the heritability of the extremes different from the normal range?

DeFries and Fulker (1985) first described

a multiple regression model for the analysis of twin data obtained from selected samples, which may help determine whether the genetic architecture of a trait (e.g., memory) is different in samples identified because one member is at the extreme of the distribution (e.g., demented). Does heritability for cognition and memory in pairs where one or both members develop dementia differ from that in pairs where both remain intact? Not only pathology but also extremes at the positive end of the distribution (e.g., "successful aging") can be addressed. Analyses of this sort represent a logical extension of the dementia and normal aging studies described previously.

## V. Summary

Perhaps one of the most notable trends in recent years concerning perspectives on aging has been a recognition of heterogeneity and a de-emphasis on "inevitable" decline. Psychological developmental theories of the life span describe a dynamic process in which the focus is on change in proportion rather than a sequence from growth to decline (Baltes, in press). Gerontological behavioral genetics elaborates on both of these perspectives: heterogeneity and change in proportion. The purpose of behavioral genetic analyses is to describe inter- and intraindividual variability in terms of genetic and environmental sources. These influences are described in terms of proportions of variation, and themselves display considerable heterogeneity. As the following summary of five principal findings indicates, there are no patent conclusions concerning the role of genetic and environmental factors for aging.

1. The relative importance of genetic and environmental effects on individual differences in the elderly is phenotype-specific. Heritability is low to moderate for personality traits and measures of well-being, moderate for health-related phenotypes, and greater for cognitive abilities. Within domains there is also considerable variability in heritability estimates (e.g., heritability for memory is lower than for verbal and spatial abilities or perceptual speed).

2. There are age differences in heritability, the pattern of which is phenotype-dependent. For some measures, particularly health-related characteristics, the relative importance of genetic effects appears to decrease across age groups. For others, heritability is stable, increases, or reflects an inverted L-shaped function. Variance changes may reflect either an increase of environmental or genetic influences, depending on the phenotype. More often, environmental effects account for the increase in variability in health-related phenotypes.

3. Across short time spans, genetic effects are more stable than environmental effects for personality and cognition. Environmental effects of importance for individual differences late in life are changing. Nevertheless, environmental influences are at least as important for phenotypic stability across short (3–6 year) spans of time.

4. The associations among and between domains are variably mediated by genetic and environmental influences. Within domains, for example, within the cognitive domain, the associations are mediated predominantly by genetic influences, that is, genetic effects for one measure of memory are highly correlated with genetic effects for another. On the other hand, associations across domains depend on the measures involved and the age and sex of the subjects studied.

5. Heritability of extreme behaviors or pathologies may differ from heritability of normal range behavior in the elderly. There may be different mechanisms influencing individual differences in memory or depressive symptoms than those

resulting in the manifestation of dementia or depression (which may require some other influence to cross the threshold).

The variability in the relative importance of genetic and environmental effects, dependent on the phenotype and the sex and age of the sample, reaffirms the need for multidimensional theories of aging that integrate interdisciplinary perspectives. Evidence from cross-sectional and longitudinal analyses suggests that maintenance of stability may be very different than change or decline. Theories of aging that rely on demonstration of genetic variance as support for claims of stability need to be modified to incorporate findings of both genetic and environmental involvement in stability. On the other hand, multivariate behavioral genetic models may be helpful tools for reassessing theories concerning the structure of individual differences within domain (e.g., the five-factor theory of personality or the fluid–crystallized distinction.)

Although there is considerable variation among the elderly, this is not necessarily a result of increased environmental variation. Nevertheless, evidence for reduced heritability for health and cognition in older subsamples might indicate an accumulation of environmental stressors ("wear and tear") or lack of activation ("use it or lose it"). Both genetic and environmental factors are mediators of associations between cognitive and health domains after the age of 65, perhaps indicating the loss of ability to alter gene expression in response to environmental challenge (Morgan, in press).

The explosion of information coming from a number of relatively recently established twin studies of aging as well as other studies of gerontologically relevant issues in genetically informative populations represents only the tip of the iceberg. Although a great deal more information will become available in the next few years, there is a clear need for following these samples longitudinally and for a greater focus on genetic analyses in generational studies. This will be the only way generalizations about age differences may be confirmed concerning the actual aging processes.

## Acknowledgments

Preparation of this chapter was supported in part by grants from the National Institute on Aging (AG-04563, AG-10175, AG-08724), the John D. and Catherine T. MacArthur Foundation, and the Swedish Council for Social Research (92–0186).

## References

Baltes, P. B. (1993). The aging mind: Potential and limits. *Gerontologist, 33,* 580–594.

Baltes, P. B. (in press). Psychological and social aspects of aging: Facts and frontiers. In D. Magnusson (Ed.), *The life-span development of individuals: Behavioral, neurobiological and psychosocial perspectives.* Cambridge, England: Cambridge University Press.

Bengtson, V. L., & Roberts, R. E. L. (1991). Intergenerational solidarity in aging families: An example of formal theory construction. *Journal of Marriage and the Family, 53,* 856–870.

Berg, S., Johansson, B., Plomin, R., Ahern, F. M., Pedersen, N. L., & McClearn, G. E. (1992). Origins of variance in the old-old: The first presentation of the OCTO-Twin Study in Sweden. *Behavior Genetics, 22,* 708–709.

Bergem, A. L. M., Engedal, K., & Kringlen, E. (1992). Twin concordance and discordance for vascular dementia and dementia of the Alzheimer type. *Neurobiology of Aging, 13*(Suppl. 1), 66.

Bergeman, C. S., Plomin, R., Pedersen, N. L., & McClearn, G. E. (1991). Genetic mediation of the relationship between social support and psychological well-being. *Psychology and Aging, 6,* 640–646.

Bergeman, C. S., Plomin, R., Pedersen, N. L., McClearn, G. E., & Nesselroade, J. R. (1990). Genetic and environmental influences on social support: The Swedish Adoption/Twin

Study of Aging. *Journal of Gerontology: Psychological Sciences, 45,* P101–P106.

Bouchard, T. J., Jr., Lykken, D. T., McGue, M., Segal, N. L., & Tellegen, A. (1990). Sources of human psychological differences: The Minnesota Study of Twins Reared Apart. *Science, 250,* 223–228.

Brandt, J., Welsh, K. A., Breitner, J. C. S., Folstein, M. F., Helms, M., & Christian, J. C. (1993). Hereditary influences on cognitive functioning in older men: A study of 4,000 twin pairs. *Archives of Neurology (Chicago), 50,* 599–603.

Breitner, J. C. S., Gatz, M., Bergem, A. L. M., Christian, J. C., Mortimer, J. A., McClearn, G. E., Heston, L. L., Welsh, K. A., Anthony, J. C., Folstein, M. F., & Radebaugh, T. S. (1993). Use of twin cohorts for research in Alzheimer's disease. *Neurology, 43,* 261–267.

Breitner, J. C. S., Welsh, K. A., Magruder-Habib, K. M., Churchill, C. M., Folstein, M. F., Murphy, E. A., Priolo, C. V., & Brandt, J. (1990). Alzheimer's disease in the NAS Registry of aging twin veterans: I. Pilot investigations. *Dementia, 1,* 297–303.

Broadhead, W. E., Kaplan, B. H., James, S. A., Wagner, E. H., Schoenback, V. J., Grimson, R., Heyden, S., Tibblin, G., & Gehlbach, S. H. (1983). The epidemiological evidence for a relationship between social support and health. *American Journal of Epidemiology, 117,* 521–537.

Carey, G. (1988). Inference about genetic correlations. *Behavior Genetics, 18,* 329–338.

Carmelli, D., Swan, G. E., & Cardon, L. R. (1995). Genetic mediation in the relationship of education to cognitive function in older people. *Psychology and Aging, 10,* 48–53.

Costa, P. T., & McCrae, R. R. (1992). 4 ways 5 factors are basic. *Personality and Individual Differences, 13,* 653–665.

DeFries, J. C., & Fulker, D. W. (1985). Multiple regression analysis of twin data. *Behavior Genetics, 15,* 467–473.

Feinleib, M., Garrison, R. J., Fabsitz, R. R., Christian, J. C., Hrubec, Z., Borhani, N. O., Kannel, W. B., Rosenman, R., Schwartz, J. T., & Wagner, J. O. (1977). The NHLBI Twin Study of cardiovascular disease risk factors: Methodology and summary of results. *American Journal of Epidemiology, 106,* 284–295.

Finkel, D., & McGue, M. (1993). The origins of individual differences in memory among the elderly: A behavior genetic analysis. *Psychology and Aging, 8,* 527–537.

Finkel, D., Pedersen, N. L., McGue, M., & McClearn, G. E. (1995). Heritability of cognitive abilities in adult twins: Comparisons of Minnesota and Swedish data. *Behavior Genetics, 25,* 421–431.

Finkel, D., Whitfield, K., & McGue, M. (1995). Genetic and environmental influences on functional age: A twin study. *Journal of Gerontology: Psychological Sciences, 50B,* 104–113.

Gatz, M., Pedersen, N. L., Plomin, R., Nesselroade, J. R., & McClearn, G. E. (1992). Importance of shared genes and shared environments for symptoms of depression in older adults. *Journal of Abnormal Psychology, 101,* 701–708.

Gatz, M., Pedersen, N. L., Reynolds, C., & Lowe, B. (1993, September). *Screening a population for dementia using a telephone interview protocol and the Mini-Mental State Examination: Data from The Study of Dementia in Swedish Twins.* Paper presented at the Sixth Congress of the International Psychogeriatric Association, Berlin.

Harris, J. R., & Pedersen, N. L. (1994). How do genes and environments contribute to the relationship between health and cognition? *Nordiska Kongressen i Gerontologi Jönköping, Sweden, 12th,* Abstraktbok, p. 43.

Harris, J. R., Pedersen, N. L., McClearn, G. E., Plomin, R., & Nesselroade, J. R. (1992). Age differences in genetic and environmental influences for health from the Swedish Adoption/Twin Study of Aging. *Journal of Gerontology: Psychological Sciences, 47,* 213–220.

Harris, J. R., Pedersen, N. L., Stacey, C., McClearn, G. E., & Nesselroade, J. R. (1992). Age differences in the etiology of the relationship between life satisfaction and self-rated health. *Journal of Aging and Health, 4,* 349–368.

Hayakawa, K., Shimizu, T., Ohba, Y., & Tomioka, S. (1992). Risk factors for cognitive aging in adult twins. *Acta Geneticae Medicae et Gemellologiae, 41,* 187–195.

Hoffman, L. (1991). The influence of the family environment on personality. *Psychological Bulletin, 110,* 187–203.

Jarvik, L. F., & Bank, L. (1983). Aging twins:

Longitudinal psychometric data. In K.W. Schaie (Ed.), *Longitudinal studies of adult psychological development* (pp. 40–63). New York: Guilford.

Kallmann, F. J., & Sander, G. (1948). Twin studies on aging and longevity. *Journal of Heredity, 39*, 349–357.

Katzman, R. (1993). Education and the prevalence of dementia and Alzheimer's disease. *Neurology, 43*, 113–120.

Kendler, K. S., Pedersen, N., Johnson, L., Neale, M. C., & Mathé, A. A. (1993). A pilot Swedish twin study of affective illness, including hospital- and population-ascertained subsamples. *Archives of General Psychiatry, 50*, 699–706.

Kessler, R. C., Kendler, K. S., Heath, A., Neale, M. C., & Eaves, L. J. (1992). Social support, depressed mood, and adjustment to stress: A genetic epidemiologic investigation. *Journal of Personality and Social Psychology, 62*, 257–272.

Lichtenstein, P., & Pedersen, N. L. (1995). Social relationships, stressful life events, and self-reported physical health: Genetic and environmental influences. *Psychology and Health, 10*, 295–319.

Magaziner, J., Bassett, S. S., & Hebel, J. R. (1987). Predicting performance on the Mini-Mental State Examination. *Journal of the American Geriatrics Society, 35*, 996–1000.

McArdle, J. (1986). Latent-variable growth within behavior genetic models. *Behavior Genetics, 16*, 79–95.

McGue, M., Hirsch, B., & Lykken, D. T. (1993). Age and the self-perception of ability: A twin study analysis. *Psychology and Aging, 8*, 72–80.

Miles, T. P., Furner, S. E., Goldberg, J., & Meyer, J. (1992). Identifying a national cohort of older twins: The health of older twins study (HOOTS) [Special issue II]. *The Gerontologist, 32*, 86.

Molenaar, P., Boomsma, D., & Dolan, C. (1991). Genetic and environmental factors in a developmental perspective. In D. Magnusson, L. Bergman, G. Rudinger, & B. Törestad (Eds.), *Problems and methods in longitudinal research: Stability and change* (pp. 250–273). Cambridge, England: Cambridge University Press.

Morgan, D. G. (in press). Aging and molecular biology. In D. Magnusson (Ed.), *The life-span development of individuals: Behavioral,* *neurobiological and psychosocial perspectives.* Cambridge, England: Cambridge University Press.

Mortimer, J. A. (1994). What are the risk factors for dementia? In F. A. Huppert, C. Brayne, & D. O'Connor (Eds.), *Dementia and normal ageing* (pp. 208–229). Cambridge, England: Cambridge University Press.

Mortimer, J. A., & Graves, A. B. (1993). Education and other socioeconomic determinants of dementia and Alzheimer's disease. *Neurology, 43*(Suppl. 4), 539–544.

Neale, M. C., & Cardon, L. R. (1992). *Methodology for genetic studies of twins and families.* Dordrecht, The Netherlands: Kluwer Academic Publishers.

Pedersen, N. L. (1991). Behavioral genetic concepts in longitudinal analyses. In D. Magnusson, L. Bergman, G. Rudinger, & B. Törestad (Eds.), *Problems and methods in longitudinal research: Stability and change* (pp. 236–249). Cambridge, England: Cambridge University Press.

Pedersen, N. L. (1993). Genetic and environmental continuity and change in personality. In T. J. Bouchard & P. Propping (Eds.), *Twins as a tool of behavioral genetics* (pp. 147–162). New York: Wiley.

Pedersen, N. L., Friberg, L., Floderus-Myrhed, B., McClearn, G. E., & Plomin, R. (1984). Swedish early separated twins: Identification and characterization. *Acta Geneticae Medicae et Gemellologiae, 33*, 243–250.

Pedersen, N. L., McClearn, G. E., Plomin, R., Nesselroade, J. R., Berg, S., & de Faire, U. (1991). The Swedish Adoption Twin Study of Aging: An update. *Acta Geneticae Medicae et Gemellologiae, 40*, 7–20.

Pedersen, N. L., Plomin, R., & McClearn, G. E. (1994). Is there G beyond g? (Is there genetic influence on specific cognitive abilities independent of genetic influence on general cognitive ability?). *Intelligence, 18*, 133–143.

Pedersen, N. L., Plomin, R., Nesselroade, J. R., & McClearn, G. E. (1992). A quantitative genetic analysis of cognitive abilities during the second half of the life span. *Psychological Science, 3*, 346–353.

Pedersen, N. L., Reynolds, C., & Gatz, M. (in press). Sources of covariation among Mini-Mental State Examination scores, education and cognitive abilities. *Journal of Gerontology: Psychological Sciences.*

Plomin, R., DeFries, J. C., & McClearn, G. E. (1990). *Behavioral genetics: A primer* (2nd ed.). New York: Freeman.

Plomin, R., & McClearn, G. E. (1990). Human behavioral genetics of aging. In J. E. Birren & K. W. Schaie (Eds.), *Handbook of the psychology of aging, 3rd ed.* (pp. 67–77). New York: Academic Press.

Plomin, R., & Nesselroade, J. R. (1990). Behavioral genetics and personality change. *Journal of Personality, 58,* 191–220.

Plomin, R., Pedersen, N. L., Lichtenstein, P., & McClearn, G. E. (1994). Variability and stability in cognitive abilities are largely genetic later in life. *Behavior Genetics, 24,* 207–215.

Schaie, K. W., Plomin, R., Willis, S. L., Gruber-Baldini, A., Dutta, R., & Bayen, U. (1993). Longitudinal studies of family similarity in intellectual abilities. In J. J. F. Schroots (Ed.), *Aging, health and competence* (pp. 183–198). New York: Elsevier.

Steuer, J., & Jarvik, L. F. (1981). Cognitive functioning in the elderly: Influence of physical health. In J. L. McGaugh & S. B. Kiesler (Eds.), *Aging: Biology and behavior* (pp. 231–253). New York: Academic Press.

Swaab, D. F. (1991). Brain aging and Alzheimer's disease: "Wear and tear" versus "use it or lose it." *Neurobiology of Aging, 12,* 317–324.

Swan, G. E., Carmelli, D., Reed, T., Harshfield, G. A., Fabsitz, R. R., & Eslinger, P. J. (1990). Heritability of cognitive performance in aging twins: The National Heart, Lung, and Blood Institute Twin Study. *Archives of Neurology, (Chicago), 47,* 259–262.

Swan, G. E., LaRue, A., Carmelli, D., Reed, T. E., & Fabsitz, R. R. (1992). Decline in cognitive performance in aging twins: Heritability and biobehavioral predictors from the National Heart, Lung, and Blood Institute twin study. *Archives of Neurology, (Chicago), 49,* 476–481.

Tambs, K., Sundet, J. M., & Magnus, P. (1984). Heritability analysis of the WAIS subtests: A study of twins. *Intelligence, 8,* 283–293.

Whitfield, K. E., Cherny, S. S., Finkel, D. G., & McGue, M. (1994). *A genetic analysis of information processing capabilities in older adults.* Manuscript submitted for publication.

Five
_____

# Brain and Life Span in Primates

Atiya Hakeem, Gisela Rodriguez Sandoval, Marvin Jones, and John Allman

## I. Introduction

Why is the brain so large in some primate species? Brain size is well correlated with body size in primates, but some primates, such as humans and cebus monkeys, have much larger brains than would be expected for their body sizes. It has long been postulated that species with larger brains tend to live longer (Friedenthal, 1910; Sacher, 1959). We have found strong quantitative support for this proposition in higher primates (Allman, in press; Allman, McLaughlin, & Hakeem, 1993a, 1993b; see Section V in this chapter). Our hypothesis is that the brain is a buffer against environmental variation. Animals that have longer life spans are likely to experience more extreme environmental fluctuations and thus be exposed during the course of their longer lives to more severe crises (such as shortages in normally used food resources) than animals with shorter life spans. Parts of the brain enable animals to store information about the environment and develop cognitive strategies that enable them to switch to alternative food resources. In this chapter we examine the ecological specializations linked to large brains and long life. The

relative sizes of some brain structures, such as the cerebellum and neocortex, are particularly closely correlated with life span. The cerebellum and some of these other highly correlated structures appear to be especially vulnerable to age-related dysfunction (see Allman, in press; Allman et al., 1993b).

## II. Longevity in the Wild

Our analysis is based on the life spans of captive primates. We have very little information on the longevity of primates in the wild, because this requires sustained observations of wild populations for many decades. One of our concerns in using life spans of captive animals was that they might vary greatly from the species' maximum life span in the wild; one might think that primates living in zoos would have longer maximum life spans than those living in the wild. The few very long-term studies of primates living under natural conditions indicate, however, that some individuals do live into extreme old age in the wild. Long-term observational data suggest that the maximum life spans for zoo-living and wild primates may be

*Handbook of the Psychology of Aging, Fourth Edition*

about the same. Kenneth Glander (personal communication, February 1, 1993) has measured tooth wear in a wild population of 580 howler monkeys (*Alouatta palliata*) in Costa Rica since 1970. Twelve of these monkeys have been under observation since 1970. In these old monkeys, the teeth are all worn down to the gum line. He estimates them to be between 24 and 28 years old. The maximum life spans recorded for captive *Alouatta* species range from 20–25 years and thus appear to be fairly close to their longevity in the wild.

Goodall (1986) observed 11 chimpanzees that she considered old at Gombe from 1965 through 1983. One of these was Flo, who was a very successful individual with high-ranking offspring, Figan and Fifi. Flo's teeth were worn down to the gum line and Goodall estimated her age four years before her death as "certainly more than 40" (p. 104; see also Zihlman, Morbeck, & Goodall, 1990). Flo's status and aggressive personality were strong factors in Figan and Fifi's achievement of high rank. Flo remained reproductive into old age, but her last two offspring, Flint and Flame, did not flourish. The infant Flame died during her mother's illness. Flint, although more than 8 years old at the time of his mother's death, was unable to survive without her support. For 8 years at Ranomafana in Madagascar, Patricia Wright (personal communication, March 1, 1993) observed a dominant female *Propithecus diadema* that she estimated on the basis of extreme tooth wear to be close to 30 years of age at the time of her death.

Thus the limited data available from primates living in natural conditions indicate that some individuals live into robust old age. Goodall's observations of Flo and her family also suggest that a parent's longevity contributes to the success of the offspring, even as adults, and is likely to be a factor in the evolution of life span–sustaining mechanisms in higher primates. The parent's longevity may be particularly important in catarrhine primates, and especially in apes and humans, because development is slow, the period of dependence on the parents is long, and even in adulthood the success of the offspring may be closely linked to parental status. Because of late reproductive age, long interbirth intervals, and long periods of dependence on the mother, female apes must live more than half the maximum reported life span for these species to maintain the population at the stable replacement level (Goodall, 1986; Ross, 1991; Smuts, Cheney, Seyfarth, Wrangham, & Struhsaker, 1987; see Table I). These factors may be responsible in part for the strong correlations between brain (and most brain structures) and life span in the group made up of gorillas, orangutans, chimpanzees, and humans (see Table II). The selective pressure for maternal longevity may also explain the predominance of females in our sample of very old primates (Table I) and the much lower female mortality rates in contemporary human populations.

## III. Brains, Life Span, and Diet

We have confirmed earlier studies that fruit-eating primates have significantly larger brains than leaf-eating primates (Clutton-Brock & Harvey, 1980). Fruit-eating bats also have larger brains for their body size than insect eaters (Eisenberg & Wilson, 1978; Pirlot & Stephan, 1970; Stephan, Nelson, & Frahm, 1981). A fruit eater's food supply is not constant because different plants bear fruit at different times and at different locations in the complex matrix of the tropical forest (MacKinnon, 1975). An animal guided by memory of the locations of fruit-bearing trees can more efficiently exploit the available fruit resources than would otherwise be possible; thus natural selection may have favored the development of capacities for visuospatial memory in frugivorous primates (Allman, 1977). This

**Table I**
Primate Life Spans

| Genus and species | Age[a] | Acquisition age[b] | Acquisition date | Death date | Sex[c] | Animal's name | Facility or source | Last response date |
|---|---|---|---|---|---|---|---|---|
| Alouatta caraya | 20.25 L | .25 | 4/9/72 | — | F | | Lincoln Park Zoo, Chicago, Illinois | 8/8/89 |
| Alouatta caraya | 20.00 L | 3 | 8/29/75 | — | F | April | Twycross Zoo, Atherstone, Warwickshire, England | 7/9/92 |
| Alouatta palliata | 25.00 L | — | — | — | B | | Observations of Ken Glander, Costa Rica, Wild population | 12/1/93 |
| Alouatta palliata | 20.00 | — | — | — | U | | Ross (1991) | 2/5/91 |
| Alouatta seniculus | 25.00 | — | — | — | U | | Ross (1991) | 2/5/91 |
| Aotus trivirgatus | 25.25 L | 7 C | 1/6/76 | 3/28/94 | F | Blanche Fleur | Born at Crandon Park Zoo, Miami, Florida | 3/28/94 |
| Aotus trivirgatus | 20.00 | — | — | — | U | | Ross (1991) | 2/5/91 |
| Aotus trivirgatus | 19.25 L | 2 | 12/1/76 | — | F | Zephyr | Allman Lab, Caltech, Pasadena, California | 1/6/94 |
| Arctocebus calabarensis | 12.17 | — | 9/16/55 | — | M | | The Zoological Society of London, England | — |
| Arctocebus calabarensis | 9.50 | — | — | — | U | | Harvey, Martin, and Clutton-Brock (1987) | — |
| Ateles belzebuth | 28.00 L | 2 | 1/1/66 | — | F | Frances | Twycross Zoo, Atherstone, Warwickshire, England | 7/9/92 |
| Ateles belzebuth | 26.00 L | 2 | 1/1/67 | — | F | Ana, tattoo #33 | The Oakland Zoo in Knowland Park, Oakland, California | 8/1/91 |
| Ateles belzebuth | 26.00 L | 2 | 1/1/67 | — | F | Sigi, tattoo #71 | The Oakland Zoo in Knowland Park, Oakland, California | 8/1/91 |
| Ateles fusciceps | 24.00 | — | — | — | U | | Ross (1991) | 2/5/91 |
| Ateles fusciceps | 21.50 L | 4.9 | 10/1/74 | — | F | Buddy, 1068 | Potter Park Zoological Gardens, Lansing, Michigan | 8/20/91 |
| Ateles fusciceps | 21.00 L | 9 C | 8/23/79 | — | M | Junior, 250 | Sequoia Park Zoo, Eureka, California | 8/14/91 |

| Species | | | | | | | | |
|---|---|---|---|---|---|---|---|---|
| *Ateles geoffroyi* | 48.00 | 4 C | 4/8/49 | 1/19/93 | F | Minnie | Born 8/4/70 at National Zoo, Washington, D.C. Taronga Zoo, Sydney, Australia | 7/10/92 |
| *Ateles geoffroyi* | 38.00 L | 3 | 2/14/57 | — | F | | Born in 1945 at Salt Lake City Zoo, Utah | |
| *Ateles paniscus* | 37.75 L | 2.75 | 3/6/57 | — | F | | Munster Zoo, Germany | — |
| *Ateles paniscus* | 34.00 L | 3 | 7/6/59 | — | F | Vicky, ISIS 21 | Artis Zoo, Amsterdam, The Netherlands Paignton Zoological & Botanical Gardens, Paignton, England | 8/1/91 |
| *Cacajao calvus* | 22.33 | 1 | 11/28/58 | 3/31/80 | F | | Bronx Zoo, New York | — |
| *Cacajao calvus* | 19.92 L | — | 6/16/72 | — | U | | San Diego Zoo, California | 5/19/92 |
| *Cacajao melanocephalus* | 18.00 L | — | 1/1/74 | — | U | | Köln Zoo, Germany | — |
| *Cacajao rubicundus* | 27.00 L | 17 C | 3/23/81 | — | M | | Los Angeles Zoo, California Born 8/3/65 at Milwaukee County Zoo, Wisconsin | 8/1/91 |
| *Cacajao rubicundus* | 23.00 L | 13 C | 3/23/81 | — | F | | Los Angeles Zoo, California Born 7/10/69 at Milwaukee County Zoo, Wisconsin | 8/1/91 |
| *Callicebus moloch* | 25.25 L | — | 12/2/65 | — | M | | University of California at Davis, California | 2/5/91 |
| *Callicebus moloch* | 20.25 L | C | 3/15/72 | — | F | | University of Kassel, Germany Born 3/15/72 at Delta Primate Center, Covington, Louisiana | — |
| *Callimico goeldii* | 17.90 | — | — | — | U | | Ross (1991) | 2/5/91 |
| *Callimico goeldii* | 16.10 | — | 4/13/69 | 5/28/85 | F | | Frankfurt Zoologischer Garten, Germany | 7/27/92 |
| *Callimico goeldii* | 15.75 L | .75 | 7/11/77 | — | M | Pepe | Brookfield Zoo, Chicago Zoological Society, Illinois | 7/21/92 |
| *Callithrix argentata* | 16.83 | 1.7 | 7/18/68 | 9/23/83 | F | | Birmingham Zoo, Alabama | — |
| *Callithrix argentata* | 8.75 | — | 6/22/51 | 3/31/60 | U | | Bronx Zoo, New York | — |
| *Callithrix humeralifer* | 15.00 | — | 1/1/65 | 7/11/80 | U | | Adelaide Zoo, Australia | — |

(*continues*)

**Table I** (Continued)

| Genus and species | Age[a] | Acquisition age[b] | Acquisition date | Death date | Sex[c] | Animal's name | Facility or source | Last response date |
|---|---|---|---|---|---|---|---|---|
| *Callithrix jacchus* | 16.75 | .58 | 7/1/66 | 9/1/82 | M | | Frank Rossi (private party), Gravesend, Kent, England | — |
| *Callithrix jacchus* | 15.66 | C | 2/1/68 | — | U | | Birmingham Zoo, Alabama | |
| *Cebuella pygmaea* | 18.10 | | 5/17/68 | 6/14/86 | M | | Japanese Primate Center, Aichi, Japan | 1/1/90 |
| *Cebuella pygmaea* | 15.08 L | — | 8/24/77 | — | F | | Stichting-Apenheul, Apeldoorn, Holland | 9/21/92 |
| *Cebus albifrons* | 44.00 | — | | — | U | | Ross (1991) | 2/5/91 |
| *Cebus albifrons* | 40.50 | .5 | 6/10/49 | 6/20/89 | F | Squeaky | Sue Norton (private party), South Pasadena, California | 6/20/89 |
| *Cebus albifrons* | 25.00 L | C | 8/10/66 | — | M | | Omaha's Henry Doorly Zoo, Omaha, Nebraska | 7/19/91 |
| *Cebus apella* | 45.10 | — | 5/12/34 | 6/16/79 | M | | Milwaukee County Zoo, Wisconsin | — |
| *Cebus apella* | 41.00 | 4 | 1/1/27 | 5/24/64 | M | Irish? | San Diego Zoo, California | — |
| *Cebus capucinus* | 54.75 | 1 | 1/1/35 | 10/4/88 | M | Bobo | Lederle Labs, Pearl River, New York | — |
| *Cebus capucinus* | 46.92 | | 5/1/29 | 4/16/76 | M | | Evansville Zoo, Indiana | |
| *Cebus nigrivittatus* | 41.00 L | 1 | 7/1/52 | — | F | | Santa Ana Zoo, California | 6/5/89 |
| *Cercocebus albigena* | 32.70 | | | — | U | | Ross (1991) | 2/5/91 |
| *Cercocebus albigena* | 32.66 | | 1/19/30 | 9/23/62 | M | | San Diego Zoo, California | |
| *Cercocebus albigena* | 21.00 | | | — | U | | Harvey, Martin, and Clutton-Brock (1987) | — |
| *Cercocebus aterrimus* | 26.75 | | 4/9/54 | 2/3/81 | M | | Baltimore Zoo, Maryland | — |
| *Cercocebus atys* | 26.75 | | | — | M | | Baltimore Zoo, Maryland | — |
| *Cercocebus atys* | 18.00 | | | — | U | | Harvey, Martin, and Clutton-Brock (1987) | — |
| *Cercocebus galeritus* | 21.00 L | 5 | 4/12/75 | — | F | June | Sacramento Zoo, California | 7/1/91 |
| *Cercocebus galeritus* | 19.00 | | | — | U | | Harvey, Martin, and Clutton-Brock (1987) | 1/1/87 |
| *Cercocebus galeritus* | 19.00 | | | — | U | | Ross (1991) | 2/5/91 |
| *Cercocebus torquatus* | 27.00 | | | — | U | | Ross (1991) | 2/5/91 |

| Species | | | | Sex | Name | Location/Source | Date |
|---|---|---|---|---|---|---|---|
| *Cercocebus torquatus* | 20.50 | — | — | U | | Harvey, Martin, and Clutton-Brock (1987) | 1/1/87 |
| *Cercocebus torquatus* | 14.70 L | 4.7 | 7/16/81 | F | | Micke Grove Zoo, Lodi, California | 7/23/91 |
| *Cercopithecus aethiops* | 31.60 L | 13 C | 4/1/74 | M | Aba | Jerusalem Biblical Zoo, Ltd., Romema, Jerusalem, Israel | 7/28/91 |
| *Cercopithecus aethiops* | 31.00 | — | — | U | | Born 1/1/60 at Haddassah Harvey, Martin, and Clutton-Brock (1987) | — |
| *Cercopithecus aethiops* | 23.00 L | 4 | 2/8/72 | M | Jonathan | The Oakland Zoo in Knowland Park, Oakland, California | 7/1/91 |
| *Cercopithecus ascanius* | 28.25 | 2.5 | 8/14/58 | F | Nosy | Birmingham Zoo, Alabama | — |
| *Cercopithecus ascanius* | 25.92 | 22.33 | 4/30/84 | F | | San Diego Zoo, California | — |
| *Cercopithecus cambelli* | 25.00 L | 2 | 5/19/55 | F | | Jardin Zoologique de Québec, Canada | 8/29/91 |
| *Cercopithecus cephus* | 23.00 L | 3.33 | 12/22/72 | F | | Louisiana Purchase Gardens and Zoo, Monroe, Louisiana | 8/19/92 |
| *Cercopithecus cephus* | 23.00 L | 3.33 | 12/22/72 | M | | Louisiana Purchase Gardens and Zoo, Monroe, Louisiana | 8/19/92 |
| *Cercopithecus diana* | 37.25 | — | 1/1/40 | U | | Miami Monkey Jungle, Florida | 11/1/77 |
| *Cercopithecus diana* | 34.80 | — | — | U | | Harvey, Martin, and Clutton-Brock (1987) | — |
| *Cercopithecus diana* | 30.00 L | 5 | 2/4/66 | F | Dora | Audubon Zoological Gardens, New Orleans, Louisiana | 7/19/91 |
| *Cercopithecus hamlyni* | 27.00 | 21 | 9/29/80 | M | | San Diego Zoo, San Diego, California | — |
| *Cercopithecus mitis* | 27.10 L | 1 | 6/21/66 | F | Sarah, 192 | Omaha's Henry Doorly Zoo, Omaha, Nebraska | 7/28/92 |
| *Cercopithecus mitis* | 25.00 L | 4.17 | 11/2/71 | F | | Lousiana Purchase Gardens and Zoo, Monroe, Louisiana | 8/19/92 |
| *Cercopithecus mona* | 22.00 | — | — | U | | Ross (1991) | 2/5/91 |

*(continues)*

**Table I** (Continued)

| Genus and species | Age[a] | Acquisition age[b] | Acquisition date | Death date | Sex[c] | Animal's name | Facility or source | Last response date |
|---|---|---|---|---|---|---|---|---|
| Cercopithecus mona | 20.50 L | 18 C | 3/24/88 | — | F | Lisa | Dallas Zoo, Texas Born 12/19/70 at Bronx Zoo, New York | 6/1/92 |
| Cercopithecus neglectus | 26.25 L | 4.7 | 5/25/70 | — | F | | Sacramento Zoo, California | 2/12/92 |
| Cercopithecus neglectus | 23.00 L | 1.5 | 7/7/70 | — | F | Countess | Denver Zoological Gardens, Colorado | 7/29/92 |
| Cercopithecus nictitans | 23.00 L | 3 | 11/19/71 | — | F | | Greater Baton Rouge Zoo, Baker, Louisiana | 7/19/91 |
| Cercopithecus nictitans | 18.92 L | 2 | 9/5/72 | — | M | Speedy Gonzalez | Jardin Zoologique de Québec, Canada | 8/29/91 |
| Cercopithecus petaurista | 19.00 | — | — | — | U | | Houston Zoological Gardens, Texas | — |
| Cercopithecus petaurista | 16.17 L | 4 | 2/28/79 | — | F | Serena, LRZ#936 | The Zoo of Arkansas | 6/1/91 |
| Cercopithecus pogonias | 24.10 L | 17 | 6/6/84 | — | F | | Cincinnati Zoo & Botanical Gardens, Ohio | 6/1/91 |
| Cercopithecus pogonias | 18.50 | C | 5/28/70 | 1/24/89 | F | | Cincinnati Zoo & Botanical Gardens, Ohio | 6/1/91 |
| Cercopithecus talapoin | 30.87 | 2.2 | 10/6/39 | 6/19/67 | M | | Philadelphia Zoological Garden, Pennsylvania | 7/30/92 |
| Cercopithecus talapoin | 23.08 L | 15.5 C | 9/13/83 | — | M | Beck, 83M136 | Buffalo Zoological Gardens, New York Born 3/9/68 at Brookfield Zoo, Illinois | 7/20/91 |
| Cheirogaleus major | 15.00 | — | — | | U | | Martin (1984) | — |
| Cheirogaleus major | 10.00 L | 3 | 1/1/84 | — | F | Rapunzel | Duke University Primate Center, Durham, North Carolina | 8/1/91 |
| Cheirogaleus major | 8.66 | — | 5/13/52 | 1/22/61 | U | | The Zoological Society of London, England | — |
| Cheirogaleus medius | 19.25 L | C | 4/13/73 | — | M | Jesse, 606 | Duke University Primate Center, Durham, North Carolina | 6/1/92 |
| Cheirogaleus medius | 17.00 L | C | 7/18/74 | — | F | Diaz, 613f | Duke University Primate | 8/1/91 |

| Species | | | | | Sex | Name/ID | Location | Date |
|---|---|---|---|---|---|---|---|---|
| | | | | | | | Center, Durham, North Carolina | |
| *Chiropotes albinasus* | 11.66 | — | — | — | F | | Köln Zoo, Germany | 1/1/77 |
| *Chiropotes satanas* | 15.00 | — | — | — | F | | San Diego Zoo, California | — |
| *Chiropotes satanas* | 12.66 | — | — | — | M | | Köln Zoo, Germany | 1/1/77 |
| *Colobus guereza* | 24.50 | 1 | 10/1/40 | 4/7/64 | M | | San Diego Zoo, California | — |
| *Colobus guereza* | 23.75 | C | 4/14/50 | 2/5/74 | F | | San Diego Zoo, California | — |
| *Colobus polykomos* | 30.50 | — | — | — | U | | Ross (1991) | 2/5/91 |
| *Colobus polykomos* | 26.00 | — | — | — | U | | Harvey, Martin, and Clutton-Brock (1987) | — |
| *Colobus polykomos* | 24.00 L | 23 | 4/4/90 | — | M | Sikasso, A1123 | The Zoological Society of London, England | 6/30/91 |
| *Cynopithecus niger* | 28.50 L | 5.4 | 5/10/69 | — | F | Faith, 613 | Omaha's Henry Doorly Zoo, Nebraska | 7/28/92 |
| *Cynopithecus niger* | 18.00 | — | — | — | U | | Harvey, Martin, and Clutton-Brock (1987) | — |
| *Daubentonia madagascariensis* | 24.25 | — | 6/3/14 | 9/15/37 | U | | Artis Zoo, Amsterdam, The Netherlands | — |
| *Daubentonia madagascariensis* | 5.40 L | 2.4 | 1/1/88 | — | F | Samantha | Duke University Primate Center, Durham, North Carolina | 8/5/91 |
| *Erythrocebus patas* | 23.92 | — | 3/31/64 | 2/25/88 | F | | Jardin Zoologique de Québec, Canada | 8/29/91 |
| *Erythrocebus patas* | 21.66 | — | 8/22/70 | 4/18/92 | F | | Artis Zoo, Amsterdam, The Netherlands | — |
| *Erythrocebus patas* | 21.66 | — | 1/5/55 | 8/12/76 | F | | Frankfurt Zoologischer Garten, Germany | 7/27/92 |
| *Galago crassicaudatus* | 18.75 | C | 10/24/68 | 7/17/87 | M | Barney | Houston Zool. Gardens, pers. pet of J. Banks, Texas | 9/15/87 |
| *Galago crassicaudatus* | 18.00 | C | 2/24/66 | 3/8/84 | M | | Artis Zoo, Amsterdam, The Netherlands | — |
| *Galago demidovii* | 14.00 | — | — | — | U | | Harvey, Martin, and Clutton-Brock (1987) | — |
| *Galago demidovii* | 9.42 | — | — | — | U | | Private | — |
| *Galago demidovii* | 9.16 | — | — | — | F | | Brookfield Zoo, Chicago Zoological Society, Illinois | — |

(continues)

**Table I** (*Continued*)

| Genus and species | Age[a] | Acquisition age[b] | Acquisition date | Death date | Sex[c] | Animal's name | Facility or source | Last response date |
|---|---|---|---|---|---|---|---|---|
| *Galago senegalensis* | 17.00 L | 13 C | 6/10/86 | — | F | | Cincinnati Zoo & Botanical Gardens, Ohio Born 7/73 at Buffalo Zoo, New York | 5/1/92 |
| *Galago senegalensis* | 16.50 | 12 | 6/21/73 | — | | | San Antonio Zoological Garden & Aquarium, Texas | — |
| *Gorilla gorilla gorilla* | 54.00 | 5 | 12/30/35 | 12/31/84 | M | Massa | Philadelphia Zoological Garden, Pennsylvania | 7/30/92 |
| *Gorilla gorilla gorilla* | 47.00 | 43 | 1/1/82 | 9/27/86 | F | Carolyn | Bronx Zoo, New York | 12/10/86 |
| *Hapalemur griseus* | 17.10 L | C | 6/23/75 | — | F | Befuddled | Duke University Primate Center, Durham, North Carolina | 6/1/92 |
| *Hapalemur griseus* | 12.75 | — | 8/20/64 | — | M | | Köln Zoo, Germany | — |
| *Homo sapiens* | 120.60 | 0 | 6/29/1865 | 2/21/86 | M | S. Isumi | The Guiness Book of Records, Japan | 1/1/92 |
| *Homo sapiens* | 105.00 | — | | — | U | | Max. life-span, sample of 1,000 obituaries in *Los Angeles Times* | — |
| *Hylobates agilis* | 44.00 L | 1 | 12/2/49 | — | M | Nippy, M10 | Wellington Zoological Gardens, New Zealand | 7/15/92 |
| *Hylobates agilis* | 28.00 L | 6 | 10/1/70 | — | F | | Twycross Zoo, Atherstone, Warwickshire, England | 7/9/92 |
| *Hylobates concolor* | 44.10 | — | 9/3/37 | 10/21/81 | U | | Vincennes-Parc Zoologique de Paris, France | — |
| *Hylobates concolor* | 25.00 L | 23 | 10/12/89 | — | F | Mizzi | Safaripark Beekse Bergen, Hilvarenbeek, The Netherlends | 1/30/92 |
| *Hylobates lar* | 40.00 L | 2 | 1/1/54 | — | M | Samson | San Antonio Zoological Garden & Aquarium, Texas | 7/13/92 |
| *Hylobates lar* | 40.00 L | 2 | 1/1/54 | — | F | Samantha | San Antonio Zoological Garden & Aquarium, Texas | 7/13/92 |

| Species | | | | | Sex | Name | Location | |
|---|---|---|---|---|---|---|---|---|
| *Hylobates moloch muelleri* | 29.00 L | 1 | 7/1/64 | — | M | Smiler | Twycross Zoo, Atherstone, Warwickshire, England | 7/9/92 |
| *Hylobates moloch muelleri* | 25.00 L | 3 | 7/11/69 | — | F | Berta, 690701 | San Antonio Zoological Garden & Aquarium, Texas | 8/5/91 |
| *Hylobates moloch muelleri* | 25.00 L | 3 | 7/11/69 | — | F | Gibby, 690702 | San Antonio Zoological Garden & Aquarium, Texas | 8/5/91 |
| *Hylobates pileatus* | 36.00 | 8 | 7/1/63 | 9/9/91 | M | Simon | Twycross Zoo, Atherstone, Warwickshire, England | 7/9/92 |
| *Hylobates pileatus* | 31.90 L | 2 | 4/19/62 | — | M | Boston Blackie | Phoenix Zoo, Arizona | 7/23/91 |
| *Hylobates pileatus x agilis* | 37.92 | C | 10/2/44 | 9/3/82 | F | | National Zoo, Washington, D.C. | — |
| *Hylobates syndactylus* | 38.00 L | 6 | 3/31/60 | — | F | Suzy | Milwaukee County Zoo, Wisconsin | 9/22/92 |
| *Hylobates syndactylus* | 37.00 | 7 | 7/20/59 | 3/23/89 | M | | Milwaukee County Zoo, Wisconsin | 9/22/92 |
| *Lagothrix lagotricha* | 30.00 | 4.5 | 1/1/61 | 3/7/87 | F | Lulu | The Monkey Sanctuary, Looe, Cornwall, England Ross (1991) | — |
| *Lagothrix lagotricha* | 25.90 | — | — | — | U | | Royal Zoological Society of Antwerp, Belgium | 2/5/91 |
| *Lagothrix lagotricha* | 24.75 | — | 11/10/51 | 8/15/77 | M | | | — |
| *Lemur catta* | 30.00 L | 3 | 7/2/65 | — | F | | Buffalo Zoological Gardens, New York | 7/14/92 |
| *Lemur catta* | 27.10 | — | — | — | U | | Harvey, Martin, and Clutton-Brock (1987) | — |
| *Lemur catta* | 26.00 L | 22.5 C | 9/4/86 | — | U | | Mesa College, San Diego, California Born 3/2/64 at San Diego Zoo, California | — |
| *Lemur coronatus* | 18.42 | — | 10/25/05 | — | U | | Giza Zoo, Egypt | — |
| *Lemur fulvus* | 37.00 | — | 8/3/10 | 2/1/46 | M | | Buffalo Zoological Gardens, New York | 8/9/88 |
| *Lemur fulvus* | 36.50 | 2.5 | 1/1/58 | 5/4/92 | F | Yvette, 521f | Duke University Primate Center, Durham, North Carolina | 6/1/92 |
| *Lemur macaco* | 28.00 | C | 8/11/54 | 7/31/82 | F | | St. Louis Zoo, Missouri | — |
| *Lemur macaco* | 27.10 | — | — | — | U | | Harvey, Martin, and Clutton-Brock (1987) | — |

*(continues)*

**Table I** (Continued)

| Genus and species | Age[a] | Acquisition age[b] | Acquisition date | Death date | Sex[c] | Animal's name | Facility or source | Last response date |
|---|---|---|---|---|---|---|---|---|
| Lemur macaco | 27.08 | — | 1/1/10 | 1/1/37 | F | | Buffalo Zoological Gardens, New York | — |
| Lemur macaco x fulvus | 39.00 | — | — | — | U | | Buffalo Zoological Gardens, New York | — |
| Lemur mongoz | 27.90 L | 1 | 8/12/64 | — | M | | Philadelphia Zoological Garden, Pennsylvania | 7/23/91 |
| Lemur mongoz | 24.25 | — | — | — | U | | St. Louis Zoo, Missouri | — |
| Lemur variegatus | 32.00 L | 2 | 6/2/62 | — | F | Saturna, 524f | Duke University Primate Center, Durham, North Carolina | 6/1/92 |
| Lemur variegatus | 28.00 | — | — | — | M | | The Zoological Society of London, England; Born 5/26/69 at San Diego Zoo, California | 5/23/89 |
| Leontopithecus rosalia | 24.75 L | 4.6 C | 4/11/72 | — | M | Houston | San Antonio Zoological Garden & Aquarium, Texas; Born 10/17/67 at Houston Zoological Gardens, Texas | 8/5/91 |
| Leontopithecus rosalia | 22.00 | — | 6/22/64 | 8/11/86 | F | | Los Angeles Zoo, California | 12/10/86 |
| Loris tardigradus | 16.40 | — | 6/9/74 | 11/24/89 | M | | The Zoological Society of London, England | 8/5/92 |
| Loris tardigradus | 14.00 L | — | 7/26/78 | — | M | | Frankfurt Zoologischer Garten, Germany | 7/9/92 |
| Macaca arctoides | 30.00 | — | — | — | U | | Ross (1991) | 2/5/91 |
| Macaca arctoides | 30.00 | — | — | — | U | | Harvey, Martin, and Clutton-Brock (1987) | — |
| Macaca arctoides | 24.00 L | — | 5/1/68 | — | F | Pat, #88063 | Catoctin Mountain Zoological Park, Thurmont, Maryland | 6/1/92 |
| Macaca arctoides | 20.08 L | 3.8 | 6/1/75 | — | F | Mandy, #66 | Racine Zoo, Wisconsin | 8/1/91 |
| Macaca fascicularis | 37.10 | — | — | — | U | | Ross (1991) | 2/5/91 |
| Macaca fascicularis | 37.08 | — | 12/23/33 | 2/11/71 | U | | Private, Germany | — |

| Species | | | | | Sex | Name | Source/Location | |
|---|---|---|---|---|---|---|---|---|
| Macaca fascicularis | 25.00 | 3.9 | 3/1/69 | 12/1/90 | F | | Charles Paddock Zoo, Atascadero, California | 6/1/91 |
| Macaca fuscata | 33.00 | — | 8/1/33 | — | U | | Kagoshima, Japan ("Primate lifespans," 1966) | — |
| Macaca fuscata | 33.00 | — | — | — | U | | Ross (1991) | 2/5/91 |
| Macaca fuscata | 22.66 L | 6 | 6/30/75 | — | F | Grandma | Folsom Children's Zoo, Lincoln, Nebraska | 6/1/91 |
| Macaca mulatta | 36.00 | — | — | — | U | | Ershler et al. (1988) | — |
| Macaca mulatta | 35.00 | — | — | — | U | | Tigges, Gordon, McClure, Hall, and Peters (1988) | — |
| Macaca mulatta | 26.00 L | C | 10/9/65 | — | U | | Micke Grove Zoo, Lodi, California | 7/23/91 |
| Macaca mulatta | 23.00 L | 2.5 | 10/9/65 | — | F | | Micke Grove Zoo, Lodi, California | 7/23/91 |
| Macaca nemestrina | 34.33 L | — | 5/11/56 | — | U | | Japanese Primate Center, Aichi, Japan | 1/1/90 |
| Macaca nemestrina | 27.07 | 3.9 | 6/1/67 | 5/12/92 | M | Joco | Reid Park Zoo, Tucson, Arizona | 5/12/92 |
| Macaca silenus | 40.00 | 37 | 12/5/86 | 4/3/89 | F | | Baltimore Zoo, Maryland | 6/1/91 |
| Macaca silenus | 38.00 | 37 | 12/5/86 | 5/1/87 | M | | Baltimore Zoo, Maryland | 6/1/91 |
| Macaca sinica | 30.00 | — | — | — | U | | Ross (1991) | — |
| Macaca sinica | 29.33 | — | — | — | U | | Colombo, Sri Lanka | — |
| Macaca sylvania | 22.00 | — | — | — | U | | Ross (1991) | — |
| Macaca sylvania | 17.00 L | C | 7/15/74 | — | M | Kenneth | Paignton Zoological & Botanical Gardens, Paignton, England | 8/1/91 |
| Microcebus murinus | 15.50 | 2.5 C | 12/21/77 | 9/10/91 | M | | The Zoological Society of London, England; Born in 1975 at Wellcom Laboratory, London, England | 7/9/92 |
| Microcebus murinus | 15.50 | — | — | — | U | | Harvey, Martin, and Clutton-Brock (1987) | — |
| Microcebus murinus | 14.00 L | C | 8/13/77 | — | M | Snout, 837m | Duke University Primate Center, Durham, North Carolina | 8/5/91 |
| Mirza (Microcebus) coquereli | 15.25 | — | — | — | U | | The Zoological Society of London, England | — |

(continues)

**Table I** (*Continued*)

| Genus and species | Age[a] | Acquisition age[b] | Acquisition date | Death date | Sex[c] | Animal's name | Facility or source | Last response date |
|---|---|---|---|---|---|---|---|---|
| *Nasalis larvatus* | 21.0 | 3 | 7/26/67 | 8/15/85 | M | Jimmy, 001116 | Dallas Zoo, Texas | 11/16/92 |
| *Nasalis larvatus* | 20.00 L | 18 | 2/6/90 | — | F | Barabara | Wilhelma Zoological Garden, Stuttgart, Germany | 7/24/92 |
| *Nycticebus coucang* | 26.50 | — | 4/23/63 | — | F | | Artis Zoo, Amsterdam, The Netherlands | — |
| *Nycticebus coucang* | 20.00 | 7 | 4/21/77 | 6/5/90 | F | BEM, 20680 | Woodland Park Zoo, Seattle, Washington | 7/9/92 |
| *Otolemur (Galago) garnetti* | 15.66 L | — | 11/20/76 | — | M | | University of Kassel, Germany | — |
| *Otolemur (Galago) garnetti* | 15.00 | 10.58 | 5/18/76 | 10/2/80 | F | | University of Kassel, Germany | — |
| *Pan troglodytes* | 59.40 | C | 9/21/32 | 2/19/92 | F | Gamma | Yerkes Reg. Primate Resrch Ctr, Emory Univ., Atlanta, Georgia | — |
| *Pan troglodytes* | 56.00 | 2 | 7/1/31 | 9/17/85 | M | Jimmy | Rochester Zoo, New York | — |
| *Papio anubis* | 25.17 | — | — | — | M | | San Diego Zoo, California | — |
| *Papio cynocephalus* | 40.00 | — | — | — | U | | Ross (1991) | 2/5/91 |
| *Papio cynocephalus* | 35.10 L | — | 8/4/44 | — | F | | Japanese Primate Center, Aichi, Japan | 1/1/90 |
| *Papio cynocephalus* | 27.66 | — | — | — | U | | Bronx Zoo, New York | — |
| *Papio hamadryas* | 37.50 | — | 6/1/35 | 12/27/72 | M | | Brookfield Zoo, Chicago Zoological Society, Illinois | — |
| *Papio hamadryas* | 35.60 | — | — | — | U | | Harvey, Martin, and Clutton-Brock (1987) | — |
| *Papio hamadryas* | 28.83 | 1.25 | 5/8/33 | 1/4/61 | U | | Calgary Zoo, Alberta, Canada | — |
| *Papio leucophaeus* | 33.42 | 2.5 | 1/1/50 | 11/1/80 | F | | Rome Zoological Garden, Italy | — |
| *Papio leucophaeus* | 28.60 | — | — | — | U | | Harvey, Martin, and Clutton-Brock (1987) | — |
| *Papio leucophaeus* | 28.42 | — | 7/3/33 | 11/22/61 | U | | Milwaukee County Zoo, Wisconsin | — |
| *Papio papio* | 40.00 | — | — | — | U | | Ross (1991) | 2/5/91 |

| Species | | | | | | | | |
|---|---|---|---|---|---|---|---|---|
| *Papio papio* | 27.00 | — | 1/1/64 | 3/1/91 | M | Uncle+ | Brookfield Zoo, Chicago Zoological Society, Illinois | 8/5/91 |
| *Papio papio* | 25.80 | — | — | — | U | | National Zool. Gardens of S. A. Pretoria, South Africa | — |
| *Papio sphinx* | 31.66 | — | 6/23/34 | 3/18/66 | F | | Kumamoto, Japan ("Primate life spans," 1966) | — |
| *Papio sphinx* | 31.41 | C | 6/24/44 | 12/1/75 | F | | Philadelphia Zoological Garden, Pennsylvania | — |
| *Papio ursinus* | 31.20 L | — | 7/1/59 | — | F | | Japanese Primate Center, Aichi, Japan | 1/1/90 |
| *Papio ursinus* | 27.58 | — | — | — | U | | Philadelphia Zoological Garden, Pennsylvania | — |
| *Perodicticus potto* | 26.00 | 1.5 | 12/1/59 | 7/16/84 | M | | Pittsburgh Zoo, Pennsylvania | — |
| *Perodicticus potto* | 22.00 | — | 1/1/52 | 6/26/74 | M | | Basel Zoological Gardens, Switzerland | — |
| *Phaner furcifer* | 12.00 | — | — | — | U | | Observations by Dr. J. Petter | — |
| *Pithecia monachus* | 24.60 | 4 | 7/14/64 | 5/10/85 | F | | San Diego Zoo, California | — |
| *Pithecia pithecia* | 20.66 L | 1 | 1/26/72 | — | M | Timmy | Denver Zoological Gardens, Colorado | 7/29/92 |
| *Pithecia pithecia* | 18.00 L | 2 | 6/25/75 | — | M | Ron, A258 | The Zoological Society of London, England | 7/30/91 |
| *Pithecia pithecia* | 18.00 L | 2 | 6/25/75 | — | F | Barbara, A259 | The Zoological Society of London, England | 7/30/91 |
| *Pongo pygmaeus* | 58.75 | 13 | 5/1/31 | 2/9/77 | M | Guas, #100001 | Philadelphia Zoological Garden, Pennsylvania | 7/30/92 |
| *Pongo pygmaeus* | 57.25 | 13 | 5/1/31 | 1/16/76 | F | Guarina, #100002 | Philadelphia Zoological Garden, Pennsylvania | 7/30/92 |
| *Presbytis cristata* | 31.08 | C | 2/2/45 | 3/1/76 | F | | San Diego Zoo, California Born 2/2/45 at San Diego Zoo, California | 7/7/94 |
| *Presbytis cristata* | 18.83 L | 7 C | 9/17/80 | — | M | | Los Angeles Zoo, California Born 10/18/73 at San Diego Zoo, California | 8/14/92 |
| *Presbytis entellus* | 25.00 | — | 1/1/42 | — | F | | Miami Monkey Jungle, Florida | — |

*(continues)*

**Table I** (*Continued*)

| Genus and species | Age[a] | Acquisition age[b] | Acquisition date | Death date | Sex[c] | Animal's name | Facility or source | Last response date |
|---|---|---|---|---|---|---|---|---|
| *Presbytis entellus* | 24.00 | 3 | 3/31/64 | 4/25/85 | M | | San Diego Zoo, California | — |
| *Presbytis melalophos* | 16.00 | — | — | — | U | | San Diego Zoo, California | — |
| *Presbytis obscura* | 25.00 L | 18.58 | 6/6/86 | — | U | | Artis Zoo, Amsterdam, The Netherlands | — |
| *Presbytis obscura* | 15.33 L | 7 C | 5/11/83 | — | F | June | Point Defiance Zoo & Aquarium, Tacoma, Washington | 7/20/91 |
| *Presbytis senex* | 23.00 L | 15 | 2/28/85 | — | M | | Greater Baton Rouge Zoo, Baker, Louisiana | 7/19/91 |
| *Propithecus verreauxi* | 20.60 L | C | 2/10/72 | — | M | Nigel, 597m | Duke University Primate Center, Durham, North Carolina | 6/1/92 |
| *Propithecus verreauxi* | 18.17 | — | — | — | F | | Duke University Primate Center, Durham, North Carolina | — |
| *Pygathrix nemaeus* | 25.00 L | — | 6/8/68 | — | M | | Köln Zoo, Germany | — |
| *Pygathrix nemaeus* | 21.00 L | — | 3/25/70 | — | M | Peter | Wilhelma Zoological Garden, Stuttgart, Germany | 7/24/91 |
| *Saguinus fuscicollis* | 24.50 | 1.17 | 8/5/69 | 3/13/92 | F | | Jersey Wildlife Preservation Trust, Jersey, Channel Islands | 1/4/93 |
| *Saguinus fuscicollis* | 20.40 | C | 2/12/68 | 7/3/88 | F | | University of Tennessee, Knoxville, Tennessee | 7/27/92 |
| *Saguinus imperator imperator* | 20.17 | — | 6/10/61 | 9/7/81 | M | | Jersey Wildlife Preservation Trust, Jersey, Channel Islands | — |
| *Saguinus imperator imperator* | 13.00 | — | 10/14/62 | 10/14/75 | M | | Frankfurt Zoologischer Garten, Germany | — |
| *Saguinus nigricollis* | 15.20 | — | 4/18/61 | 7/15/76 | F | | Brookfield Zoo, Chicago Zoological Society, Illinois | — |

| Species | Age | Value | Date | Date | Sex | Name | Location | Date |
|---|---|---|---|---|---|---|---|---|
| *Saguinus nigricollis* | 11.08 | — | 4/18/61 | 6/10/72 | U | | Brookfield Zoo, Chicago Zoological Society, Illinois | — |
| *Saguinus oedipus* | 23.08 L | 1 | 6/17/70 | — | M | Jimmy | Denver Zoological Gardens, Colorado | 7/29/92 |
| *Saguinus oedipus* | 22.95 L | .95 | 12/31/67 | — | U | | St. Paul Zoo, Minnesota | — |
| *Saguinus tamarin* | 15.40 | — | 11/9/64 | 4/14/80 | M | | Zurich Zoologischer Garten, Switzerland | — |
| *Saguinus tamarin* | 13.17 | — | — | — | F | | Zurich Zoologischer Garten, Switzerland | — |
| *Saimiri sciureus* | 27.00 | — | 1/1/67 | 11/29/84 | F | Miss Baker | Alabama Space and Rocket Center, Huntsville, Alabama | — |
| *Saimiri sciureus* | 22.66 | 2.5 | 1/5/60 | 3/19/80 | M | WD-1 | Woodland Park Zoo, Seattle, Washington | 7/9/92 |
| *Tarsius spectrum* | 12.00 | — | — | — | U | | Ross (1991) | 2/5/91 |
| *Tarsius spectrum* | 12.00 | — | — | — | U | | Harvey, Martin, and Clutton-Brock (1987) | — |
| *Tarsius syrichta* | 15.00 | 4 | 5/16/83 | 12/1/93 | M | Amos | Duke University Primate Center, Durham, North Carolina | — |
| *Tarsius syrichta* | 13.50 | — | 5/8/64 | 10/14/77 | M | | Frankfurt Zoologischer Garten, Germany | — |
| *Theropithecus gelada* | 28.00 L | 2 | 2/5/65 | — | F | | San Antonio Zoological Garden & Aquarium, Texas | 8/5/91 |
| *Theropithecus gelada* | 27.00 L | C | 10/28/65 | — | F | | Zurich Zoologischer Garten, Switzerland | — |

[a]L, the animal was still alive at the time of the last response
[b]C, Captive born
[c]F, female; B, both males and females; M, male; U, unknown sex

93

**Table II**

Correlations between Brain Structure Volume
Residuals and Life Span Residuals for Gorillas,
Orangutans, Chimpanzees, and Humans

| Brain structure | r | p |
|---|---|---|
| Brain, whole | 0.997 | 0.0008 |
| Cerebellum, whole | 0.985 | 0.0152 |
| Diencephalon | 0.990 | 0.0077 |
| Hippocampus | 0.946 | 0.0738 |
| Medulla | 0.988 | 0.0105 |
| Mesencephalon | 0.991 | 0.0064 |
| Neocortex | 0.989 | 0.0087 |
| Striatum | 0.994 | 0.0041 |

study has shown that fruit eaters also live significantly longer lives than do leaf eaters when the effect of body size is removed. Because of the ubiquitous nature of leaves, the computational and memory requirements necessary to support a leaf eater might be less than the requirements to support a fruit eater of the same body size.

There is evidence for a budgetary trade-off between energy devoted to mental activity (brain metabolism) and energy devoted to digestion. This proposition may be obvious to anyone who has felt groggy while digesting a large meal. This trade-off arises from the fact that the energy consumption of the whole organism is closely related to body mass, and therefore expansion of one energy-expensive tissue must be compensated by a reduction in other expensive tissues (Aeillo & Wheeler, 1995). In haplorhine primates, body weight–digestive organ weight residuals are significantly negatively correlated with body–brain weight residuals ($r = -0.69$, $p < 0.001$, $n = 18$; Aiello & Wheeler, 1995). Thus haplorhine primates with large guts for their body size tend to have small brains. The size of the digestive organs is in turn related to the complexity of the foods to be digested. Difficult-to-digest foods such as leaves require a large gut, whereas easy-to-digest foods such as ripe fruit and meat require a smaller gut. Thus,

to have a large brain an animal would tend to have a small gut and a correspondingly rich, easily digested diet. The greater difficulty in obtaining sufficient quantities of energy-rich, easily digested foods, in turn, would be a selective factor favoring the development of a larger brain.

In the plot of relative gut mass to relative brain mass (Aiello & Wheeler, 1995), it is striking that the primate with the largest brain and smallest gut, Homo sapiens, is also the longest lived. In this same figure from Aiello and Wheeler, the species closest to Homo sapiens is *Cebus apella*. Figure 1 plots relative life span to relative brain weight; the cluster of three data points nearest to Homo sapiens are three species of *Cebus*, which like humans also have small guts and an energy-rich diet. At the opposite (lower left) end of the graph in Figure 1, the small-brained and short-lived species are all leaf eaters, which tend to have large guts (Aiello & Wheeler, 1995; Chivers & Hladik, 1980). Thus there appears to be an energy budgetary trade-off such that an organism must devote more of its energy to the digestion of readily available, hard-to-digest foods, or alternatively to the task of acquiring foods that are less available, and easy to digest. The search for foods that are both less available and also rich and easily digested requires a larger brain. These observations led us to test the hypothesis that relative gut size would also be negatively correlated with relative life span. Using Aiello and Wheeler's gut data, we calculated the gut–body residuals and compared them with our life span–body residuals. We found they were not significantly correlated ($r = -0.169$, $p = 0.477$, $n = 19$). However, the distribution of the data revealed that there were no haplorhine primates with relatively large guts and long life spans for their body weight.

We found no relationship between basal metabolic rate (BMR) and maximum life span in primates when the effect of body weight was removed. Austad and Fischer

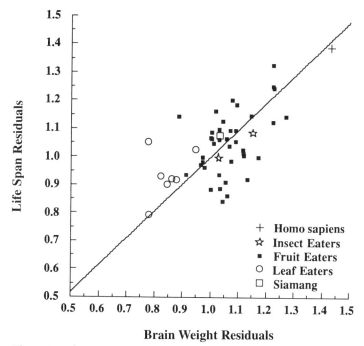

**Figure 1**   Life span residuals versus brain weight residuals for haplorhine primates (Martin data set) ($N = 50$, $r = 0.640$, $p < 0.001$, slope of major axis regression = 1.014). Species data points are labeled according to diet type. The siamang (*Hylobates syndactylus*) has dietary proportions of 43.5% fruit and 43.75% leaves (average of studies reported in Smuts et al., 1987). It was omitted from the dietary statistical analyses because its extremely similar dietary proportions made it difficult to classify.

(1991) showed that the exceptional longevity of bats relative to a large sample of nonflying eutherian mammals is not related to BMR. These authors have also shown that although marsupials have significantly lower BMRs than eutherian mammals, they have shorter life spans when the effect of body mass is taken into account. These findings contradict the popular idea that animals with high BMRs burn out more quickly, which in scientific parlance has been termed the "rate of living" hypothesis of longevity (see Finch, 1990, for a review). It is still conceivable that the well-established relationship between body mass and longevity is somehow related to the higher BMRs in smaller animals, which might, for example, result in the more rapid generation of toxic by-products and thus accelerate the aging process; however, our findings and those of Austad and Fischer (1991) provided no support for the prediction of the "rate of living" hypothesis that animals with higher BMRs than would be expected for their body masses have shorter life spans. We suspect, moreover, that the relationship between body mass and longevity is due to the greater vulnerability of smaller animals to predation, starvation, and intoxication by plant poisons (see Section IV).

## IV. Specializations Enhancing Longevity in Birds and Mammals

The relationship between brain and life span is confined to the haplorhine primates (tarsiers, monkeys, apes, and humans) and is especially strong in the group made up of the great apes and humans (Allman, in press; Allman et al., 1993a; Section V of this chapter). The lack of correlation in strepsirhines (lorises and lemurs) may be due to the fact that all strepsirhine species are nocturnal or native to the island of Madagascar (or both). Nocturnality and island habitat probably result in both less competition for food resources and less predation pressure by other animals, and this may account for the lack of correlation between brain and life span residuals in lower primates. Alternatively, the relationship between brain and life span may be a specialization in higher primates. It is important to analyze relationships between brain and life span in other groups of mammals. Austad and Fischer (1992) found that the relationship between brain and life span was much stronger for primates than other mammals. In a preliminary survey of bats and insectivores, we found no correlation between brain and life span residuals. It is possible that the strong linkage between brain and life span is unique to higher primates or conceivably limited to a few groups of animals yet to be determined.

Another biological specialization linked to longevity is flight. Francis Bacon (1638) commented extensively on the great longevity of birds. Factoring out body weight, the average maximum life span for avian species is more than twice as long as for eutherian mammals (Lindstedt & Calder, 1976). Similarly, maximum longevity in bats averages three times that of nonflying eutherian mammals; gliding mammals average 1.7 times the average maximum life span of nonflying eutherians; and arboreal marsupials have significantly longer life spans than terrestrial marsupials (Austad & Fischer, 1991). The capacity for flight, gliding, or arboreality potentially reduces the risks of predation and opens up new means for gaining access to food resources. These capacities are analogous to expanded brain size in higher primates in that they are energetically expensive adaptations that reduce vulnerability to the hazards of predation and starvation.

A recent theory of life history hypothesizes that the rate of senescence is determined by the extrinsic adult mortality rate (i.e., by deaths resulting from predation, environmental hazards, and other factors not related to the reproductive efforts of the organism) (Charnov, 1991; Hill, 1993; Promislow & Harvey, 1990). This theory is substantiated by the finding that opossums living on an island with reduced exposure to predation live longer and have a slower acceleration of age-specific mortality rates than do opossums living on the mainland where they are exposed to the full range of predators (Austad, 1993). There is also evidence that the biochemical mechanisms of senescence are retarded in the island-dwelling opossums because the age-specific deterioration of collagen fibers is slower in them than in the mainland opossums (Austad, 1993). This theoretical linkage between increased environmental hazards and accelerated senescence may also explain the shorter life spans in folivores, because they ingest large quantities of plant toxins in their diet. In conclusion, we suggest that the ability to fly and enlarged brains are specializations that reduce the vulnerability in some groups of endothermic vertebrates to the hazards of predation and starvation and that the development of these capacities is linked to the retardation of the rate of senescence and to increased longevity.

# V. Primate Brain and Life Span Database

We used the maximum recorded life span because it should measure, under ideal circumstances, the genetic potential for longevity for each species. Age-specific mortality or even average life span data are not available for a large enough sample of species to conduct this analysis. We collected a database of life spans for primate species by querying zoos and research institutions throughout the world. Our queries were guided by records from the International Species Inventory System (ISIS), and by the records of one of the authors (MJ). The ISIS database does not keep track of ages greater than 20 years, which is less than the maximum life span for most primate species. We queried zoos for ages for the oldest ISIS-listed animals where the maximum listed life span was less than 20 years, and for all animals listed in ISIS as over 20, as well as for old animals in personal records. We next sent out requests for more details (such as dates and animal IDs) about the oldest animals of each species, as identified by our preliminary questionnaires. We also used some life span data from Ross (1988, 1991) and from Harvey, Martin, and Clutton-Brock (1987) when these data gave a longer life span for a species than we otherwise had. The maximum documented human life span is 120.6 years (Matthews, 1994); however, this is based on a population about a million times larger than that for any nonhuman primate. Therefore we used a value from a contemporary human population more nearly comparable in size to the populations of nonhuman primates sampled. In a sample of 1,000 obituary notices published from August 1991 through June 1993 in the *Los Angeles Times*, the longest lived individual was 105 years old (Obituary, 1992).

The quality of the life span data is limited by three major factors. First, the sample sizes for rare species were relatively small. We believe that the extremely high correlations between brain structure and life span residuals we found in the great apes and humans (see Table II) were in part due to the large sample sizes and high quality of record keeping for this group. Second, many of the long-lived animals in our survey were born in the wild, and their age at acquisition could only be estimated. We accepted the zoo's estimate of the age

at which an animal was acquired for animals that were acquired while immature. For animals acquired from the wild as adults, we used a value for adult age as the age at acquisition. Our value of the adult age was the average age of females at first reproduction for the species, from a table by Ross (1988, 1991). If the zoo had evidence, such as extreme tooth wear or having borne several offspring, to indicate that the animal was older than the female age at first reproduction when it was acquired, we adjusted the estimated age at acquisition accordingly.

In particular, since our earlier publications we have adjusted our maximum life span for the orangutan upwards, as we learned that the record-holding animal, Guas, was a mature male with cheek pads when he was acquired by the Philadelphia Zoo. According to Dr. Biruté Galdikas (personal communication, March 1, 1994), the minimum age for a male orangutan to develop cheek pads is 13, so we used 13 as Guas's estimated age at acquisition. It is possible that he and his mate, Guarina, were older when acquired, but we prefer to use the most conservative estimate consistent with the available information. This change in our maximum life span value for the orangutan, the use of maximum human life span from a sample size comparable to that available for nonhuman primates, and changes in the maximum life span values for a few other species for which we have received additional records have slightly changed our resulting correlation values from those we have published before (Allman, 1995; Allman et al., 1993a, 1993b). The third major factor limiting the quality of the life span data is that, because of improved husbandry, in 36 species the maximum life span record is for a living animal. Thus, the maximum life spans will necessarily be underestimated for these species.

Table I is a compendium of our data including the vital statistics for the first and second longest-lived individuals for 112 primate species. In cases where the first or second record for a species was from a publication rather than from a zoo record, the top two zoo records are also listed if available. In the sample of very old primates, in the cases for which gender was known, there was a preponderance of females over males (F = 94; M = 73).

We tested the hypothesis that brain weight is correlated with life span when the effect of body weight is removed. We used brain and body weight data from an unpublished database compiled by Prof. R. D. Martin and his colleagues at the University of Zurich. We also used data from Stephan and his collaborators (Baron, Frahm, Bhatnagar, Kunwar, & Stephan, 1983; Frahm, Stephan, & Baron, 1984; Frahm, Stephan, & Stephan, 1982; Matano, Baron, Stephan, & Frahm, 1985; Stephan, Baron, & Frahm, 1982; Stephan, Frahm, & Baron, 1981, 1984, 1987) on body

weights and the volumes of various brain structures to determine which structures are correlated with life span. We obtained BMRs from an unpublished database compiled by Prof. Martin. We also used pineal volumes from Stephan, Frahm, and Baron (1981); surface areas of the posterior half of the eye (Stephan et al., 1984); and testes weights (Harrison & Lewis, 1986). Because life span, brain weight, and these other measures are all correlated with body weight (Allman et al., 1993a, 1993b), it was necessary to remove the effect of body weight to observe the net effect of variation in the size of the brain, its components, and the other measures on life span. Data on diet in primate species were obtained from Smuts et al. (1987).

Figure 2 illustrates the relationship between body and brain weight. Figure 3 illustrates the relationship between body weight and life span. To remove the effect

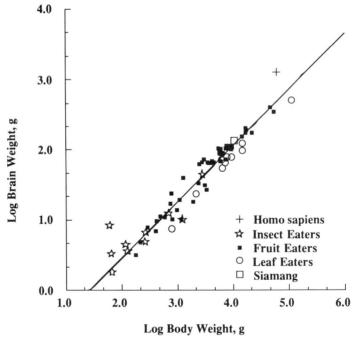

**Figure 2**  Log brain weight in grams versus log body weight for the entire set of primate species for which we have data ($N = 72$, $r = 0.970$, $p = 0.001$, slope = 0.803). The effects of body weight were removed by calculating the residuals from the least-squares regression line.

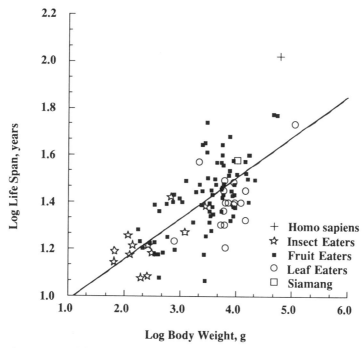

**Figure 3**   Log life span (years) versus log body weight for the entire set of primate species for which we have data ($N = 109$, $r = 0.685$, $p = 0.001$, slope $= 0.172$).

of body weight by the *residuals* method, we plotted the base 10 logarithm of the parameter in question (brain weight or life span, for example) against the base 10 logarithm of the body weight. The distance in the y dimension between the least-squares regression line and each data point was added to 1, giving a value >1 for points that fall above the line and <1 for points that fall below the line. This gives the residual value of this parameter for each species. We used the least-squares regression as the basis for calculating residuals because this procedure removes the effect of body weight plotted along the x axis (Harvey & Pagel, 1991). We sought to determine whether a species that lived longer than one would expect for its body weight had a brain or brain structure that was commensurably larger than would be expected for its body weight. We also used the method of partial correlations to remove the effect of body size on the log-

transformed brain and life span data. In virtually every case the partial correlation coefficient was equal to or higher than the residual correlation coefficient (Pearson's r). The advantage of the residuals method is that the distribution of the residuals can be graphed (see Figure 1). The data were analyzed with the assistance of the computer programs Systat and Statview.

Brain weight residuals and life span residuals are correlated in haplorhine primates (Martin data: $N = 50$, $r = 0.640$, $p = <0.001$; Stephan data: $N = 27$, $r = 0.680$, $p < 0.001$), but not in strepsirhine primates (Martin data: $N = 16$, $r = 0.107$, $p = 0.694$; Stephan data: $N = 13$, $r = 0.272$, $p = 0.369$). The distribution of the residuals for brain weight and life span in haplorhine primates reflects dietary specializations. In Figure 1, which plots relative life span against relative brain weight, species that are predominately leaf eaters are in the lower-left part of the distribution with smaller brains and shorter life spans; species that are predominately fruit eaters are in the middle and upper-right with larger brains and longer life spans; the small number of insect eaters are mixed with the fruit eaters; the omnivorous human is the extreme upper-right data point. The leaf eaters have significantly smaller brains and shorter life spans than the fruit eaters for their body sizes (brains: average for 43 frugivores = 1.072, average for 9 folivores

$= 0.874$, $p < 0.001$; life spans: average for 66 frugivores $= 1.052$, average for 17 folivores $= 0.811$, $p = 0.007$). When the data set is limited to our closest relatives (great apes and humans) the ape with the smallest brain and shortest life for its body weight, the gorilla, is a leaf eater, which is consistent with the pattern for haplorhine primates as a whole (Allman et al., 1993a).

Figure 4 shows the correlations for the brain and many of its components, as well

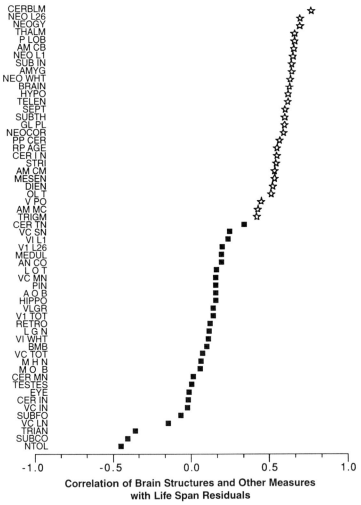

**Figure 4** Correlations of brain structures and other measures with life span, with the effect of body weight removed for haplorhine primates. The correlation coefficients for the residuals for each brain structure or other measure versus life span residuals are plotted on the scale from −1 to 1. Correlations that had $p$ values <0.05 are represented by stars. The structures

as some other measures such as reproductive maturity, BMR, pineal volume, testes weight, and eye size for haplorhine primates. In each case we calculated the residuals relative to body weight as described above for brain weight relative to body weight and then determined the correlation with life span residuals relative to body weight. The structures are plotted in descending order of *r* value from top to bottom. The data points represented by stars are statistically significant at $p < 0.05$. The data for haplorhines reveal that the brain is a mosaic with respect to life span. In haplorhines, the most strongly correlated structure is the cerebellum (CERBLM). The second and third most strongly correlated structures are different measures of neocortical volume (NEO L26, NEO GY). The fourth structure is the thalamus (THALM), which is closely connected to the neocortex. The amygdala and its components (AMYG, AM CB, AM CM), the hypothalamus (HYPO), the substantia innominata (SUB IN), globus pallidus (GL PL), and the closely connected subthalamus (SUBTH) are all well correlated with life span. The main and accessory olfactory bulbs (MOB and AOB) are not significantly correlated; however, olfac-

tory cortical structures such as the pyriform lobe (P LOB), prepyriform cortex (PP CER), and the olfactory tubercule (OL T) are significantly related to life span.

Visual structures such as the eye, the lateral geniculate nucleus (LGN), and the various measures of primary visual cortex (V1 LI, V1 L26, V1 TOT, V1 WHT) and vestibular structures (VC TOT, VC SN, VC MN, VC IN, VC LN) are not significantly related. Female reproductive maturity (RP AGE) is significantly correlated with life span but not as well as many brain structures. BMR, pineal volume (PIN), and testes size (TESTES) are not significantly correlated.

In comparison, only two brain structures, the closely connected globus pallidus and subthalamus, are significantly correlated with life span in strepsirhine primates. Reproductive age is not correlated with life span when the effect of body size is removed in lower primates, which is consistent with the lack of correlation between brain or most brain structures and life span. The results for one subset of haplorhine primates, the catarrhines (Old World monkeys, apes, and humans) are very similar to those for haplorhines as a whole, with a few highly correlated struc-

---

and other measures are plotted in descending order of correlation from top to bottom. AM BC, basolateral complex of the amygdala; AM CM, centromedial complex of the amygdala; AM MC, magnocellular part of the basolateral amygdala; AMYG, amygdala; AN CO, anterior commissure; AOB, accessory olfactory bulb; BMR, basal metabolic rate; BRAIN, Martin brain weight; CER IN, interpositus nucleus of the cerebellum; CER LN, lateral nucleus of the cerebellum; CER MN, medial nucleus of the cerebellum; CER TN, cerebellar nuclei, total; CERBLM, cerebellum, total; DIEN, diencephalon; EYE, surface area of the posterior half of the eye; GL PL, globus pallidus; HIPPO, hippocampus; HYPO, hypothalamus; LGN, lateral geniculate nucleus; LOT, lateral olfactory tract; MEDUL, medulla; MESEN, mesencephalon; MHN, medial habenular nucleus; MOB, main olfactory bulb; NEOCOR, neocortex, total; NEO GY, gray matter of the neocortex; NEO L1, layer 1 of the neocortex; NEO L26, layers 2 through 6 of the neocortex; NEO WHT, neocortical white matter; NTOL, nucleus of the lateral olfactory tract; OL T, olfactory tubercule; PIN, pineal body; P LOB, pyriform lobe; PP CER, prepyriform cortex; RETRO, retrobulbar cortex; RP AGE, average female age at first reproduction; SEPT, septum; STRI, striatum; SUBCO, subcommissural body; SUBFO, subfornical body; SUB IN, substantia innominata; SUBTH, subthalamus; TELEN, telencephalon; TESTES, testes weight; THALM, thalamus; TRIAN, triangular nucleus of the septum; TRIGM, trigeminal complex; VC, vestibular complex; VC IN, inferior nucleus of the vestibular complex; VC LN, lateral nucleus of the vestibular complex; VC MN, medial nucleus of the vestibular complex; VC SN, superior nucleus of the vestibular complex; VC TOT, total vestibular complex; V1 GR, gray matter of the primary visual cortex; V1 L1, layer 1 of the primary visual cortex; V1 L26, layers 2 through 6 of primary visual cortex; V1 TOT, total primary visual cortex; V1 WHT, white matter of the primary visual cortex; VPO, ventral pons.

tures not achieving statistical significance because of small sample size. The results for the other subset of haplorhine primates, the platyrrhines (New World monkeys), reveal that the correlation coefficients tend to be lower, and only the brain as a whole, plus the substantia innominata, the cerebellum, and the pyriform lobe, are significantly related to life span. There are 21 structures that are significantly related to life span in catarrhines, three in platyrrhines, and only two in strepsirhines. Finally, we considered the more limited set of brain structures for which data are available for humans and the closely related great apes. These results are illustrated in Table II, which indicates very strong correlations between residuals for the brain as a whole and for seven out of the eight brain structures for which data are available. Taken together these findings indicate a strong tendency for the brain and its components to become more closely correlated with life span with decreasing phylogenetic distance to humans.

## VI. Final Note

Near the completion of this work, we found through an extensive literature search an unpublished doctoral dissertation (Witkin, 1980) that performed a similar analysis of brain and life span in primates using the method of partial correlations on log-transformed data. Although the data used in this earlier study were based primarily on published records with maximum life spans that were generally shorter than those obtained in the present study (by direct inquiry from zoos and research institutions), many of the conclusions in Witkin (1980) are similar to those we obtained without knowledge of her study.

For example, Witkin found that when the effect of body weight was removed for the anthropoidea (monkeys, apes, and humans) the partial correlation between brain weight and life span was 0.617. Using the method of partial correlations to remove the effect of body weight for the haplorhines (tarsiers, monkeys, apes, and humans), we found a correlation of 0.664 for the Martin data and 0.714 for the Stephan data. However, Witkin found a significant partial correlation (0.659) between brain and life span for prosimians (lorises, lemurs, and tarsiers), whereas we did not find significant correlations for strepsirhines (Martin data, $r = 0.175$; Stephan data, $r = 0.280$). This difference is probably due to the considerably shorter life spans used by Witkin for many of the lemurs and by the absence of some lemur species from her longevity data. Witkin found that leaf-eating anthropoidea had significantly shorter lives than fruit eaters, as we have found for the haplorhines. Witkin also found that of all the brain structures, the neocortex was the best predictor of life span in both higher and lower primates. We found that the cerebellum was the best predictor in haplorhine primates, with two measures of neocortical volume being nearly as good predictors in haplorhine primates. In strepsirhine primates, we found only two brain structures that were significantly related to life span, the globus pallidus and the subthalamus.

## Acknowledgments

We thank the 138 zoos and research institutions who kindly provided primate life span data. We especially thank the Duke University Primate Center for longevity data for nine species. We thank Prof. R. D. Martin for generously providing his unpublished database of body and brain weights. We thank Dr. Leslie Aiello for providing gut and body weight data. We also thank Mr. Todd McLaughlin, Mr. Christopher Alexander, and Ms. Prista Charuworn for their valuable assistance in data collection and statistical analysis. Support for this research was provided by a grant from the Howard Hughes Medical Institute through the Undergraduate Biological Sciences Education Program and by grants from the National Institute on Aging, the McDonnell–Pew Program in Cognitive Neuroscience, and the Hixon Professorship.

# References

Aiello, L., & Wheeler, P. (1995). The expensive tissue hypothesis: The brain and the digestive system in human and primate evolution. *Current Anthropology, 36*, 199–221.

Allman, J. (1977). Evolution of the visual system in the early primates. *Progress in Psychobiology and Physiological Psychology, 7*, 1–53.

Allman, J. (1995). Brain and life span in catarrhine primates. In R. Butler & J. Brody (Eds.), *Strategies for delaying the dysfunctions of age* (pp. 221–241). New York: Springer.

Allman, J., McLaughlin, T., & Hakeem, A. (1993a). Brain weight and life-span in primate species. *Proceedings of the National Academy of Sciences of the U.S.A., 90*, 118–122.

Allman, J., McLaughlin, T., & Hakeem, A. (1993b). Brain structures and life-span in primate species. *Proceedings of the National Academy of Sciences of the U.S.A., 90*, 3559–3563.

Austad, S. (1993). Retarded senescence in an insular population of Virginia opossums *(Didelphis virginiana). Journal of Zoology, 229*, 695–708.

Austad, S., & Fischer, K. (1991). Mammalian aging, metabolism, and ecology: Evidence from the bats and marsupials. *Journal of Gerontology: Biological Sciences, 46*, B47–B53.

Austad, S., & Fischer, K. (1992). Primate longevity: Its place in the mammalian scheme. *American Journal of Primatology, 28*, 251–261.

Bacon, F. (1638). *The historie of life and death.* London: Okes.

Baron, G., Frahm, H., Bhatnagar, K., Kunwar, P., & Stephan, H. (1983). Comparison of brain structure volumes in insectivores and primates: III. Main olfactory bulb (MOB). *Journal für Hirnforschung, 24*, 551–568.

Charnov, E. (1991). Evolution of life history variation among female mammals. *Proceedings of the National Academy of Sciences of the U.S.A., 88*, 1134–1137.

Chivers, D., & Hladik, C. (1980). Morphology of the gastrointestinal tract in primates. *Journal of Morphology, 166*, 337–386.

Clutton-Brock, T., & Harvey, P. (1980). Primates, brains and ecology. *Journal of Zoology, 190*, 309–323.

Eisenberg, J., and Wilson, D. (1978). Relative brain size and feeding strategies in the Chiroptera. *Evolution, (Lawrence, Kans.), 32*, 740–751.

Ershler, W., Coe, C., Gravenstein, S., Schultz, K., Klopp, R., Meyer, M., & Houser, W. (1988). Aging and immunity in nonhuman primates: I. Effects of age and gender on cellular immune function in rhesus monkeys *(Macaca mulatta). American Journal of Primatology, 15*, 181–188.

Finch, C. (1990). *Longevity, senescence and the genome.* Chicago: University of Chicago Press.

Frahm, H., Stephan, H., & Baron, G. (1984). Comparison of brain structure volumes in insectivores and primates: V. Area striata. *Journal für Hirnforschung, 25*, 537–557.

Frahm, H., Stephan, H., & Stephan, M. (1982). Comparison of brain structure volumes in insectivores and primates: I. Neocortex. *Journal für Hirnforschung, 23*, 375–389.

Friedenthal, H. (1910). Uber die Gultigkeit der Massenwirkung für der Energieumsatz der lebendigen Substanz. *Zentral blatt fuer Physiologie, 24*, 321–327.

Goodall, J. (1986). *The chimpanzees of Gombe.* Cambridge, MA: Harvard University Press.

Harrison, R., & Lewis, R. (1986). The male reproductive tract and its fluids. In J. Erwin (Ed.), *Comparative primate biology* (Vol.3, pp. 101–148). New York: Alan R. Liss.

Harvey, P., Martin, R., & Clutton-Brock, T. (1987). Life histories in comparative perspective. In B. Smuts, D. Cheney, R. Seyfarth, R. Wrangham, & T. Struhsaker (Eds.), *Primate societies* (pp. 181–196). Chicago: University of Chicago Press.

Harvey, P., & Pagel, M. (1991). *The comparative method in evolutionary biology.* New York: Oxford University Press.

Hill, K. (1993). Life history theory and evolutionary anthropology. *Evolutionary Anthropology, 2*, 78–88.

Lindstedt, S., & Calder, W. (1976). Body size and longevity in birds. *Condor, 78*, 91–94.

MacKinnon, J. (1975). *Borneo.* New York: Time-Life Books.

Martin, R. (1984). Dwarf and mouse lemurs. In D. MacDonald (Ed.), *Encyclopedia of mammals* (p. 331). New York: Facts on File.

Matano, S., Baron, G., Stephan, H., & Frahm, H. (1985). Volume comparisons in the cerebellar complex of primates: II. Cerebellar nuclei. *Folia Primatologica, 44,* 182–203.

Matthews, P. (1994). *The Guinness book of world records.* New York: Bantam.

Obituary: Annie Lloyd Welbourn. (1992, May 31). *Los Angeles Times.*

Pirlot, P., & Stephan, H. (1970). Encephalizations in the chiroptera. *Canadian Journal of Zoology, 48,* 433–444.

Primate life span. (1966). *International Zoo News, 13*(6).

Promislow, D., & Harvey, P. (1990). Living fast and dying young: A comparative analysis of life-history variation among mammals. *Journal of Zoology, 220,* 417–437.

Ross, C. (1988). The intrinsic rate of natural increase and reproductive effort in primates. *Journal of Zoology, 214,* 199–219.

Ross, C. (1991). Life history patterns of new world monkeys. *International Journal of Primatology, 12,* 481–502.

Sacher, G. (1959). Relation of life span to brain weight and body weight in mammals. *Ciba Foundation Colloquium on Ageing, 5,* 115–133.

Smuts, B., Cheney, D., Seyfarth, R., Wrangham, R., & Struhsaker, T. (1987). *Primate societies.* Chicago: University of Chicago Press.

Stephan, H., Baron, G., & Frahm, H. (1982). Comparison of brain structure volumes in insectivores and primates: II. Accessory olfactory bulb (AOB). *Journal für Hirnforschung, 23,* 575–591.

Stephan, H., Frahm, H., & Baron, G. (1981). New and revised data on volumes of brain structures in insectivores and primates. *Folia Primatologica, 35,* 1–29.

Stephan, H., Frahm, H., & Baron, G. (1984). Comparison of brain structure volumes in insectivores and primates: IV. Non-cortical visual structures. *Journal für Hirnforschung, 25,* 385–403.

Stephan, H., Frahm, H., & Baron, G. (1987). Comparison of brain structure volumes in insectivora and primates: VII. Amygdaloid components. *Journal für Hirnforschung, 28,* 571–584.

Stephan, H., Nelson, J., & Frahm, H. (1981). Brain size comparison in chiroptera. *Zeitschrift für Zoologische Systematik und Evolutionsforschung, 19,* 195–222.

Tigges, J., Gordon, T., McClure, H., Hall, E., & Peters, A. (1988). Survival rate and life span at the Yerkes Primate Research Center. *American Journal of Primatology, 15,* 263–273.

Witkin, J. (1980). *Primate brain and life history.* Unpublished doctoral dissertation, Columbia University, New York.

Zihlman, A., Morbeck, M., & Goodall, J. (1990). Skeletal biology and individual life history of Gombe chimpanzees. *Journal of Zoology, 221,* 37–61.

Six

# Structural and Functional Changes in the Aging Brain

Arnold B. Scheibel

## I. Introduction

Within the past decade, an enormous range of information has become available on the anatomical and physiological characteristics of the aging human brain. Although the changes described are variable and idiosyncratic to the areas involved, the general direction of change could be interpreted as tending inevitably toward diminution of function and degradation or loss of the individual elements involved. However, a much more positive and constructive attitude toward this pattern of age-related change can be adapted when the following concepts are factored in:

1. Those changes characteristic of the older years are part of a continuum of alterations characterizing the maturational process.

2. The greatest loss of neurons occurs during the perinatal period and far exceeds those more gradual losses that develop with normal healthy adult aging.

3. The longevity and adaptive capacity of neurons and the entire nervous system is remarkable. Lacking the capacity to regenerate (with one exception, namely, sensory epithelial cells of the olfactory

mucosa) the great majority of neurons live through the entire life span of the organism.

4. Most neurons of the cerebral cortex maintain some degree of plasticity for the entire life of the organism, thereby providing opportunities for cognitive and emotional growth into very old age.

The remarkable increase in average longevity that has been experienced during the twentieth century, especially by inhabitants of the industrialized nations, clearly poses a challenge of major dimensions to the nervous system. With an average added life span of more than 20 years spent in an increasingly complex and polluted environment, it is not remarkable that the later years have witnessed a progressive uncovering of late-developing genetic faults as well as the appearance of stress- and environment-related brain disease.

My purpose in this chapter is to focus on patterns of aging in the healthy brain. However, aging is a coat of many colors. Some individuals, without obvious pathology, are cognitively and emotionally "showing their age" at 60, whereas others appear vigorous and intellectually vital at

*Handbook of the Psychology of Aging, Fourth Edition*
Copyright © 1996 Academic Press, Inc. All rights of reproduction in any form reserved.

85 or 90. In addition to this individual-to-individual variation, the many components of the brain itself vary in their degree of age-related change. Even portions of a single brain structure (e.g., the divisions of the cornu ammonis of the hippocampal-dentate complex) show different degrees of alteration with advancing years. My descriptions will be based on what the literature of the late 1980s and early 1990s has to say about structural and functional patterns of aging in patients without obvious neurological disease or dementia.

But even here, another caveat is in order. We have no way of knowing what kinds of lives the subjects of these many studies were living at the time of their examinations or in the years before their death. Intellectual activity and psychosocial enrichment move brain structure in one direction; retirement and deprivation lead in another (Diamond, Johnson, & Ingham, 1975; Greenough, Juraska, & Volkmar, 1979). Diet, exercise, levels of involvement, and affective stance are equally important and to a large extent equally ignored in clinical descriptions of the aged (Rowe & Kahn, 1987). Until there is sufficiently widespread realization of the continuing adaptability and plasticity of brain tissue to stimulation (or lack of it), all published data must be accepted with some degree of caution.

## II. Gross Changes

In general, the brain decreases in size with aging. Concomitantly, the leptomeninges become thickened, opaque, and increasingly adherent. The sulci widen, cerebral convolutions tend to narrow, and an excess of cerebrospinal fluid collects between the leptomeninges and the cortical surface (Greenfield et al., 1967, p. 523). Gyral atrophy (Figure 1) is most likely to be noted in the frontal and temporal regions, but varies widely and may, in some cases, be invisible to inspection. Most brain shrinkage is due to loss of mass in the white matter, although in the old-old (beyond age 75) other factors, including loss of grey matter, is also involved.

Brain weight, although idiosyncratically determined by many factors (such as gender and body size), also tends to decrease after the fourth decade. Taking the average brain weight of a 20-year-old male as 1399.8 g, it is 1360.8 g between the ages of 41 and 50; 1337.6 g between 51 and 60; 1306.4 g between 61 and 70; 1265.9 g between 71 and 80; and 1179.9 g between 81 and 90 (Greenfield et al., 1967). We must emphasize once more that these are average values and some aging brains show little or no evidence of shrinkage. These classic figures quoted from Greenfield et al. (1967) represent data gleaned more than a quarter of a century ago and may, when repeated, prove increasingly unrepresentative of the more active, dynamic, and venturesome healthy aged of the 1990s and beyond.

Noninvasive imaging techniques have added a new and exciting means of studying the living brain in situ. Using the earlier developed technology of computed tomography (CT), qualitative and semiquantitative studies of normally aging individuals have been reported by a number of investigators (e.g., Brinkman, Sarwar, Leven, & Morris, 1981; Gyldensted, 1977; M. Schwartz et al., 1985). Methods of measurement have varied but virtually all have reported some degree of age-related loss of grey or white matter and progressive dilatation of the ventricles. The volume of cerebrospinal fluid appeared to correlate positively with age while the total volume of grey matter showed a negative age-related correlation. M. Schwartz et al. (1985, p. 146) reported that "the volume of the lateral and third ventricles was elevated in the elderly and volumes of the thalamus and lenticular nuclei were reduced." A few reports refer specifically to diminished amounts of cortex in the temporal lobe in presumably normal elderly

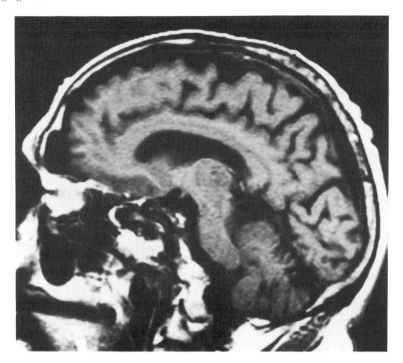

**Figure 1** Magnetic resonance image ($T_1$ weighting) of an 87-year-old subject without obvious dementia. Note the marked atrophic changes over much of the cerebral hemisphere as evidenced by the narrowing of gyri and widening of sulci. There is also widening of the space between skull and cerebral cortex and increase in size of the ventricles. Changes of this magnitude are unusual in cognitively intact individuals and it would be important to learn more about the life pattern of this subject (see text). (Courtesy of Dr. John Bentson.)

individuals with benign senescent forgetfulness.

More uncertain was a postulated relationship between ventricular enlargement and diminished cognitive performance (George et al., 1983) due in part to the amount of interindividual variation in ventricle size. A somewhat more reliable yardstick for correlation with neuropsychologic performance has been the ventricular–brain ratio, and correlation ratios of 0.725 or more have been reported by Eslinger, Damasio, Graff-Radford, and Damasio (1984).

In the last decade, magnetic resonance imaging (MRI), with its unique capability of exploring tissue resonance phenomena after radio excitation (relaxation time, $T_1, T_2$) has added both enhanced resolution and the capacity to evaluate white matter abnormalities. Although a moderately consistent picture of dementia-related brain changes has developed, attempts to establish similar correlations among dimensions of grey and white matter, ventricular size, and psychological performance with the normal aging process have proven more difficult. For one thing, the processes of maturation and regression appear to proceed simultaneously (Cowan, Fawcett, O'Leary, & Stanfield, 1984), presumably to increase functional efficiency and specificity of the remaining neurons.

In an MRI-based study of 39 normal children and young adults aged 8–35 years, Jernigan, Traines, Hesselink, and Tallal (1991) noted progressive diminution in thickness of grey matter over the frontal and parietal convexities (without similar change in inferior cortical areas), and small increases in the amount of cerebrospinal fluid, alterations that one usually conceives of as developing significantly later in life. Accompanying these changes were slight decreases in size of the posterior thalamus and basal ganglia, and increases in the anterior thalamus. Explanations for these highly area-selective alterations were speculative. In this regard it is interesting to note that Huttenlocher (1979) reported decreases in synaptic density in human frontal cortex during this period.

Some investigations report loss only of grey matter without associated changes in the white (Escalona et al., 1991; Jernigan, Archibald et al., 1991). The latter group also call attention to a continuous decrease of the grey–white ratio with age, at least through the eighth decade. Although a few investigators disagree with this view, there is some measure of consensus that loss of cerebral tissue occurs primarily in grey matter until the age of 50, after which the white matter becomes the primary site of loss.

In a more detailed examination of age-related white matter changes reported by Ylikowski et al. (1993), interest was focused on changes ($T_2$ weighted images) in hyperintensity (areas of increased opacity in the MRI image) in the white matter of periventricular areas and the centrum semiovale. A battery of neuropsychological examinations (including memory, verbal-intellectual performance, language, speed of mental processing, and simple psychomotor skills) were used as testing measures. Varying degrees of mild hyperintensity changes were seen in the white matter, which increased with age. More interesting, a consistent and significant relationship was found, controlling for age, between tests of speed and attention, together with speed of mental processing, and total white matter hyperintensity

scores. Although there was the expected variation, the speed of mental processing seemed particularly related to white matter hyperintensity patterns (leukoairosis) in the perinventricular areas.

The meaning of this apparent correlation remains unclear but the authors suggest that white matter changes such as these may reflect one or more of a number of age-related ongoing processes that include widening of perivascular spaces, vascular ectasia (dilation), atrophic perivascular demyelination, cystic or noncystic infarcts, gliosis, and so on (Figure 2). It is worth recalling that alterations in white matter are at the root of most "disconnection syndromes," which are once again being recognized as clinical, neurological, and neuropathological entities.

The significance of changes in localized white matter hyperintensity as a yardstick for the benign aging process has increasingly come into question in the last year or two (e.g., Cummings, personal communication, 1994; Erkinjuntti et al., 1994). It seems increasingly likely that such alterations are the result of underlying pathological conditions such as hypertension, diabetes, and cardiac disorders, and are not directly related to normal brain aging. The thrust of these arguments leads one to conclude that the appearance of hyperintensity changes in cerebral white matter, even in the seventh and eighth decades and beyond, cannot safely be attributed to benign age-related changes in a healthy individual.

Interestingly enough, age-related changes of *hypo*intensity (areas of increased lucency in the MRI image) have been reported in some subcortical and brain stem sites, using long TR/TE (relaxation time/ excitation time) spin-echo images. Among the loci that have been reported under these conditions of visualization are globus pallidus, substantia nigra (pars reticulata), red nucleus, and dentate nucleus. The putamen apparently becomes hypointensive after the age of 60, whereas thalamus and

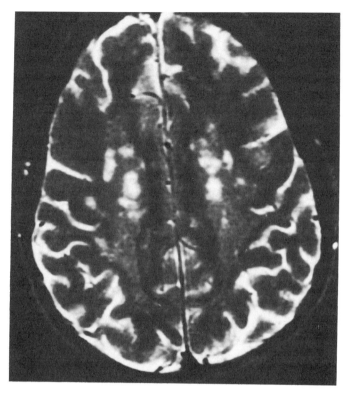

**Figure 2**  Magnetic resonance image ($T_2$ weighting) of a 76-year-old individual without obvious dementia. The sinuous peripheral markings are caused by cerebrospinal fluid in cerebral sulci. The splotchy light (hyperintense) areas in the central white matter represent patches of leukoairosis (see text). (Courtesy of Dr. John Bentson.)

caudate never show such changes. These alterations have been attributed to accumulation of ferric iron.

Attempts at a more rigorous definition of volumetric changes by MRI in the aging human brain are epitomized by the study of Coffey et al. (1992). Working with 76 healthy subjects, they reported an average decrease in volume of the cerebral hemispheres of 0.23%/year; temporal lobes, 0.28%/year; and amygdaloid-hippocampal complex, 0.30% year. On the other hand the volume of the third ventricle was found to increase by 2.8%/year, and that of the lateral ventricle by 7.7%/year. In their material, hyperintensity of subcortical white matter became increasingly apparent; for example, deep cortical white matter, 6.3%/year, and pons, 8.1%/year. Gender was not a significant factor and changes occurred symmetrically in both hemispheres. However, the data also indicated that at age 68 there was only a 50% chance for cortical atrophic changes to be present. Furthermore, 54% of their elderly patient population did not show any of the criteria for ventricular enlargement, a particularly significant observation because ventricular enlargement was reported to proceed more rapidly than cortical atrophy.

A somewhat different approach to quantifying age-related loss of grey and white matter was described by Meier-Ruge, Ulrich, Bruhlmann, and Meier (1992). Basing their study on stereological measurements of the number of capillary segments in randomly selected 40-μm fields of tissue, they computed the total length and diameter of the capillary plexus found in each sample. A higher numerical value was interpreted as due to tissue shrinkage caused by loss of myelinated nerve fibers with some increase in volume of extracellular space. Their results suggested a mean white matter loss of 16–20% between the youngest group measured (15–50 years) and the eldest (71–93 years). Corresponding differences in cortex were reported as less than 6%. A working assumption underlying this study was that the capillary plexus remains more or less constant throughout normal life.

Positron emission tomography (PET) can provide objective functional data on patterns of activity throughout the brain. Although levels of temporal and spatial resolution do not match those of the MRI, the findings are nevertheless revealing. In a typical study by Salmon et al. (1991), frontal metabolic levels were found to be decreased relative to those in other cortical or subcortical areas in a population of healthy elderly compared to young volunteers. The authors suggest that neither cortical atrophy nor neuronal depopulation are likely to explain these changes and hypothesize that subcortical deafferentation may play a role in this process. This suggestion gains credence from recent studies such as those of Boone et al. (1992) indicating that the development of leukoairosis in a healthy aging population was associated with a decline in frontal lobe function. However, progressive alterations in the structural substrate of frontal cortex may also occur.

The data presented here represent a typical selection from a much larger body of material in the literature. Clearly the new, relatively noninvasive means of studying the brain in action will continue to enrich our understanding of the process of normal, healthy aging. But the stigmata of the aging process itself are likely to change as basic ideas about the role of exercise, nutrition, and intellectual challenge become

more widely known. Supreme Court Justice Black (appointed 1937, retired 1971) was known for the passion of his liberal beliefs and the vigor of his competitive spirit. B. Schwartz (1993) provided the following quotation from Black: "When I was forty, my doctor advised me that a man in his forties shouldn't play tennis. I heeded his advice carefully and could hardly wait until I reached fifty to start again." He continued to play several sets every day until he was 83! This vignette is as revealing about medical opinions of aging, less than a half century ago, as it is of the habits of a notably successful and creative practitioner of successful aging.

## III. Microscopic Changes

The range of variations shown at macroscopic levels by the maturing and aging brain is more than matched by the spectrum of alterations reported at microscopic and submicroscopic levels. Many factors are involved in these heterogeneous data. For one thing, brain tissue seems to be inherently plastic and responsive to change, whether environmental, nutritional, or hormonal (Diamond, 1988). Idiosyncratic genetic determinants and constraints on the aging process affect the fine structure and function of each human brain, but at present investigators are familiar with them on a descriptive and anecdotal basis only. Then, too, the conditions under which brain specimens are obtained, prepared, and studied vary enormously, thereby contributing further diversity to the results reported. Even the usual "stop-frame" mode of tissue study to which one is limited by the methods of neurohistology and pathology—providing one look, frozen in time, without reference to what preceded this state or what came later—represents a powerful limitation to our interpretation of what we see. Continuous longitudinal study is still virtually impossible with present methodology. Accordingly, any description or set of descriptions must represent, at best, a set of approximations, reflective of the state of the art at the time, and subject to reinterpretation as broader experience and larger series become available over time.

One more potential problem deserves to be noted. Boundary conditions defining the limits between normal healthy aging and the beginnings of pathology remain to be determined. How much dendritic shrinkage or neuron loss can be considered to fall within "normal" limits? At what point does "benign senescent forgetfulness" grade into memory deficits with more serious prognostic import? Until we are more certain of our limits, our discussions must remain tentative.

A. Neuron Loss

No single age-related issue has generated more discussion than the problem of neuron loss. Almost everyone is familiar with the old "truism" that we lose 100,000 nerve cells every day. The source of this figure is not clear, but earlier studies certainly painted a bleak picture, equating the inevitability of continuing cell loss with aging and senescence. Even if this figure were correct, it would still represent only a fraction of the massive cell loss that occurs during the late fetal and perinatal period. Programmed cell death and axonal retraction appear central to the continued development of many forebrain structures such as the corpus callosum (Innocenti, Koppl, & Clarke, 1981) and the cerebral cortex (Schatz, Chun, & Luskin, 1988). We agree with Mesulam (1987, p. 582), who questions "why neuronal attrition which is described as 'developmental' early in life should be called 'involutional' later on." This statement is mitigated only by the fact that the mechanisms of cell loss—and presumably their consequences—probably vary through time.

Approximately 100 years ago, Hodge (1894) may have set the stage for these concerns by showing age-related nerve cell loss in both the human and the honey bee.

Some 60 years later, Brody (1955, 1970) reported decreases in neuron density in the superior temporal lobe of 50–60% between the ages of 18 and 95 with almost equivalent losses in superior frontal gyrus and somewhat less in the primary sensory and motor cortical strips.

Although significant age-related neuron loss has also been reported by Shefer (1973), Mouritzen Dam (1979), and Miller, Alston, Mountjoy, and Corsellis (1984), objections to these findings have also been raised by a number of investigators. Coleman and Flood (1987) have pointed out that two-point studies that compare cell counts at two epochs (in different brains, of course!) may not be sufficiently sensitive to pick up maturational and age-related changes that are not monotonic. Furthermore, as we have already indicated, even robust decrements in cell number that may occur in the eighth and ninth decades are still modest compared to the massive elimination of neurons during the perinatal period. Another confounding variable is the extent to which increasing physical disease or a prolonged agonal period may contribute to the overall picture of neuronal pathology and loss. In this regard, it should be remembered that detailed multi-epoch investigations of aging rat cortex reveal significant diminution in the density of neurons between 41 and 108 days of age, followed by apparent stability in number until 904 days of age (Diamond, Johnson, Protti, Ott, & Kajisa, 1985). The 900-day rat is roughly equivalent to a 90-year-old human being!

Terry, DeTeresa, and Hansen (1987) have emphasized the importance of size transitions in large neurons, in evaluating the degree of cell loss in the healthy aging brain. Through the use of automated cell-counting techniques, they described a selective decrease in the density of large neurons ($> 90 \mu m$) and an apparent increase in the density of small neurons ($41–90 \mu m$). They attributed this to age-related shrinkage of large nerve cells. Objections have been raised to this interpretation on the basis of the known increase in astrocytes with age, and an associated decrease in cortical volume (Hubbard & Anderson, 1981). Terry et al. (1987) felt that their careful editing of the computer-generated output mitigates this criticism. Associated with the decrease in size of large neurons, these authors described accompanying decrements in brain weight, cortical thickness in midfrontal and superior temporal areas, and the neuron-glial ratio in midfrontal and superior parietal areas. Total neuron number and neuronal density were unchanged. There were apparent age-associated *increases* in number of small neurons in midfrontal cortex and glia in the midfrontal and superior temporal areas. The authors concluded from their data that there is some degree of overall age-associated neuron loss (i.e., constant neuron density plus diminished cortical volume), but that the amount of loss is much smaller than previously supposed. Such a position is consonant with the somewhat earlier findings by Haug (1985) in the human cortex and by Kaplan and Scheibel (1982) in cats.

In this regard, it is worth noting a somewhat earlier group of studies centered on possible age-related changes (i.e., cell loss) in the smaller and more readily quantifiable neuronal ensembles of cerebellum and brain stem. Essentially no decrements were found in the cerebellar roof nuclei (Heidary & Tomasch, 1969), the inferior olive (Moatamed, 1966), the ventral cochlear nucleus (Konigsmark & Murphy, 1970), the seventh cranial nerve nucleus (Van Buskirk, 1945), and even in the nucleus basalis of Meynert (Chui, Bondareff, Zarow, & Slager, 1984), although this finding has not gone unchallenged.

B. Changes in the Structure of Nerve Cells and Their Immediate Environment

Despite the remarkable longevity of the majority of neurons, it is also clear that time leaves its mark. Among these age-related alterations, I will consider intrasomal inclusions, changes in the endoskeletal components of the nerve cell body and its extensions, alterations in dendrites and synaptic terminals, and the appearance in varying degrees of discrete foci of degeneration in the neuropil known as senile plaques.

## 1. Neuron Loss

The majority of neurons in the aging nervous system appear to accumulate lipochrome bodies or lipofuscins (Borst, 1992). These particulate inclusions (Figure 3) are extremely prominent in brain tissue from patients in the seventh and eighth decades of their life but may also be found very much earlier. In fact, cells of the inferior olive may show accumulations of lipofuscins as early as the sixth postnatal year. Their apparent lack of impact on the well-being and longevity of the cell is suggested by the fact that the inferior olive appears to maintain its full complement of neurons throughout life (Vijayashankar & Brody, 1977).

The nature of these inclusions remains unclear but they are believed to represent pigmented cellular waste products such as the incompletely degraded membrane fragments of endocellular organelles (e.g., lysosomes and mitochondria) (Minckler, 1968). Although there is no direct evidence of toxicity to the host cell, their gradual accumulation in the cyton may displace the endoplasmic reticulum and Golgi bodies necessary for protein synthesis and cell maintenance functions. In support of this thesis, Hyden and Lindström (1950) demonstrated an inverse relationship between ribonucleic acid (RNA) content and the amount of yellow pigment in neurons.

## 2. Granulovacuolar Degeneration

Granulovacuolar degeneration is characterized by the presence of 1-μm argyrophilic granules contained in membrane-

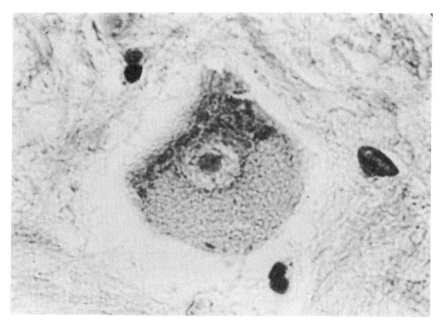

**Figure 3**   Neuron from the upper brain stem of a 75-year-old subject showing heavy loading with lipofuscin granules. The major portion of the cell body is filled with this granular material, leaving only a small area for the (dark staining) endoplasmic reticulum, the organelle system responsible for the protein-synthesizing capability of the cell. Cresyl violet stain. Original magnification × 980. (Reproduced with permission from A. Scheibel, 1992, p. 155.)

bound vacuoles, 3–5 μm in diameter. They are most frequently found in the apical end of large pyramids in the hippocampal complex and subiculum and may gradually displace intracytoplasmic RNA. Ball (1983) suggested that their regional specificity may indicate a common substrate neurotransmitter such as acetycholine. Hirano bodies, eosinophilic inclusions 15–30 μm in length, will be mentioned in passing. Also found in hippocampal pyramids, their nature and pathogenesis remain unclear (Brun, 1983).

## 3. Neurofibrillary Tangles

Neurofibrillary tangles constitute one of the pathognomic signs of Alzheimer's disease and undoubtedly represent the single most damaging cell body inclusion. The fact that these structures are also present in small numbers in brain tissue of apparently healthy aged individuals constitutes one of the more problematic aspects of geriatric neurohistology. They are found primarily in cortical pyramidal cells in hippocampus and in frontal and temporal association areas, as well as subcortically in basal forebrain, amygdala, and catecholaminergic nuclei of the brain stem (Greenfield et al., 1967, p. 532).

Tangles are easily visualized microscopically (Figure 4) with reduced silver stains or with Congo red, where their typical green birefringence is probably due to the β-pleated structure of their constituent molecules. At the ultrastructural level they consist largely of paired helical filaments (PHF), each 10–12 nM in diameter, wound round each other in a left-handed helical configuration with a half periodicity of 80 nM (Kidd 1963; Terry, Gonatas, & Weiss, 1964). The nature and pathogenesis of the PHF remains enigmatic, although a group of immunohistochemical and molecular biological studies during the past decade have begun to throw some light on the subject (e.g., Lee,

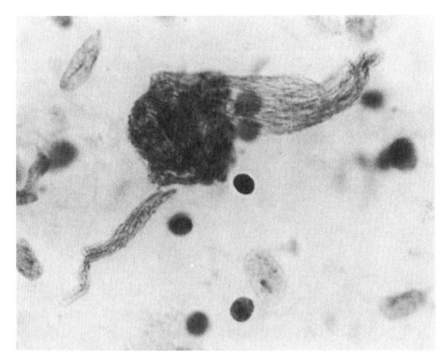

**Figure 4**  Neurofibrillary tangles in a pyramidal cell of the hippocampal cortex of a patient with senile dementia of Alzheimer's type. Note that tangles in the cell body are arranged in swirls or packets whereas those entering the apical and basilar dendrite shafts are arranged in linear ensembles. These structures are immunohistochemically stained by antibody to paired helical filaments (donated by Dr. D. J. Selkoe) and counterstained with cresyl violet. Final print magnification × 980. Neurofibrillary tangles in the neurons of healthy aged individuals are indistinguishable from these. However, the number of tangle-containing cells is greatly reduced (see text). (Courtesy of Dr. Taihung Duong.)

Balin, Otovos, & Trojanowski, 1991; Price et al., 1991; Probst, Langer, & Ulrich, 1991).

The individual filaments appear to consist of globular subunits stacked to form the twin filaments. Although the PHF are structurally different from normal endoskeletal components like microtubules and neurofilaments, they share epitopes with cytoskeletal proteins. As an example, tau protein, of which at least six isoforms have been identified, is usually associated with axonal and dendritic microtubules. In Alzheimer's disease (and presumably to a lesser extent in normal aging), a proportion of tau protein becomes abnormally phosphorylated and accumulates in paired helical filaments. Other cytoskeletal components that may also be involved include phosphorylated epitopes of the neurofilament 150– and 200–kD polypeptides, microtubule-associated protein (MAP 2), vimentin, actin, and ubiquitin. Both neurofibrillary tangles and senile plaques share the doubtful honor of serving as histological hallmarks of Alzheimer's disease and of being present in lesser quantities in the presumably healthy aging brain. In the aged nonhuman primate, a useful model of age-associated neural change, paired helical filaments appear to develop before senile plaques (Price et al., 1991). On this basis it may be assumed that neurofibrillary changes also antedate plaque formation in the human brain.

### 4. Senile Plaques

Senile plaques, initially described by Alzheimer (1907) and Simchowitz (in 1910, as cited in Blackwood, McMenemy, Meyer, Norman, & Russell, 1967, pp. 526, 575), are foci of neuropil destruction surrounding (in the mature plaque state) a central core of amyloid. The plaque itself is usually encircled by partially destroyed neurites and by microglia, all of which may be considered as parts of a progressive and slowly widening focus of tissue death (Figure 5). Plaques are easily visualized microscopically with any one of a number of staining techniques including reduced silver, PAS, Congo red, and thioflavin S. The electron microscope reveals the characteristic core to be made up of amyloid fi-

bers in the form of paired helical filaments that are somewhat differently organized than those of the neurofibrillary tangles (Wisniewski, 1983). Plaques are most likely to be found in the second and third layers of frontal and temporal association cortex and in hippocampus.

As with so many other histological components of the aging or senescent brain, the nature and pathogenesis of these structures and particularly of their amyloid core remain unclear. Until recently, discussion centered around the possible source of amyloid (i.e., from neurons and glia in situ or, alternatively, introduced from more distant sites via the capillary plexus). More recent work has focused interest on the metabolic cleavage patterns of β amyloid precursor protein (β APP), a normal constituent of all cell membranes. Aberrant processing of β APP may lead to the laying down of β amyloid (Aβ) either in excessive amounts or in insoluble forms

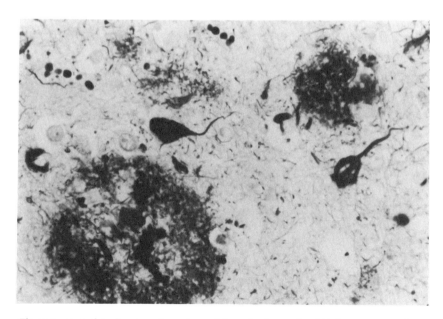

**Figure 5**   Entorhinal cortex of a patient with senile dementia of Alzheimer's type showing senile plaques and several neurons with neurofibrillary tangles. The larger plaque has a central core of amyloid. Such structures are also present in the healthy aging brain although in smaller numbers (see text). Reduced silver stain. Original magnification × 440. (Reproduced with permission from A. Scheibel, 1992, p. 158.)

(Mullan & Crawford, 1993). Several possible gene markers have been suggested as central to this process in Alzheimer's disease, but whether they may also be involved in the far more subtle version of amyloid deposition and plaque formation usually found in healthy aged brains remains unknown.

It is not possible to provide parametric limits to the "allowable number" of plaques and tangles that may be found in the healthy aging brain, beyond which the term *healthy* would have to be withdrawn (but see Khachaturian, 1985). Earlier studies by Tomlinson, Blessed, and Roth (1970) seemed to indicate an approximately linear relationship between increasing numbers of plaques and tangles per high-powered microscopic field and the development of dementia. Investigators are far less certain of such a relationship today, although it remains well accepted that, for any age group, the density of plaques and tangles in the brain of a healthy individual will usually constitute only a small fraction of those present in a demented counterpart.

## C. Dendrite Systems

Dendrite systems of neurons are one of the most significant anatomical yardsticks of neural function, because they are the primary recipient of the arrays of synaptic input impinging on each cell. Between 80 and 95% of the total synaptic receptive surface of the neuron is made up of dendritic tissue (Aitken & Bridger, 1967; Schade & Baxter, 1960), thereby virtually ensuring that the "synaptic vigor" of the neuron is a function of the state of its dendritic tree. A broad range of studies indicate the enormous variation in synapse populations on nerve cell–dendrite systems, ranging from as few as several thousand on a small spinal neuron to as many as 300,000 or more on large cerebellar Purkinje cells. Dendrite development begins during the latter part of the second trimes-

ter of pregnancy as the primitive neurons reach their final positions in the rapidly thickening walls of the neural tube (i.e., the mantle layer of the spinal cord and brain stem and the cortical plate of archicortex and neocortex). Growth continues at a rapid pace throughout infancy, childhood, and puberty (Conel, 1941–1951). During early maturity, the pace slows and further growth may then become more a function of individual neuronal system response to specific challenge and use than of continued general growth drive.

Regression becomes more noticeable in the old-old (Coleman & Flood, 1987), but even here, experimental data based on work with very old rodents indicates that some degree of dendrite plasticity in response to environmental challenge may continue into very old age (Diamond, 1988). Residual plasticity in the aged human brain has been demonstrated by Buell and Coleman (1979), who reported net dendritic growth in layer II pyramidal cells of the parahippocampal gyrus. Some of this increase may represent response to limited loss of neurons that reactively stimulates dendrite sprouting in adjacent cells (Coleman & Flood, 1987). One might almost consider neuropil (the dendritic and axonal matrix of the central nervous system) as an active, vital tapestry endeavoring to maintain its own integrity during a time of changing physiological and computational demands. Nonetheless, the differential sensitivity of such reparative phenomena to age and brain locus is illustrated in studies comparing old (18–20 years) and very old (27–28 years) macaque neocortex and subiculum (Cupp & Uemura, 1980; Uemura, 1985). The locus-specific nature of plasticity is also emphasized by Buell and Coleman (1979), who demonstrated dendritic loss in layer II pyramidal neurons of the middle frontal gyrus in apparent contradistinction to the more plastically reactive dendrites of the parahippocampus already alluded to.

It is not inappropriate to stress the dynamic interplay between dendritic growth and retraction, especially during the later part of life, because the integrity of the dendritic ensemble is a vital measure of neuronal interconnectivity. Upon the latter, in turn, depends the computational power of the nervous system and the cognitive abilities of the individual involved.

The loss of dendritic tissue seems to follow a centripetal sequence with initial disappearance of the outermost twigs of the dendritic tree followed by loss of those branches located progressively closer to the cell body of origin. Isolated patches of dendritic spine loss and nodular swellings along the course of the dendrite shaft frequently antedate disappearance of the dendrite segment itself (M. Scheibel, Lindsay,

Tomiyasu, & Scheibel, 1975; M. Scheibel, Tomiyasu, & Scheibel, 1977). Sequential alterations of this nature clearly reflect a diminution of the synaptic input to the neuron with probable changes in its capacity to integrate large amounts of afferent data. The cell appears to remain viable during at least a part of this process but it is not known whether dendritic retraction, once started, is reversible (Figure 6).

One of the most dramatic and predictable exemplars of this process is the giant pyramidal cell of Betz of the motor strip (area 4). These large layer V pyramids, which are characteristically 70–100 μm in size, are found in the largest concentrations in cortical sites that control antigravity muscles (i.e., the large extensor

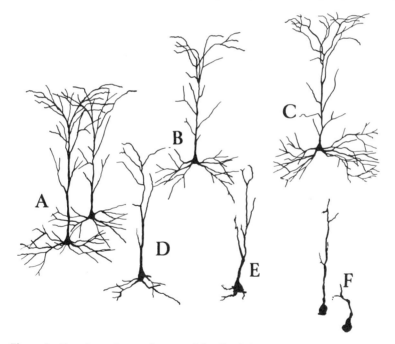

**Figure 6**  Drawings of several pyramidal cells of the cerebral neocortex, epitomizing two different aging scenarios. The sequence A, B, C represents a series of events believed to be followed during the course of normal healthy aging. One of the two neurons present in A is lost during the aging process but the remaining neuron appears to respond by developing a more extensive dendritic arbor, particularly as terminal branchlets of the basilar dendrite system, B, C. The sequence A, D, E, F represents the train of events followed during the development of senile dementing disease. The loss of one of the two neurons, A, is not followed by compensatory growth of dendritic branches in the remaining neuron. Instead, there is progressive loss of dendrite branches in the remaining neuron D, E, F with resultant impoverishment in synaptic connections.

muscles of the pelvic girdle and lower extremities, and the axial musculature of the vertebral column and shoulder girdle). They are remarkably few in number (40,000 neurons per hemisphere) and have been found to play a unique role in preparing the individual for specific motor action. Acting via a brief phasic burst of descending impulses, they appear to release antigravity tone in extensors and somewhat increase tone in large flexors immediately prior to a motor act. In this way, the individual plays out the sequence of the selected motor action upon a reduced background of antigravity tone.

Dendritic alterations in these cells appear as early as the fifth decade of life and as many as 75% of Betz cells may be destroyed or show regressive changes by the eighth decade (M. Scheibel et al., 1977). It is very possible that the increased stiffness and slowing of motor activity that characterizes most older individuals is due in part to the loss of this small but important cell population. This apparently selective loss of giant pyramidal cells of Betz may be one of the more prominent examples of the overall diminution in larger cortical cells described by Terry et al. (1987) and already alluded to.

## D. Gliosis

Gliosis (an increase in the number of neuroglial cells) is commonly found in most aging brains although not to the extent seen in Alzheimer's disease or other cortical dementias (Beach, Walker, & McGeer, 1989). In the nondemented aged individual, gliosis (primarily astrocytic) is found principally in the supragranular layers of association cortices with inconsistent patterns of perivascular gliosis in putamen, thalamus, and the periventricular white matter. In view of previously cited data on the correlative appearance of leukoairosis with hypertension, diabetes, and cardiac disorders (J. Cummings, personal communication, 1994; Erkinjuntti et al., 1994),

one questions whether some of these perivascular glial concentrations may not also represent a response to unrecognized systemwide pathology.

## IV. Regional Changes

### A. Limbic System

The limbic system shows varying degrees of age-related change depending on the subjects selected for study and the method of analysis. Noninvasive visualization techniques in the hands of Golomb et al. (1993) demonstrated some degree of hippocampal atrophy (10–40%) in approximately one-third of individuals in a cohort of 154 healthy adults aged 55–84 years. The atrophy was more obvious in males than in females and was progressively more apparent in the older members of the group. The authors also noted that those subjects with visible atrophy did more poorly on tests of recent (secondary) verbal memory but seemed unaffected in the area of immediate (primary) memory. Follow-up studies should eventually indicate whether those individuals showing both structural and memory alterations represent an early phase of senile deterioration.

At the microscopic level, normal aging appeared to have no significant effect on pyramidal cell density in any hippocampal field in a small group of subjects aged 6–87 years (Davies, Horwood, Isaacs, & Mann, 1992). Among the various sectors of the cornu amonis (CA), CA2 appeared the most resistant to cell loss (Marie, Lohr, & Jeste, 1986). These authors (Marie et al., 1986) stress the rather unique attributes of CA2 with its slightly narrower cell band, its unusually high degree of vascularization, and its robust level of resistance to ischemic insult. A possible corollary of this is its remarkable freedom from neurofibrillary tangles, in comparison with adjacent fields CA1, CA3, and CA4. However, in patients with Alzheimer's dementia, CA2 apparently becomes the most vulnerable of the hippocampal fields to tangle formation (Mizutani & Shimada, 1991).

Information on the impact of normal aging on fibers afferent to the hippocampus is incomplete. However, Powers et al. (1988) have described swollen noradrenergic afferents to hippocampus as well as to posterior commissure and pineal gland, suggesting some type of age-related process in these important fibers. Normal aging is also accompanied by "modest" loss in density of acetylcholinesterase (AChase)-containing fibers in the entorhinal and inferotemporal cortices but not in the cingulate area, according to Geula and Mesulam (1989). These changes are believed to be related to alterations in the nucleus basalis (see Section IV.B).

It is worth noting that the normal aging process seems less benign in other parts of the limbic system. West (1993) studied a group of 32 males from 13–85 years of age and reported neuronal losses up to 52% in the subiculum and 31% in the dentate gyrus.

The picture may be a little more complicated in the adjacent amygdala. Healthy aged subjects have been reported to contain a number of dystrophic neurites, although no reduction in immunolabeled fibers has been noted (Benzing, Mufson, & Armstrong, 1993). Thus there must be some degree of degradation or loss of amygdaloid neuronal processes (and possibly of neurons), but the number of afferent peptidergic and cholinergic afferent fibers does not seem to be appreciably altered.

## B. Nucleus Basalis of Meynert

The nucleus basalis of Meynert is of particular interest to us, not only as a principal source of cholinergic innervation to the cerebral cortex but also as a postulated site of major pathology in Alzheimer's disease (Whitehouse et al., 1982). As with so much of our data about the healthy aging

brain, there is considerable variation in the descriptions of this critical neuronal ensemble. De Lacalle, Iraiziz, and Gonzalo (1991) found almost 50% loss in total nucleus basalis cell numbers in individuals at the age of 90 compared to a cohort of younger subjects aged 16–29 years. They also reported an increase in average cell size by more than 17% until the age of 60, followed by a gradual decline. In contrast, Chui et al. (1984) were struck by the stability of nucleus basalis neuron counts over the years with little evidence of regression in size or number.

There appears to be a somewhat higher level of consistency in reports about the decrease of choline acetyl transferace (ChAT) activity in the nucleus basalis, as well as in the density of dopaminergic and serotonergic terminals within the nucleus. Sparks et al. (1992) suggested that the age-related decline in ChAT activity may be due either to loss of cholinergic cells or decrease in the amount of ChAT in the neurons. Flood and Coleman (1988) noted that over the lifetime of the individual (ages 4–92) there is a 65% reduction in ChAT, which is compatible with the loss of 68% of the cholinergic neurons previously reported by E. McGeer and McGeer (1982). As with so much of the rest of the data being summarized here, variations in research methodology, in the nature of the lives led by the subjects (especially in the latter years of their lives), and in the imponderables of genotypic and phenotypic diversity probably all contribute to the range of results.

## C. Hypothalamus

The hypothalamus comprises a spectrum of neuronal systems with a broad range of functional domains. It is therefore not surprising that the degree of age-related changes varies widely throughout the structure. Several cell systems have been studied in more detail than others and they will serve as models.

## 1. Suprachiasmatic Nucleus

The suprachiasmatic nucleus (SCN) has, not surprisingly, been the subject of a number of studies. Several groups report marked decreases in the number of neurons in the SCN (Mirmiran et al., 1992; Swaab et al., 1993). These changes are particularly noticeable after the age of 80 and are especially prominent in vasopressin-expressing cells (Swaab et al., 1993). In such patients, circadian rhythms are almost always disturbed with phase advance, and there is decreased stability of the diurnal rhythms (Mirmiran et al., 1992). Degenerative changes in the visual system and decreases in melatonin synthesis also contribute to this effect. It is interesting that in a companion study by some of this same group (Goudsmit, Neijmeijer-Leloux, & Swaab, 1992), vasopressin- and oxytocin-secreting cells of the supraoptic and paraventricular nuclei are described as an extremely stable cell population throughout the life span. An increase in vasopressin secretion is described in very old individuals, perhaps in compensation for deteriorating renal function. Assuming that these data will stand the test of repetition in larger population groups, they suggest that cells of presumably comparable function react differently to the aging process, depending on their site of action.

## 2. Sexually Dimorphic Nuclei

The sexually dimorphic nuclei (SDN) appear to remain unaltered until the age of 50 in males. Thereafter the number of neurons begins to decrease rapidly. In females, the most dramatic downturn in cell numbers occurs after 70, presumably accompanying hormonal changes that characterize female senescence (Hofman & Swaab, 1989). Interestingly enough, SDN neurons are noted to diminish in number at approximately the same rate in normal aging and

in Alzheimer's disease. However, the latter condition is also marked by the presence of both tau and Alz,-50 proteins, whereas cells in normally aging subjects show neither (Swaab et al., 1992).

## 3. Medial and Lateral Tuberal Nuclei

The medial and lateral tuberal nuclei at the base of the infundibular stalk appear relatively intact in the normal aging individual. Even in Alzheimer's disease, intracellular changes (neurofibrillary tangles, etc.) in these neurons are relatively subdued in their expression. This may reflect the continuing functional importance of these cell groups in vital metabolic and neurohormonal processes (Swaab et al., 1992). Nonetheless, age-related decrements in neurohormonal secretion are well documented. Zadik, Chalew, McCarter, Meisters, and Kowarski (1985) have noted decreased production of growth hormone as a function of age. The authors identify this as a probable cause of decrease in lean body mass, increase in adipose tissue, and thinning of the skin. This syndrome can be countered by administration of synthetic growth hormone, a treatment that may also lead to significant cognitive and mood improvement (McGauley, 1989).

## D. Pineal Gland

The pineal gland shows little or no structural change to routine microscopic and ultramicroscopic examination based on a study of seven patients older than 70 years compared with five younger adults (Hasegawa, Ohtaubo, Izumiyama, & Shimada, 1990). However, dense immunoreactivity for phosphorylated neurofilaments was present in the marginal plexuses associated with processes of pinealocytes, boutons, and knoblike terminals (Pardo, Martin, Trancoso, & Price, 1990). The authors suggested that the pineal begins to undergo morphological changes in the first decade of life but does not generate significant age-related alterations in cytoskeletal processes either in normal aging or in Alzheimer's disease. Iguchi, Kato, and Ibayashi (1982) suggested that age-related reduction in functional activity of pinealocytes may develop without obvious changes in neuronal cytoskeleton or afferent fibers. However, a more recent analysis by Jengelisky, Powers, O'Connor, and Price (1989) indicated that terminals in the pineal made visible by the use of a polyclonal antibody to dopamine hydroxylase show age-related swelling. This finding may be indicative of alterations in the sympathetic ganglia that are known to develop age-related neurofibrillary tangles (Kawasaki, Muregama, Tomonaga, Izumiyama, & Shimada, 1987). The reader might be reminded that the circadian rhythm-dependent link between the suprachiasmatic nucleus and the pineal gland is effected by sympathetic pre- and postganglionic fibers.

## E. Locus Caeruleus

The locus caeruleus (LC) shows moderate age-related cell loss (Marcyniuk, Mann, & Yates, 1989). In a series of 11 healthy subjects aged 79 or older, the authors noted an average of 20% fewer neurons in the LC than in a control group with a mean age of 30 years. Furthermore, the loss was diffuse rather than localized to a specific site in the nucleus. These data contrast sharply with those from a series of Alzheimer's disease patients in whom cell loss was more robust and more or less centered in the dorsal portion of the nucleus along its entire rostro-caudal extent (Marcyniuk, Mann, & Yates, 1986). In another series of cases based on immunocytochemical identification of neurons with tyrosine hydroxylase and dopamine hydroxylase antibodies (Chan-Palay & Azan, 1989), cell loss of 27–33% was noted in older, nondemented adults. This loss was found to be

highest in the rostral part and least obvious in the caudal part of the nucleus, thereby suggesting a pattern of cell dropout at variance with that described by Marcyniuk et al. (1989). However, the estimate of loss of between one-quarter and one-third of the ensemble of LC cells by both sets of investigators is fairly consistent with figures quoted earlier by Vijayashankar and Brody (1979) and should therefore be considered reasonably solid, at least by present quantitative standards.

## F. Substantia Nigra

The substantia nigra (SN) shows a modest response to normal aging. Fearnley and Lees (1990) noted loss of pigmented neurons in the pars compacta of the caudal SN with advancing age. The rate of loss was described as approximately linear at 4.7% / decade. Assuming that such a loss pattern developed by the beginning of the fifth decade of life, it would suggest a total neuronal loss of approximately 25% by the end of the ninth decade. The authors suggested that symptoms of Parkinson's disease develop at levels of 50% loss or more (68% loss in the lateral ventral segment; 48% loss in the caudal pole). If correct, these figures imply that even the healthy centenarian should not be at special risk for developing the syndrome. P. McGeer, McGeer, and Suzuki (1977) have also reported decreased nigral neurons with age. A significant correlate of this alteration is the steady decrement in the number of dopaminergic uptake sites between the ages of 19 and 88 (De Keyser, Ebinger, & Vauquelin, 1990) and an age-correlated linear decrease in fluoro-dopa uptake sites in striatal tissue as detected by PET (Martin, Palmer, Patlack, & Calne, 1989).

In this regard it might be noted that MRI studies have identified a robust negative correlation between midbrain volume and subject age, the range of differences being as much as 300%. Midbrain diameter may also show as much as a 200% change (Doraiswamy et al., 1992).

## G. Cerebellum

The cerebellum does not seem to show significant age-related gross changes (Escalona et al., 1991). However, our microscopic studies have revealed loss of both Purkinje and granule cells (Scheibel and Duong, unpublished data). The Purkinje cell dendrite ensemble is an especially sensitive index of cerebellar change, and after the seventh decade of life frequently shows patchy spine loss and disappearance of third-order dendrites. Because the Purkinje cell is the primary source of outflow from cerebellar cortex it follows that these alterations must affect cerebellar modulation of many neural systems.

## H. Brain Stem

A comprehensive evaluation of the aging human brain stem is not yet available, although scattered data on several brain stem nuclei have been reported. The inferior olive of 26 individuals aged 24–83 has been subject to densitometric analysis by Pesce, Provera, Dessanti, and Provaggi (1990). They describe age-related increase in neuronal density accompanied by regression of olivo-cerebellar contacts and loss of "supernumerary axonal collaterals." They interpret these changes as being due to decrease in the volume of the entire inferior olivary nucleus. However, the total olivary cell complement remains essentially unchanged according to Vijayashankar and Brody (1977).

## V. Vascular Changes

The cerebral vascular system may show any one of a number of changes that develop with age. Many of these are actually related to pathological states that accompany the aging process (e.g., hypertension,

diabetes, and high serum cholesterol levels) and must be conceptually disengaged from the aging process itself. In this regard, Hegedus and Molnar (1989) noted that age-related changes are mainly limited to the intima of the vessel wall. By the fourth or fifth decade, the internal elastic layer becomes thicker and the intimal cushions at branch point become more prominent. The intimal elastic layer may split into two, and, from the second decade on, the number of cellular elements under the endothelium progressively increases. After the fifth decade, the thickened intima is gradually replaced by collagen fibers. Such alterations are both subtle and modest compared to the much grosser alterations characteristic of Alzheimer's disease. Here the vessel walls become grossly tortuous and lumpy due to the presence of (a) many monocytes or pericytes and (b) lakes of amorphous material such as amyloid within reduplicated sheets of basement membrane. Coincident with (or possibly causal to) these robust changes is the loss of the perivascular neural plexus that characterizes the abluminal surface of the normally aging cerebral vessel (A. Scheibel, Duong, & Tomiyasu, 1987).

## VI. Concluding Comments

In this broad spectrum of data, the reader can hardly fail to be impressed by the variability of structural changes that have been described in the presumably normally aging human brain. Not only does the brain of one aging individual vary appreciably from that of another, but the discrete parts of each brain show idiosyncratic patterns of alteration as life continues. On the basis of the reports cited, and they are only a sample of the available literature, one might despair of developing a coherent picture of this late-life process that engages one intellectually, and ultimately involves one personally.

In the final analysis, structural changes

become important only insofar as they result in alterations in the level of behavior of the individual, whether at sensorimotor, cognitive, or psychosocial levels. Investigators have already observed that no cell loss experienced in later life is likely to match that which occurs as a normal consequence of brain maturation during the perinatal period. Cell populations in the language-involved superior temporal lobe may decrease by 30% between the ages of 2 months and 18 years, a period during which the individual's facility with language develops to its fullest extent. The corpus callosum may lose one-half of its fibers in the postnatal period (Innocenti et al., 1981) while the child is most actively absorbing the myriad aspects of its culture. It may be less productive to inquire about "what is lost" than "what can the remainder do."

Few would deny that cognitive styles change as life progresses. One has only to compare the behavior of the average 18-year-old driver behind the wheel with that of a 60- or 70-year-old to conclude that information-processing speeds decrease with age. By the same token, every parent or grandparent knows how much more expensive it will be to provide insurance coverage for the teenage driver than for himself. That lifelong accumulation of experience that we call *judgment*, or perhaps *wisdom*, may well make up for the age-related slowing of cerebral processing and recall. In fact (and I am unaware of hard data to back up this conjecture) it may be just that extra processing time that allows the distillates of previous experience to be retrieved and integrated into the final decision.

Is it possible that progressive diminution in size and loss of neuronal elements in later life represents an essential part of that continuous developmental process (which accompanies aging)? And could a significant outcome of this process lie in the continuing maturation of cognitive function where breadth and speed are sacrificed for depth and weight? Thus the process, perhaps describable as "enhancement of fi-

delity at expense of channel width" (Mesulam, 1987, p. 583) could well provide certain advantages, at a price. But the price paid in loss of agility, both cognitive and behavioral, comes at a time when those age-old biological functions of territorial defense, mating and child-rearing are no longer individual imperatives. Perhaps what is lost matters less than what is gained. (A. Scheibel, 1992, p. 169)

Although a few life-forms, such as the bristlecone pine, seem almost proof against aging and senescence, it appears unlikely, at least for the foreseeable future, that the length of human life will be extended much beyond 100–120 years. What can be done, even with the knowledge at hand, is to make the full extent of this temporal envelope increasingly rich and satisfying for increasing numbers of our population. Appropriate dietary habits, exercise, intellectual challenge, and social involvement must remain the touchstones for successful aging.

## References

Aitken, J., & Bridger, J. (1967). Neuron size and neuron population density in the lumbosacral region of the cat's spinal cord. *Journal of Anatomy, 95*, 38–53.

Alzheimer, A. (1907). Uber eine eigenartige Erkrankung der Hirnrinde. *Allgemeine Zeitschrift fuer Psychiatrie und Psychisch-Gerentliche Medicin, 64*, 146–148.

Ball, M. (1983). Granulovacular degeneration. In B. Reisman (Ed.), *Alzheimer's disease: The standard reference* (pp. 62–68). New York: Free Press.

Beach, T., Walker, R., & McGeer, E. (1989). Patterns of gliosis in Alzheimer's disease and aging cerebrum. *Glia, 2*(6), 420–436.

Benzing, W., Mufson, E., & Armstrong, D. (1993). Immunocytochemical distribution of peptidergic and cholinergic fibers in the human amygdala: Their depletion in Alzheimer's disease and morphologic alteration in non-demented elderly with numerous senile plaques. *Brain Research, 625*(1), 125–138.

Blackwood, W., McMenemy, W., Meyer, A., Norman, R., & Russell, D. (Eds.). (1967). *Greenfield's neuropathology*. Baltimore: Williams & Wilkins.

Boone, K., Miller, B., Lesser, I., Mahringer, C., Hill-Gutierrez, R., Goldberg, A., & Berman, N. (1992). Neuropsychological correlates of white-matter lesions in healthy elderly subjects. *Archives of Neurology (Chicago), 49,* 549–554.

Borst, M. (Ed.). (1992). *Pathologische histologie.* Leipzig: Vogel.

Brinkman, S., Sarwar, M., Leven, H., & Morris, H. (1981). Quantitative indexes of computed tomography in dementia and normal aging. *Radiology, 138,* 89–92.

Brody, H. (1955). Organization of the cerebral cortex. III. A study of aging in the human cerebral cortex. *Journal of Comparative Neurology, 103,* 511–556.

Brody, H. (1970). Structural changes in the aging nervous system. In H. Blumenthal (Ed.), *The regulatory role of the nervous system in aging: Vol. 7. Interdisciplinary topics in gerontology.* Basel: Karger.

Brun, A. (1983). An overview of light and electron microscopic changes. In B. Reisberg (Ed.) *Alzheimer's disease: The standard reference* (pp. 37–47). New York: The Free Press.

Buell, S., & Coleman, P. (1979). Dendritic growth in the aged human brain and failure of growth in senile dementia. *Science, 206,* 854–856.

Chan-Palay, V., & Azan, F. (1989). Quantitation of catecholamine neurons in the locus coeruleus in human brains of normal young and older adults in depression. *Journal of Comparative Neurology, 287,* 357–372.

Chui, H., Bondareff, W., Zarow, C., & Slager, U. (1984). Stability of neuronal number in the nucleus basalis of Meynert with age. *Neurobiology of Aging, 5,* 83–88.

Coffey, C., Wilkinson, W., Paraskos, I., Soady, S., Sullivan, R., Patterson, L., Figiel, W., Webb, M., Spritzer, C., & Djang, W. (1992). Quantitative cerebral anatomy of the aging human brain: A cross-sectional study using magnetic resonance imaging. *Neurology 42*(3, Pt.1), 527–536.

Coleman, P., & Flood, D. (1987). Neuron numbers and dendritic extent in normal aging and Alzheimer's disease. *Neurobiology of Aging, 8,* 521–545.

Conel, J. (1941–1951). *The postnatal development of the human cerebral cortex* (Vols. 2–4). Cambridge, MA: Harvard University Press.

Cowan, W., Fawcett, J., O'Leary, D., & Stanfield, B. (1984). Regressive events in neurogenesis. *Science, 225,* 1258–1265.

Cupp, C., & Uemura, E. (1980). Age-related changes in prefrontal cortex of *Macaca mulata*: Quantitative analysis of dendritic branching patterns. *Experimental Neurology, 69,* 69–143.

Davies, D., Horwood, N., Isaacs, S., & Mann, D. (1992). The effect of age and Alzheimer's disease on pyramidal neuron density in the individual fields of the hippocampal formation. *Acta Neuropathologica, 83*(5), 510–517.

De Keyser, J., Ebinger, G., & Vauquelin, G. (1990). Age-related changes in the human nigrostriatal dopaminergic system. *Annals of Neurology, 27,* 157–161.

de Lacalle, S., Iraiziz, I., & Gonzalo, L. (1991). Differential changes in cell size and number in topographic subdivisions of human basal nucleus in normal aging. *Neuroscience, 43*(2–3), 445–456.

Diamond, M. (1988). *Enriching heredity.* New York: Free Press/Macmillan.

Diamond, M., Johnson, R. E., & Ingham, C. A. (1975). Morphological changes in the young, adult, and aging rat cortex, hippocampus, and diencephalon. *Behavioral Biology, 14,* 163–174.

Diamond, M., Johnson, R., Protti, A., Ott, C., & Kajisa, L. (1985). Plasticity in the 904-day-old male rat cerebral cortex. *Experimental Neurology, 87,* 309–317.

Doraiswamy, P., Na, C., Husain, M., Figiel, G., McDonald, W., Ellinwood, E., Jr., Boyko, O., & Krishnan, K. (1992). Morphometric changes in the human mid-brain with normal aging: MR and stereological findings. *American Journal of Neuroradiology, 13*(1), 383–386.

Erkinjuntti, T., Gao, F., Lee, D., Eliasjiiv, M., Meishey, A., & Hachinski, V. (1994). Lack of difference in brain hyperintensities between patients in early Alzheimer's disease and control subjects. *Archives of Neurology (Chicago), 51,* 260–268.

Escalona, P., McDonald, W., Doraiswamy, P., Boyko, O., Husain, M., Figiel, G., Laskowitz, D., Ellinwood, E. Jr., & Krishnan, K. (1991). In vivo stereological assessment of human cerebellar volume: Effects of gender and age. *American Journal of Neuroradiology, 12*(5), 927–929.

Eslinger, P., Damasio, H., Graff-Radford, N., & Damasio, A. (1984). Examining the relationship between computed tomography and neuro-psychological measures in normal and demented elderly. *Journal of Neurology, Neurosurgery and Psychiatry, 47,* 1319–1325.

Fearnley J., & Lees, A. (1990). Striatonigral degeneration: A clinicopathological study. *Brain, 113*(Pt. 6), 1823–1842.

Flood, D., & Coleman, P. (1988). Neuron numbers and sizes in aging brain: Comparisons of human, monkey and rodent data. *Neurobiology of Aging, 9,* 453–463.

George, A., DeLeon, M., Rosenbloom, S., Ferris, H., Gentes, C., Emmerich, M., & Kricheff, I. (1983). Ventricular volume and cognitive deficit: A computed tomographic study. *Radiology, 149,* 493–498.

Geula, C., & Mesulam, M. (1989). Cortical cholinergic fibers in aging and Alzheimer's disease: A morphometric study. *Neuroscience, 33*(3) 469–481.

Golomb, J., de Leon, M., Kluger, A., George, A., Tarshish, G., & Ferris, S. (1993). Hippocampal atrophy in normal aging: An association with recent memory impairment. *Archives of Neurology (Chicago), 50,* 967–973.

Goudsmit, E., Neijmeijer-Leloux, A., & Swaab, D. (1992). The human hypothalamus-neurohypophysial system in relation to development, aging and Alzheimer's disease. *Progress in Brain Research, 93,* 237–247.

Greenfield, J. P., Blackwood, W., McMenemy, W., Meyer, A., Norman, R., & Russel, D. (Eds.). (1967). *Neuropathology.* Baltimore: Williams & Wilkins.

Greenough, W. T., Juraska, J. M., & Volkmar, F. R. (1979). Maze training effects on dendritic branching in occipital cortex of adult rats. *Behavioral and Neural Biology, 26,* 287–297.

Gyldensted, C. (1977). Measurements of the normal ventricular system and hemispheric sulci of 100 adults with computed tomography. *Neuroradiology, 14,* 183–192.

Hasegawa, A., Ohtaubo, E., Izumiyama, N., & Shimada, H. (1990). Ultrastructural study of the human pineal gland in aged patients including a centenarian. *Acta Pathologica Japonica, 40*(1), 30–40.

Haug, H. (1985). Are neurons of the human cerebral cortex really lost in aging? A morphometric examination. In J. Traber & W. Gaspers (Eds.), *Senile dementia of the Alzheimer type.* Berlin: Springer-Verlag.

Hegedus, K., & Molnar, P. (1989). Age-related changes in reticular fibers and other connective tissue elements in the intima of the major intracranial arteries. *Clinical Neuropathology, 8,* 92–97.

Heidary, H., & Tomasch, J. (1969). Neuron number and perikaryon size in the human cerebellar nuclei. *Acta Anatomica, 74,* 290–296.

Hodge, C. (1894). Changes in ganglion cells from birth to senile death: Observations in man and honey-bee. *Journal of Physiology (London), 17,* 129–134.

Hofman, M., & Swaab, D. (1989). The sexually dimorphic nucleus of the preoptic area in the human brain: A comparative morphometric study. *Journal of Anatomy, 164,* 55–72.

Hubbard, B., & Anderson, J. (1981). A quantitative study of cerebral atrophy in old age and senile dementia. *Journal of Neurological Science, 50,* 135–145.

Huttenlocher, P. (1979). Synaptic density in human frontal cortex: Developmental changes and effects of aging. *Brain Research, 163,* 195–205.

Hyden, H., & Lindström, B. (1950). Report. *Discussions of the Faraday Society, 9,* 436.

Iguchi, H., Kato, K.-I., & Ibayashi, H. (1982). Age-dependent reductions in serum melatonin concentrations in healthy human subjects. *Journal of Clinical Endocrinology and Metabolism, 5,* 27–29.

Innocenti, G., Koppl, H., & Clarke, S. (1981). Glial phagocytosis during the postnatal shaping of visual corpus callosum. *Neuroscience Letters Supplement, 7,* 5160.

Jengelisky, C., Powers, R., O'Connor, D., & Price, D. (1989). Noradrenergic innervations of human pineal gland: Abnormalities in aging and Alzheimer's disease. *Brain Research, 481,* 378–382.

Jernigan, T., Archibald, S., Berkow, M., Sowell, E., Foster, D., & Hesselink, J. (1991). Cerebral studies on M.R.I.: 1) Localization of age-related changes. *Biological Psychiatry, 29,* 155–167.

Jernigan, T., Traines, D., Hesselink, I., & Tallal, P. (1991). Maturation of human cerebrum observed in vivo during adolescence. *Brain, 114,* 2037–2049.

Kaplan, A., & Scheibel, A. (1982). Alterations in

neuron number and size in auditory cortex of old vs. young cats: Is chronic disease a factor? *American Aging Association, 12*, 14.

Kawasaki, H., Muregama, S., Tomonaga, M., Izumiyama, N., & Shimada, H. (1987). Neurofibrillary tangles in human upper cervical ganglia: Morphological study with immunohistochemistry and electron microscopy. *Acta Neuropathologica, 75*, 156–159.

Khachaturian, Z. (1985). Diagnosis of Alzheimer's disease. *Archives of Neurology (Chicago), 42*, 1097–1105.

Kidd, M. (1963). Paired helical filaments in electron microscopy of Alzheimer's disease. *Nature (London), 197*, 192–193.

Konigsmark, B., & Murphy, E. (1970). Neuronal populations in the human brain. *Nature (London), 228*, 1335–1336.

Lee, V., Balin, B., Otovos, L., & Trojanowski, J. (1991). A major subunit of paired helical filaments and derivatized forms of normal tau. *Science, 251*, 675–678.

Marcyniuk, B., Mann, D., & Yates, P. (1986). The topography of cell loss from locus coeruleus in Alzheimer's disease. *Journal of Neurological Sciences, 76*, 335–345.

Marcyniuk, B., Mann, D., & Yates, P. (1989). The topography of nerve cell loss from the locus coeruleus in elderly persons. *Neurobiology of Aging, 19*(1), 5–9.

Marie, R., Lohr, J., & Jeste, D. (1986). Hippocampal pyramidal cells and aging in the human: A qualitative study of neuronal loss in sectors, CA$_1$–CA$_4$. *Experimental Neurology, 94*, 29–40.

Martin, W., Palmer, M., Patlack, C., & Calne, D. (1989). Nigro-striatal function in humans studied with positron emission tomography. *Annals of Neurology, 26*, 535–542.

McGauley, G. (1989). Quality of life assessment before and after treatment in adults with growth hormone deficiency. *Acta Paediatrica Scandinavica, Supplement, 356*, 70–72.

McGeer, E., & McGeer, P. (1982). Neurotransmitters in normal aging. In D. Platt (Ed.), *Geriatrics I* (pp. 263–282). Berlin: Springer-Verlag.

McGeer, P., McGeer, E., & Suzuki, J. (1977). Aging and extrapyramidal function. *Archives of Neurology (Chicago), 34*, 33–35.

Meier-Ruge, W., Ulrich, J., Bruhlmann, M., & Meier, E. (1992). Age-related white matter atrophy in the human brain. *Annals of the New York Academy of Sciences, 673*, 260–269.

Mesulam, M. (1987). Involutional and developmental implications of age-related neuronal changes: In search of an engram for wisdom. *Neurobiology of Aging, 8*, 581–583.

Miller, A., Alston, R., Mountjoy, C., & Corsellis, J. (1984). Automated differential cell counting on a section of the normal human hippocampus: The influence of age. *Neuropathology and Applied Neurobiology, 10*, 123–141.

Minckler, J. (1968). *Pathology of the nervous system* (Vol. 1). New York: McGraw-Hill.

Mirmiran, M., Swaab, D., Kok, J., Hofman, M., Wittig, W., & Van Gool, W. (1992). Circadian rhythms and the suprachiasmatic nucleus in perinatal development, aging and Alzheimer's disease. *Progress in Brain Research, 93*, 151–162.

Mizutani, T., & Shimada, H. (1991). Quantitative study of neurofibrillary tangles in subdivisions of the hippocampus CA$_2$ as a special area in normal aging and senile dementia of the Alzheimer type. *Acta Pathologica Japonica, 41*(8), 597–603.

Moatamed, F. (1966). Cell frequencies in the human inferior olivary complex. *Journal of Comparative Neurology, 128*, 109–116.

Mouritzen Dam, A. (1979). The density of neurons in the human hippocampus. *Neuropathology and Applied Neurobiology, 5*, 249–264.

Mullan, M., & Crawford, F. (1993). Genetic and molecular advances in Alzheimer's Disease. *Trends in Neuroscience, 16*(10), 398–403.

Pardo, C., Martin, L., Trancoso, J., & Price, D. (1990). The human pineal gland in aging and Alzheimer's disease: Patterns of cytoskeletal antigen immunoreactivity. *Acta Neuropathologica, 80*, 535–540.

Pesce, C., Provera, P., Dessanti, P., & Provaggi, M. (1990). Densitometric analysis of the nerve cell population of the inferior olive in aging. *Acta Neuropathologica, 80*(1), 95–97.

Powers, R., Struble, R., Casanova, M., O'Connor, D., Kim, C., & Price, D. (1988). Innervation of human hippocampus by noradrenergic systems: Normal anatomy and structural abnormalities in aging and in Alzheimer's disease. *Neuroscience, 25*, 401–417.

Price, D., Martin, L., Sisodia, S., Wagster, M.,

Koo, E., Walker, L., Kobiatsos, V., & Cork, L. (1991). Aged non-human primates: An animal model of age-associated neurodegenerative disease. *Brain Pathology, 1,* 287–296.

Probst, A., Langer, D., & Ulrich, J. (1991). Alzheimer's disease: A description of the structural lesions. *Brain Pathology, 1,* 119–239.

Rowe, J., & Kahn, R. (1987). Human aging: Usual and successful. *Science, 237,* 143–149.

Salmon, E., Marquet, P., Sadzot, B., Degueldre, C., Lemaire, C., & Franck, G. (1991). Decrease of frontal metabolism demonstrated by positron emission tomography in a population of healthy elderly volunteers. *Acta Neurologica Belgique, 91*(5), 288–295.

Schade, J., & Baxter, C. (1960). Changes during growth in the volume and surface area of cortical neurons in the rabbit. *Experimental Neurology, 2,* 158–178.

Schatz, C., Chun, J., & Luskin, M. (1988). The role of the subplate in the development of the mammalian telencephalon. In A. Peters & E. Jones (Eds.), *Cerebral cortex* (Vol. 7, pp. 35–38). New York: Plenum.

Scheibel, A. (1992). Structural changes in the aging brain. In J. E. Birren, R. Sloane, & G. Cohen (Eds.), *Handbook of mental health and aging* (pp. 147–173). San Diego, CA: Academic Press.

Scheibel, A., Duong, T., & Tomiyasu, U. (1987). Denervation microangiopathy in senile dementia, Alzheimer type. *Alzheimer's Disease and Associated Disorders, 1,* 19–37.

Scheibel, M., Lindsay, R., Tomiyasu, U., & Scheibel, A. (1975). Progressive dendritic changes in aging human cortex. *Experimental Neurology, 47,* 392–403.

Scheibel, M., Tomiyasu, U., & Scheibel, A. (1977). The aging human Betz cell. *Experimental Neurology, 56,* 598–609.

Schwartz, B. (1993). *A history of the Supreme Court.* New York: Oxford University Press.

Schwartz, M., Creasey, H., Grady, C., De Lee, J., Frederickson, H., Cutler, N., & Rapaport, S. (1985). Computed tomographic analysis of brain morphometrics in 30 healthy men aged 21 to 81 years. *Annals of Neurology, 17,* 146–157.

Shefer, V. (1973). Absolute numbers of neurons and thickness of the cerebral cortex during aging, senile, and vascular dementia and Pick's and Alzheimer's disease. *Neuroscience and Behavioral Biology, 6,* 319–324.

Sparks, D., Hunsaker, J., Slavin, J., DeKosky, S., Kryscio R., & Markesberry, W. (1992). Monoaminergic and cholinergic synaptic markers in the nucleus basalis of Meynert (nbM): Normal age-related changes and the effect of heart disease and Alzheimer's disease. *Annals of Neurology, 31*(6), 611–620.

Swaab, D., Grunde-Iqbal, I., Iqbal, I., Kremer, H., Ravid, R., & Van de Ness, J. (1992). Tau and ubiquitin in the human hypothalamus in aging and Alzheimer's disease. *Brain Research, 590,* 239–249.

Swaab, D., Hofman, M., Lucassen, P., Purba, J., Raadsheer, F., & Van de Ness, J. (1993). Functional neuroanatomy and neuropathology of the human hypothalamus. *Anatomical Embryology, 187*(4), 317–330.

Terry, R., DeTeresa, R., & Hansen, L. (1987). Neocortical cell counts in normal human adult aging. *Annals of Neurology, 21*(6), 530–539.

Terry, R., Gonatas, N., & Weiss, M. (1964). Ultrastructural studies in Alzheimer's presenile dementia. *American Journal of Pathology, 44,* 269–297.

Tomlinson, B., Blessed, G., & Roth, M. (1970). Observations on the brains of demented old people. *Journal of Neurological Sciences, 11,* 205–242.

Uemura, E. (1985). Age-related changes in the subiculum of *Macaca mulatta:* Dendrite branching pattern. *Experimental Neurology, 87,* 412–427.

Van Buskirk, C. (1945). The seventh cranial nerve complex. *Journal of Comparative Neurology, 82,* 303–334.

Vijayashankar, N., & Brody, H. (1977). A study of aging in the human abducens nucleus. *Journal of Comparative Neurology, 173,* 433–437.

Vijayashankar, N., & Brody, H. (1979). A quantitative study of pigmented neurons in the nuclei locus coeruleus and subcoeruleus in man as related to aging. *Journal of Neuropathology and Experimental Neurology, 38,* 495–497.

West, M. (1993). Regionally specific loss of neurons in the aging human hippocampus. *Neurobiology of Aging, 14,* 287–293.

Whitehouse, P., Price, D., Struble, R., Clark, A., Coyle, J., & DeLong, M. (1982). Alzheimer's disease and senile dementia: Loss of neurons in the basal forebrain. *Science, 215,* 237–239.

Wisniewski, H. (1983). Neuritic (senile) and amyloid plaques. In B. Reisberg (Ed.), *Alzheimer's disease: The standard reference* (pp. 57–61). New York: Free Press.

Ylikoski, R., Ylikoski, A., Erkinjuntti, T., Sulkava R., Raininko, R., & Tilvis, R. (1993). White matter changes in healthy elderly persons correlate with attention and speed of mental processing. *Archives of Neurology (Chicago)*, *50*(8), 818–824.

Zadik, Z., Chalew S., McCarter, C., Meisters, M., & Kowarski, A. (1985). The influence of age on the 24 hour integrated concentration of growth hormone in individuals. *Journal of Clinical Endocrinology and Metabolism*, *60*, 513–516.

Seven

# Health, Behavior, and Aging

Dorly J. H. Deeg, Jan W. P. F. Kardaun, and James L. Fozard

## I. Introduction

This chapter reviews research that spe-
cifies how aging operates as the dynamic
dimension in the continuing interplay between health and behavior. Linking health
and behavior implies looking at individual
aging, as well as at the impact of society on
aging processes (Riley, 1987). The pertinent research findings come mostly from
behavioral medicine, social epidemiology,
and health psychology (Elias, Elias, &
Elias, 1990; Maddox, 1987; Siegler, 1990;
Siegler & Costa, 1985).

Numerous research findings show
cross-sectional age differences in health,
behavior, or both. The interpretation of
these research findings requires an understanding of life course processes as well as
cohort differences. For example, Riley
(1987) cited a study of healthy persons
aged 50–80 years in which older people
were found to associate less anger, fear, or
shame with illness than younger people
(Leventhal, 1984). Why these age differences? Over their lives, older persons may
have had more experience with successful
coping with problems, or may have developed lower aspiration levels or expectations. In addition to asking questions

about how coping strategies that have developed over the life course determine
how illness is managed, one should consider cohort differences and ask questions
about how typical social structures and
values regarding health, behavior, and
aging in different historical periods (Birren, 1988) promote age differences in particular coping strategies and aspiration
levels.

The leading question of this chapter—
How does aging affect the relation between health and behavior?—is presented
diagrammatically in Figure 1. If a health–
behavior association were stronger in
younger age, and weaker in older age, we
would say that age moderated the association, and would infer that factors associated with age mediated the association
(Baron & Kenny, 1986). Mediating factors
could be, for example, shifts in resources,
in norms and priorities, or in perceptions
of self. These age-associated mediating
factors should show changes across the
life course or be different across cohorts.
Furthermore, an age-associated mediator
should be related to both health and behavior.

The complex relation among health, behavior, and aging is summarized in two

**Figure 1**   Age-associated mediators as explanatory variables of the association between health and behavior, and between behavior and health.

sections: the behavioral consequences of ill health (Section III), and the health consequences of behavior (Section IV). In Section V, several conceptual and methodological limitations of current research and opportunities for future research are discussed.

## II. Definitions and Concepts

Health is "a state of complete physical, mental and social well-being, and not merely the absence of disease or handicap" (World Health Organization, 1948). This positive definition of health is suitable for setting policy aims, but not for disentangling physical, mental, and social functions in relation to aging (Elias et al., 1990; Siegler & Costa, 1985). For the purposes of this chapter, we will use a more narrow definition of health to indicate the absence of acute and chronic physical or mental disease and impairments. The majority of older persons would—even by this less strict definition—not be "healthy" (Fozard, Metter, & Brant, 1990). As will be described, however, even in the presence of acute or chronic disease, acceptable levels of physical, mental, and social well-being can be achieved.

Behavior primarily includes physical activities (both habitual and exceptional or strenuous), social activities with other individuals in various organizations, and leisure pursuits. Behaviors relating to health include physical exercise, substance abuse, diet, and stress management. Behavior also includes physical, mental, and social skills required to perform activities, such

as cognitive and perceptual abilities, and personality attributes.

## III. Behavioral Consequences of Ill Health

On the societal level, some adjustments to ill health or health deficits are recognized in laws and regulations. Examples are the prohibition from driving for epileptic and poor-sighted persons; the lack of access to certain jobs (e.g., aviation, railroad, and marine) for the color-blind; or the confinement to a psychiatric ward for those with severe mental disturbance.

On the individual level the behavioral consequences of ill health can be seen as a sequence of transitions. Whether a transition from a certain health deficit to, for example, impaired functional ability in fact takes place is determined by individual and environmental factors described earlier as "mediators." In the following review of research findings on pathways of chronic disease and disability, reports have been selected that inform us of the ways in which aging affects transitions as well as outcomes such as mental health, use of services, and mortality. The heterogeneity of pathways is further illustrated by considering behavioral outcomes for different levels of disability, and the role of cognitive ability in affecting behavioral outcomes.

### A. Mental Health and the Course of Chronic Disease

In groups of patients with different chronic diseases, symptoms of distress were less common in older patients in two cross-sectional studies (Cassileth et al., 1984; Leventhal, 1984). Cassileth et al. (1984) advanced four explanations:

1. Chronic illness offers social advantages such as increased involvement with others, and amount of attention and concern received.
2. Older persons may develop more effective skills with which to manage stressful life events.
3. The perspective and expectations of older persons may be more commensurate with adaptation to illness.
4. There may be a biologic advantage for older patients, enabling them to adapt to illnesses that are epidemiologically associated with older age.

Although it is not clear why (1) would be truer for older patients than for younger ones, (2) and (3) are commensurate with Neugarten's (1976) point that the onset of chronic illness in old age is more usual in that part of the life cycle, and therefore less disruptive. Since the studies by Leventhal (1984) and Cassileth et al. (1984), Norris and Murrell (1988) provided some support for (2) in the case of nonhealth events. Another explanation is a cohort effect: Currently older generations might be more tolerant of adverse health than younger generations, because they grew up with lower expectation levels.

Although older persons, on the whole, might be able to handle chronic illness better than younger adults, this may not be true for every phase of the illness. Cassileth et al. (1984) found that mental health was worse in older patients diagnosed less than three months prior than in those diagnosed over three months prior. This finding may be interpreted to mean that after adaptation to being ill, mental health improves.

Cassileth et al. (1984) further reported that older patients with cancer showed mental health differences according to functional status, whereas diabetes pa-

tients did not. These findings may be interpreted by considering the likely outcome of each disease course. Diabetes is not likely to have a fatal outcome, whereas cancer is. Cancer patients who have a poor functional status are likely to be in the terminal phase of their illness, which may be associated with poorer mental health.

Kennedy, Kelman, and Thomas (1990) studied the effect of ill health on mental health in older persons over a period of 24 months. The development of a depressive syndrome was better predicted by an increase in the number of medical conditions and activities of daily living (ADL) problems than by the number of conditions at baseline. Similar findings were reported from studies of adults of all ages (Ormel, Von Korff, van den Brink, Katon, & Oldehinkel, 1993; Von Korff, Ormel, Katon, & Lin, 1992). Possibly, each new medical condition requires an adjustment that may increase the risk of the development of a depressive syndrome.

The studies described use depressive symptoms as an outcome. However, depression may also represent pathology and thus exist as a comorbid condition with, or interact with, chronic physical disease (Cohen, 1992). Sullivan (1995), for example, reported functional disability and mortality increases in depressed as compared to nondepressed chronically ill patients. Three explanations are put forward: (a) depression decreases a patient's motivation to adequately care for their chronic illness; (b) depression alters perception of somatic symptoms, either for psychosocial reasons or based on physiological mechanisms; this may lead to assumption of the sick role, and increase disability and health-care utilization; (c) depression may have direct, physiological effects on the patient's disease that are maladaptive.

Whether viewed as pathology or as a quality-of-life outcome, a depressive syndrome frequently exists in chronically ill older adults (Beekman, Kriegsman, Deeg,

& van Tilburg, 1995). When recognized, depression is considered to be highly treatable. Interventions to improve mental health will both preserve the older person's well-being and postpone functional limitations and disability.

## B. Physical Health and Trajectories of Disability

In this section, we review findings from longitudinal studies on trajectories of disease-related disability, in particular on predictors of disability in self-care and instrumental ADLs (IADLs), and predictors of limitations in functional ability.

Frequently occurring, disabling chronic diseases are arthritis, cardiovascular conditions, diabetes, and asthma. Other predictors of disability are clinical abnormalities related to these diseases, including both obesity and weight loss, and hypertension (Guralnik & Kaplan, 1989; Harris, Kovar, Suzman, Kleinman, & Feldman, 1989; Hubert, Bloch, & Fries, 1993; Lammi et al., 1989; Launer, Harris, Rumpel, & Madans, 1994; Persson & Svanborg, 1992). Furthermore, poor self-perceived health and number of coexisting chronic conditions are associated with functional decline (Kaplan, Strawbridge, Camacho, & Cohen, 1993; Mor, Wilcox, Rakowski, & Hiris, 1994). Studies that started with an initially functionally able cohort indicate that baseline conditions such as cardiovascular diseases, stroke, and arthritis, as well as impairments in vision and hearing, are predictive of functional decline (Boult, Kane, Louis, Boult, & McCaffrey, 1994; Crimmins & Saito, 1993; Haga et al., 1991; Laforge, Spector, & Sternberg, 1992).

The occurrence during the study period of a new heart attack, stroke, cancer, hip fracture, or a serious fall was associated with a substantially greater functional loss than was the presence of these conditions at baseline (Guralnik & Simonsick, 1993; Kaplan et al., 1993). In the previous section (III.A), we noted a similar associa-

tion with the outcome of mental health. Although this finding seems obvious in initially healthy persons, for initially ill persons it can be interpreted to mean that the presence of a disease does not necessarily lead to continued functional decline and that a certain level of functioning can be maintained over a longer period of time, provided no other diseases occur.

Several authors noted that, over time, many older persons show improvements in functional ability (Branch, Katz, Kniepmann, & Papsidero, 1984; Mor et al., 1994). Crimmins and Saito (1993) found that, over a 2-year period, return to good functioning was likely when the onset of functional limitations and disability was less than one year prior.

Nonphysical factors (individual and environmental) affect trajectories of disability (Verbrugge & Jette, 1994). Lower socioeconomic status is associated with functional decline (Guralnik & Kaplan, 1989; Guralnik & Simonsick, 1993; Harris et al., 1989; Hubert et al., 1993; Kaplan et al., 1993; Lammi et al., 1989; Maddox & Clark, 1992). Lifelong poor health practices and limited access to medical care may be responsible for the poorer functional outcomes in older persons with low incomes and education. Furthermore, feelings of uselessness and nonparticipation in social activities were shown to be associated with functional decline (Grand, Grosclaude, Bocquet, Pous, & Albarede, 1988). Together, these findings illustrate the heterogeneity of trajectories of disability.

## C. Consequences of Disability

The heterogeneity of trajectories of disability is further reflected in possible outcomes, such as mortality, self-perceived health, use of services, and satisfaction with assistance received. Our review focuses on individual and environmental factors affecting these outcomes.

Greater disability both in self-care and in IADLs is associated with greater mortality in older persons (Deeg, 1989b; Grand, Grosclaude, Bocquet, Pous, & Albarede, 1990; Koyano, Shibata, Haga, & Suyama, 1986). Change over time in functional ability was shown to explain more of the age dependence of mortality than physiological factors such as blood glucose level, vital capacity, heart rate, and blood pressure (Manton, Stallard, Woodbury, & Dowd, 1994). Manton et al. (1994) further showed that both physiological factors and functional ability showed slower declines than expected based on mortality rates in those who survived beyond age 95. This suggests that in very old age, a lower level of disease severity leads to death than in younger ages.

Self-perceived health may be considered as a global outcome measure of the trajectory of disability. Liang (1986) and Johnson and Wolinsky (1993) showed that self-perceived health reflects the last stage of disability as well as the earlier stages of pathology, impairments, and functional limitations. Furthermore, self-assessment of health has its own impact on the disease course: It has been shown to be related to mortality, independent of more objective health assessments such as chronic diseases and impairments (Idler, Kasl, & Lemke, 1990; Mossey & Shapiro, 1982; see also Section IV).

Disability and functional decline have also been demonstrated to be directly associated with greater use of services (Mor et al., 1994) and institutionalization (Reuben, Siu, & Kimpau, 1992; Williams, 1987; Wolinsky, Callahan, Fitzgerald, & Johnson, 1993). These associations may be conditioned by the social network as well as by self-perceptions of older individuals (Krause, 1988). An older person's social network may be instrumental in both compensatory processes (family support substitutes for formal care) and bridging (a social network helps link the older person to services). Logan and Spitze (1994) demonstrated that persons who thought of themselves as old were found to be more

likely to use formal services than those who had a younger age identity. Availability and accessibility of services had little additional effect. Thus, inasmuch as social network and age identity change with aging, they can be viewed as mediators of the association between ill health and use of services.

Assistance from others and the use of devices are instrumental in coping with physical disability. In a study of disability, assistance, and subjective well-being (Penning & Strain, 1994), disabled women were more likely than disabled men to receive assistance from others. No sex difference was found in the use of devices. Men more often reported no assistance than women. Interestingly, men relying on devices, and especially men receiving assistance from others, reported lower levels of well-being. The same was true for women relying on devices but not for women receiving assistance from others. The authors attribute lower levels of well-being to an increase of feelings of dependency on others in men, and in both sexes to either difficulties and frustrations with the use of devices or a stigmatizing effect of technical aids.

More intensive assistance is described in studies focusing on the relationship between patients and their informal caregiver. Schulz and Williamson (1993) identified the stress of both patient and caregiver as independent contributors to the course of disease and disability. In the early, adaptive phase of the patient's disease, disease-related factors and anticipated loss of a loved relative were predominant stressors, whereas in the later, chronic phase, caregiver characteristics such as health, income, and age became more important. In the terminal phase of the disease, the physical demands of caregiving were the primary stressor. Furthermore, caregivers were less likely to be depressed when patients were optimistic about their future and not depressed. Vice versa, perceived control and optimism in caregivers were the most important personality variables for good patient adjustment.

The main intervening mechanism between stressor and stress reaction, for both caregiver and patient, was coping strategy. Other intervening variables for both caregiver and patient were perceived disease history, and resources such as amount and quality of support, adequacy of financial means, and quality of the mutual relationship between patient and caregiver (Schulz & Williamson, 1993).

## D. Disability, a Moderator of the Health–Behavior Relationship

The present section further describes the complexity of the health–behavior relationship by showing how disability itself may affect the association between physical conditions and behavioral outcomes.

In a diary study of daily activities in retired persons (M. M. Baltes, Wahl, & Schmid-Furstoss, 1990), the number and duration of obligatory activities as opposed to leisure activities were greater in persons with functional disability than in nondisabled persons. One of the explanations forwarded was the general slowing in old age, which causes obligatory activities to take more time. The general slowing in old age may be more conspicuous in the functionally disabled, because they have fewer means to compensate for a loss of speed (P. B. Baltes, 1991).

M. M. Baltes et al. (1990) further demonstrated an association between level of activity and sense of personal control. Interestingly, this association was stronger in functionally disabled persons than in functionally able persons, suggesting that when a person becomes disabled, the possibility of continuing to engage in activities seems to have greater impact on one's control beliefs, or, vice versa, that control beliefs are more closely linked to the possibility of engaging in activities in those who have more difficulty functioning (see Section IV).

In a study among the oldest-old (85+ years), Roberts, Dunkle, and Haug (1994) included ill health in a composite measure of life strain. Like others, they found a negative association between life strain and well-being. Interestingly, this negative association was attenuated in elders with high independence in IADLs, suggesting that elders with disability are more vulnerable to life strain.

## E. Cognitive Performance, a Mediator between Health and Behavior

Age-related change in cognitive functions qualifies cognitive performance as a possible mediator in the association between health and behavior. Because a mediator needs to be causally related to both health and behavior, we will attempt to find evidence for both the association between cognition and behavior and between health and cognition.

Decline in cognitive functions may result in the modification of adaptive responses to environmental challenges and thus hamper the maintenance of adequate levels of health (Schaie, 1987). For example, compliance with drug regimens may be limited by decreased comprehension and memory of medical information (Morrell, Park, & Poon, 1990). A general measure of cognitive impairment was associated with functional limitations and physical disability in several cross-sectional studies (Barberger-Gateau et al., 1992; Fried et al., 1994; Laukkanen, Kauppinen, Era, & Heikkinen, 1993). In a longitudinal study, visual memory appeared to be associated with decline in functional ability (Deeg et al., 1992). The studies cited provide some indications for a causal relation between cognition and behavior.

Research on the effect of ill health on cognitive functioning has concentrated on the effect of hypertension. Some debate exists about the likelihood of poorer cognitive performance of hypertensives as opposed to normotensives (Elias et al., 1990; King & Miller, 1990). The greatest impact was noted in response speed. Changes in learning and memory performance, however, have not been found to be associated with hypertension status (Arenberg, 1987; Elias, Schultz, Robbins, & Elias, 1989).

Neurodegenerative diseases, particularly Alzheimer's disease, have profound effects on cognitive abilities (Fozard, Mullin, Giambra, Metter, & Costa, 1992). In several cross-sectional studies of hypertension-related diseases (stroke, heart disease, diabetes) associations with general cognitive decline have been established (Hertzog, Schaie, & Gribbin, 1978; Launer, Dinkgreve, Jonker, Hooijer, & Lindeboom, 1993).

The evidence of a causal effect of ill health on cognition seems inconsistent. Direct empirical evidence on the mediating role of cognition in the relation between health and behavior is lacking. Such evidence would clarify some possible pathways of disease and disability.

## IV. Health Consequences of Behavior

The study of health consequences of behavior attempts to determine both behaviors that have an unfavorable effect on health and are modifiable, and behaviors that have a beneficial effect on health. Societal recognition of the negative effect of certain behaviors on health is reflected in the ban on smoking in most public places, and in discussions about raised health insurance premiums for smokers, similar to raised travel insurance premiums for persons engaging in high-risk sports such as deep-sea diving and skiing.

Both unfavorable and beneficial behaviors, usually termed *risk factors*, can affect each stage of the course of disease and disability (Verbrugge & Jette, 1994). The modification of risk factors may prevent premature death, and prevent or delay the onset of age-associated diseases and limitations in physical and psychological functioning. With respect to aging, risk

factors should be considered as continuous rather than dichotomous entities (Elias et al., 1990) (i.e., there is no clear-cut borderline between levels of behavior carrying a health risk and neutral levels of behavior). In different age groups, the same level of behavior may carry a different health risk.

### A. Preventable Causes of Death

Analyses of national mortality data can yield projections of life expectancy, assuming the elimination of the lethal effect of various diseases. In a meta-analysis, McGinnis and Foege (1993) attempted to reclassify the causes of death listed on U.S. death certificates according to what they consider "true" causes of death. These "true" causes, lifestyle-related modifiable risk factors, are thought to reflect long-term pathological processes more appropriately than the pathology and diagnosed diseases present at the time of death, which are officially noted on the death certificate as causes of death. Nine long-term factors contributing to the causes of death included smoking, 19%; diet and activity patterns, 14%; alcohol, 5%; microbial agents, 4%; toxic agents, 3%; firearms, 2%; sexual behavior, 1%; motor vehicles, 1%; illicit use of drugs, less than 1%—for a total of 50% of the 1990 deaths. These data suggest a strong contribution of lifestyle to mortality.

Much evidence on lifestyle-related risk factors concerns cardiovascular morbidity and mortality, and originates from longitudinal studies of middle-aged men (Truett, Cornfield, & Kannel, 1967). In the epidemiology of aging there is a long-standing debate on the issue of whether these risk factors have as strong effects in older age as they have in middle age (Deeg, 1989b; Kannel & Gordon, 1980). Obesity, high diastolic blood pressure, and high serum cholesterol do not appear to have the effect in older age that they have in middle age, although the pathology in older age is no less severe (Sorkin, Andres, Muller,

Baldwin, & Fleg, 1992). Mechanisms to explain this finding might be found in (a) a survivor effect—those more susceptible to high-risk-factor levels have died at an earlier age; (b) an aging effect—in older age, there is a natural decline of risk-factor level with aging (Wilson, Anderson, Harris, Kannel, & Castelli, 1994), and multiple risk factors may interact in different ways than at younger ages (Kane, Kane, & Arnold, 1985); or (c) a cohort effect. Studies of aging in more recent cohorts will supply the evidence needed to choose between the alternative mechanisms.

Older persons who are advised to adopt healthier lifestyles with respect to activity (American College of Sports Medicine, 1990), nutrition (Nelson & Franzi, 1989), weight control (Epstein & Wing, 1980; I.-M. Lee, Manson, Hennekens, & Paffenbarger, 1993), and use of recreational drugs (Rimer, Orleans, Keintz, Cristinzio, & Fleisher, 1990) often ask if the change is too late to make a difference; older persons and policy makers ask if a recommended change will be of much use given the existence of other health problems that provide competing risks. However, most authors agree that there is no age limit beyond which risk factors are no longer modifiable, thereby allowing for the possibility of improving health outcomes (Fries, Green, & Levine, 1989; Rowe & Kahn, 1987).

The possible improvement of health outcomes has been termed the *compression of morbidity*. Fries (1980) argued that improved treatment of the major diseases will result in a general improvement in the health of older persons such that the period of chronic illness and disability before death will be shortened. Evidence available on this hypothesis is not consistent. The opposite seems true—successful treatment of major diseases would increase the period of disability associated with most chronic diseases (Deeg, Kriegsman, & van Zonneveld, 1994; Guralnik, 1991; Robine & Mathers, 1993). In the oldest-old, however, some evidence in support of Fries's hypothesis has been reported: The observed decline in functional ability was smaller in 1984–1989 than in 1982–1984 (Manton, Corder, & Stallard, 1993).

## B. Physical Activity and Trajectories of Disability

Age-specific health risk appraisals have been developed to help individuals understand the consequences of lifestyle choices for health and longevity (see Goetz & McTyre, 1981, for a discussion). Interest has increased concerning the role of physical activity in postponing or ameliorating age-associated cardiovascular, neuromuscular, and arthritic diseases.

Pendergast, Fisher, and Calkins (1993) reviewed evidence mostly from cross-sectional studies showing a progressive decrease in cardiopulmonary, muscular, neurological, and metabolic capabilities with advancing age, which in general did not limit function until over age 80. This decline can be delayed, reduced, and sometimes reversed by training.

Heikkinen and co-workers (1993) summarized Finnish studies that demonstrated that habitual walking of 10+ km/week by men and women aged 70–79 was associated with greater 10–year survival than lower levels of walking. The association held after adjustment for differences in socioeconomic status and presence of chronic medical conditions. Sex differences were striking: 10-year survival was approximately 90% and 60% for more active and less active women, respectively; the corresponding figures for men were 55% and 30%. D. J. Lee and Markides (1990) found no association between activity and mortality over an 8-year period in a group of Mexican-American and Anglo men and women 60 years and older. The association between higher mortality and lower level of physical activity disappeared when age and self-reported health were controlled for in the analysis. The major difference between this study and the one by Heikkinen et al. is the inclusion of self-reported health instead of number of chronic conditions. Comparison of both findings suggests a mediating role for self-perceived health between physical activity and mortality.

Two longitudinal studies (Donahue, Abbott, Reed, & Yano, 1988; Leon, Connett, Jacobs, & Rauramaa, 1987) indicate that moderate or higher levels of activity are beneficial for middle-aged men at risk for coronary heart disease. Moreover, the effects of higher levels of physical activity— both during work and leisure time—are beneficial in older as well as middle-aged men. The results generally held after adjustment for other standard risk factors including smoking, cholesterol, body mass index, and other variables measured. It was noted that less than 5% of the men reported maintaining a heavy level of activity for more than 1 hr per week.

The studies cited suggest that the level of activity required to achieve the beneficial effect relative to cardiovascular functioning is modest and can be achieved by a variety of everyday activities. The range of physical activities measured in the studies reviewed were on average lower than levels recommended for cardiovascular fitness.

The intensity of activity in studies using self-reported measures, however, is difficult to establish. Controlled studies of training effects such as those by Holloszy and Blumenthal and co-workers (Blumenthal et al., 1989; Hagberg, Graves, & Limacher, 1989; Seals, Hagberg, Hurley, Ehsani, & Holloszy, 1984) provided evidence on the relation of intensity to level of fitness. The American College of Sports Medicine concluded in its review of these studies, "age in itself is not a limiting factor to exercise training" (1990, p. 270). Older men and women starting at several levels of fitness benefit from prescribed physical training programs. The rate of im-

provement with training, not the level, is lower in older adults.

The effect of exercise is generally considered to be improved aerobic capacity, albeit modest (Buchner, Beresford, Larson, LaCroix, & Wagner, 1992). However, some of the apparently conflicting findings from studies relating cardiovascular fitness to age result from the failure to control for individual differences in muscle mass when estimating aerobic capacity in men and women of different ages (Fleg & Lakatta, 1988). Aerobic capacity is not likely to be the limiting factor in mobility and independence of the frail elderly (Pendergast et al., 1993). Recent studies investigate the role of strength training in maintaining mobility and in protecting against cardiovascular disease. Through its effect on muscle tissue, strength training influences glucose utilization and activity level (Buchner et al., 1992).

Muscle dysfunction is quite common in older persons, and can lead to frailty, falls, and immobilization. A sedentary life and malnutrition contribute to muscle dysfunction (Fiatarone & Evans, 1993). Muscle dysfunction can be partially redressed by training of sufficient intensity, tailored specifically to increasing muscle strength. Weak evidence exists that exercise improves gait and balance, if these are below a threshold, or are impaired by, for example, arthritis (Buchner et al., 1992). A beneficial effect of exercise in postmenopausal women to prevent or reduce osteoporosis is supported by observational studies, but proof by randomized study is not yet available.

Evans and Campbell (1993, p. 468) concluded their review of the literature saying, "There is no pharmacological intervention that holds greater promise of improving health and promoting independence in the elderly than does exercise." The number of people engaging in exercise at the levels recommended, however, is very low, especially for resistive strength training. About 5% of adults were found to know what duration, frequency, and intensity of physical activity were needed to strengthen heart and lungs (Caspersen, Christenson, & Pollard, 1986). A further problem in behavioral change programs is attrition and failure to maintain commitment. In a study of the effectiveness of public education on adoption of lifestyles designed to reduce heart disease, older age and higher socioeconomic status were found to predict positive outcomes from the intervention (Winkleby, Flora, & Kraemer, 1994). It has been suggested that older persons will respond favorably to physician-recommended interventions.

The effect of activity and strength training can be lost, so successful intervention needs to be continuous over the adult years. It is a great challenge to behavioral scientists to devise approaches that make it possible to achieve the long-term goals of physical activity and strength training.

## C. Psychosocial Factors and Disability

Psychosocial factors are included in several studies of adults with severe musculoskeletal impairments, a group of nonfatal but certainly incapacitating diseases. Nosek and Parker (1987) reported no association between psychological and social independence and level of functional disability. A likely explanation is that psychologically and socially independent persons were able to solicit the assistance they needed, and subsequently had other priorities. This explanation is supported by earlier studies, which show that to severely disabled adults their disability is less salient than might be expected (Stensman, 1985; Weinberg & Williams, 1978).

The same was shown to be true for older adults with one or more chronic diseases. Although good health was generally rated as a high priority as compared to other aspects of life, significantly fewer chronically ill persons than nondiseased persons gave priority to good health (Deeg, 1995). Of relatively greater importance to the

chronically ill were religious faith and good family contacts. The question remains whether this reordering of priorities is favorable in terms of future disease course.

## D. Perceived Control and Self-Efficacy, Mediators between Behavior and Health

A mediator in the age-associated relation between behavior and health must satisfy the criterion of causal dependence on both behavior and health. We review the evidence on the association between personality characteristics and both behavior and health.

Several studies have demonstrated the important roles of perceived control and perceived self-efficacy in their effects on self-perceived health (Grembowksi et al., 1993; Seeman & Seeman, 1983) and health behavior (keeping a healthy diet, exercising, managing to abstain from smoking; see Bandura, 1991, and Seeman & Seeman, 1983). Perceived control indicates to what extent individuals view their lives as being under their personal control (internal vs. external locus of control; see Rotter, 1966), and perceived self-efficacy refers to individuals' assessments of their capacity to perform successfully a behavior that is required to produce a specific outcome (Bandura, 1977).

Perceived control in health may be both a result of an individual's experience with health or illness and a determinant of subsequent health activity (Seeman & Seeman, 1983). Older persons may be at risk of having a lower perceived control, because they are more likely to have a chronic illness.

Four sources have been identified for perceived self-efficacy: past and present experience of performance, observing others perform, social influence such as verbal persuasion, and states of physiological arousal (Bandura, 1991). Abler and Fretz (1988) argued that older persons run the risk of negative messages from all four sources, because (a) they generally perceive that their performances were better when they were younger; (b) they are more likely to know other people who are unable to respond adequately to environmental and personal challenges; (c) they are at increasing risk of dependency on others, which will lead to the belief that they are unable to perform independently; and (d) they will experience more negative physiological reactions, especially when they are anxious. A decrease in perceived self-efficacy across age groups ranging from 55–85 years was shown by Bosscher (1994).

Perceptions of efficacy may be related to particular behaviors. Perceived self-efficacy with respect to physical ability may be particularly pertinent to older adults. Davis-Berman (1990) showed that perceived physical self-efficacy was a stronger predictor of depressive symptoms than other types of self-efficacy or more objective measures of physical status, such as number of physical problems and physician visits. Similar to general perceived self-efficacy, perceived physical self-efficacy was found to decrease across older age groups (Bosscher, 1994). However, the association of physical self-efficacy with age did not hold in analyses that controlled for the presence of chronic illnesses. This suggests that the main source of decreases in perceived self-efficacy with aging is the onset of chronic illness.

A particular instance of low perceived self-efficacy in older persons is fear of falling (Tinetti & Powell, 1993). This is defined as a lasting concern about falling that may lead to the avoidance of activities, even to (unnecessary) dependence upon others. This concern may exist even if a fall has not actually occurred. The social environment may increase fear of falling by being overprotective. Tinetti and Powell (1993) reported that fear of falling is an independent predictor of functional decline.

One study among persons aged 55 years and over showed age differences in the associations between self-efficacy at taking care of health and functional ability, and between perceived control over future health and functional ability (Rakowski & Cryan, 1990). The associations were weaker (although still significant) in persons over age 80 than in persons aged 55–64. As did Neugarten (1976), the authors explained this moderating effect of age by the greater "relative deprivation" that illness might produce in younger as opposed to older adults.

Another explanation of the moderating effect of age may be offered by the finding that individuals over 60 years of age have a lower desire for health-related control than do younger individuals (Woodward & Wallston, 1987). When control over health is not a priority, a lower perceived self-efficacy may not affect functional ability as much as when it is a priority. One explanation of the age association of desire for health-related control given by Woodward and Wallston (1987) is a cohort effect: Older generations, as opposed to younger ones, grew up without questioning health professionals and without asserting themselves within the health-care system. If this is the case, the association of perceived control and self-efficacy with health will become more important in future generations of older persons. Woodward and Wallston also suggested a second explanation, based on an aging effect. A lower desire for control would arise from increasing difficulty in decision making and problem solving, increasing impairment in comprehension processes, and decreasing perceived self-efficacy with aging.

Perceived control and self-efficacy are of particular interest in gerontology (Elias et al., 1990; Siegler & Costa, 1985). Several studies show positive effects on health outcomes of interventions to improve these characteristics (Bandura, 1991; Langer & Rodin, 1975; McClelland, 1989). For example, Bandura (1991) reported that inclusion of spouses in a rehabilitation program of heart patients was beneficial for recovery, because the spouses were more convinced of the patients' progress and therefore less inclined to dissuade the patients from the strenuous activity intended to improve physical ability.

## V. Conceptual and Methodological Issues

This review emphasizes the heterogeneity and complexity of pathways from health to behavior and vice versa, of age-associated changes in these pathways, and of factors that may explain these changes. Numerous new research questions have been raised. Insight into health–behavior relationships would be improved if a comprehensive conceptual framework were available to integrate existing and future research findings. Two recently proposed conceptual models may provide the basis for such a framework: one describing the various stages in the trajectory of disability and the individual and environmental factors influencing each stage (Verbrugge & Jette, 1994), the other focusing on the role of time in the development and course of disease and the relation of stages in the disease course with psychosocial factors (Rolland, 1987). These two models are summarized in the next sections (V.A,B). The last section (V.C) discusses some methodological problems, recognition of which may lead to greater sophistication of future research and, thus, to greater insight in health–behavior relationships.

### A. The Disablement Process

The loss of good health and independent functioning with aging is described in "the disablement process" model (Verbrugge & Jette, 1994). Disability is viewed as a gap between personal capability and environmental demand. Disability, then, can be alleviated at either side, by increasing capability or reducing demand.

The disablement process delineates the pathway from pathology to various kinds of functional outcomes (Nagi, 1965; World Health Organization, 1980). *Pathology* includes biochemical and physiological abnormalities medically labeled as disease, injury, or congenital or developmental conditions. *Impairments* are dysfunctions and significant structural abnormalities in specific body systems. *Functional limitations* are restrictions in performing fundamental physical and mental actions used in daily life such as mobility (physical) or memory (mental). *Disability* is difficulty experienced doing ADLs in any domain of life due to a health or physical problem. Functional limitation refers to a person's *capabilities*; disability refers to a person's *behavior*. The specific effects of disability depend on the activity affected: obligatory (e.g., personal care), committed (e.g., housekeeping tasks, work), or discretionary (e.g., leisure activities).

New pathologies and dysfunctions can result from a disablement process. An older woman with painful arthritis may restrict her recreational walking (disability), thereby reducing cardiopulmonary function and increasing muscle weakness (impairment), all of which reduces her mobility (functional limitation) and social activities (disability). An ultimate effect of mobility restriction may be bedsores (pathology).

The pathway of any disablement is rendered variable because of risk factors, interventions, and exacerbators (Verbrugge & Jette, 1994). *Risk factors*, the enduring characteristics of individuals or their environments, affect outcomes at all stages of the disablement process. *Interventions* to reduce limitations include medical care, rehabilitation, assistance, modification of the environment, and changes in behavior such as psychosocial adaptation and activity accommodation. *Exacerbators* elevate the chances of disablement, including unintended side effects of drugs, adopting attitudes of behaviors that actually increase limitations and disability (e.g., fear of falling), and societal impediments (e.g., architectural barriers, social prejudice).

Aging is usually associated with late-life disability, rather than with lifelong disability (caused by congenital or developmental conditions and severe injury in childhood or youth). Late-life disability comes from chronic diseases at middle or older ages, with disability expanding over time. Late-life disabled persons try to restore their earlier capabilities or to adapt to their loss. The adaptations made are aided by previous experiences.

### B. Timing of Onset of Health Deficit in the Life Course

A typology of chronic diseases that facilitates the study of their psychosocial consequences is offered by Rolland (1987). Chronic diseases can be characterized by the following aspects: *onset* (acute vs. gradual), *course* (progressive, constant, or episodic), and *outcome* (affecting the life span or not, or uncertainty about this). A fourth characteristic is *incapacitation*, which in turn has three components: kind (movement, energy, cognition, sensation, disfigurement, social stigma), extent, and timing.

Rolland recognized three phases in the course of chronic disease: the *crisis* phase, including prediagnostic symptoms, and initial adjustment to diagnosis; the *chronic* phase, which may be constant, progressive, or episodic; and the *terminal* phase, including the inevitability of death, mourning, and the resolution of loss. Not all of these phases, it is noted, occur in every chronic disease. Each phase has unique psychosocial concomitants.

Adaptation to chronic illness is influenced by, first, the patient's and family's history of adaptation to illness, loss, and crisis, and, second, the interface of the illness with the individual and what Rolland calls the family life cycles. The life cycle refers to alternating periods of life structure building and structure maintaining. Both periods can be characterized by fami-

ly closeness (*centripetal* mode) or family disengagement (*centrifugal* mode). The onset of an illness usually has a centripetal effect. A constant course in the chronic phase of the illness will have a centrifugal effect inasmuch as the individual will reestablish autonomy to the extent possible. A relapsing course keeps the family in a state of preparedness and enhances a centripetal mode.

The two conceptual models described, the disablement process and the timing and course of chronic illness, provide a framework to understand the dynamics among health, aging, and behavior, for the definition of health adopted in this chapter. The two conceptual models lead to the following conclusions: The impact of onset of illness on an individual's adaptation depends on the nature of the illness, the time in the life cycle when it occurs, and the experience and coping style of the individual and family with illness. The elements of the model of disablement encompass all domains of life. It is just this wide range of influences and outcomes that creates the heterogeneity we observe in aging. The multiplicity of outcomes of ill health at the individual and family level were documented in the studies reviewed in the previous sections. Explication of all key elements of disablement in research designs will deepen insights into the associations between health, behavior, and aging.

### C. Methodological Problems

Evidence on the interplay among health, behavior, and aging comes mostly from cross-sectional research. This is particularly true for studies about moderating effects of age on associations between health and behavior, and about mediators of these associations. When longitudinal evidence is available, it is usually derived from studies that cover a short time span relative to the full life span of older individuals. Therefore, in most longitudinal studies the life course perspective is likely to be lacking. Of course, this is the state of research in this field. Only very few studies exist that encompass the entire lifetime. One such study is the Berkeley Older Generation Study, a continuation of the Guidance Study and the Berkeley Growth Study, which were initiated in 1928 and 1929 (Field, Minkler, Falk, & Leino, 1993). Most studies of adult aging emphasize the older years, although a few, such as the Baltimore Longitudinal Study of Aging, cover the ages from young adulthood (Deeg, 1989a).

Furthermore, although authors presenting cross-sectional findings often provide interpretations in terms of the life course or the cohort perspective, accompanied by the statement that longitudinal studies are needed to provide further evidence, authors presenting longitudinal findings tend to be less thoughtful of wider interpretations of their findings. A notable exception is the study by Idler (1993), who presented both cross-sectional and longitudinal evidence on changes in self-perceived health, and gives an exemplary review of possible explanations in terms of aging, selective survivorship, and cohort differences.

We have identified some associations between health and behavior that are likely to change with aging or across cohorts. The social environment in which cohorts grow old is changing more rapidly than ever before (Riley, 1987). The experience of aging in large numbers is new, and may itself have profound effects on the association between health and behavior.

Several studies based on surveys several years apart have shown evidence that later cohorts have better physical health and less disability than earlier cohorts (Jagger, Clarke, & Clarke, 1991; Manton et al., 1993; Svanborg, 1988). By contrast, smaller proportions of later cohorts report good health than earlier cohorts (Verbrugge, 1990). Indeed the prevalence of some major diseases of old age (heart disease, diabetes, arthritis, as well as the coexistence of several chronic diseases) has increased (Deeg et al., 1994). These contrasting trends evoke questions about the role of

diagnostic and treatment possibilities in the ascertainment of prevalences, and about historical changes in standards of what is "good health," each of which is likely to affect associations between health and behavior and their mediators.

Subjective instead of objective measurements are used in most studies on health and behavior (Siegler, 1990). Subjective health measures may show associations with behavioral factors that contrast with those shown by objective health measures (Kelly-Hayes, Jette, Wolf, D'Agostino, & Odell, 1992). Moreover, subjective health measures are not as strongly related to age as are objective health measures (Barberger-Gateau et al., 1992). These phenomena make it more difficult to draw conclusions about differential effects of aging on the association between health and behavior when different health measures are used.

A final note concerns the heterogeneity that is stressed throughout this chapter. Most research findings are reported as averages, for example, statistically significant associations between variables, or trends across age groups. This way of reporting obscures the view of interindividual differences. Some authors approach the study of heterogeneity by searching for measurements that discriminate individuals within age peer groups (Stones, Kozma, & Hannah, 1990). Others use innovative statistical techniques to model individual change over time (Brant et al., 1993; Campbell, 1993). Still other scholars attempt to define profiles of subgroups of older individuals sharing similar physical and mental characteristics (Manton, Siegler, & Woodbury, 1986; Smith & Baltes, 1993). Such approaches seem essential for obtaining further insight into the interplay between health and behavior with aging.

## VI. Summary

This chapter has reviewed evidence bearing on a generic question: How does aging affect behavioral consequence of health deficits and, vice versa, how does aging affect the health consequences of behavior? Health was defined as the absence of acute and chronic physical or mental disease and impairments. Behavior was defined as activities, and the physical, mental, and social skills required to perform activities. The overall goal of the review has been to document and explain the remarkable variability in observed trajectories of aging in relation to health and behavior.

Major behavioral consequences of disease are losses in functional ability and development of disabilities. In comparison with the functional effects of existing disease, the onset of a new chronic disease leads to a relatively greater functional loss. However, many older persons show improvements in functional ability, most likely in the first year after onset of a disease. The variability of functioning that occurs in disease results in part from nonphysical factors such as socioeconomic status, feelings of usefulness, and participation in social activities.

Many older patients show better mental health than younger patients with similar diseases. Assistance to older persons from informal caregivers, however, may lead to feelings of dependency and therefore to mental distress. Older persons who are functionally disabled have fewer means to compensate for physical losses and are more vulnerable to life strain, in particular when their sense of control is low.

The association between ill health and use of services is mediated by the social network and by age identity. Response speed may mediate between ill health and behavioral outcomes; for other aspects of cognition, however, no consistent evidence exists for a mediating effect.

A well-documented health consequence of behavior is cardiovascular morbidity. Risk factors such as low activity level, smoking, poor nutrition, and obesity remain modifiable in old age, making improvements in health outcomes possible at any age.

To a sizable number of chronically ill older persons their disability is of less salience than might be expected, because they can shift their priorities to other behavioral options. Perceived control and perceived self-efficacy are associated with positive health practices on the one hand, and with the absence of chronic disease and with good functional ability and self-perceived health on the other hand. A sense of control and self-efficacy therefore mediate between behavior and health outcomes. The associations are weaker in older than in middle-aged adults, which may indicate a lower desire for control in older persons.

Many of the adaptations by older persons to disease reflect one or more of the following mechanisms: (a) The onset of chronic illness in old age is more usual and therefore less disruptive than in younger age (an aging effect); (b) older persons may have developed more effective skills with which to manage health deficits (an aging effect); (c) those older persons more susceptible to negative disease consequences have died at an earlier age (survivor effect); (d) currently older generations might be more tolerant of adverse health than younger generations (a cohort effect). These explanations are crucial in interpreting much of the evidence reviewed, and in raising future research questions.

Major conceptual and methodological problems of current research are the lack of a life course perspective, the neglect of historical changes, and the use of statistical methods that ignore heterogeneity. Two comprehensive conceptual models have been discussed, which may offer a framework to integrate the complex research findings reviewed. Such models are needed in designing research through which further understanding of the relationships among aging, health, and behavior can be obtained.

## Acknowledgment

Thanks are owed to Dr. G. T. Baker III and Dr. E. J. Metter for their early contribution to the planning of this chapter.

## References

Abler, R. M., & Fretz, B. R. (1988). Self-efficacy and competence in independent living among oldest old persons. *Journal of Gerontology: Social Sciences, 43*, S138–S143.

American College of Sports Medicine. (1990). The recommended quantity and quality of exercise for developing and maintaining cardiorespiratory and muscular fitness in healthy adults. *Medicine and Science in Sports and Exercise, 22*, 265–274.

Arenberg, D. (1987). A note on differences and changes in memory with age. In M. W. Riley, J. D. Matarazzo, & A. Baum (Eds.), *The aging dimension. Perspectives in behavioral medicine* (pp. 39–47). Hillsdale, NJ: Erlbaum.

Baltes, M. M., Wahl, H. W., & Schmid-Furstoss, U. (1990). The daily life of elderly Germans: Activity patterns, personal control, and functional health [Special issue]. *Journal of Gerontology: Psychological Sciences, 45*, P173–P179.

Baltes, P. B. (1991). The many faces of human ageing: Toward a psychological culture of old age. *Psychological Medicine, 21*, 837–854.

Bandura, A. (1977). Towards a unifying theory of behavioral change. *Psychological Review, 84*, 191–215.

Bandura, A. (1991). Self-efficacy mechanism in physiological activation and health promoting behavior. In J. Madden, IV, S. Mathysse, & J. Barchas (Eds.), *Neurobiology of learning, emotion and affect* (pp. 229–270). New York: Raven Press.

Barberger-Gateau, P., Chaslerie, A., Dartigues, J.-F., Commenges, D., Gagnon, M., & Salamon, R. (1992). Health measures correlates in a French elderly community population: The PAQUID study. *Journal of Gerontology: Social Sciences, 47*, S588–S595.

Baron, R. M., & Kenny, D. A. (1986). The moderator-mediator variable distinction in social psychological research: Conceptual, strategic, and statistical consideration. *Journal of Personality and Social Psychology, 51*, 1173–1182.

Beekman, A. T. F., Kriegsman, D. M. W., Deeg, D. J. H., & van Tilburg, W. (1995). The association of physical health and depression in the older population: Age and sex differences. *Social Psychiatry and Psychogeriatric Epidemiology, 30*, 32–38.

Birren, J. E. (1988). Behavior as a cause and consequence of health and aging. In J. J. F. Schroots, J. E. Birren, & A. Svanborg (Eds.), *Health and aging: Perspectives and prospects* (pp. 25–41). Lisse, The Netherlands: Swets & Zeitlinger.

Blumenthal, J. A., Emery, C. F., Madden, D. J., George, L. K., Coleman, R. E., Riddle, M. W., McKee, D. C., Reasoners, J., & Williams, R. S. (1989). Cardiovascular and behavioral effects of aerobic exercise training in healthy older men and women. *Journal of Gerontology: Medical Sciences, 44*, M147–M157.

Bosscher, R. J. (1994). Self-efficacy expectations. In D. J. H. Deeg & M. Westendorp-de Serière (Eds.), *Autonomy and well-being in the aging population. I: Report from the Longitudinal Aging Study Amsterdam 1992–1993* (pp. 45–51). Amsterdam: VU University Press.

Boult, C., Kane, R. L., Louis, T. A., Boult, L., & McCaffrey, D. (1994). Chronic conditions that lead to functional limitations in the elderly. *Journal of Gerontology: Medical Sciences, 49*, M28–M36.

Branch, L. G., Katz, S., Kniepmann, K., & Papsidero, J. A. (1984). A prospective study of functional status among community elders. *American Journal of Public Health, 74*, 266–268.

Brant, L. J., Pearson, J. D., Morrell, C. H., Metter, E. J., Fozard, J. L., & Fleg, J. L. (1993). Longitudinal methods for assessing vulnerability. In D. J. H. Deeg, C. P. M. Knipscheer, & W. van Tilburg (Eds.), *Autonomy and well-being in the aging population: Concepts and design of the Longitudinal Aging Study Amsterdam* (NIG-Trend Studies No. 7, pp. 185–197). Bunnik, The Netherlands: Netherlands Institute of Gerontology.

Buchner, D. M., Beresford, S. A. A., Larson, E. B., LaCroix, A. Z., & Wagner, E. H. (1992). Effects of physical activity on health status in older adults: II. Intervention studies. *Annual Review of Public Health, 13*, 469–488.

Campbell, R. T. (1993). Design decisions in large scale longitudinal studies: Balancing precision and heterogeneity. In D. J. H. Deeg, C. P. M. Knipscheer, & W. van Tilburg (Eds.), *Autonomy and well-being in the aging population: Concepts and design of the Longitudinal Aging Study Amsterdam* (NIG-Trend Studies No. 7, pp. 161–183). Bunnik,

The Netherlands: Netherlands Institute of Gerontology.

Caspersen, C. J., Christenson, G. M., & Pollard, R. A. (1986). Status of the physical fitness and exercise objectives; Evidence from NHIS 1985. *Public Health Reports, 101,* 587–592.

Cassileth, B. R., Lusk, E. J., Strouse, T. B., Miller, D. S., Brown, L. L., Cross, P. A., & Tenaglia, A. N. (1984). Psychological status in chronic illness. *New England Journal of Medicine, 311,* 506–511.

Cohen, G. S. (1992). The future of mental health and aging. In J. E. Birren, R. B. Sloan, & G. D. Cohen (Eds.), *Handbook of mental health and aging* (2nd ed., pp. 894–914). San Diego, CA: Academic Press.

Crimmins, E. M., & Saito, Y. (1993). Getting better and getting worse: Transitions in functional status among older Americans. *Journal of Aging and Health, 5,* 3–36.

Davis-Berman, J. (1990). Physical self-efficacy, perceived physical status, and depressive symptomatology in older adults. *Journal of Psychology, 124,* 207–215.

Deeg, D. J. H. (1989a). *Experiences from longitudinal studies of aging: Conceptualization, organization, and output* (NIG-Trend Studies No. 3). Nijmegen, The Netherlands: Netherlands Institute of Gerontology.

Deeg, D. J. H. (1989b). *The feasibility of predicting longevity in the elderly: Conceptual and empirical aspects.* Delft, The Netherlands: Eburon.

Deeg, D. J. H. (1995). Research and the promotion of quality of life in older persons in the Netherlands. In E. Heikkinen, J. Kusinen, & I. Ruoppila (Eds.), *Preparation for aging* (pp. 155–163). New York: Plenum.

Deeg, D. J. H., Haga, H., Yasamura, S., Suzuki, T., Shichita, K., & Shibata, H. (1992). Predictors of 10-year change in physical, cognitive and social function in Japanese elderly. *Archives of Gerontology and Geriatrics, 15,* 163–179.

Deeg, D. J. H., Kriegsman, D. M. W., & van Zonneveld, R. J. (1994). Trends in fatal chronic diseases and disability in the Netherlands 1956–1993 and projections of active life expectancy 1993–1998. In C. J. Mathers, J. McCallum, & J.-M. Robine (Eds.), *Advances in health expectancies: Proceedings of the 7th meeting of the International Network on Health Expectancy REVES, Canberra, February 1994* (pp. 80–95). Canberra: Australian Institute of Health and Welfare.

Donahue, R. P., Abbott, R. D., Reed, D. M., & Yano, K. (1988). Physical activity and coronary heart disease in middle-aged and elderly men: The Honolulu heart program. *American Journal of Public Health, 78,* 683–685.

Elias, M. F., Elias, J. W., & Elias, P. K. (1990). Biological and health influences on behavior. In J. E. Birren & K. W. Schaie (Eds.), *Handbook of the psychology of aging* (3rd ed., pp. 79–102). San Diego, CA: Academic Press.

Elias, M. F., Schultz, N. R., Jr., Robbins, M. A., & Elias, P. K. (1989). A longitudinal study of neuropsychological performance by hypertensives and normotensives: A third measurement point. *Journal of Gerontology: Psychological Sciences, 44,* P25–P28.

Epstein, L. H., & Wing, R. R. (1980). Aerobic exercise and weight. *Addictive Behaviors, 5,* 371–388.

Evans, W. J., & Campbell, W. W. (1993). Sarcopenia and age-related changes in body composition and functional capacity. *Journal of Nutrition, 123,* 465–468.

Fiatarone, M. A., & Evans, W. J. (1993). The etiology and reversibility of muscle dysfunction in the aged [Special issue]. *Journal of Gerontology, 48,* 77–83.

Field, D., Minkler, M., Falk, F., & Leino, E. V. (1993). The influence of health on family contacts and family feelings in advanced old age: A longitudinal study. *Journal of Gerontology: Psychological Sciences, 48,* P18–P28.

Fleg, J. L., & Lakatta, E. G. (1988). Role of muscle loss in the age associated reduction in VO2 max. *Journal of Applied Physiology, 65,* 1147–1151.

Fozard, J. L., Metter, E. J., & Brant, L. J. (1990). Next steps in describing aging and disease in longitudinal studies. *Journal of Gerontology: Psychological Sciences, 45,* P116–P127.

Fozard, J. L., Mullin, P. A., Giambra, L. M., Metter, E. J., & Costa, P. T., Jr. (1992). Normal and pathological age differences in memory. In J. C. Brocklehurst, R. C. Tallis, & H. M. Fillit (Eds.), *Textbook of geriatric medicine and gerontology* (pp. 94–110). London: Churchill Livingstone.

Fried, L. P., Ettinger, W. H., Lind, B., Newman, A. B., Gardin, J., & Cardiovascular Health Study Research Group. (1994). Physical disability in older adults: A physiological approach. *Journal of Clinical Epidemiology,* 47, 747–760.

Fries, J. F. (1980). Aging, natural death and the compression of morbidity. *New England Journal of Medicine,* 303, 130–135.

Fries, J. F., Green, L. W., & Levine, S. (1989, March 4). Health promotion and the compression of morbidity. *Lancet,* pp. 481–483.

Goetz, A. A., & McTyre, R. B. (1981). Health risk appraisal: Some methodological considerations. *Nursing Research,* 30, 303–313.

Grand, A., Grosclaude, P., Bocquet, H., Pous, J., & Albarede, J. L. (1988). Predictive value of life events, psychosocial factors and self-rated health on disability in an elderly rural French population. *Social Science in Medicine,* 27, 1337–1342.

Grand, A., Grosclaude, P., Bocquet, H., Pous, J., & Albarede, J. L. (1990). Disability, psychosocial factors and mortality among the elderly in a rural French population. *Journal of Clinical Epidemiology,* 43, 773–782.

Grembowksi, D., Patrick, D., Diehr, P., Durham, M., Beresford, S., Kay, E., & Hecht, J. (1993). Self-efficacy and health behavior among older adults. *Journal of Health and Social Behavior,* 34, 89–104.

Guralnik, J. M. (1991). Prospects for the compression of morbidity. *Journal of Aging and Health,* 3, 132–154.

Guralnik, J. M., & Kaplan, G. A. (1989). Predictors of healthy aging: Prospective evidence from the Alameda County Study. *American Journal of Public Health,* 79, 703–708.

Guralnik, J. M., & Simonsick, E. M. (1993). Physical disability in older Americans [Special issue]. *Journal of Gerontology,* 48, 3–10.

Haga, H., Shibata, H., Ueno, M., Nagai, H., Suyama, Y., Matsuzaki, T., Yasumura, S., Koyano, W., & Hatano, S. (1991). Factors contributing to longitudinal changes in activities of daily living (ADL): The Koganei study. *Journal of Cross-Cultural Gerontology,* 6, 91–99.

Hagberg, J. M., Graves, J. E., & Limacher, M. (1989). Cardiovascular response of 70–79-year-old men and women to exercise training. *Journal of Applied Physiology,* 66, 2589–2594.

Harris, T., Kovar, M. G., Suzman, R., Kleinman, J. C., & Feldman, J. J. (1989). Longitudinal study of physical ability in the oldest old. *American Journal of Public Health,* 79, 698–702.

Heikkinen, E., Era, P., Jokela, J., Jylhä, M., Lyyra, A.-L., & Pohjolainen, P. (1993). Socioeconomic and life-style factors as modulators of health and functional capacity with age. In J. J. F. Schroots (Ed.), *Aging, health and competence* (pp. 65–86). Amsterdam: Elsevier.

Hertzog, C., Schaie, K. W., & Gribbin, K. (1978). Cardiovascular disease and changes in intellectual functioning from middle to old age. *Journal of Gerontology,* 33, 872–883.

Hubert, H. B., Bloch, D. A., & Fries, J. F. (1993). Risk factors for physical disability in an aging cohort: The NHANES I epidemiologic followup study. *Journal of Rheumatology,* 20, 480–488.

Idler, E. L. (1993). Age differences in self-assessments of health: Age changes, cohort differences, or survivorship? *Journal of Gerontology: Social Sciences,* 48, S289–S300.

Idler, E. L., Kasl, S. V., & Lemke, J. H. (1990). Self-evaluated health and mortality among the elderly in New Haven, Connecticut, and Iowa and Washington Counties, Iowa, 1982–1986. *American Journal of Epidemiology,* 131, 91–103.

Jagger, C., Clarke, M., & Clarke, S. J. (1991). Getting older—feeling younger: The changing health profile of the elderly. *International Journal of Epidemiology,* 20, 234–238.

Johnson, R. J., & Wolinsky, F. D. (1993). The structure of health status among older adults: Disease, disability, functional limitation, and perceived health. *Journal of Health and Social Behavior,* 34, 105–121.

Kane, R. L., Kane, R. A., & Arnold, S. B. (1985). Prevention and the elderly: Risk factors. *Health Services Research,* 19, 945–1006.

Kannel, W. B., & Gordon, T. (1980). Cardiovascular risk factors in the aged: The Framingham study. In S. G. Haynes & M. Feinleib (Eds.), *Second conference on the epidemiology of aging* (pp. 65–89). Bethesda, MD: National Institutes of Health.

Kaplan, G. A., Strawbridge, W. J., Camacho, T., & Cohen, R. D. (1993). Factors associated with change in physical functioning in the elderly. *Journal of Aging and Health,* 5, 140–153.

Kelly-Hayes, M., Jette, A. M., Wolf, P. A., D'Agostino, R. B., & Odell, P. M. (1992). Functional limitations and disability among elders in the Framingham study. *American Journal of Public Health,* 82, 841–845.

Kennedy, G. J., Kelman, H. R., & Thomas, C. (1990). The emergence of depressive symptoms in late life: The importance of declining health and increasing disability. *Journal of Community Health, 15*, 93–103.

King, H. E., & Miller, R. E. (1990). Hypertension: Cognitive and behavioral considerations. *Neuropsychology Review, 1*, 31–73.

Koyano, W., Shibata, H., Haga, H., & Suyama, Y. (1986). Prevalence and outcome of low ADL and incontinence among the elderly: Five years follow-up in a Japanese urban community. *Archives of Gerontology and Geriatrics, 5*, 197–206.

Krause, N. (1988). Stressful life events and physician utilization. *Journal of Gerontology: Social Sciences, 43*, S53–S61.

Laforge, R. G., Spector, W. D., & Sternberg, J. (1992). The relationship of vision and hearing impairment to one-year mortality and functional decline. *Journal of Aging and Health, 4*, 126–148.

Lammi, U.-K., Kivelä, S.-L., Nissinen, A., Punsar, S., Puska, P., & Karvonen, M. (1989). Predictors of disability in elderly Finnish men—a longitudinal study. *Journal of Clinical Epidemiology, 42*, 1215–1225.

Langer, E. J., & Rodin, J. (1975). The effects of choice and enhanced personal responsibility for the aged: A field experiment in an institutional setting. *Journal of Personality and Social Psychology, 34*, 191–198.

Laukkanen, P., Kauppinen, M., Era, P., & Heikkinen, E. (1993). Factors related to coping with physical and instrumental activities of daily living among people born in 1904–1923. *International Journal of Geriatric Psychiatry, 8*, 287–296.

Launer, L. J., Dinkgreve, M. H. A. M., Jonker, C., Hooijer, C., & Lindeboom, J. (1993). Are age and education independent correlates of the Mini-Mental State Exam performance of community-dwelling elderly? *Journal of Gerontology: Psychological Sciences, 48*, P271–P277.

Launer, L. J., Harris, T., Rumpel, C., & Madans, J. (1994). Body mass index, weight change, and risk of mobility disability in middle-aged and older women. *JAMA, Journal of the American Medical Association, 271*, 1093–1098.

Lee, D. J., & Markides, K. S. (1990). Activity and mortality among aged persons over an eight-year period. *Journal of Gerontology: Social Sciences, 45*, S539–S542.

Lee, I.-M., Manson, J. E., Hennekens, C. H., & Paffenbarger, R. S., Jr. (1993). Body weight and mortality: A 27-year follow-up of middle-aged men. *JAMA, Journal of the American Medical Association, 270*, 2823–2828.

Leon, A. S., Connett, J., Jacobs, D. R., Jr., & Rauramaa, R. (1987). Leisure-time physical activity levels and risk of coronary heart disease and death: The Multiple Risk Factor Intervention Trial. *JAMA, Journal of the American Medical Association, 258*, 2388–2395.

Leventhal, E. A. (1984). Aging and the perception of illness. *Research on Aging, 6*, 119–135.

Liang, J. (1986). Self-reported physical health among aged adults. *Journal of Gerontology, 41*, 248–260.

Logan, J. R., & Spitze, G. (1994). Informal support and the use of formal services by older Americans. *Journal of Gerontology: Psychological Sciences, 49*, P25–P34.

Maddox, G. L. (1987). Psychological perspectives on aging. In M. W. Riley, J. D. Matarazzo, & A. Baum (Eds.), *The aging dimension: Perspectives in behavioral medicine* (pp. 15–28). Hillsdale, NJ: Erlbaum.

Maddox, G. L., & Clark, D. O. (1992). Trajectories of functional impairment in later life. *Journal of Health and Social Behavior, 33*, 114–125.

Manton, K. G., Corder, L. S., & Stallard, E. (1993). Estimates of change in chronic disability and institutional incidence and prevalence rates in the U.S. elderly population from the 1982, 1984, and 1989 National Long Term Care survey. *Journal of Gerontology: Social Sciences, 48*, S153–S166.

Manton, K. G., Siegler, I. C., & Woodbury, M. A. (1986). Patterns of intellectual development in later life. *Journal of Gerontology, 41*, 486–499.

Manton, K. G., Stallard, E., Woodbury, M. A., & Dowd, J. E. (1994). Time-varying covariates in models of human mortality and aging: Multidimensional generalization of the Gompertz. *Journal of Gerontology: Biological Sciences, 49*, B169–B190.

McClelland, D. C. (1989). Motivational factors in health and disease. *American Psychologist, 44*, 675–683.

McGinnis, J. M., & Foege, W. H. (1993). Actual causes of death in the United States. *JAMA,*

*Journal of the American Medical Association, 270,* 2207–2212.

Mor, V., Wilcox, V., Rakowski, W., & Hiris, J. (1994). Functional transitions among the elderly: Patterns, predictors, and related hospital use. *American Journal of Public Health, 84,* 1274–1280.

Morrell, R. W., Park, D. C., & Poon, L. W. (1990). Effects of labeling techniques on memory and comprehension of prescription information in young and old adults [Special issue]. *Journal of Gerontology: Psychological Sciences, 45,* 166–172.

Mossey, J. M., & Shapiro, E. (1982). Self-rated health: A predictor of mortality among the elderly. *American Journal of Public Health, 72,* 800–808.

Nagi, S. Z. (1965). Some conceptual issues in disability and rehabilitation. In M. B. Sussman (Ed.), *Sociology and rehabilitation* (pp. 100–113). Washington, DC: American Sociological Association.

Nelson, R. C., & Franzi, L. R. (1989). Nutrition and aging. *Geriatric Medicine, 73,* 1531–1550.

Neugarten, B. (1976). Adaptation and the life cycle. *The Counseling Psychologist, 6,* 16–20.

Norris, F., & Murrell, S. (1988). Prior experience as a moderator of disaster impact on anxiety symptoms in older adults. *American Journal of Community Psychology, 16,* 665–683.

Nosek, M. A., & Parker, R. M. (1987). Psychosocial independence and functional abilities: Their relationship in adults with severe musculoskeletal impairments. *Archives of Physical Medicine and Rehabilitation, 68,* 840–845.

Ormel, J., Von Korff, M., van den Brink, W., Katon, W., & Oldehinkel, T. (1993). Depression, anxiety, and social disability show synchrony of change in primary care patients. *American Journal of Public Health, 83,* 385–390.

Pendergast, D. R., Fisher, N. M., & Calkins, E. (1993). Cardiovascular, neuromuscular, and metabolic alterations with age leading to frailty [Special issue]. *Journal of Gerontology, 48,* 61–67.

Penning, M. J., & Strain, L. A. (1994). Gender differences in disability, assistance, and subjective well-being in later life. *Journal of Gerontology: Social Sciences, 49,* S202–S208.

Persson, G., & Svanborg, A. (1992). Marital coital activity in men at the age of 75: Relation to somatic, psychiatric, and social factors at the age of 70. *Journal of the American Geriatrics Society, 40,* 439–444.

Rakowski, W., & Cryan, C. D. (1990). Associations among health perceptions and health status within three age groups. *Journal of Aging and Health, 2,* 59–80.

Reuben, D. B., Siu, A. L., & Kimpau, S. (1992). The predictive validity of self-report and performance-based measures of function and health. *Journal of Gerontology: Medical Sciences, 47,* M106–M110.

Riley, M. W. (1987). Aging, health and social change: An overview. In M. W. Riley, J. D. Matarazzo, & A. Baum (Eds.), *The aging dimension. Perspectives in behavioral medicine* (pp. 1–14). Hillsdale, NJ: Erlbaum.

Rimer, B. K., Orleans, C. T., Keintz, M. K., Cristinzio, S., & Fleisher, L. (1990). The older smoker: Status, challenges and opportunities for intervention. *Chest, 97,* 547–553.

Roberts, B. L., Dunkle, R., & Haug, M. (1994). Physical, psychological, and social resources as moderators of the relationship of stress to mental health of the very old. *Journal of Gerontology: Social Sciences, 49,* S35–S43.

Robine, J. M., & Mathers, C. D. (1993). Measuring the compression or expansion of morbidity through changes in health expectancy. In J. M. Robine, C. D. Mathers, M. R. Bone, & I. Romieu (Eds.), *Calculation of health expectancies: Harmonization, consensus achieved and future perspectives* (Vol. 226, pp. 269–286). Montrouge/London: Colloque INSERM/John Libbey Eurotext Ltd.

Rolland, J. S. (1987). Chronic illness and the life cycle: A conceptual framework. *Family Process, 26,* 203–221.

Rotter, J. B. (1966). Generalized expectancies for internal vs. external control of reinforcement. *Psychological Monographs, 80*(609), 1–28.

Rowe, J. W., & Kahn, R. L. (1987). Human aging: Usual and successful. *Science, 237,* 143–149.

Schaie, K. W. (1987). Aging and human performance. In M. W. Riley, J. D. Matarazzo, & A. Baum (Eds.), *The aging dimension. Perspectives in behavioral medicine* (pp. 29–36). Hillsdale, NJ: Erlbaum.

Schulz, R., & Williamson, G. M. (1993). Psychosocial and behavioral dimensions of physical frailty [Special issue]. *Journal of Gerontology, 48,* 39–43.

Seals, D. R., Hagberg, J. M., Hurley, A. A., Ehsani, A. A., & Holloszy, J. O. (1984). Endurance training in older men and women: I. Cardiovascular responses to exercise. *Journal of Applied Physiology, 57,* 1024–1029.

Seeman, M., & Seeman, T. E. (1983). Health behavior and personal autonomy: A longitudinal study of the sense of control in illness. *Journal of Health and Social Behavior, 24,* 144–160.

Siegler, I. C. (1990). Paradigms in developmental health psychology; from theory to applications: Introduction to a special issue. *Journal of Gerontology: Psychological Sciences, 45,* P113–P115.

Siegler, I. C., & Costa, P. T., Jr. (1985). Health behavior relationships. In J. E. Birren & K. W. Schaie (Eds.), *Handbook of the psychology of aging* (2nd ed., pp. 144–166). New York: Van Nostrand-Reinhold.

Smith, J., & Baltes, P. B. (1993). Differential psychological ageing: Profiles of the old and very old. *Ageing and Society, 13,* 551–587.

Sorkin, J. D., Andres, R., Muller, D. C., Baldwin, H. L., & Fleg, J. L. (1992). Cholesterol as a risk factor for coronary heart disease in elderly men: The Baltimore longitudinal study of aging. *Annals of Epidemiology, 2,* 59–67.

Stensman, R. (1985). Severely mobility-disabled people assess the quality of their lives. *Scandinavian Journal of Rehabilitation Medicine, 17,* 87–99.

Stones, M. J., Kozma, A., & Hannah, T. E. (1990). The measurement of individual differences in aging: The distinction between usual and successful aging. In M. L. Howe, M. J. Stones, & C. J. Brainerd (Eds.), *Cognitive and behavioral performance factors in atypical aging* (pp. 181–218). New York: Springer-Verlag.

Sullivan, M. (1995). Depression and disability from chronic medical illness. *European Journal of Public Health, 5,* 40–45.

Svanborg, A. (1988). The health of the elderly population: Results from longitudinal studies with age-cohort comparisons. In *Ciba Foundation Symposium, 134,* pp. 3–16. Chichester: Wiley.

Tinetti, M. E., & Powell, L. (1993). Fear of falling and low self-efficacy: A cause of dependence in elderly persons [Special issue]. *Journal of Gerontology, 48,* 35–38.

Truett, J., Cornfield, J., & Kannel, W. (1967). A multivariate analysis of the risk of coronary heart disease in Framingham. *Journal of Chronic Diseases, 20,* 511–524.

Verbrugge, L. M. (1990). Pathways of health and death. In R. D. Apple (Ed.), *Women, health and medicine in America: A historical handbook* (pp. 41–79). New York: Garland.

Verbrugge, L. M., & Jette, A. M. (1994). The disablement process. *Social Science in Medicine, 38,* 1–14.

Von Korff, M., Ormel, J., Katon, W., & Lin, E. H. B. (1992). Disability and depression among high utilizers of health care: A longitudinal analysis. *Archives of General Psychiatry, 49,* 91–100.

Weinberg, N., & Williams, J. (1978, July–September). How the physically disabled perceive their disabilities. *Journal of Rehabilitation,* pp. 31–33.

Williams, M. E. (1987). Identifying the older person likely to require long-term care services. *Journal of the American Geriatrics Society, 35,* 761–766.

Wilson, P. W. F., Anderson, K. M., Harris, T., Kannel, W. B., & Castelli, W. P. (1994). Determinants of change in total cholesterol and HDL-C with age: The Framingham study. *Journal of Gerontology: Medical Sciences, 49,* M252–M257.

Winkleby, M. A., Flora, J. A., & Kraemer, H. C. (1994). A community-based heart disease intervention: Predictors of change. *American Journal of Public Health, 84,* 767–772.

Wolinsky, F. D., Callahan, C. M., Fitzgerald, J. F., & Johnson, R. J. (1993). Changes in functional status and the risks of subsequent nursing home placement and death. *Journal of Gerontology: Social Sciences, 48,* S93–S101.

Woodward, N. J., & Wallston, B. S. (1987). Age and health care beliefs: Self-efficacy as a mediator of low desire for control. *Psychology and Aging, 2,* 3–8.

World Health Organization. (1948). *WHO basic documents. Constitution of the World Health Organization.* Geneva: Author.

World Health Organization. (1980). *International classification of impairments, disabilities, and handicaps.* Geneva: Author.

Eight

# Social Cognition and Aging

Fredda Blanchard-Fields and Ronald P. Abeles

## I. Introduction

There is a growing body of research on cognitive changes in adulthood and aging that places cognitive functioning within a social context (i.e., *social cognition and aging*—e.g., Baltes & Smith, 1990; Berg & Klaczynski, in press; Labouvie-Vief, 1992). Social cognition, in general, focuses on linkages between the following: life tasks and goals; representations of self and other; cognitive strategies; and outcomes related to adjustment and functioning. More specifically, the majority of mainstream social cognitive research has centered on the content and structure of social knowledge (one's understanding of social reality) and the cognitive processes involved in accessing such social information (Fiske, 1993). Social cognition research also involves a functional perspective, inquiring about the functional importance of social representations (and other variables) for actual behaviors in context. Finally, social cognition also concentrates on how and to what end individuals access and use information under particular kinds of social situational demands (i.e., sociocultural, affective, and motivational influences).

The social cognition paradigm offers an enriched understanding of competency in older adults and the aging process. In applying this paradigm, our understanding of age-related changes in cognitive competence is broadened by considering the reciprocal relationship between cognition, on the one hand, and changing environments, interactions with others, knowledge systems, goals, and emotional responses on the other. The paradigm also focuses attention on social competence as an important and valid dimension of cognition and intelligence.

The scope of social cognitive research is quite broad. It includes such areas as person perception, self-perception, memory for social events and people, social schemas, the role of affect and social motivation in cognition, collaborative memory, and causal attributions. This chapter examines specific aspects of social cognitive research conducted from an adult developmental and aging perspective. First, we discuss the importance of multiple context variables (e.g., cohort-specific and domain-specific knowledge and influences) in the study of social cognitive functioning. In other words, can age differences in social cognitive performance be explained in terms of adaptation to partic-

*Handbook of the Psychology of Aging, Fourth Edition*

ular life contexts? Second, we examine the representation of social knowledge and beliefs about others and oneself. Are there age-related differences in the content and structure of social representations (e.g., social knowledge structures of self and other, problem appraisal)? Finally, we explore how social knowledge influences behavior. How do social knowledge structures or schemas differentially influence the processing of social information, behavior, and adjustment outcomes, such as coping with stress, in older adults?

## II. Social Cognition and Context

Both social cognitive and developmental theorists emphasize the importance of considering how changing contextual demands influence how individuals process social information. Contextual factors include (a) knowledge brought to a context, (b) situational goals and demands in a particular context, (c) well-instantiated goals reflecting personal traits and accumulation of experience, (d) changing life circumstances, and (e) historical-cultural influences. All of these factors combine to influence the appraisal and interpretation of a situation or problem, and the motivation to employ specific strategies in that situation. Much of the work on social cognition and aging has examined age-related differences in context factors, such as social roles and life circumstances associated with adulthood and aging, and how these have an impact on cognitive functioning in a social context, such as intelligence, memory, and perceptions of others (Baltes, Dittmann-Kohli, & Dixon, 1984; Dixon, 1992; Hess, 1994).

A life span approach to studying social cognition and aging also considers individual social-contextual influences on cognitive performance in interpreting what are gains and what are losses in cognitive functioning. From this contextual per-

spective we would question what adaptive functioning is for older adults. One such question asks whether a match exists between the social-cognitive demands of the situation-specific task and the social-cognitive goals of the older adult (goals related to life stage, tasks perceived by older adults as integral to their everyday functioning, changes in social schemas).

For example, a prototypic cognitive task for mature adults may be to transmit sociocultural knowledge and information to younger generations (Adams, Smith, Gaden, & Perlmutter, 1994; Chinen, 1989; Mergler & Goldstein, 1983). Adams et al. (1994) examined age differences in memory for text within a storytelling context. The implicit demand of such a social situation for the older adult would be to communicate effectively. This requires an adaptive interplay between producing language representing the ideas to be communicated and simultaneously monitoring the comprehension of the listeners so that ideas can be reexpressed, elaborated, and illustrated whenever necessary. Indeed, in this context, older adults recalled more of the story than younger adults.

Expository or narrative storytelling in this context is a qualitatively different task than narrative recall in the traditional laboratory context (Adams et al., 1994). Therefore, the social-cognitive processing requirements of nominally identical cognitive tasks (narrative recall) may vary as a function of both context and age-related social roles. It is particularly important to examine how social knowledge structures (e.g., social schemas and scripts, stereotypes, belief systems) and goals (e.g., life tasks) of the individual change with increasing age along with differing social contextual demands. In this way, we can better understand developmental changes in motivational and interpretational mechanisms that influence the changes (e.g., gains and losses) seen in cognitive mechanisms and strategies with advancing age.

## III. Representations of Others and Social Situations

Social cognitive research has focused a considerable amount of attention on representations and interpretations of others and social situations. Such research has focused on content of scripted knowledge structures regarding everyday activities (e.g., going to a restaurant, going to the doctor's office); problem appraisal; attributions about others and what caused an event outcome; and the way social knowledge structures influence interpretations of social situations, person perception, and impression formation. Variations in representations of social knowledge about events or problems have implications for the pattern of responses an individual selects for problem solving, coping, memory, or making social judgments.

### A. Scripted Knowledge Structures and Memory

It is well established that scripted knowledge influences memory for everyday events (Bower, Black, & Turner, 1979; Schank & Abelson, 1977). Scripts are cognitive representations of temporal-causal sequences of specific everyday events (e.g., going to the doctor, going to a restaurant) derived from personal experience and social expectations (Schank & Abelson, 1977). Script-related and context-dependent retention may result in text distortions, because it elicits emotional, social, and motivational processes (e.g., Wyer & Srull, 1989). For example, individuals include personal dispositions or traits of actors in their memory of a written action sequence depending on (a) their identification with one of the main characters of the story (Bower, 1978; Pichert & Anderson, 1977) or (b) the congruity of their moods and wishes with those of the main character of the story (Bower, 1981).

With respect to aging research, a number of studies have concentrated on age-related differences in memory for information as a function of scripted social activities (Hess & Tate, 1992; Light & Anderson, 1983; Ross & Berg, 1992). Few age-related differences have been found in the typicality and structure of common scripts (e.g., going to a restaurant; a visit to the doctor) (Hess, Donley, & Vandermaas, 1989; Light & Anderson, 1983), whereas there are age-related differences in the content of these scripts (Hess, 1992; Ross & Berg, 1992). The nature of the situation or activity may determine the degree of across-age consensus on information that should be represented in a script (Hess, 1992). For example, age variation occurred most in a "getting up in the morning routine," where young adults produced significantly more actions than older adults in this context. By contrast, older adults produced more actions than younger adults in the "breakfast scene." This could be explained by changing life contexts, such as a concern for mate selection on the part of younger adults and a concern with relating to family for the older adults (Hess, 1992). Similarly, the nature of script reports is influenced by changes in developmental life stages such as marriage and retirement (Ross & Berg, 1992) or cohort-related events such as the women's movement of the 1960s.

Given age-related variations in script-related knowledge, age differences exist also in the type of information remembered in scripted events. For example, Ross and Berg (1992) reported that individuals, across the different age groups studied, recalled more acts from stories similar to their personal scripts than from stories that were different. In addition, young adults were more reliant than older adults on their personal scripts in story recall. It appears that older adults' personal scripts were not differentially facilitating recall of stories that were similar (versus dissimilar) to their personal scripts of the event.

Similarly, age differences in social judgments are based on age differences in social knowledge content. For example, in contrast to younger adults, older adults, when commenting about a main character in a story, tend to make judgments that correspond to a description of the person presented earlier. This occurs even after inconsistent behavioral information (with respect to the earlier description) is presented in the story (Hess & Pullen, 1994; Hess, Vandermaas, Donley, & Snyder, 1987). These differences were found despite the lack of age differences in the relative accessibility of the consistent or inconsistent behavioral information. Older adults' reliance on schematic processing also occurred in certain situations (e.g., where gender roles were involved) and not in others.

## B. Problem Appraisal and Problem Solving

Similar to script-related memory research, differences in strategies used for coping with stress and solving everyday problems are a function of age differences in the underlying interpretations of the problem or coping situation (e.g., Berg, Klaczynski, Calderone, & Strough, 1994; Blanchard-Fields & Norris, 1994; Lazarus & Folkman, 1984; Sansone & Berg, 1993). Indeed, effective coping depends on a realistic appraisal of the situation, matching or approximating the unfolding of events (Lazarus & Folkman, 1984). Furthermore, Berg et al. (1994) suggested the need to examine differences in problem appraisal between younger and older adults in order to better understand strategy use and the potential adaptive nature of such age differences.

Klaczynski and Berg (1992; Berg et al., 1994) found that younger and older adults differed in their appraisal of problems as a function of the type of situation and its relevance to their everyday functioning (e.g., a visit to the doctor's office and problems arising at a dinner party). On the one hand, older adults interpreted the doctor's

office problems as external-social (something about the social circumstances rather than themselves). On the other hand, older adults viewed the dinner party problem more as internal-cognitive (something to do with their decision making). Younger adults interpreted both problems as internal-affective (attributed to their personal emotions). In addition, the way in which both age groups interpreted the problem influenced their subsequent selection of problem-solving strategies.

## C. Causal Attributions about Event Outcomes

Another approach to examining the way individuals construct and structure social problem situations is by assessing their causal attributions. Although originally formulated without regard to aging or development, this area has recently garnered attention in the adult developmental literature. Traditional research in social psychology is replete with studies demonstrating people's tendencies to produce informational distortions when making causal attributions about problem situations (Georgoudi, 1985; Nisbett & Ross, 1980). However, an apparent limitation is that these informational biases and distortions have been documented primarily with college-aged samples (Sears, 1987). Such distortions and biases might well decrease if older adults are sampled (Blanchard-Fields, 1986a; see also Blank, 1987).

This expectation is based on the idea that both lifelong experiences and cohort-specific experiences influence social cognitive functioning (e.g., memory, problem appraisal, and attributions). Life experience and social knowledge are accumulated and provide well-instantiated heuristics that invoke problem interpretations. Moreover, the current life situations of older adults may result in their employing different social schemas, which in turn affect their attributions. Presumably, such processes as these underlie the following examples of age differences in attributions.

Blanchard-Fields (1994) found that when situations were ambiguous with respect to the causal factors of an event outcome and reflected negative, interpersonal content, older adults made more interactive attributions (viewing the cause of an event as a combination of external and internal causes) than younger adults. However, older adults also blamed the primary protagonist more than younger age groups, primarily in negative relationship situations. The first finding reflects a postformal developmental perspective. Attributional biases or distortions of information (attributing cause solely to either dispositional or situational factors) may reflect a youthful thinker's tendency to construct the solution or events in a problem situation dualistically, for example as right versus wrong (Blanchard-Fields, 1986b; Labouvie-Vief, 1992; Perry, 1970). More mature thinking, defined as a relativistic orientation (the ability to perceive and coordinate multiple perspectives), would result in more interactive attributions. However, the greater use of dispositional attributions by older adults suggests that, in some cases, they also overemphasized dispositional information, a fundamental attribution error.

To further examine this issue, Blanchard-Fields and Norris (1994) also examined dialectical attributional processing in adolescence through older adulthood using a qualitative analysis. They found that middle-aged adults scored higher than adolescents, youth, and younger and older adults on dialectical attributional reasoning (considering dispositional and situational factors in relation to each other, mutually determined and codefined). However, older adults (in particular older women) and adolescents scored lowest on dialectical reasoning. The authors took a sociocultural schema perspective in explaining why older adults (a) were more

predisposed to making the dispositional attributions (also found in the study above) and (b) engaged in less dialectical reasoning in negative relationship situations.

Social schemas are easily accessible knowledge structures that consist of a set of interrelated propositions (including rules on how to operate in particular social situations and inferred traits of an individual given a particular social situation) about a category of self, other, or events. They can reflect individualized and normative goals that guide future behavior (Cantor, 1990). Post hoc analyses revealed that social schemas appeared to be evoked as a function of the value-laden content of several of the vignettes. These social schemas may have been particularly salient for older adults, given their years of accumulated experience, stage in life, and the particular cohort in which they were socialized. Furthermore, previous work on aging suggests that the relationship between information schemas and judgments is particularly strong in older adults (Hess & Follett, 1994; Reder, Wible, & Martin, 1986).

## D. Cognitive Appraisal, Emotion, and Cognitive Strategies

Other research explores cognitive appraisal, social beliefs, and emotion in relation to effective functioning in older adults. This area of research examines cognition as an antecedent (in the form of cognitive appraisals, attributions, and belief systems) in relation to both emotion and such outcomes as everyday problem solving, coping, helping behavior, and social preferences.

There is a body of research exploring the relationship of problem-solving style and emotional salience to type of problem situation. Research indicates that older adults use a variety of strategies as a function of the type of issues they are addressing (Blanchard-Fields & Camp, 1990; Cornelius & Caspi, 1987). In interpersonal problem domains that are high in emotional salience (e.g., family and relationships)—as opposed to other domains that are lower in emotional salience (consumer, home management)—older adults displayed an awareness of when to avoid, passively accept, or use more instrumental modes of responding (Blanchard-Fields, Jahnke, & Camp, 1995). Younger adults opted more for a problem-focused or cognitive-analytical approach to all problems. These findings suggest that the relation between emotional salience and problem-solving style is moderated by age-related differences in perceived emotional involvement in the situation.

A number of studies document the relationship between cognitive appraisal and emotion (e.g., Manstead & Tetlock, 1989; Roseman, 1984; Smith & Ellsworth, 1985; Weiner, 1986). Although limited, there has been work examining whether or not changes in the relations between cognitive appraisal and emotion occur in adulthood and aging. Rather than simply focusing on the relationship between cognitive appraisal and emotion, Weiner and his colleagues (Weiner, 1986; Weiner & Graham, 1989) elaborated on the cognitive-emotion-action linkage and suggested that emotion plays a mediating role in the relationship between causal attributions and specific types of action. Overall, they found that elicited affect (degree of pity or anger) mediated the relationship between ratings of causal control and the intended helping behavior. In addition, they found that the elderly reported less anger (and more pity) than younger participants, yet were more willing to help a person in need, regardless of the cause of the need. Weiner and Graham (1989) concluded that linkages between emotion, thinking, and behavior remain stable in healthy older adults, accompanied by an increase in social concerns and tolerance.

This situation-specific conceptualization of affective expression is further ex-

emplified in the work on cognitive appraisal, emotion, and coping. Similar to Weiner and his colleagues, Folkman and Lazarus (1988) demonstrated a relationship between elicited emotion and intended action in the form of coping. Four different styles of coping (planful problem solving, positive reappraisal, confrontive coping, and distancing) were associated with changes in four types of emotions (disgust/anger, pleasure/happiness, confidence, and worry/fear).

In addition, age differences moderated the relationship between elicited emotion and coping. Whereas young adults' use of positive reappraisal was related to a decrease in feelings of disgust and anger and an increase in pleasure and confidence, older adults' use of positive reappraisal was associated with an increase in worry and fear. Young adults' use of confrontive coping was associated with an increase in disgust and anger, whereas older adults' use of confrontive coping was not related to any positive or negative emotions. Folkman and Lazarus explained these results in terms of young and old having different methods of coping or in terms of developmental and life changes affecting coping efficacy. Older adults might be more temperate with respect to negative emotional affect or might have developed their interpersonal skills in such a way that social support is more effective for them.

This explanation is further supported by the work of Carstensen (1992; Frederickson & Carstensen, 1990). She finds that reductions in social contact in older adults serve an adaptive role and reflect social preferences. Older adults appraise and construct their environment to maximize social and emotional gains and minimize social and emotional risks. Changes in older adults' interaction patterns are selective in that they maintain emotionally close relationships and relinquish less important relationships.

A number of issues are addressed in the domain of causal attributions and problem appraisal. First, age-related differences in representations of events (e.g., social schemas) are important influences on social cognitive functioning. Second, situational or context variation and emotion in changing life contexts also play a particularly salient role in social cognitive reasoning. Finally, sociocultural factors influence the above relationships by constraining life contexts, which in turn color an individual's interpretation (appraisal, attribution) of ongoing situations or problems. Sociocultural factors also play a major role in social schemas about others. The majority of research in this area has addressed negative stereotypes individuals possess about older adults.

## E. Attributions of Competency and Cognitive Performance

The majority of research examining stereotyping and attributions about older adults has been descriptive in nature, focusing on age-related differences in these belief systems. For example, Heckhausen, Dixon, and Baltes (1989) found that, in comparison to young and middle-aged adults, older adults were more differentiated in their expectations of desirable and undesirable changes across the life span. They viewed both a greater number of attributes as associated with adult development and aging and also more potential for change throughout adulthood. Similarly, both Brewer and Lui (1984) and Hummert, Garstka, Shaner, and Strahm (1994) reported that older adults have more differentiated knowledge representations of the elderly than younger adults due to the increased relevance of specific social roles found in later adulthood (Brewer & Lui, 1984). Finally, older adults also saw desirable changes in later life as more controllable than the younger age groups (Heckhausen & Baltes, 1991).

A few studies have examined the influence of social stereotypes of aging on behavior. For example, Erber and her col-

leagues (Erber, 1989; Erber, Etheart, & Szuchman, 1992; Erber, Szuchman, & Etheart, 1993) assessed evaluations of older adults in a specific domain, memory competence, and related these evaluations to subsequent social judgments. Erber assessed competence appraisals of young and old targets made by younger and older adults using a person-perception procedure (evaluating a person on competency based on a written description). A general finding across all studies suggested that there is an age-based double standard. Young adults rate everyday memory failure as more serious if experienced by an older target than by a younger target, whereas older adults rate young and old targets more equivalently. The generally negative bias toward the elderly was characterized by attributions to older targets of greater mental difficulty, need for memory training, and need for evaluation. Younger targets' memory failures were attributed to lack of effort or attention.

The influence of such perceptions on social judgment was measured by asking participants to assign older and younger adults to easy or difficult tasks after listening to a taped interview characterized by varying degrees of memory failures. This analysis produced different results (Erber et al., 1992): Both younger and older adults assigned tasks equally to younger and older targets irrespective of the target's level of forgetfulness. When individualized information was provided by the taped interviews, age played less of a focal role.

Erber et al. (1993) extended these findings by placing the memory appraisals in a social context of "neighborly interactions." Young adults were asked to rate how likely they would choose a certain type of neighbor (described in a vignette) to perform a memory task and then to rate the young and old target neighbors on desirable and relevant traits specific to performing memory tasks. Young adult raters chose unforgetful over forgetful neighbors, and older over young neighbors regardless of their forgetfulness. In addition, older neighbors were rated more highly on positive traits (e.g., dependability) than younger neighbors. These results speak not only to the importance of individuating information, but also to the importance of social aspects—not simply cognitive competence—involved in person perception within a specific context (e.g., neighborly interactions).

From this research it becomes clear that a multidimensional and contextual model of perceived competency and of evaluations is critical. When the evaluation is placed in a social context a more complete understanding of the nature of the evaluation is revealed. Although competency may be rated low, other factors (e.g., the demands of the context or situation) may override these concerns or simply interact with these concerns in an individual's evaluation of and decision to work with, associate with, or depend on an older adult.

## IV. Schemas about Self

From a social cognitive perspective, self-knowledge serves as an organizing influence on cognitive processes such as interpretation of information (e.g., about events, tasks, and others) and self-regulation. For example, Hess (1994) indicated that self-schemas have an impact on memory in terms of what is remembered about others and any type of self-relevant information (e.g., Kihlström et al., 1988; Mueller, Wonderlich, & Dugan, 1986). Age differences in cognitive processes and other behaviors may be partly explained through motivational and representational consequences of change in self-structure (Hess, 1994).

Recent theoretical discussions by Cantor provide a good illustration of research and perspectives on changes in self-structure with aging and the effect of these changes on behavior. Cantor (1990) sug-

gested that although broad dispositional or personality attributes (e.g., temperament) may remain relatively constant across the life span (McCrae & Costa, 1988), self-constructs or knowledge structures that influence the method for expressing any disposition (i.e., content of self-schemas) may change with changing demands in one's life context.

Along these lines, Markus and her colleagues (Cross & Markus, 1991; Markus & Herzog, 1991; Markus & Nurius, 1986) have demonstrated developmental changes in self-schemas and possible selves (personalized representations of future self states). They also suggested that possible selves guide future behavior and provide an interpretive context for current behavior. In a study comparing possible selves in younger and older adults, Cross and Markus (1991) found that older adults not only reported a more limited range of self categories along with fewer hoped for and feared possible selves, but also reported engaging in more actions to accomplish the goals defined by their possible selves. The older adults' possible selves were tied more closely to ongoing experience, whereas the self-goals of younger adults were situated more in the future and were more idealistic in nature. The result was less conflict between unrealized goals for older adults. Finally, age variations in content of possible selves reflected a greater emphasis on family and occupation for younger adults and on physical and personal goals for older adults. Similarly, Hooker (1992) found that older adults were more likely to report possible selves in the health domain than college students.

Such variations in self-structure have major implications for the functional significance of behavior in everyday settings. Representations of self have an impact on self-regulatory strategies, memory, decision making, coping, and psychological adjustment. However, the majority of the research has been conducted at a global level of defining self (e.g., using global categories such as family or health). More empirical work is needed on (a) developing more tightly defined domain-specific assessments of social schemas and, most importantly, (b) the relationship between operationally defined social schemas and various performance outcomes.

An area of research that takes this functional perspective on self-schemas involves self-perception and actual health behavior (as opposed to perceptions of health). Leventhal and his colleagues (E. A. Leventhal, Leventhal, Schaefer, & Easterling, 1993; H. Leventhal, Diefenbach, & Leventhal, 1992), for example, demonstrated how self-appraisals of age-related reductions in resources of physical and psychological energy affect the way an individual appraises illness risks and need for care, resulting in either a positive outcome (e.g., rapid care seeking and adherence to medical treatment) or negative outcome (e.g., avoiding health promotive exercise because it is erroneously viewed as draining or damaging resources). Another self-appraisal affecting health behavior is the perception of self as extremely sensitive. The "sensitive soma" has been shown to affect diet and use of medication (H. Leventhal et al., 1992). This line of research provides a good illustration of how current research is linking self-schemas to functional outcomes. However, not only a wider range of health behaviors, but also the influence of self-schemas on other domains of functional significance in older adults should be explored.

## V. Conclusion

The recent proliferation of research on social cognition and aging suggests that there are age-related changes in social knowledge and beliefs about others, oneself, and everyday events. Furthermore, the functional significance of social cognitive variables for behavior in context is demonstrated in areas such as coping with stress, everyday problem solving, health domains, and social partner selection. Important context variables identified in this chapter include (1) those external to the individual, such as the task and social-cultural-historical contexts; (2) those internal to the individual (social schemas, goals, and motivational characteristics); and (3) the interface between sociocultural context and social knowledge structures (e.g., cohort membership and schemas for relationships; age-related stereotypes and judgments of competency; life stage and perceptions of self).

A social cognitive approach adds to our understanding of changes in behavior throughout adulthood and old age by centering attention on cognitive functions and mechanisms with respect to social everyday functioning. Social cognitive research links social or everyday functioning to individual differences in emotional and motivational appraisal (e.g., the influence of self-perception on health behavior or interpersonal relationships).

This approach also suggests that there are significant qualitative changes in the content and structure of people's social knowledge structures with increasing age. However, social knowledge representations have been primarily descriptive in nature. We must also understand the functional significance of social representations for behavior. We find that age-related changes in social representations influence memory, attributional judgments, selection of problem-solving strategies, and judgments of cognitive competence. However, we need more information on (a) the universality of such changes, (b) which contexts age-related deficits are likely to occur in, and (c) how social knowledge may change qualitatively and adaptively across the life span.

Finally, a number of other limitations in the research still need to be addressed. First, there is a need for new research agendas with new empirical paradigms in order to move research on social cognition and aging forward. Second, an individual-differences approach to the study of social cognition promises to advance the field by acknowledging that the probabilistic association of age with social cognitive functioning can be influenced and even moderated by a host of relevant variables (e.g., beliefs, attitudes, ego level). Third, social cognition also needs to be studied as a social process (i.e., in the context of group processes, dyadic interactions, etc.). Finally, more research on emotional development in adulthood is needed, given that these changes result in differences in interpretation of social situations and problems as well as in strategy preferences. Although complex models of emotion and cognition have begun to emerge, there has been little application to research on aging.

## References

Adams, C., Smith, M. C., Gaden, C. P., & Perlmutter, M. (1994). *Memory in a storytelling context: A story recalled by young and old adults.* Unpublished manuscript.

Baltes, P. B., Dittmann-Kohli, F., & Dixon, R. A. (1984). New perspectives on the development of intelligence in adulthood: Toward a dual-process conception and a model of selective optimization with compensation. In P. B. Baltes & O. G. Brim, Jr. (Eds.), *Life-span development and behavior* (Vol. 6, pp. 33–76). New York: Academic Press.

Baltes, P. B., & Smith, J. (1990). Toward a psychology of wisdom and its ontogenesis. In R. J. Sternberg (Ed.), *Wisdom: Its nature, origins, and development* (pp. 87–120). New York: Cambridge University Press.

Berg, C., & Klaczynski, P. A. (in press). Practical intelligence and problem solving: Searching for perspectives. In F. Blanchard-Fields & T. M. Hess (Eds.), *Perspectives on cognitive change in adulthood and aging.* New York: McGraw-Hill.

Berg, C., Klaczynski, P., Calderone, K., & Strough, J. (1994). Adult age differences in cognitive strategies: Adaptive or deficient? In J. Sinnott (Ed.), *Handbook of adult lifespan learning* (pp. 371–388). Westport, CT: Greenwood.

Blanchard-Fields, F. (1986a). Attributional processes in adult development. *Educational Gerontology, 12,* 291–300.

Blanchard-Fields, F. (1986b). Reasoning on social dilemmas varying in emotional saliency: An adult developmental perspective. *Psychology and Aging, 1,* 325–333.

Blanchard-Fields, F. (1994). Age differences in causal attributions from an adult developmental perspective. *Journal of Gerontology: Psychological Sciences, 49,* P43–P51.

Blanchard-Fields, F., & Camp, C. J. (1990). Affect, individual differences, and real world problem solving across the adult life span. In T. M. Hess (Ed.), *Aging and cognition: Knowledge organization and utilization* (pp. 461–497). Amsterdam: Elsevier/North Holland.

Blanchard-Fields, F., Jahnke, H., & Camp, C. (1995). Age differences in problem solving style: The role of emotional salience. *Psychology and Aging, 10,* 173–180.

Blanchard-Fields, F., & Norris, L. (1994). Causal attributions from adolescence through adulthood: Age differences, ego level, and generalized response style. *Aging and Cognition, 1,* 67–86.

Blank, T. O. (1987). Attributions as dynamic elements in a lifespan social psychology. In R. P. Abeles (Ed.), *Life-span perspectives and social psychology* (pp. 61–84). Hillsdale, NJ: Erlbaum.

Bower, G. H. (1978). Experiments on story comprehension and recall. *Discourse Processes, 1,* 211–231.

Bower, G. H. (1981). Mood and memory. *American Psychologist, 36*(2), 129–148.

Bower, G. H., Black, J. B., & Turner T. J. (1979). Scripts in memory for text. *Cognitive Psychology, 11,* 177–220.

Brewer, M. B., & Lui, L. (1984). Categorization of the elderly by the elderly: Effects of perceiver's category membership. *Personality and Social Psychology Bulletin, 10,* 585–595.

Cantor, N. (1990). From thought to behavior: "Having" and "doing" in the study of personality and cognition. *American Psychologist, 45,* 735–750.

Carstensen, L. L. (1992). Selectivity theory: Social activity in life-span context. *Annual Review of Gerontology and Geriatrics, 11,* 195–217.

Chinen, A. B. (1989). *In the ever after: Fairy tales and the second half of life*. Wilmette, IL: Chiron.

Cornelius, S. W., & Caspi, A. (1987). Everyday problem solving in adulthood and old age. *Psychology and Aging, 2*, 144–153.

Cross, S., & Markus, H. (1991). Possible selves across the lifespan. *Human Development, 34*, 230–255.

Dixon, R. A. (1992). Contextual approaches to adult intellectual development. In R. J. Sternberg & C. A. Berg (Eds.), *Intellectual development* (pp. 350–380). New York: Cambridge University Press.

Erber, J. T. (1989). Young and older adults' appraisal of memory failures in young and older adult target persons. *Journal of Gerontology: Psychological Sciences, 44*, P170–P175.

Erber, J. T., Etheart, M. E., & Szuchman, L. T. (1992). Age and forgetfulness: Perceivers' impressions of targets' capability. *Psychology and Aging, 7*, 479–483.

Erber, J. T., Szuchman, L. T., & Etheart, M. E. (1993). Age and forgetfulness: Young perceivers' impressions of young and old neighbors. *International Journal of Aging and Human Development, 37*, 91–103.

Fiske, S. T. (1993). Social cognition and social perception. *Annual Review of Psychology, 44*, 155–194.

Folkman, S., & Lazarus, R. (1988). Coping as a mediator of emotion. *Journal of Personality and Social Psychology, 54*, 466–475.

Frederickson, B. L., & Carstensen, L. L. (1990). Choosing social partners: How old age and anticipated endings make people more selective. *Psychology and Aging, 5*, 163–171.

Georgoudi, M. (1985). Dialectics in attribution research: A reevaluation of the dispositional-situational causal dichotomy. *Journal of Personality and Social Psychology, 49*, 1678–1691.

Heckhausen, J., & Baltes, P. (1991). Perceived controllability of expected psychological change across adulthood and old age. *Journal of Gerontology: Psychological Sciences, 46*, P165–P173.

Heckhausen, J., Dixon, R. A., & Baltes, P. B. (1989). Gains and losses in development throughout adulthood as perceived by different age groups. *Developmental Psychology, 25*, 109–121.

Hess, T. M. (1992). Adult age differences in script content and structure. In R. West & J. Sinnott (Eds.), *Everyday memory and aging* (pp. 87–100). New York: Springer-Verlag.

Hess, T. M. (1994). Social cognition in adulthood: Aging-related changes in knowledge and processing mechanisms. *Developmental Review, 14*, 373–412.

Hess, T. M., Donley, J., & Vandermaas, M. O. (1989). Aging-related changes in the processing and retention of script information. *Experimental Aging Research, 15*, 89–96.

Hess, T. M., & Follett, K. J. (1994). Adult age differences in the use of schematic and episodic information in making social judgments. *Aging and Cognition, 1*, 54–66.

Hess, T. M., & Pullen, S. M. (1994). Adult age differences in impression change processes. *Psychology and Aging, 9*, 237–250.

Hess, T. M., & Tate, C. S. (1992). Direct and indirect assessments of memory for script-based narratives in young and older adults. *Cognitive Development, 7*, 467–484.

Hess, T. M., Vandermaas, M. O., Donley, J., & Snyder, S. S. (1987). Memory for sex-role consistent and inconsistent actions in young and old adults. *Journal of Gerontology, 43*, 505–511.

Hooker, K. (1992). Possible selves and perceived health in older adults and college students. *Journal of Gerontology: Psychological Sciences, 47*, P85–P95.

Hummert, M. L., Garstka, T. A., Shaner, J. L., & Strahm, S. (1994). Stereotypes of the elderly held by young, middle-aged, and elderly adults. *Journal of Gerontology: Psychological Sciences, 49*, P240–P249.

Kihlström, J., Cantor, N., Albright, J. S., Chew, B. R., Klein, S. B., & Niedenthal, P. M. (1988). Information processing and the study of the self. In L. Berkowitz (Ed.), *Advances in experimental social psychology* (Vol. 21, pp. 145–178). San Diego, CA: Academic Press.

Klaczynski, P. A., & Berg, C. A. (1992, April). *What's the real problem: Age, perceived control, and perceived difficulty as predictors of everyday problem definitions*. Paper presented at the Cognitive Aging Conference, Atlanta, GA.

Labouvie-Vief, G. (1992). A neo-Piagetian perspective on adult cognitive development. In R. J. Sternberg & C. A. Berg (Eds.), *Intellectual development* (pp. 197–228). New York: Cambridge University Press.

Lazarus, R. S., & Folkman, S. (1984). *Stress, appraisal, and coping.* New York: Springer.

Leventhal, E. A., Leventhal, H., Schaefer, P., & Easterling, D. (1993). Conservation of energy, uncertainty reduction, and swift utilization of medical care among the elderly. *Journal of Gerontology: Psychological Sciences,* 48, P78–P86.

Leventhal, H., Diefenbach, M., & Leventhal, E. A. (1992). Illness cognition: Using common sense to understand treatment adherence and affect cognition interaction. *Cognitive Therapy and Research,* 16, 143–163.

Light, L. L., & Anderson, P. A. (1983). Memory for scripts in young and older adults. *Memory & Cognition,* 11, 435–444.

Manstead, A. S. R., & Tetlock, P. E. (1989). Cognitive appraisals and emotional experience: Further evidence. *Cognition and Emotion,* 3, 225–240.

Markus, H., & Herzog, R. (1991). The role of self-concept in aging. *Annual Review of Gerontology and Geriatrics,* 11, pp. 110–143.

Markus, H., & Nurius, P. (1986). Possible selves. *American Psychologist,* 41, 954–969.

McCrae, R. R., & Costa, P. T. (1988). Age, personality, and the spontaneous self-concept. *Journal of Gerontology: Social Sciences,* 43, S177–S185.

Mergler, N., & Goldstein, M. D. (1983). Why are there old people? Senescence as biological and cultural preparedness for the transmission of information. *Human Development,* 26, 72–90.

Mueller, J. H., Wonderlich, S., & Dugan, K. (1986). Self-referent processing of age-specific material. *Psychology and Aging,* 1, 293–299.

Nisbett, R., & Ross, L. (1980). *Human inference: Strategies and shortcomings of social judgment.* Englewood Cliffs, NJ: Prentice-Hall.

Perry, W. (1970). *Forms of intellectual and ethical development in the college years.* New York: Holt, Rinehart, & Winston.

Pichert, J. W., & Anderson, R. C. (1977). Taking different perspectives on a story. *Journal of Educational Psychology,* 69, 309–315.

Reder, L. M., Wible, C., & Martin, J. (1986). Differential memory changes with age: Exact retrieval versus plausible inference. *Journal of Experimental Psychology: Learning, Memory, and Cognition,* 12, 72–81.

Roseman, I. (1984). Cognitive determinants of emotions: A structural theory. In P. Shaver (Ed.), *Review of personality and social psychology: Emotions, relationships, and health* (Vol. 5, pp. 11–36). Beverly Hills, CA: Sage.

Ross, B. L., & Berg, C. (1992). Examining idiosyncrasies in script reports across the life span: Distortions or derivations of experience. In R. West & J. Sinnott (Eds.), *Everyday memory and aging* (pp. 39–53). New York: Springer-Verlag.

Sansone, C., & Berg, C. (1993). Adapting to the environment across the life span: Different process or different inputs? *International Journal of Behavioral Development,* 16, 215–241.

Schank, R. C., & Abelson, R. (1977). *Scripts, plans, goals, and understanding.* Hillsdale, NJ: Erlbaum.

Sears, D. O. (1987). Implications of the life-span approach for research on attitudes and social cognition. In R. P. Abeles (Ed.), *Life-span perspectives and social psychology* (pp. 17–60). Hillsdale, NJ: Erlbaum.

Smith, C. A., & Ellsworth, P. C. (1985). Patterns of cognitive appraisal in emotion. *Journal of Personality and Social Psychology,* 48, 813–838.

Weiner, B. (1986). *An attributional theory of motivation and emotion.* New York: Springer.

Weiner, B., & Graham, S. (1989). Understanding the motivational role of affect: Life-span research from an attributional perspective. *Cognition and Emotion,* 3(4), 401–419.

Wyer, R. S., Jr., & Srull, T. K. (1989). *Memory and cognition in its social context.* Hillsdale, NJ: Erlbaum.

# Nine

# Religion, Spirituality, and Aging

Susan H. McFadden

## I. Introduction

Although religion is an enduring characteristic of human behavior, issues of religion and spirituality have not been widely addressed in gerontology. A review of research in three major gerontology journals from 1985 to 1991 found that of 2127 quantitative studies, 78 contained a religious variable. Only 14 used a multidimensional measure of religion (Sherrill, Larson, & Greenwold, 1993).

This situation is perplexing, because aging elicits many of the existential questions that religion has traditionally sought to answer. Also, national surveys indicate that older adults attach a high value to their religious beliefs and behaviors. According to Gallup Polls conducted by the Princeton Religion Research Center (PRRC) (1994), 76% of persons 65 and older declare that religion is very important and 16% describe it as fairly important in their lives. This is particularly true of ethnic and minority elders, who show a high degree of religious involvement (Jackson, Antonucci, & Gibson, 1990; Levin, Taylor, & Chatters, 1994). According to survey responses of older persons, over one-half (52%) attend religious services weekly (PRRC, 1994); nearly one-quarter pray at least three times a day; 27% read the Bible two to three times a week or more; and 64% watch religious television programs (PRRC, 1987).

This high level of religious behavior among older people points to the need for gerontological research on religion, but why should spirituality be included in a discussion of human aging? Answers to this question range from critiques of the materialistic perspectives of biomedical approaches to aging (Cole, 1992) to the observations of a pastoral counselor who has witnessed the despair of elders experiencing spiritual crises of meaning (Kimble, 1995). Increasingly, persons working in applied areas of gerontology are calling for acknowledgment of spiritual needs in the design of interventions that attend to physical, psychological, or social needs.

With some exceptions, the behavioral sciences have paid scant attention to religion and spirituality despite their manifest importance in the lives of many mature and older persons. However, several developments in the last decade indicate that this situation is changing. There have been noticeable improvements in both the quantity and the quality of psychological research on religion (Hunsberger, 1991), although psychologists of religion still have not paid much attention to older adults. Recent developments in gerontology include the establishment of an Interest Group on Religion and Aging within the Gerontological Society of America, support from the National Institute on Aging for research on aging and religion (Levin et al., 1994), and the reporting of empirical findings in publications like the *Journal of Religious Gerontology*. These indicators of a growing interest in research on religion and spirituality point to the timeliness of this review, the first review on the topic in the four editions of the *Handbook of the Psychology of Aging*.

This chapter begins by examining several thorny problems of definition, measurement, sampling, and research design. It then reviews findings to date about the effects of religion and spirituality on phenomena associated with aging well. Next, it presents developmental perspectives on late-life religion and spirituality. Because this is a new area of study, suggestions for future research appear throughout the chapter; the last two sections address further implications for research.

## II. Methodological Issues

### A. Definitions and Measures

Perusal of recent books and papers on the psychology of religion reveals a vexing problem: There is no scholarly consensus about definitions and measures of religion and spirituality. Yinger once wrote that "any definition of religion is likely to be satisfactory only to its author" (1967, p. 18). Similarly, in introducing an edited book with 13 chapters on the religious dimension in aging, Moody (1994) commented that there were as many definitions of spirituality as there were authors.

### 1. Religion

In general, the scientific study of religion employs two types of definition: substantive and functional (Berger, 1974). Substantive approaches to defining religion focus on the belief in a numinous dimension of experience and on efforts to relate the human to the divine. Functional definitions emphasize religion's role in providing meaning in the face of the unknown and its stabilizing effects upon social groups. Substantive definitions depict religiosity as an end in itself, whereas functional definitions portray religion as a means to some end, be it social control or psychological succor. In psychology, these perspectives have been associated with two types of religious motivation: intrinsic and extrinsic religiosity (Allport, 1966; Allport & Ross, 1967).

Because of its many research applications (Gorsuch, 1988), Allport's model of religiosity has been widely studied and criticized (Donahue, 1985; Kahoe, 1985; Kirkpatrick & Hood, 1990). For example, Pargament (1992) argued that by polarizing religious means and ends, researchers have distorted the very phenomenon they are trying to study. He suggested that religion be defined as "a search for significance in ways related to the sacred" (Pargament, 1992, p. 204). In both its personal and social dimensions, religion provides signposts describing pathways to significance. From a gerontological perspective, this image of religion as a means to an end emphasizes the strategies religion offers for responding to the exigencies of later life. However, religion also portrays the ends of the search for significance; its narratives, symbols, rituals, and belief structures depict "destinations of significance" (Pargament, 1992, p. 207). For many older persons, religion provides meaning that transcends suffering, loss, and the sure knowledge that death looms somewhere on the horizon.

Although debates over definitions will

doubtless continue in the psychology and philosophy of religion, psychologists who conduct research on religion have shown little interest in agreeing upon a universally acceptable definition (Gorsuch, 1988). Instead, most conclude that religion is multifaceted and they seek to understand how aspects of religion relate to various psychological functions and behavioral outcomes.

A multidimensional model of religion requires researchers to employ instruments that assess both subjective experience as well as the many forms of religious belief and behavior. Research on religion and aging that includes only a measure of church or synagogue attendance has been criticized for omitting important nonorganizational aspects of religious behavior (Ainlay & Smith, 1984; Mindel & Vaughan, 1978). The Springfield Religiosity Schedule (SRS) developed by Koenig for use with older persons (Koenig, Smiley, & Gonzales, 1988) acknowledges the complexity of religion by including measures of the four major dimensions of religiosity described by Glock and Stark (1965): belief, ritual (both organizational and nonorganizational religious activities), experience, and religious knowledge. In addition, the SRS contains several items from the religion subscale of the Spiritual Well-Being Scale (SWBS) (Paloutzian & Ellison, 1982). It also incorporates Hoge's (1972) intrinsic religiosity scale in order to assess the subjective domain of religious belief and practice.

Instruments like the SRS are important because they express the differentiated nature of religion and thus are useful in refining research questions utilizing religion either as a dependent or an independent variable. For example, with religion as a dependent variable, one might hypothesize that cognitive complexity partially explains the variance in religious belief structures, but not private religious behaviors like prayer. Conversely, measures of organized religious participation may not

predict levels of death anxiety as well as assessments of specific religious beliefs.

Because of the diversity of religious beliefs and the ways they differentially affect behavior, psychologists of religion (Gorsuch, 1988; Wulff, 1991) and gerontologists (Levin & Vanderpool, 1987) have challenged researchers to develop measures sensitive to varying religious beliefs. Illustrating the need for this, a study of the use of prayer in coping with illness showed a significant difference between elderly Baptists and non-Baptists in their reports of prayer in response to physical symptoms; Baptists also expressed significantly more agreement with the idea that illness can be a God-given test of faith or punishment for sin (Bearon & Koenig, 1990). This is but one example of the need to examine beliefs in order to understand the health behaviors of older adults more fully. In addition, how an elder conceives of the deity—as a "higher power," as aloof and unconcerned about humanity, as vengefully demanding retribution for human failings, or as lovingly valuing human life—can affect the way that individual responds to stressful life situations (Maton, 1989; Pargament, 1990).

## 2. Spirituality

Presently, considerable theoretical ferment is arising in discussions of aging and spirituality, largely because of disagreements over the relation of spirituality to religion. One way of resolving this dilemma psychologically is to view spirituality as the motivational and emotional foundation of the lifelong quest for meaning. This approach is strongly suggested by the work of Victor Frankl (1959), who depicted spirituality as the human drive for meaning and purpose. This motivation can be associated with a variety of experiences in which emotions signal a sense of connectedness or integration. When people speak of spiritual experiences of God, they are describing a felt connection perceived as meaningful. Likewise, a spiritual experience in nature is associated with emotions signaling unity and transcendence of ordinary subject-versus-object distinctions. Experiences of spiritual connections with others and within memory and imagination are also signaled by emotion.

Many of these experiences of spirituality lie outside the realm of religion, both in substance and function. Thus, spirituality cannot be equated with religion. However, as Pargament (1992) noted, religion provides many people with the narratives, symbols, rituals, and beliefs that not only guide the quest for meaning but also illuminate a destination of ultimate meaning.

Viewing spirituality, like religion, as multifaceted has implications for how it will be studied in the lives of older persons. The influences on the form spirituality takes in later life are unknown, as are the differential outcomes that may ensue from preference for one spiritual pathway over another. Research on these questions has important practical implications. For example, a long-term-care resident might be unimpressed with the availability of chapel services but feel spiritually impoverished if prevented from making contact with nature or art. Because psychologists have only recently begun to consider dimensions of spirituality apart from religious beliefs and behaviors, few assessment tools exist. Ellor and his associates have developed an assessment of the spiritual needs of older persons using a structured interview (Bracki, Thibault, Netting, & Ellor, 1990; Ellor & Bracki, 1995; Thibault, Ellor, & Netting, 1991). This approach is particularly useful for clergy, social workers, nurses, and others working in applied settings with elders. Its applicability to research has not been demonstrated.

A widely used measure that claims to tap aspects of spirituality is the SWBS developed by Paloutzian and Ellison (1982). Utilizing Moberg and Brusek's (1978) suggestion that spiritual well-being consists of two dimensions—a vertical dimension reaching to God and a horizontal dimension extending through ordinary life experiences—Paloutzian and Ellison designed the SWBS to incorporate a subscale of religious well-being and another of existential well-being. Although no norms for older adults exist for the SWBS, research utilizing samples of young and middle-aged adults has found that it shows good reliability and validity as an overall assessment of well-being (Bufford, Paloutzian, & Ellison, 1991). However, a study of hospice caregivers whose mean age was 62.3 years found little support for the validity of this instrument for use with an older population (Kirschling & Pittman, 1989).

The very idea of measuring so ineffable a human quality as spirituality probably strikes many as problematic. Other approaches, such as in-depth interviews with older persons, have revealed insights into the way a sense of spirituality promotes creativity (Bianchi, 1994), concern for others (Rubinstein, 1994), and hopefulness amidst the daily trials of life in a nursing home (Gubrium, 1993).

## B. Sampling

Given the many ways older persons are motivated to seek meaning, research on religion and spirituality in later life has been criticized for selecting samples of convenience that are biased in favor of certain religious traditions (Levin & Tobin, 1995) and geographical locations. Recent PRRC data indicate that 47% of adults in the South attend religious services regularly as compared to 33% in the West (PRRC, 1994). Koenig's pioneering research on religion and aging has been primarily conducted with samples from Missouri, Illinois, Iowa, and North Carolina; he has repeatedly called for studies utilizing samples from other regions to test the generalizability of his findings.

Samples that include a disproportionate

number of older women also need to be carefully scrutinized because research has consistently noted that older women display significantly higher levels of religiosity (Koenig, Kvale, & Ferrel, 1988; Levin et al., 1994). Compared to men, women rate religious activities as significantly more meaningful (Reker, 1988) and are significantly more likely to report religious coping (Koenig, Siegler, Meador, & George, 1990).

Finally, researchers should be cautious in drawing conclusions about religion, spirituality, and aging based upon samples made up of middle-class Whites. Care needs to be taken in disentangling the effects of religion, ethnicity, and social class. For example, studies show high levels of both organizational and nonorganizational religious activity among elderly Blacks (Chatters, Levin, & Taylor, 1992; Chatters & Taylor, 1989; Taylor & Chatters, 1991), whose churches offer both formal and informal support (Taylor & Chatters, 1986) to those in need. Among Hispanic elders, the Catholic church has been shown to be the most important social institution in their communities, and their religious faith has been called their most significant source of psychological support (Maldonado, 1995). Whether the Catholic faith functions differently in the lives of elders of varying racial, ethnic, and class backgrounds remains to be determined.

## C. Designs and Methods

Research on religion and spirituality in later life has been largely cross-sectional in design, often employing poorly designed measures and limited samples. Efforts to understand whether aging produces a greater level of organizational, nonorganizational, and subjective religiosity must account for the age-cohort-period problem. Today's elders were socialized into the religious life in the first half of the twentieth century, a time of high rates of active membership and participation in religious institutions (Payne, 1988). More complex designs that include longitudinal analysis are needed to address the perennial question of whether people become more religious or more spiritually aware (or both) as they age (Section IV). In addition, research that employs national probability samples, empirical evaluation of theoretical models, control for the effects of demographic variables, and structural-equation modeling promises to provide insights into important issues, such as the extent to which religious involvement acts as a stress buffer in older persons. A good example of this approach is the research of Krause and Tran (1989), which revealed that increased religious involvement counterbalances the negative effects of stress.

The empirical research methods favored by gerontologists have been criticized as limited in their ability to depict both the journeys aging adults take in pursuit of meaning and also the outcomes of these journeys (Thomas & Eisenhandler, 1994). Given the multidimensionality of religion and the ways humans experience it, as well as the complexity of human lives with their diverse, dynamic interactions of biological, psychological, and social forces across time, some suggest that the goal of studying religion, spirituality, and aging ought to be limited to understanding rather than explanation (Thomas, 1989). For example, qualitative analyses of older adults' poetry, stories, and discussions of art, music, and literature (Eisenhandler, 1994) sometimes reveal themes of religion and spirituality.

By now, gerontologists have a wealth of information that could be submitted to secondary analysis in order to detect references to religious and spiritual issues that were not noted in the original study. Archived interview transcripts and surveys could be reanalyzed to explore how spiritual experiences and religious commitments influence the organization of older adults' behavior. Through secondary analysis, researchers might discover that themes of religion and spirituality have formed a subtext in much of their work.

## III. Religion, Spirituality, and Aging Well

### A. Describing the Relationship

In calling for an epidemiology of religion, Levin noted that since the nineteenth century over 200 empirical studies have demonstrated a positive association between religion and various health indicators such as hypertension and cancer (Levin, 1994a; Levin & Vanderpool, 1987, 1992). Many of these studies employ cross-sectional designs, include primarily uncontrolled or bivariate analyses, and provide few insights into explanatory mechanisms. Nevertheless, Levin has proposed that assessment of the evidence in terms of consistency, plausibility, and analogy points in the direction of a causal relationship between religiosity and health (Levin, 1994b). Levin also observed that studies of greater health among older persons who regularly participate in organized religious activities are problematic to the extent that increased disability and poor health in later life might prevent such participation. Thus, religious attendance by older individuals may be a proxy for better functional health (Levin, 1989).

Studies of older adults' mental health indicate that religious beliefs, attitudes, and coping behaviors contribute to higher levels of adjustment as indexed by levels of depression, suicide rates, anxiety, and alcohol abuse (Idler & Kasl, 1992; Koenig, 1990; Krause, 1991). Further study of explanatory mechanisms is warranted given the complex, multidimensional nature of religion and the diversity of religious beliefs.

George and Clipp (1991) suggested that research on older adults' physical and mental health as well as their subjective well-being has tended to portray them as passively responding to life circumstances rather than as actively construing a meaningful existence. By employing spiritual and religious resources, older persons may experience their lives as meaningful even in the face of multiple, serious challenges to satisfaction with life (Tellis-Nayak, 1982; Wong, 1989). Careful study of the ways aging persons secure a sense of meaningfulness represents a major challenge for psychologists trying to understand the complex and sometimes paradoxical nature of aging well. Although research findings of the last quarter century point to salutary effects of religion, further research is needed on the effects of apathy about religious and spiritual matters as well as the effects of nonreligious and nonspiritual perspectives on life's meaning.

### B. Religious Coping

Aging presents humans with an accumulation of burdens at the same time that certain internal and external resources are diminished (Birren, 1988). Older adults must employ strategies for coping with a wide variety of demands, and the strategy they spontaneously mention most often is religious (Koenig, George, & Siegler, 1988). Manfredi and Pickett (1987) found that prayer is the coping strategy most frequently used by older persons. Asked to rate coping effectiveness, adults participating in the Baltimore Longitudinal Study of Aging selected faith as the most effective out of a list of 27 possibilities (McCrae & Costa, 1986).

More generally, the construct *spiritual support* is emerging in the literature on coping; it includes seeking pastoral care, participation in organizational and nonorganizational religious activities, and expressing faith in a God believed to care for humankind. People experiencing high levels of stress report more favorable well-being in conjunction with high levels of spiritual support (Maton, 1989; Wright,

Pratt, & Schmall, 1985). Psychologists must now determine when and why older adults turn to these types of coping responses, how effective they experience them to be, and how this approach to coping shapes and is shaped by images of the aging self.

In addition, researchers need to learn whether certain personality characteristics predict greater efficacy of religious belief and practice in coping with stress. In the only study to date to examine personality traits and religious coping in later life, nonreligious and religious copers did not differ in personality traits (Koenig et al., 1990). The authors cautiously concluded that "personality does not appear to play a major role in whether an older adult does or does not employ religious coping strategies to deal with stress" (p. 128). However, they also suggested that adherence to a religious worldview from early childhood could "affect the development of personality, moderating certain traits while stimulating the development of others" (p. 123).

The Project on Religion and Coping organized by Pargament and his colleagues has provided much useful information about the complexities of religious coping, including the observation that it may be deleterious to well-being (Pargament, Van Haitsma, & Ensing, 1995). Pargament urged researchers to pay attention to individual differences in their studies of religious coping for three reasons: (a) religious coping might help some persons more than others; (b) different kinds of problems may be more amenable to religious coping; and (c) certain types of religious coping may be more effective than others. In addition, Pargament noted that increased age may result in the need to change religious coping styles. Some individuals may abandon an active, self-directing coping style that assumes God grants people agency to solve problems, and substitute a deferring style in which the individual waits upon God's grace (Pargament et al., 1988).

The literature on well-being and coping presents a generally positive view of the role of religion in later life. However, one wonders how many studies never reached publication due to negative results. Regardless of the many findings on the positive relation between religion, well-being, and coping, it seems appropriate that researchers also consider the "seamy side" of religious coping (Pruyser, 1991), in which the freedom to confront stressors creatively is constricted by rigid belief systems.

## IV. Religious and Spiritual Development

### A. Do People Become More Religious as They Age?

The metaphor of the pathway is an ancient and rich description of the experience of human development across the life span. Fairy tales (Chinen, 1989b), drama (Kastenbaum, 1994), and other forms of narrative reveal the mapping strategies, choice points, sharp and startling turns, surprising vistas, and encounters with fellow travelers that characterize this journey. Many people tacitly assume that as the journey reaches its end, the signposts offered by religion become increasingly important to the traveler seeking to understand pathways followed, abandoned, or never selected.

Social scientists have found that evidence on the question of whether people grow more religious with age is mixed. Cross-sectional studies using multiple measures of religiosity have shown that although declining health and transportation difficulties may lower organizational religious participation, nonorganizational activities remain salient and their practice may even increase (Ainlay, Singleton, & Swigert, 1992; Ainlay & Smith, 1984; Mindel & Vaughan, 1978). A well-known longitudinal study revealed that religious activities decline with age, but positive religious attitudes remain stable (Blazer & Palmore, 1976). Other longitudinal data suggest that aging persons do not change their accustomed pathways to significance by turning to religion (Markides, 1983), specific religious beliefs and attitudes show little change (Shand, 1990), and the effects of religion on life satisfaction do not increase with age (Markides, Levin, & Ray, 1987). Additionally, the importance individuals attach to religion as they age may be less a function of aging than of their degree of religious commitment (Hunsberger, 1985; Young & Dowling, 1987).

Whether older people experience this stability of religiosity through adulthood as positive remains to be determined. One study that inquired about how people would change the amount of time spent on various activities through adulthood found that 54.1% of older people said they would not change the amount of time devoted to religion, but 35.2% indicated they would devote more time to religion; only 1.6% said they would devote less time (DeGenova, 1992). More research is needed to learn why some older people might regret having given little attention to religion through adulthood.

## B. Developmental Trajectories

Although research on adult religiosity presents a portrait of stability (Reich, 1992), it is possible that it has not been sensitive enough to individual differences that might produce change. For example, processes of change are implied in James Fowler's (1981) theory of faith development, which suggests that certain individuals reconstitute their beliefs and commitments as they grow older. In his study of older persons, Shulik (1988) found high correlations among measures of faith development, ego development, and moral development, leading him to suggest that there is a central process of development viewed from different perspectives by structural-developmental theorists.

It is also possible that cognitive development drives aspects of religious development, producing maturity in religious judgments made in response to religious dilemmas (Oser, 1991; Oser & Gmünder, 1991) and in the ways people construe their patterns of meaning making (Fowler, 1981). Employing a Piagetian paradigm, Oser's theory of the development of religious judgment and Fowler's theory of faith development both focus upon the logical, analytical character of formal operational thinking as the most advanced way of making religious judgments and of considering issues of faith. It has been suggested, however, that these theories would benefit from incorporation of recent insights of psychologists studying the relativistic, self-referential, intuitive nature of postformal thinking (Reich, 1993).

In addition, the work of Labouvie-Vief suggests that aging produces changes in people's modes of knowing and that older adults undergo a developmental shift that produces a greater ability to integrate cognitive and emotional perspectives (Labouvie-Vief, 1990; Labouvie-Vief & Hakim-Larson, 1989). Older persons' increased comfort with metaphor and subjectivity has been observed in their narrative interpretations (Labouvie-Vief, DeVoe, & Bulka, 1989). This might explain Oser and Gmünder's findings about older adults' responses to religious dilemmas of choice between conflicting values. Oser and Gmünder interpreted their data as indicating an "age-related regression" in religious judgment, but what they called regression may instead have been evidence of a more mature mode of knowing (1991, p. 186). Because their coding scheme is based upon a cognitive approach that claims development produces increasing levels of analytic sophistication, it may be insensitive to the turn toward subjectivity and affect evidenced by many older people.

Older adults have received little attention from psychologists studying religious development. The emphasis upon cognitive factors has coincided with the desire to apply insights from research on religious development to the religious education of youth. Clearly, new approaches are needed in order to understand possibilities for religious development in later life. Such approaches would pay attention to emotion.

Future research also needs to assess whether the stability of adult religiosity is to some degree an artifact of the research methods used to investigate it. Specifically, standardized instruments may not be as effective as in-depth interviews in elucidating the religious trajectories of older persons (Thun, cited in Reich, 1992). In other words, possibilities for both change and stability need to be investigated in the study of religious development in old age. In addition, research is needed on influences that shape individual differences in religious development.

Some people may remain stable in their belief or unbelief either because they are satisfied with the role of religion in their lives or because they are unmotivated to change. Perhaps they are "cognitively impoverished and rigid" (Kastenbaum, 1993, p. 180), thus unable to contemplate the mysteries and paradoxes religion sets before them. Their stability might also be explained by examining their needs for attachment, as the dynamics of attachment have been shown to figure prominently in religious development (Kirkpatrick, 1992). On the other hand, some older persons may experience an increase in religious commitment in later life due to an awakening to new combinations of thoughts and feelings. Still others may find that religious development brings a rejection of long-held religious beliefs and practices that overemphasize a logical, analytical stance toward religion (Wulff, 1993). Movement toward a more reflective, emotionally shaped attitude toward religion—an attitude comfortable with mystery and uncertainty—can diminish the need for adherence to specific dogmas and forms of piety (Birren, 1990; Pruyser, 1987).

Researchers need to determine whether changes in modes of knowing have the same effects upon men's and women's religious development. Given the repeated findings of higher levels of religiosity in the present cohort of older women (Section II.B), it is important to examine the effects of gender on religious development in later life. A recent review of the literature on Fowler's (1981) theory of faith development as applied to aging men found no major gender differences, although men appear to experience a more uneven trajectory of faith development (Payne, 1994); this observation requires further research scrutiny.

Future study of religious development in later life holds much promise. It should incorporate insights from the developmental psychology of cognition and of emotion, address explanatory mechanisms for stability and change, employ longitudinal designs, and examine both individual differences and normative trends.

## C. Spiritual Development

Observations of an age-related shift to an "intuitive, unitary mode of thinking" (Chinen, 1989a, p. 50) has prompted speculation that there may be a spiritual element in emerging research on cognition in late life. Specifically, theoretical and empirical work on postformal thinking has investigated elder wisdom, unitative states of consciousness, transcendence, and awareness of multiple realities, all of which point in the direction of spirituality. Although some believe that spiritual development is noncognitive and therefore should not be linked with postformal cognitive styles (Koplowitz, 1990), others urge empirical investigation into the convergence of spiritual and cognitive development (Sinnott, 1994).

Sinnott (1994) suggested that psychologists should locate persons actively engaged in spiritual questing and study their memory, problem solving, and logic to see if they are operating at a postformal level of thought. Conversely, he urged researchers to test the hypothesis that cognitive skill "allows the unitative state to be *conscious* and reportable" (p. 96). Recognizing the perils awaiting empirical psychologists who approach the issue of spirituality, Sinnott nevertheless stated it is possible to conduct "innovative and 'clean' research on cognitive aspects of spiritual development" (p. 97).

## V. Future Directions for Research

Given the importance of religion for many older adults and the ways spirituality motivates people to seek meaning, it is now reasonable to suggest that religion and spirituality variables be included in future studies of aging. For example, the report of the Vitality for Life Committee of the Human Capital Initiative contains many research questions that could be better framed if religious and spiritual issues were studied (Human Capital Initiative Coordinating Committee [HCICC], 1993). The committee stated the need for more information about the "relationships among age, beliefs, and illness outcomes" (HCICC, 1993, p. 8), and yet it did not suggest research on religion as a possible strategy for pain management or as an influence upon the conceptualization of illness.

Although aspects of religiosity will continue to appear as independent variables in research on differential outcomes in older people's lives, research should also attend to religious and spiritual orientations and experiences as dependent variables, particularly in studies of influences on development. In addition, there is a continuing need for well-designed qualitative studies of religion, spirituality, and aging. These approaches can reveal the stories behind the numbers in quantitative research.

Psychologists need to learn more about the dimensionality of religion and spirituality in adults of all ages. For example, researchers could identify the dimensions people employ in making judgments about persons they evaluate as high or low in religiosity or spirituality. Comparisons of these dimensions for young, middle-aged, and older adults could then indicate whether age affects perceptions of other persons' presentations of themselves as religious or spiritual.

Most research—both quantitative and qualitative—conducted on religion, spirituality, and aging has focused upon community-dwelling, cognitively intact elders. However, there is much yet to be learned from persons suffering from various forms of dementia. This is particularly true if emotion is acknowledged as a key factor influencing religious behaviors and spiritual experiences of meaningful connection with others, the environment, and God. Conversely, the effects of religious activities upon emotion should be investigated.

Persons with Alzheimer's disease are capable of experiencing and communicating emotional experiences (Jansson, Norbert, Sandman, Athlin, & Asplund, 1992–1993). They also do not appear to be impaired in their ability to perceive facial expression of emotion (Albert, Cohen, & Koff, 1991). There is considerable anecdotal evidence from chaplains in long-term-care facilities that persons with dementing illnesses respond positively to religious services and spiritual care (Friedman, 1995; Richards & Seicol, 1991). Clearly, there are important implications here for both research and improving the care given to these persons and their families.

## VI. Conclusion

Psychologists who study aging should pay closer attention to religion and spirituality not only because these areas are of theoretical and practical importance, but also because they stimulate reformulations of questions about aging and its meaning for individuals and societies. For example,

Chinen (1989b) depicted the mediating roles of certain wise elders who link "youth to transcendent realities and practical realities" (p. 112). Similarly, Gutmann (1985) observed that in traditional cultures elders function as bridgeheads to the sacred. As Achenbaum (1985) suggested, increased awareness of the religious and spiritual dimensions of aging could support changes in social attitudes that would make it possible for older adults to contribute more meaningfully to their communities.

On an individual level, the study of religion and spirituality directs psychologists toward a more holistic approach to the phenomenal structure of human lives. Throughout much of its history, psychology has dealt with elemental processes and has avoided complex—and controversial—phenomena like religion and spirituality. Furthermore, in observing only objective indicators of behavior, psychologists have sometimes portrayed humans as passively reactive to their environments. This approach is particularly problematic in studies of aging persons because it supports common stereotypes about the old.

An alternative view regards humans as strategic decision makers who actively coordinate internal representations of the world with external behaviors (Birren, 1988). For example, older people may recognize that religious involvement produces an increase in both the quantity and quality of social ties (Ellison & George, 1994) and thus decide to optimize their emotional connections with others through organizational religious involvement. This selective optimization, a phenomenon noted even among the very old (Lang & Carstensen, 1994), may also explain the nonorganizational religious behaviors of aging persons. Just as organizational religious involvement can be interpreted as a strategic approach to the maintenance of emotional connections with others, older persons' nonorganizational behaviors may

represent proactive efforts to retain emotional ties with God.

Older persons' religious beliefs along with behaviors like public worship, private prayer and meditation, and multiple approaches to nurturing spirituality not only represent adaptive efforts at self regulation, but also express acknowledgement of a sense of ultimate meaning and purpose. For those who decide to investigate these complex human phenomena, many challenges lie ahead in formulating good questions and selecting appropriate methods. Although the antipathy of psychology to the inclusion of religion and spirituality in research on human behavior is slowly fading, researchers may continue to encounter obstacles in persuading others of the importance and legitimacy of their work (Sherrill & Larson, 1994). Nevertheless, the emerging study of religion and spirituality promises to stimulate new thinking about many of the persistent problems in the psychology of aging.

## References

Achenbaum, W. A. (1985). Religion in the lives of the elderly: Contemporary and historical perspectives. In G. Lesnof-Caravaglia (Ed.), *Values, ethics, and aging* (Vol. 4, pp. 98–115). New York: Human Sciences Press.

Ainlay, S. C., Singleton, R., & Swigert, V. L. (1992). Aging and religious participation: Reconsidering the effects of health. *Journal for the Scientific Study of Religion, 31*, 175–188.

Ainlay, S. C., & Smith, D. R. (1984). Aging and religious participation. *Journal of Gerontology, 39*, 357–363.

Albert, M. S., Cohen, C., & Koff, E. (1991). Perception of affect in patients with dementia of the Alzheimer type. *Archives of Neurology (Chicago), 48*, 791–795.

Allport, G. W. (1966). The religious context of prejudice. *Journal for the Scientific Study of Religion, 5*, 447–457.

Allport, G. W., & Ross, J. M. (1967). Personal religious orientation and prejudice. *Journal of Personality and Social Psychology, 5*, 432–443.

Bearon, L., & Koenig, H. G. (1990). Religious

cognitions and use of prayer in health and illness. *Gerontologist, 30,* 249–253.

Berger, P. L. (1974). Some second thoughts on substantive versus functional definitions of religion. *Journal for the Scientific Study of Religion, 13,* 125–133.

Bianchi, E. (1994). *Elder wisdom: Crafting your own elderhood.* New York: Crossroad.

Birren, J. E. (1988). A contribution to the theory of the psychology of aging: As a counterpart of development. In J. E. Birren & V. L. Bengtson (Eds.), *Emergent theories of aging* (pp. 153–176). New York: Springer.

Birren, J. E. (1990). Spiritual maturity in psychological development. In J. J. Seeber (Ed.), *Spiritual maturity in the later years* (pp. 41–53). New York: Haworth.

Blazer, D., & Palmore, E. (1976). Religion and aging in a longitudinal panel. *Gerontologist, 16,* 82–85.

Bracki, M. A., Thibault, J. M., Netting, F. E., & Ellor, J. W. (1990). Principles of integrating spiritual assessment into counseling with older adults. *Generations, 14,* 55–58.

Bufford, R. K., Paloutzian, R. F., & Ellison, C. W. (1991). Norms for the Spiritual Well-Being Scale. *Journal of Psychology and Theology, 19,* 56–70.

Chatters, L. M., Levin, J. S., & Taylor, R. J. (1992). Antecedents and dimensions of religious involvement among older black adults. *Journal of Gerontology: Social Sciences, 47,* S269–S278.

Chatters, L. M., & Taylor, R. J. (1989). Age differences in religious participation among black adults. *Journal of Gerontology: Social Sciences, 44,* S183–S189.

Chinen, A. B. (1989a). From quantitative to qualitative reasoning: A developmental perspective. In L. E. Thomas (Ed.), *Research on adulthood and aging: The human science approach* (pp. 37–61). Albany: State University of New York Press.

Chinen, A. B. (1989b). *In the ever after: Fairy tales and the second half of life.* Wilmette, IL: Chiron Publications.

Cole, T. R. (1992). *The journey of life: A cultural history of aging in America.* Cambridge, England: Cambridge University Press.

DeGenova, M. K. (1992). If you had your life to live over again: What would you do differently? *International Journal of Aging and Human Development, 34,* 135–143.

Donahue, M. J. (1985). Intrinsic and extrinsic religiousness: Review and meta-analysis. *Journal of Personality and Social Psychology, 48,* 400–419.

Eisenhandler, S. A. (1994). A social milieu for spirituality in the lives of older adults. In L. E. Thomas & S. A. Eisenhandler (Eds.), *Aging and the religious dimension* (pp. 133–145). Westport, CT: Auburn House.

Ellison, C. G., & George, L. K. (1994). Religious involvement, social ties, and social support in a southeastern community. *Journal for the Scientific Study of Religion, 33,* 46–61.

Ellor, J. W., & Bracki, M. A. (1995). Assessment, referral and networking in pastoral care. In M. Kimble, S. H. McFadden, J. W. Ellor, & J. J. Seeber (Eds.), *Aging, spirituality, and religion: A handbook* (pp. 148–160). Minneapolis, MN: Fortress Press.

Fowler, J. W. (1981). *Stages of faith.* San Francisco: Harper & Row.

Frankl, V. (1959). *Man's search for meaning.* Boston: Beacon Press.

Friedman, D. (1995). A life of celebration, meaning, and connection: Facilitating religious life in long-term institutions. In M. Kimble, S. McFadden, J. Ellor, & J. Seeber (Eds.), *Aging, spirituality, and religion: A handbook* (pp. 362–373). Minneapolis, MN: Fortress Press.

George, L. K., & Clipp, E. C. (1991). Subjective components of aging well. *Generations, 15,* 57–60.

Glock, C. Y., & Stark, R. (1965). *Religion and society in tension.* Chicago: Rand McNally.

Gorsuch, R. L. (1988). Psychology of religion. *Annual Review of Psychology, 39,* 201–221.

Gubrium, J. F. (1993). *Speaking of life.* New York: de Gruyter.

Gutmann, D. (1985). Culture and mental health in later life. In J. E. Birren, R. B. Sloane, & G. D. Cohen (Eds.), *Handbook of mental health and aging* (2nd ed., pp. 75–97). San Diego, CA: Academic Press.

Hoge, D. R. (1972). A validated intrinsic religious motivation scale. *Journal for the Scientific Study of Religion, 11,* 369–376.

Human Capital Initiative Coordinating Committee (HCICC). (1993, December). HCI report 2: Vitality for life [Special issue]. *American Psychological Society Observer.*

Hunsberger, B. (1985). Religion, age, life satisfaction, and perceived sources of religiousness: A study of older persons. *Journal of Gerontology, 40*, 615–620.

Hunsberger, B. (1991). Empirical work in the psychology of religion. *Canadian Psychology, 32*, 497–504.

Idler, E. L., & Kasl, S. V. (1992). Religion, disability, depression, and the timing of death. *American Journal of Sociology, 97*, 1052–1079.

Jackson, J. S., Antonucci, T. C., & Gibson, R. C. (1990). Cultural, racial, and ethnic minority influences on aging. In J. E. Birren & K. W. Schaie (Eds.), *Handbook of the psychology of aging* (3rd ed., pp. 103–123). San Diego, CA: Academic Press.

Jansson, L., Norbert, A., Sandman, P., Athlin, E., & Asplund, K. (1992–1993). Interpreting facial expressions in patients in the terminal stage of the alzheimer disease. *Omega, 26*, 309–324.

Kahoe, R. D. (1985). The development of intrinsic and extrinsic religious orientations. *Journal for the Scientific Study of Religion, 24*, 408–412.

Kastenbaum, R. (1993). Encrusted elders: Arizona and the political spirit of postmodern aging. In T. R. Cole, W. A. Achenbaum, P. L. Jakobi, & R. Kastenbaum (Eds.), *Voices and visions of aging: Toward a critical gerontology* (pp. 160–183). New York: Springer.

Kastenbaum, R. (1994). *Defining acts: Aging as drama*. Amityville, NY: Baywood Publishing.

Kimble, M. A. (1995). Pastoral care with the aging. In M. A. Kimble, S. H. McFadden, J. W. Ellor, & J. J. Seeber (Eds.), *Aging, spirituality, and religion: A handbook* (pp. 131–147). Minneapolis, MN: Fortress Press.

Kirkpatrick, L. A. (1992). An attachment-theory proposal to the psychology of religion. *International Journal for the Psychology of Religion, 2*, 3–28.

Kirkpatrick, L. A., & Hood, R. W., Jr. (1990). Intrinsic-extrinsic religious orientation: The boon or bane of contemporary psychology of religion? *Journal for the Scientific Study of Religion, 29*, 442–462.

Kirschling, J. M., & Pittman, J. F. (1989). Measurement of spiritual well-being: A hospice caregiver sample. *The Hospice Journal, 5*, 1–11.

Koenig, H. G. (1990). Research on religion and mental health in later life: A review and commentary. *Journal of Geriatric Psychiatry, 23*, 23–53.

Koenig, H. G., George, L. K., & Siegler, I. C. (1988). The use of religion and other emotion-regulating coping strategies among older adults. *Gerontologist, 28*, 303–310.

Koenig, H. G., Kvale, J. N., & Ferrel, C. (1988). Religion and well-being in later life. *Gerontologist, 28*, 18–28.

Koenig, H. G., Siegler, I. C., Meador, K. G., & George, L. K. (1990). Religious coping and personality in later life. *International Journal of Geriatric Psychiatry, 5*, 123–131.

Koenig, H. G., Smiley, M., & Gonzales, J. A. P. (1988). *Religion, health, and aging*. New York: Greenwood Press.

Koplowitz, H. (1990). Unitary consciousness and the highest development of mind: The relation between spiritual development and cognitive development. In M. L. Commons, C. Armon, L. Kohlberg, F. A. Richards, T. A. Grotzer, & J. D. Sinnott (Eds.), *Adult development: Vol. 2. Models and methods in the study of adolescent and adult thought* (pp. 105–111). New York: Praeger.

Krause, N. (1991). Stress, religiosity, and abstinence from alcohol. *Psychology and Aging, 6*, 134–144.

Krause, N., & Tran, T. V. (1989). Stress and religious involvement among older Blacks. *Journal of Gerontology: Social Sciences, 44*, S4–S13.

Labouvie-Vief, G. (1990). Modes of knowledge and the organization of development. In M. L. Commons, C. Armon, L. Kohlberg, F. A. Richards, T. A. Grotzer, & J. D. Sinnott (Eds.), *Adult development: Vol 2. Models and methods in the study of adolescent and adult thought* (pp. 43–62). New York: Praeger.

Labouvie-Vief, G., DeVoe, M., & Bulka, D. (1989). Speaking about feelings: Conceptions of emotion across the life span. *Psychology and Aging, 4*, 425–437.

Labouvie-Vief, G., & Hakim-Larson, J. (1989). Developmental shifts in adult thought. In S. Hunter & M. Sundel (Eds.), *Midlife myths: Issues, findings, and practice implications* (pp. 69–96). Newbury Park, CA: Sage.

Lang, F. R., & Carstensen, L. L. (1994). Close emotional relationships in late life: Further support for proactive aging in the social domain. *Psychology and Aging, 9*, 315–524.

Levin, J. S. (1989). Religious factors in aging, adjustment, and health: A theoretical overview. In W. M. Clements (Ed.), *Religion, aging and health: A global perspective* (pp. 133–146). New York: Haworth.

Levin, J. S. (1994a). Introduction: Religion in aging and health. In J. S. Levin (Ed.), *Religion in aging and health* (pp. xv-xxiv). Thousand Oaks, CA: Sage.

Levin, J. S. (1994b). Religion and health: Is there an association, is it valid, and is it causal? *Social Science and Medicine, 38,* 1475–1482.

Levin, J. S., Taylor, R. J., & Chatters, L. M. (1994). Race and gender differences in religiosity among older adults: Findings from four national surveys. *Journal of Gerontology: Social Sciences, 49,* S137–S145.

Levin, J. S., & Tobin, S. S. (1995). Religion and psychological well-being. In M. A. Kimble, S. H. McFadden, J. W. Ellor, & J. J. Seeber (Eds.), *Aging, spirituality, and religion: A handbook* (pp. 30–46). Minneapolis, MN: Fortress Press.

Levin, J. S., & Vanderpool, H. Y. (1987). Is frequent religious attendance *really* conducive to better health?: Toward an epidemiology of religion. *Social Science and Medicine, 24,* 589–600.

Levin, J. S., & Vanderpool, H. Y. (1992). Religious factors in physical health and the prevention of illness. In K. I. Pargament, K. I. Maton, & R. E. Hess (Eds.), *Religion and prevention in mental health: Research, vision, and action* (pp. 83–103). New York: Haworth.

Maldonado, D. (1995). Religion and racial/ethnic minority elderly populations. In M. A. Kimble, S. H. McFadden, J. W. Ellor, & J. J. Seeber (Eds.), *Aging, spirituality, and religion: A handbook.* Minneapolis, MN: Fortress Press.

Manfredi, C., & Pickett, M. (1987). Perceived stressful situations and coping strategies utilized by the elderly. *Journal of Community Health Nursing, 4,* 99–110.

Markides, K. S. (1983). Aging, religiosity, and adjustment: A longitudinal analysis. *Journal of Gerontology, 38,* 621–625.

Markides, K. S., Levin, J. S., & Ray, L. A. (1987). Religion, aging, and life satisfaction: An eight-year, three-wave longitudinal study. *Gerontologist, 27,* 660–665.

Maton, K. I. (1989). The stress-buffering role of spiritual support: Cross-sectional and prospective investigations. *Journal for the Scientific Study of Religion, 28,* 310–323.

McCrae, R. R., & Costa, P. T., Jr. (1986). Personality, coping, and coping effectiveness in an adult sample. *Journal of Personality, 54,* 385–405.

Mindel, C. H., & Vaughan, C. E. (1978). A multidimensional approach to religiosity and disengagement. *Journal of Gerontology, 33,* 103–108.

Moberg, D. O., & Brusek, P. M. (1978). Spiritual well-being: A neglected subject in quality of life research. *Social Indicators Research, 5,* 303–323.

Moody, H. R. (1994). Foreword: The owl of Minerva. In L. E. Thomas & S. A. Eisenhandler (Eds.), *Aging and the religious dimension* (pp. ix-xv). Westport, CT: Auburn House.

Oser, F. K. (1991). The development of religious judgment. In F. K. Oser & W. G. Scarlett (Eds.), *Religious development in childhood and adolescence* (pp. 5–25). San Francisco: Jossey-Bass.

Oser, F. K., & Gmünder, P. (1991). *Religious judgement: A developmental approach.* Birmingham, AL: Religious Education Press.

Paloutzian, R. G., & Ellison, C. W. (1982). Loneliness, spiritual well-being, and quality of life. In A. Peplau & D. Perlman (Eds.), *Loneliness: A sourcebook of current theory, research and therapy* (pp. 224–237). New York: Wiley.

Pargament, K. I. (1990). God help me: Toward a theoretical framework of coping for the psychology of religion. *Research in the Social Scientific Study of Religion, 2,* 195–244.

Pargament, K. I. (1992). Of means and ends: Religion and the search for significance. *International Journal for the Psychology of Religion, 2,* 201–229.

Pargament, K. I., Kennell, J., Hathaway, W., Grevengoed, N., Newman, J., & Jones, W. (1988). Religion and the problem-solving process: Three styles of coping. *Journal for the Scientific Study of Religion, 27,* 90–104.

Pargament, K. I., Van Haitsma, K., & Ensing, D. S. (1995). When age meets adversity: Religion and coping in the later years. In M. A. Kimble, S. H. McFadden, J. W. Ellor, & J. J. Seeber (Eds.), *Aging, spirituality, and religion: A handbook* (pp. 47–67). Minneapolis, MN: Fortress Press.

Payne, B. P. (1988). Religious patterns and participation of older adults: A sociological perspective. *Educational Gerontology, 14,* 255–267.

Payne, B. P. (1994). Faith development in older men. In E. H. Thompson, Jr. (Ed.), *Older men's lives* (pp. 85–103). Thousand Oaks, CA: Sage.

Princeton Religion Research Center (PRRC). (1987). *Religion in America.* Princeton, NJ: Gallup Poll.

Princeton Religion Research Center (PRRC). (1994). Importance of religion. *PRRC Emerging Trends, 16,* 4.

Pruyser, P. W. (1987). Where do we go from here? Scenarios for the psychology of religion. *Journal for the Scientific Study of Religion, 26,* 173–181.

Pruyser, P. W. (1991). The seamy side of current religious beliefs. In H. N. Malony & B. Spilka (Eds.), *Religion in psychodynamic perspective: The contributions of Paul W. Pruyser* (pp. 47–65). New York: Oxford University Press.

Reich, K. H. (1992). Religious development across the life span: Conventional and cognitive developmental approaches. In D. L. Featherman, R. M. Lerner, & M. Perlmutter (Eds.), *Life span development and behavior* (pp. 145–188). Hillsdale, NJ: Erlbaum.

Reich, K. H. (1993). Cognitive developmental approaches to religiousness: Which version for which purpose? *International Journal for the Psychology of Religion, 3,* 145–171.

Reker, G. T. (1988, November). *Sources of personal meaning among young, middle-aged and older adults: A replication.* Paper presented at the annual meeting of the Gerontological Society of America, San Francisco.

Richards, M., & Seicol, S. (1991). The challenge of maintaining spiritual connectedness for persons institutionalized with dementia. *Journal of Religious Gerontology, 7,* 27–40.

Rubinstein, R. L. (1994). Generativity as pragmatic spirituality. In L. E. Thomas & S. A. Eisenhandler (Eds.), *Aging and the religious dimension* (pp. 169–181). Westport, CT: Auburn House.

Shand, J. D. (1990). A forty year follow-up of the religious beliefs and attitudes of a sample of Amherst College grads. *Research in the Social Scientific Study of Religion, 2,* 117–136.

Sherrill, K. A., & Larson, D. B. (1994). The anti-tenure factor in religious research in clinical epidemiology and aging. In J. S. Levin (Ed.), *Religion in aging and health* (pp. 149–177). Thousand Oaks, CA: Sage.

Sherrill, K. A., Larson, D. B., & Greenwold, M. (1993). Is religion taboo in gerontology? Systematic review of research on religion in three major gerontology journals, 1985–1991. *American Journal of Geriatric Psychiatry, 1,* 109–117.

Shulik, R. N. (1988). Faith development in older adults. *Educational Gerontology, 14,* 291–301.

Sinnott, J. D. (1994). Development and yearning: Cognitive aspects of spiritual development. *Journal of Adult Development, 1,* 91–99.

Taylor, R. J., & Chatters, L. M. (1986). Church-based informal support among elderly blacks. *Gerontologist, 26,* 637–642.

Taylor, R. J., & Chatters, L. M. (1991). Nonorganizational religious participation among elderly black adults. *Journal of Gerontology: Social Sciences, 46,* S103–S111.

Tellis-Nayak, V. (1982). The transcendent standard: The religious ethos of the rural elderly. *Gerontologist, 22,* 359–363.

Thibault, J. M., Ellor, J. W., & Netting, F. W. (1991). A conceptual framework for assessing the spiritual functioning and fulfillment of older adults in long-term care settings. *Journal of Religious Gerontology, 7,* 29–45.

Thomas, L. E. (1989). The human science approach to understanding adulthood and aging. In L. E. Thomas (Ed.), *Research on adulthood and aging: The human science approach* (pp. 1–7). Albany: State University of New York Press.

Thomas, L. E., & Eisenhandler, S. A. (1994). Introduction: A human science perspective on aging and the religious dimension. In L. E. Thomas & S. A. Eisenhandler (Eds.), *Aging and the religious dimension* (pp. xvii–xxi). Westport, CT: Auburn House.

Wong, P. T. P. (1989). Personal meaning and successful aging. *Canadian Psychology, 30,* 516–525.

Wright, S. D., Pratt, C. C., & Schmall, V. L. (1985). Spiritual support for caregivers of dementia patients. *Journal of Religion and Health, 24,* 31–38.

Wulff, D. M. (1991). *Psychology of religion: Classic and contemporary views.* New York: Wiley.

Wulff, D. M. (1993). On the origins and goals of religious development. *International Journal for the Psychology of Religion, 3,* 181–186.

Yinger, J. M. (1967). Pluralism, religion, and secularism. *Journal for the Scientific Study of Religion, 6,* 17–28.

Young, G., & Dowling, W. (1987). Dimensions of religiosity in old age: Accounting for variation in types of participation. *Journal of Gerontology, 42,* 376–380.

# Part Three

# Behavioral Processes

Ten

# Visual and Auditory Aging

Donald W. Kline and Charles T. Scialfa

## I. Introduction

Even in the absence of pathology, age-related visual and auditory losses can adversely affect performance on daily tasks (e.g., Kline et al., 1992; Kosnik, Winslow, Kline, Rasinski, & Sekuler, 1988; Rumsey, 1993; Slawinski, Hartel, & Kline, 1993). This review of visual and auditory aging research emphasizes studies published since the third edition of the *Handbook of the Psychology of Aging*. For additional information on these topics, the reader is referred to other recent reviews (e.g., Corso, 1987; Fozard, 1990; Garzia & Trick, 1992; Kline, 1991; Owsley & Sloane, 1990; Schieber, 1992; Spear, 1993; Willott, 1991).

## II. Aging and Vision

Due to the sequential organization of the visual system, isolating the effects due to aging of higher level sensorineural functions from those attributable to earlier components (e.g., the ocular media) is a primary challenge in visual aging research. Our discussion follows the "bottom-up" order of visual processing, and where they

are known, notes the contributions of aging effects at each level to overall visual functioning.

### A. Ocular Media

#### 1. Cornea

The cornea, the primary refractive element in focusing a retinal image, thickens (Weale, 1982) and becomes more yellow with age (Lerman, 1984). There are also declines in its cell density (Wilson & Roper-Hall, 1982). Normally, the direct effects of these changes on visual functioning are negligible.

#### 2. Aqueous Humor

The aqueous humor, the clear liquid that fills the eye's anterior chamber, is the principal metabolic support for the lens. Aqueous production, a function of the ciliary body, falls with age (Kupfer, 1973), as does aqueous outflow (Linner, 1976), a change that may contribute to the increase in intraocular pressure associated with glaucoma.

### 3. Iris and Pupil

The iris adjusts the pupillary aperture to maximize the eye's depth of focus, decrease optical aberration, and control the level of light reaching the retina. Pupil size declines with adult aging (*senile miosis*), reducing retinal illuminance proportionately (e.g., Loewenfeld, 1979). This change is most pronounced and most adversely effects visual performance of older observers under low-illumination conditions (Winn, Whitaker, Elliot, & Phillips, 1994).

### 4. Lens

With age, the lens yellows, becoming thicker, less flexible (i.e., *sclerotic*), and more opaque (Kashima, Trus, Unser, Edwards, & Datiles, 1993). At least some of the increase in opacity is due to exposure to sunlight (Schein et al., 1994). Changes in the lens (Wyatt, 1993) diminish linearly its ability to adjust focus, or *accommodate* (Charman, 1989; Sun et al., 1988); this loss is virtually complete by age 60. Although the latency of accommodation changes little with age, its speed declines (Schaeffel, Wilhelm, & Zrenner, 1993), particularly under degraded viewing conditions (Elworth, Larry, & Malmström, 1986).

### 5. Vitreous Humor

Although it remains clear, the vitreous liquefies with age (Spear, 1993), a change that infrequently can lead to retinal detachment (Garzia & Trick, 1992).

### 6. The Retinal Image

Light reaching the senescent retina is attenuated, scattered, and altered spectrally (e.g., Kline, 1991). Senile miosis and lenticular opacification contribute about .3 and .2 log units, respectively, to the estimated .5-log-unit reduction in retinal illuminance from age 20 to 60 (Elliot, Whitaker, &

MacVeigh, 1990; Weale, 1961). Light scatter is increased in the older eye (Ijspeert, de Waard, van den Berg, & de Jong, 1990), reducing contrast (Block & Rosenblum, 1987) independently of refractive state and pupil size (Artal, Ferro, Miranda, & Navarro, 1993). Although light scatter has been attributed primarily to refractive inhomogeneities in the lens (Garzia & Trick, 1992), Ijspeert et al. (1990) reported considerable variability between individuals, associated in part with differences in ocular pigment.

### B. Retina

The *cones*, which operate at high-light (i.e., *photopic*) levels and are responsible for acuity and color vision, are most densely concentrated in the central 5° to 7° of the retina. In its center, the *fovea*, the most central 1°, contains only cones. *Rods*, located more eccentrically, are responsible for low-illumination (i.e., *scotopic*) sensitivity.

There is minimal age-related loss of foveal cones, but some decline has been noted in the far periphery (Curcio, Millican, Allen, & Kalina, 1993; Gao & Hollyfield, 1992). Curcio et al. (1993) reported a 30% decline in rod density near the central retina. Due to an increase in their size, the remaining rods appear to maintain a fairly constant photon capture ability. Gao and Hollyfield (1992) also found a decline in rod density by the fourth decade. *Retinal pigment epithelium* cells that provide for the metabolic needs of photoreceptors appear to decline in parallel with them, suggesting a possible causal link (Gao & Hollyfield, 1992).

C. E. Wright, Williams, Drasdo, and Harding (1985) found an age-related decrease in the light-adapted amplitude of both the a- and b-waves of the flash *electroretinogram* (ERG), suggestive of declines in cones and *bipolar* cells or *Mueller* cells, respectively. Birch and Fish (1988) observed a decline in ERG amplitude for foveal but not parafoveal flashes, the reverse of what might be expected from the anatomical evidence cited above. When Birch and Anderson (1992) assessed full-field ERGs, they found that by age 70 rod and cone amplitudes decreased to one-half those of young adults. Consistent with prior research (e.g., Elsner, Berk, Burns, & Rosenberg, 1988), this difference could not be attributed to a decline in photopigment density.

There is a decline with age in the number of retinal ganglion cell axons (e.g., Jonas, Schmidt, Muller-Bergh, Schlotzer-Schrehardt, & Naumann, 1992) which may be steeper in the periphery (Gao & Hollyfield, 1992). Curcio and Drucker (1993), however, observed a relatively uniform decline of about 25% in both the central and nasal retina. This finding is generally consistent with Grunwald, Piltz, Patel, Bose, and Riva's (1993) finding of a 20% decrease in the velocity of macular blood flow.

Few studies have evaluated age differences in the pattern-evoked ERG, which is thought to be generated by retinal ganglion cells. Trick, Trick, and Haywood (1986) found that the amplitude of the photopic pattern ERG was reduced in older observers, but unlike Celesia, Kaufman, and Cone (1987), no age difference in ERG latency was observed. Porciatti, Burr, Morrone, and Fiorentini (1992) found a reduction of about 40% in the amplitude of the photopic ERG elicited by sinusoidal gratings of varied spatial and temporal frequency. Scotopic ERGs were not examined.

## C. Visual Pathways

Named after the layers in the *lateral geniculate nucleus* (LGN) to which *retinal ganglion* cells project, two parallel pathways from the retina to the visual cortex have been identified (cf. Shapley, 1990). About 90% of ganglion cells lead to the color-sensitive *parvocellular geniculo-*

*striate* pathway responsible for detailed pattern perception; the balance contributes to the contrast-sensitive *magnocellular* pathway that is most responsive to stimulus change. Most of what is known about aging of these pathways comes from animal studies. Ahmad and Spear (1993) reported a 29% decrease in LGN magnocellular density in old monkeys, with an even greater loss (41%) in parvocellular density. In contrast, Spear (1993) found little difference between parvocellular or magnocellular neurons of young and old monkeys on a range of neurophysiological and contrast-processing measures.

## D. Visual Cortex

Contrary to the reports of earlier studies, recent research indicates that there is little decline with age in neuronal density of human or monkey *striate cortex* (e.g., Leuba & Garey, 1987; Vincent, Peters, & Tigges, 1989). However, some evidence of dendritic degeneration in the monkey striate cortex has been reported (Vincent et al., 1989).

Most studies of cortical visually evoked potentials (VEPs) indicate that the latency of the first positive component (P100) increases with age (e.g., Morrison & Reilly, 1989). Many studies, but not all, also report a reduction in P100 amplitude that is most pronounced at high spatial frequencies (e.g., Bobak, Bodis-Wollner, Guillory, & Anderson, 1989; Tomoda, Celesia, Brigell, & Toleikis, 1991) and low temporal frequencies (Porciatti et al., 1992). Their findings suggested to the latter authors that the parvocellular pathway is more greatly affected by aging.

Few studies have examined age differences beyond the primary visual cortex. The results of one that did so are fascinating. Grady et al. (1992) compared *positron emission tomography* (PET) scans of cerebral blood flow in striate and extrastriate cortex in young and elderly men as they carried out discrimination (face-matching) and spatial processing (dot location) tasks. In both groups, blood flow increased most in occipitotemporal cortex during face matching, and in superior parietal cortex during dot location. However, cortical segregation was reduced among the older participants, suggesting reduced effectiveness of the areas primarily responsible for each task.

## E. Binocular Summation

With two eyes, task performance may exceed that using one eye to a greater degree than can be accounted for by probability summation, an outcome that presumably reflects cortical integration of binocular information. Owsley and Sloane's (1990) reanalysis of the monocular and binocular contrast sensitivity data of Ross, Clarke, and Bron (1985) suggested that binocular summation is greater in young than old observers.

## F. Eye Movements and Ocular Control

Smooth-pursuit eye movements (PEMs), which enable moving objects to be tracked, show age decrements in gain, presaccadic acceleration, postsaccadic velocity, and peak velocity (e.g., Morrow & Sharpe, 1993; Zakon & Sharpe, 1987). Older adults' PEMs are also more likely to be interrupted when performing a concurrent cognitive task (Lapidot, 1987).

Declines in the pursuit system and a reduced useful field of view (see Section II.J) mean that a larger number of saccadic eye movements (SEMs) may be required for elderly observers to foveate a target. Additionally, saccadic latency increases with age (e.g., Huaman & Sharpe, 1993; Sharpe & Zackon, 1987; L. A. Whitaker, Shoptaugh, & Haywood, 1986). Peak saccadic velocity and accuracy are also reduced in the elderly (Huaman & Sharpe, 1993), a finding that may be related to atrophy of cerebral cortical neurons (Creasy & Rapoport, 1985), Purkinje cells in the cerebel-

lum (Hall, Miller, & Corsellis, 1975), and the extraocular musculature (Doig & Boylan, 1989). Fixational stability, at least up to durations of about 13 s, appears to be relatively independent of age (Kosnik, Kline, Fikre, & Sekuler, 1987).

## G. Sensitivity to Light

### 1. Dark Adaptation

Among older persons, differential absorption elevates dark adaptation thresholds for short wavelength light (see Pitts, 1982). To avoid this, Eisner, Fleming, Klein, and Mauldin (1987) used a long wavelength (660 nm) test patch to establish photopic dark adaptation functions for older observers with good acuity. A threshold elevation of 0.09 log units per decade was observed, but there was no age difference in adaptation rate.

The increase in minimum light threshold is due largely to a decline in retinal illuminance, but deficits in retinal metabolism or the neural pathways may also be involved (Weale, 1982). Coile and Baker (1992) found that photopic sensitivity and photopigment regeneration, which exhibited parallel slowing of recovery with age, were significantly correlated among individuals. Additionally, even after adjustment for the effects of senile miosis, lens opacity, and rod pigment density, Sturr, Hannon, Zhang, and Vaidya (1992) found a significant age difference in scotopic sensitivity, suggesting the involvement of postreceptor mechanisms.

### 2. Suprathreshold Contrast Discrimination

Because contrast matching at levels well above absolute threshold was not affected among observers who manifested threshold losses of spatial-frequency contrast sensitivity, Tulunay-Keesey, ver Hoeve, and Terkla-McGrane (1988) concluded that the contrast gain mechanism was less steep for old observers. Leat and Millodot (1990) arrived at a similar conclusion after finding elevated contrast discrimination thresholds among elderly observers.

### 3. Color Discrimination

With aging, color discrimination declines modestly, more so for shorter wavelengths. Knoblauch et al. (1987) found that errors on the Farnsworth-Munsell 100 Hue Test increased with age along the tritan (i.e., blue/yellow) axis, particularly under reduced illumination. Using the Lanthony New Color Test, Cooper, Ward, Gowland, and McIntosh (1991) found that the ability to discriminate desaturated blues and greens declined past age 60, followed to a lesser extent by deficits in the discrimination of reds and yellows. Eisner et al. (1987) reported that performance on a 588–nm color-matching task declined about 0.01 log units per decade, a deficit consistent with the decline in foveal cone photopigment density (Kilbride, Hutman, Fishman, & Read, 1986). Both the optic media (Weale, 1986) and sensorineural mechanisms (Werner & Steele, 1988) appear to be involved.

### 4. Glare and Glare Recovery

Aging is associated with increased susceptibility to glare (e.g., Pulling, Wolf, Sturgis, Vaillancourt, & Dolliver, 1980), and an extended recovery period after exposure to strong glare (e.g., Collins & Brown, 1989). After controlling for retinal illumination, Elliott and Whitaker (1991) found photostress recovery time increased from 20 years of age onward, and argued that aging compromises glare recovery in the macular photoreceptors, the retinal pigment epithelium, or both. Schieber and Williams (1990) compared young and old observers on the effects of strong glare on contrast sensitivity as a function of spatial frequency and rate of motion. Glare reduced sensitivity for stationary gratings

more in older adults, particularly at lower spatial frequencies. An age-related decrease was also found in the magnitude of the motion enhancement effect at low spatial frequencies, suggesting the contribution of neural mechanisms.

### H. Spatial Vision

### 1. Static Acuity

Gittings and Fozard (1986) found age changes in both uncorrected and presenting *static visual acuity* (SVA), the minimum detail that can be discriminated in stationary, high-contrast targets. Changes in the former were noticeable by age 30; those in the latter were not evident until the 70s. Similar results have been found cross-sectionally (Yang, Elliot, & Whitaker, 1993).

Age deficits in acuity are increased by low light levels. For example, Sturr, Kline, and Taub (1990) found that about 77% of drivers <65 years of age had an acuity of 20/40 or better at 2.4 cd/m²; the corresponding proportions were 28% for those 65–75, and 4% for those over 75. Sensorineural factors, in addition to a decline in retinal illuminance, appear to be involved in this loss (Weale, 1982). Acuity is improved in older observers after lens removal (Jay, Mammo, & Allan, 1987), with optical correction (e.g., Klein, Klein, Linton, & de Mets, 1991), or when the effects of the optical media are bypassed using laser interferometry to present acuity targets (Jay et al., 1987). Adams, Wong, Wong, and Gould (1988) found that the low-contrast acuity of healthy, visually screened older subjects was worse than that of young observers, even though the two groups were similar at high contrast. Owsley, Sloane, Skalka, and Jackson (1990) reported a similar finding. There is evidence that tests of acuity at low luminance and contrast might be useful in identifying the unhealthy elderly (Taub & Sturr, 1991).

Recent findings that foveal cone density is little changed with age (Curcio et al., 1993; Gao & Hollyfield, 1992) suggest neural rather than photoreceptor contributions to the diminished acuity of the elderly. One such possibility is the random loss of neurons from the retina or central pathways (Weale, 1982). Spear (1993), noting its primary role in acuity, speculated that the parvocellular pathway might decline selectively with age.

## 2. Static Spatial Contrast Sensitivity

Spatial contrast sensitivity, the ability to discern luminance differences, is typically determined for sinusoidal gratings of varied spatial frequency, and is represented by the *contrast sensitivity function* (CSF). Age-related declines on the CSF are most evident at intermediate and higher spatial frequencies (e.g., Crassini, Brown, & Bowman, 1988; Elliott, 1987; Elliott et al., 1990; Scialfa, Adams, & Giovanetto, 1991; Scialfa et al., 1988; Scialfa, Garvey, Tyrell, & Leibowitz, 1992). These losses are not attributable to "yellowing" of the cornea and lens (Kelly, Goldberg, & Banton, 1984), optical blur (Scialfa et al., 1992), or *senile miosis* (Sloane, Owsley, & Alvarez, 1988, Experiment 2). Reduced retinal illuminance appears to be involved (Owsley, Sekuler, & Siemsen, 1983), but interferometric research also implicates neural mechanisms (Elliott, 1987; Elliott et al., 1990, Experiment 2). Although Morrison and Reilly (1986) concluded that neither reduced retinal illumination nor differences in decision criteria can account for these losses, a response criterion contribution cannot be ruled out (Burton, Owsley, & Sloane, 1993; Higgins, Jaffe, Caruso, & de Monasterio, 1988).

## 3. Dynamic Acuity and Spatial Contrast Sensitivity

The inverse relation between target velocity and *dynamic visual acuity* (DVA) appears to be a consequence of a reduction in the contrast of critical details due to inadequate smooth pursuit gain (Murphy, 1978). Because retinal image motion decreases high-spatial-frequency contrast disproportionately, age deficits in PEMs should be most deleterious for such stimuli. DVA data from Burg (1966) and Reading (1972) are consistent with this. Long and Crambert (1990), however, have asserted that age-based declines in DVA are energy dependent because adjustments in target luminance eliminated age differences in threshold critical detail.

Scialfa et al. (1992) examined age differences in CSFs for static and dynamic sine-wave gratings. Older adults had higher thresholds for static gratings of intermediate and higher spatial frequency, a deficit exacerbated by motion. Inadequate smooth pursuit gain and protracted temporal summation (e.g., Royer & Gilmore, 1985) have been suggested as causal mechanisms. As well, Scialfa et al. (1988) demonstrated that age deficits in dynamic sensitivity are related directly to declines in static sensitivity.

## 4. Processing in the Visual Periphery

Although peripheral refractive error is unchanged with age (Scialfa, Leibowitz, & Gish, 1989), peripheral acuity (Collins, Brown, & Bowman, 1989) and edge detection are poorer among the elderly (Crassini et al., 1988). These findings have implications for visual search studies in which targets are often presented at some distance from fixation.

The spatial extent of visual function is most commonly assessed using the visual field test, also known as *perimetry*. Binocular visual fields (Goldman II/4e target) drop to 140° from 180° by the age of 70 years (Johnson, 1986). Loss of peripheral S-type cones is implicated by the finding that age-related field deficits are greater for short wavelength targets (Johnson, Adams, Twelker, & Quigg, 1988; Sample

& Weinreb, 1990). Johnson, Adams, and Lewis (1989) argued for a neural contribution as well, because age deficits are not reduced at very high luminance levels or with targets passed through a high-pass spectral filter. Neural mechanisms are also implicated by studies using temporal modulation perimetry (Casson, Johnson, & Nelson-Quigg, 1993).

## 5. Depth Perception

Gerontological research in depth perception has concentrated on stereopsis, the depth information available from perspective differences in the two retinal images. Although failure rates on tests of stereopsis increase with age (e.g., C. E. Wright & Wormald, 1992), stereopsis thresholds show relatively small declines (e.g., Gittings & Fozard, 1986). Greene and Madden (1987) found higher thresholds among their older participants on the Randot test, but when data were excluded from four elderly participants without measurable depth perception, the age difference was eliminated. Yekta, Pickwell, and Jenkins (1989) also found no difference in stereopsis thresholds in observers aged 10 to 65 years.

## 6. Hyperacuity

Hyperacuity, the ability to make position discriminations within a few seconds of arc, a level considerably finer than the diameter of a foveal cone (Westheimer, 1975), depends on neural integration in the visual system. Odom, Vasquez, Schwartz, and Linberg (1989) found an age-related difference in hyperacuity response bias (mean error) but not threshold (the standard deviation of adjustment). Both Lakshminarayanan, Aziz, and Enoch (1992) and D. Whitaker, Elliott, and MacVeigh (1992) found that static vernier thresholds were unaffected by age. Hypothesizing that age-related increases in ocular blur impair local feature detection, Lynk, Kline,

and Culham (1994) assessed age differences in vernier acuity as a function of feature separation. The performance of the old participants improved markedly from 0 to 3.5 min of separation, such that their thresholds were below those of the young. These findings suggest that the neural processes mediating static vernier acuity are unaffected by age. In contrast, hyperacuity tasks using temporally modulated targets show pronounced age effects. Elliott, Whitaker, and Thompson (1989) found that displacement thresholds for targets oscillating at 2 Hz more than doubled from the youngest to oldest participants. Because thresholds were independent of luminance at all but the very lowest luminance levels, the authors concluded that the age differences observed were due to neural changes. Kline, Culham, Bartel, and Lynk (1994) compared the vernier thresholds of young and old observers as a function of oscillation rate and contrast. Static displacement thresholds of both age groups were virtually identical at both high and low contrast. With oscillation, a marked age deficit emerged that increased with modulation rate, a finding that the authors interpreted as evidence for a neural decline in the temporal resolution of hyperacuity mechanisms.

## I. Temporal Resolution and Motion Perception

The senescent visual system is compromised in its ability to track stimulus change. Recent research has attempted to determine the degree to which this reflects diminished sensitivity to temporal modulation, an increase in the visual system's time constant, or both.

### 1. Flicker

Age differences in flicker sensitivity have been assessed using the *temporal contrast sensitivity* (*de Lange*) function, which determines the minimum contrast needed to

detect a light source modulated sinusoi-
dally at varied rates. Although some early
studies (e.g., Tyler, 1981; Tyler, Ryu, &
Stamper, 1984) reported that temporal
contrast sensitivity was unaffected by age,
subsequent investigations indicate that
the temporal contrast sensitivity function
(TCSF) of older observers is impaired at intermediate and high temporal frequencies.
C. E. Wright and Drasdo (1985) found a
progressive age decline in contrast sensitivity at temporal rates from 10 to 30 Hz, a
result that they attributed to reduced retinal illuminance. Mayer, Kim, Svingos, and
Glucs (1988) compared observers 65 years
and over with those of a young group
matched for pupil size. Older observers
were less sensitive to flicker between 10
and 45 Hz. The authors concluded that,
although temporal contrast sensitivity
was diminished, there was little evidence
of age-related visual slowing.

To minimize retinal illuminance effects, Tyler (1989) assessed age differences
on TCSFs for a 660-nm, 5° light patch. After age 15, a high-frequency decline in sensitivity was seen, as well as a shift of the
overall function to lower frequencies, indicative of an increase in the visual system's time constant. Kuyk and Wesson
(1991) reported a similar finding. Lachenmayr et al. (1994) found a linear loss of
about .38 dB/decade in *critical flicker fusion* (CFF) over the entire age range tested,
but light difference sensitivity declined
only slightly to age 46 (−.015 dB/decade),
and at a much faster rate (2.06 dB/de-
cade) thereafter. Two possibilities were offered to account for the divergent effects of
age on CFF and light-difference sensitivity: CFF thresholds are independent of
preretinal effects and those for light sensitivity are not, or both thresholds depend on age-related neuronal losses that
differ in degree and site along the visual
pathway.

The temporal CSF may be a useful diagnostic tool for separating aging effects
from those due to disease. Mayer et al.

(1994), for example, have shown that sensitivity to flicker modulation can discriminate with 100% accuracy healthy eyes
from those with exudative age-related
maculopathy (ARM).

Age differences in temporal resolution
vary with the spatial characteristics of the
stimulus. In a study of contrast sensitivity for gratings as a function of temporal
modulation, Tulunay-Keesey et al. (1988)
found that age had no effect at low spatial
frequencies, but a progressive age-related
loss was seen at high spatial and temporal
frequencies. This finding contrasts somewhat with that of Elliott et al. (1990), who
found that the age difference in sensitivity
moved to lower spatial frequencies as
counterphase flicker rate was increased.
Simulating the effects of pupillary and lenticular aging in young observers did not
affect their sensitivity. The authors concluded that their results were consistent
with greater loss in the sustained (i.e., parvocellular) rather than transient (i.e., magnocellular) pathways.

## 2. Perception of Motion

Most motion perception tasks are sensitive to aging effects. Buckingham, Whitaker, and Banford (1987) determined that
oscillatory displacement thresholds increase markedly past middle age. Trick
and Silverman (1991) found that the coherence thresholds for the perception of motion in random dots increased directly
with age. Gilmore, Wenk, Naylor, and
Stuve (1992), however, found an age deficit
for elderly females but not males on a correlated motion paradigm.

Recognizing that an age-related deficit
in sensitivity to optical flow could impair
the mobility of older persons and increase
the likelihood of falls, Warren, Blackwell,
and Morris (1989) compared young and
old observers on their ability to estimate
their apparent direction of motion from
computer-presented, random-dot optical
flow patterns that simulated translational

or curvilinear motion. Small but significant age differences were found in the magnitude of estimation errors for motion of both types, a difference thought to reflect deficits in the higher level mechanisms that mediate the perception of complex flow fields.

## J. Attention and Visual Search

The selective aspect of attention has interested gerontological researchers since Rabbitt's (1965) demonstration of an age decrement in the ability to "ignore irrelevant information" (p. 233) in visual search. Subsequent research has replicated his finding of larger display-size effects among the elderly (Plude & Doussard-Roosevelt, 1989; Plude & Hoyer, 1986; Scialfa & Esau, 1993; Scialfa, Kline, & Lyman, 1987; Sekuler & Ball, 1986), which increase with target-distractor similarity (Plude & Doussard-Roosevelt, 1989; Scialfa & Esau, 1993). This effect may be related to increased internal noise (Allen, Groth, Weber, & Madden, 1993; Allen, Madden, Groth, & Crozier, 1992; Baracat & Marquié, 1992), slower feature extraction (Madden & Allen, 1991; Scialfa & Harpur, 1994; Zacks & Zacks, 1993), slower featural comparisons (Scialfa & Thomas, 1994), or activation of incorrect response channels (Harpur, Scialfa, & Thomas, 1995; Zeef & Kok, 1993).

Display-size effects are reduced by consistently mapped (CM) practice, wherein targets gain and distractors lose the ability to attract attention. Fisk and his colleagues (Fisk & Rogers, 1991; Fisk, Rogers, & Giambra, 1990; Rogers, 1992) have consistently found attenuated CM learning in the elderly, perhaps due to a diminished ability to inhibit processing of distractors (Hasher, Stoltzfus, Zacks, & Rympa, 1991; Kane, Hasher, Stoltzfus, Zacks, & Connelly, 1994; Stoltzfus, Hasher, Zacks, Ulivi, & Goldstein, 1993).

The costs and benefits of advance cuing provide additional indices of attentional selectivity. Although only small age differences occur in the magnitude and time course of attentional allocation (Folk & Hoyer, 1992; Hartley, Kieley, & Slabach, 1990; Madden, 1992), and the elderly often show greater benefit from advance information, misdirection of attentional resources entails a greater cost for older observers (Madden, 1992).

Sustained attention, such as that involved in driving or industrial inspection is examined in vigilance tasks, which require attentional control and continued arousal. Unlike Surwillo and Quilter (1964), neither Giambra and Quilter (1988) nor Monk, Buysse, Reynolds, Jarrett, and Kupfer (1992) found that the vigilance decrement (i.e., lower hit rates later in the task) were age related. Age-related decrements in vigilance are seen, however, when the stimuli are degraded optically (Parasuraman, Nestor, & Greenwood, 1989) or temporally (Parasuraman & Giambra, 1992; Parasuraman et al., 1989).

Attention can be selective only to the extent that the observer is capable of perceiving the features comprising task-relevant objects. As such, age deficits in the useful field of view (UFOV) (e.g., Cerella, 1985; Scialfa & Kline, 1988; Scialfa et al., 1987; Sekuler & Ball, 1986) have implications for the study of nonsearch detection (Cerella, 1985, Experiment 3; but see L. L. Wright & Elias, 1979) as well as visual search (Plude & Doussard-Roosevelt, 1989). Recently, Scialfa, Thomas, and Joffe (1994) demonstrated that, compared to the young, older adults were more likely to make a saccade prior to identifying an eccentric feature search target, but only if the target was presented in noise. Finally, after Anandam (1994) trained young and old observers in CM visual search, older adults still showed reliable display-size effects; younger adults did not. These age deficits were eliminated, however, when the analyses were restricted to the central 2 degrees of the display.

## K. What Older People Say about Their Vision

The self-reports of older observers can provide an assessment of visual dysfunction that is not readily accessible by objective laboratory or clinical tests. Morgan (1988) noted four areas of particular concern in his own visual aging: difficulties with visual search, driving at twilight, seeing in shadowed areas in conditions of high illuminance, and entering and leaving dark areas. Questionnaire studies have yielded similar self-reports. Kosnik et al. (1988) found that self-reported, age-related visual problems were of five types: visual processing, light sensitivity, dynamic vision, near vision, and visual search. A follow-up study (Kosnik, Sekuler, & Kline, 1990) found that those reporting more difficulties with routine visual tasks were more likely to have given up driving. Relatedly, Branch, Horowitz, and Carr (1989) found that self-reported vision loss among the elderly was associated with unmet needs in daily activities, as well as physical and emotional disabilities. Kline et al. (1992) surveyed participants from the Baltimore Longitudinal Study on Aging regarding their visual problems on a wide range of driving and everyday tasks. Several of the visual problems of drivers increased with age—unexpected vehicles, vehicle speed, dim displays, windshield problems, and sign reading—and were consistent with the types of accidents that are more common among older drivers. Rumsey (1993) explored the relationship between the visual complaints of middle-aged and elderly respondents and their performance on objective visual measures. Visual complaints were common among the older group, as were decrements on acuity, contrast sensitivity, stereopsis, glare sensitivity, and color vision. Only the reported complaint of decreased vision, however, was directly related to visual test performance.

## III. Aging and Hearing

### A. The Auditory System

The *pinna* and the auditory canal amplify and direct acoustic signals to the ear's internal structures. Collapse of the auditory canal is associated with increased pure-tone thresholds, particularly at 4000 Hz (Schow & Goldblum, 1980), and excess wax in the canal of the older listener diminishes pure tone sensitivity (Corso, 1963). The *tympanic ring* becomes calcified with age, and collagen replaces elastic tissue in the eardrum itself, causing a reduction in signal amplitude (Belal, 1975). Calcification of the *ossicles* of the middle ear (Etholm & Belal, 1974) may diminish absolute sensitivity.

Relative displacement of the *tectorial* and *basilar membranes* of the inner ear stimulate the *inner* and *outer hair cells*, the sensory receptors for hearing. Both membranes become less compliant with age (Hansen & Reske-Nielsen, 1965) and hair cell loss is well documented (Bhattacharyya & Dayal, 1989; Bohne, Gruner, & Harding, 1990; Tarnowski, Schmiedt, Hellström, Lee, & Adams, 1991), especially in the basal regions responsible for coding higher frequencies (Johnsson & Hawkins, 1972), and in outer hair cells (Bohne et al., 1990). The decline in outer hair cells may cause an age-related reduction in the magnitude of *otoacoustic* emissions (Collet, Garner, Moulin, & Morgon, 1990; Lonsbury-Martin, Cutler, & Martin, 1991; Quaranta, Salonna, & Longo, 1991) and the *cochlear microphonic* (Crowley, Swain, Schram, & Swanson, 1972), both of which index cochlear transfer functions. Behaviorally, hair cell loss may be responsible for declines in psycho-acoustic selectivity for higher frequencies (Matschke, 1990).

The inner and outer hair cells synapse, respectively, with the radial and outer spiral ganglia whose axons form the auditory nerve. Ganglia are less numerous in older ears (Ryals & Westbrook, 1988), with attendant increases in the amplitude thresholds of single fibers (Hellström & Schmiedt, 1991), and shallower input–output functions of auditory nerve action potentials (Hellström & Schmiedt, 1990). Research on higher centers, limited largely to gross anatomical studies (Vaughan & Vincent, 1979), reveals cell loss and damage, but little about functional changes.

## B. Auditory Functions

### 1. Hearing Thresholds

The sound pressure needed to hear a tone is expressed as a hearing level (HL) in decibels (dB). The audiogram graphically represents HL across a range of frequencies, typically 250 to 8000 Hz (Lloyd & Kaplan, 1978).

With advancing age, sensitivity for tones of higher frequency is diminished (a condition known as *presbycusis*). This has been observed in both cross-sectional (Gates, Cooper, Kannel, & Miller, 1990) and longitudinal (Brant & Fozard, 1990) studies. Davis, Ostri, and Parving (1991) also reported a marked increase in the rate of hearing loss among older listeners—about 3 dB/decade for those under age 55 and about 9 dB/decade thereafter. A primary goal of auditory aging research has been to determine the degree to which this change is related intrinsically to aging (i.e., "pure" presbycusis), and how much of it is attributable to exogenous factors, particularly noise exposure.

At higher frequencies men have poorer hearing sensitivity than women, a difference that increases with age (e.g., Pedersen, Rosenhall, & Moller, 1989); the increased difference has been attributed to differential noise exposure (e.g., Moscicki, Elkins, Baum, & McNamara, 1985). A recent longitudinal study by Pearson et al. (in press), however, has shown that declines in hearing sensitivity of men are detectable at age 30, and proceeds twice as fast as those observed in women, even though both groups in that study came from low-noise occupations and showed no evidence of noise-induced hearing loss. The gender difference among the elderly may be reversed below 1 kHz, perhaps because women exhibit greater atrophy of the stria vascularis due to cardiovascular disease (Jerger, Chmiel, Stach, & Spretnjak, 1993).

Studies have differed on whether the effects of noise on sensitivity are additive to or interactive with presbycusis (Shone, Altschuler, Miller, & Nuttall, 1991). Consistent with the interactive hypothesis, Shone et al. found that mice with an age-related hearing deficit were more susceptible to noise-induced hearing loss. They suggested that diminished metabolic responsiveness might compromise the older ear's ability to recover from noise-induced stress.

Frequency discrimination, which contributes importantly to speech perception, has been examined in only a few studies. Cranford and Stream (1991) found that frequency discrimination thresholds for short tones increased with age. Elevations in threshold were not related to audiometric hearing level, leading the authors to speculate that the discrimination deficit reflected a central neural deficit. Matschke (1990) evaluated the ability to discriminate between sounds in the speech range (.5 and 4 kHz) that differed in spectral composition. A deficit in frequency selectivity became evident at about age 60.

Lutman, Gatehouse, and Worthington (1991) studied age differences in frequency resolution for a 2-kHz tone. Even after accounting for hearing level differences, frequency resolution remained modestly related to age. Moore and Peters (1992) measured frequency difference thresholds for both pure and complex tones in young and elderly listeners for whom they had previously established frequency-selectivity filter functions. Difference thresholds for both pure and complex tones were only weakly related to filter sharpness. Difference thresholds for complex tones were smaller for elderly listeners with normal hearing than among hearing-impaired young or elderly, but larger than among the normal young.

## 2. Temporal Resolution

Age differences in auditory temporal discrimination, critical to speech perception and sound localization, have been assessed on a wide range of measures. Robin and Royer (1989) presented young and elderly listeners with two tones separated by a silent, variable interstimulus interval (ISI). For older listeners, fusion occurred at longer first-tone durations for all ISIs. However, Moore, Peters, and Glasberg (1992), using a temporal gap-detection procedure, concluded that reduced temporal resolution is not an inevitable consequence of aging.

Time compression degrades the ability of older listeners to discriminate or comprehend speech material (Schmitt & Carroll, 1985). Rastatter, Watson, and Strauss-Simmons (1989) had older listeners with normal hearing discriminate phonemic contrasts in sentences presented at a 50% time-compression rate. Consistent with prior studies, performance decreased significantly over the age range tested.

Raz, Millman, and Moberg (1990) compared young and old listeners on the ability to discriminate two target tones in a backward masking task. The greater masking evidenced in older adults was attributed to increased stimulus persistence, rather than slowing.

## 3. Speech Perception

Older persons express considerable concern about declines in their communicative abilities (Jacobs-Condit, 1984). Such disabilities are more likely to be experienced by the 25–40% of those over 65 years of age who are diagnosed as being hearing impaired (National Center for Health Statistics, 1986). Age-related deficits in speech perception (Abel, Krever, & Alberti, 1990; Gatehouse, 1991; Helfer & Huntley, 1991; Helfer & Wilber, 1990; Humes & Roberts, 1990; Lutman, 1991; Nábêlek, 1988; Schum, Matthews, & Lee, 1991; van Rooij & Plomp, 1990, 1991; van Rooij, Plomp, & Orlebeke, 1989) increase markedly in noisy or reverberant environments (Abel et al., 1990; Helfer, 1992; Schum et al., 1991). The correlations between measures of pure-tone sensitivity and speech perception vary from 0.5 to 0.9 (e.g., Cokely & Humes, 1992; Helfer & Huntley, 1991; Lutman, 1991). Once age-related differences in pure-tone sensitivity are taken into account, either statistically or by sampling, age deficits in speech recognition are minimal (Helfer, 1992; Lutman, 1991; van Rooij & Plomp, 1992). Other lines of research are also consistent with an *auditive* (Humes, 1991; van Rooij & Plomp, 1992) versus *central hypothesis* (Jerger, Oliver, & Pirozzola, 1990) of age deficits in speech perception. Older hearing-impaired persons obtain higher speech recognition scores than younger hearing-impaired listeners (Helfer & Wilber, 1990), suggesting that age per se does not account for age-related losses in speech perception. The central hypothesis also has difficulty accounting for the finding that, relative to the young, older adults make as much or more use of context to facilitate speech recognition (Craig, Kim, Rhyner, & Chirillo, 1993; Holtzman, Familant, Deptula, & Hoyer, 1986; Hutchinson, 1989; Nittrouer & Boothroyd, 1990; van Rooij & Plomp, 1991).

## 4. Auditory Attention

Studies of age differences in dichotic listening, wherein the listener "shadows" the information presented in one ear while receiving information in both (e.g., see Tun & Wingfield, 1993) indicate that older adults have difficulty with shadowing if competing information is presented to the other ear (Barr & Giambra, 1990; Wickens, Braune, & Stokes, 1987). This suggests a divided attention deficit. McDowd (1988) and McDowd and Craik (1988) found that older listeners are slowed in searching an auditory stream for acoustic or semantic content only if required to perform a visual task simultaneously. They also require more time to switch attention between ears, and consequently, miss information that is heard by younger persons (Wickens et al., 1987).

## C. What Older Persons Say about Their Hearing

Although audiometric data and hearing problems are related, the former may explain only partly the hearing handicap of elderly persons (e.g., Dancer, Pryor, & Rozema, 1989; Garstecki, 1987; Weinstein & Ventry, 1983). When Garstecki (1987) administered the Hearing Handicap Inventory for the Elderly (Ventry & Weinstein, 1982), about 30% of those who passed pure-tone screening appeared to be handicapped, and 20–25% of those who failed the screening test did not appear to be handicappped. Slawinski and Kline (1989) developed the *Your Hearing* self-report instrument to discern possible relationships between age-related changes in auditory functioning and problems in the natural environment. Administration of this instrument to respondents of varied age (Slawinski et al., 1993) revealed five types of age-related auditory problems: temporal resolution, hearing in background noise, understanding distorted speech, understanding normal speech, and hearing high-pitched sounds. Such problems were more prominent among those who reported that their hearing was poor.

# IV. Future Directions in Visual and Auditory Aging Research

Recent strides in our understanding of visual and auditory aging suggest several areas in which research is particularly promising or conspicuously overdue. In vision, these include studies of (a) optical and neural contributors to visual aging within the same individuals; (b) suprathreshold performance; (c) peripheral and scotopic visual functions; (d) possible disjunctive changes in the parvocellular and magnocellular pathways; (e) extrastriate visual functioning; (f) monocular and binocular depth cues other than stereopsis; (g) binocular integration; and (h) the impact of visual aging on the performance of everyday tasks. Promising areas for auditory research include (a) a determination of how exogenous factors contribute to age-related hearing loss; (b) the effects of aging on high-level auditory processes and temporal resolution; (c) the contribution of temporal sensitivity deficits to speech perception under adverse listening conditions; and (d) how hearing impairment and handicap relate to the well-being of hearing-impaired elderly.

Finally, given that some degree of change is likely across sensory systems, there is a need for increased understanding of the interactive nature of age-related sensory losses. Such research might examine the degree to which handicap is exacerbated by multisensory deficits, and conversely, the extent to which intersensory compensation is possible, especially when the degree of decline is disjunctive. These studies would be particularly informative if they included an interdisciplinary assessment of higher level cognitive processes, health status, and social circumstances in mediating the effects of loss, both within and across sensory systems.

## Acknowledgment

Appreciation is extended to Lisa Lynk for her assistance with the literature search and the preparation of references.

## References

Abel, S. M., Krever, E. M., & Alberti, P. W. (1990). Auditory detection, discrimination, and speech processing in ageing, noise-sensitive and hearing-impaired listeners. *Scandinavian Audiology, 19,* 43–54.

Adams, A. J., Wong, L. S., Wong, L., & Gould, B. (1988). Visual acuity changes with age: Some new perspectives. *American Journal of Optometry and Physiological Optics, 65,* 403–406.

Ahmad, A., & Spear, P. D. (1993). Effects of aging on the size, density, and number of Rhesus-Monkey lateral geniculate neurons. *Journal of Comparative Neurology, 334,* 631–643.

Allen, P. A., Groth, K. E., Weber, T. A., & Madden, D. J. (1993). Influence of response selection and noise similarity on age differences in redundancy gain. *Journal of Gerontology: Psychological Sciences, 48,* P189–P198.

Allen, P. A., Madden, D. J., Groth, K. E., & Crozier, L. C. (1992). Impact of age, redundancy, and perceptual noise on visual search. *Journal of Gerontology: Psychological Sciences, 47,* P69–P74.

Anandam, B. (1994). *Ageing and visual search.* Unpublished master's thesis, University of Calgary, Calgary, Canada.

Artal, P., Ferro, M., Miranda, I., & Navarro, R. (1993). Effects of aging in retinal image quality. *Journal of the Optical Society of America A, 10,* 1656–1662.

Baracat, B., & Marquié, J. C. (1992). Age differences in sensitivity, response bias, and reaction time on a visual discrimination task. *Experimental Aging Research, 18,* 59–66.

Barr, R. A., & Giambra, L. M. (1990). Age-related decrement in auditory selective attention. *Psychology and Aging, 5,* 597–599.

Belal, A. (1975). Presbycusis: Physiological or pathological. *Journal of Laryngology, 89,* 1011–1025.

Bhattacharyya, T. K., & Dayal, V. S. (1989). Influence of age on inner hair cell loss in the rabbit cochlea. *Hearing Research, 40,* 179–184.

Birch, D. G., & Anderson, J. L. (1992). Standardized full-field electroretinography: Normal values and their variation with age. *Archives of Ophthalmology (Chicago), 110,* 1571–1576.

Birch, D. G., & Fish, G. E. (1988). Focal cone electrograms: Aging and macular disease. *Documenta Ophthalmologica, 69,* 211–220.

Block, M. G., & Rosenblum, W. M. (1987). MTF measurements on the human lens. *Journal of the Optical Society of America A, 4,* 7.

Bobak, P., Bodis-Wollner, I., Guillory, S., & Anderson, R. (1989). Aging differentially delays visual evoked potentials to checks and grating. *Clinical Vision Sciences, 4,* 269–274.

Bohne, B. A., Gruner, M. M., & Harding, G. W. (1990). Morphological correlates of aging in the chinchilla cochlea. *Hearing Research, 48,* 79–92.

Branch, L. G., Horowitz, A., & Carr, C. (1989). The implications for everyday life of incident self-reported visual decline among people over age 65 living in the community. *Gerontologist, 29,* 359–365.

Brant, L. J., & Fozard, J. L. (1990). Age changes in pure-tone hearing thresholds in a longitudinal study of normal human aging. *Journal of the Acoustical Society of America, 88,* 813–820.

Buckingham, T., Whitaker, D., & Banford, D. (1987). Movement in decline? Oscillatory movement displacement thresholds increase with ageing. *Ophthalmic and Physiological Optics, 7,* 411–413.

Burg, A. (1966). Visual acuity as measured by static and dynamic tests: A comparative evaluation. *Journal of Applied Psychology, 50,* 460–466.

Burton, K. B., Owsley, C., & Sloane, M. E. (1993). Aging and neural spatial contrast sensitivity: Photopic vision. *Vision Research, 33,* 939–946.

Casson, E. J., Johnson, C. A., & Nelson-Quigg, J. M. (1993). Temporal modulation perimetry: The effects of aging and eccentricity on sensitivity in normals. *Investigative Ophthalmology & Visual Science, 34,* 3096–3102.

Celesia, G. G., Kaufman, D., & Cone, S. (1987). Effects of age and sex on pattern electroretinograms and visual evoked potentials. *Electroencephalography and Clinical Neurophysiology, 68,* 161–171.

Cerella, J. (1985). Age-related decline in extra-foveal letter perception. *Journal of Gerontology, 40,* 727–736.

Charman, W. N. (1989). The path to presbyopia: Straight or crooked? *Ophthalmic and Physiological Optics, 9,* 424–430.

Coile, D. C., & Baker, H. D. (1992). Foveal dark adaptation, photopigment regeneration, and aging. *Visual Neuroscience, 8,* 27–39.

Cokely, C. G., & Humes, L. E. (1992). Reliability of two measures of speech recognition in elderly people. *Journal of Speech and Hearing Research, 35,* 654–660.

Collet, L., Gartner, M., Moulin, A., & Morgon, A. (1990). Age-related changes in evoked otoacoustic emissions. *Annals of Otology, Rhinology, & Laryngology, 99*, 993–997.

Collins, M., & Brown, B. (1989). Glare recovery and age-related maculopathy. *Clinical Vision Sciences, 4*, 145–153.

Collins, M. J., Brown, B., & Bowman, K. J. (1989). Peripheral visual acuity and age. *Ophthalmic and Physiological Optics, 9*, 314–316.

Cooper, B. A., Ward, M., Gowland, C. A., & McIntosh, J. M. (1991). The use of the Lanthony New Color Test in determining the effects of aging on color vision. *Journal of Gerontology: Psychological Sciences, 46*, P320–P324.

Corso, J. F. (1963). Age and sex differences in pure tone thresholds. *Archives of Otolaryngology, 77*, 385–105.

Corso, J. F. (1987). Sensory-perceptual processes and aging. *Annual Review of Gerontology and Geriatrics, 7*, 29–55.

Craig, C. H., Kim, B. W., Rhyner, P. M. P., & Chirillo, T. K. B. (1993). Effects of word predictability, child development, and aging on time-gated speech recognition performance. *Journal of Speech and Hearing Research, 36*, 832–841.

Cranford, J. L., & Stream, R. W. (1991). Discrimination of short duration tones by elderly subjects. *Journal of Gerontology, 46*, 37–41.

Crassini, B., Brown, B, & Bowman, K. (1988). Age-related changes in contrast sensitivity in central and peripheral retina. *Perception, 17*, 315–332.

Creasy, H., & Rapoport, S. I. (1985). The aging human brain. *Annals of Neurology, 17*, 2–10.

Crowley, D. E., Swain, R. E., Schram, V. L., & Swanson, S. N. (1972). Analysis of age-related changes in electrical responses from the inner ear of rats. *Annals of Otology, Rhinology, & Laryngology, 81*, 739–746.

Curcio, C. A., & Drucker, D. N. (1993). Retinal ganglion cells in Alzheimer's disease and aging. *Annals of Neurology, 33*, 248–257.

Curcio, C. A., Millican, C. L., Allen, K. A., & Kalina, R. E. (1993). Aging of the human photoreceptor mosaic: Evidence for selective vulnerability of rods in central retina. *Investigative Ophthalmology & Visual Science, 34*, 3278–3296.

Dancer, J., Pryor, B., & Rozema, H. (1989). Hearing screening in a well elderly population: Implications for gerontologists. *Educational Gerontology, 15*, 41–47.

Davis, A. C., Ostri, B., & Parving, A. (1991). Longitudinal study of hearing. *Acta Otolaryngologica, 476*, 12–22.

Doig, H. R., & Boylan, C. (1989). Changes in the presaccadic spike potential with age. *Electroencephalography and Clinical Neurophysiology, 73*, 549–551.

Eisner, A., Fleming, S. A., Klein, M. L., & Mauldin, W. M. (1987). Sensitivities in older eyes with good acuity: Cross-sectional norms. *Investigative Ophthalmology & Visual Science, 28*, 1824–1831.

Elliott, D. B. (1987). Contrast sensitivity decline with ageing: A neural or optical phenomenon? *Ophthalmic and Physiological Optics, 7*, 415–419.

Elliott, D. B., & Whitaker, D. (1991). Changes in macular function throughout adulthood. *Documenta Ophthalmologica, 76*, 251–259.

Elliott, D. B., Whitaker, D., & MacVeigh, D. (1990). Neural contribution to spatiotemporal contrast sensitivity decline in healthy ageing eyes. *Vision Research, 30*, 541–547.

Elliott, D. B., Whitaker, D., & Thompson, P. (1989). Use of displacement threshold hyperacuity to isolate the neural component of senile vision loss. *Applied Optics, 28*, 1914–1918.

Elsner, A. E., Berk, L., Burns, S. A., & Rosenberg, P. R. (1988). Aging and human cone photopigments. *Journal of the Optical Society of America A, 5*, 2106–2112.

Elworth, C. L., Larry, C., & Malmström, F. V. (1986). Age, degraded viewing environments, and the speed of accommodation. *Aviation, Space and Environmental Medicine, 57*, 54–58.

Etholm, B, & Belal, A. (1974). Senile changes in the middle ear joints. *Annals of Otology, Rhinology, & Laryngology, 83*, 49–64.

Fisk, A. D., & Rogers, W. A. (1991). Toward an understanding of age-related memory and visual search effects. *Journal of Experimental Psychology: General, 120*, 131–149.

Fisk, A. D., Rogers, W. A., & Giambra, L. M. (1990). Consistent and varied memory/visual search: Is there an interaction between age and response-set effects? *Journal of Gerontology: Psychological Sciences, 45*, P81–P87.

Folk, C. L., & Hoyer, W. J. (1992). Aging and shifts of spatial attention. *Psychology and Aging, 7*, 453–465.

Fozard, J. L. (1990). Vision and hearing in aging. In J. E. Birren & K. W. Schaie (Eds.), *Handbook of the psychology of aging* (3rd ed., pp. 150–170). San Diego, CA: Academic Press.

Gao, H., & Hollyfield, J. G. (1992). Aging of the human retina—differential loss of neurons and retinal pigment epithelial cells. *Investigative Ophthalmology & Visual Science, 33*, 1–17.

Garstecki, D. C. (1987). Self-perceived hearing difficulty in aging adults with acquired hearing loss. *Journal of the Academy of Rehabilitative Audiology, 20*, 49–60.

Garzia, R. P., & Trick, L. R. (1992). Vision in the 90's: The aging eye. *Journal of Optometric Vision Development, 23*, 4–41.

Gatehouse, S. (1991). The role of non-auditory factors in measured and self-reported disability. *Acta Oto-Laryngologica, Supplement, 476*, 249–256.

Gates, G. A., Cooper, J. C., Kannel, W. B., & Miller, N. J. (1990). Hearing in the elderly: The Framingham cohort, 1983–1985: Part I. Basic audiometric test results. *Ear and Hearing, 11*, 247–256.

Giambra, L. M., & Quilter, R. E.(1988). Sustained attention in adulthood: A unique, large-sample, longitudinal and multicohort analysis using the Mackworth Clock Test. *Psychology and Aging, 3*, 75–83.

Gilmore, G. C., Wenk, H. E., Naylor, L. A., & Stuve, T. A. (1992). Motion perception and aging. *Psychology and Aging, 7*, 654–660.

Gittings, N. S., & Fozard, J. L. (1986). Age changes in visual acuity. *Experimental Gerontology, 21*, 423–434.

Grady, C. L., Haxby, J. V., Horwitz, B., Shapiro, M. B., Rapoport, S. I., Ungerleider, L. G., Mishkin, M., Carson, R. E., & Herscovitch, P. (1992). Dissociation of object and spatial vision in human extrastriate cortex: Age-related changes in activation of regional cerebral blood flow measured with (-sup-1-sup-50) water and positron emission tomography. *Journal of Cognitive Neuroscience, 4*, 23–34.

Greene, H. A., & Madden, D. J. (1987). Adult age differences in visual acuity, stereopsis, and contrast sensitivity. *American Journal of Optometry and Physiological Optics, 64*, 749–753.

Grunwald, J. E., Piltz, J., Patel, N., Bose, S., & Riva, C. E. (1993). Effect of aging on retinal macular microcirculation: A blue field simulation study. *Investigative Ophthalmology & Visual Science, 34*, 3609–3613.

Hall, T. C., Miller, A. K. H., & Corsellis, J. A. N. (1975). Variations in human purkinje cell population according to age and sex. *Neuropathology and Applied Neurobiology, 1*, 267–292.

Hansen, C. C., & Reske-Nielsen, E. (1965). Pathological studies in presbycusis. *Archives of Otolaryngology, 82*, 115–132.

Harpur, L. L., Scialfa, C. T., & Thomas, D. M. (1995). Age differences in feature search as a function of exposure duration. *Experimental Aging Research, 21*, 1–15.

Hartley, A. A., Kieley, J. M., & Slabach, E. H. (1990). Age differences and similarities in the effects of cues and prompts. *Journal of Experimental Psychology: Human Perception and Performance, 16*, 523–537.

Hasher, L., Stoltzfus, E. R., Zacks, R. T., & Rympa, B. (1991). Age and inhibition. *Journal of Experimental Psychology: Learning, Memory, and Cognition, 17*, 163–169.

Helfer, K. S. (1992). Aging and the binaural advantage in reverberation and noise. *Journal of Speech and Hearing Research, 35*, 1394–1401.

Helfer, K. S., & Huntley, R. A. (1991). Aging and consonant errors in reverberation and noise. *Journal of the Acoustical Society of America, 90*, 1786–1796.

Helfer, K. S., & Wilber, L. A. (1990). Hearing loss, aging, and speech perception in reverberation and noise. *Journal of Speech and Hearing Research, 33*, 149–155.

Hellström, L. I., & Schmiedt, R. A. (1990). Compound action potential input/output functions in young and quiet-aged gerbils. *Hearing Research, 50*, 163–174.

Hellström, L. I., & Schmiedt, R. A. (1991). Rate/level functions of auditory-nerve fibers in young and quiet-aged gerbils. *Hearing Research, 53*, 217–222.

Higgins, K. E., Jaffe, M. J., Caruso, R. C., & de Monasterio, F. M. (1988). Spatial contrast sensitivity: Effects of age, test-retest and psychophysical method. *Journal of the Optical Society of America A, 5*, 2173–2180.

Holtzman, R. E., Familant, M. E., Deptula, P., & Hoyer, W. J. (1986). Aging and the use of sentential structure to facilitate word recognition. *Experimental Aging Research, 12,* 85–88.

Huaman, A. G., & Sharpe, J. A. (1993). Vertical saccades in senescence. *Investigative Ophthalmology & Visual Science, 34,* 2588–2595.

Humes, L. E. (1991). Understanding the speech-understanding problems of the hearing impaired. *Journal of the American Academy of Audiology, 2,* 59–69.

Humes, L. E., & Roberts, L. (1990). Speech-recognition difficulties of the hearing-impaired elderly: The contributions of audibility. *Journal of Speech and Hearing Research, 33,* 726–735.

Hutchinson, K. M. (1989). Influence of sentence context on speech perception in young and older adults. *Journal of Gerontology: Psychological Sciences, 44,* P36–P44.

Ijspeert, J. K., de Waard, P. T. W., van den Berg, T. J. T. P., & de Jong, P. T. W. M. (1990). The intraocular straylight function in 129 healthy volunteers: Dependence on angle, age and pigmentation. *Vision Research, 30,* 699–707.

Jacobs-Condit, L. (Ed.). (1984). *Gerontology and communication disorders.* Rockville, MD: American Speech-Language-Hearing Association.

Jay, J. L., Mammo, R. B., & Allan, D. (1987). Effect of age on visual acuity after cataract extraction. *British Journal of Ophthalmology, 71,* 112–115.

Jerger, J., Chmiel, R., Stach, B., & Spretnjak, M. (1993). Gender affects audiometric shape in presbycusis. *Journal of the American Academy of Audiology, 4,* 42–49.

Jerger, J., Oliver, T., & Pirozzola, F. (1990). Impact of central auditory processing disorder and cognitive deficit on the self-assessment of hearing handicap in the elderly. *Journal of American Audiology, 1,* 75–80.

Johnson, C. A. (1986, February). *Peripheral visual fields and driving in an aging population.* Paper presented at the Invitational Conference on Work, Aging, and Vision, National Research Council, Washington, DC.

Johnson, C. A., Adams, A. J., & Lewis, R. A. (1989). Evidence for a neural basis of age-related visual field loss in normal observers. *Investigative Ophthalmology & Visual Science, 30,* 2056–2064.

Johnson, C. A., Adams, A. J., Twelker, J. D., & Quigg, J. M. (1988). Age-related changes in the central visual field for short wavelength sensitive (SWS) pathways. *Journal of the Optical Society of America A, 5,* 2131–2139.

Johnsson, L. G., & Hawkins, J. E., Jr. (1972). Sensory and neural degeneration with aging, as seen in microdissections of the human inner ear. *Annals of Otology, Rhinology, & Laryngology, 81,* 179–193.

Jonas, J. B., Schmidt, A. M., Muller-Bergh, J. A., Schlotzer-Schrehardt, U. M., & Naumann, G. O. H. (1992). Human optic nerve fiber count and optic disc size. *Investigative Ophthalmology & Visual Science, 33,* 2012–2018.

Kane, M. J., Hasher, L., Stoltzfus, E. R., Zacks, R. T., & Connelly, S. L. (1994). Inhibitory attentional mechanisms and aging. *Psychology and Aging, 9,* 103–112.

Kashima, K., Trus, B. L., Unser, M., Edwards, P. A., & Datiles, M. B. (1993). Aging studies on normal lens using the Scheimpflug slit-lamp camera. *Investigative Ophthalmology & Visual Science, 34,* 293–269.

Kelly, S. A., Goldberg, S. E., & Banton, T. A. (1984). Effect of yellow-tinted lenses on contrast sensitivity. *American Journal of Optometry and Physiological Optics, 61,* 657–662.

Kilbride, P. E., Hutman, L. P., Fishman, M., & Read, J. S. (1986). Foveal cone pigment density difference in the aging human eye. *Vision Research, 26,* 321–325.

Klein, R., Klein, D. E. K., Linton, K. L. P., & de Mets, D. L. (1991). The Beaver Dam eye study: Visual acuity. *Ophthalmology (Rochester, Minnesota), 98,* 1310–1315.

Kline, D. W. (1991). Light, ageing and visual performance. In J. Marshall & J. R. Cronly-Dillon (Eds.), *Vision and visual dysfunction: Vol. 16. The susceptible visual apparatus* (pp. 150–161). London: Macmillan.

Kline, D. W., Culham, J., Bartel, P., & Lynk, L. (1994). Aging and hyperacuity thresholds as a function of contrast and oscillation rate. *Canadian Psychology, 35*(2a), 14.

Kline, D. W., Kline, T. J. B., Fozard, J. L., Kosnik, W., Schieber, F., & Sekuler, R. (1992). Vision, aging and driving: The problems of older drivers. *Journal of Gerontology: Psychological Sciences, 47*, P27–P34.

Knoblauch, K., Saunders, F., Kusuda, M., Hynes, R., Podgor, M., Higgins, K. E., & de Monasterio, F. M. (1987). Age and illuminance effects in the Farnsworth-Munsell 100–hue test. *Applied Optics, 26*, 1441–1448.

Kosnik, W. D., Kline, D. W., Fikre, J., & Sekuler, R. (1987). Ocular fixation control as a function of age and exposure duration. *Psychology and Aging, 2*, 302–305.

Kosnik, W. D., Sekuler, R., & Kline, D. W. (1990). Self-reported problems of older drivers. *Human Factors, 32*, 597–608.

Kosnik, W. D., Winslow, L., Kline, D. W., Rasinski, K., & Sekuler, R. (1988). Visual changes throughout adulthood. *Journal of Gerontology: Psychology of Aging, 2*, P302–P305.

Kupfer, C. (1973). Clinical significance of pseudofacility. *American Journal of Ophthalmology, 75*, 193–204.

Kuyk, T. K., & Wesson, M. D. (1991). Aging-related foveal flicker sensitivity losses in normal observers. *Optometry and Visual Science, 68*, 786–789.

Lachenmayr, B. J., Kojetinsky, S., Ostermaier, N., Angstwurm, K., Vivell, P. M. O., & Schaumberger, M. (1994). The different effects of aging on normal sensitivity in flicker and light-sense perimetry. *Investigative Ophthalmology & Visual Science, 35*, 2741–2748.

Lakshminarayanan, V., Aziz, S., & Enoch, J. M. (1992). Variation of the hyperacuity gap function with age. *Optometry and Vision Science, 69*, 423–426.

Lapidot, M. B. (1987). Does the brain age uniformly? Evidence from effects of smooth pursuit eye movements on verbal and visual tasks. *Journal of Gerontology, 42*, 329–331.

Leat, S. J., & Millodot, M. (1990). Contrast discrimination in normal and impaired human vision. *Clinical Vision Sciences, 5*, 37–43.

Lerman, S. (1984). Biophysical aspects of corneal and lenticular transparency. *Current Eye Research, 3*, 3–14.

Leuba, G., & Garey, L. J. (1987). Evolution of neuronal numerical density in the developing and aging human visual cortex. *Human Neurobiology, 6*, 11–18.

Linner, E. (1976). Ocular hypertension: 1. The clinical course during ten years without therapy. Aqueous humor dynamics. *Acta Ophthalmologica, 54*, 707–720.

Lloyd, L. L., & Kaplan, H. (1978). *Audiometric interpretation: A manual of basic audiometry*. Baltimore: University Park Press.

Loewenfeld, I. E. (1979). Pupillary changes related to age. In H. S. Thompson (Ed.), *Topics in neuro-ophthalmology* (pp.124–150). Baltimore: Williams & Wilkins.

Long, G. M., & Crambert, R. F. (1990). The nature and basis of age-related changes in dynamic visual acuity. *Psychology and Aging, 5*, 138–143.

Lonsbury-Martin, B. L., Cutler, W. M., & Martin, G. K. (1991). Evidence for the influence of aging on distortion-product otoacoustic emissions in humans. *Journal of the Acoustical Society of America, 89*, 1749–1759.

Lutman, M. E. (1991). Degradations in frequency and temporal resolution with age and their impact on speech identification. *Acta Oto-Laryngologia, 476*(Suppl.), 120–126.

Lutman, M. E., Gatehouse, S., & Worthington, A. G. (1991). Frequency resolution as a function of hearing threshold level and age. *Journal of the Acoustical Society of America, 89*, 320–328.

Lynk, L., Kline, D. W., & Culham, J. (1994). Adult age differences in vernier acuity as a function of target separation. *Canadian Psychology, 35*(2a), 15.

Madden, D. J. (1992). Selective attention and visual search: Revision of an allocation model and application to age differences. *Journal of Experimental Psychology: Human Perception and Performance, 18*, 821–836.

Madden, D. J., & Allen, P. A. (1991). Adults' age differences in the rate of information extraction during visual search. *Journal of Gerontology: Psychological Sciences, 46*, P124–P126.

Matschke, R. G. (1990). Frequency selectivity and psychoacoustic tuning curves in old age. *Acta Oto-Laryngologica, 476*(Suppl.), 114–119.

Mayer, M. J., Kim, C. B. Y., Svingos, A., & Glucs, A. (1988). Foveal flicker sensitivity in healthy aging eyes: I. Compensating for pupil variation. *Journal of the Optical Society of America A, 5*, 2201–2209.

Mayer, M. J., Ward, B., Klein, R., Talcott, J. B., Dougherty, R. F., & Glucs, A. (1994). Flicker sensitivity and fundus appearance in pre-exudative age-related maculopathy. *Investigative Ophthalmology & Visual Science, 35,* 1138–1149.

McDowd, J. M. (1988). The effects of age and extended practice on divided attention performance. *Journal of Gerontology, 41,* 764–769.

McDowd, J. M., & Craik, F. M. (1988). Effects of aging and task difficulty on divided attention performance. *Journal of Experimental Psychology: Human Perception and Performance, 14,* 267–280.

Monk, T. H., Buysse, D. J., Reynolds, C. F., Jarrett, D. B., & Kupfer, D. J. (1992). Rhythmic and homeostatic influences on mood, activation, and performance in young and old men. *Journal of Gerontology: Psychological Sciences, 47,* P221–P227.

Moore, B. C. J., & Peters, R. W. (1992). Pitch discrimination and phase sensitivity in young and elderly subjects and its relationship to frequency selectivity. *Journal of the Acoustical Society of America, 91,* 2881–2893.

Moore, B. C. J., Peters, R. W., & Glasberg, B. R. (1992). Detection of temporal gaps in sinusoids by elderly subjects with and without hearing loss. *Journal of the Acoustical Society of America, 92,* 1923–1932.

Morgan, M. (1988). Vision through my aging eyes. *Journal of the American Optometric Association, 59,* 278–280.

Morrison, J. D., & Reilly, J. (1986). An assessment of decision-making as a possible factor in the age-related loss of contrast sensitivity. *Perception, 15,* 541–552.

Morrison, J. D., & Reilly, J. (1989). The pattern visual evoked cortical response in human ageing. *Quarterly Journal of Experimental Physiology and Cognate Medical Sciences, 74,* 311–328.

Morrow, M. J., & Sharpe, J. A. (1993). Smooth pursuit initiation in young and elderly observers. *Vision Research, 33,* 203–210.

Moscicki, E. K., Elkins, E. F., Baum, H. M., & McNamara, P. M. (1985). Hearing loss in the elderly: An epidemiologic study of the Framingham Heart Study cohort. *Ear and Hearing, 6,* 184–190.

Murphy, B. J. (1978). Pattern thresholds for moving and stationary gratings during smooth pursuit eye movements. *Vision Research, 18,* 521–530.

Nábêlek, A. K. (1988). Identification of vowels in quiet, noise, and reverberation: Relationships with age and hearing loss. *Journal of the Acoustical Society of America, 84,* 476–484.

National Center for Health Statistics. (1986). *Current estimates for the National Health Interview Survey, U.S., 1985* (Vital and Health Statistics, Series 10, No. 160, DHHS Publication No. PHS 86–1588). Washington, DC: U.S. Government Printing Office.

Nittrouer, S., & Boothroyd, A. (1990). Context effects in phoneme and word recognition by young children and older adults. *Journal of the Acoustical Society of America, 87,* 2705–2715.

Odom, J. V., Vasquez, R. J., Schwartz, T. L., and Linberg, J. V. (1989). Adult vernier thresholds do not increase with age; Vernier bias does. *Investigative Ophthalmology & Visual Science, 30,* 1004–1008.

Owsley, C., Sekuler, R., & Siemsen, D. (1983). Contrast sensitivity throughout adulthood. *Vision Research, 23,* 689–699.

Owsley, C., & Sloane, M. E. (1990). Vision and aging. In F. Boller & J. Grafman (Eds.), *Handbook of neuropsychology* (Vol. 4, pp. 229–249). Amsterdam: Elsevier.

Owsley, C., Sloane, M. E., Skalka, H. W., & Jackson, C. A. (1990). A comparison of the Regan Low-Contrast Letter Charts and contrast sensitivity testing in older patients. *Clinical Vision Science, 5,* 325–334.

Parasuraman, R., & Giambra, L. (1992). Skill development in vigilance: Effects of event rate and age. *Psychology and Aging, 6,* 155–169.

Parasuraman, R., Nestor, P., & Greenwood, P. (1989). Sustained-attention capacity in young and older adults. *Psychology and Aging, 4,* 339–345.

Pearson, J. D., Morell, C. H., Gordon-Salant, S., Brant, L. J., Metter, E. J., Klein, L., & Fozard, J. L. (1995). Gender differences in a longitudinal study of age-associated hearing loss. *Journal of the Acoustical Society of America, 97,* 1196–1205.

Pedersen, K. E., Rosenhall, U., & Moller, M. B. (1989). Changes in pure-tone thresholds in individuals aged 70–81: Results from a longitudinal study. *Audiology, 28,* 194–204.

Pitts, D. G. (1982). The effect of aging on selected visual functions: Dark adaptation, visual acuity, stereopsis, and brightness contrast. In R. Sekuler, D. W. Kline, & K. Dismukes (Eds.), *Aging and the human visual function* (pp. 131–159). New York: Alan R. Liss.

Plude, D. J., & Doussard-Roosevelt, J. A. (1989). Aging, selective attention and feature integration. *Psychology and Aging, 4,* 1–7.

Plude, D. J., & Hoyer, W. J. (1986). Age and the selectivity of visual information processing. *Psychology and Aging, 1,* 1–16.

Porciatti, V., Burr, D. C., Morrone, C., & Fiorentini, A. (1992). The effects of ageing on the pattern electroretinogram and visual evoked potential in humans. *Vision Research, 32,* 1199–1209.

Pulling, N. H., Wolf, E., Sturgis, S. P., Vaillancourt, D. R., & Dolliver, J. J. (1980). Headlight glare resistance and driver age. *Human Factors, 22,* 103–112.

Quaranta, A., Salonna, I., & Longo, G. (1991). Subclinical changes of auditory function in the aged. *Acta Oto-Laryngology, 476*(Suppl.), 91–96.

Rabbitt, P. M. A. (1965). An age decrement in the ability to ignore irrelevant information. *Journal of Gerontology, 20,* 233–237.

Rastatter, M., Watson, M., & Strauss-Simmons, D. (1989). Effects of time-compression on feature and frequency discrimination in aged listeners. *Perceptual and Motor Skills, 68,* 367–372.

Raz, N., Millman, D., & Moberg, P. J. (1990). Mechanism of age-related differences in frequency discrimination with backward masking: Speed of processing or stimulus persistence? *Psychology and Aging, 5,* 475–481.

Reading, V. M. (1972). Visual resolution as measured by dynamic and static tests. *Pfluegers Archives, 333,* 17–26.

Robin, D. A., & Royer, F. L. (1989). Age-related changes in auditory temporal processing. *Psychology and Aging, 4,* 144–149.

Rogers, W. A. (1992). Age differences in visual search: Target and distractor learning. *Psychology and Aging, 7,* 526–535.

Ross, J. E., Clarke, D. D., & Bron, A. J. (1985). Effect of age on contrast sensitivity function: Uniocular and binocluar findings. *British Journal of Ophthalmology, 69,* 51–56.

Royer, F., & Gilmore, C. (1985). Spatiotemporal

factors and developmental changes in visual processes. *Bulletin of the Psychonomic Society, 23,* 404–406.

Rumsey, K. E. (1993). Redefining the optometric examination: Addressing the vision needs of older adults. *Optometry and Visual Science, 70,* 587–591.

Ryals, B. M., & Westbrook, E. W. (1988). Ganglion cell and hair cell loss in *Coturnix* quail associated with aging. *Hearing Research, 36,* 1–8.

Sample, P. A., & Weinreb, R. N. (1990). Color perimetry for the assessment of primary open angle glaucoma. *Investigative Ophthalmology & Visual Science, 31,* 1869–1875.

Schaeffel, F., Wilhelm, H., & Zrenner, E. (1993). Interindividual variability in the dynamics of natural accommodation in humans: Relation to age and refractive errors. *Journal of Physiology (London), 461,* 301–320.

Schein, O. D., West, S., Muñoz, B., Vitale, S., Maguire, M., Taylor, H., & Bressler, N. M. (1994). Cortical lenticular opacification: Distribution and location in a longitudinal study. *Investigative Ophthalmology & Visual Science, 35,* 363–366.

Schieber, F. (1992). Aging and the senses. In J. E. Birren, R. B. Sloane, & G. D. Cohen (Eds.), *Handbook of mental health and aging* (2nd ed., pp. 251–306). San Diego, CA: Academic Press.

Schieber, F., & Williams, M. J. (1990). The effects of age and glare upon spatiotemporal contrast thresholds [Special issue]. *Gerontologist, 30,* 64A.

Schmitt, J. F., & Carroll, M. R. (1985). Older listeners' ability to comprehend speaker-generated rate alteration of passages. *Journal of Speech and Hearing Research, 28,* 309–312.

Schow, R. L., & Goldblum, D. E. (1980). Collapsed ear canals in the elderly nursing home population. *Journal of Speech and Hearing Disease, 45,* 259–267.

Schum, D. J., Matthews, L. J., & Lee, F. (1991). Actual and predicted word-recognition performance in elderly hearing-impaired listeners. *Journal of Speech and Hearing Research, 34,* 636–642.

Scialfa, C. T., Adams, E. M., & Giovanetto, M. (1991). Reliability of the Vistech Contrast Test System in a life-span adult sample. *Optometry and Vision Science, 66,* 270–274.

Scialfa, C. T., & Esau, S. (1993, November). *Age differences in feature and conjunction search as a function of display size and target-distractor similarity.* Paper presented at the meeting of the Gerontological Society of America, New Orleans, LA.

Scialfa, C. T., Garvey, P. M., Gish, K. W., Deering, L., Leibowitz, H. W., & Goebel, C. C. (1988). Relationships among measures of static and dynamic visual sensitivity. *Human Factors, 30,* 677–687.

Scialfa, C. T., Garvey, P. M., Tyrrell, R. A., & Leibowitz, H. W. (1992). Age differences in dynamic contrast thresholds. *Journal of Gerontology: Psychological Sciences, 47,* P172–P175.

Scialfa, C. T., & Harpur, L. L. (1994). Effects of similarity and duration on age differences in visual search. *Canadian Journal on Aging, 13,* 51–65.

Scialfa, C. T., & Kline, D. W. (1988). Effects of noise type and retinal eccentricity on age differences in identification and localization. *Journal of Gerontology: Psychological Science, 43,* P91–P99.

Scialfa, C. T., Kline, D. W., & Lyman, B. J. (1987). Age differences in target identification as a function of retinal location and noise level: An examination of the useful field of view. *Psychology and Aging, 2,* 14–19.

Scialfa, C. T., Leibowitz, H. W., & Gish, K. W. (1989). Age differences in peripheral refractive error. *Psychology and Aging, 4,* 372–375.

Scialfa, C. T., & Thomas, D. M. (1994). Age differences in same-different judgments as a function of multi-dimensional similarity. *Journal of Gerontology: Psychological Sciences, 49,* P173–P178.

Scialfa, C. T., Thomas, D. M., & Joffe, K. M. (1994). Age-related changes in the eye movements subserving feature search. *Optometry and Vision Science, 71,* 736–742.

Sekuler, R., & Ball, K. (1986). Visual localization: Age and practice. *Journal of the Optical Society of America A, 3,* 864–867.

Shapley, R. (1990). Visual sensitivity and parallel retinocortical channels. *Annual Review of Psychology, 41,* 635–658.

Sharpe, J. A., & Zackon, D. H. (1987). Senescent saccades. *Acta Oto-Laryngologica, 104,* 422–428.

Shone, G., Altschuler, R. A., Miller, J. M., & Nuttall, A. L. (1991). The effect of noise exposure on the aging ear. *Hearing Research, 56,* 173–178.

Slawinski, E. B., Hartel, D. M., & Kline, D. W. (1993). Self-reported hearing problems in daily life throughout adulthood. *Psychology and Aging, 8,* 552–561.

Slawinski, E., & Kline, D. W. (1989). *Your hearing: A survey by the Audition/Speech and Vision/Aging Laboratories of the University of Calgary.* Calgary: University of Calgary, Department of Psychology.

Sloane, M. E., Owsley, C., & Alvarez, S. L. (1988). Aging, senile miosis and spatial contrast sensitivity at low luminance. *Vision Research, 28,* 1235–1246.

Spear, P. D. (1993). Neural bases of visual deficits during aging. *Vision Research, 33,* 2589–2609.

Stoltzfus, E. R., Hasher, L., Zacks, R. T., Ulivi, M. S., & Goldstein, D. (1993). Investigations of inhibition and interference in younger and older adults. *Journal of Gerontology: Psychological Sciences, 48,* P179–P188.

Sturr, J. F., Hannon, D. J., Zhang, L., & Vaidya, C. (1992). Psychophysical evidence for neural losses in the rod systems of older observers in good ocular health. *Investigative Ophthalmology & Visual Science, 33,* 1414.

Sturr, J. F., Kline, G. E., & Taub, H. A. (1990). Performance of young and older drivers on a static acuity test under photopic and mesopic luminance conditions. *Human Factors, 32,* 1–8.

Sun, F., Stark, L., Nguyen, A., Wong, J., Lakshminarayanan, S., & Mueller, E. (1988). Changes in accommodation with age: Static and dynamic. *American Journal of Optomology and Physiological Optics, 65,* 492–498.

Surwillo, W. W., & Quilter, R. E. (1964). Vigilance, age and response time. *American Journal of Psychology, 77,* 614–620.

Tarnowski, B. I., Schmiedt, R. A., Hellström, L. I., Lee, F. S., & Adams, J. C. (1991). Age-related changes in the cochleas of Mongolian gerbils. *Hearing Research, 54,* 123–134.

Taub, H. A., & Sturr, J. F. (1991). The effect of age and ocular health on letter contrast sensitivity and high and medium contrast acuity as a function of luminance. *Clinical Vision Sciences, 6,* 181–189.

Tomoda, H., Celesia, G. G., Brigell, M. G., &

Toleikis, S. (1991). The effects of age on steady-state pattern electroretinograms and visual evoked potentials. *Documenta Ophthalmologica*, 77, 201–211.

Trick, G. L., & Silverman, S. E. (1991). Visual sensitivity to motion: Age-related changes and deficits in senile dementia of the Alzheimer type. *Neurology*, 41, 1437–1440.

Trick, G. L., Trick, L. R., & Haywood, K. M. (1986). Altered pattern evoked retinal and cortical potentials with human senescence. *Current Eye Research*, 5, 717–724.

Tulunay-Keesey, U., ver Hoeve, J. N., & Terkla-McGrane, C. (1988). Threshold and suprathreshold spatiotemporal response throughout adulthood. *Journal of the Optical Society of America A*, 5, 2191–2200.

Tun, P. A., & Wingfield, A. (1993). Is speech special? Perception and recall of spoken language in complex environments. In J. Cerella (Ed.), *Adult information processing: Limits on loss* (pp. 425–457). San Diego, CA: Academic Press.

Tyler, C. W. (1981). Specific deficits of flicker sensitivity in glaucoma and ocular hypertension. *Investigative Ophthalmology & Visual Science*, 20, 204–212.

Tyler, C. W. (1989). Two processes control variations in flicker sensitivity over the lifespan. *Journal of the Optical Society of America A*, 6, 481–490.

Tyler, C. W., Ryu, S., & Stamper, R. (1984). The relation between visual sensitivity and intraocular pressure in normal eyes. *Investigative Ophthalmology & Visual Science*, 25, 103–105.

van Rooij, J. C. G. M., & Plomp, R. (1990). Auditive and cognitive factors in speech perception by elderly listeners. II: Multivariate analyses. *Journal of the Acoustical Society of America*, 88, 2611–2624.

van Rooij, J. C. G. M., & Plomp, R. (1991). The effects of linguistic entropy on speech perception in noise in young and elderly listeners. *Journal of the Acoustical Society of America*, 90, 2985–2991.

van Rooij, J. C. G. M., & Plomp, R. (1992). Auditive and cognitive factors in speech perception by elderly listeners. III: Additional data and final discussion. *Journal of the Acoustical Society of America*, 91, 1028–1033.

van Rooij, J. C. G. M., Plomp, R., & Orlebeke, J. F. (1989). Auditive and cognitive factors in speech perception by elderly listeners. I: Development of test battery. *Journal of the Acoustical Society of America*, 86, 1294–1309.

Vaughan, P. W., & Vincent, J. M. (1979). Ultra structure of neurons in the auditory cortex of aging rats: Morphometric study. *Journal of Neurocytology*, 8, 215–228.

Ventry, I. M., & Weinstein, B. E. (1982). The Hearing Handicap Inventory for the Elderly: A new tool. *Ear and Hearing*, 3, 128–134.

Vincent, S. L., Peters, A., & Tigges, J. (1989). Effects of aging on the neurons within area 17 of rhesus monkey cerebral cortex. *Anatomical Record*, 223, 329–341.

Warren, W. H., Blackwell, A. W., & Morris, M. W. (1989). Age differences in perceiving the direction of self-motion from optical flow. *Journal of Gerontology: Psychological Sciences*, 44, P147–P153.

Weale, R. A. (1961). Retinal illumination and age. *Transactions of the Illuminating Engineering Society*, 26, 95–100.

Weale, R. A. (1982). Senile ocular changes, cell death, and vision. In R. Sekuler, D. W. Kline, & K. Dismukes (Eds.), *Aging and human visual function* (pp. 161–171). New York: Alan R. Liss.

Weale, R. A. (1986). Senescence and color vision. *Journal of Gerontology*, 41, 635–640.

Weinstein, B., & Ventry, I. (1983). Audiometric correlates of the Hearing Handicap Inventory for the Elderly. *Journal of Speech and Hearing Disorders*, 48, 379–384.

Werner, J. S., & Steele, V. G. (1988). Sensitivity of human foveal color mechanisms throughout the life span. *Journal of the Optical Society of America A*, 5, 2122–2130.

Westheimer, G. (1975). Visual acuity and hyperacuity. *Investigative Ophthalmology & Visual Science*, 14, 570–571.

Whitaker, D., Elliott, D. B., & MacVeigh, D. (1992). Variations in hyperacuity performance with age. *Ophthalmic and Physiological Optics*, 12, 29–32.

Whitaker, L. A., Shoptaugh, C. F., & Haywood, K. M. (1986). Effect of age on horizontal eye movement latency. *American Journal of Optometry and Physiological Optics*, 63, 152–155.

Wickens, C. D., Braune, R., & Stokes, A. (1987). Age differences in the speed and capacity of information processing: 1. A dual-task approach. *Psychology and Aging, 2,* 70–78.

Willott, J. (1991). *Aging and the auditory system.* San Diego, CA: Singular Publishing Group.

Wilson, R. S., & Roper-Hall, M. J. (1982). Effect of age on the endothelial cell count in the normal eye. *British Journal of Ophthalmology, 66,* 513–515.

Winn, B., Whitaker, D., Elliott, D. B., & Phillips, N. J. (1994). Factors affecting light-adapted pupil size in normal human subjects. *Investigative Ophthalmology & Visual Science, 35,* 1132–1137.

Wright, C. E., & Drasdo, N. (1985). The influence of age on the spatial and temporal contrast sensitivity function. *Documenta Ophthalmologica, 59,* 385–395.

Wright, C. E., Williams, D. E., Drasdo, N., & Harding, G. F. A. (1985). The influence of age on the electroretinogram and visual evoked potential. *Documenta Ophthalmologica, 59,* 365–384.

Wright, C. E., & Wormald, R. P. (1992). Stereopsis and ageing. *Eye, 6,* 473–476.

Wright, L. L., & Elias, J. W. (1979). Age differences in the effects of perceptual noise. *Journal of Gerontology, 34,* 704–708.

Wyatt, H. J. (1993). Application of a simple mechanical model of accommodation to the aging eye. *Vision Research, 33*(5/6), 731–738.

Yang, K. C. H., Elliott, D. B., & Whitaker, D. (1993). Does logMAR VA change linearly with age? *Investigative Ophthalmology & Visual Science, 34,* 1422.

Yekta, A. A., Pickwell, L. D., & Jenkins, T. C. A. (1989). Binocular vision, age and symptoms. *Ophthalmic and Physiological Optics, 9,* 115–120.

Zacks, J. L., & Zacks, R. T. (1993). Visual search times without reaction times: A new method and application to aging. *Journal of Experimental Psychology: Human Perception and Performance, 15,* 419–433.

Zakon, D. H., & Sharpe, J. A. (1987). Smooth pursuit in senescence: Effects of target acceleration and velocity. *Acta Oto-Laryngologica, 104,* 290–297.

Zeef, E. J., & Kok, A. (1993). Age-related differences in the timing of stimulus and response processes during visual selective attention: Performance and psychophysiological analyses. *Psychophysiology, 30,* 138–151.

# Eleven

# Posture, Gait, and Falls

Guy G. Simoneau and Herschel W. Leibowitz

This chapter is divided into four sections. First, a brief overview of the anatomical and functional characteristics of the sensory, motor, and information-processing systems that contribute to the control of posture, gait, and other mobility skills associated with ambulation (e.g., stepping over obstacles) are reviewed. In the second section, the impact of aging on the functional control of posture and gait is discussed. The third section examines falls and their related physical and psychological adverse effects. The final section of this chapter presents general intervention strategies designed to maintain physical mobility and decrease the risk of falls in the elderly.

## I. The Control of Posture and Gait

### A. The Balance System

Within the context of this chapter, posture refers to the position of the body when standing upright. Maintaining an upright stance position can be simplistically characterized as controlling the position and orientation of each individual body segment so that the line of gravity of the cen-ter of mass of the entire body falls within the supporting surface delimited by the position of the feet. A balanced *static* stance position is therefore obtained as long as this criterion is met and muscular action to overcome gravitational pull is present.

Conversely, walking is characterized by successive *loss of balance* episodes where a fall is avoided by repositioning each foot alternately in a manner such that the body is displaced in a controlled fashion along a preintended path. Unlike the relatively stable stance position, gait is characterized by instability because the center of mass of the body is almost always outside the base of support represented by the feet (Winter, Patla, Frank, & Walt, 1990).

Although standing upright could be considered a static task and walking a dynamic function, both require proper control of balance. Isaacs (1982, p. 135) defined the concept of balance as the "set of functions which maintains man upright during stance and locomotion by detecting and correcting displacements of the line of gravity beyond the support base."

Maintaining optimal balance while standing, walking, or performing other active mobility tasks, such as moving from

*Handbook of the Psychology of Aging, Fourth Edition*

a bed to a chair, requires a close working relationship between sensory and motor functions. The afferent information (from the periphery to the central nervous system) helpful for the control of balance arises from three complementary and interconnected sensory systems: the vestibular organs, the visual apparatus, and the somatosensory receptors. After efficient and rapid processing of the afferent sensory information takes place, an appropriate motor response must be generated to maintain balance during stance, adjust to the change in body position that occurs during undisturbed gait, or recover from an unforeseen disturbance, such as tripping over an object. Therefore, difficulty with balance, resulting in falls, may arise from impaired sensory perception, inaccurate movement planning, or inappropriate motor response.

## B. Sensory Function

### 1. The Vestibular System

The primary functions of the vestibular organs, located within the temporal bones, are to assist in the production of postural corrections and to provide awareness of head position and motion in space. The vestibular system provides information on the static position and linear as well as angular acceleration of the head. Information from these receptor organs also generates the vestibulo-ocular reflex that maintains image stability on the retina during head and body movement.

During the aging process, the vestibular organs deteriorate progressively. Anatomically, there is a reduction in the number of nerve fibers in the vestibular nerve and the number of hair cells (vestibular receptor organs) in the otoliths and semicircular canals (Richter, 1980). Functionally, deficits in vestibular function have been demonstrated (under experimental conditions) by the decreased ability of older subjects to maintain postural equilibrium in the ab-

sence of somatosensory and visual feedback (Horak, Mirka, & Shupert, 1989).

### 2. The Visual System

The visual system has two distinct functions that contribute to the control of balance: spatial orientation (which provides information on the location, orientation, and movement of the body in relationship to its environment) and recognition (which assists in the identification of environmental hazards during gait) (Post & Leibowitz, 1986).

The control of balance through visual sensory information necessitates the detection of image movements on the retina. While head–body movement provides the image displacement (assuming a moving individual and a fixed visual environment), the actual perception of this displacement depends on several factors, such as the ambient lighting, the distance between the visual stimuli and the eye, and the orientation and level of contrast of the visual cues (Paulus, Straube, & Brandt, 1987). Therefore, the degree of visual assistance in the control of balance is not simply a function of good vision but also of the quality of the visual environment. This is best exemplified by comparing the sense of balance obtained from standing near vertical objects that contrast greatly with the surroundings (good visual input) and standing at the edge of a cliff looking into a cloudless blue sky (poor visual input).

Visual detection of information for the purpose of controlling upright posture and gait also depends on the quality of the visual system. During the aging process, various components of the visual system undergo physiological and anatomical changes that result in decreased visual function. The visual deficits most likely to have a negative effect on posture and locomotion are decreased light transmissivity, visual acuity, contrast threshold sensitivity, and the ability to adapt to sudden changes in ambient light. The culmination of the deficits may reduce a person's ability to rely on vision to use stable orientation cues and, most importantly, to identify obstacles or conditions that may cause a fall.

### 3. The Somatosensory System

The somatosensory system provides afferent information from nerve endings located in the skin, joints, and muscles throughout the body. Mechanoreceptors located in the cutaneous and subcutaneous structures of the plantar surface of the foot contribute to the control of balance during stance and gait by mediating the perception of touch, pressure, and shear taking place under the feet during these movements. Information about body segment orientation, joint position, and joint angular movement is mediated by mechanoreceptors located in the joint capsule and articular ligaments (Wyke, 1972). Sensory end organs of tendons and muscles, principally the Golgi tendon organs and muscle spindle receptors, also contribute information necessary for optimal kinesthetic sense (Wyke, 1972).

During the aging process, the somatosensory system's ability to detect stimuli and provide sensory information progressively declines. Of perhaps greatest importance to the process of postural control and gait in the elderly is the progressive decline in a person's ability to perceive joint movement and position (Stelmach, Meeuwsen, & Zelaznik, 1990).

### C. Motor Function

The muscular action needed to maintain posture and to achieve mobility for daily activities requires proper function of the cerebellar motor system, the lower motor neurons, the neuromuscular junctions, and the muscle contractile units.

There is overwhelming evidence in the literature that a loss of muscle strength and mass typically occurs with aging in humans. Just how much of this atrophy is due to aging and how much is due to disease or sedentary lifestyle remains to be clearly established. Regardless, there is evidence in the literature that a decrease in strength of specific muscles active in the control of balance and gait (e.g., ankle dorsiflexors) may be related to an increased occurrence of fall events (Whipple, Wolfson, & Amerman, 1987).

From a disease perspective, there are a number of neurological and neuromuscular diseases that may affect an individual's ability to walk and maintain balance. Specific gait characteristics related to these dysfunctions have been described elsewhere (Rubino, 1993; Sudarsky & Ronthal, 1983).

### D. Information Processing

The sensory inputs originating from the somatosensory, visual, and vestibular sensory organs provide highly redundant information on the position and movement of the body. These systems also provide information on the conditions of the surrounding environment. This complex sensory information needs to be analyzed and integrated in a manner that will generate an efficient functional motor output required to maintain balance and perform tasks such as standing or walking. How and at what level of the central nervous system this information is processed is not completely understood. More recent views on the control of posture stress the functionality of the system (Reed, 1989). Because a multitude of optional actions (from the motor planning phase to the execution of the task) are typically available to accomplish a given mobility task, the control of posture shows both great resiliency and flexibility. It is still unclear to what extent the "skills" involved in the integration of sensory information and the production of an adequate motor response are influenced by the processes of aging.

## II. Functional Age-Related Changes in Posture and Gait

### A. Posture

Standing is an unstable position that is characterized by constant micromotions and postural adjustments of the body's center of mass. Clinically, the subjective assessment of standing balance, known as the *Romberg test*, is routinely performed in the evaluation of patients with vestibular, neurological, or balance deficits. Quantification of this clinical test (which consists of the subjective observation of body movement while standing with feet together and eyes closed or open) has been the subject of much research interest since the late nineteenth century (e.g., Hinsdale, 1887, 1890, and Hancock, 1894, both of whom are cited in Sheldon, 1963).

Objective quantification of stability during stance has been achieved through several methods. These include the measurement of movement of a specific body segment such as the trunk via a pen recorder, movement of the estimated center of mass of the body through kinematic analysis, and the path of the center of pressure recorded using a force platform. It must be pointed out that although the intent of each technique is to quantify body movement during stance, each measures a slightly different phenomenon and has different inherent assumptions (Patla, Frank, & Winter, 1990).

It is well known that the elderly exhibit a greater amount of body movement (sway) when standing quietly with eyes open or closed than do young adults (Overstall, Extol-Smith, Imms, & Johnson, 1977; Sheldon, 1963). Most often cited is the classic work of Sheldon (1963), who measured body sway on 268 subjects whose ages ranged from 6 to more than 80 years. The result of Sheldon's work illustrated that childhood (ages 6–14 years) and advanced age (>60 years) are characterized by greater body movement than early adulthood.

Based on his findings, Sheldon suggested that childhood can be considered as a period of refinement of the control of posture, whereas the increased sway seen from the sixth decade onward is evidence of a progressive deterioration of the control of balance to maintain upright stance.

It is often assumed that individuals who demonstrate greater sway during stance have difficulty with balance, which would lead to an increased likelihood of falling. In the elderly, it may be tempting to link increased body movement during quiet stance with the increased likelihood of falls because both phenomena are present in this age group. A number of studies have attempted to confirm this relationship between increased postural sway and falls in the older population in an attempt to provide an assessment tool to identify individuals at greater risks for falls.

A few prospective studies provide some evidence to support the suggestion that the amount of sway during standing may be a predictor of the likelihood of falling in older individuals. Fernie, Gryfe, Holliday, and Llewellyn (1982) recorded the number of fall events for 205 institutionalized subjects for a period of 1 year following the assessment of posture. Their data demonstrated that, overall, the residents who fell during that 1-year period exhibited more sway than those who did not fall. But within the group who experienced at least one fall, there was no association between the frequency of falls and body sway measurements. Campbell, Borrie, & Spears (1989) investigated the relationship between sway and falls by studying 761 community-living subjects over a 1-year period. Body sway was one of several factors identified as being associated with falls for both men and women. A direct relationship between fall events and poor postural control was also found by Topper, Maki, and Holliday (1993); the authors suggested that a test of static standing balance may help identify individuals who are at a high risk of falling.

Retrospective studies offer only limited evidence of a positive association between increased sway and falls. Brocklehurst, Robertson, and James-Groom (1982) found a limited relationship between falls in the year prior to the test and amount of sway in the age group between 75 and 84 years of age, but no relationship was found for the age group between 65 and 74 or for the age group 85 and older. Based on a sample group of 243 elderly individuals aged 60 to 96, Overstall et al. (1977) concluded that no difference in sway existed between elderly individuals who did not fall and those who fell due to tripping during the year prior to the assessment of posture. But, those who fell due to reasons other than tripping (for example, giddiness, turning the head, drop attacks, loss of balance, and rising from a chair) had more body sway than the individuals who did not fall. Lichtenstein, Shields, Shiavi, and Burger (1988), in a study of independently living women, also established a positive relationship between a measure of increased sway and a history of falling during the prior year.

Imms and Edholm (1981), who retrospectively surveyed a group of 71 subjects between the ages of 60 and 99 years, failed to demonstrate that significantly greater sway was present in a group of older individuals who had a history of falls compared to a group who did not.

When taken all together, the above studies provide only marginal support for the presumed relationship between increased sway and falls. Patla et al. (1990) suggested that increased body sway is not necessarily an indication of a lesser ability to control upright posture and is not predictive of falls. Instead, the greater sway noticed in the elderly may be in response to a shift in the primary sensory system relied upon to control posture. It is hypothesized that, in the older population, increased sway may serve to augment proprioceptive input through the increase in joint movement at the ankle.

Although the Romberg test and its variations are widely used clinically to identify individuals with instability, the most compelling argument against the use of static stance tests to predict the likelihood of falls is derived from the fact that most fall events occur as a result of slips or trips (Patla et al., 1990). Because the task of maintaining a static stance position is quite different from the requirements needed to recover from a trip or slip, static balance tests have been viewed as inadequate to predict functional abilities and the future occurrence of fall events. Therefore, functional mobility tests should be included in the evaluation of balance deficits. As will become clear in Section III, the difficulty in establishing any single factor such as body sway as a valid predictor of fall events is due in part to the multifactorial nature of falls.

## B. Gait

Several authors who compared the gait patterns of young and older individuals have identified progressive idiopathic age-related changes in the gait pattern of the healthy elderly (Murray, Kory, & Clarkson, 1969; Wall, Hogan, Turnbull, & Fox, 1991). These age-related changes, starting in the sixth decade, prompted Murray et al. (1969) to adopt the term *presenile gait* to describe this idiopathic condition.

The most commonly reported changes in the gait pattern of older individuals are a decrease in gait velocity, an increase in the double-support stance period (when both feet are on the ground simultaneously), a decrease in step length, and a larger stride width. The elderly also make contact with the ground using a more flat-footed contact pattern. It appears that all these age-related gait modifications have a common goal: improving stability and safety during gait (Wall et al., 1991).

The majority of the earlier studies comparing gait between young and older individuals concentrated almost exclusively on the movement pattern characteristics and speed of walking. Winter et al. (1990) expanded this analysis by measuring and comparing the forces and moments present at the joints of the lower extremities during ambulation. Their findings indicated that healthy and fit elderly individuals demonstrate a decreased power during the push-off phase of gait. Because power at push-off is directly related to the forward propulsion of the body, this finding is consistent with the lower walking velocity exhibited in the older population.

The second significant finding of the study by Winter et al. was that, contrary to the overall age-related kinematic changes that are aimed at providing increased stability during gait, the older individuals had a lower *index of dynamic balance*. This index provides an indication of the level of cohesion between the motor activity patterns occurring at the hip and knee. This reduction would suggest a deterioration in the system providing dynamic support of the body against gravity. The authors suggested that this decrease in active support may be one factor participating in the increased frequency of falls seen in the elderly. It is also possible that the kinematic adjustments seen in the elderly are compensatory strategies resulting from this decreased active balance function.

Although several studies have demonstrated a gradual decline of the quality of gait with aging, the underlying causes of these changes (in the absence of a pathology) are yet unknown. In most cases, these changes are presumed to be the result of progressive age-related deterioration in the musculoskeletal and central and peripheral nervous systems. It has also been proposed that behavioral changes, such as fear of falling and depression, may be important contributing factors leading to progressive adaptive gait changes in the older population. Fear of falling is often seen in older individuals who have fallen or have friends who were injured (and possibly died) as a result of a fall (Tideiksaar,

1989). Rehabilitation therapists work only a short time in direct contact with older patients before this fear is voiced to them.

In some cases, the progressive changes seen in the gait pattern of older individuals may culminate in a clinically significant gait disorder of idiopathic origin. In the elderly male, idiopathic senile gait is characterized by walking with a broad base, small steps, diminished arm swing, and a stooped posture. In females, senile gait is characterized by a narrow base and increased side-to-side movement (Rubino, 1993). Both genders also show a much slower gait velocity. Sudarsky and Ronthal (1983) reported that 8 of 50 (16%) consecutive elderly patients seen in their clinic for previously undiagnosed gait disorders had no identifiable cause for these changes.

But in most cases, as in the remaining 42 patients studied by Sudarsky and Ronthal (1983), gait dysfunction seen in the elderly can be attributed to neurological or orthopedic disorders. Because there is a high incidence of neurological and orthopedic problems in the older population, it is not always possible to distinguish between gait changes that are due to aging and those that are due to a specific or unspecified disease process. In fact, it is likely that changes in gait pattern, including those described above, are not the result of chronological age alone but rather of a disease process or physical inactivity (Imms and Edholm, 1981). Several specific dysfunctional gait patterns related to neurological diseases have been described (Rubino, 1993; Sudarsky, 1990; Sudarsky & Ronthal, 1983).

Whether from idiopathic origin or the result of well-diagnosed neurological or orthopedic dysfunctions, decreased mobility afflicts a significant percentage of the elderly population. In 1987, the National Center for Health Statistics issued a report stating that "the elderly were more likely to have problems with walking than with any other personal care activity"

(Dawson, Hendershot, & Fulton, 1987, p. 2). Of 26.4 million community-living individuals aged 65 and over, 4.9 million (19%) had difficulty walking. This percentage increased from 12% in the 66–69 age range to 40% in the group 85 years and over.

Lundgren-Lindquist, Aniansson, and Rundgren (1983) reported that, in the Swedish population over the age of 79 that they studied, 25% required an assistive device to walk and none of the subjects could walk comfortably at a speed of 1.4 m/s. This speed is of particular interest because it corresponds to the standard speed for timing pedestrian crossing signals in Sweden. Therefore, unexpectedly, the time allowed for crossing a street may represent a hazard to the elderly, who may not have adequate time to cross the street. To compensate, they may adopt an unusually fast speed of walking that could result in an increased chance of falling. This inability to walk safely across an intersection is a good example of a deterrent sufficient to limit the social interactions of individuals who have difficulty walking.

Anywhere from 40 to 50% of nursing home residents have major problems with mobility (Sudarsky, 1990). A fall experience is a contributing factor in 40% of nursing home admissions (Tinetti, Speechley, & Ginter, 1988). Actually, mobility dysfunction is one of three most often cited factors for admission to the nursing home, along with incontinence and decline in cognitive function. In addition to its negative impact on physical health, the consequences of decreased mobility include personality changes, decreased interaction with family and peers, decreased participation in activities, and loss of social contact—all of which can lead to depression and decreased physical function.

Based on the outcome of functional stability and mobility tests, elderly individuals who demonstrate an increased difficulty with walking appear to be more prone to experience fall events (Campbell

et al., 1989; Tinetti et al., 1988). Because of this, gait and mobility rating scales have been developed in order to identify individuals who are at a greater risk of falls (Berg, Wood-Dauphinee, Williams, & Gayton, 1989; Tinetti, Williams, & Mayewski, 1986).

## III. Falls

### A. Contributing Factors

A review of the literature on falls in the elderly reveals an extensive list of risk factors that may participate in causing a fall event. These risk factors can be categorized into two larger groups: *predisposing* risk factors and *situational* risk factors (Speechley & Tinetti, 1990).

Predisposing risk factors are factors directly related to the physical and cognitive function of the individual. These risk factors are considered to be of either intrinsic or extrinsic origin. Intrinsic factors directly relate to cognitive, sensory, neurological, or musculoskeletal deficits occurring as the result of the normal aging process or the presence of disease. Extrinsic predisposing risk factors are due to physical or cognitive changes caused by short- or long-term external influences such as medication and alcohol. Several predisposing risk factors have been shown to be directly related to an increased risk of falls. These include (to name only a few) the use of medication (namely, sedatives and psychotropics), cognitive impairment, disability of the lower extremities, abnormality of balance and gait, poor vision, decreased sensory function, and foot problems (Tinetti, 1990; Tinetti et al., 1988).

Situational risk factors include everyday environmental hazards and hazards related to the activity in which the individual is involved. Environmental factors may contribute to more than 40% of fall events. They include, for example, stairs, snow, ice, and loose objects on the floor.

The use of walking aids is also an important risk factor for falls in the elderly: Tinetti (1987) reported that incorrect use of walking aids accounted for 10% of the reported falls in a population of ambulatory nursing home residents.

Most falls in the elderly have a multifactorial etiology, with predisposing and situational risk factors often coexisting, to result in a situation where falling is likely. For example, the poor balance function of an older individual may be adequate for walking on level surfaces but may contribute to falling when stepping over an object. Speechley and Tinetti (1990) suggested that risk factors are likely to be additive and that reduction or elimination of one risk factor may lead to a significant positive intervention in reducing the frequency of falls. The cumulative effect of risk factors on falls was clearly demonstrated by Tinetti et al. (1986), who studied a group of 79 elderly residents of an intermediate care facility over a 3-month period. None of the older individuals who had three or fewer of the nine risk factors (assessed by the authors at admission) fell during that time period. Strikingly, all subjects who had seven or more risk factors and 31% of the group with four to six risk factors fell. These findings are also supported by the greater incidence of falls found in the community-living frail elderly (50% fell over a 1-year period) as compared to the vigorous elderly (17% fell over a 1-year period) (Speechley & Tinetti, 1991).

Therefore, once the risk factors for an individual have been established, any partial or total correction of one or more of the risk factors could lead to a significant reduction in the risk of falling. Further discussion of specific intervention strategies can be found in Section IV.

## B. Incidence of Falls in the Elderly

Our knowledge of the frequency of falls in the elderly population living independently at home is limited because, with the exception of studies using a firm reporting routine and guidelines, most reported falls are limited to those that have resulted in an injury. Because falls are forgotten, denied, or explained as being normal based on the surrounding events, it is most likely that the reported numbers of falls are underestimates.

The proportion of people who experience a fall event increases with age. It is estimated that one-third of all individuals over the age of 65 and 40% of those over 80 fall at least once each year (Prudham & Evans, 1981; Sorock, 1988). Although fall occurrence statistics are most often reported in relationship to chronological age, this reporting approach may be an oversimplification of the problem. As described earlier, an individual's risk of a fall is directly related to the number of situational and predisposing risk factors present.

Surveys of falls taking place in medical institutions, including nursing homes and skilled care facilities, are more likely to be accurate than those of falls taking place in the home. Gryfe, Amies, and Ashley (1977) reported an annual fall rate of 668 incidents per 1000 in a population aged over 65 and living in a residential care facility, with 45% of all subjects falling at least once during the 5-year study. Frequency of falls rose with age, and women fell more often than men. In nursing homes, nearly 60% of ambulatory residents may fall at least once each year (Tinetti, 1987).

## C. Complications of Falls

Four discrete complications of falls are usually suggested: injury, fear, decreased mobility, and morbidity. In reality, these consequences often represent a continuum (from injury to morbidity) in the events following a fall. Therefore, although death may occur as a sudden result of a fall, it may also occur as the end result of a fall-related injury that is followed by increased fear of falling and concomitant decreased mobility.

## 1. Injuries

The incidence of serious injuries such as fractures and head trauma sustained as a result of a fall is reported to be between 6 and 11% (Nevitt, Cummings, & Hudes, 1991; Tinetti et al., 1988). Risk of serious injuries increases for falls that are the result of loss of consciousness or when lower extremity weakness or decreased cognitive function is present (Nevitt et al., 1991; Tinetti, 1987).

Hip fracture is one of the most common serious injuries resulting from a fall, and its incidence is directly related to age. For individuals between the ages of 65 and 69 years, only 1 out of 200 falls occurring at home results in a hip fracture. In the population older than 85 years of age, 10% of falls result in a hip fracture (Prudham & Evans, 1981).

Although the incidence of serious injuries is relatively small (roughly 10%), the approximate number of individuals affected is quite large if we consider that one-third of the population over the age of 65 fall each year. Using these data, 3.3% (10% of the 33% that fell) of all individuals over the age of 65 would suffer a serious injury related to a fall every year. Because it is projected that, by the year 2000, the number of individuals in the age group 65 years and older will reach 35 million (13% of the total population of the United States; Department of Health and Human Services, 1991), we can therefore speculate that serious injuries from falls would afflict 1.15 million individuals in this age group each year.

In contrast to the low incidence of major injuries, a large proportion of reported falls (approximately 55%) result in minor soft tissue injuries (Nevitt et al., 1991). Minor injuries (when compared to no injury) are more likely in individuals who have slower hand reaction time and decreased grip strength (Nevitt et al., 1991; Tinetti, 1987). Clearly, it appears that the likelihood of a severe or minor injury as a result of a fall is directly related to the presence of impairments that affect the individuals' ability to protect themselves when they fall.

The type of falls and the circumstances surrounding falls also influence the rate of injuries. Tinetti (1987), in a study of older individuals living independently in the community, reports that the vigorous elderly—who are more likely to fall when walking, when environmental hazards are present, and when on stairs—suffer a greater likelihood of serious injury (22% of fall events) than the frail elderly (6% of fall events).

## 2. Fear

Fear of falling itself may represent a problem for the elderly. Although the injurious consequences of falls can be measured with relative ease based on the percentage of reported falls, the psychosocial aftermath of a fall is more difficult to assess with respect to both incidence and severity. Tinetti et al. (1988) reported that almost 50% of fallers admit a fear of falling and one out of four individuals with a fear of falling purposefully avoids activities because of this fear.

Murphy and Isaacs (1982, p. 265) have coined the term *postfall syndrome* to describe the general characteristics of older individuals who, following a fall, "expressed great fear of falling when they stood erect, tending to grab and clutch at objects within their view, and showing remarkable hesitancy and irregularity in their walking attempts." Fear of falling has also been observed by other authors who have proposed terms such as *ptophobia* (Bhala, O'Donnell, & Thoppil, 1982) and *fallaphobia* (Tideiksaar, 1989).

In Murphy and Isaacs's study (1982), 26 of 36 patients over the age of 65 who were admitted to the hospital following a fall without significant injuries developed a postfall syndrome. Of these 26 patients, 10 were judged to be severely affected and were unable to walk unsupported. Of these 10 patients, 6 died and 3 were still in the hospital 4 months after admission. Of the 16 patients who had a moderate postfall syndrome and were able to walk independently, 3 died and 2 were still in the hospital 4 months after admission. Out of the 10 subjects who did not demonstrate signs of the syndrome, 1 died and none was still in the hospital 4 months postadmission. Factors that were related to the severity of the postfall syndrome included being housebound prior to the last fall event, having had previous falls, and being on the floor for more than 1 hour following the last fall event.

To help measure fear of falling in individuals who have fallen and those who have not, Tinetti, Richman, and Powell (1990) developed a measure of *falls efficacy*. Fall-related self-efficacy refers to an individual's perception of his or her ability to avoid falls during daily activities. Fear was therefore operationally defined as "low perceived self-efficacy or confidence at avoiding falls." The test consisted of participants rating their perceived confidence to perform 10 commonly accomplished tasks of daily living such as walking, taking a bath, getting in and out of a chair, and reaching into cabinets. Perceived confidence is self-rated on a continuous scale from 1 to 10 for each task.

Results obtained on a relatively small group of community residents indicate that the test appears to be valid and reliable. Strong correlation with measures of balance and a direct measure of fear support the validity of the test questionnaire. This test may be helpful in identifying individuals in the earlier stages of functional decline related to a self-perceived decreased efficacy in dealing with tasks of daily living without falling.

### 3. Decreased Mobility

Decreased mobility refers to the difficulty of moving from one place to another, ranging from difficulty in driving a car to the inability to move from a bed to a chair. The short-term or permanent mobility status of the older person can be severely threatened by injuries, fear, and temporary periods of bed rest (or immobility) resulting from falls.

Wild, Nayak, and Isaacs (1981) reported a greater deterioration of mobility and independence in a group of older individuals who fell at home as compared to age- and gender-matched individuals who had not fallen when followed over the same period of time. In a study by Clark, Dion, and Barker (1990) of a nursing home population, "taking to bed" was reported to occur at a rate of 13 per 1,000 resident-months, with 58% of those taking to bed doing so after a fall.

Although no specific numbers have been reported, self-imposed reduction of mobility even without a previous history of falls may be a common cause of the general deconditioning observed in some elderly individuals. This sedentary lifestyle is often self-imposed and based on fall events that have happened to friends or family members. Decreased walking and standing abilities have been reported to have a profound negative impact on health, emotional well-being, and quality of life (Dawson et al., 1987).

An active lifestyle may directly imply a more frequent exposure to events and situations causing a fall, but the health and mental benefits of an active lifestyle are believed to far outweigh this increased risk of falls.

### 4. Morbidity

Falling is the sixth leading cause of death among the elderly (Tinetti, 1990). Of the 11,000 deaths due to falls that occurred in 1986, 56% were sustained by individuals 75 years of age and older, making falls the leading cause of accidental death in the population over 77 years of age (National Safety Council, 1987). The mortality rate for falls and fall-related injuries in the age group over 65 years is reported to be 18 per 100,000 falls. The rate is especially high in the segment of this population that is over the age of 85 years, where rates are reported to be as high as 131.2 per 100,000 (Department of Health and Human Services, 1991). Fife (1987) reported that the estimates of death secondary to falls in the older population are likely to be underestimated because only 40% of death certificates mentioning a fall injury actually code the cause of death as *fall*.

In addition to the risk of death related to immediate complications of injuries sustained with a fall, the death toll associated with long-term physical and psychological complications of falls must be considered. The mortality rate within a 1-year period following a fall was found to be four times higher than for a gender–age match group of nonfallers (Wild et al., 1981).

## IV. Optimization of Function and Prevention of Falls

The increasing number of individuals growing older, the high incidence of falls in the older population, the morbidity and mortality subsequent to fall events, and the growing health-care costs associated with the treatment of injuries sustained from falls all provide the impetus for developing effective clinical intervention programs aimed at reducing the incidence of frailty and falls in the older population.

The most important intervention strategy may be in establishing an early screening and prevention program. As the individual gets older, efforts should be made to screen and identify specific predisposing and situational risk factors that may cause a fall. This screening should include an inspection of the living environment and a medical evaluation. The medical screening should include the evaluation of functions—sensory (visual, vestibular, and somatosensory functions); motor (strength and endurance); psychosocial (cognition, depression, anxiety, and fear of falling); and cardiovascular (blood pressure)—as well as a review of the medication taken. In addition, the individual's functional and mobility status (e.g., sit-to-stand transfers, posture, and gait) should be assessed using available assessment tools (Berg et al., 1989; Tinetti et al., 1986).

This screening should be followed up by effective strategies to address risk factors that have been identified. Examples of interventions include strength training for individuals with strength deficits, balance training for individuals with balance dysfunction, correction of visual deficits, and review of the medication taken. Predisposing risk factors that cannot be altered should be closely monitored and interventions providing coping strategies should be established. Examples of coping strategies include better lighting and visual orientational cues for individuals with permanent or partial vision loss, walking aids for marked balance deficits, and behavioral instructions for individuals who have postural hypotension or are taking medications that affect the central nervous system.

Environmental and situational accommodations, specific to the individual, should also be part of the overall intervention strategies. These may include grab bars in the bathroom, proper footwear, removal or securing of loose area rugs, and improved lighting in the stairways.

Individuals who have a history of falls deserve special attention. In addition to the intervention strategies outlined above, a psychosocial profile of the individual should be obtained in order to identify specific fall-related problems such as the fear of falling.

The implementation of a postfall assessment program followed by an appropriate intervention strategy is strongly suggested by the work of Rubenstein, Robbins, Josephson, Schulman, and Osterweil (1990). In their study of individuals residing in a long-term-care facility, the group who received the evaluation and treatment program following a fall event had 26% fewer hospitalizations, 52% fewer hospital days, 9% fewer falls, and 17% fewer deaths than the control group over a 2-year follow-up period.

Although a number of intervention strategies have been proposed and are already being used clinically to prevent frailty and fall-related injuries, strong research evidence of the efficacy of these interventions is still lacking. The next few years should provide important information on this topic because much effort is currently invested in this area of research, as exemplified by a set of eight collaborative intervention studies known as the *FICSIT* (Frailty and Injuries: Cooperative Studies of Intervention Techniques) trials (Ory et al., 1993). Some of the clinical trials being tested include strengthening and endurance training, the use of nutritional supplements, the use of hip protection garments, balance training, improving the safety of living environments, instruction on environmental hazards, and specific physical therapy intervention.

The variety of intervention strategies suggested to prevent or reduce the problem of falls in the elderly population reflects not only the multifactorial nature of the problem but also the fact that the underlying fundamental mechanisms through which falls occur are not completely understood. Future research should strive to determine the role of age-related changes in the etiology of falls, including changes that are musculoskeletal (loss of strength, endurance, or flexibility), sensorial (decreased function of visual, vestibular, or proprioceptive systems), and related to the central nervous system (changes in central processing ability or changes in cerebellar function).

## References

Berg, K., Wood-Dauphinée, S., Williams, J. I., & Gayton, D. (1989). Measuring balance in the elderly: Preliminary development of an instrument. *Physiotherapy Canada, 41*, 304–311.

Bhala, R. P., O'Donnell, J., & Thoppil, E. (1982). Ptophobia: Phobic fear of falling and its clinical management. *Physical Therapy, 62*, 187–190.

Brocklehurst, J. C., Robertson, D., & James-Groom, P. (1982). Clinical correlates of sway in old age-sensory modalities. *Age and Ageing, 11*, 1–10.

Campbell, A. J., Borrie, M. J., & Spears, G. F. (1989). Risk factors for falls in a community-based prospective study of people 70 years and older. *Journal of Gerontology: Medical Sciences, 44*, M112–M117.

Clark, L. P., Dion, D. M., & Barker, W. H. (1990). Taking to bed. *Journal of the American Geriatrics Society, 38*, 967–972.

Dawson, D., Hendershot, G., & Fulton, J. (1987). Aging in the eighties: Functional limitations of individuals age 65 and over. *Advancedata, 133*, 1–12.

Department of Health and Human Services. (1991). *Healthy people 2000* (DHHS Publication No. PHS 91–50212). Washington, DC: U.S. Government Printing Office.

Fernie, G. R., Gryfe, C. I., Holliday, P. J., & Llewellyn, A. (1982). The relationship of postural sway in standing to the incidence of falls in geriatric subjects. *Age and Ageing, 11*, 11–16.

Fife, D. (1987). Injuries and deaths among elderly persons. *American Journal of Epidemiology, 126*, 936–941.

Gryfe, C. I., Amies, A., & Ashley, M. J. (1977). A longitudinal study of falls in an elderly population: I. Incidence and morbidity. *Age and Ageing, 6*, 201–210.

Horak, F. B., Mirka, A., & Shupert, C. L. (1989). The role of peripheral vestibular disorders in postural dyscontrol in the elderly. In M. H. Woollacott & A. Shumway-Cook (Eds.), *Development of posture and gait across the life span* (pp. 253–279). Columbia: University of South Carolina Press.

Imms, F. J., & Edholm, O. G. (1981). Studies of gait and mobility in the elderly. *Age and Ageing, 10*, 147–156.

Isaacs, B. (1982). Disorders of balance. In F. I. Caird (Ed.), *Neurological disorders in the elderly* (pp. 135–145). Littleton, MA: John Wright PSG.

Lichtenstein, M. J., Shields, S. L., Shiavi, R. G., & Burger, M. C. (1988). Clinical determinants of biomechanics platform measures of balance in aged women. *Journal of the American Geriatrics Society, 36,* 996–1002.

Lundgren-Lindquist, B., Aniansson, A., & Rundgren, A. (1983). Functional studies in 79-year-olds: III. Walking performance and climbing capacity. *Scandinavian Journal of Rehabilitation Medicine, 15,* 125–131.

Murphy, J., & Isaacs, B. (1982). The post-fall syndrome: A study of 36 elderly patients. *Gerontology, 28,* 265–270.

Murray, M. P., Kory, R. C., & Clarkson, B. H. (1969). Walking patterns in healthy old men. *Journal of Gerontology, 24,* 169–178.

National Safety Council. (1987). *Accident facts.* Chicago: Author.

Nevitt, M. C., Cummings, S. R., & Hudes, E. S. (1991). Risk factors for injurious falls: A prospective study. *Journal of Gerontology: Medical Sciences, 46,* M164–M170.

Ory, M. G., Schechtman, K. B., Miller, J. P., Hadley, E. C., Fiatarone, M. A., Province, M. A., Arfken, C. L., Morgan, D., Weiss, S., Kaplan, M., & The FICSIT Group. (1993). Frailty and injuries in later life: The FICSIT trials. *Journal of the American Geriatrics Society, 41,* 283–296.

Overstall, P. W., Extol-Smith, A. N., Imms, F. J., & Johnson A. L. (1977). Falls in the elderly related to postural imbalance. *British Medical Journal, 1,* 261–264.

Patla, A., Frank, J., & Winter, D. (1990). Assessment of balance control in the elderly: Major issues. *Physiotherapy Canada, 42,* 89–97.

Paulus, W., Straube, A., & Brandt, T. H. (1987). Visual postural performance after loss of somatosensory and vestibular function. *Journal of Neurology, Neurosurgery and Psychiatry, 50,* 1542–1545.

Post, R. B., & Leibowitz, H. W. (1986). Two modes of processing visual information: Implications for assessing visual impairment. *American Journal of Optometry and Physiological Optics, 63,* 94–96.

Prudham, D., & Evans, J. G. (1981). Factors associated with falls in the elderly: A community study. *Age and Ageing, 10,* 141–146.

Reed, E. S. (1989). Changing theories of postural development. In M. H. Woollacott & A. Shumway-Cook (Eds.), *Development of posture and gait across the life span* (pp. 3–24). Columbia: University of South Carolina Press.

Richter, E. (1980). Quantitative study of human Scarpa's ganglion and vestibular sensory epithelia. *Acta Oto-Laryngologia, 90,* 199–208.

Rubenstein, L. Z., Robbins, A. S., Josephson, K. R., Schulman, B. L., & Osterweil, D. (1990). The value of assessing falls in an elderly population: A randomized clinical trial. *Annals of Internal Medicine, 113,* 308–316.

Rubino, F. A. (1993). Gait disorders in the elderly: Distinguishing between normal and dysfunctional gaits. *Postgraduate Medicine, 93,* 185–190.

Sheldon, J. H. (1963). The effect of age on the control of sway. *Gerontologia Clinica, 5,* 129–138.

Sorock, G. S. (1988). Falls among the elderly: Epidemiology and prevention. *American Journal of Preventive Medicine, 4,* 282–288.

Speechley, M., & Tinetti, M. (1990). Assessment of risk and prevention of falls among elderly persons: Role of the physiotherapist. *Physiotherapy Canada, 42,* 75–87.

Speechley, M., & Tinetti, M. (1991). Falls and injuries in frail and vigorous community elderly persons. *Journal of the American Geriatrics Society, 39,* 46–52.

Stelmach, G. E., Meeuwsen, H., & Zelaznik, H. (1990). Control deficits in the elderly. In T. Brandt, W. Paulus, W. Bles, M. Dieterich, S. Krafczyk, & A. Straube (Eds.), *Disorders of posture and gait* (pp. 253–256). Stuttgart and New York: Thieme.

Sudarsky, L. (1990). Geriatrics: Gait disorders in the elderly. *New England Journal of Medicine, 322,* 1441–1446.

Sudarsky, L., & Ronthal, M. (1983). Gait disorders among elderly patients: A survey study of 50 patients. *Archives of Neurology (Chicago), 40,* 740–743.

Tideiksaar, R. (1989). *Falling in old age: Its prevention and treatment.* New York: Springer.

Tinetti, M. E. (1987). Factors associated with serious injury during falls by ambulatory nursing home residents. *Journal of the American Geriatrics Society, 35,* 644–648.

Tinetti, M. E. (1990). Falls. In C. K. Cassel, D. E. Riesenberg, L. B. Sorensen, & J. R. Walsh

(Eds.), *Geriatric medicine* (2nd ed., pp. 528–534). New York: Springer-Verlag.

Tinetti, M. E., Richman, D., & Powell, L. (1990). Falls efficacy as a measure of fear of falling. *Journal of Gerontology: Psychological Sciences, 45,* P239–P243

Tinetti, M. E., Speechley, M., & Ginter, S. F. (1988). Risk factors for falls among elderly persons living in the community. *New England Journal of Medicine, 319,* 1701–1707.

Tinetti, M. E., Williams, T. F., & Mayewski, R. (1986). Fall risk index for elderly patients based on number of chronic disabilities. *American Journal of Medicine, 80,* 429–434.

Topper, A. K., Maki, B. E., & Holliday, P. J. (1993). Are activity-based assessments of balance and gait in the elderly predictive of risk of falling and/or type of fall? *Journal of the American Geriatrics Society, 41,* 479–487.

Wall, J. C., Hogan, D. B., Turnbull, G. I., & Fox, R. A. (1991). The kinematics of idiopathic gait disorder. *Scandinavian Journal of Rehabilitation Medicine, 23,* 159–164.

Whipple, R. H., Wolfson, L. I., & Amerman, P. M. (1987) The relationship of knee and ankle weakness to falls in nursing home residents: An isokinetic study. *Journal of the American Geriatrics Society, 35,* 13–20.

Wild, D., Nayak, U. S. L., & Isaacs, B. (1981). How dangerous are falls in old people at home? *British Medical Journal, 282,* 266–268.

Winter, D. A., Patla, A. E., Frank, J. S., & Walt, S. E. (1990). Biomechanical walking pattern changes in the fit and healthy elderly. *Physical Therapy, 70,* 340–347.

Wyke, B. (1972). Articular neurology: A review. *Physiotherapy, 58,* 94–99.

# Twelve

# Motivation and Emotion

Sigrun-Heide Filipp

Much research within the psychology of aging has focused on cognitive changes, mental health, or living environments, and this research has significantly increased the understanding of old age. Nonetheless, psychologists know comparatively little about motivation and emotion in the aged, and many textbooks or handbooks on aging do not even have special chapters devoted to this topic; instead, phenomena *related* to motivation or emotion are often indexed under special terms (e.g., life satisfaction). Yet, motivation and emotion in the aged deserve closer attention for a number of reasons: First, researchers need to understand the factors that regulate behavior in the aged in order to know how far motivational and emotional phenomena generalize across various ages. Second, because old age is a period characterized by physical decline, cognitive changes, and changing social roles, one needs to understand the role of motivation in these changes as well as their implications for emotional well-being. Third, mental and physical health, as crucial issues in the study of aging, can be understood completely only if motivational phenomena are taken into consideration as well. Finally, a better grasp of the

motivational and emotional changes that take place across age might also be useful in developing programs to promote successful aging or to prevent pathological aging (see Vallerand & O'Connor, 1989).

## I. Approaches to the Study of Motivation and Emotion

The study of motivation centers on the question of why people initiate, terminate, and persist in specific actions under particular circumstances. A multitude of answers can be given to this question, of course, reflecting more general differences in (meta)theoretical approaches to the study of human behavior. These answers refer to goals or drives, current concerns, uncompleted intentions, or self- or control-related belief systems; that is, they usually involve some type of "internally rooted" need or motive, such as to achieve, to affiliate, to avoid pain, but also to hold a positive view of the self or to be in control of one's life. Similarly, no single, satisfactory conceptualization of *emotion* or other affective phenomena is agreed upon (Frijda, 1993). Nonetheless, there seems to be a consensus that emotion and affect constitute a primary motivational system that underlies memory, perception, thought, and action just as much as, for example, drives. Thus, emotional and motivational phenomena are seen to be most closely interrelated, if not even indistinguishable; they are also seen as intertwined with neurophysiological and endocrinological processes. Despite the variation in conceptualizations, two major theoretical perspectives have been adopted in order to account for what arouses emotions and motivational states.

*Cognitive theories* maintain that emotions and motivational states are primarily rooted in and regulated by cognitive activity. For example, to anticipate desired outcomes having instrumental value for higher order goals is at the heart of expectancy-by-value theories; causal reasoning and attributions are seen to mediate emotions and motivated acts, or cognitive appraisals of internal or external data are conceived of as the crucial determinants of particular emotions (see Weiner, 1980, for an overview). In addition, because humans continuously develop knowledge about their environment and their selves, motivational and emotional processes are seen to operate in conjunction with or directly implicate these knowledge structures.

On the other hand, emotion and motivation have been viewed from the perspective of *arousal* or *activation* theory. Usually, the term arousal refers to a variety of psychophysiological states that are characterized by high degrees of excitation, activation, or energy mobilization. It is often maintained that high levels of arousal are a *prerequisite* for the experience of emotion. Most prominent is the idea that changes in neural activity are affecting particular innately determined facial expressions, which, in turn, generate the subjective experience of a particular emotion through sensory feedback from muscular activity (Izard & Buechler, 1980).

For the purpose of this chapter, it is im-portant to note that both approaches also differ in their openness toward a developmental focus. Given the obvious relevance of biological functioning to the experience of emotion and many motivational phenomena, arousal theory has gained particular attention. One of the most robust and repeatedly replicated findings is that there is a general slowing of the aging organism in both biological and psychological processes (cf. Salthouse, 1991; Schaie, 1989), an idea reflected in one of the metaphors of aging in which life is thought of as a journey on which the young appear as restless explorers of life and the aged as those who know all about life (Birren & Fisher, 1992).

Research based on cognitive theories, on the other hand, has been less explicit with regard to old age. Instead, studies have often been linked to general or differential psychology, although some researchers have referred to aging as bringing about, for example, significant changes in goals and values or an increased desire for personal growth (Ryff, 1985). These changes have often been conceived of from a clearly developmental perspective, as indicated, for example, by emotional *maturation* (cf. Labouvie-Vief, DeVoe, & Bulka, 1989), rather than from a contextual view of aging, which would focus more on changing social roles or living conditions that shape motives and emotions across the life span.

In the following sections, quite divergent issues are addressed. First, studies on emotion and affect in old age that are predominantly based on a noncognitive view of emotions are presented. Second, a closer look is taken at motives that are related to two frequently studied behavioral domains, achievement and affiliation. Some of these studies have clearly adopted a cognitive view of motivation, although many social motives are not considered to be mediated cognitively. Hence, the cognitive versus noncognitive distinction of motivation and emotion cannot be strictly maintained in organizing this chapter.

## II. Studies of Emotion and Affect in Old Age

Interest from developmentalists in emotions and affect was often centered on the ontogenesis of emotion in the early years, and it is only a few years since Levenson, Carstensen, Friesen, and Ekman (1991) pointed out that studies of the various manifestations of emotion in old age are almost completely lacking. Meanwhile, quite a few studies with aged samples are available in which emotions were investigated as individual phenomena (i.e., in their subjective and physiological manifestations) as well as social phenomena (i.e., expressed in faces, voices, and postures).

### A. The Experience of Emotion in Old Age

There have been various attempts to describe emotions in terms of their quality as well as their intensity. Some authors have focused on distinct "basic" emotions (e.g., fear, anger, and disgust) and have tried to elaborate their very distinct motivational, experiential, and physiological aspects (Izard & Buechler, 1980). Others have argued that emotions can be satisfactorily classified as either *positive* or *negative*, particularly when used as indicators of subjective well-being. Diener, Sandvik, and Pavot (1991) assessed the intensity and frequency with which positive or negative affect was experienced and were able to show that it is the relative frequency of positive over negative affect, and not its intensity, that predicts subjective well-being and happiness.

From a developmental perspective, however, the intensity parameter was of particular interest, and divergent predictions were delineated with regard to the nature of age-related changes. Because aging is associated with a decrease in parasympathetic and sympathetic innervation, an emotional blunting and diminu-

tion in the intensity of affective experience was expected. In contrast, Schulz (1985) concluded from the scarce evidence at that time that elderly people may experience emotions more intensely and over a longer duration than younger people due to an age-related decrease in the efficiency of homeostatic mechanisms that restore equilibrium following autonomic activation. Since then, quite a few studies have assessed arousal and intensity of affect, both via self-report measures as well as physiological indicators.

Diener, Sandvik, and Larsen (1985) conducted an age-comparative study (age range 16–68) that revealed distinct decreases in affect intensity as age increased. Although old age was not represented adequately in this study, these authors discussed their results from a contextual as well as a developmental point of view by noting (a) age-related differences in current life conditions (e.g., young people being more likely than older people to be exposed to stimulating "fun events" and stressful experiences); and (b) the exposure of elderly people to many more emotional incidents in their entire lives by which they could have become "habituated." This is quite in line with Schulz's (1985) proposition that an accumulated storage of emotion-related experiences might create higher thresholds for experiencing emotions of comparable intensity when people are exposed to similar emotion-arousing events in later years.

Instead of relying solely on self-report measures, Levenson et al. (1991) were among the first to directly examine arousal of the autonomic nervous system (ANS) elicited by different emotions in a sample of healthy aged adults (mean age 77). Two tasks were used to instigate these emotions: Subjects had to relive emotional memories and also voluntarily construct representations of emotional facial expressions. Results indicated both differences and similarities when compared to results reported for younger samples from other studies. Similarities were observed in the patterns of autonomic differentiation of emotions found in both age groups, particularly when the aged were asked to relive emotional memories; self-reports of emotions and the spontaneous production of emotional facial expressions during recall of these memories were comparable, as well. However, differences were observed in the intensity of emotion-specific ANS activity, which proved to be much reduced in the aged sample. Similar results were recently reported from a study of marital interaction observed in older and middle-aged couples, in that physiological arousal assessed during various types of conversation proved to be significantly lower in the older couples (Levenson, Carstensen, & Gottman, 1994).

These findings, in sum, support the notion that hypoarousal is much more characteristic of emotionality in old age than hyperarousal, although contradictory evidence has been reported as well (cf. Malatesta & Kalnok, 1984). Despite measurement issues, which are always considered to account for the heterogeneity of results, the various neurophysiological and endocrinological changes in late life do not follow a consistent path, thus leaving room for considerably high degrees of interindividual variance.

Researchers were also interested in issues related to *affect prevalence* in elderly people, old age being seen to bear the risk of predominantly negative affect. However, empirical evidence has proved to be quite in contrast to these predictions. Smith and Baltes (1993) reported from the Berlin Aging Study, with a representative sample of old and very old subjects (age groups 70–74 to over 95), that although frequency of positive affect (emotions associated with mental alertness, energy, and enthusiasm) proved to decrease slightly with age, frequency of negative affect (fear, distress, anger, guilt, and shame) did not differ across age groups. A similar picture is drawn by results from the longi-

tudinal study on comparison processes in old age[1] (see Ferring & Filipp, 1995). Frequency as well as intensity of positive and negative affect were assessed in a sample of "young old" (N = 264, aged 65–75) and "old old" (N = 88, aged 75–92) at two measurement occasions using a MANOVA design (time span: 10 months). With regard to affect *intensity*, positive affect proved to be lowered and to decrease significantly over time within the older as compared to the younger group; yet, again intensity of negative affect was similar in both age groups as well as stable over time. With regard to *frequency* of affect, significant age differences emerged, old olds scoring lower on positive, though also scoring higher on negative affect, accompanied by a significant decrease in frequency of positive affect over time which was not observed in the group of young olds. Recently, Levenson et al. (1994) added evidence from their age-comparative study of couples in long-term marriages (aged 40–50 or 60–70). Subjects were asked to engage in three types of conversation, discussing topics that were mutually agreed-upon pleasant, continuously disagreed upon, and neutral. The amount of negative and positive affect was calculated for each couple; results indicated that marital positivity increased with age and, more generally, confirmed the view that aging is not necessarily accompanied by an increase in negative affect.

## B. The Expression of Emotion in Old Age

There have been several attempts to investigate how functional and structural changes in the aging organism might also affect the expression of emotion in old age. It has been speculated that emotional expressivity should be characterized either by a delayed onset of, or by reductions in, the "clarity" of emotional expressions in

[1]The study is supported by a grant from the German Research Foundation (Fi 343/3-2).

elderly people. This hypothesis was based on assumptions that autonomic reactions to emotionally relevant stimuli (e.g., blushing or facial muscle activity) become less marked, or wrinkles and sagging skin interfere with the signals related to the emotion actually experienced. Consequently, the aged were seen as having difficulties in adequately expressing emotional information, and, in turn, their partners as having difficulties in decoding emotional signals from them. Moreover, the aged were seen to perform poorly in decoding the emotional signals of others, ostensibly due to a lowered interest in others' emotional cues.

Malatesta, Izard, Culver, and Nicolich (1987) conducted an age-comparative study of the accuracy of young, middle-aged, and aged women in understanding the emotion expressed in the faces of similarly aged other women. Emotional arousal was induced experimentally by having these subjects ("encoders") recall personally significant events that elicited distinct, strong emotions (e.g., anger, happiness). Facial expressions of emotion during these induction procedures were recorded on videotapes and were subsequently presented to the other group of subjects ("decoders"), who were asked to judge the dominant emotion displayed by the "encoders." The results of this study indicate, first, that the ability to express emotional information adequately (as reflected in decoders' judgments) does not decrease with age. However, the nature of the emotion-eliciting task might have played an important role, as can be concluded from a comparison with results reported by Levenson et al. (1991). These authors also used a relived emotions task and were equally unable to find age differences in the expression of emotions. They had, however, also asked their subjects to voluntarily construct representations of emotional facial expressions. Age-related differences became clearly observable in this task: The quality of the various facial configurations (as indicated by ratings on a facial action coding system) proved to be much lower in their aged sam-

ple compared to younger subjects, presumably due to a lessening of voluntary muscular control with age.

A second set of results reported by Malatesta et al. (1987) refers to accuracy in decoding emotions. Here, their older subjects proved to be less accurate in decoding the emotions that had been experimentally elicited in the encoder group, but a strong interaction effect was obtained, indicating that the aged have high capabilities of understanding emotions in same-aged partners, whereas they perform poorly in decoding emotions in younger or middle-aged people. Although this heightened accuracy in decoding emotions in age peers was found for all age groups, the effect was most pronounced in the oldest group. More recently, Malatesta-Magai, Jonas, Shepard, and Culver (1992), who attempted to link emotion expressivity to personality traits, reported that older subjects proved to be less inhibited than younger subjects in expressing emotion in an interview session (during anger mood recollections), as well as in a fear and sadness induction.

Thus, in sum, one can conclude that—as Levenson et al. (1991, p. 9) put it—the basic emotional "machinery" is still intact in old age. If aged people sometimes appear to be "less emotional" in their natural environment, this might be due in part to particular affect-regulation strategies they have learned to use. Although people of all ages employ tactics and strategies to control their emotions, these are seen to become more prominent in old age and to result in a lessening of negative affect. Of course, these strategies have deserved particular interest in explaining the "paradox" of positive affect in old age.

## C. Perspectives on the Paradox of Well-Being in Old Age

A variety of theoretical conceptions has been proposed to account for the often noted picture of contentment and positive affect amidst threat and loss in old age, and hypotheses derived from various theories have been presented in the literature.

According to social integration theory, social networks and convoys serve as effective buffers against the detriments of aging (Antonucci & Jackson, 1987). This idea was recently stated more explicitly with regard to old age by Carstensen (1993) in her *Social Emotional Selectivity Theory* (see Section IV). In this "energy conservation" view, elderly people are seen to conserve their emotions better, as an adaptive response to the reductions in physical stamina that accompany old age. In particular, they are seen to afford fewer and fewer persons the power to affect them profoundly, and thus may have also made progress throughout their lives in their ability to limit the experience of negative emotions.

In addition, selectivity in choosing others as *comparison targets* to provide feelings of self-worth ("downward comparisons") has been posited by social comparison theory; downward comparisons might be a mechanism that is applicable to people of all ages. Nonetheless, social comparison processes were reported to be less salient in old age and the aged to be generally less sensitive to social comparison feedback (Suls & Mullen, 1982). Instead, it has been proposed that temporal comparisons (comparisons between present and past self) become more prominent, along with a shift in orientation away from social demands toward the "inner life" and toward self-fulfillment based on personal standards and goals. Yet only preliminary results are available, so far. Filipp and Buch-Bartos (1994) reported from a study of elderly women (aged 70–89) that self-rated frequency of being engaged in social comparisons proved to be completely unrelated to all measures of well-being, whereas frequency of *temporal* comparisons was negatively related. This finding seems to indicate that temporal comparisons are comprised mainly of *upward* comparisons

that can neither be equated, on a priori grounds, with opportunities to fortify current self-esteem, nor be adequately compensated for by *downward* social comparisons. Obviously, attempts to distinguish the various ways of "looking back" and their diverging implications for well-being in old age are the crucial issue here (Wong & Watt, 1991).

Another perspective in explaining the maintenance of well-being is adopted within the dual-process model of development proposed by Brandtstädter and Renner (1990). This model claims a shift from *assimilative* to *accommodative* coping styles during middle and late adulthood. Examples of the assimilative style are instrumental activities; the accommodative style (comprising a broad spectrum of coping responses) includes, for example, the devaluation of and disengagement from blocked goals, the (re)adjustment of aspirations, and positive reappraisals of what has been initially threatening. One of the results in support of this model was that high scores on a measure of accommodative style moderated the relationship between perceived developmental losses and depressive mood in a large sample of aged subjects (see also Brandtstädter & Greve, 1994).

From the perspective of control theory, Heckhausen and Schulz (1995) have presented a similar argument, that morale in old age can be understood adequately only if developmental transitions in the employment of control strategies are considered. According to their proposition of the *primacy of primary control*, individuals of all ages have clear preferences for primary control, that is, for engaging in behaviors that shape their environment to fit their particular needs and potentials. This "built-in motivational system," which can be inferred even from the behaviors of toddlers, does not seem to lose its force up to late life, as reflected, for example, in the strong desire of the aged for autonomy. Nevertheless, because more and more biological and societal constraints on primary control accompany aging, these are considered to be compensated for only by a heightened investment in secondary control strategies (e.g., "palliative" coping behaviors).

The shift from assimilative to accommodative modes of coping or from primary to secondary strategies of control, respectively, is nicely paralleled by results reported within the traditional *stress and coping paradigm*, in which older subjects have repeatedly scored higher on distancing, positive reappraisal, or seeking social support (e.g., Aldwin, 1991). Similarly, within the Trier Longitudinal Study on Coping with Chronic Disease,[2] middle-aged (45–60) and old-aged (over 60 years) patients scored significantly higher on Threat Minimization than patients younger than 45 years—despite a significant decline in Threat Minimization over the time span of 1 year that was observed in *all* age groups (Filipp, 1992). Furthermore, some results do suggest that personal resources are invested in with increased efficiency by aged people (Meeks, Carstensen, Tamsky, Wright, & Pellegrini, 1989); other results point to an age-related increase in the "goodness of fit" between coping strategies and the nature of the stressor (for a review, see Blanchard-Fields, 1989).

In sum, a number of models have been proposed that aim to describe how gains and losses can be balanced and how resources and vulnerabilities appear to be coordinated in order to maintain positive affect in later life and to achieve successful aging. From this point of view, it seems as if research has been dominated too long by the presumed problems among the aged of "long-term" affective states, like emotional adjustment, suicidal state, or depression (see Kessler, Foster, Webster, & House, 1992). Aging clearly means *differential* aging, and one has to pay attention

to the resilience in late adulthood that might account for the preservation of well-being into old age in many people (Staudinger, Marsiske, & Baltes, 1995).

## III. Achievement-Related Motivation in Old Age

If one were to compile a comprehensive list of human motivations, the achievement motive would certainly appear as the best-documented example. Studies have focused on traditional achievement-related contexts, like schools or work settings, in which elderly are only rarely to be found as subjects. Yet, a few hypotheses on age-related changes in achievement motivation have been proposed. Raynor and Entin (1983), for example, argued that people, as they age, change from a more extrinsic to a more intrinsic orientation; and goals related to striving and getting ahead are assumed to change to goals related to preserving their accomplishments and integrating the various aspects of their lives. Empirical evidence, so far, is scarce. Veroff, Reuman, and Feld (1984) reported from two national representative surveys in the United States in 1957 and 1976 a decisive age-related decline in the achievement motive with age, but only for the subsample of women, not for men. Moreover, when controlling for age and education effects, women in the 1976 sample scored higher than women in the 1957 sample, whereas there were no differences among men. In general, it was concluded that the achievement motive should not be considered a stable trait, and it is obvious from these and other studies that assessments of motive strength at various points of the life span need to be related to work and family patterns rather than to age per se.

By far the greatest interest in motivational processes in the aged has emerged from the psychology of *cognitive* aging. This research has, in general, reported

[2]The study was supported by a grant from the German Research Foundation (Fi 343/1-2).

declines in psychometric intelligence on the statistical level of means, and has thus resulted in a negative portrayal of aging (see Schaie, Ch. 15, this volume). However, the interindividual variance in the cognitive performance of the aged has been reported to be impressive, and differences in health, prior level of cognitive functioning, and lifestyle have been considered in order to account for this variance (e.g., Willis, Jay, Diehl, & Marsiske, 1992). In addition, the complex interactions between ability and motivation processes in cognitive performance have become increasingly evident. Thus, the study of motivation in the aged became somehow confined to the study of motivational influences on cognitive performance. Again, these motivational influences can be conceptualized differently and can be addressed from the *arousal* and *cognitive* perspective as well.

## A. Achievement Motivation from the Perspective of Arousal Theory

Research in the tradition of arousal theory has emphasized the level of vigilance, alertness, and speed of response among the aged (Salthouse, 1991; Schaie, 1989). Very broadly speaking, it has been assumed that a less energized or activated organism should exhibit less interaction with its environment, thus reducing the opportunity for all psychological processes (like perception, acquisition, or storage) to take place as individuals age. Accordingly, age-related decrements in various indicators of vigilance were reported, although the relationship between age and vigilance also proved to be moderated by task characteristics. For example, Giambra and Quilter (1988), although unable to obtain age-related differences or changes in detection accuracy, reported that response speed in such detections was clearly affected by age, as evidenced in longitudinal changes (18-year time span) as well as in cross-sectional differences. In fact, age-related slowing has

repeatedly been referred to as one of the most reliable psychological markers of aging. The role of speed in explaining age differences in psychometric intelligence has also been recently confirmed by Lindenberger, Mayr, and Kliegl (1993) within an age-comparative study of old (aged 70–84) and very old (aged 85–103) adults. They were able to show that, even within those age spans, the speed-mediated effect of age fully explained differences in general abilities as well as in specific measures (e.g., reasoning and memory). When discussing these results, proponents of the general slowing hypothesis of cognitive aging refer to a decrease in processing rate with age. Other researchers refer to the *attentional block hypothesis* by pointing to lapses of concentration in the aged due to a lowered ability to inhibit or suppress task-irrelevant information. This lowered ability, in turn, prevents access to target information and rapid response (for an overview, see Salthouse, 1991).

Other researchers have tried to consider age-related slowing from a slightly different point of view, by using *physical fitness* as the marker variable. Findings in fact have indicated repeatedly that reaction times were faster and performance on various cognitive tasks was enhanced in those elderly who were physically fit, as opposed to nonexercisers or less physically fit aged (Plante & Rodin, 1990). Because field studies cannot disentangle the combined effects of physical fitness and other factors on cognitive performance, quasi-experimental studies have been conducted, as well. For example, Dustman, Emmerson, and Shearer (in press) placed older adults in an aerobic exercise, an exercise control, or a nonexercise group for 4 months; response time and performance measures on various cognitive tasks served as criteria. It was reported that exercise had a considerable positive effect on these measures, presumably by counteracting some of the degeneration of the nervous system that occurs with age. Given the complexity of the processes involved, it is not surprising that others were unable to obtain similar effects (see Blumenthal & Madden, 1988, on a 3–month exercise training program on memory-search performance).

Finally, one could also speculate that cognitive tasks are more anxiety provoking in aged as opposed to younger subjects, due to, for example, their lowered self-perceptions of ability. In this case, *high* levels of arousal that are associated with anxiety should reduce the capacity of the working memory and interfere with the processing of task-relevant information. Whereas trait measures of anxiety have not proved to be age related in either cross-sectional or longitudinal studies (Costa & McCrae, 1988), divergent results have been obtained for test anxiety. Significant interactions were reported between age and anxiety level on performance, indicating a much larger negative correlation between anxiety level and performance in *middle-aged* than in elderly subjects (La-Rue & D'Elia, 1985). Other studies have reported anxiety level to be an important moderator of intervention effects (Yesavage, Sheikh, Tanke, & Hill, 1988) in that aged subjects with high levels of anxiety benefit more from a mnemonic training in combination with relaxation pretraining than those with low anxiety. Nonetheless, Willis (1990), in her review of relevant intervention studies, questioned whether performance can, in fact, be enhanced by reducing anxiety, given that researchers have often been unable to demonstrate reductions in anxiety level itself.

A quite different view has been adopted in arguing that vigilance decrements in the aged could be equally attributable to a decrease in *willingness*, rather than in ability, to engage in task-related behavior. Hence, motivational factors in the maintenance of efficiency were likely to be addressed from a more cognitively oriented view on motivation.

## B. Achievement Motivation from the Perspective of Cognitive Theories

Cognitive theories of motivation differ in which "cognitions" are considered to be crucial—anticipations of desired outcomes that serve as incentives, self-perceptions of ability, or control-related beliefs. Some studies have attempted to highlight the role of *incentives* and to enhance the effectiveness of cognitive intervention programs by manipulating them. For example, Hill, Storandt, and Simeone (1990) studied an aged sample in a two-by-two factorial design (skills training versus placebo, by incentive versus no incentive). Skills training focused on categorizing tasks, whereas the placebo group was given attention training on map-reading skills. The incentive was the chance to win a lottery for a round-trip airline ticket. (In order to ensure that this really was an incentive, participants were selected according to their high interest in airline traveling!) Results indicated that both training groups performed better than the placebo group, and that adding the incentive to skills training did not produce any further advantage.

A similar result was reported by Robinson and Ross (1987), who used monetary incentives (or equivalents, such as candies) in order to facilitate performance on concrete Piagetian tasks in a sample aged 59–94. Although the incentive groups scored higher than the no-incentive groups on all tasks, these differences failed to reach statistical significance. Warren, Butler, Katholi, and Halsey (1985) asked younger, middle-aged, and older subjects to solve arithmetic tasks under a monetary incentive or a no-incentive condition. Rather than measuring performance, physiological indicators of arousal were assessed. It was shown that the incentive actually did increase arousal, although in a similar way at *all* age levels. In addition, the physiological responses to the task condition (as compared to a control condition of rest) did not differ between these age groups. This was taken as a clue that elderly subjects might tackle task-related behavior in a similar way to younger subjects—as is also reflected in the finding that older and younger subjects, competing on a physical-skills task, did not differ in increments in arousal (Backman & Molander, 1986).

In general, it appears that the kind of incentives used in these studies was not very powerful in enhancing motivation and performance in the aged. One can even question why an increase in these types of rewards should in fact enhance motivation, or whether they might even decrease intrinsic motivation. Perlmuter and Monty (1989) have argued that the individual's level of engagement in the task is the crucial motivational factor, and that it depends mainly on *choice* and *perceptions of control*.

It is quite obvious that old age is characterized by diminished opportunities for and restrictions on control (Heckhausen & Schulz, 1995). What is more, it has been reported repeatedly that professional helpers prefer "manageable" aged individuals, that is, those who withdraw from efforts to control their lives themselves (M. M. Baltes, Wahl, & Reichert, 1991), and such helpers thus contribute remarkably to decrements in control. On the other hand, because internal control beliefs have consistently proved to be related to effective cognitive functioning in old age (as well as to health and well-being), attempts to prevent loss of control or enhance feelings of control in elderly subjects have a long history in the psychology of aging (Schulz, 1985). Such programs have been seen— more than any other type of intervention—to lead to generalized and pronounced effects in the cognitive domain, in particular to provide elderly subjects with opportunities to make choices that had not been available before. Perlmuter and Monty (1989) illustrated this by findings from an unpublished study aimed at

determining whether choice during a memory task would attenuate background interference (to which the aged are seen to be more susceptible than young people). Half of the task consisted of to-be-learned target words chosen by the subjects and the other half consisted of assigned words. Memory performance proved to be significantly enhanced for the choice part of the task as opposed to the assigned part. Moreover, under the choice condition, recognition of both target words and background words improved significantly; thus, choice obviously facilitated incidental learning as well. Although these experiments do not permit any conclusions on whether people of different ages benefit differently from choice, the results at least indicate that choice does have beneficial effects on performance in old age.

Other research has focused on measures of generalized as well as domain-specific control beliefs and their role in cognitive functioning. Recently, Gatz and Karel (1993) reported findings from their impressively large data set: Longitudinal results revealed an age-related increase in internality over the time span of 20 years; cross-sectional results indicated that older groups were relatively external at all times of measurement; time-sequential comparisons, finally, revealed that the oldest generation of women consistently scored highest on externality, suggesting sociocultural and contextual influences on control beliefs.

Remarkable inconsistencies, however, characterize the results on control beliefs as predictors of subsequent task-related behavior and cognitive performance (Lachman, 1991). The role of control beliefs might even be seen quite differently, as one can conclude from the 5-year longitudinal study by Lachman and Leff (1989); control beliefs assessed in a sample of elderly adults did not prove to affect performance in cognitive tests; rather, initial level of cognitive functioning proved to be a significant predictor of changes in control beliefs.

This might be viewed as supporting the more general notion that individuals come to perceive control primarily through feedback intrinsic to their own behavior.

On the other hand, perceptions of control or self-efficacy often diverge from what people, in fact, actually do and can do. This is most clearly evidenced in studies on *metamemory*, in particular on personal beliefs about one's intellectual capabilities and abilities to exercise control over one's memory (see Hertzog, Dixon, Schulenberg, & Hultsch, 1987). It is reported not infrequently that memory training programs, although having proved to be effective on performance measures, hardly influence the negative perceptions by the elderly of their memory capabilities, as can be seen in a study by Rebok and Balcerak (1989). These authors investigated the effects of short-term mnemonic training on both memory performance and two facets of memory self-efficacy in a group of young (aged 17–19) as compared to a group of old adults (aged 60–78). As expected, age differences in recall performance and memory self-efficacy were observed, both in favor of the younger group. In addition, results provided support for the effectiveness of the training in enhancing recall; yet, it failed both to reduce initial age-related performance differences and to increase both measures of self-efficacy in the elderly subjects. On the contrary, a significant interaction effect revealed that the young subjects benefited most in terms of increments in self-efficacy. Dittmann-Kohli, Lachman, Kliegl, and Baltes (1991) assigned their subjects, aged 63 to 89 years, to one of four treatment groups in order to investigate differential effects of these treatments on measures of self-efficacy. Only ability training (rather than, for example, a simple retest condition) resulted in positive changes in self-efficacy. However, these effects were restricted to test-specific self-efficacy and did not appear to generalize.

Based on these findings, attempts were made to restructure the self-perceptions of the aged of memory capabilities directly and to integrate these attempts into traditional intervention programs. In most cases, these attempts consisted of training aged subjects to reattribute the causes of success and failure in order to encourage further mastery attempts. Such a focus on *attribution patterns* has, more generally, emerged from studies of normative conceptions about the life span (e.g., about age-related decrements in the cognitive domain) and about controllability of change across adulthood (Heckhausen & Baltes, 1991). The types of causal attributions made for good versus poor performance were seen to reflect these normative conceptions and thus were expected to favor the young.

This was demonstrated in a study by Lachman and McArthur (1986), who asked young and aged subjects to make causal attributions for their own, for a same-aged, or for a different-aged other person's hypothetical good or poor performance. When self-attributions were compared with attributions for another person's performance, a similar pattern emerged: Young subjects discounted good performance in the elderly, that is, were less likely to relate it to ability factors and more likely to relate poor performance to inability; elderly subjects confirmed their expectancies for poor performance in themselves and in same-age others by attributing it to inability, as well. Various attempts to alter this attributional pattern have been based on an increasing consensus in the literature that individuals may be taught to reattribute failures or successes in a way that leads to positive effects on subsequent mastery attempts. For example, Lachman and Dick (reported in Lachman, 1991) combined memory training with an attributional persuasion retraining technique and were able to improve memory self-efficacy, whereas memory training alone was ineffective in altering these beliefs. Yet, an independent positive impact of reattribution training on performance still needs to be proved.

In sum, it seems highly likely that the maintenance and generalization of gains resulting from cognitive training may require the use of motivational techniques, because these were shown to increase older adults' compliance in other areas of functioning (e.g., health; see Rodin, 1986). Nevertheless, it is still necessary to examine the types of training and the types of task that together produce the greatest desirable changes in both memory performance and personal beliefs about one's cognitive capabilities (for a critical review, see Willis, 1990). In addition, research is still scarce with regard to how the elderly differ from younger people (as well as within their age group) in their desire to succeed and to avoid failure in achievement-related settings.

## IV. Social Motivation in Old Age

Social interactions, at all stages of the life span, are based on and driven by a variety of motives, such as the need for belongingness, the power motive, sexual desires, and altruism. It appears that a focus on interindividual differences in these motives has dominated research up to now, rather than systematically linking research to the psychology of aging. Nonetheless, there are a few remarkable exceptions, which deal with social activity, social support, or with the issue of dependence and autonomy in old age. Given the fact that excellent reviews of relevant research are available (M. M. Baltes & Silverberg, 1994; Carstensen, 1993), these issues are addressed here only briefly.

One popular notion (borrowed from disengagement theory) holds that elderly people withdraw from *social activity* and responsibilities; moreover, social withdrawal is not seen primarily as a result of a progression of losses in old age, but as a preparatory response to impending death, thus serving adaptive functions. A focus solely on the amount of social activity, of

course, does not provide any insight into the needs and desires underlying affiliative behaviors in aged people. This has been addressed more explicitly by Carstensen (1993). She proposed that elderly individuals may have fewer relationships, yet have selected those in which they can be meaningfully understood, share intimacy, and express emotions; people in later life are seen to seek fewer instrumental outcomes and to be more concerned with intrinsically meaningful aspects of interactions. Greater selectivity regarding which social contacts to engage in, and which to avoid or give up, may thus compensate for reductions in network size. Yet, to argue that relationships have more instrumental significance early in life, whereas they increase in emotional significance in later life, implies that needs for emotional sharing and intimacy grow during adult development. This is an important and far-reaching proposition, which certainly needs to be supported by more systematic research.

Interest in the social activities of the elderly was nurtured from yet another perspective, namely, from research on *social support*, defined as those interpersonal transactions that involve aid, affirmation, or affect (Antonucci & Jackson, 1987). Just as social activity is not found to be related consistently to indicators of adjustment, findings on social support also fail to reveal a simple pattern of "the more, the better." Instead, reciprocity in supportive relationships has been considered to be the crucial variable; in addition, research has pointed to unintended negative side effects of social support, and has questioned its beneficial effects on well-being; in particular, support may contribute to diminished autonomy and lessened feelings of control in many elderly people as well as victims of life crises (cf. Aymanns, Filipp, & Klauer, 1995).

Other studies have focused on whether the *adaptive value* of social support might change with age. For example, Calsyn and

Roades (1991) recruited a sample of young-old (aged 60–74) and old-old (aged 75+) subjects in order to investigate whether a self-report measure of social support yielded a more pronounced stress-buffering effect on morale in the older than in the younger sample. This, in fact, was not the case: Social support proved to be positively related to morale in both age groups and to be independent of amount of stress as well. On the other hand, moderator effects of age have been found. For example, Blazer, Hughes, and George (1992) investigated young, middle-aged, and old adults suffering a major depressive episode. Impaired social support proved to be more predictive of decreases in life satisfaction (over a 12-month period) in the middle-aged than in the older group. Hansson (1986) compared measures of social support in young-old and old-old subjects and found that those measures were related positively to indicators of morale and self-esteem, but only in the young-old group. Nonetheless, given the multitude of measures used, and given the many other factors that might account for differences (but not controlled for in these studies), the diversity of results is not at all surprising.

Of greater interest is the shift in emphasis that has been made, meanwhile. Instead of viewing elderly people as needy recipients of social support, research has focused on elderly people as providers of social support and on their altruistic motivation. Initially, developmentally oriented research revealed positive, linear relationships between age and indicators of altruistic motives, although only a few studies have addressed the adult years (e.g., Rushton, Fuller, Neale, Nias, & Eysenck, 1986). Elderly samples have been of less interest, presumably due to old age being considered either as a period in which individuals aim to extricate themselves from social demands and obligations or as a period that brings about frailness and dependency.

Quite in contrast, one could assume that providing support to others is a strong desire, particularly in elderly people. Not only may they wish to maintain reciprocity in supportive relationships, as do people of all ages; but helping may also restore or maintain well-being particularly in the aged, by providing a distraction from current troubles, by ensuring social acquaintances, or by lending a sense of meaning to life. In fact, Midlarsky (1991) reported from a series of studies with community-dwelling elderly that helping was the most powerful predictor of social integration as well as of self-esteem. To investigate the causal role of helping, an intervention study was conducted, for which two groups of participants were selected from an earlier study. An intervention group was exposed to information about volunteer opportunities through in-depth personalized conversations containing explicit encouragements to volunteer; no such information was given to the control group. Results indicated that intervention led to increases in both helping and volunteer activities; these, in turn, proved to be predictive of increases in well-being, controlling for prior level of well-being.

Moreover, findings from a field study by Midlarsky and Hannah (1989) conducted in public places (e.g., malls) are illustrative here. Two types of solicitors, namely either a pregnant or a nonpregnant woman, were asking for donations to a fund for infants with birth defects. Money was assumed to be potentially less available to retired adults than to middle-aged people in this study and observers were trained in estimating the ages of persons in these settings and were instructed to register the ages of all donors and nondonors. People of all ages were donating to the pregnant more than to the nonpregnant solicitor, yet remarkable age differences in generosity emerged in terms of significantly more older persons donating to either solicitor: Whereas 59% of those judged to be 25–34 years old were donating, this percentage jumped to 93% percent in the group judged to be 65–74, and was still 85% percent among those judged to be 75 years and older. Of course, because donations had to be made in public settings, the potential impact of these settings on prosocial behavior may vary with age, a possibility that certainly needs to be addressed by further studies. Nevertheless, Midlarsky (1991) concluded from her research that the ability of the elderly to express compassion and engage in altruistic behaviors ultimately serves as a pathway to successful coping in old age.

## V. Summary and Conclusions

This chapter has presented a highly selective review of research from the large domain of "motivation and emotion." This selectivity was guided by the idea of focusing particularly on those domains of research in which interesting data have been reported within the last years or stimulating propositions have been formulated that might guide further research.

First, evidence has been presented on how aged people experience and express emotions. Data seem to converge on the observation that there is a lowered intensity of emotion and affect in the elderly, as indicated by various physiological measures obtained under particular experimental conditions, such as reliving emotionally tuned experiences. Nonetheless, it is clear that even in old age the various distinct emotions are experienced differently and do have emotion-specific manifestations in autonomous activity. In general, research in this domain either has been confined to studying the various basic emotions or else has reduced the richness of emotional life to a single "pleasure versus pain" distinction; in addition, studies have been aimed, more or less explicitly, at relating these observations to neurophysiological and endocrinological changes in

the aging organism. In contrast, more "complex" emotions have remained widely unattended in research—those emotions that may arise from such cognitive activity as interpreting other people's interactive behavior, appraising the threat inherent in symptom perception, or ruminating on what one has or has not accomplished in life (to name just a few not uncommon instigators of emotions in old age). More generally, this relates to the question of whether the types of internal and external events that elicit particular emotions do change with age or whether particular events (e.g., loss of spouse) are associated with a lessened impact in old age because they are then appraised as being "on time."

In addition, propositions have been formulated on how emotions in old age might have evolved from individuals' lifelong histories of emotional experiences. Accordingly, rather than looking for the average effects of aging on emotion and affect, a differential perspective certainly needs to be adopted in research by looking, for example, at individuals' "emotional biases" in appraising events or by investigating how emotions are linked to autobiographical memory and the self-system. Although such approaches might be considered to represent a truly developmental perspective, they certainly pose a heavy burden on researchers in collecting and interpreting relevant data.

A second domain of research was addressed, namely motivational factors as they might underlie task-related behaviors in old age. Researchers seem to have little interest in measuring the achievement motive itself in the elderly or in investigating how they approach achievement situations, for example, from an expectancy-by-value view. Rather, studies have aimed mostly at ruling out the impact of motivational factors on cognitive functioning in aged people, paralleling the common distinction of "can" versus "try" in explaining behavioral outcomes. As has been reported over and over in the literature, age-related decrements in vigilance and speed prove to be the crucial factors here. When motivational processes are conceptualized differently, for example in terms of (generalized) self-efficacy or control beliefs as intervening cognitions, their contribution to explaining the variance in cognitive performance appears to be far less than their contribution to explaining well-being and morale. In addition, it is still far from clear whether it is a challenge for elderly people to strive for success or to avoid failure in the cognitive domain, given that aging is equated with cognitive decline in most people's developmental conceptions. Thus, the empirical picture is highly incomplete regarding what types of situation may indeed arouse what is usually called the *achievement motive*, and in whom this might occur. One could speculate here, as well, that the conceptual meaning and scope of motivational constructs need to be reformulated in order to allow for the implementation of the perspective on aging (Filipp & Olbrich, 1986).

Finally, a brief look has been given to research related to social motivation and affiliative behaviors in the aged. It appears that long-standing notions of social withdrawal or decreased social integration in old age have given way to perspectives that focus on the active role of the aged in selecting and shaping their social world. These affiliative behaviors have been conceived as highly adaptive strategies in coping with the detriments of old age. In addition, research has been enriched by a different perspective that views the elderly as providers of social support and help rather than as dependent on and cared for by others. Research on the nature of altruistic motives in the elderly is in its infancy, although it is stimulating to conceive of helping as a means of coping that might be peculiar to old age. This again reflects a shift away from describing various age-related phenomena (e.g., maintenance of morale) and toward investigating the mechanisms underlying them.

As in many other domains in the psychology of aging, it is insufficient to confine research to age-comparative and cross-sectional studies, for a number of reasons that are now well known. In addition, one of the principles of research on aging is that almost all data—physiological and psychological—show tremendous variability across individuals. Accordingly, it is extremely difficult to characterize the "typical" older person or "normal" aging. In fact, it seems to be far more promising to focus on variance rather than on means in studying old age. So far, this differential aging perspective has not been satisfactorily applied to the study of emotion and motivation in the elderly. Furthermore, although some changes do appear to be related to biological aging (like intensity of affect), many other changes may result from factors that are associated with being old, such as increased disease or loss of significant others. How these events are related to and account for variance is still an open question.

In addition, much research has not been linked explicitly enough to life-span models of development (e.g., models using notions like developmental tasks or crises), nor has it attempted to account for the various results from the perspective of successful aging. The model of selective optimization with compensation, proposed by P. B. Baltes and Baltes (1990), offers a conceptual tool for the study of motivation and emotion in old age, as well. Salient concerns or "motives" can be seen to be selectively related to domains that still permit the subjective experience of satisfaction and control, and aged people may strive to become primarily engaged in those behaviors that enrich and augment their reserves; thus, viewed from a metamodel of motivation in elderly people, motives can be equated with personal strivings toward compensation for what has been lost and the optimization of what has been left.

## References

Aldwin, C. M. (1991). Does age affect the stress and coping process? Implications of age differences in perceived control. *Journal of Gerontology: Psychological Sciences, 46,* P174–P180.

Antonucci, T. C., & Jackson, J. S. (1987). Social support, interpersonal efficacy, and health: A life course perspective. In L. L. Carstensen & B. A. Edelstein (Eds.), *Handbook of clinical gerontology* (pp. 291–311). New York: Pergamon.

Aymanns, P., Filipp, S. H., & Klauer, T. (1995). Family support and coping with cancer: Some determinants and adaptive correlates. *British Journal of Social Psychology, 34,* 107–124.

Backman, L., & Molander, B. (1986). Adult age differences in the ability to cope with situations of high arousal in a precision sport. *Psychology and Aging, 1,* 133–139.

Baltes, M. M., & Silverberg, S. B. (1994). The dynamics between dependency and autonomy: Illustrations across the life-span. In D. Featherman, R. Lerner, & M. Perlmutter (Eds.), *Life-span development and behavior* (Vol. 12, pp. 42–91). Hillsdale, NJ: Erlbaum.

Baltes, M. M., Wahl, H. W., & Reichert, M. (1991). Successful aging in long-term care institutions. *Annual Review of Gerontology and Geriatrics, 11,* 311–337.

Baltes, P. B., & Baltes, M. M. (1990). *Successful aging: Perspectives from the behavioral sciences.* Cambridge, England: Cambridge University Press.

Birren, J. E., & Fisher, L. M. (1992). Aging and slowing of behavior: Consequences for cognition and survival. In T. B. Sonderegger (Ed.), *Psychology and aging* (pp. 1–37). Lincoln: University of Nebraska Press.

Blanchard-Fields, F. (1989). Controllability and adaptive coping in the elderly: An adult developmental perspective. In P. S. Fry (Ed.), *Psychological perspectives of helplessness and control in the elderly* (pp. 43–61). Amsterdam: North-Holland.

Blazer, D. G., Hughes, D. C., & George, L. K. (1992). Age and impaired subjective support: Predictors of depressive symptoms at one-

year follow-up. *Journal of Nervous and Mental Disease, 180,* 172–178.

Blumenthal, J. A., & Madden, D. J. (1988). Effects of aerobic exercise training, age, and physical fitness on memory-search performance. *Psychology and Aging, 3,* 280–285.

Brandtstädter, J., & Greve, W. (1994). The aging self: Stabilizing and protective processes. *Developmental Review, 14,* 52–80.

Brandtstädter, J., & Renner, G. (1990). Tenacious goal pursuit and flexible goal adjustment: Explication and age-related analysis of assimilative and accommodative strategies of coping. *Psychology and Aging, 5,* 58–67.

Calsyn, R. J., & Roades, L. A. (1991). Stress, social support, and morale: Failure to replicate age effects. *Journal of Community Psychology, 19,* 373–377.

Carstensen, L. L. (1993). Motivation for social contact across the life span. In J. E. Jacobs (Ed.), *Developmental perspectives on motivation* (pp. 209–254). Lincoln: Nebraska University Press.

Costa, P. T., & McCrae, R. R. (1988). Personality in adulthood: A six-year longitudinal study of self-reports and spouse ratings on the NEO Personality Inventory. *Journal of Personality and Social Psychology, 54,* 853–863.

Diener, E., Sandvik, E., & Larsen, R. J. (1985). Age and sex differences for emotional intensity. *Developmental Psychology, 21,* 542–546.

Diener, E., Sandvik, E., & Pavot, W. (1991). Happiness is the frequency, not the intensity, of positive versus negative affect. In F. Strack, M. Argyle, & N. Schwarz (Eds.), *Subjective well-being* (pp. 119–137). Oxford: Pergamon.

Dittmann-Kohli, F., Lachman, M. E., Kliegl, R., & Baltes, P. B. (1991). Effects of cognitive training and testing on intellectual efficacy beliefs in elderly adults. *Journal of Gerontology, 46,* 62–164.

Dustman, R., Emmerson, R., & Shearer, D. (in press). Electrophysiology and aging: Slowing, inhibition, and aerobic fitness. In M. Howe, M. Stones, & C. J. Brainerd (Eds.), *Factors in atypical aging.* New York: Springer.

Ferring, D., & Filipp, S.-H. (1995). The structure of subjective well-being in the elderly: A test of different models by structural equation modeling. *European Journal of Psychological Assessment, 11,* 32.

Filipp, S.-H. (1992). Could it be worse? The diagnosis of cancer as a prototype of traumatic life events. In L. Montada, S.-H. Filipp, & M. J. Lerner (Eds.), *Life crises and experiences of loss in adulthood*. Hillsdale, NJ: Erlbaum.

Filipp, S. H., & Buch-Bartos, K. (1994). Vergleichsprozesse und Lebenszufriedenheit im Alter: Ergebnisse einer Pilotstudie. *Zeitschrift für Entwicklungspsychologie und Pädagogische Psychologie, 26*, 22–34.

Filipp, S. H., & Olbrich, E. (1986). Human development across the life span: Overview and highlights of the psychological perspective. In A. Sorensen, F. Weinert, & L. Sherrod (Eds.), *Human development and the life course: Multidisciplinary perspectives* (pp. 343–377). Hillsdale, NJ: Erlbaum.

Frijda, N. H. (1993). Moods, emotion episodes, and emotions. In M. Lewis & J. M. Haviland (Eds.), *Handbook of emotions* (pp. 381–404). New York: Guilford.

Gatz, M., & Karel, M. J. (1993). Individual change in perceived control over 20 years. *International Journal of Behavioral Development, 16*, 305–322.

Giambra, L. M., & Quilter, R. E. (1988). Sustained attention in adulthood: A unique, large-sample, longitudinal and multicohort analysis using the Mackworth Clock Test. *Psychology and Aging, 3*, 75–83.

Hansson, R. O. (1986). Relational competence, relationships, and adjustment in old age. *Journal of Personality and Social Psychology, 50*, 1050–1058.

Heckhausen, J., & Baltes, P. B. (1991). Perceived controllability of expected psychological change across adulthood and old age. *Journal of Gerontology, 46*, 165–173.

Heckhausen, J., & Schulz, R. (1995). A life-span theory of control. *Psychological Review, 102*, 284–304.

Hertzog, C., Dixon, R. A., Schulenberg, J. E., & Hultsch, D. F. (1987). On the differentiation of memory beliefs from memory knowledge: The factor structure of the metamemory in adulthood scale. *Experimental Aging Research, 13*, 101–107.

Hill, R. D., Storandt, M., & Simeone, C. (1990). The effects of memory skills training and incentive on free recall in older learners. *Journal of Gerontology, 45*, 227–232.

Izard, C. E., & Buechler, S. (1980). Aspects of consciousness and personality in terms of differential emotions theory. In R. Plutchik & H. Kellerman (Eds.), *Emotion: Theory, research and experience* (pp. 165–188). New York: Academic Press.

Kessler, R. C., Foster, C., Webster, P. S., & House, J. S. (1992). The relationship between age and depression in two national surveys. *Psychology and Aging, 7*, 119–126.

Labouvie-Vief, G., DeVoe, M., & Bulka, D. (1989). Speaking about feelings: Conceptions of emotion across the life span. *Psychology and Aging, 4*, 425–437.

Lachman, M. E. (1991). Perceived control over memory aging: Developmental and intervention perspectives. *Journal of Social Issues, 47*, 159–175.

Lachman, M. E., & Leff, R. (1989). Perceived control and intellectual functioning in the elderly: A 5-year longitudinal study. *Developmental Psychology, 25*, 722–728.

Lachman, M. E., & McArthur, L. Z. (1986). Adulthood age differences in causal attributions for cognitive, physical, and social performance. *Psychology and Aging, 1*, 127–132.

LaRue, A., & D'Elia, L. F. (1985). Anxiety and problem solving in middle-aged and elderly adults. *Experimental Aging Research, 11*, 215–220.

Levenson, R. W., Carstensen, L. L., Friesen, W. V., & Ekman, P. (1991). Emotion, physiology, and expression in old age. *Psychology and Aging, 6*, 28–35.

Levenson, R. W., Carstensen, L. L., & Gottman, J. M. (1994). The influence of age and gender on affect, physiology, and their interrelations: A study of long-term marriages. *Journal of Personality and Social Psychology, 67*, 56–68.

Lindenberger, U., Mayr, U., & Kliegl, R. (1993). Speed and intelligence in old age. *Psychology and Aging, 8*, 207–220.

Malatesta, C. Z., Izard, C. E., Culver, C., & Nicolich, M. (1987). Emotion communication skills in young, middle-aged, and older women. *Psychology and Aging, 2*, 193–203.

Malatesta, C. Z., & Kalnok, M. (1984). Emotional experience in younger and older adults. *Journal of Gerontology, 39*, 301–308.

Malatesta-Magai, C. Z., Jonas, R., Shepard, B., & Culver, L. C. (1992). Type A behavior pattern and emotion expression in younger and older adults. *Psychology and Aging, 7*, 331–561.

Meeks, S., Carstensen, L. L., Tamsky, B. F.,

Wright, T. L., & Pellegrini, D. (1989). Age differences in coping: Does less mean worse? *International Journal of Aging and Human Development, 28,* 127–140.

Midlarsky, E. (1991). Helping as coping. *Review of Personality and Social Psychology, 12,* 238–264.

Midlarsky, E., & Hannah, M. E. (1989). The generous elderly: Naturalistic studies of donations across the life span. *Psychology and Aging,* 346–351.

Perlmuter, L. L., & Monty, R. A. (1989). Motivation and aging. In L. H. Poon, D. C. Rubin, & B. A. Wilson (Eds.), *Everyday cognition in adulthood and late life* (pp. 373–393). Cambridge, England: Cambridge University Press.

Plante, T. G., & Rodin, J. (1990). Physical fitness and enhanced psychological health. *Current Psychology: Research & Reviews, 9,* 3–24.

Raynor, J. E., & Entin, E. E. (1983). The function of future orientation as a determinant of human behavior in step-path theory of action. *International Journal of Psychology, 18,* 463–487.

Rebok, G. W., & Balcerak, L. J. (1989). Memory self-efficacy and performance differences in young and old adults: The effect of mnemonic training. *Developmental Psychology, 25,* 714–721.

Robinson, K., & Ross, S. M. (1987). Incentives as a treatment variable for facilitation performance of elderly adults on concrete Piagetian tasks. *International Journal of Behavioral Development, 10,* 501–508.

Rodin, J. (1986). Health, control, and aging. In M. M. Baltes & P. B. Baltes (Eds.), *The psychology of control and aging* (pp. 139–167). Hillsdale, NJ: Erlbaum.

Rushton, J., Fuller, D., Neale, M., Nias, D., & Eysenck, J. (1986). Altruism and aggression: The heritability of individual differences. *Journal of Personality and Social Psychology, 50,* 1192–1198.

Ryff, C. D. (1985). Adult personality development and the motivation for personal growth. In D. A. Kleiber & M. L. Maehr (Eds.), *Advances in motivation and achievement* (Vol. 4, pp. 55–92). Greenwich, CT: JAI Press.

Salthouse, T. A. (1991). *Theoretical perspectives on cognitive aging.* Hillsdale, NJ: Erlbaum.

Schaie, K. W. (1989). Perceptual speed in adult-

hood: Cross-sectional and longitudinal studies. *Psychology and Aging, 4,* 443–453.

Schulz, R. (1985). Emotion and affect. In J. E. Birren & K. W. Schaie (Eds.), *Handbook of the psychology of aging* (2nd ed., pp. 531–543). New York: Van Nostrand-Reinhold.

Smith, J., & Baltes, P. B. (1993). Differential psychological ageing: Profiles of the old and very old. *Ageing and Society, 13,* 551–587.

Staudinger, U. M., Marsiske, M., & Baltes, P. B. (1995). Resilience and reserve capacity in later adulthood: Potentials and limits of development across the life span. In D. Cicchetti & D. Cohen (Eds.), *Developmental psychopathology* (Vol. 2: Risk, disorder, and adaptation, pp. 801–847). New York: Wiley.

Suls, J. M., & Mullen, B. (1982). From the cradle to the grave: Comparison and self-evaluation across the life-span. In J. M. Suls (Ed.), *Psychological perspectives on the self* (Vol. 1, pp. 97–128). Hillsdale, NJ: Erlbaum.

Vallerand, R. J., & O'Connor, B. P. (1989). Motivation in the elderly: A theoretical framework and some promising findings. *Canadian Psychology, 30,* 538–550.

Veroff, J., Reuman, D., & Feld, S. (1984). Motives in American men and women across the adult life span. *Developmental Psychology, 20,* 1142–1158.

Warren, L. R., Butler, R. W., Katholi, C. R., & Halsey, J. H. J. (1985). Age differences in cerebral blood flow during rest and during mental activation measurements with and without monetary incentive. *Journal of Gerontology, 40,* 53–59.

Weiner, B. (1980). *Human motivation.* New York: Holt, Rinehart & Winston.

Willis, S. L. (1990). Current issues in cognitive training research. In E. A. Lovelace (Ed.), *Aging and cognition: Mental processes, self-awareness, and interventions* (pp. 263–280). Amsterdam: North-Holland.

Willis, S. L., Jay, G. M., Diehl, M., & Marsiske, M. (1992). Longitudinal change and prediction of everyday task competence in the elderly. *Research on Aging, 14,* 68–91.

Wong, P. T. P., & Watt, L. M. (1991). What types of reminiscence are associated with successful aging? *Psychology and Aging, 6,* 272–279.

Yesavage, J. A., Sheikh, J. I., Tanke, E. D., & Hill, R. (1988). Response to memory training and individual differences in verbal intelligence and state anxiety. *American Journal of Psychiatry, 145,* 636–639.

# Thirteen

# Memory

Anderson D. Smith

Most older adults report that their memories have gotten worse as they have grown older (Ryan, 1992). These reports have been validated by a large number of laboratory studies showing differences in memory performance between young and old adults. It is also clear, however, that the nature of these memory differences is complex, and many factors seem to be important in determining the size of age effects. Because of this complexity, the laboratory study of memory remains one of the most popular research topics in the psychology of aging. For three of the years (1991–1993) since the publication of the last *Handbook* chapter on memory (Hultsch & Dixon, 1990), memory and aging research studies have represented 34% of all the published papers in the two journals, *Psychology and Aging* and *Journal of Gerontology: Psychological Sciences*.

In this chapter, major methodological and theoretical issues in the study of memory and aging are reviewed. Unfortunately, the literature cited will be very selective given the limitation of a single handbook chapter. Studies will be discussed only to illustrate methodological and theoretical issues. Fortunately, in the past few years, major substantive reviews of the memory and aging literature have appeared (e.g., Craik, 1994; Craik & Jennings, 1992; Kausler, 1994; L. L. Light, 1991; Salthouse, 1991), and these reviews provide a more comprehensive picture of the state of the field.

## I. Methodological Strategies

There are basically two research strategies used to understand age differences in memory. One method has been to manipulate task or stimulus variables with different age groups and look for statistical interactions between the manipulated variables and age. Interactions showing age differences in one condition and no age differences in another condition, or large age differences in one condition and small age differences in the other, are then interpreted as specifying what aspects of memory are affected by age and what aspects are not. Unfortunately, the cognitive mechanisms responsible for the interactions typically are only inferred because few studies include independent measures of the explanatory constructs.

A second research strategy uses correlational and individual-difference techniques that have been used more prevalently when examining complex cognitive processes like intelligence or reasoning (see Ch. 15 by Schaie and Ch. 16 by Willis, this volume). Recently, laboratory memory researchers have used the statistical control procedures of individual-difference research to identify cognitive mechanisms responsible for age-related variance in memory performance. Independent measures of potential mechanisms are developed and then used to predict age-related variance on different memory criterion tasks.

## A. Interaction Research

The research goal of traditional interaction research is to find conditions that bring about differences in the size of age effects. The "holy grail" of interaction research over the years has been to find memory conditions that produce no age differences, even though this quest has proven to be difficult at best. First, the finding of "no difference" always begs the power question. Early reports of no age differences in implicit memory, for example, were later replaced by significant age differences in implicit memory when larger samples of subjects were used (Hultsch, Masson, & Small, 1991). As discussed by Salthouse (1991), interaction research also has problems with the measurement scale used for the different conditions, and he suggested that performance levels need to be expressed in units of sample variability rather than in the original units of measurement or raw scores. Rarely is this done in aging memory research, however.

The greatest problem with interaction research is that memory is just too complex to be catalogued by simple two-way interactions. As soon as a two-way interaction is described, it is often modified later by a third factor that attenuates or amplifies age effects when it is included in the experimental equation. Published studies have claimed no age differences in recogni-

tion memory (as compared to recall), implicit memory (as compared to explicit memory), semantic memory (as compared to episodic memory), picture memory (as compared to memory for words), prospective memory (as compared to retrospective memory), and short-term memory (as compared to long-term memory). Later, each of these conclusions was shown to be too simplistic given a more complex analysis. Under certain conditions there can be age differences in recognition memory (White & Cunningham, 1982), implicit memory (Chiarello & Hoyer, 1988), semantic memory (Bowles & Poon, 1985), picture memory (Smith, Park, Cherry, & Berkovsky, 1990), prospective memory (Einstein, Holland, McDaniel, & Guynn, 1992), and short-term memory (Salthouse & Babcock, 1991). These conclusion reversals do not involve a failure to replicate. Instead, the two-way interaction between age and conditions assumed to vary along some memory dimension was simply modified by another condition or variable that produced a triple interaction.

As can be seen with even a cursory review of the memory-aging literature, the results of interaction research, even with the problems listed above, have provided further and further refinements in the specification of age differences in memory. The results thus far, however, should caution investigators not to overinterpret age-invariant memory findings or simple two-way interactions with age.

## B. Individual-Difference Research

Through various methods of statistical control, recent investigators have used individual-difference techniques to identify factors that can account for the age-related variance seen in memory tasks. Independent measures of some theoretical construct that is assumed to underlie age differences in memory are collected. Then, the extent to which these measures covary with memory performance is determined.

Regression techniques have been used to see if age-related differences in memory performance remain after the variance associated with the construct of interest has been controlled (e.g., Salthouse, 1994b). Regression, path analytic techniques, and structural equation modeling are used to determine if the factor of interest mediates the relationship between age and memory performance (e.g., Lindenberger, Mayr, & Kliegl, 1993). Although the systematic application of these techniques to different memory tasks is a relatively new research endeavor, the promise of this research is to directly relate different cognitive factors (e.g., working memory, verbal ability) and noncognitive factors (e.g., health, education) to age-related differences in memory, and to determine how different task and stimulus variables relate to possible underlying memory mechanisms. This research is discussed throughout the chapter as these topics are covered. Of course, this research is only as good as the reliability and validity of the measures used to operationalize the constructs.

## II. Resource Theories of Age Differences in Memory

Several different mechanisms have been proposed to account for age differences in memory. These proposed mechanisms share an assumption that there are limitations in the cognitive resources that older adults can use in memory tasks, but frame these resources in different ways. Different forms of the resource hypothesis predict that age differences will be found to the extent that the memory task (a) does not provide sufficient environmental support; (b) requires deliberate processing; (c) involves integration of the to-be-remembered information with context; (d) requires inhibition of irrelevant information; (e) has significant working-memory requirements; or (f) can be affected by perceptual speed.

### A. Environmental Support

Craik proposed a functional account for age differences in memory, suggesting that older adults are penalized more when the memory task involves less support, thus requiring more self-initiated processing resources to be devoted to remembering (see Craik, 1994). For example, in a recognition test the subject only has to pick out the words that were seen earlier. Free recall, on the other hand, offers less environmental support and more self-initiated processing at retrieval because the subject has to actively generate the items experienced earlier. Craik and McDowd (1987) had subjects perform a choice reaction time secondary task at the same time they performed a series of either recall or recognition paired-associate tasks. The two retrieval conditions were equated in difficulty by having the recognition tasks delayed until after the lists had been presented. Even when the performance levels on recall and recognition were equated, large age differences were found in recall but none were found in recognition. Supporting the idea that recall involves less environmental support and thus more self-initiated processing, there were longer reaction times in the secondary task with the recall task, and this effect was amplified in the old group.

### B. Deliberate Processing

Similar to the concept of self-initiated processing is the hypothesis that the size of age differences on memory tasks depends on the extent to which the tasks involve deliberate processing. Hasher and Zacks (1979) distinguished between effortful (i.e., deliberate) processing and automatic processing. Although deliberate processing requires effort and the use of self-initiated cognitive resources, automatic processing functions independently of attention or effort. Hasher and Zacks suggested that age differences would be found only on tasks that involved deliberate processing.

This hypothesis has had considerable support from the priming literature. In general, implicit or indirect memory measures of priming, such as filling in a word fragment (e.g., _ar_d_gm) with a word experienced earlier or completing a word stem (e.g., bec___), are assumed to be automatic indirect memory measures, and not acts of deliberate recollection. In fact, priming effects occur even in the absence of conscious awareness of the memory effects. A large body of literature suggests that age differences in implicit memory are much smaller than differences seen with explicit memory measures. Whether or not significant priming effects are found at all for older subjects seems to depend on the number of subjects used (Hultsch et al., 1991), or with the particular indirect memory test used (Chiarello & Hoyer, 1988). Good reviews of aging and implicit memory literature can be found in Graf (1990) and Kausler (1994).

One problem with the variety of indirect tests of memory is determining the extent to which the tasks are controlled by automatic and deliberate processing requirements. Park and Shaw (1992), for example, found no age differences in implicit memory when using a word-stem completion test, even though performance improved in both groups when environmental support increased by providing more letters in the stem (either two, three, or four letters). In other words, the environmental support manipulation affected the implicit task in the same way as it did a comparison explicit task in which the subjects were told to complete the stems with words seen earlier. Does this mean that environmental support operates on the automatic processes involved in both explicit memory tasks and implicit memory tasks? Unfortunately, it has been difficult to directly measure the extent of deliberate and automatic processes in any given task. Clearly, deliberate processing can contaminate implicit test performance, and automatic activation or familiarity is a component of most explicit tasks.

A new procedure for separating the deliberate and automatic components of memory tasks has been developed by Jacoby and his colleagues (Jacoby, 1991; Jacoby, Toth, & Yonelinas, 1993). Jacoby suggested that performance on most memory tasks, both explicit and implicit, are influenced by both processes, familiarity and deliberate recollection. Jacoby and his colleagues also have argued that older adults have deficits in deliberate recollection, but have no deficits in memory performance when only familiarity is involved.

Jennings and Jacoby (1993) measured both familiarity and deliberate recollection in an experiment examining age differences in a recognition memory task. In this experiment, young and old subjects were presented with a list of words and told either to read the words or to generate words when the items were represented as anagrams. After the presentation of the first list, they heard a second list of words for which they expected a later memory test. They then had two forced-choice recognition tests. On both tests, one word in each word pair was new and the other word was either presented in list 1 or heard in list 2. On the first test, subjects were incorrectly told that one word in each pair had been presented auditorily on list 2, and the other word was either new or one presented in list 1. They were to pick the word they heard in list 2. If they picked a list 1 word when it was paired with a new word, it had to be on the basis of familiarity, because if they had actively recollected the word, they would have rejected it and picked the other new word.

On the second test, they were told that one word was new and they had to pick the other word that they either saw in list 1 or heard in list 2. In the second memory test, recognition could be based on either familiarity or deliberate recollection. For an estimate of deliberate processing, the estimate of familiarity from the first recognition test was subtracted from the scores on the second test. The estimate of familiarity showed no age effects, whereas large age differences were found in the estimate of deliberate processing. Furthermore, when the recognition decision involved one of the words for which an anagram was solved in the first list, the recollection component was much larger than for the words only read, because of the more elaborate processing for those words. The familiarity component, however, was relatively unaffected by solving the anagrams (but see Jacoby, 1991).

## C. Failure to Integrate Context

Similar but more specific than the deliberate processing hypothesis is a hypothesis that suggests that older adults have greater problems actively integrating the memory context with the information they are trying to remember. This context is necessary to provide adequate retrieval cues for later remembering (Craik & Jennings, 1992; Park, Smith, Morrell, Puglisi, & Dudley, 1990). The hypothesis that older adults cannot take advantage of contextual cues was first systematically proposed almost 15 years ago (Burke & Light, 1981), but evidence supporting this hypothesis has been mixed. There are many studies showing age differences in memory for context. For example, older subjects have greater problems when trying to identify whether a word was presented visually or auditorily (Lehman & Mellinger, 1986), or when trying to identify which voice presented an auditory list (Ferguson, Hashtroudi, & Johnson, 1992).

If older adults are deficient in remembering and using context, they should show smaller "encoding specificity" effects. In other words, if they encode fewer contextual details, they should be less affected when there are changes in the contextual details between encoding and retrieval. In a series of experiments, however, Park and her colleagues have shown no age differences in the relative effects of encoding specificity between young and old subjects in either picture recognition

(Park, Puglisi, Smith, & Dudley, 1987) or word recall (Puglisi, Park, Smith, & Dudley, 1988). Again, however, the situation is more complex in that older adults failed to show encoding specificity if they had to perform a secondary digit-monitoring task during the memory task (Puglisi et al., 1988, Experiment 2). Rabinowitz, Craik, and Ackerman (1982) also showed less encoding specificity in older adults when weakly associated cues at encoding were changed to strongly related cues at retrieval. In both experiments, older adults had context-utilization problems when integration of the context with the targets was difficult, either because of a competing secondary task, or because the cues were weak and self-initiated integration was required.

The degree of self-initiated integration required in a task was manipulated directly by Park et al. (1990). A context picture was either unrelated to the target, perceptually related to the target (the two objects interacting in a single picture), or semantically related (two separate pictures of objects from the same category). The older adults' memory performance on recall of the unrelated targets was only 36% of the performance of the young groups. The performance of the older group relative to the younger group was greatly improved, however, when the pairs were already integrated (66% with perceptually interacting items and 70% with semantically related items).

The extent to which deliberate processing is required to integrate context with the to-be-remembered information, therefore, seems to be an important determinant of whether age differences are observed. If deliberate integration is required, age differences are found, and if less subject-initiated integration is required because of already existing integrations, age differences are smaller.

## D. Failures of Inhibition

Hasher and Zacks (1988) proposed a hypothesis that the reduced processing resources in older adults are due to the presence of task-irrelevant thoughts because of inefficient inhibition during working-memory processing. Because task-irrelevant information cannot be inhibited as effectively, older adults have less working memory for on-task processing. For example, Hartman and Hasher (1991) had different aged subjects finish a sentence with a final word (e.g., "She ladled the soup into her ___."). Then, sentences were presented that either contained the generated word (confirmed) or contained a different unexpected word (nonconfirmed). On a later implicit memory test, older subjects showed equal repetition priming (responding faster to the primed word) for both the confirmed and nonconfirmed words whereas the younger adults showed repetition priming only for the confirmed words. The interpretation provided for these findings was that older adults failed to inhibit the nonconfirmed words.

Similar results have been found with "negative priming," the ability of subjects to inhibit a nontarget on one trial so that a response to it when it is a target on the next trial is not slower than would be expected. A number of studies have shown that older adults have reduced negative priming, as would be expected, if they have failed to effectively inhibit the word on the earlier trial when it was a nontarget (Hasher, Stoltzfus, Zacks, & Rypma, 1991; Tipper, 1991). In other studies, significant negative priming effects can be demonstrated in older adults, but they are typically smaller than seen in younger adults (see review by McDowd, Oseas-Kreger, & Filion, 1995).

One study not supporting the inhibition hypothesis was reported by Giambra (1989). Giambra directly measured task-irrelevant thoughts during a boring vigilance task performed by both young and old adults. When subjects reported task-irrelevant thoughts either when they occurred, or when they were probed for the thoughts during the visual detection task, older adults actually reported fewer, not more, task irrelevant thoughts than did younger adults.

A problem with both the integration and inhibition hypothesis is the absence of independent measures of the constructs that then can be related to memory task performance (McDowd et al., in press). For example, Park et al. (1994) tried to use an index of negative priming as an independent difference measure for inhibition in a large multivariate study of memory performance. Even though significant negative priming was found for both young and old subjects in two very different tasks, constructed individual indices of inhibitory function proved much too low in reliability to use statistically.

E. Working Memory

A more general working-memory hypothesis suggests that age differences in memory tasks are caused by older adults' reduced capacity to simultaneously perform a cognitive task while trying to remember some of the information for a later memory task. It is clear that large, reliable age differences exist in working memory (e.g., Salthouse, 1991; Salthouse & Babcock, 1991). This finding contrasts with other measures of short-term memory, such as digit span, that are more passive and reflect only the ability to store information without accompanying processing. Both Dobbs and Rule (1989) and Wingfield, Stine, Lahar, and Aberdeen (1988) have found large age differences when working-memory measures are used, but little or no differences on simple span storage tests. The importance of processing to working-memory differences was confirmed by Salthouse and Babcock (1991) when they decomposed working-memory performance into storage, processing, and the coordination of storage and processing, or executive function. They concluded that age differences in working memory are primarily due to the processing component of the tasks.

Because of the reliability of the working-memory measures, they can be used in individual-difference studies to see if they account for age-related differences in different memory tasks. Hultsch, Hertzog, and Dixon (1990), for example, found that working memory was related to both memory for words and memory for text. Using structural equation models, Park et al. (1994) found that an indirect path from age through working memory was strongest to free recall, a little less strong to cued recall, and not reliable to spatial memory. Free recall is often assumed to involve the most processing resources (self-initiated processing); cued recall is assumed to involve somewhat less deliberate processing; and spatial memory is assumed to involve the least. The relationship of working memory to these three memory tasks supports this hypothesis.

## F. Perceptual Speed

A long-held hypothesis suggests that older adults' reduction in perceptual speed can account for most age-related differences in cognition, including memory performance (e.g., Welford, 1958). There is no doubt that older adults are slower, and no doubt that the slower responses are not simply due to motor slowing, because older adults get relatively much slower when the cognitive complexity of the task increases (K. E. Light & Spirduso, 1990; Salthouse, 1991).

The work of Salthouse has consistently shown that perceptual speed, measured by such tasks as digit-symbol substitution, accounts for a significant portion of the age-related variance in memory performance. For example, Salthouse has shown that when perceptual speed is statistically controlled, age differences in free recall and paired-associate recall (Salthouse, 1993, 1994b) and serial recall (Salthouse & Coon, 1993) are all significantly attenuated. In Salthouse's (1993)

study, perceptual speed accounted for over 80% of the age-related variance in the recall measures. And even when subjects were given all the time they needed to complete the memory tasks, perceptual speed still accounted for over 70% of the total age-related variance (Salthouse, 1994b).

Earlier (Section II.E), the Hultsch et al. (1990) study was discussed to indicate the influence of working memory on memory performance. Actually, perceptual speed in that study accounted for the most age-related variance. Although working memory accounted for a significant amount of the variance, most of the effect was indirect, mediated through perceptual speed. Likewise, the Park et al. (1994) study found that perceptual speed mediated most of the working-memory effects, and speed was the major contributor to age-related variance in all memory tasks they examined. Using a sample of older adults (70–100 years old), Lindenberger et al. (1993) also found no direct effect of age on memory performance that was not mediated by speed. For paired-associate recall, memory for activities, and text recall, only 3% of the age-related memory variance remained after controlling for perceptual speed.

Working memory and speed have been shown to be very important constructs to account for age differences in memory performance. In fact, they may be basic constructs that underlie cognitive performance in general. For example, working memory correlates moderately well with the construct of inductive reasoning and may be a good index of many fluid intelligence measures (see Salthouse, 1994a).

## G. Conclusions for Resource Hypotheses

Six different hypotheses for age-related differences in memory performance have been discussed. When L. L. Light (1991) reviewed the theoretical perspectives in memory-aging research, she painted a pessimistic picture of current hypotheses. One problem, however, is the tendency to put the various hypotheses in opposition to each other. In fact, the similarities in the various hypotheses seem more salient than their differences. Older adults most likely have deficits in processing resources, probably because of reduced processing efficiency in working memory or inhibitory deficits or both. The primary mechanism for these processing difficulties involves perceptual speed. Because of the importance of processing efficiency to the ability to use working memory effectively, these reduced resources make it more difficult to engage in deliberate processing, but do not affect automatic processing. The problems of deliberate processing mean that older adults would have more problems in integrating context with to-be-remembered information, and in engaging in the self-initiated semantic processing important for effective remembering. Environmental support provided by the memory materials or tasks themselves can compensate for these processing deficiencies. In fact, Salthouse (1991) pointed out that context integration is simply a resource efficiency problem because its effects can be measured as an outcome of processing.

What is clearly needed, as acknowledged by the proponents of the various hypotheses, are reliable independent measures for these various constructs so that their relationships with each other, with various memory situations, and with age can be better specified. There are good measures for working memory and perceptual speed, and because of this, an understanding of their relationship, and their relationship to episodic memory, is beginning to emerge. Unfortunately, there are no good independent measures for environmental support, inhibition, and integration. Although Jacoby's work (e.g., 1991) on separately measuring deliberate processing and familiarity is very promising, it is still too early to judge the impact of these techniques.

## III. Systems or Structural Theories of Memory and Aging

Obviously, how one conceptualizes memory determines how one theoretically and empirically addresses the important research questions dealing with age differences in memory. Traditionally, there have been two conceptualizations of memory that have captured most of the attention of researchers in aging and memory. As just discussed, the first assumes that there are age differences in processing efficiency because of differences in processing resources. The second conceptualization assumes that age differences are specific to various memory structures or systems, and the research goal therefore is to determine whether the different systems are affected differently by aging. Memory is usually divided into sensory memory, short-term memory (current information processing), and long-term memory (memory based on past experiences). Short-term memory can then be divided into primary memory (memory span) and working memory (simultaneous storage and processing). Long-term memory is divided into episodic memory (memory for specific experiences), semantic memory (memory for knowledge), and procedural memory (automatic activation).

The common research strategy with different systems or structures is to find age dissociations, age effects that are limited to one memory system and not another. For example, Wingfield et al. (1988) found age effects in working memory (reading span) but not primary memory (digit span). Park and Shaw (1992) found no age differences in procedural memory (implicit memory) but significant age differences in explicit memory (recall).

As mentioned earlier, however, problems arise when complete dissociation is found (i.e., age invariance in one memory system and age effects in another). More often than not, conditions exist for which age differences are found, and not found, within a single memory system. For example, there are instances of age differences in implicit memory (e.g., Chiarello & Hoyer, 1988; Hultsch et al., 1991), even though they are always smaller than those found with explicit memory tasks. It is not clear, however, how a memory systems approach handles findings of smaller or larger age differences between memory systems.

## IV. Stage Theories of Memory and Aging

In the 1970s and 1980s, a popular hypothesis was to attribute age differences in memory to one or more of the memory stages of encoding, storage, or retrieval. Little contemporary research tries to attribute age effects to one stage or another. Instead, research has focused specifically on one or another of the stages themselves.

### A. Encoding

One assumption of encoding research is that older adults engage in less elaborate processing, and that age differences should be reduced if the nature of the processing was controlled during encoding. As recently concluded by Craik and Jennings (1992), this literature is full of apparently conflicting findings. Some studies show that increased elaboration at encoding produces disproportionately larger benefit for older adults (e.g., Park et al., 1990); some studies show equal effects for young and old subjects (e.g., Park, Puglisi, & Smith, 1986); whereas others show greater effects for the young subjects (e.g., Puglisi & Park, 1987). Note that the divergent examples listed were all conducted by the same research team. Craik and Jennings (1992) concluded from this state of affairs that the relationship between elaboration at encoding and age may not be linear and equivalent between age groups. Younger

adults may improve initially but level off at asymptote, whereas older subjects do not show improvement initially, then start to improve and eventually reach the same level of asymptote. This would result in very different patterns of results depending on where on the memory elaboration dimension sampling took place.

### B. Storage

Other research has focused on whether there are age differences in the manner in which information is represented or stored in memory. There is essentially no support, however, for an argument that the organization of long-term memory storage is different between young and old adults (L. L. Light, 1992). For example, one method of assessing semantic organization is a free-association test. Differences in the pattern of semantic associations would indicate differences in the way information is stored or represented in memory. Old and young adults are very similar in the associations they give to words (Burke & Peters, 1986) or pictures (Puglisi, Park, & Smith, 1987).

There is some evidence that older adults have problems with word finding or verbal fluency, but this seems to be due more to lexical access than to organizational deficits (see L. L. Light, 1992).

### C. Retrieval

It is difficult to look at retrieval effects independent of potential encoding differences in aging research. For example, the fact that age differences in free recall are much larger than age differences in recognition often has been interpreted as demonstrating retrieval difficulty in older adults, because recall is assumed to have greater retrieval requirements. If older adults bring processing deficiencies into the task, however, the effect could be due to deficits in processing during the presentation of the memory items. For example, some have suggested that older adults have greater problems with relational or organizational processing than do younger adults (e.g., Witte, Freund, & Brown-Whistler, 1993). If this is the case, then the better performance on recognition may be due to the greater requirement for organizational encoding for recall than for recognition.

An interesting phenomenon associated with retrieval difficulty is the tip-of-the-tongue experience, a problem with retrieving a well-known word given its definition or in naming a familiar face (see MacKay, Ch. 14, this volume). Older adults seem to experience a greater number of tip-of-the-tongue experiences (Burke & Laver, 1990). Evidence suggests that the effect is temporary because older adults are eventually able to retrieve the word in most cases (Burke, MacKay, Wothley, & Wade, 1991).

## D. Conclusion about Stage Theories

Although stage theories were once popular in memory aging research, resource hypotheses that more appropriately emphasize the nature and amount of processing in different age groups seem to provide a better description of effects seen both at encoding and retrieval.

# V. Other Memory Distinctions

Most research on memory and aging has been conducted with verbal materials (e.g., lists of words), but there are some other memory distinctions to consider. Materials in a memory task can be nonverbal rather than verbal; the memory task can involve a list of actions or activities rather than a list of words; and the memory task can involve remembering to do something in the future rather than remembering something from the past.

## A. Nonverbal Memory

### 1. Memory for Spatial Location

One way to determine if the age differences seen with remembering verbal information are also found with nonverbal tasks is to examine memory for spatial location. With few exceptions, older adults show memory deficits with spatial memory in a variety of different tasks. Denney, Dew, and Kihlström (1992), for example, found that older adults were worse in remembering on which quadrant of the screen a word appeared. Likewise, age differences were found when subjects were asked to replace objects in a three-dimensional model (Cherry, Park, & Donaldson, 1993). Age differences were even found when subjects were asked to replace office objects in a real-world office after performing various tasks in the office (Uttl & Graf, 1993). Summarizing spatial memory studies conducted between 1980 and 1990, age differences were found in 12 out of 14 studies reviewed (Smith & Park, 1990).

### 2. Nonverbal Materials

Age differences are also found when the to-be-remembered materials are nonverbal, such as faces (Crook & Larrabee, 1992) or map routes (Lipman & Caplan, 1992). As an exception to this finding, Park and her colleagues have consistently shown that older and younger adults show equal memory performance in memory for complex scenes (e.g., Park et al., 1986, 1990). However, this age invariance can be disrupted easily by changing the organizational structure of the scenes (Frieske & Park, 1993), changing the semantic character of the picture by rearranging the perceptual details to make the pictures abstract, or simply taking out perceptual details (Smith et al., 1990). The failure to find age differences in scene memory, therefore, seems to be due to the rich environmental support provided by the complex scenes themselves.

## B. Memory for Actions and Activities

Older adults also have problems when trying to remember which complex cognitive activities they had performed earlier, such as a battery of psychometric cognitive tests (e.g., Earles & Coon, 1994). Unlike complex activities, however, there are conflicting findings on whether age differences are found with simple actions (e.g., wave your hand, stomp your foot). Some studies have found age differences in the recall of these brief actions (e.g., Nyberg, Nilsson & Bäckman, 1992), whereas others have not (e.g., Bäckman & Nilsson, 1985). In a review of action memory studies, Kausler (1994) found that all the studies failing to find significant age differences in memory for simple actions did show some difference favoring the younger adults. It also has been repeatedly demonstrated that age differences in recalling performed activities or actions are smaller than differences in recalling verbal labels for the activities that were not performed (e.g., Bäckman & Nilsson, 1985). Kausler (1994) suggested that the reason for smaller age differences in memory for actions and activities when compared to verbal materials is the rehearsal independence inherent in performed activities or actions. Performing an action automatically encodes it. Because little deliberate processing is required for encoding, age differences are small. Age differences exist, however, because deliberate recollection would still be necessary at retrieval when attempting to recall the activities.

## C. Prospective Memory

Instead of remembering the past, memory often involves remembering to do something in the future. Einstein and McDaniel (1990) studied this in the laboratory by having subjects press a computer key when they saw a particular word while performing several other tasks. They found no age differences in the prospective memory task of remembering to press the key. Age differences have been found, however, when the to-be-performed task becomes more complex, such as when several target words can serve as the cue for pressing the computer key (Einstein et al., 1992) or when seeing a beard while looking at pictures of faces (Maylor, 1993). Age differences are also found when the prospective task is time-based rather than event-based. McDaniel and Einstein (1993) found age differences when the task was to do something every 10 minutes (no explicit environmental cue). Again, age differences seem to be found to the extent that processing resources are required to perform the task.

## D. Conclusion about Other Memory Distinctions

Rather than showing that age differences are different with nonverbal materials than with verbal materials, different with activity memory than with verbal memory, or different with prospective memory than with retrospective memory, the literature instead suggests that the processing requirements of the task are the primary determinant of finding age differences in memory. This conclusion is only speculative, however, until it is demonstrated that processing resource variables can account for differences in age-related variance among the various tasks.

## VI. Is It Aging, or Something Else?

One popular set of hypotheses attempts to attribute age differences on memory tasks to factors other than aging. Variables that may correlate with age such as education, health, metamemory, everyday experiences, or motivation have been implicated as possible factors that can account for age differences on memory tasks. Although it is clear that these factors can influence memory, they do not seem to account for a significant portion of the age-related variance on memory tasks (see Salthouse, 1991, for a full discussion of these hypotheses).

For example, increasing age is correlated with increased probability of health problems, and maybe these health problems are the cause for the memory deficits rather than age itself. Salthouse, Kausler, and Saults (1990), however, failed to find any change in the memory decline across the life span on a paired-associate task, verbal memory task, or spatial memory task in a subgroup of their sample that rated their health as "excellent" when compared to the total sample. Salthouse (1991) also reviewed several studies that had included health status and cognition, and found essentially no evidence for attenuation of the age–cognition relationship after statistically controlling for self-rated health. Of course, although self-rated health has been shown to be reliable, it may be different from actual health status. More research is clearly needed with multivariate health measures. Others have argued that laboratory memory tasks are too contrived and lack ecological validity to assess older adults' everyday memory capabilities. Evidence suggests, however, that even when the memory tasks are designed to assess only relevant everyday memory tasks, age remains the most predictive from a list of individual-difference variables (West, Crook, & Barron, 1992). In fact, Salthouse (1991) listed over 35 ecologically valid, everyday tasks in which older adults do worse than younger adults.

Finally, there is a great deal of evidence suggesting that metamemory (knowledge and attitudes about memory) cannot account for differences in memory performance (see L. L. Light, 1991, and Salthouse, 1991, for reviews).

## VII. Conclusion and Future Directions for Memory Research

In the past, memory aging researchers often have relied on ad hoc explanations for their findings. Although these explanations have led to hypothesis-driven research that has been productive in generating a large and rich body of literature, only recently have investigators taken a different research tack. Now, there are attempts to develop reliable and valid independent measures of mechanisms that are assumed to account for memory performance (e.g., resource mechanisms). In the future, the systematic use of these measures should allow a better determination of the relationship of different memory tasks and conditions, and then, their relationship to age. This trend will meld experimental and psychometric approaches to the study of memory and aging.

Another clear trend is the melding of the behavioral study of remembering with neuropsychological research examining underlying brain mechanisms. Both the frontal cortical areas of the brain (working memory) and the hippocampus and its associated medial temporal cortex (memory encoding and explicit retrieval) have been implicated in memory changes associated with normal aging (see Moscovitch & Winocur, 1992, for a review of this research). These findings come primarily from research that examines older adults' memory performance on neuropsychological tests that have been shown to differentiate patients with various brain lesions (e.g., Shimamura & Jurica, 1994). More recently, neuroimaging studies are beginning to appear that examine brain structure and brain activity while older adults are actually performing various memory tasks (e.g., Grady, Haxby, Horwitz, Schapiro, & Rapoport, 1992).

## Acknowledgment

The preparation of this chapter was supported in part by an NIH grant from the National Institute on Aging (RO1 AGO6265–09).

## References

Bäckman, L., & Nilsson, L.-G. (1985). Prerequisites for lack of age differences in memory performance. *Experimental Aging Research,* *11*, 67–73.

Bowles, N. L., & Poon, L. W. (1985). Aging and retrieval of words in semantic memory. *Journal of Gerontology, 40*, 71–77.

Burke, D. M., & Laver, G. D. (1990). Aging and word retrieval: Selective age deficits in language. In E. A. Lovelace (Ed.), *Aging and cognition: Mental processes, self-awareness, and interventions* (pp. 281–300). Amsterdam: North Holland.

Burke, D. M., & Light, L. L. (1981). Memory and aging: The role of retrieval processes. *Psychological Bulletin, 90*, 513–546.

Burke, D. M., MacKay, D., Worthley, J., & Wade, E. (1991). On the tip of the tongue: What causes word finding failures in young and old adults? *Journal of Memory and Language, 30*, 542–579.

Burke, D. M., & Peters, L. (1986). Word associations in old age: Evidence for consistency in semantic encoding during adulthood. *Psychology and Aging, 1*, 283–296.

Cherry, K. E., Park, D. C., & Donaldson, H. (1993). Adult age differences in spatial memory: Effects of structural context and practice. *Experimental Aging Research, 19*, 333–350.

Chiarello, C., & Hoyer, W. J. (1988). Adult age differences in implicit and explicit memory: Time course and encoding effects. *Psychology and Aging, 3*, 358–366.

Craik, F. I. M. (1994). Memory changes in normal aging. *Current Directions in Psychological Science, 3*, 155–158.

Craik, F. I. M., & Jennings, J. M. (1992). Human memory. In F. I. M. Craik & T. A. Salthouse (Eds.), *The handbook of aging and cognition* (pp. 51–110). Hillsdale, NJ: Erlbaum.

Craik, F. I. M., & McDowd, J. M. (1987). Age differences in recall and recognition. *Journal of Experimental Psychology: Learning, Memory, and Cognition, 13*, 474–479.

Crook, T. H., & Larrabee, G. J. (1992). Changes in facial recognition memory across the adult lifespan. *Journal of Gerontology: Psychological Sciences, 47*, P138–P141.

Denney, N. W., Dew, J. R., & Kihlström, J. F. (1992). An adult developmental study of encoding of spatial location. *Experimental Aging Research, 18*, 25–32.

Dobbs, A. R., & Rule, B. G. (1989). Adult age differences in working memory. *Psychology and Aging, 4*, 500–503.

Earles, J. E., & Coon, V. E. (1994). Adult age differences in long-term memory for performed activities. *Journal of Gerontology: Psychological Sciences, 49*, P32–P34.

Einstein, G. O., Holland, L. J., McDaniel, M. A., & Guynn, M. J. (1992). Age-related deficits in prospective memory: The influence of task complexity. *Psychology and Aging, 7*, 471–478.

Einstein, G. O., & McDaniel, M. A. (1990). Normal aging and prospective memory. *Journal of Experimental Psychology: Learning, Memory, and Cognition, 16*, 717–726.

Ferguson, S. A., Hashtroudi, S., & Johnson, M. K. (1992). Age differences in using source-relevant cues. *Psychology and Aging, 7*, 443–452.

Frieske, D. A., & Park, D. C. (1993). Effects of organization and working memory on age differences in memory for scene information. *Experimental Aging Research, 19*, 321–332.

Giambra, L. M. (1989). Task-unrelated-thought frequency as a function of age: A laboratory study. *Psychology and Aging, 4*, 136–143.

Grady, C. L., Haxby, J. V., Horwitz, B., Schapiro, M. B., & Rapoport, S. I. (1992). Dissociation of object and spatial vision in human extrastriate cortex: Age-related changes in activation of regional cerebral blood flow measured with [$^{15}$O]Water and PET. *Journal of Cognitive Neuroscience, 4*, 23–34.

Graf, P. (1990). Life-span changes in implicit and explicit memory. *Bulletin of the Psychonomic Society, 28*, 353–358.

Hartman, M., & Hasher, L. (1991). Aging and suppression: Memory for previously irrelevant information. *Psychology and Aging, 6*, 587–594.

Hasher, L., Stoltzfus, E. R., Zacks, R. T., & Rypma, B. (1991). Age and inhibition. *Journal of Experimental Psychology: Learning, Memory, and Cognition, 17*, 163–169.

Hasher, L., & Zacks, R. T. (1979). Automatic and effortful processes in memory. *Journal of Experimental Psychology: General, 108*, 356–388.

Hasher, L., & Zacks, R. T. (1988). Working memory, comprehension, and aging: A review and a new view. In G. Bower (Ed.), *The psychology of learning and motivation: Advances in research and theory* (Vol. 22, pp. 193–225). San Diego, CA: Academic Press.

Hultsch, D. F., & Dixon, R. A. (1990). Learning

and memory in aging. In J. E. Birren & K. W. Schaie (Eds.), *Handbook of the psychology of aging* (3rd ed., pp. 258–274). San Diego, CA: Academic Press.

Hultsch, D. F., Hertzog, C., & Dixon, R. A. (1990). Ability correlates of memory performance in adulthood and aging. *Psychology and Aging, 5,* 356–368.

Hultsch, D. F., Masson, M., & Small, B. (1991). Adult age differences in direct and indirect tests of memory. *Journal of Gerontology: Psychological Sciences, 46,* P22–P30.

Jacoby, L. L. (1991). A process dissociation framework: Separating automatic from intentional uses of memory. *Journal of Memory and Language, 30,* 513–541.

Jacoby, L. L., Toth, J. P., & Yonelinas, A. P. (1993). Separating conscious and unconscious influences of memory: Measuring recollection. *Journal of Experimental Psychology: General, 122,* 139–154.

Jennings, J. M., & Jacoby, L. L. (1993). Automatic versus intentional uses of memory: Aging, attention, and control. *Psychology and Aging, 8,* 283–293.

Kausler, D. H. (1994). *Learning and memory in normal aging.* San Diego, CA: Academic Press.

Lehman, E. B., & Mellinger, J. C. (1986). Forgetting rates in modality memory for young, mid-life, and older women. *Psychology and Aging, 1,* 178–179.

Light, K. E., & Spirduso, W. W. (1990). Effects of adult aging on the movement complexity factor of response programming. *Journal of Gerontology: Psychological Sciences, 45,* P107–P109.

Light, L. L. (1991). Memory and aging: Four hypotheses in search of data. *Annual Review of Psychology, 43,* 333–376.

Light, L. L. (1992). The organization of memory in old age. In F. I. M. Craik & T. A. Salthouse (Eds.), *The handbook of aging and cognition* (pp. 111–165). Hillsdale, NJ: Erlbaum.

Lindenberger, U., Mayr, U., & Kliegl, R. (1993). Speed and intelligence in old age. *Psychology and Aging, 8,* 207–220.

Lipman, P. D., & Caplan, L. J. (1992). Adult age differences in memory for routes: Effects of instructions and spatial diagram. *Psychology and Aging, 7,* 435–442.

Maylor, E. A. (1993). Aging and forgetting in prospective and retrospective memory tasks. *Psychology and Aging, 8,* 420–428.

McDaniel, M. A., & Einstein, G. O. (1993). The importance of cue familiarity and cue distinctiveness in prospective memory. *Memory, 1,* 23–41.

McDowd, J. M., Oseas-Kreger, D. M., & Filion, D. L. (1995). Inhibitory processes in cognition and aging. In F. Dempster & C. Brainerd (Eds.), *New perspectives on interference and inhibition in cognition* (pp. 363–400). San Diego, CA: Academic Press.

Moscovitch, M., & Winocur, G. (1992). The neuropsychology of memory and aging. In F. I. M. Craik & T. A. Salthouse (Eds.), *The handbook of aging and cognition* (pp. 315–372). Hillsdale, NJ: Erlbaum.

Nyberg, L., Nilsson, L.-G., & Bäckman, L. (1992). Recall of actions, sentences, and nouns: Influence of adult age and passage of time. *Acta Psychologica, 79,* 245–254.

Park, D. C., Puglisi, J. T., & Smith, A. D. (1986). Memory for pictures: Does an age-related decline exist? *Psychology and Aging, 1,* 11–17.

Park, D. C., Puglisi, J. T., Smith, A. D., & Dudley, W. N. (1987). Cue utilization and encoding specificity in picture recognition by older adults. *Journal of Gerontology, 42,* 423–425.

Park, D. C., & Shaw, R. J. (1992). Effect of environmental support on implicit and explicit memory in younger and older adults. *Psychology and Aging, 7,* 632–642.

Park, D. C., Smith, A. D., Lautenschlager, G., Earles, J. Frieske, D., Zwahr, M., & Gaines, C. (1994, April). *Mediation of long-term memory performance across the life span.* Paper presented at the Cognitive Aging Conference, Atlanta, GA.

Park, D. C., Smith, A. D., Morrell, R. W., Puglisi, J. T., & Dudley, W. N. (1990). Effects of contextual integration on recall of pictures by older adults. *Journal of Gerontology: Psychological Sciences, 45,* P52–P57.

Puglisi, J. T., & Park, D. C. (1987). Perceptual elaboration and memory in older adults. *Journal of Gerontology, 42,* 160–162.

Puglisi, J. T., Park, D. C., & Smith, A. D. (1987). Picture associations among old and young and old adults. *Experimental Aging Research, 13,* 115–116.

Puglisi, J. T., Park, D. C., Smith, A. D., & Dudley, W. N. (1988). Age differences in encoding specificity. *Journal of Gerontology: Psychological Sciences, 43,* P145–P150.

Rabinowitz, J. C., Craik, F. I. M., & Ackerman, B. P. (1982). A processing resource account of age differences in recall. *Canadian Journal of Psychology, 36,* 325–344.

Ryan, E. B. (1992). Beliefs about memory changes across the adult life span. *Journal of Gerontology: Psychological Sciences, 47,* P41–P61.

Salthouse, T. A. (1991). *Theoretical perspectives on cognitive aging.* Hillsdale, NJ: Erlbaum.

Salthouse, T. A. (1993) Speed and knowledge as determinants of adult age differences in verbal tasks. *Journal of Gerontology: Psychological Sciences, 48,* P29–P36.

Salthouse, T. A. (1994a). The nature of the influence of speed on adult age differences in cognition. *Developmental Psychology, 30,* 240–259.

Salthouse, T. A. (1994b). The aging of working memory. *Neuropsychology, 8,* 535–543.

Salthouse, T. A., & Babcock, R. L. (1991). Decomposing adult age differences in working memory. *Developmental Psychology, 27,* 763–776.

Salthouse, T. A., & Coon, V. E. (1993). Influence of task-specific processing speed on age differences in memory. *Journal of Gerontology: Psychological Sciences, 48,* P245–P255.

Salthouse, T. A., Kausler, D. H., & Saults, J. S. (1990). Age, self-assessed health status, and cognition. *Journal of Gerontology: Psychological Sciences, 45,* P156–P160.

Shimamura, A. P., & Jurica, P. J. (1994). Memory interference effects and aging: Findings from a test of frontal lobe function. *Neuropsychology, 8,* 408–412.

Smith, A. D., & Park, D. C. (1990). Adult age differences in memory for pictures and images. In E. A. Lovelace (Ed.), *Aging and cognition: Mental processes, self awareness, and interventions* (pp. 69–96). Amsterdam: North-Holland.

Smith, A. D., Park, D. C., Cherry, K., & Berkovsky, K. (1990). Age differences in memory for concrete and abstract pictures. *Journal of Gerontology: Psychological Sciences, 45,* P205–P209.

Tipper, S. P. (1991). Less attentional selectivity as a result of declining inhibition in older adults. *Bulletin of the Psychonomic Society, 29,* 45–47.

Uttl, B., & Graf, P. (1993). Episodic spatial memory in adulthood. *Psychology and Aging, 8,* 257–273.

Welford, A. T. (1958). *Aging and human skill.* Oxford: Oxford University Press.

West, R. L., Crook, T. H., & Barron, K. L. (1992). Everyday memory performance across the life span: Effects of age and noncognitive individual differences. *Psychology and Aging, 7,* 72–82.

White, N., & Cunningham, W. R. (1982). What is the evidence for retrieval problems in the elderly? *Experimental Aging Research, 8,* 169–171.

Wingfield, A., Stine, E. L., Lahar, C. J., & Aberdeen, J. S. (1988). Does the capacity of working memory change with age? *Experimental Aging Research, 14,* 103–107.

Witte, K. L., Freund, J. S., & Brown-Whistler, S. (1993). Age differences in free recall and category clustering. *Experimental Aging Research, 19,* 15–28.

Fourteen

# Language, Memory, and Aging: Distributed Deficits and the Structure of New-versus-Old Connections

Donald G. MacKay and Lise Abrams

This chapter reviews recent theory and data on language, memory, and aging while attempting to avoid overlap with other recent reviews (e.g., Kemper, 1992b; Light, 1992). Findings in four broad and seemingly disparate categories are reviewed: language production, direct versus indirect tests of memory, language comprehension, and encoding under time pressure. Across these four areas emerge three closely interrelated themes or hypotheses: the language-memory hypothesis, the new-versus-old connection hypothesis, and the distributed defect hypothesis. We first outline these hypotheses and then show how they stem from data in each of the four categories.

## I. Language, Memory, and Aging: Three Hypotheses

Under the *language-memory* hypothesis, functionally identical mechanisms underlie the acquisition, comprehension, and production of words on the one hand, and the encoding, storage, and recall of words in studies of verbal memory, on the other. That is, processes for encoding and retrieving experimentally constructed verbal materials, and processes required for acquiring, comprehending, and producing written and spoken language, at any age, are not just dependent on or related to one another, but are identical and impossible to distinguish. Language abilities and memory abilities involving verbal materials are not separate, but unitary, even though different verbal memory tasks tap into these unitary language-memory abilities in different ways (see, e.g., MacKay & Burke, 1990).

This language-memory view of the relation between language and memory is genuinely new and contrasts sharply with traditional views of memory, where words are comprehended, stored, retrieved, and produced in four distinct, independent, and sequentially ordered stages. In this traditional view, the storage stage begins only after comprehension is complete, and the word production stage begins only after the word retrieval stage is complete (see, e.g., Gordon, 1989, pp. 196–216). The traditional view receives its first detailed critique in this review.

Our second hypothesis, concerning *new-versus-old connections*, originated in the observation that older adults exhibit differential decline in tasks that involve

*Handbook of the Psychology of Aging, Fourth Edition*

new versus old learning or fluid versus crystallized intelligence (e.g., Salthouse, 1988), and typically require more time than young adults to form the new connections for representing novel combinations of words (see, e.g., Burke & Harrold, 1988; also MacKay & Burke, 1990, for a review). What is new about the present treatment of this hypothesis is how it applies to recent studies of encoding under time pressure, to detailed aspects of language production, and to recent data from direct versus indirect tests of memory.

The third hypothesis, *distributed defects*, combines a new idea with an old one. The old idea is the connectionist point that cognition and memory reflect processes operating within a network of nodes linked to one another via connections of varying strengths (see, e.g., MacKay, 1987; Salthouse, 1985). The new idea is that aging causes nodes or the connections between them to become universally defective, resulting in processing deficits that are distributed throughout the information processing network rather than limited to a particular type of component or process within it (see, e.g., Salthouse, 1985). Examples are the general suggestions that cognitive aging resembles a home computer with a progressively increasing cycle time (Salthouse, 1985), or reflects "defects of some sort distributed throughout a neural network of some sort" (Cerella, 1990, p. 202). More detailed suggestions are that cognitive aging reflects declines in short-term memory (e.g., Stine, 1994) or in how much information can be processed, as in Cerella's complexity hypothesis, where age-linked deficits are "tied to the amount, not the type, of information processing" (1990, p. 201; also Myerson, Hale, Wagstaff, Poon, & Smith, 1990).

Although discovery of distributed defects constitutes a major goal of the field, not all recent theories assume a distributed defect. For example, the Inhibition Deficit hypothesis of Hasher and others (e.g., Hart-man & Hasher, 1991; see McDowd, Oseas-Kreger, & Filion, 1994, for an excellent review) assumes that age-linked deficits are limited to a particular aspect of processing (inhibition) rather than being universal or distributed across all aspects.

## II. Language Production, Memory, and Aging

Although it was once widely believed that verbal abilities are universally preserved in old age, recent data indicate that two fundamental aspects of language production exhibit age-related deficits: retrieval of particular words, and the process of planning what to say, and where, when, and how to say it. Both processes are relevant to the language-memory and new-versus-old connection hypotheses. For example, retrieving familiar words involves use of old connections (see Burke, Mac-Kay, Worthley, & Wade, 1991), unlike planning what we want to say, and where, when, and how to say it, which invariably requires formation of new connections.

### A. Word Retrieval Deficits

Older adults often report difficulties in retrieving familiar words (Burke et al., 1991; Cohen & Faulkner, 1984), and recent studies both document and expand on these reports. For example, picture naming exhibits age-related decrements in accuracy (e.g., Bowles, Obler, & Poon, 1989), and in naming time (e.g., Mitchell, 1989), and spontaneous speech exhibits similar age-linked word retrieval problems. For example, older adults produce more pronouns and other ambiguous references when describing a picture, when recalling a sequence of videotaped events (Heller, Dobbs, & Rule, 1992), and when recalling a memorable personal experience (Ulatowska, Hayashi, Cannito, & Flemming, 1986). When instructed to provide single-word names for pictures, older adults also generate more circumlocutions and multi-word responses than do young adults (e.g., Albert, Heller, & Milberg, 1988), and are slower and less accurate in producing words that start with a specified letter, or match an experimenter-provided definition (e.g., Bowles & Poon, 1985) or semantic category (e.g., McCrae, Arenberg, & Costa, 1987). Older adults even take longer than young adults to begin to read a visually presented word (e.g., Balota & Duchek, 1988), and spontaneously speak more slowly than young adults (e.g., Duchin & Mysak, 1987), due to longer and more frequent pausing as well as to word lengthening per se (e.g., Balota & Duchek, 1988). This age-linked slowing may reflect changes at the speech muscle level (Kahane, 1981), or at the phonological level (Burke et al., 1991), or both.

## 1. Tip-of-the-Tongue Phenomenon

The tip-of-the-tongue (TOT) phenomenon is an age-linked word-finding difficulty that is so dramatic, informative, and extensively studied as to require separate treatment. TOTs occur when speakers are temporarily unable to retrieve some or all phonological aspects of a word that they later rate as highly familiar. The most striking general finding is that laboratory-induced and naturally occurring TOTs exhibit remarkably similar characteristics. Diary procedures and retrospective questionnaires indicate that naturally occurring TOTs usually involve familiar words that are used relatively rarely, and have not been used recently, and experimental TOTs are easier to induce in response to definitions of words that are infrequent in the language (Burke et al., 1991). The aspects of words that speakers become aware of are also similar for naturally occurring and experimentally induced TOTs: Speakers can typically report the number of syllables, the stress pattern, and the initial sounds or letters of an otherwise irretrievable word during both naturally occurring

and laboratory-induced TOTs (see, e.g., Burke et al., 1991).

Aging (beginning at about age 37) significantly increases the frequency of both naturally occurring and laboratory-induced TOTs (Burke et al., 1991). Once in the TOT state, older adults also report less partial information about the target (number of syllables, stress pattern, initial sounds or letters) than do young adults, and take more time to finally retrieve the target word, both in everyday life and in the laboratory (e.g., Burke et al., 1991). The largest category of naturally occurring TOTs for both young and older subjects is proper names (e.g., the family name of an acquaintance; Burke et al., 1991), and this effect interacts with age: Controlled for familiarity, relatively more of the naturally occurring TOTs of older than younger adults involve proper rather than common nouns, a finding that Burke at al. (1991) replicated in the laboratory.

These TOT findings support the language-memory hypothesis: Language production and retrieval from long-term memory are indistinguishable in the case of TOTs and are impossible to segregate into separate stages. The similarity of TOT data derived from retrospective questionnaires, everyday speech, and laboratory word retrieval tasks likewise suggests identical processing principles for language and memory. TOTs also indicate that even highly familiar information can become more difficult to retrieve with age, providing an important counterexample to the once popular view that only the ability to use or remember new information (fluid intelligence) exhibits age-related declines. TOTs also contradict Cerella's (1990) complexity hypothesis, that only the amount of information processed is relevant to aging: TOTs clearly indicate that the type of information processed (e.g., common versus proper nouns) determines whether age-linked deficits are small or large.

Effects of aging on TOTs also challenge

the popular hypothesis that inhibition causes TOTs (see, e.g., Jones, 1989). The focus of this inhibitory hypothesis is on persistent alternates (also known as *blockers* or *interlopers*; see Jones, 1989), that is, words that the speaker knows are inappropriate, but nevertheless come repeatedly and spontaneously to mind and often resemble the TOT word in sound, meaning, and syntax. An example from Burke et al. (1991) is *dacron*, a persistent alternate that the speaker rejected as inappropriate, but that came repeatedly and involuntarily to mind instead of the TOT target, *velcro*, a word similar in sound, meaning, and syntax (both are common nouns).

Occurrence of persistent alternates covaries with how long it takes to spontaneously resolve or come up with a TOT word (Burke et al., 1991), further suggesting that persistent alternates may inhibit or somehow block retrieval of TOT words. However, early evidence said to support this inhibitory account has encountered a string of empirical challenges and methodological criticisms (see, e.g., Burke et al., 1991). For example, older adults report fewer persistent alternates and less phonological information about the target (number of syllables, stress pattern, initial sounds, or letters), both in everyday life (e.g., Burke et al., 1991; Cohen & Faulkner, 1984) and in the laboratory (Burke et al., 1991). However, if inhibition from alternates causes TOTs, then one would expect more alternates for older adults, and fewer TOTs, because inhibitory processes tend to decline with age (see, e.g., McDowd et al., 1994). Inhibitory accounts also have difficulty explaining why persistent alternates accompany TOTs only *sometimes* (less than 50% of laboratory-induced TOTs have alternates) and why TOTs involve proper names more often than other word types, especially in the case of older adults.

However, all available TOT data fit the Transmission Deficit hypothesis, the distributed defect account of MacKay and Burke (1990). Under this account, the amount of priming transmitted across connections between all nodes in the network decreases with age, and TOTs originate when the lexical node for a target word becomes activated (providing access to its semantic information), but at least some of its connected phonological nodes remain unactivated because of the deficit in transmission of priming. Such transmission deficits are distributed throughout the interactive activation network, and increase in probability with aging and infrequent or nonrecent use of a connection; however, the *structure* of connections underlying, for example, proper versus common names, and phonological versus semantic nodes, modulate the degree to which transmission deficits become manifest in behavior (see Burke et al., 1991).

## B. Language Planning Deficits

Major age-linked deficits have been repeatedly demonstrated in planning what one intends to say and how to say it during language production. The classic indicators of language planning problems are disfluencies (hesitations, false starts, and word repetitions), which consistently increase with age (e.g., Kemper, 1992a; Valencia-Laver, 1992). This link between age and disfluency carries practical significance because both young and elderly listeners use fluency as a cue to a speaker's competence (e.g., Kemper, 1992a).

Why do older adults speak less fluently? Further research into three interrelated issues is needed: Do age-linked fluency deficits differ in type and frequency for language versus other cognitive skills? Do age-linked fluency deficits reflect problems of older adults in remembering nonlinguistic information that they want to communicate? Do age-linked increases in disfluency reflect the usual decline in the ability of older adults to encode new information (see, e.g., Burke & Harrold, 1988)? Research on recall of stories from memory (e.g., Bayles, Tomoeda, & Boone, 1985) clearly illustrates this last issue. Recalling story episodes involves retrieval of new information, that is, the new connection aspect of memory known to be problematic in older adults (see, e.g., MacKay & Burke, 1990). Consequently, age-linked disfluencies in story recall may reflect a general deficit in connection formation abilities rather than in a specific ability to communicate.

Free speech tasks (e.g., Glosser & Deser, 1992) avoid the problems of story recall, but introduce other methodological problems of their own. For example, accuracy in communicating one's intentions is typically unknown and uncontrolled in spontaneous speech, and may vary with age. Moreover, older subjects are free to compensate for retrieval deficits in spontaneous speech, or to voluntarily simplify one dimension (e.g., sentence syntax) while complicating another (e.g., narrative or plot structure; see Kemper, 1992a). As a result, reported age effects are often complex and difficult to interpret. For example, both false starts and filled pauses (*um* and *er*) interact with syntax (occurring more in embedded than in main clauses), which in turn interacts with age; that is, older subjects generate fewer embedded clauses than young subjects, a not uncommon baseline problem in free speech tasks (see Kemper, 1992b).

Lack of control in observations of spontaneous speech may also account for some conflicting reports in the literature. For example, differing effects of age on the disfluencies known as word repetitions have been reported. Valencia-Laver (1992) reported more word repetitions for older than young adults describing novel patterns of interconnected colored dots for a hypothetical listener to reconstruct, sight unseen. In contrast, Yairi and Clifton (1972) reported no more repetitions and *fewer* false starts and incomplete phrases for older than young adults creating stories appropriate for preschool children. The problem with this curious inverse deficit is that older subjects may have more extensive experience than young subjects in creating stories suitable for young children. To overcome such problems with story recall and free speech tasks, Heller et al. (1992) recommended use of on-line tasks, for example, having subjects describe filmed events as they unfold on a video monitor. However, such "modified free speech" tasks are also problematic. Video description may unfairly disadvantage older subjects by forcing them to describe unfolding events at an unnatural pace. In short, further research on fluency as a potential index of age-linked planning deficits is sorely needed.

## III. Language Memory Tested via Direct versus Indirect Means

Indirect tests of memory involve either language production (e.g., word production time) or language perception (e.g., word recognition time) and show effects of prior presentation of a word (i.e., repetition priming) without seeming to require conscious recollection of the prior experience, whereas direct tests of memory (e.g., cued recall, recognition, and free recall) involve conscious recollection of the prior experience. Recent data from direct versus indirect tests support the language-memory hypothesis, and undermine the traditional basis for separating language from memory, namely the occurrence of language disorders without concomitant memory disorders and vice versa. For example, patients who show Wernicke comprehension deficits on direct tests show no deficits via tests that are on-line and indirect (Tyler, 1988), suggesting that a memory problem underlies this classic language comprehension deficit.

Recently demonstrated age differences for direct versus indirect tests further reinforce this general conclusion. Although older adults consistently perform more poorly than young adults on direct tests such as recognition and recall, they perform as well or nearly as well as young adults on many indirect tests (see, e.g., Howard, 1991, and Light & LaVoie, 1993, for extensive recent reviews). The practical significance of such age-linked dissociations in performance on direct-versus-indirect memory tasks has been widely recognized. As Howard and Wiggs (1993) pointed out, small or nonexistent age effects recommend indirect tests for facilitating morale in education programs designed for older adults. However, the theoretical import of these age effects remains controversial.

Some view the evidence as indicating the existence of explicit versus implicit memory systems that are separate and fundamentally different (e.g., Mitchell, 1989), whereas others argue that direct and indirect tasks tap into different aspects of a unitary language-memory system. For example, age differences between direct versus indirect tests may simply reiterate the old-versus-new connection theme (MacKay & Burke, 1990). Most direct measures test whether new connections have been formed at a relatively high level in the system, for example, between a stimulus word and its time, place, or context of use, a connection formation process that provides the basis for awareness and is especially subject to age-linked decline. However, most indirect measures test whether old connections have been activated and automatically strengthened, an unconscious process known as *engrainment learning* (MacKay, 1990) that is less subject to age-linked decline (see MacKay & Burke, 1990).

For example, when a subject hears a particular speaker repeat a familiar word in the repetition priming paradigm, no new connections are required to identify and say the word, but time to pronunciation is shortened because dozens of existing connections representing word phonology and acoustic characteristics of the voice have become automatically strengthened in both young and older adults. Repeated visual pre-

sentation of a word in the same familiar font likewise strengthens large numbers of existing connections at phonological and orthographic levels in both young and older subjects, a perceptual process that also requires no new connections. Age-linked dissociations between direct versus indirect tests may therefore reflect the greater age deficits for forming new connections than for using and strengthening old connections via engrainment learning.

Consistent with this hypothesis, a recent meta-analysis (Light & LaVoie, 1993) indicated that age differences for indirect tests were smaller than those for direct tests, but nevertheless did exist, with young adults showing larger repetition priming effects than older adults. However, Light and LaVoie urged caution in interpreting these results, especially for associative priming tasks, where a "temporally adjacent" stimulus (e.g., the first word in a familiar and recently presented phrase) facilitates recognition of the subsequent word. Indeed, many conflicting age effects have been reported for repetition priming tasks, and at least five different classes of explanation for these conflicting results have been suggested. One is that conscious or deliberate recollection processes may intrude and contaminate results for indirect tests, although two recent studies found that intrusion of conscious recall processes into an indirect test involving word completion was not responsible for age-related differences (Howard, Fry, & Brune, 1991) or lack of age-related differences (Park & Shaw, 1992).

A second explanation for age differences on indirect tasks invokes reduced elaborative encoding in older adults (Howard, 1991), but Moscovitch, Winocur, and McLachlan (1986) and Light and LaVoie (1993) found age effects using indirect tasks that require virtually no elaborative encoding.

A third suggested explanation is that older adults can form new connections assumed necessary for associative priming effects, but simply require more time, that is, self-paced tasks (Howard et al., 1991). However, Moscovitch et al. (1986) found age differences even when older subjects received more processing time than young adults in an associative priming task. A fourth suggested explanation is that age effects are found when older adults must form an associative connection in only one trial, but not when they receive repeated trials (Howard, 1988b; Light & LaVoie, 1993). Again, however, exceptions exist (see, e.g., Davis et al., 1990). Moreover, repeated trials may enable use of conscious recall strategies, especially by young subjects, an age-linked contamination of indirect measures with an explicit or conscious process.

The fifth and most basic explanation of the conflicting results concerns power and sensitivity of the tests. Because studies to date have not adopted highly sensitive indirect measures (for example, reaction times), noneffects of age are difficult to interpret. More sensitive measures also seem essential in view of statistical power problems noted by Light and LaVoie (1993): Indirect tests seem to show age differences only for unusually large subject samples (e.g., Davis et al., 1990; Howard, 1991) or unusually powerful meta-analytic procedures (Light & LaVoie, 1993). Even this claim is controversial, however; Howard (1988b) found age differences with a relatively small sample, whereas Park and Shaw (1992) found no age differences with a relatively large sample.

The solution to these controversies may lie in developing a viable theory of how direct versus indirect measures tap into the information processing network. Future work in this area must become embedded within a detailed theory of language-memory that specifies how young and older subjects comprehend and produce words and connect words to one another and to aspects of the context. The recent study of Light, LaVoie, Valencia-Laver, Albertson-Owens, and Mead (1992) clearly

illustrates this point. Light et al. presented words to subjects either visually or auditorily, and tested memory for the words or their modality of presentation either directly or indirectly. One direct test required yes–no recognition of the presented words versus foils, and a second direct test required recognition of what modality the words had been presented in. As is usual for such direct tests, recognition accuracy was much lower for older than young adults.

The indirect tests required subjects to identify words that had been presented either visually (with brief exposure) or auditorily (in noise), and subjects showed slightly greater repetition priming when test words appeared in the same modality as previously. These small effects were significant but equivalent in magnitude for young and older subjects, a surprising finding because Light and LaVoie (1993) labeled this an associative priming task of the sort that generally requires the age-sensitive process of forming new connections, here between the words and their cotemporal modality of presentation.

However, a strong case can be made that the assumption of Light et al. (1992) does not apply to this perception task because new connections play no role in identifying familiar words. When a word is presented, say, auditorily in a particular voice, preexisting connections between the many low-level nodes representing acoustic characteristics of the voice are automatically strengthened in both young and older adults. These strengthened acoustic-node connections will help both young and older subjects perceive this word when it is subsequently presented auditorily in noise, as Light et al. (1992) observed. They are inaccessible to awareness via direct tests of memory, however, and cannot facilitate perception when the word is presented visually, also as Light et al. observed. The situation is very different when subjects must directly recognize or recall the original modality of presentation for the word. Here, new consciously formed connections are needed to represent the high level proposition that this particular word had been presented auditorily. The large age differences on this direct test may therefore reflect the more extensive age-linked deficit in forming new connections.

## IV. Language Comprehension, Memory, and Aging

Many findings suggest that, for older adults, tests of language comprehension often resemble indirect tests of memory. Both show slight if any decline with age, independent of declines in the ability to encode new information (e.g., Burke & Harrold, 1988; Howard & Wiggs, 1993). However, language comprehension is complex (see MacKay, 1987, for details): Here we contrast comprehension in semantic priming studies, where age-linked improvement has been conclusively demonstrated, versus comprehension in studies of negation, where a deficit seems likely.

### A. Semantic Priming Effects

Semantic priming refers to the fact that words such as *doctor* can be pronounced or recognized as words more rapidly when immediately preceded by a semantically related word such as *nurse*, than by an unrelated word such as *truck*. This semantic priming effect has been demonstrated for a wide variety of visual and auditory tasks in both young and older adults (see, e.g., Burke, White, & Diaz, 1987). The usual explanation for semantic priming postulates facilitated transmission of priming across links between associated words in memory, which temporarily makes information about the target word more accessible. This priming may reduce the amount of sensory processing needed for word recognition (see, e.g., Stanovich & West, 1983), so that factors that slow word

recognition (e.g., aging) should decrease the size of semantic priming effects.

However, recent evidence has challenged this view of cognitive aging. Although a large number of studies, taken individually, indicated no statistically reliable age differences in the size of semantic priming effects (see, e.g., Balota & Duchek, 1988), a recent meta-analysis across 15 studies (Laver & Burke, 1993) indicated reliably smaller semantic priming effects for young than older subjects. This inverse age deficit holds across lexical decision and pronunciation tasks, and across a wide range of prime-target intervals.

Theories must therefore explain why semantic priming exhibits age-linked facilitation rather than decline or slowing, as is typically found in studies of cognitive aging. One hypothesis is that age-linked practice effects explain age-linked facilitation in semantic priming tasks. That is, semantic connections are formed between related words during youth and receive greater practice during the longer lifetime of older adults, thereby causing greater spread of priming, and therefore greater facilitation effects in older adults. However, this differential practice hypothesis requires additional assumptions to explain why older adults exhibit deficits rather than facilitation at phonological levels (see Burke et al., 1991).

A second hypothesis holds that conditions associated with increased latency (e.g., unrelated contexts) should increase latency more for older than young adults because all cognitive processes slow down with aging (Cerella, 1990; Lima, Hale, & Myerson, 1991). That is, older adults typically respond more slowly than young adults in semantic priming tasks, and this causes age-linked facilitation by providing a longer time interval during which priming can spread from the prime to the target word, even when the time between prime and target is controlled and varied over a wide range, as in Howard (1988a). However, Laver (1992) used a deadline procedure (where subjects respond at particular points in time following presentation of the target) to show that the longer interval from prime presentation to target response in older adults was not responsible for the age-linked facilitation in semantic priming tasks.

A third and more likely hypothesis focuses on age-linked differences in the structure of the semantic system (see MacKay & Burke, 1990). Because of their greater experience, older adults know more about concepts such as *doctor* and *nurse*, and have formed more connections that link these semantically related words in memory. Priming will therefore summate across these additional connections in the language-memory system of older adults, causing age-linked facilitation in semantic priming tasks by offsetting transmission deficits across single connections. However, when a task requires transmission of priming across a single critical connection, priming summation cannot compensate for age-linked deficits in priming transmission.

The concept of a single critical connection is best illustrated via the top-down priming of phonological nodes that occurs during word retrieval. In general, phonological nodes are hierarchically linked to one another via only a single or critical top-down connection and so receive a single source of priming without the possibility of summation typically seen in the semantic system. Syllable nodes, for example, receive top-down priming from the single node that represents the word that a speaker is attempting to retrieve. As Burke et al. (1991) pointed out, this limitation in the number of connections that can deliver priming to phonological nodes during language production may explain why production tends to be more vulnerable to age-related deficits than comprehension. When comprehending a word, priming converges or summates bottom-up from many phonological nodes onto the single node that represents the word

(see, e.g., MacKay, Wulf, Yin, & Abrams, 1993).

## B. Aging and the Processing of Negation

The processing of negation is a theoretically important area where age constancy in comprehension seems unlikely. If negative words (e.g., *no, not*) trigger an inhibitory process, as MacDonald and Just (1989) suggested, then under the Inhibition Deficit hypothesis, older adults should exhibit reduced effects of negation relative to young adults. Although the on-line processing of negation has never been systematically studied in older adults, current data seem to support this prediction. Morris, Gick, and Craik (1988) reported an Age × Negation interaction in the times to verify negative versus affirmative sentences. Although Morris et al. attributed this interaction to syntactic complexity, the semantics of negation provides a more plausible account because a different manipulation of syntactic complexity (active versus passive structures) did not interact with age.

## V. Encoding and Immediate Recall under Time Pressure

Age-linked deficits are the rule for comprehension and immediate recall of rapidly presented sentences and lists (e.g., MacKay, Miller, & Schuster, 1994; Miller & MacKay, 1994; Wingfield, Wayland, & Stine, 1992). Why is the comprehension system of older adults so vulnerable to time pressure? We examine recent evidence relevant to two contrasting distributed-defect accounts: reduced encoding speed and reduced short-term memory capacity.

### A. Reduced Speed of Encoding

As presentation rate increases, immediate recall declines disproportionately for older relative to young adults, especially for lists as compared to sentences (see, e.g., Wingfield, Poon, Lombardi, & Lowe, 1985; Wingfield & Stine, 1987), and especially for prosodically disrupted sentences as compared to prosodically normal sentences (see, e.g., Wingfield et al., 1992). It is as if lists require too many new connections for older adults to form at rapid rates of presentation, whereas the familiar syntactic and prosodic cues that help in linking words to phrases in normal sentences enable older adults to compensate for their reduced speed of encoding (see MacKay & Abrams, 1994).

This Connection Formation hypothesis has received strong support from studies of repetition blindness. These studies compare immediate recall of a single "target word" that is either repeated or unrepeated in almost identical sentences presented via RSVP (rapid serial visual presentation). For example, recall of the word *one* is compared in "He is the man who one day will be famous" (unrepeated target version) with the second *one* in "He is the one who one day will be famous" (repeated target version). Subjects experiencing repetition blindness fail to encode repeated targets more often than unrepeated targets and report seeing, "He is the one who day will be famous" (see, e.g., MacKay, Miller, & Schuster, 1994).

Older adults exhibit significantly greater repetition blindness than young adults across a wide range of presentation rates, an age-linked effect that rules out alternative accounts of repetition blindness based on inhibition, refractory periods, and perceptual fusion of the repeated words (see MacKay, Miller, & Schuster, 1994). For example, if repetition blindness reflects an inhibitory process, then it should decrease with age because inhibitory processes tend to decrease with age (see, e.g., McDowd et al., 1994). Rather, the increase in repetition blindness with age indicates an age-linked difficulty in forming a single theoretically specified connection: To encode a repeated word, one and the same word node must connect in sequence with two phrase nodes, and these two time-consuming instances of connection formation make the repeated word more difficult to encode under time pressure than an unrepeated word. Thus, older adults exhibit more repetition blindness than young adults because forming the double connection from a repeated word to its phrase nodes takes more time, thereby exacerbating the age-linked difficulty in forming new connections (see, e.g., MacKay & Burke, 1990).

Other recent experiments using the repetition blindness paradigm have extended these findings by showing that old or already established connections exhibit similar age-linked effects. Specifically, subjects in MacKay, Abrams, and Miller (1994) and MacKay and Abrams (1994) immediately recalled lists containing repeated versus unrepeated words in familiar chunks (e.g., *good night* and *night owl* in "people good night mind night owl pile"), which increased repetition blindness for both young and older adults, that is, reduced the probability of encoding and immediately recalling repeated words relative to unrepeated words.

These results raise a question with important practical as well as theoretical implications: Do existing or highly practiced connections interfere with the ability to form new connections, especially in older adults? An affirmative answer to this question would suggest that older adults may experience encoding difficulties in part because, relative to young adults, they have acquired many more highly practiced connections that can interfere with their ability to form new ones. Other questions of practical and theoretical importance concern the onset and universality of the new learning problem: At about what age do difficulties in forming new connections become of substantial importance? And what other individual differences besides age contribute to difficulties in forming new connections?

## B. The Chunk Capacity Hypothesis

Many aspects of cognitive aging have been attributed to age-linked declines in memory capacity, processing resources, or working memory that are independent of language per se. For example, Light (1988) suggested that language competence may remain intact in older adults, even though memory factors such as short-term capacity "set limits on older adults' ability to understand and produce language" (p. 178; see also Craik, 1983; Kemper, 1992a; Stine, 1994). Although lack of formal specification has prevented definitive tests of most theories of this type (see, e.g., Mac-Kay & Burke, 1990; Salthouse, 1988), Mac-Kay, Abrams, and Miller (1994) both formalized and tested the claim that short-term memory has a fixed capacity measured in chunks. This *Chunk Capacity* hypothesis predicted better immediate recall of unrelated words in rapidly presented lists that also contain familiar chunks (e.g., *good night*) than in otherwise similar lists with no chunks.

Results of two experiments contradicted this and other Chunk Capacity predictions, and a subsequent study (MacKay & Abrams, 1994) obtained corroborating results for older adults. However, data from both studies supported the Connection Formation hypothesis, that the limiting factor in immediate recall for both young and older subjects is how many connections must be formed or strengthened, or both, during available encoding time.

## VI. Summary and Conclusions

Our conclusions focus on the three hypotheses that emerged from our review (as stated in the introduction to this chapter), beginning with the new-versus-old connection hypothesis. Age-linked differences between new-versus-old connections surfaced repeatedly in every area of our review, especially language planning, direct versus indirect tests of memory, and language comprehension. We also reviewed recent findings that suggest a new and more detailed direction for future research into the new-versus-old connection issue: Effects of age on the formation of single connections in the repetition blindness paradigm go significantly beyond previously studied encoding effects that have involved hundreds of unspecified new and old connections.

Turning to the language-memory hypothesis, comprehension data from both direct and indirect tests supported the claim that identical mechanisms underlie the encoding and short-term storage of verbal materials on the one hand and language comprehension on the other. As Light (1992) noted, where language comprehension leaves off and where memory storage begins is very difficult to determine, for both everyday behavior and experimental tasks alike. However, the language-memory hypothesis goes beyond such observations to suggest that no memory-specific processes exist independently of mechanisms and processes that have evolved for learning, comprehending, and producing language. MacKay, Abrams, and Miller (1994) exemplified this position in a study of limitations on the amount of verbal information that can be encoded and retrieved as a function of time, chunking, and other "memory variables." Their conclusion strongly supported the language-memory hypothesis, that short-term memory limitations reflect the same everyday processes of node activation and connection formation that underlie the highly refined everyday skill of language comprehension (see MacKay, 1987).

Production data from both direct and indirect tests also supported the language-memory hypothesis (e.g., the close parallels between TOTs in laboratory tasks versus everyday language production). To-gether with the fact that no theory of production has established a convincing dividing line between where memory re-trieval ends and where word production begins, such close parallels suggest that language production mechanisms and word retrieval mechanisms are not just dependent on or related to one another, and therefore difficult to distinguish, but are identical and impossible to distin-guish. This strong form of the language-memory hypothesis carries potential im-plications for the field at large. For example, if there are no articulatory loops or special memory buffers for verbal informa-tion that are separate from the mecha-nisms for acquiring, comprehending, and producing language per se, it makes no sense to ask whether working memory constraints are responsible for age differ-ences in language perception or produc-tion. By the same token, asking whether processes for perceiving or producing lan-guage introduce constraints that are re-sponsible for age differences in working memory likewise makes no sense. Instead, the language-memory hypothesis raises a whole new set of much more detailed questions, and as we have seen, recent data and theory (e.g., MacKay & Abrams, 1994) are already answering some of these ques-tions for both new and old connections.

As to the distributed defect theme, data reviewed here on semantic priming in comprehension and on TOTs in produc-tion directly contradicted the complexity hypothesis, indicating that the type rather than just the amount of information being processed can determine whether one ob-serves large age-linked deficits, small age-linked deficits, no age-linked deficits, or, indeed, age-linked facilitation. The diver-sity of these aging effects warns against dis-tributed defect hypotheses that are overly simple. To be successful, distributed defect hypotheses must be embedded within a de-tailed theory of language-memory that spe-cifies how words are processed and how

concepts become connected to one another in the everyday use of language. The Trans-mission Deficit hypothesis exemplifies such an approach.

Under the Transmission Deficit hy-pothesis, general patterns of decline, for example, general slowing and problems in forming new connections (MacKay & Burke, 1990), reflect a truly distributed de-fect in transmission of excitatory and in-hibitory priming across every connection between every node in the information processing network. However, the de-tailed nature of processes in the larger the-ory of language-memory within which the distributed defect known as transmission deficits is embedded plays a role in differ-ential declines such as the age-linked dif-ferences between new-versus-old connec-tions. Thus, the old connections for re-trieving familiar but rare and not recently used words exhibit small but reliable age-linked declines because even highly prac-ticed connections undergo deficits in pri-ming transmission due to age and disuse. However, new connection formation ex-hibits much greater age-linked declines because the connection formation process is priming-intensive, and is therefore espe-cially susceptible to transmission deficits (see MacKay & Burke, 1990).

The detailed structure of interconnec-tions in a language-memory network con-taining transmission deficits also contrib-utes to differential declines, such as the age-linked differences in learning and re-trieving common versus proper nouns (see, e.g., Burke et al., 1991). Similarly, as we have seen, transmission deficits, to-gether with age-linked differences in the number of connections that link seman-tically related words in memory, make sense of the fact that age-linked facilita-tion occurs under some conditions such as semantic priming tasks, but not others such as phonological retrieval tasks. Whether transmission deficits are the true underlying cause of such age-linked changes in behavior remains to be seen.

However, developing this or some other account that integrates the new-versus-old connection hypothesis, the language-memory hypothesis, and the distributed defect hypothesis into a single, unified theory seems likely to shape the course of research on language, memory, and aging into the next century.

## References

Albert, M. S., Heller, H. S., & Milberg, W. (1988). Changes in naming ability with age. *Psychology and Aging, 33,* 173–178.

Balota, D. A., & Duchek, J. M. (1988). Age-related differences in lexical access, spreading activation, and simple pronunciation. *Psychology and Aging, 3,* 84–93.

Bayles, K. A., Tomoeda, C. K., & Boone, D. R. (1985). A view of age-related changes in language function. *Developmental Neuropsychology, 1,* 231–264.

Bowles, N. L., Obler, L. K., & Poon, L. W. (1989). Aging and word retrieval: Naturalistic, clinical and laboratory data. In L. W. Poon, D. C. Rubin, & B. A. Wilson (Eds.), *Everyday cognition in adulthood and late life* (pp. 244–264). Cambridge, England: Cambridge University Press.

Bowles, N. L., & Poon, L. W. (1985). Aging and retrieval of words in semantic memory. *Journal of Gerontology, 40,* 71–77.

Burke, D. M., & Harrold, R. M. (1988). Automatic and effortful semantic processes in old age: Experimental and naturalistic approaches. In L. L. Light & D. M. Burke (Eds.), *Language, memory and aging* (pp.100–116). New York: Cambridge University Press.

Burke, D. M., MacKay, D. G., Worthley, J. S., & Wade, E. (1991). On the tip of the tongue: What causes word finding failures in young and older adults? *Journal of Memory and Language, 30,* 542–579.

Burke, D. M., White, H., & Diaz, D. L. (1987). Semantic priming in young and older adults: Evidence for age constancy in automatic and attentional processes. *Journal of Experimental Psychology: Human Perception and Performance, 13,* 79–88.

Cerella, J. (1990). Aging and information processing rate. In J. Birren & K. W. Schaie (Eds.), *Handbook of the psychology of aging* (3rd ed., pp. 201–221). San Diego, CA: Academic Press.

Cohen, G., & Faulkner, D. (1984). Memory in old age: "Good in parts." *New Scientist, 11,* 49–51.

Craik, F. I. M. (1983). On the transfer of information from temporary to permanent memory. *Philosophical Transactions of the Royal Society of London, Series B 302,* 341–359.

Davis, H. P., Cohen, A., Gandy, M., Colombo, P., VanDusseldorp, G., Simolke, N., & Romano, J. (1990). Lexical priming effects as a function of age. *Behavioral Neuroscience, 104,* 288–297.

Duchin, S. W., & Mysak, E. D. (1987). Disfluency and rate characteristics of young adult, middle-aged, and older males. *Journal of Communication Disorders, 20,* 245–257.

Glosser, G., & Deser, T. (1992). A comparison of changes in macrolinguistic and microlinguistic aspects of discourse production in normal aging. *Journal of Gerontology: Psychological Sciences, 47,* P266–P272.

Gordon, W. C. (1989). *Learning and memory.* Pacific Grove, CA: Brooks/Cole.

Hartman, M., & Hasher, L. (1991). Aging and suppression: Memory for previously relevant information. *Psychology and Aging, 6,* 587–594.

Heller, R. B., Dobbs, A. R., & Rule, B. G. (1992, April). *Age differences in communication: Evidence from an on-line video description task.* Paper presented at the 4th biennial Cognitive Aging Conference, Atlanta.

Howard, D. V. (1988a). Aging and memory activation: The priming of semantic and episodic memories. In L. L. Light & D. M. Burke (Eds.), *Language, memory and aging* (pp. 77–99). New York: Cambridge University Press.

Howard, D. V. (1988b). Implicit and explicit assessment of cognitive aging. In. M. L. Howe & C. J. Brainerd (Eds.), *Cognitive development in adulthood* (pp. 3–37). New York: Springer-Verlag.

Howard, D. V. (1991). Implicit memory: An expanding picture of cognitive aging. *Annual Review of Gerontology and Geriatrics, 11,* 1–22.

Howard, D. V., Fry, A. F., & Brune, C. M. (1991). Aging and memory for new associations: Direct and indirect measures. *Journal of Experimental Psychology: Learning, Memory and Cognition, 17,* 779–792.

Howard, D. V., & Wiggs, C. L. (1993). Aging and learning: Insights from implicit and explicit tests. In J. Cerella, W. J. Hoyer, J. Rybash, & M. Commons (Eds.), *Adult information processing: Limits on loss* (pp. 511–527). San Diego, CA: Academic Press.

Jones, G. V. (1989). Back to Woodworth: Role of interlopers in the tip of the tongue phenomenon. *Memory & Cognition, 17,* 69–76.

Kahane, J. C. (1981). Anatomic and physiologic changes in the aging peripheral speech mechanism. In D. S. Beasley & G. A. Davis (Eds.), *Aging: Communication processes and disorders.* New York: Grune & Stratton.

Kemper, S. (1992a). Adults' sentence fragments: Who, what, when, where, and why. *Communication Research, 19,* 444–458.

Kemper, S. (1992b). Language and aging. In F. I. M. Craik & T. A. Salthouse (Eds.), *The handbook of aging and cognition* (pp. 213–270). Hillsdale, NJ: Erlbaum.

Laver, G. D. (1992, April). *A speed-accuracy analysis of semantic priming effects in young and older adults.* Paper presented at the 4th biennial Cognitive Aging Conference, Atlanta.

Laver, G. D., & Burke, D. M. (1993). Why do semantic priming effects increase in old age? A meta-analysis. *Psychology and Aging, 8,* 34–43.

Light, L. L. (1988). Language and aging: Competence versus performance. In J. E. Birren & V. L. Bengston (Eds.), *Emergent theories of aging* (pp. 177–213). New York: Springer.

Light, L. L. (1992). Memory and aging: Four hypotheses in search of data. *Annual Review of Psychology, 42,* 333–376.

Light, L. L., & LaVoie, D. (1993). Direct and indirect measures of memory in old age. In P. Graf & M. Mason (Eds.), *Implicit memory: New directions in cognition, development and neuropsychology* (pp. 207–230). Hillsdale, NJ: Erlbaum.

Light, L. L., LaVoie, D., Valencia-Laver, D., Albertson-Owens, S. A., & Mead, G. (1992). Direct and indirect measures of memory for modality in young and older adults. *Journal of Experimental Psychology: Learning, Memory, and Cognition, 18,* 1284–1297.

Lima, S. D., Hale, S., & Myerson, J. (1991). How general is general slowing? Evidence from the lexical domain. *Psychology and Aging, 6,* 416–425.

MacDonald, M. C., & Just, M. A. (1989). Changes in activation levels with negation. *Journal of Experimental Psychology, 15,* 633–642.

MacKay, D. G. (1987). *The organization of perception and action: A theory for language and other cognitive skills.* New York: Springer Verlag.

MacKay, D. G. (1990). Perception, action, and awareness: A three body problem. In W. Prinz & O. Neumann (Eds.), *Relationships between perception and action* (pp. 269–303). Berlin: Springer-Verlag.

MacKay, D. G., & Abrams, L. (1994, April). *Chunking, repetition deficits, and the Single Attachment principle: Further evidence for age-linked deficits in forming single, theoretically-specified connections.* Poster presented at the 5th biennial Cognitive Aging Conference, Atlanta, GA.

MacKay, D. G., Abrams, L., & Miller, M. D. (1994). *Chunking and repetition deficits challenge capacity theories and the single attachment principle.* Unpublished manuscript.

MacKay, D. G., & Burke, D. M. (1990). Cognition and aging: A theory of new learning and the use of old connections. In T. Hess (Ed.), *Aging and cognition: Knowledge organization and utilization* (pp. 281–300). Amsterdam: North-Holland.

MacKay, D. G., Miller, M. D., & Schuster, S. P. (1994). Effects of repetition blindness on aging: Evidence for a binding deficit involving a single, theoretically specified connection. *Psychology and Aging, 9,* 251–258.

MacKay, D. G., Wulf, G., Yin, C., & Abrams, L. (1993). Relations between word perception and production: New theory and data on the verbal transformation effect. *Language and Memory, 32,* 624–646.

McCrae, R. R., Arenberg, D., & Costa, P. T. (1987). Declines in divergent thinking with age: Cross-sectional, longitudinal, and cross-sequential analyses. *Psychology and Aging, 2,* 130–137.

McDowd, J. M., Oseas-Kreger, D. M., & Filion, D. L. (1994). Inhibitory processes in selective attention and aging. In F. Demster (Ed.), *New perspectives on interference and inhibition in cognition* (pp. 1–24). San Diego, CA: Academic Press.

Miller, M., & MacKay, D. G. (1994). Repetition

deafness: Repeated words in computer compressed speech are difficult to encode and recall. *Psychological Science, 5,* 47–51.

Mitchell, D. B. (1989). How many memory systems? Evidence from aging. *Journal of Experimental Psychology: Learning, Memory, and Cognition, 15,* 31–49.

Morris, R. G., Gick, M. L., & Craik, F. I. M. (1988). Processing resources and age differences in working memory. *Memory & Cognition, 16,* 362–366.

Moscovitch, M., Winocur, G., & McLachlan, D. (1986). A neuropsychological approach to perception and memory in normal and pathological aging. In F. I. M. Craik & S. Trehub (Eds.), *Aging and cognitive processes* (pp. 55–78). New York: Plenum.

Myerson, J., Hale, S., Wagstaff, D., Poon, L. W., & Smith, G. A. (1990). The information-loss model: A mathematical theory of age-related cognitive slowing. *Psychological Review, 97,* 475–487.

Park, D. C., & Shaw, R. J. (1992). Effect of environmental support on implicit and explicit memory in young and older adults. *Psychology and Aging, 7,* 632–642.

Salthouse, T. A. (1985). *A theory of cognitive aging.* Amsterdam: North-Holland.

Salthouse, T. A. (1988). Initiating the formalization of theories of cognitive aging. *Psychology and Aging, 3,* 3–16.

Stanovich, K. E., & West, R. F. (1983). On priming by a sentence context. *Journal of Experimental Psychology: General, 112,* 1–36.

Stine, E. A. L. (1994, April). *Aging and the distribution of resources in working memory.* Paper presented at the 5th biennial Cognitive Aging Conference, Atlanta, GA.

Tyler, L. (1988). Spoken language comprehension in a fluent aphasic patient. *Journal of Cognitive Neuropsychology, 5,* 375–400.

Ulatowska, H. K., Hayashi, M. M., Cannito, M. P., & Flemming, S. G. (1986). Disruption of reference in aging. *Brain and Language, 28,* 24–41.

Valencia-Laver, D. L. (1992). *Adult age differences in the production, detection, and repair of speech errors.* Unpublished doctoral dissertation, Claremont Graduate School, Claremont, CA.

Wingfield, A., Poon, L. W., Lombardi, L., & Lowe, D. (1985). Speed of processing in normal aging: Effects of speech rate, linguistic structure, and processing time. *Journal of Gerontology, 40,* 579–585.

Wingfield, A., & Stine, E. L. (1987). Organizational strategies in immediate recall of rapid speech by young and elderly adults. *Experimental Aging Research, 12,* 79–83.

Wingfield, A., Wayland, S. C., & Stine, E. L. (1992). Adult age differences in the use of prosody for syntactic parsing and recall of spoken sentences. *Journal of Gerontology: Psychological Sciences, 47,* P350–P356.

Yairi, E., & Clifton, N. F. (1972). Disfluent speech behavior of preschool children, high school seniors, and geriatric persons. *Journal of Speech and Hearing Research, 15,* 714–719.

Fifteen

# Intellectual Development in Adulthood

K. Warner Schaie

## I. Introduction

This chapter is designed to bring up to date the literature on adult intellectual development and to review new directions of research on this topic that have become apparent since the last edition of this *Handbook*, emphasizing material published since 1988. Other extensive reviews of topics covered in this chapter can be found in Carroll (1993), Cunningham (1987), Lindenberger (1994), and Schaie (1990a, 1995).

I open with a review of metatheoretical issues concerned with the definition and implications of theories of intelligence for the study of adult development. Next, I consider differential patterns of intellectual aging, and then I address independent variables that affect the aging of intellectual abilities. Attention is given also to reversibility of intellectual deficit by educational training, because this topic bears upon the question of whether intellectual decline is normative or simply due to disuse. The chapter closes with some "prescriptions" for research and theory building on adult intelligence.

## A. Intelligence and Cognition: Some Definitions

In this chapter I deal with the literature for what some describe as cognitive products rather than the cognitive mechanisms treated in the information-processing context (e.g., Rybash, Hoyer, & Roodin, 1986). Measurement of intelligence has traditionally been concerned with operationalizing laboratory operations that are thought to represent intelligent behaviors in the real world. Alfred Binet already argued in 1905 that "To judge well, to comprehend well, to reason well, these are the essentials of intelligence. A person may be a moron or an imbecile if he lacks judgment; but with judgment he could not be either" (Binet & Simon, 1905, p. 106). This definition remains a classic to this day.

I would argue that there is a natural hierarchy in the study of intelligence leading from information processing, through the products measured in tests of intelligence, to practical or everyday intelligence (e.g., Baltes, 1987; Sternberg & Berg, 1987; Willis & Schaie, 1993). Understanding of the mechanisms of intelligent behavior are, of course, important, and theoretical models that attempt to account for the aging of such mechanisms (e.g., Salthouse, 1988a) are highly relevant to the study of intelligence. But the literature on information processing and the development of expertise is treated elsewhere in this handbook (see Ch. 13 by Smith and Ch. 20 by Salthouse & Maurer, this volume). Likewise, I will not deal with the topic of practical intelligence or everyday competence, because this material is covered in the chapter by Willis (Ch. 16, this volume), nor with the burgeoning topic of wisdom (cf. Sternberg, 1990).

The products or intellectual skills that characterize psychometric intelligence are likely to represent the most appropriate level for the direct prediction of many socially desirable outcomes (Willis & Schaie, 1993). The entire age span from young adulthood to advanced old age must be included, because it is not enough to compare young and old adults. Instead, we need to know at what point intellectual development peaks as well as determine the rate and pattern of decline (cf. Schaie, 1994). This is particularly important when basic work on intelligence is related to capability for industrial work and maintenance of societal productivity (cf. Avolio, 1991; Rabbitt, 1991; Welford, 1992).

## B. How Do Theories of Intelligence Affect the Study of Adult Development?

At least four influential theoretical positions have informed empirical research on intelligence conceptualized as products or performance indices. The earliest theoretical influence comes from Sir Charles Spearman's work (1904) that suggested a general dimension of intelligence (g) to underlie all purposeful intellectual products. All other components of such products were viewed as task or item specific (s). This view provides the theoretical foundation for the family of assessment devices that originate from the work of Binet and Simon (1905). The concept of a single general form of intelligence may be appropriate in childhood when there exists an isomorphic and unidimensional validity criterion: scholastic performance. But it is not useful beyond adolescence, because of the lack of a unidimensional criterion in adults and because convincing empirical evidence supports the presence of multiple dimensions of intelligence displaying a different life course (cf. Horn, 1982; Schaie, 1994, 1995).

The first influential theory that was multidimensional in nature was E. L. Thorndike's view suggesting different dimensions of intelligence, which he contended would display similar levels of performance within individuals. Thorndike also suggested that all categories of intelligence possessed three attributes: power, speed, and altitude (cf. Thorndike & Woodworth, 1901). This approach is exemplified by Wechsler's work (see Matarazzo, 1972), which specified 11 distinct scales derived from clinical observation and earlier mental tests; these are combined into two broad dimensions: Verbal and Performance (nonverbal-manipulative) intelligence. These dimensions are then combined to form a total global IQ.

The Wechsler scales have had great importance for use in the clinical assessment of adults with psychopathology. Although the Wechsler verbal and performance scales are highly reliable in older persons, the difference between the two, often used as a rough estimate of age decline, is far less reliable (Snow, Tierney, Zorzitto, Fisher, & Reid, 1989). A major limitation of the test for research on intellectual aging, however, has been the fact that the factorial structure of the scales does not remain invariant across age (McArdle & Prescott, 1992; Meredith, 1993; Sands, Terry, & Meredith, 1989). As a consequence, most recent studies of intellectual aging in community-dwelling populations have utilized subsets of the primary mental abilities (cf. Cunningham, 1987; Hultsch, Hertzog, Small, McDonald-Miszlak, & Dixon, 1992).

Factorially far simpler multiple dimensions of intelligence were identified in the classical work of L. L. Thurstone (1938), which was further expanded by Guilford (1967). The primary mental abilities described by Thurstone have formed the basis for my own work, which has utilized measurement instruments developed by Thurstone and Thurstone (1949) and by the Educational Testing Service (Ekström, French, Harman, & Derman, 1976), based on the work of Thurstone and of Guilford (1967), as well as parallel forms developed in my laboratory (Schaie, 1995).

The original work on the primary mental abilities was conducted with children (Thurstone, 1938), but the factorial structure of various subsets of the primary abilities in adults has been well described in numerous investigations of adults. Second-order factor analyses of the primary abilities have identified several higher order dimensions, including those of fluid intelligence (applied to novel/eductive tasks) and crystallized intelligence (applied to acculturated information), popularized by Cattell and Horn (e.g., Carroll, 1993; Cunningham, 1987; Horn & Hofer, 1992; Schaie, Willis, Hertzog, & Schulenberg, 1987; Schaie, Willis, Jay, & Chipuer, 1989).

The introduction of Piagetian thought into American psychology led some investigators to consider the application of Piagetian methods to adult development. The Genevan approach, however, has contributed only sparsely to the study of adult cognition (but see Alexander & Langer, 1990; Commons, Sinnott, Richards, & Armon, 1989; Kuhn, 1992; Labouvie-Vief, 1992; Schaie, 1977–1978).

Cutting across these theoretical positions there are also discernable secular trends in relative emphases on different aspects of adult intelligence. Woodruff-Pak (1989) identified four stages: In the first,

lasting until the mid-1950s, concerns were predominantly with identifying steep and apparently inevitable age-related decline. The second stage (in the late 1950s to mid-1960s) involved the discovery that there was stability as well as decline. External social and experiential effects influencing cohort differences in ability levels identified during this period led to a third stage (beginning with the mid-1970s) in which the field was dominated by attempts to alter experience and manipulate age differences. In the latest stage, the impact of successful demonstrations of the modifiability of intellectual performance has led investigators to expand definitions of intelligence and explore new methods of measurement.

## C. The Role of Longitudinal Studies

The study of adult intelligence presents us with two related but nevertheless distinct objectives. The objective of most age-comparative studies is to determine whether adults at different age levels also differ in intellectual performance at a particular moment in historical time. When such information is needed for policy-relevant determinations, cross-sectional methods will suffice. But cross-sectional data are not directly relevant to the question of how intelligence changes with age *within* individuals, nor will such data help discover the antecedents of individual differences in the course of adult development. Increased attention has therefore been given to the role of longitudinal data in understanding adult intellectual development. A respectable number of longitudinal studies have been conducted in the United States and in Europe that cover substantial age ranges (Busse, 1993; Costa & McCrae, 1993; Cunningham & Owens, 1983; Eichorn, Clausen, Haan, Honzik, & Mussen, 1981; Jarvik & Bank, 1983; Rott, 1990; Schaie, 1995; Shanan, 1993; Steen & Djurfeldt, 1993).

An important new addition is provided

by the initiation of longitudinal studies in the very old, providing hope that we will soon have better information on age changes in the 90s and beyond (e.g., Baltes, Mayer, Helmchen, & Steinhagen-Thiessen, 1993; Poon, Sweaney, Clayton, & Merriam, 1992). There have also been recent proposals for multivariate models that jointly examine cross-sectional and longitudinal data (McArdle, Hamagami, Elias, & Robbins, 1991; McArdle & Prescott, 1992). Their promise remains to be demonstrated.

## D. Observed and Latent Variables

Most research on intelligence is not so much concerned with age changes or differences in specific measures but rather with understanding the effects of intellectual aging on the underlying ability dimensions. Within the primary mental ability framework, the question has been raised whether specific abilities or second-order constructs are of greater importance. For adult development, however, assessment would seem to be optimal at the primary level, because the role of $g$ becomes less central as expertise is developed in specific skills and because most age-related change in cognitive processes requires more than a single component to explain individual differences (Salthouse, 1988b, 1992).

Aging patterns differ between the various primary mental abilities (Schaie, 1995; Schaie & Willis, 1993) and the various second-order ability factors (Horn & Hofer, 1992), and measures of intellectual functioning are not necessarily factorially invariant across age and time (Schaie et al., 1989). Although the factor structure of abilities may be fairly stable across age, differences in factor covariances, particularly in the regression of the observed marker variables on the factors, have been reported (cf. Hertzog, 1987; Horn & McArdle, 1992; Schaie et al., 1989). Although most factor scores based on multiple

markers provide valid comparisons across age, the same cannot be said for individual scales whose regression on a given ability factor may vary markedly from young adulthood into old age.

## II. The Course of Adult Intellectual Development

In this section, I review briefly what seem to me to be the substantive conclusions that can be reached from the current literature. I utilize information from a broad array of current studies, but caution the reader that I lean heavily on results from my own work.

### A. What Do We Know about Population Parameters for Age Changes and Age Differences in Adult Intellectual Aging?

Intellectual aging as a multidimensional process in normal community-dwelling populations has been studied most intensively in the Seattle Longitudinal Study (SLS; Schaie, 1993, 1994, 1995). The principal variables in this study, which has extended thus far over a 35-year period, were five measures of psychological competence known as *primary mental abilities* (Schaie, 1985; Thurstone & Thurstone, 1949): Verbal Meaning, Space, Reasoning, Number, and Word Fluency (the ability to recall words according to a lexical rule). During the last two test occasions, six multiply-marked abilities were assessed at the factor level: Inductive Reasoning, Spatial Orientation, Perceptual Speed, Numeric Ability, Verbal Ability, and Verbal Memory.

Various combinations of the primary mental abilities are represented in all meaningful activities of a person's daily living and work (Willis, Jay, Diehl, & Marsiske, 1992; Willis & Schaie, 1986a, 1994a). The SLS has followed large numbers of individuals over each 7-year interval over the age range from 25–88 years. On average, there is gain until the late 30s or early 40s are reached, and then there is stability until the mid-50s or early 60s are reached. Beginning with the late 60s, however, 7-year decrements are statistically significant throughout. These data suggest that average decline in psychological competence may begin for some as early as the mid-50s, but that early decrement is of small magnitude until the mid-70s are reached. Because of the modest gains from young adulthood to middle age, longitudinal comparisons from a young adult base (age 25) show significant cumulative decline from that base only by the mid-70s.

At the factor level, longitudinal decline is noted by the mid-50s for Perceptual Speed and Numeric Ability, by the late 60s for Inductive Reasoning and Spatial Orien-

tation, and by the late 70s for Verbal Ability and Verbal Memory. Figures 1 and 2 show longitudinal gradients for the five observed mental abilities and six derived ability factors.

A number of recent short-term longitudinal studies confirm that age change in cognitive functions is a rather slow process. Thus at least two studies have found virtual stability over a 3-year period (Hultsch et al., 1992; Zelinski, Gilewski, & Schaie, 1993).

Substantial intellectual changes within individuals occur only late in life and tend to occur for abilities that were less central to the individuals' life experiences and thus perhaps less practiced. Nevertheless, in our community-based studies we found that virtually everyone had declined modestly on at least one of five mental abilities

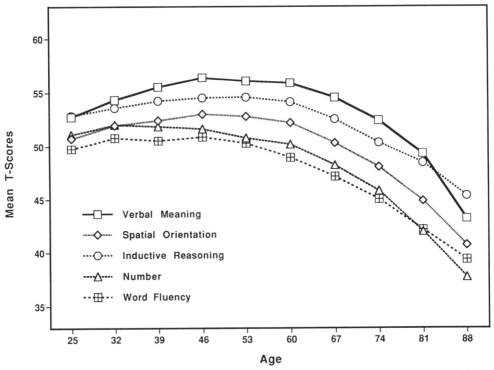

**Figure 1**  Longitudinal estimates of age changes on observed measures of five primary mental abilities. (From "The Course of Adult Intellectual Development" by K. W. Schaie, 1994, *American Psychologist*, *49*, pp. 304–313. Copyright 1994 by the American Psychological Association. Reproduced by permission of the publisher.)

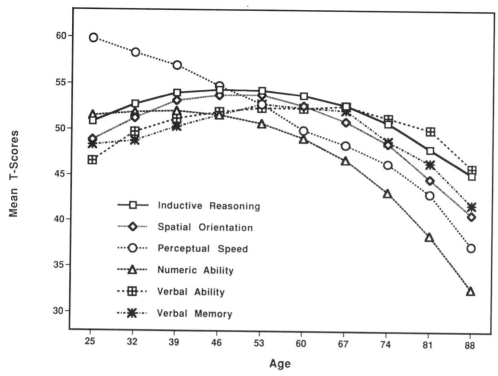

**Figure 2**  Longitudinal estimates of age changes in factor scores on six primary mental abilities at the latent construct level. (From "The Course of Adult Intellectual Development" by K. W. Schaie, 1994, *American Psychologist, 49*, pp. 304–313. Copyright 1994 by the American Psychological Association. Reproduced by permission of the publisher.)

by age 60, but that none of the study participants had declined on all five abilities even by age 88 (Schaie, 1989a).

But what about findings from age-comparative (cross-sectional) studies of intellectual performance in which young and old adults are compared at a single point in time? Due to substantial cohort differences (see Section II.B), these studies show far greater age differences than do longitudinal data. Typically, ages of peak performance occur earlier (for later-born cohorts), and modest age differences are found by the early 50s for some and by the 60s for most dimensions of intelligence. Because of the slowing in the rate of positive cohort differences, age difference profiles have begun to converge somewhat more with the age change data from longi-

tudinal studies. Figure 3 shows age difference patterns from the SLS over the age range from 25–81 in 1970 and 1991. As can be seen, both peak performance and beginning decline seem to be shifting to later ages for most variables.

Recent work on the Wechsler Adult Intelligence Scale (WAIS) with data sets based on normal individuals has shifted to approaches that involve latent variable models (see Horn & McArdle, 1992; McArdle & Prescott, 1992; Millsap & Meredith, 1992; Rott, 1993). Alternatively, analyses have been conducted at the item level. An example of the latter approach is a study by Sands et al. (1989) of two cohorts spanning the age range from 18–61. Consistent improvement in performance was found between the ages of 18 and 40

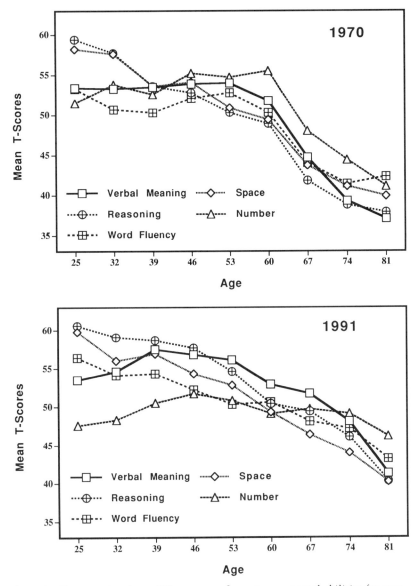

**Figure 3**  Cross-sectional age differences on five primary mental abilities for samples tested in 1970 and 1991. (Adapted from Schaie, 1995.)

and between 18 and 54. Between ages 40 and 61 improvement was found for the Information, Comprehension, and Vocabulary subtests; mixed change (gain on the easy items and decline on the difficult items) on Picture Completion; and decline on Digit Symbol and Block Design (with decline only for the most difficult items of the latter test).

### B. Individual Differences in Level and Rate of Change

Is decline in psychological competence a global or a highly specific event? SLS data

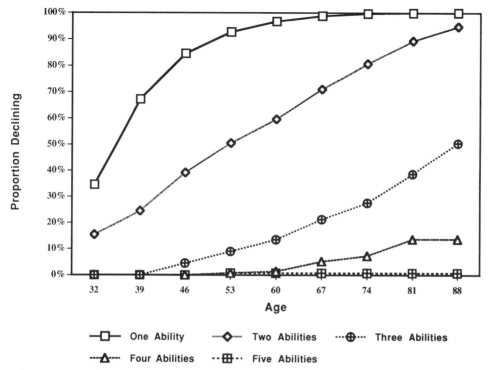

**Figure 4**  Cumulative proportion by age of individuals who show significant decline on one or more primary mental abilities. (From "The Hazards of Cognitive Aging" by K. W. Schaie, 1989, *Gerontologist*, 29, pp. 484–493. Copyright the Gerontological Society of America. Reproduced with permission of the publisher).

graphed in Figure 4 show cumulative proportions by age of subjects whose level of cognitive functioning had declined on one or more abilities. Although by age 60 virtually every subject had declined on one ability, few individuals showed global decline. Virtually no one showed universal decline on all abilities monitored, even by the 80s. Optimization of cognitive functioning in old age may well involve selective maintenance of some abilities but not others (cf. Baltes & Baltes, 1990). Moreover, such optimization seems to be a highly individualized phenomenon (cf. Rabbitt, 1993; Schaie, l989a, 1990b).

Despite these encouraging data, it is clear that significant reductions in psychological competence occur in most persons as the 80s and 90s are reached. However, even at such advanced ages, compe-tent behavior can be expected by many persons in familiar circumstances. Much of the observed loss occurs in highly challenging, complex, or stressful situations that require activation of reserve capacities (cf. Baltes, 1993; Raykov, 1989). The often voiced hope that the more able are also more resistant to intellectual decline remains generally unsupported (cf. Christensen & Henderson, 1991). But those who start out at high levels remain advantaged even after suffering some decline.

## C. Why Do Cohort Effects Matter?

There have been marked generational shifts in levels of performance on tests of mental abilities (Schaie, 1989b, 1995; Willis, 1989a). Empirical findings suggest that later-born cohorts are generally advantaged when compared with earlier cohorts at the same ages. This phenomenon has been explained by increased educational opportunities and improved lifestyles, including nutrition and the conquest of childhood disease, which have enabled successive generations to reach ever higher ability asymptotes, similar to the observed secular trends of improvement for anthropometric and other biological markers (Shock et al., 1984). Although linear trends have been found for some variables, there seems to be contrary evidence that such trends may have been time limited and domain or even variable specific (cf. Schaie, 1990c; Willis, 1989a).

Accurate descriptions of patterns of cohort change in mental ability are important because they provide the foundation for a better understanding of how intellectual productivity and competence shift over time in our society. These data also help us understand how cohort differences in performance can lead to erroneous conclusions from age-comparative cross-sectional studies (cf. Schaie, 1988). The changing demographic composition of the population makes it necessary to assess differences in performance level at comparable ages for individuals representing eras characterized by differential fertility rates (e.g., contrasts of the pre-baby boom, baby boom, and baby bust generations). Cohort shifts at older ages, moreover, are directly relevant to policy considerations regarding the maintenance of a competent workforce that will contain increasing proportions of older workers, as mandatory retirement has become a relic of a biased past, and unfavorable changes in dependency ratios will require many to work to later ages than most people now contemplate. Cohort trends over time have been reported that are likely to influence the proportion of individuals of advanced age who will remain capable of significant late-life accomplishments; these trends

may reflect the ability of older individuals to take advantage of recent technological developments (Schaie, 1989a; Willis, 1989a).

Figure 5 shows cohort gradients for the same abilities for which age trends were given above. The negative shift in some abilities for more recent cohorts may make many older persons appear to be more competitive with their younger peers than has been true in the past. Because of the recent leveling off of cohort differences for some abilities and the curvilinear nature of cohort differences for other abilities, it may be expected that the large ability differences between young and old adults observed currently will be much reduced in the future. For numerical skill, in particular, we may expect a period of time when older adults will be advantaged as compared to younger persons. Conversely, the level reached by recent cohorts in educational attainment and positive lifestyles may well be close to the limits possible within our society's resources and structures. The positive shifts in potential experienced in early old age by successive cohorts (Schaie, 1990b) may therefore come to a halt by the end of this century.

Although cohort differences in intelligence have generally been studied in random population samples, we have recently supplemented this literature by investigating cohort differences in 531 adult parent–offspring pairs. Significant within-family cohort ability differences were found in favor of the offspring generation in about the same magnitude as shown in the previous studies, but generational differences became smaller for more recently born parent–offspring pairs (Schaie, Plomin, Willis, Gruber-Baldini, & Dutta, 1992).

## D. Is the Structure of Intelligence Invariant across Adulthood?

Much attention has been given to age changes and differences in level of performance,

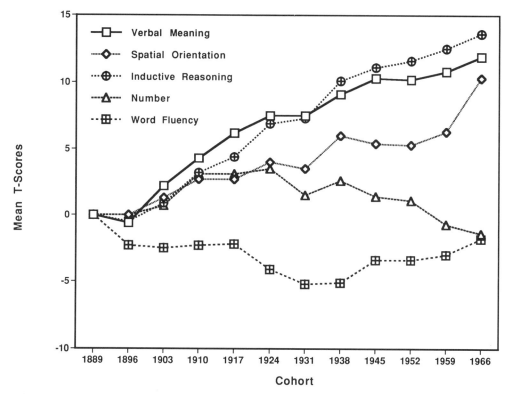

**Figure 5**  Cohort gradients showing cumulative cohort differences on five primary mental abilities for cohorts born 1889 to 1966. (From "The Course of Adult Intellectual Development" by K. W. Schaie, 1994, *American Psychologist, 49*, pp. 304–313. Copyright 1994 by the American Psychological Association. Reproduced by permission of the publisher.)

but another fundamental question is whether the structure of intelligence remains constant across adulthood. Heinz Werner (1948) was an early proponent of a differentiation–dedifferentiation hypothesis, which suggested differentiation of dimensions of human behavior during the growth stage, and eventual dedifferentiation or reintegration as individuals aged. This hypothesis was explicitly extended to intellectual development by Reinert (1970).

The introduction of confirmatory factor analysis permitted testing of the above hypothesis by designing studies that formally assess factorial invariance across age (cf. Alwin, 1988; Horn & McArdle, 1992;

Millsap & Meredith, 1992). The same number of dimensions generally suffice to describe the abilities domain across adulthood, but the relative importance of observed measures as estimates of the underlying latent constructs changes across age. In my own work, my colleagues and I have found configural invariance across adulthood into the 80s in cross-sectional data, but could not accept complete metric invariance (Schaie et al., 1989). This means that in age-comparative studies one should not compare means for observed variables, but should instead compare estimated factor scores on the latent constructs. Most recently I have conducted longitudinal within-cohort factor analyses and found that metric invariance can be demonstrated over 7 years, except for subjects now in their 80s (Schaie, 1994, 1995).

# III. Antecedents of Differential Age Changes in Adult Intellectual Development

Why is it that some maintain high levels of intellectual functioning into advanced old age whereas others tend to decline early? In this context we must distinguish between the effects of normal and pathological aging, consider the impact of behavioral slowing, and explore the effects of social context and personality differences.

## A. How to Distinguish Normal versus Pathological Aging

In order to identify declines in intellectual functioning caused by acute or chronic disease (cf. Anstey, Stankov, & Lord, 1993), many investigators have attempted to control for or measure the impact of such disease. Simple questionnaires on subjective health status often suffice to adduce fairly strong relationships with levels of cognitive functioning (cf. Field, Schaie, & Leino, 1988; Hultsch, Hammer, & Small, 1993; Perlmutter & Nyquist, 1990). More ambitious efforts have involved intensive studies of health history data or the inclusion of partial or complete medical work-ups in some studies of intellectual development.

## 1. Impact of Cardiovascular Disease

One might suspect that the presence or absence of cardiovascular disease ought to be related to the rate of intellectual aging. Such analyses have been undertaken in the Duke Longitudinal Study (Manton, Siegler, & Woodbury, 1986; Palmore, Busse, Maddox, Nowlin, & Siegler, 1985) and in the SLS. In the latter, it was found that individuals who were at risk from cardiovascular disease tended to decline earlier on average on all mental abilities studied than did individuals not so affected (cf. Gruber-Baldini, 1991). Those who declined had significantly greater numbers of illness diagnoses, as well as clinic visits for cardiovascular disease.

It should be noted, however, that the effects of hypertension have been far more complicated than those of other cardiovascular conditions. When distinctions are made between moderate or medically controlled and severe hypertension, it is often found that mild hypertension may actually have positive effects on intellectual functioning (e.g., Elias, Elias, & Elias, 1990; Sands & Meredith, 1992; Schultz, Elias, Robbins, & Streeten, 1989).

## 2. Impact of Other Chronic Diseases

Other chronic diseases that affect maintenance of intellectual functioning include arthritis, neoplasms (tumors), osteoporosis, and sensory deficits. In one study of the very old, visual and hearing deficits accounted for almost half of the total individual-differences variance, and for more than 90% of the age-related portion of those differences (Lindenberger & Baltes, 1994).

Data from the SLS suggest that arthritics have lower functioning and greater decline on Verbal Meaning, Spatial Orientation, and Inductive Reasoning. When malignant and benign neoplasms are distinguished, persons with benign neoplasms (other than skin tumors) were found to have earlier onset of intellectual decline, but less overall decline. Persons with malignant neoplasms and benign skin neoplasms had indirect negative influences on performance (through reduced activity). Results of the influence of neoplasms on cognition might be specific to type of tumor (malignant versus nonmalignant) as well as location (skin, bone, etc.). Osteoporosis and hip fractures were predictive of earlier decline on Word Fluency. Hearing impairment was associated with an increased risk of experiencing Verbal Meaning decline, but was associated with better performance and later decline on Space. Vision difficulties predicted later age at onset of decline for Verbal Meaning and Space (Gruber-Baldini, 1991).

Some caution is urged, however, not to overinterpret the relationship between disease and intellectual functioning. This relationship may be exaggerated by the fact that the more able are more likely to engage in appropriate health maintenance behavior and seek competent help earlier, and hence are more likely to postpone the onset of serious disease.

## B. The Impact of Behavioral Slowing on Intellectual Aging

It is quite evident that decline in reaction time with age adversely affects performance on tests of intellectual abilities. Many questions remain, however, as to whether the behavioral slowing involves a single mechanism or multiple ones (cf. Salthouse, 1988a, 1993c, 1994). Slowing of performance seems to have differential effects depending not only on the cognitive processes or abilities involved but also on the format involved in the presentation of test materials (Hertzog, 1989). Although group data on age changes in reaction time or perceptual speed take quite linear form, analyses of individual differences tend to support patterns of change that are more likely to follow a stair-step pattern (Schaie, l989b). Birren has argued for a long time that loss in speed is a species-specific characteristic of normal aging, and has concluded that if one cannot think quickly, one cannot think well (Birren & Botwinick, 1951; Birren & Fisher, 1992). Stankov (1988), moreover, showed that speed of search is related to processing information. When statistical adjustments were made for the effects of individual differ-

ences in attention, age differences in fluid abilities were markedly reduced, whereas crystallized abilities tended to show increases into later life.

A number of studies have investigated the specific impact of level of performance on measures of perceptual speed. The usual method has been to partial out perceptual speed from the correlations between age and intellectual performance. Most studies report that age differences are markedly reduced or completely eliminated after such adjustment (Hertzog, 1989; Lindenberger, Mayr, & Kliegl, 1993; Salthouse, 1993c; Schaie, 1989b). Other possible adjustments of speed-mediated age differences in intelligence have involved measures of psychomotor speed (cf. Hertzog, 1989; Schaie & Willis, 1991).

If cognitive decrement with age is seen as a diminution of resources of which speed of behavior is a prime component (Salthouse 1988b), then other cognitive mechanisms may also be implicated. For example, reduction in the efficiency of verbal memory occurring with increasing age would reduce the preservation of information during processing of any complex cognitive task (Salthouse, 1993a). On the other hand, superior resources, such as crystallized knowledge, might reduce age differences on verbal tasks even when older subjects display slower processing speed (Salthouse, 1993b).

## C. The Social Context of Intellectual Aging

Needless to say, intellectual aging occurs within a social context. Hence, a number of demographic dimensions have been identified that tend to affect the rate of cognitive decline (cf. Schaie, 1994; Willis, l989a).

Because of different socialization patterns, gender roles result in differential performance levels on certain mental abilities. On the primary mental abilities women consistently excel over men on reasoning and verbal skills, whereas men do better on spatial skills (Schaie, 1995). On the WAIS, adult gender differences have been found to favor men on Arithmetic, Information, and Block Design, with women excelling on Digit Symbol (Kaufman, Kaufman, McLean, & Reynolds, 1991). Because of women's greater life expectancy, men are always closer to death. At comparable advanced ages, therefore, women tend to do better (also see Berg, Ch. 18, this volume). Gender differences in rates of decline, moreover, are greater for those skills where each gender excels in young adulthood (Feingold, 1993; Schaie, 1995).

Not only are high levels of education implicated in slower rates of intellectual decline (Schaie, 1989a), but a lengthy marriage to a well-educated and intelligent spouse has also been identified as a positive risk factor (Gruber & Schaie, 1986). High occupational status and its more subtle aspects (such as high workplace complexity) are positive predictors of maintenance of intellectual functioning into old age (Dutta, 1992; Miller, Slomczynski, & Kohn, 1987; Schooler, 1987). Moreover, retirement seems to have favorable cognitive sequelae for those retiring from routinized jobs but to accelerate decrement for those retiring from highly complex jobs. Other contextual variables that have favorable impact on cognitive aging include an intact marriage, exposure to stimulating environments, and the utilization of cultural and educational resources throughout adulthood (Schaie, 1984). Lifestyle variables such as those mentioned above were also identified as positive risk factors in the Boston Normative Aging study (Jones, Albert, Duffy, & Hyde, 1991), and in studies of memory functioning in older Canadian men (Arbuckle, Gold, Andres, & Schwartzman, 1992).

## D. Personality, Cognitive Styles, and Motivation

Certain personality traits and cognitive style variables have also been found to af-fect maintenance of intellectual functioning. There seems to be a modest positive relationship between self-efficacy and intellectual functioning, although it remains to be resolved whether this relationship is unidirectional or reciprocal (Dittman-Kohli, Lachman, Kliegl, & Baltes, 1991; Grover & Hertzog, 1991; Lachman & Leff, 1989).

Intellectual performance might also be affected by the subjects' self-appraisal of changes with age. This question has been studied empirically by assessing perceived change in performance with objectively measured change (Schaie, Willis, & O'Hanlon, 1994). Study participants were categorized, based on their actual performance, into those who had maintained earlier performance level, significantly increased their performance, or declined in performance. A typology linking actual and perceived change in performance was created: *Realists* (those who accurately estimated change in their performance); *Optimists* (those who overestimated positive change); and *Pessimists* (those who overestimated negative change). The majority of subjects made realistic appraisals of changes in intellectual functioning. However, women were more likely to be pessimists on Spatial Orientation than men, and older individuals were more likely to be pessimists on Verbal Meaning and Inductive Reasoning Abilities and to be realists on Number ability compared to younger participants. By contrast, Rabbitt and Abson (1991) found that their subjects failed to predict objective performance on simple memory tasks, although their predictions were related to the Beck Depression Inventory. They suggested that their subjects rated their memory relative to reduced memory requirements in their current environment.

More securely established is the antecedent status of the personality characteristic of rigidity or flexibility. There are two aspects of this trait: motor-cognitive flexibility and attitudinal flexibility.

Longitudinal studies suggest that one's lifelong standing on flexible *behaviors* is maintained for most persons into the 70s, whereas, on average, people develop more rigid *attitudes* by the early 60s (cf. Schaie, 1995). It has also been shown that those with flexible attitudes in midlife tend to experience less decline in psychological competence with advancing age than those who were observed to be fairly rigid at that life stage (Schaie, 1984, 1995). These studies also concluded that high levels of motor-cognitive flexibility at the young-old stage are highly predictive of one's standing on numerical and verbal skills as well as psychological energy when reaching the old-old stage (also see O'Hanlon, 1993; Schaie, Dutta, & Willis, 1991).

## IV. Interventions in Adult Intellectual Development

### A. Is Adult Intellectual Decline Irreversible or Remediable?

Findings on individual differences in intellectual change and the identification of antecedents for differential intellectual aging cast at least some doubt on the inevitability of general intellectual decline for all individuals. More substantive evidence for such doubt is provided by cognitive intervention research that has successfully remediated some intellectual decline in the elderly. Longitudinal studies make it possible to distinguish effects of training that remediate age deficits from improvement in the performance of individuals above earlier levels. The former outcome, however, is of particular theoretical interest because it suggests that much of the intellectual aging seen in community-dwelling elderly may be experiential in nature. Training studies conducted in a longitudinal context also permit the identification of antecedent conditions that predict the likelihood of training success or failure (Willis, 1989b, 1990).

### B. Remediation of Deficit versus Reduction of Cohort Effects

Much of the work on cognitive training was conducted in the context of the Adult Development and Enrichment Project (ADEPT, Baltes & Willis, 1982) and the SLS (Schaie & Willis, 1986; Willis & Schaie, 1986b). Both of these studies involved pre-posttest designs, with 5 hr of instruction in strategies at the ability level, given in small groups in the ADEPT study and individually in the SLS. In the former study, significant training gains were demonstrated for subjects over age 60 for the primaries of figural relations and induction, whereas in the latter study, significant training gains occurred for inductive reasoning and spatial orientation. In the SLS, moreover, significant gain occurred for subjects who had declined as well as for those who had remained stable. Women experienced greater training effects on spatial orientation, and training benefited both speed and accuracy in women but primarily accuracy in men (Willis & Schaie, 1988). In both studies, near transfer was shown to occur for alternate markers within each ability, but there was no far transfer to other primary abilities.

Variations of the ADEPT study, introducing multiple training conditions, or conditions involving self-programmed training conditions, have for the most part replicated the original findings in a German sample (Baltes & Lindenberger, 1988; Baltes, Sowarka, & Kliegl, 1989), and in American studies by Blackburn, Papalia-Finley, Foye, and Serlin (1988) and Hayslip (1989). A study of figural relations training by Denney and Heidrich (1990) showed equal magnitudes of improvement for young, middle-aged, and old subjects.

Does cognitive training change the structural characteristics of the primary abilities (i.e., convert a pretraining fluid ability to a crystallized ability—cf. Donaldson, 1981)? In the SLS, invariance of factor structure across training was confirmed in the training groups. Minor shifts occurred in the factor loadings of the individual markers of the abilities trained, but training did not result in any of the markers loading on factors other than those hypothesized (Schaie et al., 1987).

## C. Long-Term Effects of Cognitive Interventions on Adult Intellectual Development

Cognitive training will clearly yield significant improvement in the performance of older persons on the targeted abilities, but skepticism has remained whether such training produces any lasting effects. Long-term follow-up over a 7-year period has been conducted for both the ADEPT and SLS training studies. Significantly lower decline over 7 years was shown in the ADEPT study for those individuals trained on figural relations as compared to the control group (Willis & Nesselroade, 1990). In the SLS, similar findings occurred for both Inductive Reasoning and Spatial Orientation abilities (Willis & Schaie, 1994b). In the latter study, those who had declined prior to the initial training were at the greatest comparative advantage upon follow-up. Both studies also examined effects of booster training. As would be expected, as subjects entered advanced old age, booster training, although yielding significant effects, resulted in somewhat lower magnitudes of training effects. It seems then that periodic reactivation of specific mental skills is likely to reduce the magnitude of intellectual decline in community-dwelling persons.

## V. Conclusions: Future Directions for Research on Intellectual Aging

In my 1990 review I concluded that there had been a turning away from studies that simply defined the extent and ability specificity of age differences and age changes in

intelligence, toward a greater preoccupation with individual patterns of change and with the identification of antecedent variables that might account for the vast array of individual differences. I also identified much progress in the study of practical intelligence, a field that has expanded so much in the most recent period that an entire chapter is devoted to it in this volume (see Willis, Ch. 16).

Progress has continued also in identifying the social structural, health, and personality variables that account for such differences. No longer are contextual variables treated as methodological confounds; rather, increasing efforts are being made to identify the precise influences that will eventually predict individual hazards of intellectual decline and maintenance. Important theoretical efforts therefore have been directed toward replacing index variables, such as age or cohort, with more direct explanations of individual differences (also see Salthouse and Maurer, Ch. 20, this volume, and Anstey et al., 1993).

Findings presented in this chapter lead to the prediction that intellectual age differences in adulthood will become more compressed over the next decade because of the apparent plateauing of positive cohort differences for some abilities, and the occurrence of negative effects for others. The baby-boom cohort is now in midlife, and given the enormous demographic pressures affecting this group, monitoring of its cognitive functioning as it ages attains greater importance (cf. Willis & Schaie, in press).

More work is needed on the role of lifelong experience in the maintenance of intellectual functions and productive performance in societal roles. Information gathered with retrospective questionnaires indicates that the role of experience may be less than common sense would suggest (e.g., Salthouse & Mitchell, 1990). But the sparse relations found between age and job performance (Avolio & Waldman, 1990; Salthouse & Maurer, this volume) suggest to me that experience cannot yet be written off as an important source of compensation for loss of speed and cognitive efficiency.

I have previously called attention to the lack of comparative work on intellectual aging within minority groups in the United States; also lacking are informative cross-cultural comparisons with intellectual aging in other societies (but see Dai, Xie, & Zheng, 1993). Life course sociologists have taken advantage of substantial environmental interventions (e.g., the Great Depression, farm crises, cultural revolution, and so on) that may have differential effects upon human development (e.g., Elder, Rudkin, & Conger, 1994). Adult cognitive psychologists have yet to emulate this useful approach in their work.

Further progress has been made in work on cognitive intervention to show that intellectual decline in old age is not necessarily irreversible and that formal intervention strategies are available that might allow longer maintenance of high levels of intellectual function in community-dwelling older persons. The data on successful cognitive interventions have now been supplemented by evidence of positive long-term effects of these interventions. It is still necessary, however, to remove these techniques from the laboratory to a broader social context. This would require the implementation of "clinical trials" as well as the investigation of modes of intervention that are indigenous to the daily experience of older persons (such as games and other activities that may be cognitively challenging; see, e.g., Tosti-Vasey, Person, Maier, & Willis, 1992). Also needed are efforts to relate the effect of cognitive training to specific activities of daily living.

The field of adult intelligence has matured from a descriptive science toward one that increasingly calls for the identification of precise mechanisms and the identification of antecedents of individual differences. It has also progressed to the stage of interventions informed by basic science in the interest of improving intellectual competence in old age.

## References

Alexander, C., & Langer, E. J. (Eds.). (1990). *Beyond formal operations: Alternative endpoints to human development.* New York: Oxford University Press.

Alwin, D. F. (1988). Structural equation models in research on human development and aging. In K. W. Schaie, R. T. Campbell, W. Meredith, & S. C. Rawlings (Eds.), *Methodological issues in aging research* (pp. 71–170). New York: Springer.

Anstey, K., Stankov, L., & Lord, S. (1993). Primary aging, secondary aging, and intelligence. *Psychology and Aging, 8,* 562–570.

Arbuckle, T. Y., Gold, D. P., Andres, D., & Schwartzman, A. (1992). The role of psychosocial context, age, and intelligence in memory performance of older men. *Psychology and Aging, 7,* 25–36.

Avolio, B. J. (1991). Levels of analysis. *Annual Review of Gerontology and Geriatrics, 11,* 239–260.

Avolio, B. J., & Waldman, D. A. (1990). An examination of age and cognitive test performance across job complexity and occupational types. *Journal of Applied Psychology, 75,* 43–50.

Baltes, P. B. (1987). Theoretical propositions of life-span developmental psychology: On the dynamics between growth and decline. *Developmental Psychology, 23,* 611–626.

Baltes, P. B. (1993). The aging mind: Potential and limits. *Gerontologist, 33,* 580–594.

Baltes, P. B., & Baltes, M. M. (1990). Psychological perspectives on successful aging: The model of selective optimization with compensation. In P. B. Baltes & M. M. Baltes (Eds.), *Successful aging: Perspectives from the behavioral sciences* (pp. 1–34). Cambridge, England: Cambridge University Press.

Baltes, P. B., & Lindenberger, U. (1988). On the range of cognitive plasticity in old age as a function of experience: 15 years of intervention research. *Behavior Therapy, 19,* 283–300.

Baltes, P. B., Mayer, K. U., Helmchen, H., & Steinhagen-Thiessen, E. (1993). The Berlin Aging Study (BASE): Overview and design. *Ageing and Society, 13,* 483–533.

Baltes, P. B., Sowarka, D., & Kliegl, R. (1989). Cognitive training research on fluid intelligence in old age: What can older adults achieve by themselves? *Psychology and Aging, 4*, 217–221.

Baltes, P. B., & Willis, S. L. (1982). Enhancement (plasticity) of intellectual functioning in old age: Penn State's Adult Development and Enrichment Project (ADEPT). In F. I. M. Craik & S. Trehub (Eds.), *Aging and cognitive processes* (pp. 353–389). New York: Plenum.

Binet, A., & Simon, T. (1905). Méthodes nouvelles pour le diagnostique du niveau intellectuel des anormaux. *Année Psychologique, 11*, 102–191.

Birren, J. E., & Botwinick, J. (1951). Rate of addition as a function of difficulty and age. *Psychometrika, 16*, 219–232.

Birren, J. E., & Fisher, L. M. (1992). Aging and slowing of behavior: Consequences for cognition and survival. In T. Sonderegger (Eds.), *Psychology and aging: Nebraska Symposium on Motivation: Vol. 39* (pp. 1–37). Lincoln: University of Nebraska Press.

Blackburn, J. A., Papalia-Finley, D., Foye, B. F., & Serlin, R. C. (1988). Modifiability of figural relations performance among elderly adults. *Journal of Gerontology: Psychological Sciences, 43*, P87–P89.

Busse, E. W. (1993). Duke longitudinal studies of aging. *Zeitschrift für Gerontologie, 26*, 123–128.

Carroll, J. B. (1993). *Human cognitive abilities: A survey of factor-analytic studies.* New York: Cambridge University Press.

Christensen, H., & Henderson, A. S. (1991). Is age kinder to the initially more able? A study of eminent scientists and academics. *Psychological Medicine, 21*, 935–946.

Commons, M. L., Sinnott, J. D., Richards, F. A., & Armon, C. (Eds.). (1989). *Beyond formal operations: Vol. 2. Adolescent and adult development models.* New York: Praeger.

Costa, P. T., & McCrae, R. R. (1993). Psychological research in the Baltimore Longitudinal Study of Aging. *Zeitschrift für Gerontologie, 26*, 138–141.

Cunningham, W. R. (1987). Intellectual abilities and age. *Annual Review of Gerontology and Geriatrics, 7*, 117–134.

Cunningham, W. R., & Owens, W. A., Jr. (1983). The Iowa State Study of the adult develop-ment of intellectual abilities. In K. W. Schaie (Ed.), *Longitudinal studies of adult psychological development* (pp. 20–39). New York: Guilford.

Dai, X., Xie, Y., & Zheng, L. (1993). Age, education and intelligence declining in adulthood. *Chinese Mental Health Journal, 7*, 215–217.

Denney, N. W., & Heidrich, S. M. (1990). Training effects on Raven's Progressive Matrices in young, middle-aged, and elderly adults. *Psychology and Aging, 5*, 144–145.

Dittmann-Kohli, F., Lachman, M. E., Kliegl, R., & Baltes, P. B. (1991). Effects of cognitive training and testing on intellectual efficacy beliefs in elderly adults. *Journal of Gerontology: Psychological Sciences, 46*, P162–P164.

Donaldson, G. (1981). Letter to the editor. *Journal of Gerontology, 36*, 634–636.

Dutta, R. (1992). *The relationship between flexibility-rigidity and the Primary Mental Abilities.* Unpublished doctoral dissertation, Pennsylvania State University, University Park.

Eichorn, D. H., Clausen, J. A., Haan, N., Honzik, M. P., & Mussen, P. H. (1981). *Present and past in middle life.* New York: Academic Press.

Ekström, R. B., French, J. W., Harman, H., & Derman, D. (1976). *Kit of factor-referenced cognitive tests* (rev. ed.). Princeton, NJ: Educational Testing Service.

Elder, G. H., Jr., Rudkin, L., & Conger, R. D. (1994). Inter-generational continuity and change in rural America. In V. L. Bengtson, K. W. Schaie, & L. Burton (Eds.), *Adult intergenerational relations: Effects of societal change* (pp. 30–60). New York: Springer.

Elias, M. F., Elias, J. W., & Elias, P. K. (1990). Biological and health influences on behavior. In J. E. Birren & K. W. Schaie (Eds.), *Handbook of the psychology of aging* (3rd ed., pp. 80–102). San Diego, CA: Academic Press.

Feingold, A. (1993). Cognitive gender differences: A developmental perspective. *Sex Roles, 29*, 91–112.

Field, D., Schaie, K. W., & Leino, E. V. (1988). Continuity in intellectual functioning: The role of self-reported health. *Psychology and Aging, 3*, 385–392.

Grover, D. R., & Hertzog, C. (1991). Relationships between intellectual control beliefs and psychometric intelligence in adulthood. *Journal of Gerontology: Psychological Sciences, 46*, P109–P115.

Gruber, A. L., & Schaie, K. W. (1986, November). *Longitudinal-sequential studies of marital assortativity.* Paper presented at the annual meeting of the Gerontological Society of America, Chicago.

Gruber-Baldini, A. L. (1991). *The impact of health and disease on cognitive ability in adulthood and old age in the Seattle Longitudinal Study.* Unpublished doctoral dissertation, Pennsylvania State University, University Park.

Guilford, J. P. (1967). *The nature of human intelligence.* New York: McGraw-Hill.

Hayslip, B. (1989). Alternative mechanisms for improvements in fluid ability performance among older adults. *Psychology and Aging, 4,* 122–124.

Hertzog, C. (1987). Applications of structural equation models in gerontological research. *Annual Review of Gerontology and Geriatrics, 7,* 265–293.

Hertzog, C. (1989). The influence of cognitive slowing on age differences in intelligence. *Developmental Psychology, 25,* 636–651.

Horn, J. L. (1982). The theory of fluid and crystallized intelligence in relation to concepts of cognitive psychology and aging in adulthood. In F. I. M. Craik & S. Trehub (Eds.), *Aging and cognitive processes* (pp. 237–278). New York: Plenum.

Horn, J. L., & Hofer, S. M. (1992). Major abilities and development in the adult period. In R. J. Sternberg & C. A. Berg (Eds.), Intellectual development (pp. 44–99). Cambridge, England: Cambridge University Press.

Horn, J. L., & McArdle, J. J. (1992). A practical and theoretical guide to measurement invariance in aging research. *Experimental Aging Research, 18,* 117–144.

Hultsch, D. F., Hammer, M., & Small, B. J. (1993). Age differences in cognitive performance in later life: Relationships to self-reported health and activity life style. *Journal of Gerontology: Psychological Sciences, 48,* P1–P11.

Hultsch, D. F., Hertzog, C., Small, B. J., McDonald-Miszlak, L., & Dixon, R. A. (1992). Short-term longitudinal change in cognitive performance in later life. *Psychology and Aging, 7,* 571–584.

Jarvik, L. F., & Bank, L. (1983). Aging twins: Longitudinal psychometric data. In K. W. Schaie (Ed.), *Longitudinal studies of adult psychological development* (pp. 40–63). New York: Guilford.

Jones, K. J., Albert, M. S, Duffy, F. H., & Hyde, M. R. (1991). Modeling age using cognitive, psychosocial and physiological variables: The Boston Normative Aging study. *Experimental Aging Research, 17,* 227–242.

Kaufman, A. S., Kaufman, J. L., McLean, J. E., & Reynolds, C. R. (1991). Is the pattern of intellectual growth and decline across the adult life span different for men and women? *Journal of Clinical Psychology, 47,* 801–812.

Kuhn, D. (1992). Thinking as argument. *Harvard Educational Review, 62,* 155–178.

Labouvie-Vief, G. (1992). A neo-Piagetian perspective on adult cognitive development. In R. J. Sternberg & C. A. Berg (Eds.), *Intellectual development* (pp. 197–228). Cambridge, England: Cambridge University Press.

Lachman, M. E., & Leff, R. (1989). Perceived control and intellectual functioning in the elderly: A 5-year longitudinal study. *Developmental Psychology, 25,* 722–728.

Lindenberger, U. (1994). Intellectual aging. In R. J. Sternberg (Ed.), *Encyclopedia of intelligence* (pp. 52–60). New York: Macmillan.

Lindenberger, U., & Baltes, P. B. (1994). Sensory functioning and intelligence in old age. *Psychology and Aging, 9,* 339–355.

Lindenberger, U., Mayr, U., & Kliegl, R. (1993). Speed and intelligence in old age. *Psychology and Aging, 8,* 207–220.

Manton, K. G., Siegler, I. C., & Woodbury, M. A. (1986). Patterns of intellectual development in later life. *Journal of Gerontology, 41,* 486–499.

Matarazzo, J. D. (1972). *Wechsler's measurement and appraisal of adult intelligence* (5th ed.). Baltimore: Williams & Wilkins.

McArdle, J. J., Hamagami, F., Elias, M. F., & Robbins, M. A. (1991). Structural modeling of mixed longitudinal and cross-sectional data. *Experimental Aging Research, 17,* 29–52.

McArdle, J. J., & Prescott, C. A. (1992). Age-based construct validation using structural equation modeling. *Experimental Aging Research, 18,* 87–115.

Meredith, W. (1993). Measurement invariance, factor analysis and factorial invariance. *Psychometrika, 58,* 525–543.

Miller, J., Slomczynski, K. M., & Kohn, M. L. (1987). Continuity of learning-generalization through the life span: The effect of job on men's intellectual process in the United States and Poland. In C. Schooler & K. W. Schaie (Eds.), *Cognitive functioning and social structure over the life course* (pp. 176–202). New York: Ablex.

Millsap, R. E., & Meredith, W. (1992). Component analysis in multivariate aging research. *Experimental Aging Research, 18,* 203–212.

O'Hanlon, A. M. (1993). *Inter-individual patterns of intellectual change: The influence of environmental factors.* Unpublished doctoral dissertation, Pennsylvania State University, University Park.

Palmore, E., Busse, E. W., Maddox, G. L., Nowlin, J. B., & Siegler, I. L. (Eds.). (1985). *Normal aging III.* Durham, NC: Duke University Press.

Perlmutter, M., & Nyquist, L. (1990). Relationships between self-reported physical and mental health and intelligence performance across adulthood. *Journal of Gerontology: Psychological Sciences, 45,* P145–P155.

Poon, L. W., Sweaney, A. L., Clayton, G. M., & Merriam, S. B. (1992). The Georgia Centenarian Study. *International Journal of Aging and Human Development, 34,* 1–17.

Rabbitt, P. (1991). Management of the working population. *Ergonomics, 34,* 775–790.

Rabbitt, P. (1993). Does it all go together when it goes? *Quarterly Journal of Experimental Psychology: Human Experimental Psychology, 46A,* 385–434.

Rabbitt, P., & Abson, V. (1991). Do older people know how good they are? *British Journal of Psychology, 82,* 137–151.

Raykov, T. (1989). Reserve capacity of the elderly in aging sensitive tests of fluid intelligence: A reanalysis via a structural equation modelling approach. *Zeitschrift für Psychologie, 197,* 263–282.

Reinert, G. (1970). Comparative factor analytic studies of intelligence through the human life-span. In L. R. Goulet & P. B. Baltes (Eds.), *Life-span developmental psychology: Research and theory* (pp. 468–485). New York: Academic Press.

Rott, C. (1990). Intelligenzentwicklung im Alter [Development of intelligence in old age]. *Zeitschrift für Gerontologie, 23,* 252–261.

Rott, C. (1993). Ein Drei-Komponenten-Modell der Intelligenzentwicklung im Alter: Ergebnisse aus der Bonner Gerontologischen Langsschnittstudie [Three components of intellectual development in old age: Results from the Bonn Longitudinal Study on Aging]. *Zeitschrift für Gerontologie, 26,* 184–190.

Rybash, J. M., Hoyer, W. J., & Roodin, P. A. (1986). *Adult cognition and aging.* New York: Pergamon.

Salthouse, T. A. (1988a). Initiating the formalization of theories of cognitive aging. *Psychology and Aging, 3,* 3–16.

Salthouse, T. A. (1988b). Resource-reduction interpretations of cognitive aging. *Developmental Review, 8,* 238–272.

Salthouse, T. A. (1992). Shifting levels of analysis in the investigation of cognitive aging. *Human Development, 35,* 321–342.

Salthouse, T. A. (1993a). Influence of working memory on adult age differences in matrix reasoning. *British Journal of Psychology, 84,* 171–199.

Salthouse, T. A. (1993b). Speed and knowledge as determinants of adult age differences in verbal tasks. *Journal of Gerontology: Psychological Sciences, 48,* P29–P36.

Salthouse, T. A. (1993c). Speed mediation of adult age differences in cognition. *Developmental Psychology, 29,* 722–738.

Salthouse, T. A. (1994). The nature of the influence of speed on adult age differences in cognition. *Developmental Psychology, 30,* 240–259.

Salthouse, T. A., & Mitchell, D. R. (1990). Effects of age and naturally occurring experience on spatial visualization performance. *Developmental Psychology, 26,* 845–854.

Sands, L. P., & Meredith, W. (1992). Blood pressure and intellectual functioning in late midlife. *Journal of Gerontology: Psychological Sciences, 47,* P81–P84.

Sands, L. P., Terry, H., & Meredith, W. (1989). Change and stability in adult intellectual functioning assessed by Wechsler item responses. *Psychology and Aging, 4,* 79–87.

Schaie, K. W. (1977–1978). Toward a stage theory of adult cognitive development. *Aging and Human Development, 9,* 129–138.

Schaie, K. W. (1984). Midlife influences upon intellectual functioning in old age. *International Journal of Behavioral Development, 7,* 463–478.

Schaie, K. W. (1985). *Manual for the Schaie-Thurstone Adult Mental Abilities Text (STAMAT).* Palo Alto, CA: Consulting Psychologists Press.

Schaie, K. W. (1988). Internal validity threats in studies of adult cognitive development. In M. L. Howe & C. J. Brainerd (Eds.), *Cognitive development in adulthood: Progress in cognitive development research* (pp. 241–272). New York: Springer-Verlag.

Schaie, K. W. (1989a). The hazards of cognitive aging. *Gerontologist, 29,* 484–493.

Schaie, K. W. (1989b). Perceptual speed in adulthood: Cross-sectional and longitudinal studies. *Psychology and Aging, 4,* 443–453.

Schaie, K. W. (1990a). Intellectual development in adulthood. In J. E. Birren & K. W. Schaie (Eds.), *Handbook of the psychology of aging* (3rd ed., pp. 291–319). San Diego, CA: Academic Press.

Schaie, K. W. (1990b). Late life potential and cohort differences in mental abilities. In M. Perlmutter (Ed.), *Late life potential* (pp. 43–62). Washington, DC: Gerontological Society of America.

Schaie, K. W. (1990c). The optimization of cognitive functioning in old age: Predictions based on cohort-sequential and longitudinal data. In P. B. Baltes & M. M. Baltes (Eds.), *Successful aging: Perspectives from the behavioral sciences* (pp. 94–117). Cambridge, England: Cambridge University Press.

Schaie, K. W. (1993). The Seattle Longitudinal Study: A thirty-five year inquiry of adult intellectual development. *Zeitschrift für Gerontologie, 26,* 129–137.

Schaie, K. W. (1994). The course of adult intellectual development. *American Psychologist, 49,* 304–313.

Schaie, K. W. (1995). *Intellectual development in adulthood: The Seattle Longitudinal Study.* New York: Cambridge University Press.

Schaie, K. W., Dutta, R., & Willis, S. L. (1991). The relationship between rigidity-flexibility and cognitive abilities in adulthood. *Psychology and Aging, 6,* 371–383.

Schaie, K. W., Plomin, R., Willis, S. L., Gruber-Baldini, A., & Dutta, R. (1992). Natural cohorts: Family similarity in adult cognition. In T. Sonderegger (Eds.), *Psychology and aging: Nebraska Symposium on Motivation, 1991* (pp. 205–243). Lincoln: University of Nebraska Press.

Schaie, K. W., & Willis, S. L. (1986). Can intellectual decline in the elderly be reversed? *Developmental Psychology, 22,* 223–232.

Schaie, K. W., & Willis, S. L. (1991). Adult personality and psycho-motor performance: Cross-sectional and longitudinal analyses. *Journal of Gerontology: Psychological Sciences, 46,* P275–284.

Schaie, K. W., & Willis, S. L. (1993). Age difference patterns of psychometric intelligence in adulthood: Generalizability within and across ability domains. *Psychology and Aging, 8,* 44–55.

Schaie, K. W., Willis, S. L., Hertzog, C., & Schulenberg, J. E. (1987). Effects of cognitive training upon primary mental ability structure. *Psychology and Aging, 2,* 233–242.

Schaie, K. W., Willis, S. L., Jay, C., & Chipuer, H. (1989). Structural invariance of cognitive abilities across the adult life span: A cross-sectional study. *Developmental Psychology, 25,* 652–662.

Schaie, K. W., Willis, S. L., & O'Hanlon, A. M. (1994). Perceived intellectual performance change over seven years. *Journal of Gerontology: Psychological Sciences, 49,* P108–P118.

Schooler, C. (1987). Cognitive effects of complex environments during the life span: A review and theory. In C. Schooler & K. W. Schaie (Eds.), *Cognitive functioning and social structure over the life course* (pp. 24–49). New York: Ablex.

Schultz, N. R., Elias, M. F., Robbins, M. A., & Streeten, D. H. (1989). A longitudinal study of the performance of hypertensive and normotensive subjects on the Wechsler Adult Intelligence Scale. *Psychology and Aging, 4,* 496–499.

Shanan, J. (1993). Die Jerusalemer Langsschnittuntersuchungen der mittleren Lebensjahre und des Alterns—JESMA [The Jerusalem Longitudinal Study on Mid-adulthood and Aging (JESMA)]. *Zeitschrift für Gerontologie, 26,* 151–155.

Shock, N. W., Greulick, R. C., Andres, R., Arenberg, D., Costa, P. T., Lakatta, E. G., & Tobin, J. D. (1984). *Normal human aging: The Baltimore Longitudinal Study of Aging.* Washington, DC: U.S. Government Printing Office.

Snow, W. G., Tierney, M. C., Zorzitto, M. L., Fisher, R. H., & Reid, D. W. (1989). WAIS-R test-retest reliability in a normal elderly sample. *Journal of Clinical and Experimental Neuropsychology, 11,* P423–428.

Spearman, C. (1904). "General intelligence": Objectively determined and measured. *American Journal of Psychology, 15,* 201–292.

Stankov, L. (1988). Aging, attention and intelligence. *Psychology and Aging, 3,* 59–74.

Steen, B., & Djurfeldt, H. (1993). The gerontological and geriatric population studies in Gothenburg, Sweden. *Zeitschrift für Gerontologie, 26,* 163–169.

Sternberg, R. J. (1990). *Wisdom, its nature, origins, and development.* New York: Cambridge University Press.

Sternberg, R. J., & Berg, C. (1987). What are the theories of adult intellectual development theories of? In C. Schooler & K. W. Schaie (Eds.), *Cognitive functioning and social structure over the life course* (pp. 3–23). New York: Ablex.

Thorndike, E. L., & Woodworth, R. S. (1901). Influence of improvement in one mental function upon the efficiency of other mental functions. *Psychological Review, 8,* 247–261, 384–395, 553–564.

Thurstone, L. L. (1938). *Primary mental abilities.* Chicago: University of Chicago Press.

Thurstone, L. L., & Thurstone, T. G. (1949). *Examiner manual for the SRA Primary Mental Abilities Test.* Chicago: Science Research Associates.

Tosti-Vasey, J. L., Person, D. C., Maier, H., & Willis, S. L. (1992, November). *The relationship of game playing to intellectual ability in old age.* Paper presented at the annual meeting of the Gerontological Society of America, Washington, DC.

Welford, A. T. (1992). Psychological studies of aging: Their origins, development and present challenge. *International Journal of Aging and Human Development, 34,* 185–197.

Werner, H. (1948). *Comparative psychology of mental development.* New York: International Universities Press.

Willis, S. L. (1989a). Cohort differences in cognitive aging: A sample case. In K. W. Schaie & C. Schooler (Eds.), *Social structure and aging: Psychological processes* (pp. 95–112). New York: Erlbaum.

Willis, S. L. (1989b). Improvement with cognitive training: Which old dogs learn what tricks? In L. Poon, D. Rubin, & B. Wilson (Eds.), *Everyday cognition in adulthood and late life* (pp. 545–569). Cambridge, MA: Cambridge University Press.

Willis, S. L. (1990). Contributions of cognitive training research to understanding late life potential. In M. Perlmutter (Ed.), *Late life potential* (pp. 25–42). Washington, DC: Gerontological Society of America.

Willis, S. L., Jay, G. M., Diehl, M., & Marsiske, M. (1992). Longitudinal change and prediction of everyday task competence in the elderly. *Research on Aging, 14,* 68–91.

Willis, S. L., & Nesselroade, C. S. (1990). Long term effects of fluid ability training in old-old age. *Developmental Psychology, 26,* 905–910.

Willis, S. L., & Schaie, K. W. (1986a). Practical intelligence in later adulthood. In R. Sternberg & R. Wagner (Eds.), *Practical intelligence: Origins of competence in the everyday world* (pp. 236–270). New York: Cambridge University Press.

Willis, S. L., & Schaie, K. W. (1986b). Training the elderly on the ability factors of spatial orientation and inductive reasoning. *Psychology and Aging, 1,* 239–247.

Willis, S. L., & Schaie, K. W. (1988). Gender differences in spatial ability in old age: Longitudinal and intervention findings. *Sex Roles, 8,* 189–203.

Willis, S. L., & Schaie, K. W. (1993). Everyday cognition: Taxonomic and methodological considerations. In J. M. Puckett & H. W. Reese (Eds.), *Mechanisms of everyday cognition* (pp. 33–54). Hillsdale, NJ: Erlbaum.

Willis, S. L., & Schaie, K. W. (1994a). Assessing competence in the elderly. In C. E. Fisher & R. M. Lerner (Eds.), *Applied developmental psychology* (pp. 339–372). New York: Macmillan.

Willis, S. L., & Schaie, K. W. (1994b). Cognitive training in the normal elderly. In F. Forette, Y. Christensen, & F. Boller (Eds.), *Plasticité cérébrale et stimulation cognitive* [Cerebral plasticity and cognitive stimulation] (pp. 91–113). Paris: Fondation Nationale de Gérontologie.

Willis, S. L., & Schaie, K. W. (in press). Cognitive functioning in middle age. In S. W. Willis & J. Reid (Eds.), *Middle aging.* San Diego, CA: Academic Press.

Woodruff-Pak, D. S. (1989). Aging and intelligence: Changing perspectives in the twentieth century. *Journal of Aging Studies, 3,* 91–118.

Zelinski, E. M., Gilewski, M. J., & Schaie, K. W. (1993). Individual differences in cross-sectional and 3-year longitudinal memory performance across the adult life span. *Psychology and Aging, 8,* P176–P186.

Sixteen

# Everyday Problem Solving

Sherry L. Willis

## I. Definitions and Conceptual Issues

A major shift in the study of cognitive aging occurring in the past two decades has been the increased attention given to *contexts*, beyond the experimental laboratory. A corollary of this movement has been a focus on *real-world* problem solving. In the study of real-world problem solving, Kuhn (1992) suggested that researchers need to identify the problems that arise in people's lives and the kinds of thinking they have developed to deal with them. The focus of this chapter is on reasoning and problem solving as it occurs in the everyday lives and real-world contexts of older adults. The first section of this chapter considers definitions of problem solving and characteristics of everyday problem solving derived from the research literature (Section I). In the second part of the chapter, a model for the study of everyday problem solving is presented; the components of the model and relationships among components are briefly discussed (Section II). In the third part of the chapter, the components of the model provide a structure for reviewing the research litera-

ture on everyday problem solving (Sections III, IV, and V).

In their 1985 handbook review of problem-solving research, Reese and Rodeheaver (1985) concluded that all problems refer to a transformation of the situation from an initial state to some other state. Problem solving involves assessing the present state, defining the desired state, and finding ways to transform the former to the latter. Decision making refers to the evaluation of these possible solutions and the selection of one for implementation (Reese and Rodeheaver, 1985). The early problem-solving research that addressed issues of external validity often involved little more than substituting more "real life" stimuli within traditional laboratory-based problem-solving paradigms (Rabbitt, 1977; Reese & Rodeheaver, 1985). However, in the past decade cognitive aging researchers have begun to mount major research programs on real-life problem solving in older populations (M. M. Baltes, Mayr, Borchelt, Maas, & Wilms, 1993; Denney, 1990; Park, 1992; Sinnott, 1989; Willis & Schaie, 1993; Willis, Schaie, & Hayward, in press).

Although problem solving has traditionally

been categorized as a complex cognitive activity, *noncognitive* factors have been given greater attention in recent applied cognitive aging research. Our position is that to understand the role of intellectual processes in problem solving about real-life issues, it is critical to examine the phenomenon as an entity, including the *context* and *noncognitive* factors, as well as component cognitive processes (Gauvain, 1993).

## A. Characteristics of Everyday Problem Solving

Several distinctions have been made between the study of problem solving in the real world and laboratory-driven research approaches to problem solving.

### 1. Cognitive and Noncognitive Factors

First, everyday problem solving cannot be studied as an isolated act of pure cognition (Labouvie-Vief & Hakim-Larson, 1989; Park & Mayhorn, in press). To understand the role of intellectual processes in everyday problem solving, their relationship with other factors influencing problem outcomes must be studied (Blanchard-Fields, 1986; Park, 1992; Willis, 1991). These factors include belief systems, efficacy, emotionality, and the physical and social environment.

### 2. The Context

Human problem solving occurs within meaningful contexts, as people conduct purposeful goal-directed activity (Lawton, 1982). The context is salient not only in its influence on the problem-solving process, but also in *defining* the problem itself (Berg & Sternberg, 1985; Hartley, 1989; Kuhn, 1992). The very nature of the challenges and problems encountered by the elderly in their daily lives is defined in part by the sociocultural context, and thus varies with historical time. Likewise, the

problem-solving process involves an interaction of environmental demands and the problem-solving strategies of the individual. Resolution of everyday problems requires a fit or match between the competence of the individual and the environmental demands and resources (Grisso, 1986; Lawton, 1982; Willis, 1995).

### 3. Temporal Duration

Problem solving in the real world is often a temporally lengthier and more iterative process than is represented in laboratory problem-solving tasks (H. Leventhal & Cameron, 1987; Willis & Schaie, 1993). For example, Park and Mayhorn (in press) have described medication compliance as a multiphase process involving comprehension of the instructions regarding the medications, storage of the information in long-term memory, use of working memory to integrate information related to multiple medications, and employment of prospective memory in order to take the medication at the appropriate schedule. Medications for chronic diseases involve problem solving that spans many years.

## B. Goal-Directed Everyday Problem Solving

### 1. Maintaining Independence

Problem solving that occurs in the real world is largely defined and guided by the goals of daily living (Gauvain, 1993). Toward what goals, then, are many of the daily activities of the elderly directed? A major concern for many elderly is the maintenance of an *independent lifestyle*. What many elderly fear most is dependence —the inability to care for oneself and the subsequent need for institutionalization. What are the domains of competence that are associated with an independent lifestyle? Interestingly, both psychologists (Lawton & Brody, 1969) and those who provide legal definitions of competence

(Grisso, 1986) have focused on two broad domains: (a) caring for *oneself*, and (b) managing one's *property*. The Uniform Probate Code (1989) distinguishes between legal proceedings regarding care of the person (guardianship) and those related to property (conservatorship).

### 2. Instrumental Activities of Daily Living

Social scientists have identified a set of competencies associated with these two broad domains (Fillenbaum, 1985; Kane & Kane, 1981). *Activities of daily living,* commonly known as ADLs, focus primarily on self-care, including feeding, bathing, toileting, and basic mobility (Katz, Ford, Moskowitz, Jackson, & Jaffee, 1963). *Instrumental activities of daily living,* commonly known as IADLs (Fillenbaum, 1985), are viewed as more complex but essential abilities required in order to live independently. Seven IADL activity domains are commonly cited: managing medications, shopping for necessities, managing one's finances, using transportation, using the telephone, maintaining one's household (housekeeping), and meal preparation and nutrition (Fillenbaum, 1985; Lawton & Brody, 1969).

The majority of real-world problem solving should occur in relation to the type of activities in which the elderly spend considerable amounts of time. Studies in both the United States and Germany indicate that community-dwelling elderly spend more time on IADLs (e.g., meal preparation, shopping, housekeeping, health care) than on any other type of activity. Older adults in Germany reported spending more than half of a typical day on obligatory activities; these activities were usually performed at home and in the morning (M. M. Baltes, Wahl, & Schmid-Furstoss, 1990). In a study in the United States, community-dwelling elderly reported spending a total of 5–6 hr per day in IADLs (Lawton, Moss, & Fulcomer, 1986–1987; Moss & Lawton,

1982). Given the salience of IADL-type tasks for maintenance of independent living and the amount of time spent on these activities by the elderly, our literature review of everyday problem solving will concentrate on these task domains.

## II. A Model for Studying Everyday Problem Solving

Most models of problem solving have focused almost exclusively on cognitive aspects and have considered a singular problem domain. Figure 1 presents a more comprehensive model for studying everyday problem solving. The model is based on several assumptions: (a) *Antecedent* characteristics of the problem solver and the sociocultural context must be taken into account; (b) the elderly are active problem solvers who construct a *representation* of the problem and its solution. Representation of the problem includes *cognitive* and *noncognitive* aspects; (c) *task* (problem) characteristics interact with antecedent person variables to influence the problem-solving process; (d) problem-solving competence reflects a *match* between the *individual's* problem-solving skills and the demands and resources of the immediate *environment.*

### A. Antecedent Variables

Each individual comes to a problem with his or her own unique developmental history, which influences how the adult defines the problem and selects and utilizes strategies for resolving the problem. Moreover, any problem arises within a particular sociocultural context and historical period. The first domain of antecedents, thus, includes individual-difference variables, such as the adult's (a) objective and subjective health; (b) basic cognitive abilities and skills; (c) personality characteristics; and (d) belief systems. These variables often represent stable or enduring

| *ANTECEDENTS* | *THE PROBLEM* | *OUTCOMES* |
|---|---|---|
| Individual Factors | Individual Factors: Problem Representation | |
| Health | Declarative knowledge | Physical well-being |
| Cognition | Procedural knowledge | |
| Personality | Beliefs and self-regulation | |
| Belief systems | | |
| | Task Characteristics | |
| | Novelty | |
| | Complexity | Psychological well-being |
| | Structure | |
| Sociocultural Factors | Contextual Demands and Resources | |
| Historical period | Social environment | |
| Subcultures | Physical environment | |

**Figure 1**   A model for the study of everyday problem solving in old age.

characteristics of the individual that pre-date a particular problem, but influence how the individual represents the problem and its solution.

The second domain frames the problem and problem solver within a particular sociocultural context and historical period. The sociocultural context influences what a particular society defines as a problem, and the specific tasks of everyday problem solving will vary across historical time (Willis, 1991, 1995). For example, recent technological advances are both contributing to the emergence of particular types of problems as well as providing new forms of solutions. Likewise, the historical period will influence what are considered the most appropriate and socially responsible means of resolving a given problem.

## B. The Problem

Adults are seen as active problem solvers who construct a representation of both the problem and the process or strategies involved in solving the problem (Abelson, 1981; Chi, 1985; H. Leventhal & Cameron, 1987). The adult's representation of the problem and its solution involves factors that may vary with the type of problem being solved. For example, studies of *well-structured* problems (Simon, 1978) focus on (a) declarative knowledge, the body of domain-specific knowledge possessed by the adult; and (b) procedural knowledge, the problem-solving strategies and skills that are relevant to the particular problem. In *ill-structured* problems, on the other hand, the problem is not well defined, allowing alternative solution strategies. Research on ill-structured problems has often focused on the adults' cognitions and beliefs about the problem and about solution or treatment alternatives (Voss & Post, 1988).

The problem solver's efficacy and control beliefs influence the manner in which the individual represents the problem and possible solutions. Likewise, the emotional saliency of the problem and of alternative solutions are important in the study of ill-structured problems (Blanchard-Fields, 1986; Labouvie-Vief & Hakim-Larson, 1989).

### C. Contextual Demands

Problem solving does not occur within a vacuum. The context, including the physical and social environment, are important in defining the problem and in either facilitating or hindering problem solutions (Gauvain, 1993; Lawton, 1982). Within the model, the context is considered from two perspectives. When considered under antecedents, the concern is with the macrolevel *sociocultural* context that defines the types of problems and challenges experienced by the elderly within a specific historical period.

When considering the representation and solution of a particular problem, the focus shifts to the individual's *immediate environment*. The concern is with factors such as social support systems and the "user friendliness" of the physical environment. Problem-solving competence represents the *congruence* between the knowledge and skills of the individual and the demands of the immediate environment (Grisso, 1986; Willis, 1995). An individual who appears to be competent in a resource-rich context may appear less able in a deprived environment. Thus, assessment of competence needs to consider both the individual and the resources in the immediate environment.

### D. Solution Outcomes

Finally, successful resolution of real-world problems should enhance the physical and the psychological well-being of the problem solver.

## III. Literature on Antecedents of Problem Solving

### A. Health

Sensory impairment is a major aspect of health as it affects everyday problem solving. Branch, Horowitz, and Carr (1989) studied the relationship between ability to perform tasks of daily living and visual impairment. Changes in self-reports of everyday competence were compared over a 5-year period for a group of elderly who reported good vision at both interviews versus a group of elderly reporting a decline in vision. Those reporting a decline in vision were significantly more likely to report needing assistance with shopping and paying bills. Those suffering visual impairment were 1.5 times less likely to leave their residence and were only half as likely to travel by car.

Physical health is also related to medication compliance, an important task of daily living. Elderly with multiple disease pathologies who were taking multiple drugs with complicated regimens were found to be less compliant (Fincham, 1988).

### B. Cognitive Abilities

Several theorists propose multiple forms of intelligence, including a practical intelligence domain and a mechanistic domain. The "mechanics" of intelligence involve basic mental abilities and processes, and the "pragmatics" of intelligence are concerned with everyday cognition and problem solving (P. B. Baltes, Dittman-Kohli, & Dixon, 1984; Berg & Sternberg, 1985). A major issue for multiple intelligence theories is the definition of the inter-relationship among the various forms. According to Berg and Sternberg, "a mechanistic theory is needed to specify the cognitive processes by which contextually appropriate behavior is carried out" (1985, p. 348). The question then arises whether the mechanistic constructs and variables traditionally studied by cognitive aging researchers are relevant to the study of real-world problem solving. There exists considerable debate regarding the relationship between traditional cognitive constructs and practical intelligence (P. B. Baltes, Smith, & Staudinger, 1992; Heidrich & Denney, 1994; Salthouse, 1990; Sternberg & Wagner, 1986).

We have proposed a hierarchical relationship, such that traditional abilities and processes are necessary but not sufficient antecedents for competence in tasks of practical intelligence (Willis, 1991; Willis & Schaie, 1986, 1993). We have conducted a program of research examining older adults' ability to solve everyday problems involving printed material (Marsiske & Willis, 1995; Willis & Marsiske, 1991; Willis & Schaie, 1993). Tasks in each of the seven IADL domains were examined: meal preparation (e.g., nutrition label of food package), transportation (e.g., bus schedule), financial management (e.g., Medicare form), medications (e.g., prescription drug label), shopping (e.g., mail order catalog form), and telephone (e.g., emergency phone listing).

Because different psychometric abilities exhibit different patterns of age-related change in later adulthood (see Schaie, Ch. 15, this volume), it has been of particular interest to determine the specific mental abilities that relate to everyday task performance. Cattell (1987) differentiated between two broad domains of mental abilities. Crystallized abilities (e.g., verbal, social reasoning) are said to reflect acculturation influences, such as level of schooling; in healthy older adults crystal-lized abilities remain stable, on average, showing little or no decline until old-old age. In contrast, fluid abilities involve abstract reasoning and speeded responding; fluid abilities are said to be affected by neurological assault and to exhibit earlier patterns of decline, beginning, on average, in the mid-60s or earlier. Hence, older adults' performance on everyday tasks would be expected to show different patterns of developmental change, depending on whether such tasks are more closely related to underlying fluid or crystallized abilities.

In research on concurrent relationships between mental abilities and everyday tasks, my colleagues and I found that over half of the variance in older adults' performance on everyday tasks could be accounted for by mental ability performance (Willis & Marsiske, 1991; Willis & Schaie, 1986). Both fluid and crystallized abilities accounted for everyday task performance, although a somewhat greater portion of the variance was accounted for by fluid abilities. However, causal relationships among variables cannot be determined by examination of concurrent relationships. In our hierarchical model of relationships between ability and everyday competence, basic mental abilities have been hypothesized to be salient antecedents of performance on complex tasks of daily living.

To test this hypothesis, my colleagues and I examined whether performance on fluid and crystallized abilities at the first assessment occasion were significant predictors of everyday task performance 7 years later. Both fluid and crystallized abilities were indeed found to be significant predictors. A series of structural equation analyses were conducted to further examine the reciprocal relationship between abilities and everyday task performance (Willis, Jay, Diehl, & Marsiske, 1992). That is, the directionality of the relationship between abilities and everyday tasks was examined by contrasting models of abilities as predictors of everyday task performance against models of everyday task performance as predictors of abilities. These analyses indicated that fluid ability at the first assessment occasion predicted everyday task performance at the second assessment occasion 7 years later. But everyday task performance predicted abilities at the second occasion less well. These findings were taken as support for our hypothesis that level of functioning on basic mental abilities is a significant antecedent of performance on everyday tasks involving printed materials.

Park has similarly proposed that multiple cognitive components are involved in adherence to a medication regimen (Park, 1992; Park & Kidder, 1995; Park & Mayhorn, in press). Based on prior laboratory-based research on various forms of memory, Park argued that the comprehension and retrospective aspects of memory should be problematic. With regard to comprehension of information on actual prescription drug labels, Morrell, Park, and Poon (1989) found that older adults made significantly more errors on comprehension (21%) than young adults (14%). Likewise, older adults had considerable difficulty with long-term recall of medication information when it was presented in an experimental setting (Morrell et al., 1989). On the other hand, when older subjects were given organizational devices that supported the comprehension, working-memory, and long-term memory aspects of medication cognition, the adherence behaviors of old-old adults were facilitated significantly (Park, Morrell, Frieske, & Kincaid, 1992). Of interest was the finding that the young-old evidenced high adherence rates and were not facilitated by the devices supporting these aspects of memory; it is likely that this finding occurred because the young-old adults already had sufficient cognitive resources to accurately handle the comprehension and retrospective aspects of medication cognition.

## C. Personality Characteristics

Longitudinal research has shown that personality traits exhibit considerable stability across the adult life course (McCrae & Costa, 1990). Hence, the inclusion of personality or cognitive-style variables should provide important information on individual differences associated with representation of, coping with, or resolving the problem.

Research on consumer behavior has examined the association between personality characteristics, such as tolerance for ambiguity and cognitive style, and consumers' approach to investigating new products and their willingness to try innovative products (Cox, 1967). When faced with the comparison of new products, those tolerant of ambiguity engaged in more extensive information searches, particularly when ambiguous or discrepant information about products was involved (Schaninger & Schiglimpaglia, 1981). Those intolerant of ambiguity or high in trait anxiety were less likely to be attracted to or to buy products that were novel, complex, or innovative (i.e., having many unfamiliar attributes).

Cox (1967) examined the cognitive styles of simplifiers versus clarifiers in relation to problem solving in the consumer context. Simplifiers tended to react to uncertain or inconsistent product information by avoiding the incongruent information, whereas clarifiers actively sought new and additional information in order to reduce the ambiguity or inconsistencies. Simplifiers resisted changing their product preferences when presented with additional information on products.

The salience of personality characteristics, such as tolerance for ambiguity, has also been noted in medical decision making (E. A. Leventhal, Leventhal, Schaefer, & Easterling, 1993). Compared to middle-aged adults, older patients made quicker decisions about whether they were ill and also sought medical care sooner when they judged the condition to be serious. Quicker decision making was interpreted as being due to less tolerance of ambiguity and the need to reduce uncertainty on the part of the old. By contrast, middle-aged individuals were characterized as more likely to use the coping defenses of distraction and denial; that is, they were more willing to live with uncertainty and more likely to develop a "wait and see" approach to health problems, even when thought to be serious.

### D. Beliefs about Knowledge and Ways of Knowing

Kuhn (1992) suggested that individuals' beliefs about knowledge and ways of knowing influence their approaches to problem solving. Individuals were identified with three types of belief systems, regarding the certainty of knowledge and the process by which knowledge is acquired. First, the *absolutists* believe that knowledge is certain and cumulative. Absolutists hold that even complex questions such as why prisoners become repeat offenders can be answered with complete certainty. Fifty percent of subjects could be classified as absolutists. In contrast, *multiplists* or *relativists* hold that no knowledge is absolutely certain, and that all opinions are of equal validity. Approximately 35% of subjects when reasoning about complex societal problems held that everyone had a right to his or her opinion and hence all opinions could be considered equally valid. The third type was labeled *evaluative*. Knowing was viewed as a process, rather than a certainty, and the focus was on use of thinking, evaluation, and argument in order to examine the relative merits of various types of information.

Kuhn and others (Krammer & Woodruff, 1986) argued that individuals' beliefs about the certainty of knowledge and ways of knowing may be more salient in their approach to the problem than the charac-

teristics of the problem as defined by the investigator. The distinctions between well- and ill-structured problems held by the investigator may be of little relevance, for example, to an absolutist, who approaches all problems with a belief in the certainty of knowledge.

## IV. Literature Related to the Problem-Solving Process

### A. Task Characteristics

The characteristics of real-life tasks can interact with long-term individual differences to influence the problem-solving process. Three salient task characteristics, novelty, complexity, and structure, are frequently cited in the general problem-solving literature (Chi, 1985; Simon, 1978) and in the aging literature (Hershey, Walsh, Read, & Chulef, 1990; Park & Kidder, 1995; Park & Mayhorn, in press).

### 1. Task Novelty

The novelty of a task can have either a facilitative or a negative influence on problem solving. In the previous section, the interaction was noted between personal characteristics, such as tolerance for ambiguity and cognitive styles (simplifiers versus clarifiers), and willingness to engage in informational searches associated with problem solving. That is, adult consumers high in tolerance for ambiguity and characterized as clarifiers were more likely to explore and to find attractive new or innovative products with large numbers of unfamiliar features (Cox, 1967; Schaninger & Schiglimpaglia, 1981).

Task novelty may *limit* individuals, particularly experts, in their use of well-honed declarative or procedural knowledge bases. For example, although chess experts were much quicker and more adept at recalling placement of pieces when the placement subscribed to well-known plays, chess experts were at no advantage compared to novices when placement of pieces was random (Charness, 1981).

Novelty may, on the other hand, *facilitate* problem solutions that require planning and implementing an action. This is particularly evident when the individual is involved in multiple activities and must monitor progress in each activity. Cohen and Faulkner (1989) found that novel, high-priority plans were more likely to be recalled and implemented. In contrast, highly routinized and repetitive everyday tasks become less distinct and less likely to be remembered at the appropriate time. Park and Kidder (1995) suggest that repetitive medication schedules, particularly those with multiple dosages within 24 hours, contribute to failures of prospective memory in medication adherence.

## 2. Task Complexity

Task complexity is related to (a) the *amount* of information needed to solve a problem, and (b) the *search* processes required to obtain information. The search process may involve information retrieval from external sources or from one's own knowledge store.

We have examined older adults' ability to use information from everyday documents (Willis, 1991; Willis & Schaie, 1993). For example, older adults were asked to utilize information on a cereal nutrition label to determine the difference in calories when adding whole versus low-fat milk. We examined what task characteristics contributed to problem-solving complexity (Meyer, Marsiske, & Willis, 1993). Several characteristics of the document contributed to complexity, including (a) the number of propositions in the document; (b) the number of places in the document from which relevant information had to be abstracted; and (c) the number of plausible alternative solution choices available to the subject. As the complexity of the task increased, so did the difficulty of solving the problem.

The interaction between the person characteristics and task attributes were of importance. Older adults with higher levels of functioning on fluid reasoning and verbal ability were more likely to solve tasks of greater complexity.

Task complexity also interacts with the procedural strategies used in problem solving. As the complexity of the task increases, experts use procedural strategies that minimize the informational search process. The demands on working memory and long-term memory increase so that the expert becomes increasingly *selective* in the information that he or she focuses on in the task (Hershey et al., 1990). In contrast, the novice reacts to increases in task complexity by seeking more and more information, thus risking memory overload and inefficiency in executing the problem-solving strategies.

## 3. Structure of the Task

Some in the cognitive sciences (Chapman, 1993; Galotti, 1989; Sinnott, 1989; Sternberg & Wagner, 1986) have argued that the distinction between well- and ill-structured problems is useful in defining real-world versus academic or laboratory problem-solving tasks. Laboratory tasks are said to involve almost exclusively well-structured problems, whereas real-world problems are viewed as almost always ill structured in nature. In well-structured problems, the initial state, the goal state, and the necessary task information are available to the subject (Simon, 1978). Well-structured problems may also have singular solutions (e.g., goal clarity) and an optimal solution path (e.g., use of heuristics and algorithms, Sinnott, 1989). In contrast, ill-structured problems involve (a) a high degree of complexity and minimal definition (e.g., lack of goal clarity); (b) a failure to specify necessary procedural information in instructions; and (c) lack of a set of prescribed rules leading to solution as part of the initial problem statement.

We believe, however, that the realm of real-world problem solving includes *both* well- and ill-structured problems (Willis & Schaie, 1993). For example, tasks such as comparison of medigap insurance plans, programming of a microwave oven, or call-forwarding mechanisms on a phone meet the criteria for well-structured problems. Yet these are activities experienced by many older adults in their daily lives. Although both well- and ill-structured problems are involved in daily living, the distinction between them is a useful one in studying the cognitive processes and strategies that are involved in problem solution. As Chapman (1993) noted, the above definitions of well- and ill-structured problems simply describe the characteristics of the tasks, but they do not provide information on the *cognitive demands* of the two types of problems. According to Chapman (1993),

Everyday reasoning is 'ill-defined' to the extent that the information given, the permitted operations, or the desired end-states are left relatively unspecified . . . to the extent that heuristics for 'everyday reasoning' have been codified, one might argue that the distinction between formal and everyday reasoning becomes blurred. (pp. 96–97)

Sinnott (1989) suggested that two features (clarity of goals; use and availability of heuristics or algorithms) are particularly salient to the problem-solving process. These are two characteristics that distinguish well- and ill-structured problems. In problems that have clearly defined goals, but in which well-defined strategies are either not available or unknown to the subject, considerable time is spent on identifying or constructing a strategy for solving the problem. In contrast, when the goal is unclear but there is an available, well-defined solution strategy, there is the tendency to apply the heuristic or algorithm in a routinized manner and assume that the goal is "whatever is yielded by the process." In this instance the problem may appear to have been "solved" very quickly. Sinnott (1989) sug-

gested that the tendency to apply an available heuristic in a routinized manner when the goal is unclear is often characteristic of age-related decline in problem solving.

## B. Problem Representation and Knowledge Systems

### 1. Declarative Knowledge

Declarative knowledge, defined as knowing which facts are relevant in a particular situation, has been of most concern in the study of well-structured problems (Chi, 1985). Experts have a large body of domain-specific (declarative) knowledge (Hershey et al., 1990; Staudinger, Smith, & Baltes, 1992). Experts' knowledge, compared to that of novices, is stored in larger and sometimes more abstract memory chunks, leading to a more integrated, cohesive understanding of the problem domain. The knowledge domains of experts are organized hierarchically with information indexed in terms of meaningful interrelations, allowing experts to scan their memory of a topic quickly and efficiently.

*a. Experts versus Novices*   One of the most interesting distinctions between experts and novices is that experts attend to fewer pieces of information when engaged in problem solving, compared to novices. However, the information attended to by experts is usually higher order information within the hierarchy of the knowledge base (Hershey et al., 1990). Because experts have both well-organized knowledge hierarchies and well-honed strategies for solving a particular problem, they are more efficient in selecting only the most relevant information and "plugging" it into the problem-solving strategy.

A number of studies have found that novices, in contrast, engage in more complex and time-consuming information searches, and amass large amounts of data in the early stages of problem solving. Hershey et al. (1990) found novices requested more information and engaged in more complicated information searches in a financial problem-solving task. Having accumulated a mass of information, novices were more likely to reexamine the same information more than once. However, the information sought by novices was at a lower level in the hierarchical structure of domain-specific knowledge constructed by experts. Hershey et al. (1990) suggested that use of lower order information forced novices to engage in more steps in the problem-solving process than experts.

*b. Aging and Use of Declarative Knowledge*  Given their extensive lifetime experiences, the old might be expected to organize and utilize their declarative knowledge in a manner similar to that of experts. The elderly would, thus, have hierarchically organized knowledge bases that were well integrated and that utilized less, but higher order information. Findings in support of these hypotheses are mixed.

Meyer, Russo, and Talbot (1995) examined decision making with respect to a health scenario about breast cancer. Young, middle-aged, and older women were presented with increasing amounts of information about an individual with suspected breast cancer in an unfolding scenario and asked to make decisions about treatment at three stages in the scenario. Older women had no greater prior domain-specific knowledge about breast cancer. They, moreover, sought less information before making a treatment decision. When given further information as part of the unfolding scenario, older women typically did not change their initial treatment decision. In contrast, younger women were more likely to seek additional information, while delaying a decision about treatment, and were more likely to compare and contrast various types and sources of information in making a decision.

For all age groups, the treatment decision was related to (a) the type of information that was remembered about various treatment options from the material presented; and (b) the particular material that individuals considered important and underlined in the material presented. Treatment decisions were only weakly related to information about cancer treatments that subjects had prior to the study. Older adults remembered less information presented during the study. In spite of these differences in use and recall of information related to treatment options, older women made the same decision regarding treatment as the young and middle-aged. The older women reached the same decision based on less information and earlier in the decision-making process than younger women.

A study of managerial decision making reported a somewhat similar pattern of findings (Streufert, Pogash, Piasecki, & Post, 1990). Age differences in a simulated complex decision-making task involving managerial functioning were examined. The youngest management teams engaged in the greatest information seeking; this resulted in a greater number of decisions and a wider range of approaches taken to resolve problems. In contrast, the older managerial teams were less responsive to incoming information and made fewer decisions throughout the course of the task. The older teams spent larger amounts of time discussing issues before implementing decisions. However, again, when an emergency situation was introduced into the ongoing problem-solving task, there were no age differences in the decisiveness or adequacy of responding to the emergency. Although across the whole simulation the old made fewer decisions, there were no age differences in decisions made in the emergency situation.

Several other studies have also reported age-related reductions in the amount of information used and the extensiveness of the information search process undertaken by the old. In studies of consumer behavior involving new and innovative products, younger shoppers were more actively engaged in a search for greater amounts of information, whereas the old sought less information and considered fewer alternatives in making product choices (Schaninger & Schiglimpaglia, 1981). Likewise, in a study of age differences in seeking of medical care, the elderly were less likely to seek information from outside sources prior to contacting their physician (E. A. Leventhal et al., 1993).

### 2. Procedural Knowledge

Procedural knowledge represents the individual's understanding of how to go about solving a particular problem—how facts relevant in a particular situation can be combined to produce a solution (Chi, 1985). Procedural knowledge has often been represented in the form of a problem-solving *script* that involves a game plan for the organization of the set of operations leading to the solution (Hershey et al., 1990). Abelson (1981) defined a script as "a hypothesized cognitive structure that when activated organizes comprehension of event-based situations" (p. 717). The script may involve a set of rule-based mental operations into which the relevant parameters for a particular problem can be inserted.

Although experts and novices may differ in both declarative and procedural knowledge, deficits in procedural knowledge are considered more limiting. Experts and novices differ in the sequence of steps used to obtain a solution. Experts use information to work forward through a problem; they quickly identify a plan (e.g., script) and work forward from the starting point of the plan to a solution. In contrast, novices, lacking a precise plan, work backward, starting at the goal and trying to develop a plan as they work backward.

*a. Speed of Reaching Problem Solutions* Experts have been found to arrive at problem solutions faster than novices across a number of problem-solving stud-

ies. This finding appears to be due not only to the more extensive declarative and procedural knowledge of experts, but also to the greater efficiency in use of procedural knowledge.

There is, again, a somewhat puzzling similarity with findings from problem-solving research with older adults. That is, older adults reached decisions or problem solutions faster than young adults in several studies. In the Meyer et al. (1995) study of decision making regarding treatments for breast cancer, older women reached their decisions faster or earlier in the problem-solving process than young or middle-aged subjects, although the nature of the decision reached did not differ by age group.

E. A. Leventhal et al. (1993) examined age differences in timing of decisions to seek medical care. The timing of two decision points was examined: (a) time until persons decided they were ill; (b) time from decision of illness until they sought medical care. Older adults reached the decision that they were ill much sooner than did middle-aged adults. In addition, when the condition was thought to be serious, the old sought medical care sooner than the middle-aged. All age groups had equal access to medical care, and the actual or perceived severity of the medical condition for which treatment was sought did not vary by age group. The middle-aged group reported more pain associated with the medical condition, but they were more likely to delay seeking care. Moreover, working outside the home was not related to delay in seeking care.

In their study of managerial functioning and decision making, Streufert et al. (1990) found that older management teams responded as efficiently and as quickly in responding to an emergency situation as young teams. In nonemergency situations, however, the older teams often ignored relevant information and were less responsive to incoming information.

The quicker response of the old in

problem-solving and decision-making situations is particularly interesting, given that a focus on age-related slowing has characterized much of the cognitive aging literature (Salthouse, 1985). A closer examination of procedural strategies employed more frequently by the elderly may be instructive.

*b. Top-Down versus Bottom-Up Processing Style*   Age-related changes in styles of processing information and solving problems have been reported (Labouvie-Vief & Hakim-Larson, 1989; Sinnott, 1989). Researchers, however, differ in their interpretation of the efficacy of these changes. Labouvie-Vief and Hakim-Larson (1989) proposed that there are two modes of thinking and knowing—a youthful ability to think about reality in a formalistic, abstract, and objectified manner, in contrast to a more pragmatic, concrete, and subjective approach to reality sometimes favored in adulthood. The latter mode of thinking reflects sensitivity to the interpersonal context and thus focuses on inner, personal experience as the way of thinking and knowing. Study of cognitive aging until recently has focused almost exclusively on the mode more common in youth, and, in judging mature thought solely in terms of a single mode, has focused on deficits or regression in aging. A vertical or hierarchical, rather than balanced or integrated, ordering of the two modes of thought was imposed. Pragmatic, emotive modes of thinking were devalued and subjugated. Labouvie-Vief suggests that in adulthood there is the unique potential to integrate optimal use of both modes of thought; she proposes that the concept of wisdom reflects this integration.

Labouvie-Vief stated that "as individuals acquire expertise, their knowledge becomes too complex and richly organized to conform to a simple rule-oriented system, and flexible functioning is enhanced by a less explicit and more intuitive approach" (Labouvie-Vief & Hakim-Larson, 1989,

p. 80; see also Rybash, Hoyer, & Roodin, 1986). As adults become experts at processing information relating to subjective processes and inner dynamics, this processing style may result in deficits in tasks that require more objective and formal ways of processing. Young adults focus on literal, text-based features of information, whereas older adults summarize the gist along with its psychological and metaphorical meaning. These researchers argue that these changes in modes of thinking do not reflect deficit or compensation, as an integrative response style begins to emerge in middle adulthood—when there is no loss in recall of objective information.

*c. Age-Related Processing Styles*   Sinnott (1989) proposed three age-related processing styles. The *Youthful* style involves intense data gathering and "bottom-up" processing. Young adults possess fewer relevant knowledge structures and compensate by gathering and focusing on data. There is little reliance on past experience, and the approach is largely noncontextual. The *Mature* style, reflected in middle age, is characterized by a balance of "top-down" and "bottom-up" processing modes. The top-down mode makes use of the well-integrated, relevant knowledge bases (e.g., declarative knowledge, heuristics, and algorithms), whereas the bottom-up mode reflects a recognition of the need to seek further information when called for. The *Old* style represents solely or primarily a top-down approach. The old are characterized as utilizing in a somewhat indiscriminate manner the extensive knowledge acquired through a lifetime of experience and heuristics that have proven useful in prior problem-solving situations but may not be optimal in the present situation. Sinnott (1989, p. 96) said that the old style is suited for "rapid, low energy-demand solutions done by the experienced solver with many available structures of knowledge. It was top-down in style with little attention to data, probably because of poor memory capacities." Meyer et al. (1995) suggested that the quicker decisions regarding breast cancer treatment made by older women may reflect a decrease in the utilization of bottom-up processing even when they were presented with additional relevant information, and a reliance almost solely on the top-down approach.

The issue of "balance" is critical in considering the relative merits of the proposed shifts in processing style suggested by Labouvie-Vief and Sinnott. Effective problem solving involves both types of processing; maturity or wisdom is reflected in achieving an optimal balance of the styles in a particular problem-solving situation.

### 3. Cognitions, Beliefs, and Self-Regulation

Concepts such as declarative and procedural knowledge have more frequently been used in the study of well-structured problems involving formal reasoning processes. In the study of ill-structured problems, there has been recognition of the salience of another type of knowledge—the adult's personal experiences, beliefs, and understanding of the problem and of alternative solution strategies.

*a. Personalized Knowledge* H. Leventhal and Cameron (1987) argued that a distinction should be made between two types of declarative knowledge, based on their work on a self-regulatory model of medical compliance. Leventhal distinguished between semantic memories, which represent the individual's conceptual knowledge about the problem and episodic memories, or autobiographical information, based on the subject's prior experiences with respect to a particular problem domain. The former type (i.e., semantic memories) is similar to the typical usage of the term *declarative knowledge*. However, the more personalized knowledge (i.e., episodic memories) may be particularly relevant for the elderly, given that

they would be expected to have a more extensive bank of experiences and thus would be more disposed to employ this personalized knowledge in problem-solving situations.

Leventhal, moreover, argued that there may be a conflict between the two types of knowledge that may influence the problem-solving process. For example, with regard to medical decision making, the more objective, semantic knowledge may inform a person that certain diseases (e.g., heart disease) are asymptomatic and hence one cannot rely on how one feels in making decisions regarding the efficacy of medications or when to see a doctor. In contrast, the personalized knowledge based on episodic memories may argue that, in the past, sickness was related to not feeling well (e.g., symptoms); hence, if there are no symptoms, then one is not sick. Different decisions and problem solutions will be reached depending on which knowledge system is utilized. Leventhal argued that personalized knowledge (episodic memories), in contrast to the more objective declarative knowledge, is the more critical and predictive of compliance in health problem solving. The primacy of episodic memories is supported in the study by Meyer et al. (1995) in that older women based their rapid decision making on their personal beliefs and fears that quick action was needed before the cancer spread, although information provided to the subjects indicated that cancer spreads more slowly in the old and therefore the elderly had more time for considering alternative treatments.

The individual's own personal belief system or representation of the problem becomes increasingly salient, when the goal of the problem is less clearly defined and there are less well-determined heuristics or algorithms (i.e., procedural knowledge) to employ in solving the problem. This more personalized and contextualized knowledge base is also relevant to the second mode of thinking discussed by

Labouvie-Vief and characterized by Sinnott's old processing style.

b. *Self-Regulation and Problem Solving*  In his research on medical compliance, Leventhal has conceptualized problem solving as a self-regulatory behavior employed by the patient (problem solver) in order to manage a health-related problem (H. Leventhal & Cameron, 1987). A self-regulatory perspective conceptualizes individuals as active problem solvers engaged in attempting to close the perceived gap between their current status and a goal or ideal state. Behavior, such as compliance to a health recommendation, depends on the person's cognitive representations of the current status and goal state, plans for changing the current state, and techniques or rules for appraising progress. Leventhal's self-regulation model of illness involves three stages: (a) cognitive representations of the health threat; (b) formulation and initiation of a plan of action (action or coping stage); and (c) utilization of specific criteria to gauge the success of one's actions (appraisal stage). This leads to modifications in the representation or coping plan, or both.

c. *Cognitive Representation of Problem*  Of particular interest here is the cognitive representation of the problem. This representation includes the individual's *perception* of the severity of the health problem, the potential causes of the health problem, the possible consequences and the perceived benefits or efficacy of treatment, and how the problem manifests itself over time (H. Leventhal & Cameron, 1987). This cognitive representation of illness and treatment is dynamic, evolving over time, and can be modified by feedback from the coping and appraisal stages in the model.

Multiple illness representations may be developed if the individual has multiple illness conditions, as is common with chronic diseases in the elderly. Park has reported considerable intraindividual variability in medication compliance; the same individual may be highly adherent for one drug, but not for another (Park & Kidder, 1995). Park suggests that variability in illness representations for the same individual may account for intraindividual differences in adherence patterns.

What are the possible linkages between cognition and the self-regulatory model of compliance? The self-regulatory model suggests that it must first be determined whether the illness representation is congruent with medical adherence; if the illness representation is not congruent with compliance, then examination of predictors (e.g., cognition) of compliance may be less salient. If one perceives the health problem to be of concern and to have possible serious consequences, and also believes a treatment to be beneficial, then congruency between one's belief systems and adherence is likely.

d. *Coping and Appraisal*  E. A. Leventhal et al. (1993) argued that the speed of seeking medical attention is associated with the elderly's increased need to conserve physical and emotional resources with accompanying age. The strategies that adults use in dealing with health threats are believed to change and to become more efficient with age. These strategies include being strongly motivated to detect and avoid threat as soon as possible, and to do so with minimal expenditure of personal resources. By moving more quickly and efficiently, the older person avoids anxiety and tension that might sap diminishing physical and emotional resources. Older persons have been found to be more active in confronting and coping with health threats (Folkman, Lazarus, Pimley, & Novacek, 1987) and are likely to report adoption of preventive behaviors that require little expenditure of physical energy, such as eating a balanced diet, avoiding salted foods, getting regular medical check-ups, and avoiding excessive drinking (Costa & McCrae, 1980; Prohaska, Leventhal,

Leventhal, & Keller, 1985). Young-old adults were also found to be more compliant than younger age groups with regard to medications and medical treatments (Nerenz, Love, Leventhal, & Easterling, 1986; Park et al., 1992).

## V. Literature Related to Contextual Demands and Resources

It has been argued that competence does not reside solely in the individual but represents the *congruence* between the abilities of the individual and the demands and resources in the context (Grisso, 1986; Lawton, 1982). A loss of competence resulting from incongruence between the individual and environment may reflect decreases in the abilities of the individual, changes in the environmental demands or resources, or a combination of these. In this final section I consider a few possible ways in which the immediate social and physical environment influence the problem-solving process.

### A. Social Environment

The work of Antonucci (1990) suggests that, across the life course, individuals experience multiple convoys of social networks. The individuals within the social support network change across the life course. Given the gender differences in average life expectancy, the social support network of older women often shifts from spouses to adult children and close neighbors or friends. Although the particular individuals within the support network may change, findings from research suggest that perceived level of support does not decline in old age (Antonucci, 1990).

The problem-solving process may be influenced by the older adult's social context in a number of ways. First, one's social contacts may be an important source of declarative knowledge in the problem-

solving process. A fundamental aspect of perceived social support is instrumental support, including individuals from whom one can obtain information or advice. Second, individuals in the primary support network may significantly influence one's personalized knowledge and beliefs, which are considered critical in development and modification of illness representations.

Antonucci and Jackson (1987) suggested that efficacy beliefs may be an important mechanism by which one's social support system influences the development and maintenance of competence. These authors proposed that it is through continuous interactions with a successive array of significant or supportive others that the elderly develop and maintain beliefs that they have the ability to meet the demands of the situation and to successfully mount the challenges of daily life.

Significant others in one's social network may serve as a cognitive prosthesis in problem-solving situations, such as medication adherence. Men in a coronary primary prevention trial were found to be more adherent to a medical regimen when they had highly supportive wives. Husbands' compliance was related to wives serving as reminders to take their medication (Doherty, Schrott, Metcalf, & Iasiello-Vailas, 1983). On the other hand, more medication errors were made by elderly living alone.

### B. Physical Environment

Features of the physical environment can serve as external aids for memory and problem-solving activities. Natural events may serve as aids. For example, memory for prospective events can be significantly enhanced by the use of ongoing activities as external supports for remembering to perform an action. A prospective memory which is time based (take medications three times a day) may be converted to an event-based memory by linking the taking of medications to meal time (take medications after meals).

Alternatively, external memory aids may be introduced into the environment. Low-tech items in the environment, such as timers, pill reminders, and calendars, have been found to significantly enhance the memory component in a problem-solving task.

## VI. Conclusions and Recommendations

The focus of this chapter has been on everyday problem solving. Problem solving that occurs in the real world is largely defined and guided by the goals and everyday activities of the elderly. Because maintenance of independent living is a primary goal of most elderly, special attention has been given to problem solving in domains considered essential for independent living, commonly known as IADLs. Although these are necessary domains of problem solving, few elderly would consider themselves to have a high quality of life if activities were limited to these domains. Thus, everyday problem solving should also be expanded to include such domains as leisure activities, social relationships, and volunteer activities.

In this chapter, I presented a model for the study of everyday problem solving. The model is based on four assumptions: (a) *antecedent* characteristics of the problem solver and the sociocultural context must be taken into account; (b) the elderly are active problem solvers who construct a *representation* of the problem and its solution; (c) characteristics of the *task* (problem) interact with antecedent characteristics of the individual, and they influence the problem-solving process; (d) the elderly's competence to solve a given problem reflects a *match* between the *individual's* problem-solving skills and the demands and resources of the immediate *environment*.

A useful mechanism for studying problem solving is the individual's representation of the problem. In studying problems in which the goals and procedures for solving the problem are well defined, problem representation has focused largely on the individual's declarative knowledge and procedural knowledge. With regard to declarative knowledge, a consistent finding from several studies is that older adults engage in less extensive information searches than younger adults. Older adults also utilize fewer pieces of information in reaching a decision related to a problem. Interestingly, research on expertise also indicates that experts, compared to novices, engage in less extensive information searches, drawing instead on extensive, well-organized knowledge bases related to the domain of study. Likewise, experts are able to identify the few, most relevant pieces of information and utilize these in problem solution. Both the elderly and experts have been found to make a decision (reach a solution) faster and earlier in the problem-solving process, compared to the young and novices, respectively.

Researchers working in quite different fields (e.g., self-regulatory models of medical compliance, postformal reasoning) have suggested that two forms of knowledge or modes of thinking should be considered in studying problem solving and reasoning in later adulthood. Labouvie-Vief contrasted two modes of thought as formalistic, abstract, and objectified versus pragmatic, concrete, and subjective. Leventhal and colleagues in research on medical compliance have contrasted objective knowledge regarding one's health condition and treatment versus personalized knowledge acquired through the adult's experience in prior illness situations. Labouvie-Vief argues that developmental shifts in adult thought involve more balance in the use of these two modes of thought in middle age and old age. Leventhal proposed that there may be conflict between the two forms of knowledge in health-related problem solving; the more personalized episodic knowledge may be particularly critical in medical compliance.

The procedural strategies of the old may more often be characterized as top-down processing. The elderly increasingly utilize prior experiential knowledge and well-honed procedural strategies to solve problems of daily living. They are less likely to engage in bottom-up processing requiring extensive information searches and inductive reasoning strategies. A major challenge for the elderly appears to be determining the appropriate balance between the two modes of thought and evaluating the utility of top-down versus bottom-up processing strategies. When there appears on the surface to be considerable familiarity with prior problem-solving situations, the elderly often inappropriately apply personalized knowledge and top-down processing procedures in a routinized manner.

The seeming efficiency of the elderly's problem-solving approach (limited information search, utilization of fewer pieces of information, emphasis on personalized knowledge, top-down processing) may represent a coping strategy based on their increased need to conserve physical and emotional resources. Quicker decision making in health situations may be based on the elderly being strongly motivated to detect and avoid threat as soon as possible, to reduce anxiety and tension, and to minimize ambiguity.

The above discussion has suggested *age-related* differences in approaches to problem solving. However, the wide variability in problem-solving competence in the elderly suggests that characteristics other than age are necessary to explain the phenomenon described. The lack of longitudinal studies of everyday problem solving precludes an examination of cohort differences. Moreover, individual-difference variables such as education and domains of expertise need further consideration.

Finally, it is argued that everyday problem solving does not occur in a vacuum. Competence in everyday problem solving represents the congruence of the abilities of the problem solver and the demands of the environment. Competence does not reside solely in either the individual or the environment. Hence, the role of the social and physical context in facilitating or hindering problem solving is an essential component in the study of everyday problem solving.

The study of everyday problem solving represents an exciting addition to the field of cognitive aging. Salient characteristics of research in this area include a focus on personalized knowledge bases, noncognitive factors, and the importance of the context. Given these characteristics, research on everyday problem solving will need to involve not only those with expertise in cognitive aging, but also our colleagues involved in social, emotional, and environmental studies. Psychogerontology and the elderly have much to gain from these interdisciplinary efforts.

## References

Abelson, R. P. (1981). Psychological status of the script concept. *American Psychologist, 36,* 715–729.

Antonucci, T. C. (1990). Social supports and social relationships. In R. H. Binstock & L. K. George (Eds.), *Handbook of aging and the social sciences* (3rd ed., pp. 205–226). San Diego, CA: Academic Press.

Antonucci, T. C., & Jackson, J. S. (1987). Social support, interpersonal efficacy and health. In L. L. Carstensen & B. A. Edelstein (Eds.), *Handbook of clinical gerontology* (pp. 291–311). New York: Pergamon.

Baltes, M. M., Mayr, U., Borchelt, M., Maas, I., & Wilms, H. (1993). Everyday competence in old and very old age: An interdisciplinary perspective. *Aging and Society, 13,* 657–680.

Baltes, M. M., Wahl, H. W., & Schmid-Furstoss, U. (1990). The daily life of elderly humans: Activity patterns, personal control, and functional health. *Journal of Gerontology: Psychological Sciences, 45,* P173–P179.

Baltes, P. B., Dittman-Kohli, F., & Dixon, R. (1984). New perspective on the development of intelligence in adulthood: Toward a dual-process conception and a model of selective optimization with compensation. In P. Baltes & O. Brim, Jr. (Eds.), *Life-span development and behavior* (Vol. 6, pp. 33–76). New York: Academic Press.

Baltes, P. B., Smith, J., & Staudinger, U. (1992). Wisdom and successful aging. In T. Sonderegger (Ed.), *Nebraska Symposium on Motivation: Vol. 39. Psychology and aging* (pp. 123–167). Lincoln: University of Nebraska Press.

Berg, C., & Sternberg, R. (1985). A triarchic theory of intellectual development during adulthood. *Developmental Review, 5,* 334–370.

Blanchard-Fields, F. (1986). Reasoning in adolescence and adults on social dilemmas varying in emotional saliency: An adult developmental perspective. *Psychology and Aging, 1,* 325–333.

Branch, L. G., Horowitz, A., & Carr, C. (1989). The implications for everyday life of incidents of self-reported visual decline among people over age 65 living in the community. *Gerontologist, 29,* 359–365.

Cattell, R. B. (Ed.). (1987). *Intelligence: Its structure, growth and action.* Amsterdam: North-Holland.

Chapman, M. (1993). Everyday reasoning and the revision of belief. In J. M. Puckett & H. W. Reese (Eds.), *Mechanisms of everyday cognition* (pp. 91–102). Hillsdale, NJ: Erlbaum.

Charness, N. (1981). Search in chess: Age and skill differences. *Journal of Experimental Psychology: Human Perception and Performance, 7,* 467–476.

Chi, M. T. H. (1985). Interactive roles of knowledge and strategies in the development of organized sorting and recall. In S. Chipman, J. Segal, & R. Glaser (Eds.), *Thinking and learning skills: Current research and open questions* (Vol. 2, pp. 85–95). Hillsdale, NJ: Erlbaum.

Cohen, G., & Faulkner, D. (1989). Age differences in source forgetting: Effects on reality monitoring and on eyewitness testimony. *Psychology and Aging, 4,* 10–17.

Costa, P. T., & McCrae, R. R. (1980). Somatic complaints in males as a function of age and neuroticism: A longitudinal analysis. *Journal of Behavioral Medicine, 3,* 245–257.

Cox, D. F. (Ed.). (1967). *Risk taking and information handling in consumer behavior.* Boston: Harvard University Press.

Denney, N. W. (1990). Adult age differences in traditional and practical problem solving. In E. A. Lovelace (Ed.), *Aging and cognition: Mental process, self awareness and interventions* (pp. 329–349). Amsterdam: Elsevier.

Doherty, W. J., Schrott, H. G., Metcalf, L., & Iasiello-Vailas, L. (1983). Effect of spouse support and health beliefs on medication adherence. *Journal of Family Practice, 17,* 837–841.

Fillenbaum, G. G. (1985). Screening the elderly: A brief instrumental activities of daily living measure. *Journal of the American Geriatrics Society, 33,* 698–706.

Fincham, J. E. (1988). Patient compliance in the ambulatory elderly: A review of the literature. *Journal of the Geriatric Drug Therapy, 2,* 31–52.

Folkman, S., Lazarus, R., Pimley, S., & Novacek, J. (1987). Age differences in stress and coping processes. *Psychology and Aging, 2,* 171–184.

Galotti, K. (1989). Approaches to studying formal and everyday reasoning. *Psychological Bulletin, 105,* 331–351.

Gauvain, M. (1993). The development of spatial thinking in everyday activity. *Developmental Review, 13,* 92–121.

Grisso, T. (1986). *Evaluating competencies: Forensic assessments and instruments.* New York: Plenum.

Hartley, A. A. (1989). The cognitive ecology of problem solving. In L. W. Poon, D. C. Rubin, & B. A. Wilson (Eds.), *Everyday cognition in adulthood and late life* (pp. 300–329). Cambridge, England: Cambridge University Press.

Heidrich, S. M., & Denney, N. W. (1994). Does social problem solving differ from other types of problem solving during the adult years? *Experimental Aging Research, 20,* 105–126.

Hershey, D. A., Walsh, D. A., Read, S. J., & Chulef, A. S. (1990). The effects of expertise on financial problem solving: Evidence for goal directed problem solving scripts. *Organizational Behavior and Human Decision Processes, 46,* 77–101.

Kane, R. A., & Kane, R. L. (1981). *Assessing the elderly: A practical guide to measurement.* Lexington, MA: Lexington Books.

Katz, S., Ford, A. Moskowitz, R., Jackson, B., & Jaffee, M. (1963). Studies of illness in the aged: The Index of ADL, a standardized measure of biological and psychological function. *JAMA, Journal of the American Medical Association, 185,* 94–99.

Krammer, D., & Woodruff, D. (1986). Relativistic and dialectical thought in three adult age groups. *Human Development, 29,* 280–290.

Kuhn, D. (1992). Thinking as argument. *Harvard Educational Review, 62,* 155–178.

Labouvie-Vief, G., & Hakim-Larson, J. (1989). Developmental shifts in adult thought. In S. Hunter & M. Sundel (Eds.), *Midlife myths* (pp. 69–96). Newbury Park, CA: Sage.

Lawton, M. P. (1982). Competence, environmental press, and adaptation of older people. In M. P. Lawton, P. Windley, & T. Byerts (Eds.), *Aging and the environment: Theoretical approaches* (pp. 33–59). New York: Springer.

Lawton, M. P., & Brody, E. M. (1969). Assessment of older people: Self-maintaining and instrumental activities of daily living. *Gerontologist, 9,* 179–185.

Lawton, M. P., Moss, M., & Fulcomer, M. (1986–1987). Objective and subjective uses of time by older people. *International Journal of Aging and Human Development, 24,* 171–188.

Leventhal, E. A., Leventhal, H., Schaefer, P. M., & Easterling, D. (1993). Conservation of energy, uncertainty reduction, and swift utilization of medical care among the elderly. *Journal of Gerontology: Psychological Sciences, 48,* 78–86.

Leventhal, H., & Cameron, L. (1987). Behavioral theories and the problem of compliance. *Patient Education and Counseling, 10,* 117–138.

Marsiske, M., & Willis, S. L. (1995). Dimensionality of everyday problem solving in older adults. *Psychology and Aging, 10,* 269–283.

McCrae, R. R., & Costa, P. T. (1990). *Personality in adulthood.* New York: Guilford.

Meyer, B. J. F., Marsiske, M., & Willis, S. L. (1993). Text processing variables predict the readability of everyday documents read by older adults. *Reading Research Quarterly, 28,* 234–249.

Meyer, B. J. F., Russo, C., & Talbot, A. (1995). Discourse comprehension and problem solving: Decisions about the treatment of breast cancer by women across the life-span. *Psychology and Aging, 10,* 84–103.

Morrell, R. W., Park, D. C., & Poon, L. W. (1989). Quality of instructions on prescription drug labels: Effects on memory and comprehension in young and old adults. *Gerontologist, 29,* 345–354.

Moss, M., & Lawton, M. P. (1982). Time budgets of older people: A window on four lifestyles. *Journal of Gerontology, 37,* 576–582.

Nerenz, D. R., Love, R. R., Leventhal, H., & Easterling, D. V. (1986). Psychosocial consequences of cancer chemotherapy for elderly patients. *Health Services Research, 20,* 961–976.

Park, D. C. (1992). Applied cognitive aging research. In F. I. M. Craik & T. A. Salthouse (Eds.), *Handbook of cognition and aging* (pp. 449–493). Hillsdale, NJ: Erlbaum.

Park, D. C., & Kidder, K. (1995). Prospective memory and medication adherence. In M. Brandimonte, G. Einstein, & M. McDaniel (Eds.), *Prospective memory: Theory and applications* (pp. 369–390). Hillsdale, NJ: Erlbaum.

Park, D. C., & Mayhorn, C. B. (in press). Remembering to take medications: The importance of nonmemory variables. In D. Herrmann, M. Johnson, C. McEvoy, C. Hertzog, & P. Hertel (Eds.), *Research on practical aspects of memory* (Vol. 2). Hillsdale, NJ: Erlbaum.

Park, D. C., Morrell, R. W., Frieske, D., & Kincaid, D. (1992). Medication adherence behaviors in older adults: Effects of external cognitive supports. *Psychology and Aging, 7,* 252–256.

Prohaska, T. R., Leventhal, E. A., Leventhal, H., & Keller, M. L. (1985). Health practices and illness cognition in young, middle aged, and elderly adults *Journal of Gerontology, 40,* 569–578.

Rabbitt, P. (1977). Changes in problem solving ability in old age. In J. E. Birren & K. W. Schaie (Eds.), *Handbook of the psychology of aging* (pp. 606–625). New York: Van Nostrand-Reinhold.

Reese, H. W., & Rodeheaver, D. (1985). Problem solving and complex decision making. In J. E. Birren & K. W. Schaie (Eds.), *Handbook of the psychology of aging* (2nd ed., pp. 474–499). New York: Van Nostrand-Reinhold.

Rybash, J. M., Hoyer, W. J., & Roodin, P. A. (1986). *Adult cognition and aging: Developmental changes in processing, knowing, and thinking.* New York: Pergamon.

Salthouse, T. A. (1985). Speed of behavior and

the implications for cognition. In J. E. Birren & K. W. Schaie (Eds.), *Handbook of the psychology of aging* (2nd ed., pp. 400–426). New York: Van Nostrand-Reinhold.

Salthouse, T. A. (1990). Cognitive competence and expertise in aging. In J. E. Birren & K. W. Schaie (Eds.), *Handbook of the psychology of aging* (3rd ed., pp. 310–319). San Diego, CA: Academic Press.

Schaninger, D. M., & Schiglimpaglia, D. (1981). The influence of cognitive personality traits and demographics on consumer information acquisition. *Journal of Consumer Research, 8,* 208–216.

Simon, H. A. (1978). Information-processing theory of human problem solving. In W. K. Estes (Ed.), *Handbook of learning and cognitive processes* (Vol. 5, pp. 271–296). Hillsdale, NJ: Erlbaum.

Sinnott, J. D. (1989). A model for solution of ill-structured problems: Implications for everyday and abstract problem solving. In J. D. Sinnott (Ed.), *Everyday problem solving: Theory and applications* (pp. 72–99). New York: Praeger.

Staudinger, U. M., Smith, J., & Baltes, P. B. (1992). Wisdom-related knowledge in a life review task: Age differences and the role of professional specialization. *Psychology and Aging, 2,* 271–281.

Sternberg, R., & Wagner, R. (1986). *Practical intelligence.* New York: Cambridge University Press.

Streufert, S., Pogash, R., Piasecki, M., & Post, G. M. (1990). Age and management team performance. *Psychology and Aging, 5,* 551–559.

Uniform Probate Code. (1989). Chicago: National Conference of Commissioners on Uniform State Laws.

Voss, J. F., & Post, T. A. (1988). On the solving of ill-structured problems. In M. T. H. Chi, R. Glaser, & M. Farr (Eds.), *The nature of expertise* (pp. 261–285). Hillsdale, NJ: Erlbaum.

Willis, S. L. (1991). Cognition and everyday competence. *Annual Review of Gerontology and Geriatrics, 11,* 80–109.

Willis, S. L. (1995). Everyday problem solving in the cognitive challenged elderly. In M. Smyer, M. B. Kapp, & K. W. Schaie (Eds.), *The impact of the law on aging* (pp. 87–126). New York: Springer.

Willis, S. L., Jay, G. M., Diehl, M., & Marsiske, M. (1992). Longitudinal change and prediction of everyday task competence in the elderly. *Research on Aging, 14,* 68–91.

Willis, S. L., & Marsiske, M. (1991). A life-span perspective on practical intelligence. In D. Tupper & K. Cicerone (Eds.), *The neuropsychology of everyday life* (pp. 183–198). Boston: Kluwer Academic Publishers.

Willis, S. L., & Schaie, K. W. (1986). Practical intelligence in later adulthood. In R. Sternberg & R. Wagner (Eds.), *Practical intelligence* (pp. 236–270). New York: Cambridge University Press.

Willis, S. L., & Schaie, K. W. (1993). Everyday cognition: Taxonomic and methodological considerations. In J. M. Puckett & H. W. Reese (Eds.), *Lifespan developmental psychology: Mechanisms of everyday cognition* (pp. 33–53). Hillsdale, NJ: Erlbaum.

Willis, S. L., Schaie, K. W., & Hayward, M. (in press). *Societal mechanisms for maintaining competence in old age.* New York: Springer.

Seventeen

# Personality and Aging: Coping and Management of the Self in Later Life

Jan-Erik Ruth and Peter Coleman*

## I. Introduction

As Neugarten (1977) stated in the first *Handbook of the Psychology of Aging*, personality research is an area without borders and without consensus on which methods to employ. The metaphor of personality that scientists have created is an intriguing but nebulous construct encompassing a multitude of research topics, theoretical concepts, and research methods. A presentation within the limits of a single chapter of this vast and vigorous field of work and its relevance to aging must be very selective.

This review of personality-linked issues centers on two basic questions: (a) How does the aging individual cope with life events typically encountered in old age; what are the resources available in this encounter? and (b) How can an aging individual maintain and develop a self-image in spite of obstacles, like illness, that tend to accompany aging? Consideration both of previous reviews in these handbooks and of current innovative research has deter-

mined the choice of questions for treatment in this chapter.

In the third edition of the *Handbook*, Kogan (1990) provided a comprehensive review of major theoretical conceptualizations and empirical findings on the established trait and developmental stage models, as well as on recent contextual models. A discussion of personality as a predictor of life outcomes, such as satisfaction or happiness, was deliberately omitted, however, and coping in old age has been addressed specifically in only one presentation in the earlier handbooks (Whitbourne, 1985). Consequently, coping was also chosen for discussion in this chapter because of its importance to the adaptation and well-being of the aging individual. A number of extensive studies on this concept have been published recently, some of which are longitudinal, and others that depict coping and aging in different cultural contexts.

In many of these studies, the aging individual is still viewed as a rather passive and reactive agent whose life course is shaped by the life events he or she encounters. However, in our search for a related area within personality research, one that pictured a more proactive and dynam-

* The authors wish to thank Donald Polkinghorne, Jean A. Radecki and Susan McFadden for insightful comments on earlier versions of this chapter.

ically developing aging individual, we chose recent conceptions of the self. Especially noteworthy is the trend to view the self as a process recreating itself through life, as described in the story (or stories) of life the individual narrates (see Birren, Kenyon, Ruth, Schroots, & Svensson, 1995).

For the 1985 edition of this handbook, Bengtson, Reedy, and Gordon reviewed a large number of studies on stability and change in self-concept with age. In the succeeding 11 years, although relatively little new data have been collected, conceptual, theoretical, and methodological advances have answered some of the questions raised in their review.

## II. Definitions of Coping and Adaptation

Lazarus and Folkman defined *coping* as "constantly changing cognitive and behavioral efforts to manage specific external and/or internal demands that are appraised as taxing or exceeding the resources of the person" (1984, p. 141). Even in this early definition, the main factors of later coping research can be found, namely: demands, appraisal, resources, and mastering life strains.

Coping has been defined in developmental studies as a state of congruence between the individual and the environment in which the individual maintains a sense of well-being or quality of life (George, 1980). The term *adaptation* is broader in its scope than the notion of coping with stress. Adaptation pertains to a range of behaviors to meet demands, from developing habits to meeting problems and frustrations through managing intense anxiety (Whitbourne, 1985). Recently, existentialist constructs, such as goal setting, meaning, and purpose in life, have been used in definitions of adaptation and well-being across the life span (Reker, Peacock, & Wong, 1987).

## III. Basic Patterns of Coping

### A. Cognitive Processes

In many studies the concept of coping is cognitively conceived. Folkman, Lazarus, Pimley, and Novacek (1987), for example, employed a transactional frame of reference in studying the individual and his or her relation to the environment. Through the cognitive mediating processes called *primary* and *secondary appraisal*, the mastery of a stressful life situation can be achieved. Primary appraisal pertains to the assessment of a situation as stressful or benign. Secondary appraisal pertains to the perceived ways of mastering the situation.

The basic idea is that by gaining control, or even a perception of control, and by coping either in cognition or behavior, mastering is possible (Folkman et al., 1987). Some researchers, such as Thomae (1990) and Markus and Herzog (1991), posit that the impact of the past, present, and future on the individual's self and its coping efforts must be acknowledged. The individual's inner feelings or outer behavior is affected by his or her perception of a situation, earlier experiences, and the future consequences of a way of coping (Thomae, 1990).

### B. Ways of Coping

Basic distinctions have been made between problem-focused and emotion-focused (palliative) coping, approach and avoidance coping, and active or passive mastery, as described by Feifel and Strack (1989). The active, confrontative, and planful ways of coping are usually described as successful, whereas avoidance, minimization of the threat, or resignation are described as less successful (Folkman et al., 1987).

In an overview of coping research, Stone, Helder, and Schneider (1988) argued for seven basic dimensions in coping strategies: social support, information seeking, religiosity, situation redefinition, avoidance, tension reduction, and problem solving. The validity of the factors is still problematic because they have not always been replicated in reanalyses. One reason for this may be the vastly diverging situations or life events with which subjects are coping in these studies (Suutama, 1994; Thoits, 1991). Another reason may pertain to the personality resources or social resources of the copers, or the interaction among these.

## IV. Old Age—A Stressful or Nonstressful Period of Life?

Three different conceptions of the basic nature of old age can be found in the literature. Negative perceptions of old age depict it as a period of multiple losses, as often found in psychiatric studies. Pfeiffer (1977), for example, described adaptation to the loss of spouse, friends, roles, income, and health; such losses, according to Pfeiffer, are the source of major distress in old age.

In studies on personality and social psychology of old age, overtly positive descriptions can be found. Murrell, Norris, and Grots (1988), Cohler (1991), Markus and Herzog (1991), and Costa and McCrae (1993) argued for the normative nature of aging, whereby changes can be well anticipated. Gerontologists who depict retirement and old age as more stressful than earlier periods of life are said to be clinging to scientific myths that seldom are empirically supported (Tornstam, 1992).

A middle position is presently taken in life span studies, acknowledging both stressful and stress-free development in old age. Some individuals encounter losses, some gains. Declines can be found in some areas of individual adjustment, growth in others (Baltes, 1987; Carstensen, 1991). Both stability and change can be found in the self-concept in aging (Bengtson et al., 1985). Life span psychologists have used the

terms *differential aging, plasticity,* and *reserve capacity* in their arguments for this view (Featherman, Smith, & Peterson, 1990; Smith & Baltes, 1993).

## V. Major Life Events in Old Age

According to the life-event model of adaptation, the homeostasis of everyday life is disturbed by daily hassles or turning points in life, and excess demands are placed on the physical or psychological system of the individual. It is often assumed that both negative and positive events induce stress and that the stress accumulates if encountered within a short period of time (Holmes & Rahe, 1967). What then can be said about the impact of the major life events on the well-being of an aging individual?

### A. Events of Transition into Old Age

Five major life events were identified in a 6-year follow-up study of Americans aged 40–70: retirement, the retirement of the spouse, medical problems, widowhood, and the empty-nest syndrome (Palmore, Cleveland, Nowlin, Ramm, & Siegler, 1985). But none of these transition events from middle age to old age produced major stress reactions demanding an adaptation that would fit the cumulative-losses perspective.

In a study in the United States by George and Siegler (1982), based on interview data, the stressful situations encountered by 100 men and women aged 55–80 were classified as health, family, self, economics, and work. There seemed to be more problems within the personal than within the interpersonal sphere, and more economic problems in old age than at earlier ages. Men mentioned work-related and health-related personal events more, whereas women were more likely to mention interpersonal ones, such as husband's illness. The stresses reported were not viewed as overwhelming, and only the negative life events were experienced as adaptive challenges, not the positive ones (in contrast to Holmes & Rahe, 1967). The use of ready-made checklists in stress studies has also been criticized. One-third of the stress situations found by George and Siegler (1982) would have been missed if interview procedures had not been used.

## B. Life Events in Old Age

Over 900 Danish noninstitutionalized persons aged 70–95 were asked which life events they had encountered during the last year (Holstein, Due, Holst, & Almind, 1992). The most common events were death of a close person, own illness, and the illness of a close person. Only about 20% of the aged Danes had experienced more than one of the losses within a year, however. Some had experienced accidents, conflicts with a close person, being a victim of crime, or housing problems. In a Finnish study by Suutama (1994) of 300 persons aged 75+ the most common events were death of a spouse (especially for women) and encountering a serious illness. Giving up activities due to medical problems was also often reported by both women and men. Involuntary relocation and breaks between close persons were less commonly reported in the study. Only about half of the events had occurred in the last part of the life span, however.

In a study in Finland by Ruth and Öberg (1995), based on life stories and thematic interviews with an urban sample aged 73–83, the loss of one's own health at some point in life and the loss of a spouse's health in old age, along with difficulties in coping, were two of the most decisive turning points in a way of life called "life as a trapping pit." On the other hand, feelings of mastering one's health by active coping with and transcending illness restrictions, and by pursuing a healthy lifestyle in old age, characterized the optimal ways of life named "life as a job career" and "the sweet life."

These results clearly show some effects of cultural influences, and point to the importance of the notion of the "social construction of aging." Some of the less common problems in the Scandinavian studies (such as accidents, being a victim of crime, or housing problems) would be expected to occur more frequently among American older persons, especially in the big cities.

## C. Coping with Events of Illness and Institutionalization

Situational conditions and contexts are central factors affecting the perception of stress. This is clear in stress and coping studies performed within an institutional setting during an ongoing stressful period. Meeks, Carstensen, Tamsky, Wright, and Pellegrini (1989), in a study of 68 patients in an orthopedic ward, both young and old, found the following stressors: pain and discomfort, inactivity, lack of control, anxiety, missing personal attachments, and missing objects. Studies show that elderly people use predominantly active strategies in coping with health stresses and are satisfied with them (Keller, Leventhal, & Larson, 1989; Rott & Thomae, 1991). Particularly noteworthy are the studies of the Leventhals (Leventhal, Leventhal, & Schaefer, 1992), which show older persons to be more vigilant and responsive to health threats than middle-aged or younger persons. This does not seem to be because of greater emotional responsiveness but because of enhanced motivation to reduce the distress resulting from illness. The findings of the Bonn longitudinal study also suggest that older women's coping with health problems increased with aging (Rott & Thomae, 1991).

Few studies have yet been carried out on coping of frail elderly people in institutional settings. American studies indicate the importance to survival of instrumental coping behavior, assertiveness, and a strong sense of internal control (Lieberman & Tobin, 1983). However, it is not clear to what extent these findings are specific to American institutions and generalizable elsewhere.

## D. Issues Raised by the Studies

The review on stress in relation to age raises some research issues and theoretical considerations. The first concerns the issue of the potential stressfulness of all life events. In studies using subjective accounts as data sources, the elderly refute the idea that positive events elicit stress, contradicting earlier theories (George & Siegler, 1982).

The second issue concerns the notion of cumulative harmful life events in old age. According to empirical findings, relatively few major life events occur solely in old age. Many have occurred earlier, such as health-related events. Neither does the occurrence of events seem to be condensed into very short time periods (Suutama, 1994). Daily hassles seem to show stronger correlates to physical and psychological well-being than life events in the elderly (Landrevill & Vezina, 1992).

A third issue pertains to individuals as agents in coping situations. In earlier studies individuals were seen as passive in encountering stresses elicited by life events. In more recent studies, however, individuals are seen as active agents seeking challenges, purposefully steering their lives, and transcending limits using available resources (Ryff & Essex, 1991).

## VI. Internal and External Resources in Coping

It is to be expected that physical, mental, and social resources affect the way in which the individual copes with stressful life events, as demonstrated in the Duke Longitudinal Study of Aging (Palmore et al., 1985). One would further assume that education, cognitive capacities, life experiences, knowledge, social abilities, social networks, motivation, energy, biological capacity, health, gender, economic resources, and living conditions in old age would make a difference in coping strategies (Ruth & Kenyon, 1995). Mediating factors that further influence the coping strategies would be differentiation and personality-linked factors such as values, goals, attitudes, commitments, self-concept, and self-esteem (Labouvie-Vief, Hakim-Larson, & Hobart, 1987; Markus & Herzog, 1991).

## A. Internal Resources

In a discussion of internal resources in coping, reference must be made to the pioneering work of Vaillant (1977) and Haan (1977), who emphasized that the maturity of the copers can be evaluated according to the defense mechanisms they use. The less mature, mostly younger copers rely on denial and projection, whereas the more mature, usually older copers are more likely to use sublimation, suppression, and humor. The younger copers also more often show hostile reactions or escapist fantasies, which older copers seldom show (Costa & McCrae, 1993).

Neuroticism is a personality disposition that negatively affects the perception of stress and ways of coping, leading to lower levels of well-being and more somatic complaints (Costa & McCrae, 1993). An easy-going or an optimistic disposition, on the other hand, is related to more favorable outcomes (Moos & Schaefer, 1993; Scheier & Carver, 1987). According to Antonowsky (1987), an important aspect of adjustment is the coherence an individual experiences in distressing life situations. The coherence encompasses a sense of comprehensibility, manageability, and meaningfulness, and these factors all enhance coping and well-being.

It has been shown that persons with an internal locus of control are more likely to use more direct coping and less suppression, whereas persons with an external locus of control show the reverse patterns (Holahan & Moos, 1987). A personal disposition of commitment, control, and challenge (called *hardiness*) can form a buffer against stress (Kobasa, Maddi, & Kahn, 1982), and self-efficacious persons are more active copers (Bandura, 1989). Gatz and Karel (1993) reported an impressive 20-year longitudinal study of perceived control employing cross-sectional, longitudinal, and sequential analytic strategies. Mean levels became more internal but the oldest generation remained the most external, which may be a cohort rather than developmental effect. According to Brandtstädter and Baltes-Götz (1990), there is no indication of a significant age-related decrement in perceived autonomous control of life events, but an inconsistency of findings still plagues this field. In retrospective accounts of adaptation in a life span perspective, maintained control, lost control, and regained control in the course of development have all been reported (Ruth & Öberg, 1995).

The dispositions of autonomous control may be functional in many situations in which adults and middle-aged persons find themselves, but it is still unclear if aged copers are best helped by these personality features. Labouvie-Vief et al. (1987) argued that older adults sometimes are better served by accommodating to negative life events (such as severe illness) and by reassessing the events in a more positive way —using "passive or inner mastery" (Gutmann, 1977)—than by overt action. Thomae (1992) pointed out that accepting a situation (such as divorce of a child) in old age is not necessarily passive behavior. It is only making an unfavorable and uncontrollable situation internally acceptable. The meaning ascribed by the individual to a life situation or daily hassles as well as the individual's view of the outcome of coping efforts must also be considered. Studies on stress

must incorporate the biographical context of the individual in the research designs; otherwise they will lack contact with the lives of aging individuals (Thomae, 1992).

Labouvie-Vief et al. (1987) argued that there is continued personality differentiation among adults and that coping strategies are linked not only to situations or to the age of the coper, but to ego level as well. Impulsive, self-protective, and conformist strategies are considered as more immature ego levels while conscientious, autonomous, and integrated strategies are considered as more mature ones. The less differentiated (younger) copers are further hypothesized to be hampered by age-related cognitive limitations in coping. In an ongoing study, Featherman et al. (1990) coined the term *adaptive competence* for an individual's ability to draw upon gained knowledge in functioning in the world. This adaptive competence pertains to problem-solving heuristics and is hypothesized to benefit from earlier professional training in which reflective planning is a central element. (For a recent conception of adaptive competence and life satisfaction see Svensson, 1995.)

## B. External Resources

Not surprisingly, some published studies have found a connection between socioeconomic status, education, and coping strategies. Highly educated individuals are less likely to ignore and postpone dealing with marital or occupational problems and more likely to use problem-focused coping rather than avoidance coping (Holahan & Moos, 1987). Individuals with higher socioeconomic status are more inclined to use adaptive forms of coping based on logical choice and flexibility and less inclined to rely on irrational and rigid solutions (Haan, 1977).

In studies of social networks as an external resource, it has been shown that individuals with more social resources are less likely to use avoidance coping (Moos & Shaefer, 1993). Individuals with family support use more problem-focused coping. Men who have social support use confrontation more and acceptance or resignation less, and women with supportive husbands increase their information seeking and restructuring of the problem in an illness situation, whereas women who lack family support often engage in avoidance coping (Feifel & Strack, 1989; Holahan & Moos, 1987).

## C. Limitations of Studies and Models

Stable personality traits and ego defenses are the so-called internal resources that have received most of the attention in coping research, whereas factors that may show some change during the life span through education and maturation (such as values, goals, motives, and attitudes) have received less attention (Holahan, 1988; Ryff, 1989). This is one of the reasons for the argument that personality dispositions seem stable over the life span (see Costa & McCrae, 1993).

In some studies aimed at personality development, cognitive reasoning as well as personality-linked variables are used to explain coping behavior (Baltes & Smith, 1990; Labouvie-Vief et al., 1987). More studies of the relationships between these two domains would clearly be fruitful.

Emotionally grounded coping resources have received scarce attention in the research even as the affective dimension gains importance in old age (Carstensen, 1991). Finding purpose and meaningfulness in life and having positive future perspectives concerning personal growth also constitute neglected resources in the research (Ryff & Essex, 1991). The use of more humanistic or existentialist models may lead to new conceptualizations of the resources older individuals possess and their possibilities for environmental mastery.

In developmental studies on personality

and coping resources, cross-sectional research design is generally used, which confounds age effects with cohort effects. More longitudinal and cross-sequential studies are needed to partial out these effects (Cohler, 1991).

The physical dimension, or the health of the individual, has usually been included in coping studies as a stressing life event but not as a resource—or a hindrance—of the individual, as Suutama pointed out (1994). Thus one of the most important of the resources in old age has not been sufficiently taken into consideration in studies on coping and aging.

# VII. Conceptualizations of the Self

## A. Self-Concept and Personality

One way of relating self-concept to personality is to see the former as a subset of the latter, as comprising "those motivations, attitudes and behaviors which are relevant to self-definition and the meaning of one's life" (McAdams, 1993, p. 266). However, it is also possible to define personality in a way that does not overlap with self-concept, "as the set of characteristic dispositions that determine emotional, interpersonal, experiential, attitudinal and motivational styles" (McCrae and Costa, 1988, p. 177).

McCrae and Costa (1988) noted both the logical and theoretical reasons for this interrelation: Personality traits form part of the content of self-concept, and personality is most often measured through self-report; evidence supports the hypotheses that neurotics are more dissatisfied with their lives and that extroverts are more optimistic (although these links are not high). But an important indicator of functional difference is the growing consensus that personality traits tend to be stable with age whereas key aspects of self (such as goals, values, coping styles, and control beliefs) are more amenable to change (Dittmann-Kohli, 1990; Ryff, 1991).

## B. Structure of the Self

As far as the structure of the self is concerned, the distinction articulated by William James (1890) between *I* and *me*, the self as awareness and the self as object in awareness, has been commonly repeated. James did not refer to two separate things, but to separate aspects of the same process (Sherman & Webb, 1994). It is the objective self that can be thought of as structure and can be analyzed. James referred to the *material Me*, the *social Me*, and the *spiritual Me*, the first two being most accessible to objective study, whereas the spiritual Me is more subjective and closer to the primary consciousness of the I.

The objective self has been traditionally differentiated into actual self, ideal self, and self-esteem. These are the concepts most often utilized in the earlier studies cited by Bengtson et al. (1985). However, a far greater variety of past, present, and future self-referent conceptions are now being utilized, including the good, the bad, the hoped-for, the feared, the not-me, and the ought-to selves (Markus & Herzog, 1991), and greater attention is being paid to domain-specific self-concepts as well as to overarching self or life themes (Kaufman, 1986; Ruth & Öberg, 1995).

## C. The Self as Active

The new emphasis on the self as active, competent, and creative owes much to Atchley's work on management of identity and the achievement of continuity through the role changes, stigma, and threats of aging (Atchley, 1989). Research has continued to employ the framework of principles first set out by Rosenberg (1979) to explain regulation of the self (feedback from others, social comparison with them or with the previous self, observation of one's own behavior, and centrality/peripherality of self aspects involved), but in addition acknowledges the importance of goal setting (reconsideration and revision of history and plans). Although responses from others are essential to these processes, it is the active self who chooses what to select and to attend to.

Contemporary critique of the passive and deterministic model of the development of the self as it results from societal and organismic processes is well represented by the writings of Dannefer (e.g., Dannefer, 1989; Dannefer & Perlmutter, 1990). He noted not only that aging is sensitive to processes that are at least partially under the control or mediated by the self, such as values, beliefs, and intentional decisions, but also that the self is active in the "production and reproduction of social institutions and practices from which the social forces that impact individual aging derive" (1989, p. 3). The life course itself is not part of the "natural order" but of a "humanly produced order" and it can be conceived as a "text" that is open to revision and reinterpretation (1989, p. 12–13). To understand the construction and ongoing changes in the self requires careful interpretation because we are beings housed in language, culture, and history (Bruner, 1990; Freeman, 1993; Gergen, 1991).

## D. Motivations of the Self

Another set of assumptions about the self that have been unquestioned until recently concern its basic motivations to look good and to preserve consistency and continuity. A number of researchers have followed Whitbourne (1986) in detailing the various ways in which adults maintain continued positive self-evaluation in the face of threats (e.g., attributing failures to external causes, de-emphasizing certain goals for those more attainable, and making social comparisons with those doing less well) (Atchley, 1989; Dittmann-Kohli, 1990; Heidrich & Ryff, 1993).

But recent studies on late life have questioned whether there is an overemphasis on continuity and positive evaluation of individual performance in isolation (Johnson, 1993). The oldest-old may benefit from adapting by accepting change. Control over circumstances may become less important, internal controls over meaning more so. It is significant that Ryff (1989) found that middle-aged people stressed the importance of self-acceptance as important to well-being, but that older people stressed accepting change.

### E. Methodological Issues

As is the case for coping studies, rating scales provide only limited information on management of the aging self (Atchley, 1991). What are required are models of analysis that integrate a complex array of information into a whole. The growing emphasis on self as process requires more descriptive, ethnographic studies of spontaneous messages about the self in everyday life, and qualitative analysis of stories told about the self in social interaction. Because one is dealing with personal constructions, longitudinal studies that take the person's earlier self as baseline are essential.

## VIII. Stability and Change in the Self with Aging

### A. Explaining Observed Stability

Studies using subjective rating scales and content analysis of responses to self-completion stems have confirmed a picture evident in the literature (Bengtson et al., 1985) of relative stability of self-concept (and self-esteem with aging (Atchley, 1991; Baltes & Baltes, 1990; Dittmann-Kohli, 1990; Markus & Herzog, 1991; McCrae & Costa, 1988). However, with some exceptions (e.g., Coleman, Ivani-Chalian, & Robinson, 1993; Field & Millsap, 1991; Gatz & Karel, 1993), reported research has continued to be cross-sectional in nature. This raises difficulties for interpreting dif-

ferences in self-representation as cohort or age effects.

The resilience of the self with aging requires fresh theoretical perspectives. Earlier theoretical reviews now seem unnecessarily negative. Interpretive processes as social comparisons and reflected appraisals, far from being less significant factors in maintenance of the self in old age, appear to be of considerable importance (Baltes & Baltes, 1990; Ryff & Essex, 1991). It is also to older people's advantage that they show increased self-acceptance (Ryff, 1991), a more realistic ideal self, and lowered expectations in life (Dittmann-Kohli, 1990). In his review of the subject, Atchley (1991) articulated a theoretical position in which normal aging influences the self, mostly for good, until the point of frailty. Older people could be expected to have a more tested, stable set of processes for managing the self, and more robust self-concepts.

### B. Applications of the Life Story Model of Identity

A number of theoreticians have followed Cohler (1982) in postulating a growing coherence of life-story with age (Freeman, 1993; McAdams, 1993; Munnichs, 1992). McAdams's studies of age differences in generativity in narrative accounts are particularly pertinent (McAdams & de St. Aubin, 1992; McAdams, de St. Aubin, & Logan, 1993). They add significantly to empirical research on Erikson's midlife and old-age stages, the paucity of which was emphasized in the previous review (Kogan, 1990). By late life, the life-history report is a significant indicator of well-being (Coleman, 1986; Hagberg, 1995). Old values can take on new meanings appropriate to present circumstances (Kaufman, 1986; Ruth & Kenyon, 1995). Tobin (1991) cited evidence that institutionalized elderly people strive hard to keep their story in good shape, and make it more vivid and striking to defend against challenges. But opportunities may also need to be provided to help old people reassert integrity (Haight, Coleman, & Lord, 1995).

Success is not guaranteed. Ruth and Öberg (1992) reported an analysis of elderly women's life histories in which the narrating self is often more contradictory and less integrated. Their accounts reflect a view of themselves more as objects than subjects in their own lives. This analysis may provide a corrective to some theoretical writing, which seems to assume that people have little difficulty in seeing their lives as a story, and as something continuous and coherent. Both clinical and nonclinical observation suggests rather that some older individuals do not have a sense of having lived a "coherent life," but rather feel confused, hurt, or depressed—a satisfactory identity has not yet been constructed. Even some older individuals may still need to reflect on themselves, and to compose a story they can call their own (Cohler & Cole, 1995; Gergen, 1995).

### C. Queries on the Adequacy of the Life-Story Model

McAdams (1990) suggested that people in old age may finally move beyond story making. Having accepted their lived lives they come to live in the present, the "eternal now." A number of authors in gerontology refer to the possibilities of a shift from a materialistic-rational to a transcendent perspective on self and life (Reker & Wong, 1988; Tornstam, 1994). William James (1890) described the material and social Me as strongly appropriative (i.e., not only my body, my possessions, but also my family, my friends), whereas the spiritual Me is constituted by my states of consciousness with "the more active-feeling states" at its core (p. 48). Sherman and Webb (1994) commented that these are useful concepts for describing a spiritual process in which some older persons are able to live without the more appropria-

tive aspects of the self and engage in an inward journey in which the duality of subject and object is transcended. The notion of *gero-transcendence* recently formulated by Tornstam (1994, pp. 207–211) also implies that a maturation process will occur in old age in which the self is more occupied with philosophical pondering on life; with a redefinition of time (blurring of the borders between the past, present, and future); and with reality (feeling of affinity with both past generations and the unknown). There are affinities with the theoretical concepts of *ego integrity, disengagement*, and *passive and magical mastery*.

## IX. Conclusions

This review of coping and management of the self in old age has suggested some new avenues of investigation and referred to limitations in research. In our concluding remarks we point to some emerging trends and comment upon their relevance for future research.

According to many pieces of research reviewed here, the stressfulness of old age can be questioned. For most individuals, life events are not more taxing than in earlier life and they do not seem to accumulate in a negative sense in old age. Many studies show no clear trend of older people using less successful coping strategies. There are several individual and social resources to draw upon in the coping process for many older individuals. A reevaluation of the meaning of threats to the self also seems to occur. The results are not without contradictions, however. In some studies decrement and deficiency have been reported in coping in old age; many of these studies have used ready-made instruments, hypothetical coping situations, and cross-sectional designs.

Research on the self, coping, and aging has consisted, for the greater part, of the study of different age groups. Some commentators argue that the age differences found are probably tied to the particular cohort studied and do not reflect ontogenetic age changes. It would add to clarification of the results if the explanations of age differences were consistently sought in sociohistorical circumstances surrounding different cohorts. If age effects are to be assessed in future research, such research designs as repeated-cross-sectional, longitudinal, or cross-sequential techniques should be employed (Schaie & Hertzog, 1985).

Many studies focus on middle-aged or newly retired individuals. In order to learn how the self and models of coping are changing, there is a need for more studies on old-old age samples. These samples have been initiated, although little data are available at present (Baltes, Mayer, Helmchen, & Steinhagen-Thiessen, 1993; Poon, 1992). Clear differences in life events and daily hassles encountered in old age, and coping strategies used by the elderly, can be found between the American and European studies reviewed here.

It is becoming more evident that there are only a few psychological aging effects that are general to all individuals irrespective of social contexts and times (Dannefer & Perlmutter, 1990). What now seems fruitful is to describe and explain patterns of aging coconstituted by social and cultural circumstances. The assumption of unidirectional and general aging effects has been questioned repeatedly by researchers, lately in Baltes's (1987) and Carstensen's (1991) remarks on the necessity to look for both gains and losses in aging and to apply an inter- as well as intraindividual perspective in gerontological research. The methods and the design in studies examining personality-related constructs must be based on these insights.

It is clear that a significant part of gerontological research on personality-linked constructs is moving away from the "mean level stability or change" approach. Even if trait psychology is alive and well (Schaie & Willis, 1995), an increased interest in the study of individual lives can now be seen. Thus, contrary to the predictions of Bengtson et al. in their review of 1985, much of the innovative research moves away from a narrowing of focus in already known personality-linked concepts to the study of newly formulated constructs, many of which are of a more holistic and dialectic nature. These constructs often reflect aspects of "the ego's involvement in the world" (Allport, 1955), such as possible selves, goal setting, values, meaning, and purpose in life (Ryff, 1989).

The trend first pointed to by Kogan in 1990 of studying development in the sociocultural and historic context in which older people are living out their lives, and of following the trajectories of individuals or groups of individuals, has become a vigorous area of research. Making use of narratives as mirrors of development is considered a particularly promising way of enfolding individuals' perceptions of their lives, as Gergen (1991) has illustrated. An examination of an individual's biography is considered essential both to capture stability and change and to understand the perceived precedents and consequences of development (Markus & Herzog, 1991).

Criticisms of abstract or restricted ways of mapping presumed stress events, coping mechanisms, and reformulations of self have led to recommendations to use more observations and interview techniques. The use of fictive situations also adds to problems of ecological validity (i.e., generalizing the results). We need studies that are more closely tied to real-life situations where stressful events or daily hassles are encountered and resources or developmental reserves used (Cohler, 1991).

The passive image of the aging person found in many coping studies, but refuted in recent studies of management of the self, has increased self-reflection among researchers. If the hypotheses predict restrictions, if decline is made probable by the research designs used, only the losses of old age will be delineated but the gains will remain uncovered (Ryff & Essex,

1991). The proactive individual, overriding restrictions and re-creating situations and circumstances, emanates from the "adaptive competence" and the "management of the self" domains. Research from this point of view produces pictures of a more differentiated aging individual who shows gains and losses in mental capacities as well as plasticity in behavior.

## References

Allport, G. W. (1955). *Becoming: Basic considerations for a psychology of personality.* New Haven, CT: Yale University Press.

Antonowsky, A. (1987). *Unraveling the mystery of health: How people manage stress and stay well.* San Francisco: Jossey-Bass.

Atchley, R. C. (1989). A continuity theory of normal aging. *Gerontologist, 29,* 183–190.

Atchley, R. C. (1991). The influence of aging or frailty on perceptions and expressions of the self: Theoretical and methodological issues. In J. E. Birren & I. Lubben (Eds.), *The concept and measurement of quality of life in the frail elderly* (pp. 207–225). San Diego, CA: Academic Press.

Baltes, P. B. (1987). Theoretical propositions of life-span developmental psychology. *Developmental Psychology, 23,* 611–626.

Baltes, P. B., & Baltes, M. M. (1990). Psychological perspectives on successful aging: The model of selective optimization with compensation. In P. B. Baltes & M. M. Baltes (Eds.), *Successful aging: Perspectives from the behavioral sciences* (pp. 1–34). New York: Cambridge University Press.

Baltes, P. B., Mayer, K. U., Helmchen, H., & Steinhagen-Thiessen, E. (1993). The Berlin Aging Study (BASE): Overview and design. *Ageing and Society, 13,* 483–515.

Baltes, P. B., & Smith, J. (1990). Toward a psychology of wisdom and its ontogenesis. In R. J. Sternberg (Ed.), *Wisdom: Its nature, origins, and development* (pp. 87–120). New York: Cambridge University Press.

Bandura, A. (1989). Self regulation of motivation and action through internal standards and goal systems. In L. A. Pervin (Ed.), *Goal concepts in personality and social psychology* (pp. 69–164). Hillsdale, NJ: Erlbaum.

Bengtson, V. L., Reedy, M. N., & Gordon, C. (1985). Aging and self-conceptions: Personality processes and social contexts. In J. E. Birren & K. W. Schaie (Eds.), *Handbook of the psychology of aging* (2nd ed., pp. 544–593). New York: Van Nostrand-Reinhold.

Birren, J. E., Kenyon, G., Ruth, J.-E., Schroots, J. J. F., & Svensson, T. (Eds.). (1995). *Aging and biography: Explorations in adult development.* New York: Springer.

Brandtstädter, J., & Baltes-Götz, B. (1990). Personal control over development and quality of life perspectives in adulthood. In P. B. Baltes & M. M. Baltes (Eds.), *Successful aging: Perspectives from the behavioral sciences* (pp. 197–224). New York: Cambridge University Press.

Bruner, J. (1990). *Acts of meaning.* London: Harvard University Press.

Carstensen, L. (1991). Selectivity theory: Social activity in life-span context. *Annual Review of Gerontology and Geriatrics, 11,* 195–217.

Cohler, B. J. (1982). Personal narrative and the life course. In P. B. Baltes & O. G. Brim, Jr. (Eds.), *Life-span development and behavior* (Vol. 4, pp. 205–241). New York: Academic Press.

Cohler, B. J. (1991). Life course perspectives on the study of adversity, stress and coping: Discussion of papers from the West Virginia Conference. In E. M. Cummings, A. L. Greene, & K. H. Karraker (Eds.), *Life-span developmental psychology: Perspectives on stress and coping* (pp. 297–326). Hillsdale, NJ: Erlbaum.

Cohler, B. J., & Cole, T. (1995). Studying older lives: Reciprocal acts of telling and listening. In J. E. Birren, G. Kenyon, J.-E. Ruth, J. J. F. Schroots, & T. Svensson (Eds.), *Aging and biography: Explorations in adult development* (pp. 61–76). New York: Springer.

Coleman, P. G. (1986). *Ageing and reminiscence processes: Social and clinical implications.* Chichester, UK: Wiley.

Coleman, P. G., Ivani-Chalian, C., & Robinson, M. (1993). Self-esteem and its sources: Stability and change in later life. *Ageing and Society, 13,* 171–192.

Costa, P. T., & McCrae, R. R. (1993). Psychological stress and coping in old age. In L. Goldberger & S. Breznitz (Eds.), *Handbook of stress: Theoretical and clinical aspects* (2nd ed., pp. 403–412). New York: Free Press.

Dannefer, D. (1989). Human action and its place in theories of aging. *Journal of Aging Studies, 3,* 1–20.

Dannefer, D., & Perlmutter, M. (1990). Development as a multidimensional process: Individual and social constituents. *Human Development, 33*, 108–137.

Dittmann-Kohli, F. (1990). The construction of meaning in old age: Possibilities and constraints. *Ageing and Society, 10*, 279–294.

Featherman, D. L., Smith, J., & Peterson, J. G. (1990). Successful aging in a post-retired society. In P. B. Baltes & M. M. Baltes (Eds.), *Successful aging: Perspectives from the behavioral sciences* pp. 50–93. New York: Cambridge University Press.

Feifel, H., & Strack, S. (1989). Coping with conflict situations: Middle-aged and elderly men. *Psychology and Aging, 4*(1), 26–33.

Field, D., & Millsap, R. E. (1991). Personality in advanced old age: Continuity or change. *Journal of Gerontology: Psychological Sciences, 46*, P299–P308.

Folkman, S., Lazarus, R. S., Pimley, S., & Novacek, I. (1987). Age differences in stress and coping processes. *Psychology and Aging, 2*, 171–184.

Freeman, M. (1993). *Rewriting the self: History, memory, narrative.* London: Routledge.

Gatz, M., & Karel, M. J. (1993). Individual change in perceived control over 20 years. *International Journal of Behavioral Development, 16*, 305–322.

George, L. K. (1980). *Role transitions in later life.* Monterey, CA: Brooks/Cole.

George, L. K., & Siegler, I. C. (1982). Stress and coping in later life. *Educational Horizons, 60*, 147–154.

Gergen, K. (1991). *The saturated self: Dilemmas of identity in contemporary life.* New York: Basic Books.

Gergen, K. (1995). Beyond narrative: Biography in therapy. In J. E. Birren, G. Kenyon, J.-E. Ruth, J. J. F. Schroots, & T. Svensson (Eds.), *Aging and biography: Explorations in adult development* (pp. 205–223). New York: Springer.

Gutmann, D. (1977). The cross-cultural perspective: Notes toward a comparative psychology of aging. In J. E. Birren & K. W. Schaie (Eds.), *Handbook of the psychology of aging* (pp. 302–326). New York: Van Nostrand-Reinhold.

Haan, N. (1977). *Coping and defending: Process of self-environment organization.* New York: Academic Press.

Hagberg, B. (1995). The individual's life history as a formative experience to ageing. In B. Haight & J. Webster (Eds.), *The art and science of reminiscing: Theory, research, methods and application.* Washington, DC: Taylor & Francis.

Haight, B. K., Coleman, P., & Lord, K. (1995). The linchpins of a successful life review: Structure, evaluation and individuality. In B. K. Haight & J. Webster (Eds.), *The art and science of reminiscing: Theory, research, methods and applications.* Washington, DC: Taylor & Francis.

Heidrich, S. M., & Ryff, C. D. (1993). The role of social comparisons processes in the psychological adaptation of elderly adults. *Journal of Gerontology: Psychological Sciences, 48*, P127–P136.

Holahan, C. K. (1988). Relations of life goals at age 70 to activity participation and health and psychological well-being among Terman's gifted men and women. *Psychology and Aging, 3*, 268–291.

Holahan, C. K., & Moos, R. H. (1987). Personal and contextual determinants of coping strategies. *Journal of Personality and Social Psychology, 52*, 946–955.

Holmes, T., & Rahe, R. (1967). The social readjustment scale. *Journal of Psychosomatic Research, 14*, 213–218.

Holstein, B. E., Due, P., Holst, E., & Almind, G. (1992, June). *Elderly people's coping with strainful events.* Paper presented at the 11th Scandinavian Congress of Gerontology, Odense, Denmark.

James, W. (1890). *Principles of psychology.* New York: Holt.

Johnson, C. L. (1993, November). *Personal meanings and long-term survivorship.* Paper presented at the meeting of the Gerontological Society of America, New Orleans, LA.

Kaufman, S. (1986). *The ageless self: Sources of meaning in late life.* Madison: University of Wisconsin Press.

Keller, M. L., Leventhal, E. A., & Larson, B. (1989). Aging: The lived experience. *International Journal of Aging and Human Development, 29*, 67–82.

Kobasa, S. C., Maddi, S. R., & Kahn, S. (1982). Hardiness and health: A prospective study. *Journal of Personality and Social Psychology, 42*, 168–172.

Kogan, N. (1990). Personality and aging. In J. E.

Birren & K. W. Schaie (Eds.), *Handbook of the psychology of aging* (3rd ed., pp. 330–346). San Diego, CA: Academic Press.

Labouvie-Vief, G., Hakim-Larson, J., & Hobart, C. J. (1987). Age, ego level and life span development of coping and defense processes. *Psychology and Aging, 3,* 286–293.

Landrevill, P., & Vezina, J. (1992). A comparison between daily hassles and major life events as correlates of well-being in older adults. *Canadian Journal on Aging, 2,* 137–149.

Lazarus, R. S., & Folkman, S. (1984). *Stress, appraisal and coping.* New York: Springer.

Leventhal, H., Leventhal, E. A., & Schaefer, P. M. (1992). Vigilant coping and health behavior. In M. G. Ory, R. P. Abeles, & P. D. Lipman (Eds.), *Aging, health and behavior* (pp. 109–140). Newbury Park, CA: Sage.

Lieberman, M. A., & Tobin, S. S. (1983). *The experience of old age: Stress, coping and survival.* New York: Basic Books.

Markus, H. R., & Herzog, R. A. (1991). The role of the self-concept in aging. In K. W. Schaie & M. P. Lawton (Eds.), *Annual review of gerontology and geriatrics* (Vol. 11, pp. 110–143). New York: Springer.

McAdams, D. P. (1990). Unity and purpose in human lives: The emergence of identity as a life story. In A. I. Rabin, R. A. Zucker, R. A. Emmons, & S. Frank (Eds.), *Studying persons and lives* (pp. 148–200). New York: Springer.

McAdams, D. P. (1993). *The stories we live by: Personal myths and the making of the self.* New York: William Morrow.

McAdams, D. P., & de St. Aubin, E. (1992). A theory of generativity and its assessment through self-report, behavioral acts, and narrative themes in autobiography. *Journal of Personality and Social Psychology, 62,* 1003–1015.

McAdams, D. P., de St. Aubin, E., & Logan, R. L. (1993). Generativity among young, midlife, and older adults. *Psychology and Aging, 8,* 221–230.

McCrae, R. R., & Costa, P. T. (1988). Age, personality and the spontaneous self-concept. *Journal of Gerontology: Social Sciences, 43,* S177–S185.

Meeks, S., Carstensen, L., Tamsky, B. F., Wright, T., & Pellegrini, D. (1989). Age differences in coping: Does less mean worse? *International Journal of Aging and Human Development, 28,* 127–140.

Moos, R., & Schaefer, J. A. (1993). Coping resources and processes: Current concepts and measures. In L. Goldberger & S. Breznitz (Eds.), *Handbook of stress: Theoretical and clinical aspects* (2nd ed., pp. 234–257). New York: Free Press.

Munnichs, J. M. A. (1992). Ageing: A kind of autobiography. *European Journal of Gerontology, 1,* 244–250.

Murrell, S. A., Norris, F. H., & Grots, C. (1988). Life events in older adults. In L. H. Cohen (Ed.), *Life events and psychological functioning: Theoretical and methodological issues* (pp. 96–122). Newbury Park, CA: Sage.

Neugarten, B. L. (1977). Personality and aging. In J. E. Birren & K. W. Schaie (Eds.), *Handbook of the psychology of aging* (pp. 626–649). New York: Van Nostrand-Reinhold.

Palmore, E. B., Cleveland, W. P., Nowlin, J. P., Ramm, D., & Siegler, I. C. (1985). Stress and adaptation in later life. *Journal of Gerontology, 34,* 841–851.

Pfeiffer, E. (1977). Psychopathology and social pathology. In J. E. Birren & K. W. Schaie (Eds.), *Handbook of the psychology of aging* (pp. 650–671). New York: Van Nostrand-Reinhold.

Poon, L. W. (Ed.). (1992). The Georgia centenarian study [Special issue]. *International Journal of Aging and Human Development, 34*(1).

Reker, G. T., Peacock, E. S., & Wong, P. T. P. (1987). Meaning and purpose in life and well-being: A life span perspective. *Journal of Gerontology, 42,* 44–49.

Reker, G. T., & Wong, P. T. P. (1988). Aging as an individual process: Toward a theory of personal meaning. In J. E. Birren & V. L. Bengtson (Eds.), *Emergent theories of aging* (pp. 214–246). New York: Springer.

Rosenberg, M. (1979). *Conceiving the self.* New York: Basic Books.

Rott, C., & Thomae, H. (1991). Coping in longitudinal perspective: Findings from the Bonn Longitudinal Study on Aging. *Journal of Cross-Cultural Gerontology, 6,* 23–40.

Ruth, J.-E., & Kenyon, G. (1995). Biography in adult development and aging. In J. E. Birren, G. Kenyon, J.-E. Ruth, J. J. F. Schroots, & T. Svensson (Eds.), *Aging and biography: Explorations in adult development* (pp. 1–20). New York: Springer.

Ruth, J.-E., & Öberg, P. (1992). Expressions of aggression in the life stories of aged women. In K. Björkqvist & P. Niemelä (Eds.), *Of mice and women: Aspects of female aggression* (pp. 133–146). San Diego, CA: Academic Press.

Ruth, J.-E., & Öberg, P. (1995). Ways of life: Old age in life history perspective. In J. E. Birren, G. Kenyon, J.-E. Ruth, J. J. F. Schroots, & T. Svensson (Eds.), *Aging and biography: Explorations in adult development* (pp. 167–186). New York: Springer.

Ryff, C. D. (1989). In the eye of the beholder: Views of psychological well-being among middle-aged and older adults. *Psychology and Aging, 4*, 195–210.

Ryff, C. D. (1991). Possible selves in adulthood and old age: A tale of shifting horizons. *Psychology and Aging, 6*, 286–295.

Ryff, C. D., & Essex, M. J. (1991). Psychological well-being in adulthood and old age: Descriptive markers and explanatory processes. In K. W. Schaie & M. P. Lawton (Eds.), *Annual review of gerontology and geriatrics*, Vol. 11, 144–171. New York: Springer.

Schaie, K. W., & Hertzog, C. (1985). Measurement in the psychology of adulthood and aging. In J. E. Birren & K. W. Schaie (Eds.), *Handbook of the psychology of aging* (pp. 61–92). New York: Van Nostrand-Reinhold.

Schaie, K. W., & Willis, S. (1995). *Adult development and aging* (4th ed.). New York: Harper Collins.

Scheier, M. F., & Carver, C. S. (1987). Dispositional optimism and physical well-being: The influence of generalized outcome expectancies on health. *Journal of Personality, 55*, 169–210.

Sherman, E., & Webb, T. A. (1994). The self as process in late-life reminiscence: Spiritual attributes. *Ageing and Society, 14*, 255–267.

Smith, J., & Baltes, P. B. (1993). Differential psychological ageing: Profiles of the old and very old. *Ageing and Society, 13*, 551–587.

Stone, A. A., Helder, L., & Schneider, M. S. (1988). Coping with stressful events: Coping dimensions and issues. In L. H. Cohen (Ed.), *Life events and psychological functioning: Theoretical and methodological issues* (pp. 182–210). Newbury Park, CA: Sage.

Suutama, T. (1994). Life events, stress and coping of elderly people. In P. Öberg, P. Pohjolainen, & I. Ruoppila (Eds.), *Experiencing aging: Festschrift to J.-E. Ruth* (pp. 198–214). Helsinki: Svenska social-och kommunal högskolan.

Svensson, T. (1995). Competence and quality of lives: Theoretical views of biography. In J. E. Birren, G. Kenyon, J.-E. Ruth, J. J. F. Schroots, & T. Svensson (Eds.), *Aging and biography: Explorations in adult development* (pp. 100–116). New York: Springer.

Thoits, P. A. (1991). Patterns in coping with controllable and uncontrollable events. In E. M. Cummings, A. L. Greene, & K. H. Karraker (Eds.), *Life-span developmental psychology: Perspectives on stress and coping* (pp. 235–258). Hillsdale, NJ: Erlbaum.

Thomae, H. (1990). Stress, satisfaction, competence: Findings from the Bonn longitudinal study of aging. In M. Bergner & S. Finkel (Eds.), *Clinical and scientific psychogeriatrics* (Vol. 1, pp. 117–134). New York: Springer.

Thomae, H. (1992). Emotion and personality. In J. E. Birren, B. Shane, & G. Cohen (Eds.), *Handbook of mental health and aging* (2nd ed., pp. 355–375). San Diego, CA: Academic Press.

Tobin, S. S. (1991). *Personhood in advanced old age: Implications for practice*. New York: Springer.

Tornstam, L. (1992). The quo vadis of gerontology: On the gerontological research paradigm. *Gerontologist, 32*, 318–326.

Tornstam, L. (1994). Gero-transcendence: A theoretical and empirical exploration. In L. E. Thomas & S. A. Eisenhandler (Eds.), *Aging and the religious dimension* (pp. 203–225). Westport, CT: Greenwood.

Vaillant, G. E. (1977). *Adaptation to life*. Boston: Little, Brown.

Whitbourne, S. K. (1985). The psychological construction of the life span. In J. E. Birren & K. W. Schaie (Eds.), *Handbook of the psychology of aging* (2nd ed., pp. 594–618). New York: Van Nostrand-Reinhold.

Whitbourne, S. K. (1986). *The me I know: A study of adult identity*. New York: Springer.

Eighteen

# Aging, Behavior, and Terminal Decline

Stig Berg

## I. Introduction

Developmental aging research has indicated that in the process of aging there are patterns that are related more to distance to death or length of survival than to age per se; these patterns are important for the understanding of individual variations in late life and are of practical consequence for clinical practice. Many studies during the last three decades have revealed a complex picture involving a broad range of behaviors including cognition, personality, and adjustment, as well as different psychosocial variables.

This chapter is intended as a selective review of research relating behavior to different aspects of survival, and especially to what has been termed *terminal decline* and *terminal drop*. The focus is largely on different aspects of cognitive functioning but also on results from studies of personality, perceived health, and social networks in relation to survival. There are in addition a large number of studies relating diseases and functional capacity to survival, but they are not included in this chapter.

Among the earliest prominent investigations within the field of behavior and survival were the studies of terminal decline and terminal drop. The general hypothesis states that changes in many functions are not correlated primarily with chronological age as such but instead are related to distance to death. According to this hypothesis, most people maintain stable or only slightly declining functions into old age, and more marked decline is an indication of impending death.

The terminal decline concept was first developed by Kleemeier (1962), who concluded from the results of a longitudinal analysis of intelligence test scores that there are great individual differences in intelligence test performance in old age and that "these differences may be accounted for to a substantial degree by the presence of terminal drop or decline in performance associated with the death of the subject, but are not directly related to age in the senium" (p. 294). Although many studies have used the terminal decline model, there are different and somewhat unclear concepts used in various reports when analyzing and describing the terminal decline phenomena.

There are two main methodological approaches used in the terminal decline research. One of these can be described as cross-sectional analysis of longitudinal information (Siegler, 1975). Data from one measurement point are divided into two or several groups on the basis of distance from death or survival or nonsurvival through a certain time span. The basic assumption here is that low scores or low functioning in the nonsurviving group are due to a decline related to death. The truth of this assumption can, however, be questioned because the low scores among the nonsurvivors could sometimes be just a lifelong low level of functioning that is related to a short life span and not to a process of decline before death. The cross-sectional terminal decline design is in general the same as what are called *mortality*, *survival*, or *longevity* studies, where individuals are partitioned into groups in relation, for instance, to differences in illnesses, functional capacity, or self-rated health, and the data are then analyzed in survival curves or in multivariate approaches, such as the Cox regression method and other hazard regression survival models (Allison, 1984).

The second type of terminal drop or terminal decline analysis involves longitudinal analysis of longitudinal data. Here changes in the behavior of individuals are followed over time and can then be related to length of survival or distance to death. This type of design can detect a linear or curvilinear decline related to death, whereas a cross-sectional analysis of longitudinal data is a much weaker design that can address only problems of distance to death and its relation to behavioral or other variables.

Palmore and Cleveland (1976) suggested that the term *terminal decline* should be used for a steady linear decline prior to death, and only curvilinear or accelerated decline before death should be called *terminal drop*. In most studies that have been carried out, terminal decline and terminal drop have been used without any consideration of the problem of linear or curvilinear development as two separate aspects.

In this chapter the term *terminal decline* is used for both more general cross-sectional longitudinal analysis and for longitudinal analysis of changes prior to death in longitudinal studies. *Terminal drop* will, in accordance with Palmore and Cleveland's (1976) suggestion, be reserved for a curvilinear decline related to death. In those studies where the cross-sectional longitudinal methods are called *longevity* or *survival analysis*, those terms have been kept here.

There are different opinions among researchers concerning how long before death the terminal decline pattern can be observed. An important related question is whether terminal decline is in fact a specific phenomenon seen only in selected variables, or whether it is a more pervasive aspect of aging related to vitality in general.

Studies of behavior and mortality can be divided into two main streams. Cognitive functioning and personality have traditionally been analyzed within a conceptual framework of terminal decline and terminal drop, whereas more social-psychological domains like social networks and perceived health have been studied with multivariate survival analysis. There has also been a change over time in the approach to the study of death and behavior. The terminal decline and terminal drop methods were most frequently used up to the 1980s, whereas the broad multivariate survival models are now more predominant. The early crude cross-sectional terminal decline designs have been superseded by the more sophisticated survival analysis models.

## II. Cognitive Functioning

### A. Intelligence

The concepts of terminal decline and terminal drop have their origins in studies of intellectual functioning in middle and old age. The terminal decline and terminal drop phenomenon was used in the early studies as an explanation for the frequently observed discrepancies in cognitive test scores between cross-sectional and longitudinal studies; that is, analysis revealed a clear decline in intelligence test scores with increasing age in the cross-sectional designs but usually a more stable level of functioning in longitudinal studies. The decrement in the cross-sectional scores, according to the terminal decline hypothesis, can be explained by the greater proportion of subjects who had poor test scores due to being in a terminal phase rather than due to aging itself. The same kind of logic also explains the dip that can be seen at the last measurement point in many longitudinal studies. Since the first study was published (Kleemeier, 1962), there have been at least 20 studies that have reported on terminal decline and terminal drop in intellectual abilities.

Kleemeier's (1962) sample was made up of 70 men who lived in an institution for the aged. After 12 years about half of them had died; the mean age at the last testing point was 79 years among both the survivors and nonsurvivors. They had been tested with the Wechsler-Bellevue intelligence test battery two or more times during the follow-up period, and there was no change from the group's test performance at the start of the study. Because the period of time between successive tests was different for each subject, a mean annual rate of change was calculated for each individual. A significant decline in the change scores among the nonsurvivors, compared to survivors, was found only in the performance part of the test battery.

There were 13 subjects who had been tested four times. Four of them had died shortly after the last testing and their curves were characterized by a marked decline compared to the curves for the survivors. For only two of the nonsurvivors, however, the curves can be said to be examples of terminal drop, that is, a curvilinear decline. It was emphasized that the results were conservative estimates of terminal decline, as some of the survivors were also approaching death, and in fact died within a relatively short time after the arbitrary date chosen for the analysis.

Another early investigation of the terminal decline phenomenon used information from the New York State Psychiatric Institute Study of Aging, which started in 1946. From a 12-year longitudinal follow-up of twin pairs, Jarvik and Falek (1963) analyzed survival 5 years after the last test session in relation to stability or decline during earlier measurement points. They found a positive relationship between 5-year survival and stability scores on Vocabulary, Digit Symbol, and Similarities from the Wechsler-Bellevue Intelligence test battery. Individuals who showed a critical loss on two or three tests had higher mortality than subjects with loss in only one or none of the tests. A special formula for the calculation of the annual rate of decline was used in order to define stability and critical loss. A yearly decrement of 10% on Similarities, 2% on Digit Symbols, and any decline on Vocabulary were defined as a critical loss, and decline less than these was regarded as stability.

Relatively few studies have correctly tried to address the problem of terminal drop, that is, by a longitudinal analysis of curvilinear decline related to distance to death. One such example is the research of Palmore and Cleveland (1976), who in an analysis based on the Duke Longitudinal Study reported a large aging decline and a small but significant linear terminal decline, but practically no terminal drop in the intelligence test scores. Similar results have been obtained in the Bonn Longitudinal Study of Aging (Lehr, Schmitz-Scherzer, & Zimmerman, 1987; Schmitz-Scherzer, 1987). In this study, clear differences were found in Wechsler test scores between survivors and nonsurvivors, but few signs of a terminal drop except during the year of death itself, when a decisive decline was observed.

I reported from the Gothenburg Longitudinal Study a relationship between distance to death and vocabulary and inductive reasoning test scores during an 11-year follow-up (Berg, 1987). There was a tendency toward a terminal drop pattern, but it was relatively weak because the study had only three measurement points (see Figure 1). This study, however, differs from most others: It included 280 subjects, all 70 years old when the study started, which means that there is no confounding effect from age differences among the subjects, as in many other terminal decline studies.

It is difficult to find clear terminal drop patterns in studies in mainly noninstitutionalized populations over a long time span. It is, perhaps, during a near-death stage that a more pronounced terminal drop pattern can first be seen, as a few studies suggest. A small group of institutionalized persons were regularly tested during a 30-month period with brief performance tasks like the Bender-Gestalt test and the Draw-A-Person Test (Lieberman, 1965). It was found that those who died less than 3 months after the last measurement occasion had more or less curvilinear declines in several psychological tests, whereas those who survived a year or more did not show that form. The results indicate that the changes that preceded death could be viewed as a lessened ability to cope adequately with environmental demands because of a lowered ability to integrate stimuli. Schmitz-Scherzer (1987) maintained that more comprehensive drops in individual functioning can be found only during the last year before death and that these changes should be interpreted in the context of the psychosocial components of the terminal stage.

## B. Memory

There are only a few studies that have specifically analyzed memory in relation to survival. In some of the investigations that have used the Wechsler intelligence test battery, the Digit Span subtest has been reported separately. The test is usually seen as an indicator of immediate memory and is simply the longest sequence of digits that the subject can repeat in the same and reversed order immediately following presentation.

Jarvik and Falek (1963) found no significant relationship between the annual rate of decline in the Digit Span tests and survival or nonsurvival. In contrast to this, a terminal decline effect was found in the Gothenburg Longitudinal Study (Johansson & Berg, 1989), both for the forward and backward versions of the test. The investigation included four groups, all 70 years old when the study started. The results demonstrated a typical terminal decline pattern in which the survivors showed a superior performance and the decline in nonsurvivors emerged several years prior to death. There was also a tendency to a terminal drop in the group that was measured between the ages of 70 and 79 and then died before 85, compared to those who were alive at 85. (These results are shown in Figure 2.) Comparisons in this study between participants and retest-resisters suggest that the stability in the survivors was not merely an artifact of selective attrition or an underestimation of developmental change. The discrepancy with Jarvik and Falek's study might be due to their relatively small sample size and wide age range.

Figure 1 (A) The relation between survival and scores on an intelligence test of verbal meaning. The Gothenburg Longitudinal Study. (B) The relation between survival and scores on an intelligence test of inductive reasoning. The Gothenburg Longitudinal Study. (From "Intelligence and Terminal Decline," by S. Berg, 1987. In G. L. Maddox and E. W. Busse (Eds.), *Aging: The Universal Experience* (pp. 414–415), New York: Springer Publishing Company. Copyright 1987 by Springer Publishing Company, Inc., New York 10012. Used by permission.)

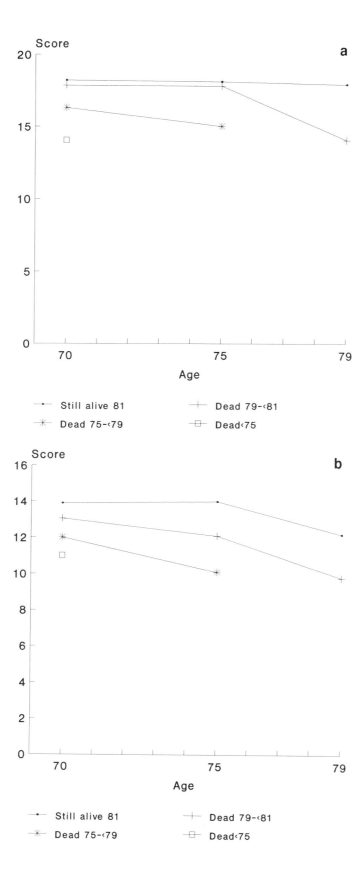

The relationship between distance to death and memory has been studied in the Duke First Longitudinal Study (Siegler, McCarty, & Logue, 1982). Logical memory and paired associates subtests in the Wechsler Memory Scale were combined into a memory score called *verbal memory*. In addition, the Visual Reproduction subtest was used. The subjects were categorized into three groups on the basis of distance to death: individuals who died within 7 years of testing, those who died between 8 and 13 years of testing, and those who were alive 14 years or longer after the testing. The results indicated that distance to death was significantly related to the test scores both for the verbal memory composite and the Visual Reproduction Test. In a study using a composite score based on the Wechsler Memory Scale (Deeg, Hofman, & van Zonneveld, 1990) it was found that the rate of decline during an 8-year period was strongly associated with survival. Thus, it seems that the memory component of cognitive functioning does not differ from the general results obtained in the intelligence and survival studies.

## C. Age and Survival

In the terminal decline literature there has been some discussion of whether the relationship between survival and cognitive test scores is stronger among the middle-aged and young-old than for those in the old-old age group. Riegel and Riegel (1972) suggested that death at higher ages is more random and that psychological differences between survivors and nonsurvivors is less marked, whereas death among the young-old strikes individuals who clearly are psychologically different from the survivors. In line with this are the data

from the New York State Psychiatric twin study, in which Jarvik and Falek (1963) found a critical loss related to survival when most of the twins were in the young-old age group, but not when they were old-old (Steuer, LaRue, Blum, & Jarvik, 1981).

There are, however, a number of studies that contradict the suggestion of Riegel and Riegel and the data in Steuer et al. For example, in a 2-year follow-up of a sample of 68-year-old males, no differences were found in cognitive test scores when those who had died were compared with the survivors (Steen, Hagberg, Johnson, & Steen, 1987). Deeg et al. (1990) could prove terminal decline among individuals at age 70 and over but not in a group between age 65 and 69. In the Gothenburg Longitudinal Study the terminal decline patterns are seen well into the eighth decade (Berg, 1992; Johansson & Berg, 1989).

The results relating terminal decline and age are conflicting, and the discrepancies might be due to differences in the sampling procedures of the different studies. The number of deceased is also relatively low in several of the studies; for example, in the New York twin study 12 out of 22 had died, and even if the sample is large, as in some studies, the proportion of nonsurvivors can be relatively small. The general impression, however, from the vast literature on cognition and survival, is that the terminal decline pattern can be found over a large age range among both the young-old and the old-old.

A special problem in many studies, especially the early investigations, is that they have not controlled for age. Sometimes age differences between survivors and nonsurvivors are not accounted for, or the age groupings are very wide. In order to control for age more effectively in studies that try to find predictors of longevity, Pal-

**Figure 2** Performance of the digit span test in relation to survival. (A) Forward digit span; (B) backward digit span. The Gothenburg Longitudinal Study. (Data from Johansson and Berg, 1989.)

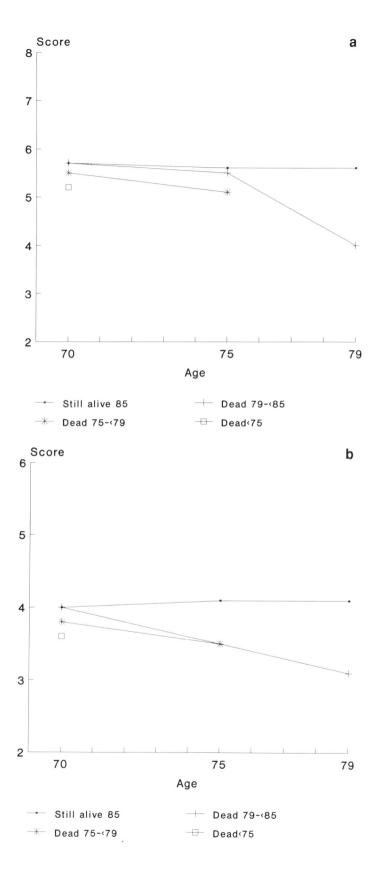

more (1969) suggested a parameter called *longevity quotient* or later called *longevity difference* (Palmore, 1982). It consists of the observed number of years lived after examination, divided by the expected number of years that would be remaining after examination according to appropriate actuarial life expectancy tables. The advantage of the longevity difference is that in survival studies it becomes possible to control for confounding effects on longevity from demographic characteristics such as women's lower mortality and the increased risk of death with age.

### D. Global or Specific Predictors of Survival

It is often stated in the reports of survival and cognition that terminal drop and terminal decline involve only selected abilities rather than global intellectual functioning. There is, however, conflicting evidence, as some studies give support to the hypothesis that terminal decline is seen only in verbal abilities, and others show that it is seen only in fluid abilities; still other studies demonstrate a relation of terminal decline to both fluid and crystallized functions. Birren (1968), in a 5-year follow-up of individuals in very good health at the study's outset, reported that differences between survivors and nonsurvivors were primarily seen in verbal information skills. In a later 11-year follow-up (Granick, 1971) it was concluded that both low performance scores and low verbal scores were related to nonsurvival, although the verbal scores seemed to have a somewhat better power of differentiation. A study of independently living volunteers from an organization of retired persons (White & Cunningham, 1988) showed that survival was related only to vocabulary test scores and only for those who died at age 70 or earlier.

Others, however, have found the opposite results. Savage, Britton, Bolton, and Hall (1973), in their study from Newcastle upon Tyne, found that subtests influenced by fluid intelligence differentiated most between survival or nonsurvival. Botwinick, West, and Storandt (1978) found that low scores on psychomotor tests predicted death, whereas subtests included in the verbal part of the Wechsler scale showed no relation to terminal decline. It is noteworthy that even in the first terminal decline study (Kleemeier, 1962) it was only the performance scores that were predictive of survival. In a large number of both verbal and performance studies, however, tests of crystallized and fluid functions have been found to be related to survival (e.g., Berg, 1987; Palmore, 1982; Siegler et al., 1982).

It is still difficult to say if terminal decline is a global or specific cognitive phenomenon, but the contradictory evidence is probably due to differences in methodology, health profiles, age, gender, and so on. It is remarkable that the health status of the subjects in nearly all of the studies is not reported and usually just perfunctorily discussed.

### E. How Long Is the Predictive Period?

It is nearly an axiom in the description of the terminal decline phenomenon that death is preceded by a decrease in cognitive functioning over roughly a 5-year period before death. A look into the different studies, however, reveals that there are very great variations in the length of time before death that cognitive decline can be detected. Reimanis and Green (1971) reported that males with a mean age of 68 years living in a Veterans Administration domiciliary who died within 1 year after the last test showed greater intellectual decrement compared to subjects who died later or were still living. Similar results were presented by White and Cunningham (1988) who found an effect only for those who died at age 70 or less and within 2 years of testing, but there are also studies that report terminal decline patterns for 10 or more years (Berg, 1987; Siegler et al., 1982).

## III. Adjustment and Survival

### A. Personality

According to a number of aging and personality studies, especially the trait-oriented longitudinal investigations, there is a predominant pattern of stability in personality with increasing age (Field, 1991). A deviation from this stable pattern might therefore be an indication of individuals' psychosocial problems, declining health, or impending death. Compared to the cognitive domain, however, there are only a few studies that relate personality and survival.

In a personality inventory study based on Murray's theory of psychogenic needs (Nilsson & Persson, 1984), it was found that men who died before the age of 79 had, when they were tested at age 70, higher scores on the defense of status subscale and lower scores on the exhibition subscale. In other words, men who tended to have low self-evaluation, show sensitivity to the opinions of others, refrain from actions in order to avoid failures, defend mistakes, and keep in the background had increased mortality. Field and Schaie (1985) reported similar results from the Berkeley Older Generation Study. Based on interviewers' ratings of people aged 59–81, it was found that those persons who died during a 12-year follow-up were more withdrawn than those who survived.

Cognitive personality style and terminal decline has in a very unusual way been examined by Suedfeld and Piedrahita (1984). Their research material consists of published letters written during the last 10 years of life by 18 eminent individuals, among them Sigmund Freud, Napoleon, Robert Browning, Queen Victoria, and Franz Liszt. Paragraphs from the letters were sampled and scored for integrative complexity, which is a measure that assesses the degree to which individuals process information in complex or simple ways. Low scores on this dimension mean rigid, close-ended, and crude differentiations among stimuli in the cognitive processes, whereas high scores mean that the subjects' information processing is more open-ended, flexible, and differentiated. Individuals were also divided into two groups, those who died of protracted illness or "old age" and those who died suddenly. The sudden death group included accidents, death within a month after the contraction of an ailment, or death after a discrete event such as a heart attack. The results showed that the protracted group on average had a decline in complexity scores 5 years before death, but decline was seen only in the year immediately prior to death among those who died suddenly. There was, however, no correlation between age and the cognitive style and complexity measure.

A few studies do report significant correlations between rigidity scales and survival. Riegel, Riegel, and Meyer (1967) showed that high scores on measures of rigidity and dogmatism, especially in their middle-aged and young-old groups (55–64), were predictors of death. From the Bonn Longitudinal Study using the same scale it has been reported that nonsurviving men showed more rigidity and more intolerance than survivors (Lehr et al., 1987).

Cognitive style has been investigated in a Swedish longitudinal study using the Rod-and-Frame Test, which measures the field independence–dependence dimension (Hagberg, Samuelsson, Lindberg, & Dehlin, 1991). The test was administered during every second year during a 6-year period when the subjects were between the ages of 67 and 73. At each measurement point a series of 20 consecutive observations was obtained in order to emphasize cognitive style. Stability in the test scores predicted survival to age 83, whereas destabilization was related to nonsurvival during the same period. The general trend in the destabilization was a move from field independence to field dependence. It is noteworthy that although the Rod-and-Frame Test scores were related to survival at the age of 67, they did not predict survival up to age 83. Thus the stability in the test scores was a more important indicator of survival than whether a person was field dependent or independent.

The results from studies on personality and survival are limited and often vague. Significant correlates have been found for only a few personality dimensions, often related to different aspects of psychic energy or to the rigidity–flexibility dimension. Usually the investigations have not been specifically designed to test a terminal decline or survival hypothesis but are parts of wider studies on aging. There are also very large differences in personality assessment methods used in the various investigations, and the analyses are to a great extent without theoretical depth. One plausible hypothesis is that the relations found between survival and personality traits are to a large degree just reflecting cognitive functioning. The connections between nonsurvival and decline in psychic energy and flexibility are probably also a reflection of health problems.

## B. Social Networks and Social Support

Social networks and social support are, according to a number of studies, related to health and survival, but there are also some studies that have not been able to demonstrate such a connection. As an example, data from the Alameda County study showed that social ties are significant predictors of survival after controlling for demographic and health factors (Seeman, Kaplan, Knudsen, Cohen, & Guralnik, 1987). The importance of different types of social ties for survival varied across age groups; for example, ties with friends and relatives assumed greater sig-

nificance for those aged 60 and older, whereas marital status was important for survival only for those less than 60 years old. After a review of five major studies, House, Landis, and Umberson (1988) concluded that prospective studies, which control for baseline health status, consistently show a higher mortality rate among individuals with a low quantity, and sometimes a low quality, of social relationships.

Widowhood seems to be related to increased mortality when comparing widows to the general population of the same age, especially for men (Bowling, 1987). For instance, using 1968–1978 census data from Sweden for adults ages 50–90, Mellström, Nilsson, Odén, Rundgren, and Svanborg (1982) tested mortality following loss of spouse. They reported excess mortality among both women and men: At 3 months the excess was 22% for women and 48% for men, with a trend toward increased risk persisting up to 11 years, especially for men. However, this pattern is not unchallenged insofar as some studies do not reveal excess mortality among the bereaved (Murrell, Himmelfarb, & Phifer, 1988). According to one study, close intergenerational relations with adult children seem to buffer elevated mortality risks associated with becoming widowed (Silverstein & Bengtson, 1991).

The relationships between social networks and survival have been questioned in some studies. In a report of data from a longitudinal study of the elderly in rural North Wales (Shahtahmasebi, Davies, & Wenger, 1992), it was concluded after multivariate analyses that many of the relationships were spurious and that there is no prima facie evidence that survival is affected by social networks or quality-of-life factors. Similar results have also been found in studies from Denmark (Olsen, Olsen, Gunner-Svensson, & Waldström, 1991) and Finland (Jylhä & Aro, 1989).

There is no obvious explanation of why some studies find relationships between social networks and social support and mortality, whereas other investigations do not. The studies are of good quality and quite similar in methodology; the explanation might be that this kind of relation is sensitive to differences in populations, baseline age, and the length of the follow-up period. In a short-term perspective, for example, it might be that there is a high frequency of social contacts during a short illness period before death, whereas isolation and lack of social support are more related to nonsurvival in the long run.

There have also been some proposals regarding explanation of the association between social relationships and survival. Sabin (1993), in summarizing a number of studies, suggested that social interaction may strengthen the endocrine system and the immune system, enhancing the defense against disease and environmental hazards. Other explanations have been that belonging to a social network provides access to better health information and that it is easier to obtain vital help and support in addition to assistance from the health-care system. Social networks might also be protective against different kinds of stressful events through psychological mechanisms such as feelings of belonging and intimacy. These views, however, are only tentative and not proven, and there is a lack of studies that show the mechanisms behind the relationship between social networks and mortality more definitively. Unfortunately, social network studies that have a longitudinal terminal decline design are also scant.

## C. Perceived Health

Self-rated or perceived health has been included in many of the major epidemiological and longitudinal health surveys. It is usually measured in a simple, straightforward fashion using a question such as "At the present time, how would you rate your health?" or sometimes with an age-related question like "Compared to other people in your own age would you say that your health is . . . ?" and with predetermined response alternatives such as, "excellent, good, fair, poor, and bad." Research has demonstrated that such feelings or perceptions are an important component of overall health, but also that these very simple questions have complex relations with other aspects of physical and psychological functioning. For instance, self-rated health is more strongly associated with recovery of physical function after a serious medical event (Wilcox & Kasl, 1992) and life satisfaction and well-being (Larsson, 1978) than are objective measures of health.

A number of large epidemiological surveys have found that self-rated health is an important predictor of survival in old age. Mossey and Shapiro (1982), in a 6-year follow-up of noninstitutionalized elderly Canadians, reported that individuals who assessed their health to be poor were much more likely to die than individuals who assessed their health as excellent. In a study based on the Yale Health and Aging Project, Idler and Kasl (1991) in a 4-year follow-up study showed that self-evaluations of health status predicted mortality above and beyond the contribution to prediction made by a number of indices of physical disability, prescience of health problems, and biological or lifestyle factors.

Similar results have also been presented in other studies (Idler & Angel, 1990; Idler, Kasl, & Lemke, 1990; Kaplan, Barell, & Lusky, 1988; Kaplan & Camacho, 1983; Wolinsky & Johnson, 1992). A consistent finding in all these studies is that self-rating represents a distinct aspect of health that has significant implications for survival independent of a number of other factors.

Self-evaluated health seems to be both a short-term and a long-term predictor of mortality. There have been reports of significant associations between survival and self-perception of health during follow-up periods of 4 years (Wolinsky & Johnson,

1992), 9 years (Kaplan & Camacho, 1983), and 12 years (Idler & Angel, 1990).

Nearly all studies of self-rated health report that the relation with mortality is higher among men than among women; the odds ratios are sometimes doubled for men compared to women. For instance, Idler and Kasl (1991) showed that men whose perception of their health state was poor were more than six times more likely to die than those who perceived their health as excellent. For the women who rated their health as poor, the risk of nonsurvival was around three times higher.

A problem in several of the studies of self-rated health and survival is the lack of independent health indicators, and it is sometimes not clear whether objective health status and functional impairment have been controlled for. The fact is that in most of the studies diagnoses and other health data are based on reports by the respondents themselves. There are, however, a few studies that have used independent assessments of health; for example, Idler and Angel (1990) reported that when comprehensive clinical and laboratory data were available, self-rated health was an independent predictor of survival only among middle-aged men but not among women or elderly men. It seems that the more comprehensive medical and functional data are controlled for, the weaker is the independent predictive power of perceived health for survival.

A study including separate health examinations as well as medications (Pijls, Feskens, & Kromhout, 1993) showed an independent effect of self-rated health on all-cause and cancer mortality, but not on death related to cardiovascular disease. This finding suggests that data should be analyzed more often in relation to cause-specific mortality to determine if the net effect of perceived health on mortality differs by disease.

Why is such a "soft" variable like self-rated health a fairly good predictor of survival? Very little information exists on the underlying mechanisms that determine the relationship. In their review Idler and Kasl (1991) suggested three possible explanations: (a) a number of the earlier studies have methodological shortcomings, including inadequate controls for physical health and other variables, and the use of nonrandom samples resulted in spurious relations; (b) different psychosocial variables that influence mortality account for the association between self-rated health and mortality; and (c) self-evaluations of health status have a direct and independent effect of their own on survival. An addition to the last statement might be that the self-ratings by themselves do not affect mortality, but self-perceived health could be seen as a unique summary and conclusion of an individual's total beliefs and information on his or her health, a kind of information that cannot be obtained by other means. Many people apparently know when they are entering their years of more general decline and, eventually, their terminal drop.

## IV. Conclusions

The terminal decline studies have a long tradition in gerontological psychology and they display a broad analysis of development, aging, and death. For years, psychological researchers have used methods of analysis of individual differences that help to sort out clusters of related variables leading to the identification of complex patterns in aging and vitality. It is also remarkable how powerful behavioral variables are in such a complex biological field as the study of aging and vitality.

A general conclusion from terminal decline and survival investigations is that relationships do exist between distance to death and a wide range of behavioral variables. It is also clear that these relationships are somewhat elusive, as there are a number of studies that fail to detect this pattern. The contradictory findings are probably due to methodological differ-ences among various studies, both within the same main area of behavior and among different main areas. The populations stud-ied vary considerably, and there are large differences in age ranges and baseline age, thus complicating analyses and compari-sons. The inconsistency in results may also be due to different design models or the use of different statistical methods.

An interesting observation from many of the survival and terminal decline stud-ies is that decrements or low scores in re-markably simple behavior variables can predict survival or nonsurvival for 5, 10, or even more years. Examples of such vari-ables are single self-rated health questions and the simple Digit Span test measuring immediate memory.

Some of the inconsistency in results in studies of behavior and mortality might be caused by a confusion of long-term and short-term changes. Terminal drop could be seen mainly as a short-term effect close-ly related to just a short time before death, whereas terminal decline and other mortality-related mechanisms might in-volve long-term developmental changes caused by both genetic and environmental influences during life.

The correlates of survival in the later part of life are of special interest as many industrialized countries approach a situa-tion where an overwhelming proportion of a cohort will reach old age. It could be ar-gued that a survival or terminal decline analysis should always be included in de-velopmental studies, especially among older adults in order to get a more compre-hensive understanding of the aging pro-cess. After all, illness or death is nothing abnormal in late life! A direct practical consequence of terminal decline is that it can be mistaken for dementia or some oth-er kind of psychological dysfunction. A better awareness of the terminal decline patterns on an individual level might be important for early detection of people at risk.

Most studies do not discuss possible mechanisms behind the relationship be-tween behavior variables and survival or do so only in a perfunctory or speculative way. One such mechanism is, obviously, basic biological aging factors and health, but in the reports from the different surviv-al and terminal decline studies there has been very little discussion about the roles of general health and specific illnesses. Many studies do not include health vari-ables or use only various self-reports on health, and do not have independent health assessments.

It could also be asked if there are differ-ent subtypes of behavioral terminal de-cline and terminal drop. One type, for ex-ample, could be related more to various disease processes, whereas another type could be part of a more general biological system breakdown—a breakdown due to basic aging processes resulting in de-creased organ reserve capacity and failure in homeostatic systems. The disease-related terminal decline might be more typical among the young-old, whereas the breakdown type might be more frequent among the old-old.

It is important for future studies to look more specifically into both the question of mechanisms and the role of different dis-eases. Until now there is no study that has been specifically designed to analyze the relationship between behavior and dis-tance to death. The interpretations of ter-minal decline and terminal drop might also be improved if some studies had a qualitative aspect.

Studies using a broad range of variables indicate, however, that there are large in-tercorrelations among biological, psycho-logical, and social variables. There is no one specific set of variables that are the overall best predictors of survival, and it seems that correlated variables can be ex-changed without much loss of power in the prediction. It is probably futile to search for the specific predictor or predic-tors of survival, and it is better to see them as indicators of general survival patterns or what could be called *vitality*.

## References

Allison, P. D. (1984). *Event history analysis: Regression for longitudinal event data.* Beverly Hills, CA: Sage.

Berg, S. (1987). Intelligence and terminal decline. In G. L. Maddox & E. W. Busse (Eds.), *Aging: The universal human experience* (pp. 411–416). New York: Springer.

Berg, S. (1992). Åldrande, sjukdom och intelligens: Resultat från H70–undersökningen. *Gerontologia, 6,* 22–31.

Birren, J. E. (1968). Increments and decrements in the intellectual status of the aged. *Psychiatric Research Reports, 23,* 207–214.

Botwinick, J., West, R., & Storandt, M. (1978). Predicting death from behavioral test performance. *Journal of Gerontology, 33,* 755–762.

Bowling, A. (1987). Mortality after bereavement: A review of the literature on survival periods and factors affecting survival. *Social Science Medicine, 24,* 117–124.

Deeg, J. H., Hofman, A., & van Zonneveld, R. J. (1990). The association between change in cognitive function and longevity in Dutch elderly. *American Journal of Epidemiology, 132,* 973–982.

Field, D. (1991). Continuity and change in personality in old age—Evidence from five longitudinal studies: Introduction to a special issue. *Journal of Gerontology: Psychological Sciences, 46,* P271–P274.

Field D., & Schaie, K. W. (1985, November). *Personal and social indicators of survivorship in old-old age in the Berkeley older generation study.* Paper presented at the meeting of the Gerontological Society of America, New Orleans, LA.

Granick, S. (1971). Cognitive aspects of longevity. In E. Palmore & F. C. Jeffers (Eds.), *Prediction of life span* (109–122). Lexington, MA: Heath Lexington Books.

Hagberg, B., Samuelsson, G., Lindberg, B., & Dehlin, O. (1991). Stability and change of personality in old age and its relation to survival. *Journal of Gerontology: Psychological Sciences, 46,* P285–P291.

House, J. S., Landis, K. R., & Umberson, D. (1988). Social relationships and health. *Science, 241,* 540–545.

Idler, E. L., & Angel, R. (1990). Self-rated health and mortality in the NHANES-I epidemiologic follow-up study. *American Journal of Public Health, 80,* 446–452.

Idler, E. L., & Kasl, S. (1991). Health perceptions and survival: Do global evaluations of health status really predict mortality? *Journal of Gerontology: Social Sciences, 46,* S55–S65.

Idler, E. L., Kasl, S. V., & Lemke, J. H. (1990). Self-evaluated health and mortality among the elderly in New Haven, Connecticut, and Iowa, and Washington Counties, Iowa, 1982–1986. *American Journal of Epidemiology, 131,* 91–103.

Jarvik, L. F., & Falek, A. (1963). Intellectual stability and survival in the aged. *Journal of Gerontology, 18,* 173–176.

Johansson, B., & Berg, S. (1989). The robustness of the terminal decline phenomenon: Longitudinal data from the Digit-Span memory test. *Journal of Gerontology: Psychological Sciences, 44,* P184–P186.

Jylhä, M., & Aro, S. (1989). Social ties and survival among the elderly in Tampere, Finland. *International Journal of Epidemiology, 18,* 158–164.

Kaplan, G., Barell, V., & Lusky, A. (1988). Subjective state of health and survival in elderly adults. *Journal of Gerontology: Social Sciences, 43,* S114–S120.

Kaplan, G. A., & Camacho, T. (1983). Perceived health and mortality: A nine-year follow-up of the human population laboratory cohort. *American Journal of Epidemiology, 117,* 292–304.

Kleemeier, R. W. (1962). Intellectual changes in the senium. *Proceedings of the American Statistical Association, 1,* 290–295.

Larsson, R. (1978). Thirty years of research on the subjective well-being of older Americans. *Journal of Gerontology, 33,* 109–125.

Lehr, U., Schmitz-Scherzer, R., & Zimmerman, E. J. (1987). Vergleiche von Überlebenden und Verstorbenen in der Bonner Gerontologischen Längsschnittstudie (BOLSA). In U. Lehr & H. Thomae (Eds.), *Formen seelischen Alterns* (pp. 228–249). Stuttgart: Ferdinand Enke Verlag.

Lieberman, M. A. (1965). Psychological correlates of impending death: Some preliminary observations. *Journal of Gerontology, 20,* 181–190.

Mellström, D., Nilsson, Å., Odén, A., Rundgren, Å., & Svanborg, A. (1982). Mortality among the widowed in Sweden. *Scandinavian Journal of Social Medicine, 10*, 33–41.

Mossey, J. M., & Shapiro, J. W. (1982). Self-rated health: A predictor of mortality among the elderly. *American Journal of Public Health, 72*, 800–808.

Murrell, S. A., Himmelfarb, S., & Phifer, J. F. (1988). Effects of bereavement/loss and pre-event status on subsequent physical health in older adults. *International Journal of Aging and Human Development, 27*, 89–107.

Nilsson, L. V., & Persson, G. (1984). Personality changes in the aged: A longitudinal study of psychogenic needs with the CMPS. *Acta Psychiatrica Scandinavica, 69*, 182–189.

Olsen, R. B., Olsen, J., Gunner-Svensson, F., & Waldström, B. (1991). Social networks and longevity: A 14 year follow-up study among elderly in Denmark. *Social Sciences Medicine, 33*, 1189–1195.

Palmore, E. (1969). Physical, mental and social factors in predicting longevity. *Gerontologist, 9*, 103–108.

Palmore, E. (1982). Predictors of the longevity difference. *Gerontologist, 22*, 513–518.

Palmore, E., & Cleveland, W. (1976). Aging, terminal decline, and terminal drop. *Journal of Gerontology, 31*, 76–81.

Pijls, L. J. T., Feskens, E. J., & Kromhout, D. (1993). Self-rated health, mortality and chronic diseases in elderly men: The Zutphen Study, 1985–1990. *American Journal of Epidemiology, 138*, 840–848.

Reimanis, G., & Green, R. F. (1971). Imminence of death and intellectual decrement in the aging. *Developmental Psychology, 5*, 270–272.

Riegel, K. F., & Riegel, R. M. (1972). Development, drop and death. *Developmental Psychology, 6*, 306–319.

Riegel, K. F., Riegel, R. M., & Meyer, G. (1967). *Journal of Personality and Social Psychology, 5*, 342–348.

Sabin, P. E. (1993). Social relationships and mortality among the elderly. *Journal of Applied Gerontology, 12*, 44–60.

Savage, R. D., Britton, P. G., Bolton, N., & Hall, E. H. (1973). *Intellectual functioning in the aged.* London: Methuen.

Schmitz-Scherzer, R. (1987). Zum Konstrukt des "Terminal Decline." In U. Lehr & H. Thomae (Eds.), *Formen seelischen Alterns* (pp. 256–259). Stuttgart: Ferdinand Enke Verlag.

Seeman, T. E., Kaplan, G. A., Knudsen, L., Cohen, R., & Guralnik, A. (1987). Social network ties and mortality among the elderly in the Alameda county study. *American Journal of Epidemiology, 126*, 714–723.

Shahtahmasebi, S., Davies, R., & Wenger, G. C. (1992). A longitudinal analysis of factors related to survival in old age. *Gerontologist, 32*, 404–413.

Siegler, I. C. (1975). The terminal drop hypothesis: Fact or artifact. *Experimental Aging Research, 1*, 169–185.

Siegler, I. C., McCarty, S. M., & Logue, P. E. (1982). Wechsler memory scale scores, selective attrition, and distance from death. *Journal of Gerontology, 37*, 176–181.

Silverstein, M., & Bengtson, V. (1991). Do close parent-child relations reduce the mortality risk of older parents? *Journal of Health and Social Behavior, 32*, 382–395.

Steen, G., Hagberg, B., Johnson, G., & Steen, B. (1987). Cognitive function, cognitive style and life satisfaction in a 68-year-old male population. *Comprehensive Gerontology, B, 1*, 54–61.

Steuer, J., LaRue, A., Blum, J. E., & Jarvik, L. F. (1981). "Critical loss" in the eighth and ninth decades. *Journal of Gerontology, 36*, 211–213.

Suedfeld, P., & Piedrahita, L. E. (1984). Intimations of mortality: Integrative simplification as a precursor of death. *Journal of Personality and Social Psychology, 47*, 848–852.

White, N., & Cunningham, W. R. (1988). Is terminal drop pervasive or specific? *Journal of Gerontology: Psychological Sciences, 43*, P141–P144.

Wilcox, V., & Kasl, S. V. (1992). Self-rated health predicts recovery of physical functioning in older people after hospitalization [Abstract]. *Gerontologist, 32*, 15.

Wolinsky, F. D., & Johnson, R. D. (1992). Perceived health status and mortality among older men and women. *Journal of Gerontology: Social Sciences, 47*, S304–S312.

Nineteen

# Activity, Exercise, and Behavior

Michael J. Stones and Albert Kozma

Physical conduct refers to habitual levels of physical activity. Physical performance, defined as the outcome of coordinated locomotor activity in gross bodily movement or when doing physical work, measures an aspect of competence. This chapter examines the relationship of age to physical conduct, physical competence, and the consequences of activity for physical and psychological performance. The emphases throughout will be on measurement and modeling.

## I. Physical Conduct at Different Age Levels

Epidemiological measures of physical activity include retrospective interviews, retrospective questionnaires, and current time budget diaries (Andersen, Masironi, Rutenfranz, & Seliger, 1978). Although the time spent in physical activity provides one measure of participation, more frequently used indexes combine time with energy cost. Expressions of energy cost include rates of energy expenditure (e.g., kilocalories, kilojoules), oxygen consumption, relative load (e.g., actual to maximal oxygen consumption), multiples of the basal metabolic rate (METs), and changes in the heart rate (Andersen et al., 1978). Cooper (1977) provided popular tables of total energy cost for various durations and intensities of physical activity.

Andersen et al. (1978) cited pre-1970 evidence that the time spent exercising and total energy costs decline with age in both genders. After the twenties and thirties, participation in sport and exercise declines in favor of gentler pursuits, such as gardening and walking. Shephard in 1969 compared then-recent American data on cardiorespiratory fitness with 1938 findings by Robinson to show a decrease in fitness during the intervening 30 years. This decrease seems to relate to generally lower levels of exercising for some decades after World War II.

Post-1980 data from countries including Canada and Japan show more frequent exercising during the past two decades, and particularly by older people. Stephens, Craig, and Ferris (1986) and Kozma, Stones, and Hannah (1991) reported findings from more than 6000 participants in the Canada Fitness Survey of household residents. Harada (1994) included Japanese data on the frequency of persons who participate in ex-

*Handbook of the Psychology of Aging, Fourth Edition*

ercise or sport at least weekly. Both the Canadian and Japanese data show higher exercising by people in their sixties than in their forties and fifties. The number of "inactive" people is low at all ages, although the frequency doubles between the twenties and sixties.

The evidence is incomplete on the reasons why older people continue or cease participation in exercise and athletic pursuits. One approach examines drop-out among elderly exercisers (Shephard, Berridge, Montelpare, Daniel, & Flowers, 1987; Stacey, Kozma, & Stones, 1985). Stacey et al. (1985) found drop-outs from an exercise program for older adults to be relatively unhappy people with high trait anxiety, suggesting the relevance of personality. Other evidence suggests that participants continue because of established habits: People with early life or prior adult experience in athleticism participate in sport and exercise more frequently than people without such experience (Harada, 1994; Kuh & Cooper, 1992). Both athletes and exercisers cite health as a main reason for continued participation (Harada, 1994; Stones, Kozma, & Stones, 1987). However, whereas exercisers also cite such benefits as stress reduction, the athletes obtain enjoyment from activities that test their competence (Gobbi, 1993; Harada, 1994).

## II. Measures and Models of Physical Competence

Physical competence is a broader construct than physical fitness, but encompasses attributes of the latter within its scope (e.g., endurance, flexibility, and strength). At a molar level, competence combines fitness with expertise derived from practice.

### A. Measurement of Physical Competence

Measurement poses problems because of the high between-subject variability in lat-er life. Chodzko-Zajko (1994) stated how difficult it is to obtain tests with adequate discriminatory power over the full range of the physical functioning continuum. Although he recommended as a long-term solution the development of tasks that can discriminate over the full range of functioning, their attainment awaits the future. The existing measures have limited ranges because of concerns about safety and practicality. The three examples that follow illustrate limitations to sensitivity and generalizability.

First, some tasks are beyond the capabilities of frailer subjects. Static balance measures of postural control provide one such example. Performance shows increasing heterogeneity after young adulthood when measured either by the time balanced or the extent of sway (Hellebraun & Braun, 1939; Stones, Kozma, & Hannah, 1990). Many researchers measure the time a subject can balance on one leg (i.e., unipedal balance) (MacCrae, Feltner, & Reinsch, 1994; Stones & Kozma, 1987). Because this test is beyond the capabilities of frail people, they must instead be tested with alternative measures, such as bipedal balance. However, even this task cannot be performed by many frail elderly: Lord, Clark, and Webster (1991) found more than 20% of residents of a hostel to be unable to balance on a compliant surface. Consequently, no single task has sensitively measured the full range of competencies within this cohort.

A second issue concerns the conditions under which different indexes of the same function converge. Chodzko-Zajko (1994) pointed out that laboratory-based exercise stress testing provides a *gold standard* for measuring cardiorespiratory fitness in physically fit people. However, considerations of expense, safety, and practicality have led to the development of indirect tests. Although the indirect tests may measure adequately at younger ages, they can underestimate aerobic power in older people. Warren, Dotson, Nieman, and

Butterworth (1993) examined the possibility that sedentary old people are unaccustomed to the brisk walking required by several indirect tests. They found only a moderate correlation between direct and indirect measures at baseline and following 3-months calisthenics training. However, the correlations were high after a 12-week program ·of brisk walking. These findings show that convergent validity varies with practice on the function measured in indirect testing.

Third, field researchers can monitor performance but cannot necessarily stipulate equivalency in tasks. Throwing performances by veteran athletes provide an example of task variation with age. For authenticating records and for reasons of safety, the weight of the projectile is lower for the older categories (Mundle, 1993). Although a procedure is available that allows correction for variation in projectile weight, this example illustrates task differences with age even among the fittest people in their respective cohorts.

## B. Measures of Physical Competence

The measures in the literature permit classification into four main categories—activities of daily living (ADL), physical fitness, psychophysiological fitness, and measures used in field research.

### 1. ADL Indexes

These indexes measure physical competencies for independent daily living (Fillenbaum, 1984). Because ADL indexes are designed to measure physical competence within frail and dependent populations, they lack discriminatory power above the lower bounds of physical functioning.

### 2. Physical Fitness Measures

The purpose of these measures is to discriminate among physical performance capabilities over wide ranges of age and ability. Typical tests include grip strength,

trunk flexibility, sit-ups, push-ups, and endurance capability (Canada Department of Fitness and Amateur Sport, 1981). A limitation is that they are beyond the capability of many frail old people.

### 3. Psychophysiological Fitness

Several studies have combined psychological and physical function measures within the same index. Although the name originally given to such indexes became known as *functional age* (Heron & Chown, 1967), a more accurate term may be *psychophysiological fitness*.

Recent evidence suggests that some such indexes are reliable and discriminative over a wide range of abilities. Stones and Kozma (1988) found a simple four-function index (combining flexibility, vital capacity, balance, and Digit Symbol) to have an internal consistency of .76, even with age and gender controlled. Reanalysis produced similar findings with a six-function index extracted from data by Heron and Chown (1967). The internal consistency was $\approx$.75 despite age and gender (Stones & Kozma, 1988). Moreover, the four-function index of Stones and Kozma (1988) showed greater sensitivity to the effects of physical activity than any of its component measures in cross-sectional and 1-year longitudinal designs. If physical activity has generalized effects on the brain and body, composite indexes may provide greater discrimination than discrete measures.

### 4. Field Research Indexes

The competence indexes most commonly used in field research derive from occupations and sport. We review performances in competitive sport later in this chapter (Section II.D).

## C. Issues in Modeling

The heterogeneity among older people also presents problems for modeling. Different authors approach this issue in either of two ways. First, a *process* approach distinguishes between age-intrinsic and age-extrinsic factors that affect performance (i.e., the types-of-aging paradigm). Examples include Rowe and Kahn (1987), who differentiated between successful and usual aging, where the former refers to age-intrinsic effects and the latter to non-pathological age-extrinsic effects. Both these types exclude pathology, although usual aging effects may subsequently produce pathology. Birren and Cunningham (1985) extended the typology by differentiating secondary aging (i.e., pathology-related) from the tertiary changes frequently preceding death. Investigations compatible with this paradigm include studies of lifestyle and illness that contribute to age-extrinsic effects.

Second, a *categorical* approach distinguishes among categories of people rather than types of process. Spirduso (1994) provided a five-way classification comprising physically elite, fit, independent, frail, and dependent persons. The deployment of this paradigm includes the study of elderly subpopulations, particularly people at risk.

Both paradigms distinguish the elite from the normal, and the normal from the diseased. However, these distinctions are not without confounding. The following points are germane: Elite status combines talent with training but does not preclude pathology; some disease processes seem continuous with normal aging but show augmentation due to lifestyle effects. A clarification follows.

First, elite performers have two essential attributes: They are gifted people who overpractice their skills. Although some nonelite people may possess equivalent natural gifts, they can develop expertise only if given the opportunity and motivation to practice. Consequently, the elite include persons selected from among the talented, but it is practice that sets them apart. However, an elite performer need not be healthy, as long as the disease process does not interfere with the expression of skill. An example from sport is Evander Holyfield, the recently deposed world heavyweight boxing champion, reputedly diagnosed with a long-standing cardiac disorder.

Second, usual age change and pathology sometimes appear continuous. Osteoporosis is a pathology and public health concern costing billions of dollars yearly. Bone loss with age is a consistent finding in cross-sectional research, with greater losses in physically inactive men and women (Going, Williams, Lohman, & Hewitt, 1994). Because some controlled interventions show bone accretion after a few months of weight bearing or resistance exercise, a continuity between osteoporotic change and behavioral change seems probable. Consequently, the distinction between usual and secondary aging may sometimes be more a matter of severity of consequence than kind of process.

## D. Modeling Elite Physical Performances

Elite physical performers are those at the pinnacle of their respective skills. They are talented and overpracticed, with any ongoing pathology unlikely to have a significant impact on performance. Competitive sports that compile age–class records include track and field and swimming. These field data, collected with a care and rigor rivaling that of laboratory conditions, are an invaluable resource for the gerontologist.

Stones and Kozma (1986) evaluated athletic records in relation to three models described up to that time. The models propose age deterioration to be greater in those events requiring higher power, higher endurance, or a higher power-by-endurance interaction. It was the latter model, named using the acronym *POrPA* (power output relative to power available), that received most support. The following describes its components.

First, movements that tap more power involve larger unit displacements of the body. Examples from track and field include larger stride displacements in jumping than in hurdling, in hurdling than in running, and in running than in race walking. Throwing events also use high power, although for projectile propulsion rather than bodily displacement. Of the four competitive swimming strokes, oxygen uptake and tethered motion techniques suggest the peak power cost to be highest for the butterfly followed by the breast-stroke (Astrand & Rodahl, 1977, pp. 586–589).

Second, the available power is not constant but decreases with the period of high effort. Astrand and Rodahl (1977) estimated as follows: If 10 s of maximal performance requires $x$ units of energy, the corresponding expenditures over efforts lasting 1, 4, 10, and 30 min are $.35x$, $.21x$, $.16x$, and $.14x$, respectively. Consequently, the power available for prolonged effort seems to reach a low asymptote at approximately 15% of that for immediate effort.

The POrPA model expresses the numerator (power output) and the denominator (power available) using the same metric. This usage permits strong but clear predictions. An index of power output is the displacement (horizontal, vertical, or both) per unit movement, which relates to the effort expended in propelling projectiles or the body. Power available is simply the reciprocal of endurance demand, with the latter increasing with the duration of effort. Because age effects are predicted to vary with the power-by-endurance interaction, the model successfully anticipated the following trends among veteran athletes (aged over 40 years): (a) minimal age effects on the sprints and race walks and maximal effects on the obstacle races and power events; (b) higher age effects on the butterfly than on other strokes in swimming; and (c) greater age effects on longer races within a given category (e.g., running, freestyle swimming) (Stones & Kozma, 1986).

The following analyses are of 1993 world records compiled by international regulatory bodies. The data include records for open-class (Matthews, 1993) and veteran athletes (compiled by the World Association of Veteran Athletes [WAVA] and published in *National Masters News*, Mundle, 1993).

## 1. Open-Class Track and Field

The POrPA model predicted earlier findings with veterans that loss with age was lowest in the sprints and race walks. Extrapolation to the ages of record holders in open-class competition allows the following prediction: If age least affects sprinting and race walking, these events should have more older world-record holders than the other categories. The prediction is a strong one, given that some commentators suggest sprint champions to be getting younger, and the winners of endurance races to be getting older (Rybash, Roodin, & Santrock, 1991, pp. 92–95).

Figure 1 shows the mean ages of the 1993 world-record holders at the times the records were broken. The records are for all track and field and road walking events in which both genders compete. The ages for the sprints and race walks are significantly older than for the other categories. The youngest ages are in the hurdles, jumps, and throws, with distance runners being intermediate. (Gender has nonsignificant effects.)

## 2. Open-Class Swimming

Earlier findings with veterans showed performance loss to be highest in the butterfly stroke and over longer distances. If the POrPA model holds, an extrapolation to open-class competition should show younger ages of the record holders in the power strokes (i.e., the butterfly followed by the breaststroke) and over longer races.

Figure 1 gives the ages of the 1993 world-record holders at 100 and 200 m collapsed over event distance and gender. The trend

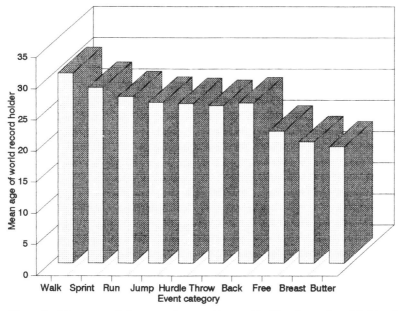

**Figure 1** Mean ages of the open-class world-record holders in track and field and swimming.

across strokes is significant, with the butterfly associated with the youngest age. Findings with freestyle swimming confirm the prediction with respect to distance. This stroke is the only one to have world records over a wide range of distances (from 50 to 500 m). The ages at breaking the records show a negative monotonic trend in both genders, decreasing with distance from 25 to 18 years in males and from 20 to 16 years in females. Consequently, open-class records in each of track, field, and swimming events confirm predictions of the POrPA model that relate age loss to the interactive demands on power and endurance.

### 3. Cross-Sectional Trends in Veteran Athletes

The following analyses use 1993 age–class world records in track, field, and walking events. Only events in which both genders compete were included. An approximate estimate of age deficit is given by the percentage discrepancy between age–class records and open-class records, with a WAVA correction applied where necessary to adjust for any difference with age in the implements used (Mundle, 1993).

Figure 2 shows the findings for veterans aged over 75 years. The findings for males accord with predictions from the POrPA model. The highest deficits are in the hurdles, jumps, and throws. The lowest deficits are in the sprints and race walks, with the middle-distance runs showing intermediate loss. A comparable pattern is present in females for all events except the race walks. A probable reason for the latter is that race walking was not a recognized female event until just over a decade ago, with the older walkers having inefficient styles.

### 4. Longitudinal Trends in Veteran Athletes

Longitudinal trends in athletic performance are unlikely to show the consistency of cross-sectional trends for several reasons. First, not many athletes remain elite

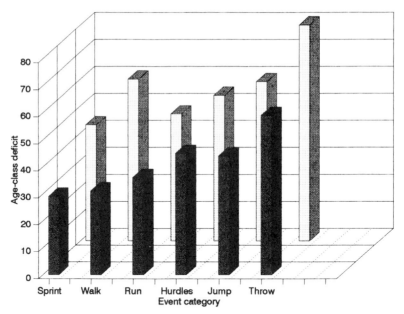

**Figure 2** Mean proportionate deficits in age-class (i.e., 75+) over open-class records for males (darker bars) and females (lighter bars) in six event categories.

over long periods. Second, performances may vary due to injury, training, and competitive opportunity. Third, longitudinal effects may vary with the age of the athlete. Despite these sources of error, discernable trends are present in the data. Figure 3 shows longitudinal changes for middle-aged and older male athletes selected because they continue to hold age–class world records over a minimal span of 7 years. Although other athletes also meet this criterion, space limitations force us to restrict our selection to one event per category.

Figure 3 shows the percentage performance loss per decade. The findings show effects due to age and event. First, older veterans show approximately twice the performance loss of younger veterans. Second, the loss across events accords with expectations from the POrPA model. From least to most loss, the order of events in the younger veterans is the race walk, 100 m, hurdles, 800 m, pole vault, and javelin. The comparable order in the older veterans is the race walk, 100 m, hurdles, pole vault, 800 m, and javelin. These find-

ings show the predictions from the POrPA model to generalize to longitudinal data, with the race walk and sprint having the lowest losses. Comparisons across events for two record holders in multiple events provide further support. A. E. Pitcher had a lower loss in the 100 m (29%) than in the pole vault (39%). Similarly, Herbert Anderson had less loss in the 100 m (25%) than in the javelin (40%).

### E. Expertise and Compensation in Elite Performance

The POrPA model is limited in scope to age effects on effortful performance that relies little on strategy. High-strategy sports include individual and team games in which the skill is more open than closed (e.g., baseball, golf, soccer, and tennis). Such sports require adaptive expertise to enable a competitor to react quickly to ongoing change in (the immediate situation. Although some high-strategy sports are physically strenuous (e.g., boxing), others are less so (e.g., golf).

Stones and Kozma (1995) applied Bäck-

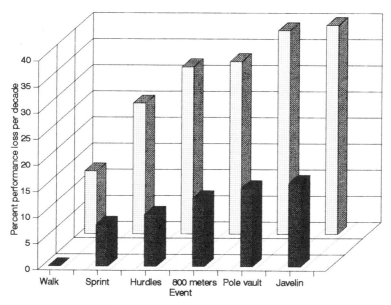

**Figure 3** Percent performance loss per decade by younger (darker bars) and older (lighter bars) veteran athletes in six events.

man and Dixon's (1992) compensation theory to age effects in high-strategy sports. They reported that proficiency remains intact longer in sports emphasizing expertise rather than effort or endurance, as evidenced by the ages of champion performers and the respective lengths of career. They also cited quantified examples of compensation, including increased aggression in response to declining skill in ice hockey players (higher penalty minutes coincides with lower points scoring), and the selection of longer races by endurance athletes experiencing declines in speed. They concluded that compensation theory may provide a useful framework for discussing retained competence with age.

## III. The Consequences of Physical Conduct for Competence

There are five main models of the effects of physical activity on competence (Stones & Kozma, 1988). The first is the *health mediation* model. This model originated with Xenophon in the fourth century B.C. He suggested that physical exercise can promote health, with retained competence being a secondary manifestation. The model has the following specification: *activity→health→competence*.

A second is the *activity moderator* model, in which activity moderates age trends in competence. Spirduso (1982) cited Cornaro in the thirteenth century A.D. as an early exponent. Cornaro thought that sloth and extravagance contributed more to functional decline than aging. Spirduso (1980, 1982) suggested that activity maintains metabolic and circulatory demands within the brain, and thereby postpones the damage to neuronal tissue that otherwise occurs with disuse. The form of the model is as follows: *age\*activity→competence*.

Third, *overpractice* models refer to the *use-it-or-lose-it* principle (Kozma & Stones, 1991; Stones & Kozma, 1988). This model proposes that competencies remain intact longer in overpracticed physical skills. Kozma and Stones (1991) reinterpreted Spirduso and Clifford's (1978) findings accordingly (p. 10): The quick reactions practiced in racquet sports may delay age losses in reaction time relative to runners and controls. Practice, rather than activity, is proposed to moderate age loss in competence: *age\*overpractice→competence*.

Fourth, *tonic effect* models refer to the generalized and beneficial effects of activity despite age (Kozma et al., 1991; Stones & Kozma, 1988). Dustman, Emmerson, and Shearer (1990) described *hypokinetic disease* as nonspecific somatic and cognitive deficits due to inactivity. This includes electrophysiological slowing with age and inactivity and a loss of inhibitory potential. Any increase in activity should mainly benefit people with such deficits. Kozma et al. (1991) provided supporting evidence with findings that fitness indexes show diminishing gains as activity levels rise beyond the midrange. Consequently, the inverse of fitness should moderate the effects of activity change ($\delta$activity) on change in competence ($\delta$competence): $\delta activity*fitness^{-1} \to \delta$ (*competence*).

Finally, *trait* models interpret any association between activity and competence as spuriously due to self-selection. For example, people physically active in leisure are more often from the upper socioeconomic strata (Hartung & Farge, 1977). Such factors could also affect competence. The model has the following form: *activity←traits→competence*.

## A. Consequences of Activity for Fitness and Physical Performance

Activity programs intended to promote strength, endurance, flexibility, or balance generally work well in older men and women. Neither resistance nor aerobic exercise needs to be unduly strenuous to produce training effects. Jones, Rikli, Benedict, and Williams (1994) found gains in strength and strength endurance with a self-regulated program of moderate intensity. Similarly, Dustman et al. (1984) reported aerobic power gains of one-fifth the baseline value in a walking program for sedentary subjects. Stones and Kozma (1987) and Binder, Brown, Craft, Schechtman, and Birge (1994) obtained gains up to 50% in balance, gait speed, and knee strength following participation in multifaceted exercise. Such findings show that exercise can benefit competence without recourse to interpretations based on health mediation or self-selection traits.

Of the other three models, only the tonic effects model addresses changes in competence following brief interventions. It suggests activity to have generalized and beneficial effects across a range of competencies. Three predictions follow. The first is that activity has effects on competence depending on the degree to which elements of the skill are practiced within a program. It is for this reason that endurance training has a minimum impact on strength and vice versa, whereas balance benefits from nonspecific programs that subsume its component skills.

Second, the benefits from increased activity should vary negatively with baseline fitness. A law of diminishing returns receives support from a perusal of interventions reviewed by Dustman, Emmerson, and Shearer (1994). Several studies gave information on pre–post levels of maximal oxygen uptake with walk–run training programs, with six having baseline levels within 25% of the normative age means (from the Canada Fitness Survey). We computed a correlation between baseline means (expressed proportionately to normative means) and percentage change in aerobic power after training. The data are from Blumenthal and Madden (1988), Dustman et al. (1984), Hassmen, Ceci, and Backman (1992), Hill, Storandt, and Malley (1993), Panton, Graves, Pollock, Hagberg, and Chen (1990), and Pierce, Madden, Siegel, and Blumenthal (1993). There was a strong negative relationship between the baseline index and training effect ($r < -.9$). Because the activity programs were of similar intensity (i.e., based on heart rate reserve), the findings confirm a law of diminishing returns.

A third prediction is that decreased activity should result in decreased fitness. Saltin, Grover, Blomqvist, Hartley, and Johnson (1968) provided a dramatic example of a 27% decrease in maximal oxygen uptake when training was followed by 20 days of bedrest.

The activity moderator and overpractice models address the more long-term effects of activity. The former proposes age-by-activity interactions, such that activity lowers the effects of aging. Kozma et al. (1991) compared the activity moderator and tonic effects models with data from 6,000 representatively sampled subjects (aged 20–70 years) on five fitness measures (aerobic power, flexibility, handgrip strength, push-ups, and sit-ups). They computed activity indexes based on reported activities over the preceding half decade. They found age and activity main effects, but no age-by-activity interaction. These findings disconfirm predictions from the activity moderator model, but suggest activity to have tonic effects on fitness.

The overpractice model makes more specific predictions than the activity moderator model: Age effects should be lower only on overpracticed skills. A prediction from this model is that age losses in the physical performance of trained athletes should be lower than the normative age loss for comparable skills. For example, aerobic power norms from the Canada Fitness Survey and age–class records in the 800 and 1500 m respectively provide estimates of endurance capability. Although the normative data show a decline of approximately 40% between the twenties and sixties for males, the athletic record data show a decline of only 25%. Longitudinal data also show lower than expected losses on endurance measures among runners (Dill, Robinson, & Ross, 1967; Pollock, Foster, Rod, Hall, & Schmidt, 1982),

thereby providing further evidence that continued practice can postpone age decline in physical performance capabilities.

## B. Consequences of Activity for Cognitive and Psychomotor Competence

The studies reviewed in this section use either intervention or cross-sectional designs. Because intervention studies with humans are typically of short duration, the findings are usually interpreted using variants of the tonic effects model. Activity moderation and overpractice models can be applied to cross-sectional research, but with the caution that self-selection effects may confound the findings.

### 1. Acute Interventions

Even a single dose of very low-intensity exercise may benefit cognitive performance in the very old. Diesfeldt and Diesfeldt-Groenendijk (1977) and Stones and Dawe (1993) obtained such effects on verbal memory with nursing-home residents in their eighties. In the latter study, the activity raised heart rate from the baseline by only two beats per minute, but prompted a gain exceeding 20% in semantic memory performance. In the Diesfeldt and Diesfeldt-Groenendijk (1977) study, the gain was 35%. Molloy, Beerschoten, Borrie, Crilly, and Cape (1988) similarly found improved performance on some tasks following a bout of acute exercise by hospital outpatients mainly in their sixties. All these studies used controlled designs with random assignment to conditions, but the effects were limited to tests of verbal memory. At present, parameters related to the effectiveness of the single-dose paradigm remain unclear: How long do the effects last? What is a requisite dose of exercise? What physiological processes underlie the effects? Future work may provide answers to these questions.

## 2. Chronic Interventions

The paradigm that predominates in research examines chronic exercising. The rationale is that improved cardiorespiratory fitness should benefit the central nervous system (e.g., decreased hypoxia, increased processing speed) and result in improved neuropsychological performance. Animal studies consistently provide supportive evidence, with findings of improved performance and changes within the brain (Dustman et al., 1994). Dustman et al. (1994) reviewed 12 controlled studies of aerobic training effects on human neuropsychological performance. However, the findings are disappointing, particularly when compared to the gains reported with the acute intervention paradigm. Only the study by Dustman et al. (1984) showed substantial gains over a range of tasks following aerobic training, with most of the remaining studies showing no strong effects.

The discrepancy in findings between animal and human studies may relate to the duration of exercise. Compared with interventions typically lasting 3–12 months in rodents, the 3- to 4-month training period used in human study is less than 1/200 of the life span. We also referred previously (Section III and III.A) to the diminishing returns of training with higher baseline fitness levels. The same principle may have relevance to neuropsychological performance. In the Dustman et al. (1984) study, the pre-post measures of aerobic power rose from 80 to 100% of the normative mean. By comparison, the only other study to include subjects equally unfit at the baseline was much less successful in promoting fitness (Blumenthal et al., 1989; Madden, Blumenthal, Allen, & Emery, 1989). Consequently, it is plausible that exercise may benefit performance mainly in persons very unfit at baseline for whom the effects of exercise are either immediate (the single dose studies) or very substantial.

## 3. Cross-Sectional Studies

Comparisons of active and inactive people of different ages can encompass significant chunks of the life span. Typical designs include comparisons of young and old subjects classified as regularly active or inactive. The classifications derive from behavior styles (e.g., participation in sport), activity indexes, and fitness measures (Dustman et al., 1990; Spirduso & Clifford, 1978; Stones & Kozma, 1989). Because the subjects clearly select their own activity in these designs, the data are possibly confounded with the effects of self-selection. However, most researchers attempt to account for such effects by equating the groups on measures like verbal intelligence.

Reviews of the findings consistently show main effects of age and activity, with age-by-activity interactions sometimes in evidence (Dustman et al., 1994; Stones & Kozma, 1988). A sample of findings follows. An early study by Spirduso (1975) found age-by-activity interactions using reaction time, with lower age differences in the active than the inactive subjects. Stones and Kozma (1989) obtained a similar interaction with symbol-digit coding but not digit-symbol coding. Dustman et al. (1990) and Spirduso, MacCrae, MacCrae, Prewitt, and Osborne (1988) failed to obtain any interactions using a range of cognitive and motor tasks.

Age-by-activity interactions arise too frequently in the literature to dismiss but too infrequently to be robust occurrences. They are theoretically important because of a supposed relevance to activity moderator models: Lower age differences with higher activity might suggest that the latter postpones losses in competence (Spirduso, 1980). However, other interpretations are possible.

The first alternative interpretation suggests that some age-by-activity interactions are really age-by-overpractice interactions. Kozma and Stones (1991) reinterpreted Spirduso's findings with racquet sport players accordingly (Spirduso, 1975; Spirduso & Clifford, 1978): Fast reactions and movements are practiced in racquet sports; the practice, rather than the high activity, might delay age losses on those tasks. Stones and Kozma (1988) also supported an overpractice interpretation with data on tapping. In two studies, they compared age differences in active and inactive groups on up-and-down and back-and-forth tapping with the hands or feet. The only overpracticed task is up-and-down tapping with the feet, which comprises a component movement of normal walking. This task was the only one to show no age difference. The other tasks showed age and activity main effects but no interactions. They concluded that the findings with up-and-down foot tapping fit an overpractice model, whereas the findings with the other tasks fit a tonic effects model.

A second alternative is that age-by-activity interactions are by-products of effects anticipated by the tonic effects model. The reasoning is as follows: First, assume that a curve of fitness on activity shows asymptote, as predicted by a law of diminishing returns. Second, it follows that activity should benefit the fitness of older people proportionally more than that of younger people, given that fitness declines with age. Third, if fitness has generalized effects on other performance despite age, it follows that the performances by older people should benefit more from activity than that of younger people, thereby giving rise to age-by-activity interactions. It may be that those age-by-activity interactions not demonstrably due to over-practice arise from tonic benefit rather than any postponement of the aging process.

## IV. Summary

This review has shown that physical conduct at different ages has differed through-

out the century. Although older people may exercise less strenuously than younger people, recent data show that people in their sixties exercise more than middle-aged people, with perceived health benefits and previous habits being strong predictors of participation.

Difficulties in the measurement and modeling of physical competence arise from the heterogeneity among older people. The measures mainly have applicability either to the lower or mid- to upper ranges of the competence continuum, with evidence of covariation across nominally disparate functions despite age. One topic in which modeling encompasses consistent findings concerns the performances of elite athletes. The ages of open-class world-record holders and cross-sectional and longitudinal effects on age-class records are substantially anticipated by the interactive demands on power and endurance.

The consequences of physical activity include effects on fitness, physical performance, and neuropsychological performance. The effects on fitness and physical performance show either specificity or generalization, depending on the degree to which the elements of performance are incorporated into training. The gains through training conform to a law of diminishing returns, with the extent of gain varying negatively with the baseline level. Robust findings on neuropsychological performance include gains following a single dose of exercise in elderly institutionalized or outpatient populations and superior performance by older chronic exercisers. Fitness training of a few months duration failed to provide consistent findings in human subjects.

Different models of the benefits of exercise for performance postulate tonic effects, overpractice, and delayed aging. A combination of overpractice and tonic effects provides a plausible account of (a) the low age losses on familiar (overpracticed) psychomotor performances and (b) the differences between active and inactive older people on physical and neuropsychological tasks. Both principles are well supported in other areas of scientific inquiry. The overuse principle finds expression in early work on age loss in writing speed (La Riviere & Simonson, 1965), later to become embedded within a range of expert–novice paradigms. The tonic effects model, which incorporates the principle of diminishing returns as fitness rises, is solidly established in psychology and exercise physiology. It may parsimoniously explain those findings of performance gain with activity that are not easily explained by practice. Consequently, the notion that activity moderates performance loss with age appears to be redundant.

# References

Andersen, K. L., Masironi, R., Rutenfranz, J., & Seliger, V. (1978). *Habitual physical activity and aging.* Copenhagen: World Health Organization.

Astrand, P.-O., & Rodahl, K. (1977). *Textbook of work physiology: Physiological bases of behavior* (2nd ed.). New York: McGraw-Hill.

Bäckman, L., & Dixon, R. A. (1992). Psychological compensation: A theoretical framework. *Psychological Bulletin, 112,* 259–283.

Binder, E. K., Brown, M., Craft, S., Schechtman, K. B., & Birge, S. J. (1994). Effects of a group exercise program on risk factors for falls in frail older adults. *Journal of Aging and Physical Activity, 2,* 25–37.

Birren, J. E., & Cunningham, W. (1985). Research on the psychology of aging: Principles, concepts and theory. In J. E. Birren & K. W. Schaie (Eds.), *Handbook of the psychology of aging* (2nd ed., pp. 3–34). New York: Van Nostrand-Reinhold.

Blumenthal, J. A., Emery, C. F., Madden, D. J., George, L. K., Coleman, R. E., Riddle, M. W., McKee, D. C., Reasoner, J., & Williams, R. S. (1989). Cardiovascular and behavioral effects of aerobic exercise training in healthy older men and women. *Journal of Gerontology: Medical Sciences, 44,* M147–M157.

Blumenthal, J. A., & Madden, D. J. (1988). Effects of aerobic exercise training, age, and

physical fitness on memory-search performance. *Psychology and Aging, 3,* 280–285.

Canada Department of Fitness and Amateur Sport. (1981). *Standardized test of fitness.* Ottawa: Government of Canada.

Chodzko-Zajko, W. J. (1994). Assessing physical performance in older adult populations. *Journal of Aging and Physical Activity, 2,* 103–104.

Cooper, K. H. (1977). *The aerobics way.* New York: M. Evans.

Diesfeldt, H. F. A., & Diesfeldt-Groenendijk, H. (1977). Improving cognitive performance in psychogeriatric patients: The influence of physical exercise. *Age and Ageing, 6,* 58–64.

Dill, D. B., Robinson, S., & Ross, J. C. (1967). A longitudinal study of 16 champion runners. *Journal of Sports Medicine, 7,* 4–27.

Dustman, R. E., Emmerson, R. Y., & Shearer, D. E. (1990). Electrophysiology and aging: Slowing, inhibition, and aerobic fitness. In M. L. Howe, M. J. Stones, & C. J. Brainerd (Eds.), *Cognitive and behavioral performance factors in atypical aging* (pp. 103–149). New York: Springer-Verlag.

Dustman, R. E., Emmerson, R. Y., & Shearer, D. E. (1994). Physical activity, age, and cognitive-neuropsychological function. *Journal of Aging and Physical Activity, 2,* 143–181.

Dustman, R. E., Ruhling, R. O., Russell, D. M., Shearer, D. E., Bonekat, H. W., Shigeoka, J. W., Wood, D. S., & Bradford, D. C. (1984). Aerobic exercise training and improved neuropsychological function in older individuals. *Neurobiology of Aging, 5,* 35–42.

Fillenbaum, G. G. (1984). *The well being of the elderly: Approaches to multidimensional assessment.* Geneva: World Health Organization.

Gobbi, S. (1993). Profile of Masters track and field participants in Sao Paulo State, Brazil. *Journal of Aging and Physical Activity, 1,* 98.

Going, S. B., Williams, D. P., Lohman, T. G., & Hewitt, M. J. (1994). Age, body composition, and physical activity: A review. *Journal of Aging and Physical Activity, 2,* 38–66.

Harada, M. (1994). Early and later life sport participation patterns among the active elderly in Japan. *Journal of Aging and Physical Activity, 2,* 105–114.

Hartung, G. H., & Farge, E. J. (1977). Personality and physiological traits in middle-aged joggers and runners. *Journal of Gerontology, 32,* 541–548.

Hassmen, P., Ceci, R., & Bäckman, L. (1992). Exercise for older women: A training method and its influences on physical and cognitive performance. *European Journal of Applied Physiology, 64,* 460–466.

Hellebraun, F. A., & Braun, G. L. (1939). The influence of sex and age on the postural sway of man. *American Journal of Physical Anthropology, 24,* 347–360.

Heron, A., & Chown, S. (1967). *Age and function.* Boston: Little, Brown.

Hill, R. D., Storandt, M., & Malley, M. (1993). The impact of long-term exercise training on psychological function in older adults. *Journal of Gerontology: Psychological Sciences, 48,* P12–P17.

Jones, C. J. J., Rikli, R. E., Benedict, J., & Williams, P. (1994). Effects of a resistance training program on leg strength and muscular function of older women. *Journal of Aging and Physical Activity, 2,* 182–185.

Kozma, A., & Stones, M. J. (1991). Decrements in habitual and maximal performance with age. In M. Perlmutter (Ed.), *Late life potential* (pp. 1–23). Washington, DC: The Gerontological Society of America.

Kozma, A., Stones, M. J., & Hannah, T. E. (1991). Age, activity, and physical performance: An evaluation of performance models. *Psychology and Aging, 6,* 43–49.

Kuh, D. J. L., & Cooper, C. (1992). Physical activity at 36 years: Patterns and childhood predictors in a longitudinal study. *Journal of Epidemiology and Community Health, 46,* 114–119.

La Riviere, J.E., & Simonson, E. (1965). The effects of age and occupation on speed of writing. *Journal of Gerontology, 20,* 415–416.

Lord, S. R., Clark, R. D., & Webster, I. W. (1991). Postural stability and associated physiological factors in a population of aged persons. *Journal of Gerontology: Medical Sciences, 46,* M69–M76.

MacCrae, P. G., Feltner, M. E., & Reinsch, S. (1994). A 1–year exercise program for older women: Effects on falls, injuries, and physical performance. *Journal of Aging and Physical Activity, 2,* 127–142.

Madden, D. J., Blumenthal, J. A., Allen, P. A., & Emery, C. F. (1989). Improving aerobic capacity in healthy older adults does not necessarily lead to improved cognitive performance. *Psychology and Aging, 4,* 307–320.

Matthews, P. (1993). *The Guinness book of records 1994.* London: Guinness.

Molloy, D. W., Beerschoten, D. A., Borrie, M. J., Crilly, R. G., & Cape, R. D. T. (1988). Acute effects of exercise on neuropsychological function in elderly subjects. *Journal of the American Geriatrics Society, 36,* 29–33.

Mundle, P. (1993). World track and field age-group records. *National Masters News,* No. 117, pp. 18–20.

Panton, L. B., Graves, J. E., Pollock, M. L., Hagberg, J. M., & Chen, W. (1990). Effect of aerobic and resistance training on fractionated reaction time and speed of movement. *Journal of Gerontology: Medical Sciences, 45,* M26–M31.

Pierce, T. W., Madden, D. J., Siegel, W. C., & Blumenthal, J. A. (1993). Effects of aerobic exercise on cognitive and psychosocial functioning in patients with mild hypertension. *Health Psychology, 12,* 286–291.

Pollock, M. L., Foster, C., Rod, J., Hall, J., & Schmidt, D. H. (1982). Ten-year follow-up upon the aerobic capacity of champion masters athletes. *Medicine and Science in Sports, 14,* 105.

Robinson, S. (1938). Physical fitness in relation to age. *Arbeitsphysiologie, 4,* 251–255.

Rowe, J. W., & Kahn, R. L. (1987). Human aging: Usual and successful. *Science, 237,* 143–149.

Rybash, J. M., Roodin, P. A., & Santrock, J. W. (1991). *Adult development and aging* (2nd ed.). Dubuque, IA: Wm. C. Brown.

Saltin, B., Grover, R. F., Blomqvist, C. G., Hartley, L. H., & Johnson, R. L. (1968). Maximal oxygen uptake and cardiac output after two weeks at 4,300 metres. *Journal of Applied Physiology, 25,* 400.

Shephard, R. J. (1969). *Endurance fitness.* Toronto: University of Toronto Press.

Shephard, R. J., Berridge, M., Montelpare, W., Daniel, J. V., & Flowers, J. F. (1987). Exercise compliance of elderly volunteers. *Journal of Sports Medicine and Physical Fitness, 27,* 410–418.

Spirduso, W. W. (1975). Reaction time and movement time as a function of age and physical activity level. *Journal of Gerontology, 30,* 435–440.

Spirduso, W. W. (1980). Physical fitness, aging,

and psychomotor speed. *Journal of Gerontology*, *35*, 850–865.

Spirduso, W. W. (1982). Exercise and the aging brain. *Research Quarterly for Exercise and Sport*, *35*, 850–865.

Spirduso, W. W. (1994). *Physical dimensions of aging*. Champaign, IL: Human Kinetics Publishers.

Spirduso, W. W., & Clifford, P. (1978). Neuromuscular speed and consistency of performance as a function of age, physical activity level and type of physical activity. *Journal of Gerontology*, *33*, 26–30.

Spirduso, W. W., MacCrae, H. H., MacCrae, P. G., Prewitt, J., & Osborne, L. (1988). Exercise effects on aged motor function. *Annals of the New York Academy of Sciences*, *515*, 363–375.

Stacey, C., Kozma, A., & Stones, M. J. (1985). Simple cognitive and performance changes resulting from improved physical fitness in persons over 50 years of age. *Canadian Journal on Aging*, *4*, 67–73.

Stephens, T., Craig, C. L., & Ferris, B. F. (1986). Adult physical activity in Canada: Findings from the Canada Fitness Survey. *Canadian Journal of Public Health*, *77*, 285–290.

Stones, M. J., & Dawe, D. (1993). Acute exercise facilitates semantically cued memory in nursing home residents. *Journal of the American Geriatrics Society*, *41*, 531–534.

Stones, M. J., & Kozma, A. (1986). Age trends in maximal physical performance: Comparison and evaluation of models. *Experimental Aging Research*, *12*, 207–215.

Stones, M. J. & Kozma, A. (1987) Balance and age in the sighted and blind. *Archives of Physical Medicine and Rehabilitation*, *66*, 85–89.

Stones, M. J., & Kozma, A. (1988). Physical activity, age, and cognitive/motor performance. In M. L. Howe & C. J. Brainerd (Eds.), *Cognitive development in adulthood: Progress in cognitive development research* (pp. 273–321). New York: Springer-Verlag.

Stones, M. J., & Kozma, A. (1989). Age, exercise, and coding performance. *Psychology and Aging*, *4*, 190–194.

Stones, M. J., & Kozma, A. (1995). Compensation in athletic sport. In R. Dixon & C. Bäckman (Eds.), *Psychological compensation: Managing losses and promoting gains*. Hillsdale, NJ: Erlbaum.

Stones, M. J., Kozma, A., & Hannah, T. E. (1990). Measurement of individual differences in aging: The distinction between usual and successful aging. In M. L. Howe, M. J. Stones, & C. J. Brainerd (Eds.), *Cognitive and behavioral performance factors in atypical aging* (pp. 181–218). New York: Springer-Verlag.

Stones, M. J., Kozma, A., & Stones, L. (1987). Fitness and health evaluations by older exercisers. *Canadian Journal of Public Health*, *78*, 18–20.

Warren, B. J., Dotson, R. G., Nieman, D. C., & Butterworth, D. E. (1993). Validation of a 1-mile walk test in elderly women. *Journal of Aging and Physical Activity*, *1*, 13–21.

Twenty

# Aging, Job Performance, and Career Development

Timothy A. Salthouse and Todd J. Maurer

## I. Introduction

One implication of the changing demographic composition of the United States population is that the number of older workers will increase dramatically in coming years in both absolute and relative terms. Particularly in light of the virtual elimination of mandatory retirement ages in the United States, questions will inevitably arise regarding the productivity of older workers. Although in recent decades the trend has been toward retirement at earlier ages, this pattern may not continue if the large baby boom cohort is confronted with the possibility of reduced or delayed benefits, and if concerns about financial security lead to decisions to postpone retirement. Interest in relations between aging and work behavior will therefore almost certainly grow in importance in the next several decades.

Because of space limitations, the focus in this chapter is restricted to two major topics concerned with aging and work. Although there are obviously many aspects of work behavior that could be addressed, the two emphasized here are job performance and career development. Job performance is clearly a fundamental topic in

the field of work, and in fact it has recently been suggested that job performance is the most important dependent variable in industrial and organizational psychology (Schmidt & Hunter, 1992). Career development is important as a factor affecting job performance, especially when there is a shift in occupation or responsibilities, and retraining or skill upgrading is needed. It is also a work-related variable likely to be of interest both to the employer, because career development relates to issues of staffing (e.g., transfer, promotion, retention), and also to the employee.

The framework for our discussion is portrayed in Figure 1. Knowledge and skills in this diagram refer both to domain-specific aspects (e.g., information and procedures relevant to a particular occupation), and to broader aspects derived from general life experience. Abilities refer to individual capabilities ranging from physical (including sensory and motor) to cognitive in nature. They correspond to trans-situational, rather than job-specific, capacities of the individual. The category labeled *Other* includes, but is not restricted to, motivation (e.g., need for achievement or self-actualization) and personality (e.g., self-efficacy beliefs, attitudes, and traits, such

*Handbook of the Psychology of Aging, Fourth Edition*

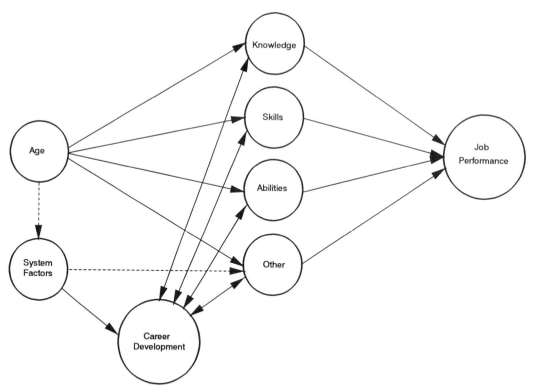

**Figure 1**   Framework illustrating hypothesized relations among age, career development, and job performance.

as conscientiousness and internal locus of control). System factors refer to situation or environment variables external to the individual such as organizational structure, supervisor style, appraisal or evaluation procedures, and social processes.

A relation, albeit weak, is postulated between age and system factors because informal policies and socially shared stereotypes or norms may rely on age as a classification variable. A relation is also postulated between system factors and career development because system factors are presumed to affect access to, or opportunity for, career development. Finally, a weak relation is represented between system factors and aspects within the *Other* category in the form of motivations, expectations about success, and self-efficacy beliefs.

This framework is obviously incom-

plete because many more variables and relations could be included in this type of diagram. The labels for the mediators are also somewhat vague, and inclusion of a category labeled *Other* imposes few constraints on the range of mediators. Despite these caveats, Figure 1 illustrates our fundamental assumption that various types of proximal characteristics, rather than age, are the important determinants of career development and job performance (see also Avolio, Barrett, & Sterns, 1984; Salthouse, 1986; Waldman & Avolio, 1986). That is, Figure 1 does not contain any direct relations between age and either the career development or the job performance criterion variables. This is a key aspect of our perspective because we view age as a dimension along which factors exert their influence, rather than an influence in and of itself.

In this respect we agree with Birren and Renner (1977), who suggested that age is a surrogate variable that ultimately should be replaced by true causal variables. As long as age is directly linked to the criterion measures, then the level of understanding is incomplete and inadequate. Further implications of this view are discussed at the end of the chapter in Section IV. At this point we turn to the application of the framework to two work-related criterion variables—job performance and career development.

## II. Job Performance

Most reviews of the relevant research literature have concluded that there is little or no relation between age and work performance or job proficiency (e.g., D. R. Davies & Sparrow, 1985; McEvoy & Cascio, 1989; Rhodes, 1983; Waldman & Avolio, 1986; Warr, 1994; also see Hunter, 1980, cited in Hunter & Hunter, 1984). The absence of a relation is somewhat surprising because negative relations might have been expected based on the relations between age and ability, and between ability and job performance. That is, if job performance is determined by KSAOs (i.e., knowledge, skills, abilities, and other factors) and there are age-related declines in some of the A variables, then why is there not a negative relation between age and job performance? The framework in Figure 1 is useful for identifying possible explanations of this puzzling discrepancy. We begin by discussing the evidence establishing the existence of this paradox, and then consider potential hypotheses that might account for it.

One relevant type of evidence is the existence of negative relations between age and various measures of cognitive ability that have been documented in many types of assessments, including a wide range of standardized tests (e.g., see Salthouse, 1991, for a review). Negative relations have been reported for measures as simple as immediate memory and as complex as abstract reasoning, with correlations typically ranging from about −.2 to −.5.

A second type of relevant evidence is the presence of positive relations between measures of cognitive ability and measures of work performance (e.g., Hunter, 1986; Hunter & Hunter, 1984; Schmidt & Hunter, 1992). The average validity coefficient for cognitive ability as a predictor of job performance (usually assessed by supervisor rating) was estimated to be .24 by Ghiselli (1973). After adjustments were made for restriction of range and measurement error, however, Hunter and Hunter (1984) estimated that the value was closer to .45. Regardless of the absolute magnitude of the relation, cognitive ability has been reported to be one of the best predictors of job performance.

The research just summarized clearly leads to the expectation of a negative relation between age and job performance. For example, if the age-cognition correlation is −.5 and the validity coefficient is .5, then path analysis logic leads to an expected correlation between age and job performance of −.25. (Of course, if the correlation between age and cognitive ability is only −.3 and the validity coefficient is only .3, then the correlation between age and job performance might be expected to be as small as −.09.)

### A. Methodological Issues

The key question that emerges from the preceding discussion is why is there not a relation between age and measures of work performance? Before considering interpretations of theoretical interest, a variety of methodological factors that could contribute to the lack of observed relations between age and job performance are briefly discussed here. Not all of the following problems are likely to be operating in every study, but for the reasons mentioned, each could contribute to distorted relations between age and job performance.

## 1. Limited Data

One major limitation of the existing literature is the paucity of relevant studies. As an example, only 13 studies were included in the meta-analysis reported by Waldman and Avolio (1986). More studies were included in a later meta-analysis by McEvoy and Cascio (1989), but the number of data sets was still relatively small. Moreover, the range of occupations was somewhat restricted because relatively few studies have been conducted examining age relations in managerial and professional occupations. Strong conclusions are not warranted if there is little pertinent evidence, and even weak conclusions are risky if one is not confident that the available studies employed representative samples, sensitive methods of assessment, and so on. Furthermore, analyses of moderator effects are not very meaningful if only a few studies are included within each moderator classification (e.g., job category and assessment type).

## 2. Weak Power

There is often a tendency to accept null results involving age comparisons without consideration of the statistical power of the comparisons to have detected effects of small to moderate magnitude. As an illustration of the magnitude of the problem, Cohen (1992) reported that a sample of 783 individuals would be needed to have .8 power to detect a correlation of .10 as statistically significant with an alpha of .05. This is admittedly a relatively small correlation, but as noted above, values within this range might be expected based on the reported relations between age and ability, and between ability and job performance. Because many of the studies in the literature have involved relatively small samples, they may have had

low power to detect small to moderate relations that might have existed.

## 3. Restricted Age Range

Another limitation of some studies is that very few adults in the sample were above the age of 40. This restricted age range is a potential problem because small, or nonlinear, age relations may not be detectable when the distribution of ages is skewed or curtailed. As an example, Avolio, Waldman, and McDaniel (1990) reported analyses of a very impressive data set with a large sample of workers ($n = 20,632$), a wide variety of job categories, and reliable assessments of job performance. However, the mean ages were less than 35 in each job category, and only 27% of the total sample was above the age of 40. It is therefore possible that the age relations in this study may have been underestimated relative to what might have been obtained in a more rectangular distribution of worker ages.

## 4. Selective Attrition

Differential dropout is a potential problem in age comparisons for two reasons. On the one hand, only the most competent may survive in some occupations because employers are unlikely to retain employees who perform poorly. On the other hand, only the least competent may survive in other occupations because the competent workers may be promoted into positions of greater responsibility and reward. For both of these reasons, comparisons involving workers of different ages may not be meaningful unless the turnover and internal transfer and promotion rates are low (D. R. Davies & Sparrow, 1985).

## 5. Nonequivalent Responsibilities

Although most comparisons involving age are made up of people with the same nominal job title, employees having the same title do not always have identical responsibilities. In particular, because older and more experienced workers tend to have greater seniority, they may have more desirable or more lucrative positions (e.g., assembly-line position and sales territory). To the extent that the actual work, or the level of potential reward, is not equivalent for people of different ages, age comparisons may be meaningless.

### 6. Biased Assessment

Many types of performance appraisals have the potential to be subjectively influenced by aspects that are not directly relevant to job performance. Unfortunately, the direction of the bias is not always easy to predict. For example, attributes such as loyalty, reliability, and past achievements or experience may operate to the advantage of older workers, whereas dimensions such as likelihood for advancement or potential for promotion will probably favor younger workers. Work sample evaluations are usually more objective, but they are also not ideal because they could reflect optimum or potential performance rather than normal performance. That is, work sample evaluations may be misleading if people are capable of high performance for short durations, but are unable to sustain that level over prolonged periods. If these characteristics are more true of older adults than of younger adults, then work sample evaluations may overestimate the true capabilities or typical performance levels of older workers.

### 7. Insensitive Assessment

One of the major concerns within the field of industrial psychology is the reliability and validity of criterion measures of job performance. Although a great deal of development and refinement of measurement properties has occurred in the area of ability assessment, the assessment of job performance (and particularly performance in complex jobs) is sometimes not

as reliable, valid, or sensitive as desired. The lack of significant relations involving age could therefore reflect inadequacies of measurement as much as, or more than, a genuine absence of an age relation.

### 8. Job Type

The relation between age and job performance could also vary according to job type. In particular, because Hunter and Hunter (1984) and Hunter (1986) have reported stronger relations between cognitive ability and job performance as the complexity of the job increased, one might expect larger age effects on cognitively demanding jobs in which novel problem solving is required. Mixed results have been found when job type has been used as a moderator of age-performance relations in meta-analyses (McEvoy & Cascio, 1989; Waldman & Avolio, 1986), but it is possible that the classification of job type in these studies did not adequately reflect the actual cognitive complexity of the jobs. Furthermore, the number of entries within certain job categories may have been so small as to preclude powerful analyses of the moderating effects of job type.

### B. Possible Explanations for the Discrepancy

Schmidt, Hunter, Outerbridge, and Goff (1988) suggested that the two most critical individual-difference determinants of job performance are general mental ability and job experience. Because some aspects of mental ability are negatively related to age, whereas job experience is often positively related to age, the question arises as to the net effect of these two relations. Warr (1994) provided an informative discussion of how the relation between age and job performance depends on the degree to which job-relevant abilities and knowledge are influenced both by age and by experience. However, an unresolved issue in this area is how experience affects job performance. That is, what are the specific mechanisms by which increased experience leads to improved levels of job performance?

One possibility is that many of the relations between experience and job performance are mediated through greater amounts of job knowledge (i.e., the K in the KSAO framework). In fact, there is some evidence that job experience is positively related to job knowledge, and that job knowledge is positively related to job performance (e.g., Schmidt & Hunter, 1992; Schmidt, Hunter, & Outerbridge, 1986; Schmidt et al., 1988). Furthermore, the stable or increasing relations between age and measures of knowledge, or crystallized cognitive ability (see Salthouse, 1991, for a review), could be viewed as consistent with the suggestion that older workers maintain high levels of job performance because they have acquired greater amounts of job-relevant knowledge or skills. One potential example of this type of mechanism is apparent in research on transcription typists (Salthouse, 1984), where skilled older typists have been found to rely on greater anticipation of forthcoming keystrokes (i.e., a form of procedural knowledge) than younger typists.

It is also possible that high levels of functioning in one's occupation might be achieved by different combinations of characteristics at different ages. For example, a successful older worker may rely more on his or her accumulated knowledge or store of prior solutions compared to a younger worker, who must rely on reasoning to develop fresh solutions to each situation or problem that is encountered. To the extent that a trade-off of this type occurs, it could be considered a form of compensation. However, there is still relatively little evidence regarding the existence of compensation as a phenomenon, and there is even disagreement about the type of evidence that would be relevant and convincing to demonstrate the existence of compensation (Salthouse, 1995).

Nevertheless, the possibility that the composition of competence varies as a function of age is intriguing, and clearly warrants further investigation.

Although the focus in this section has been on job performance, it is worth mentioning that older workers have been reported to have lower rates of absenteeism, fewer accidents, and higher levels of job satisfaction than younger workers (D. R. Davies & Sparrow, 1985; Rhodes, 1983; Warr, 1994). In some circumstances, therefore, the overall value of the older worker to the employer may be equal to, or possibly even greater than, that of a younger worker, regardless of any relation that might exist between age and job performance. In other words, even if an older worker is not compensating to maintain the same, or a higher, level of job performance as a younger worker, his or her value to the company may remain high because of these other characteristics.

## III. Career Development

The focus within this section is on the relation between age and participation in career development experiences that enhance the learning and growth of an employee within his or her career. These experiences include activities such as on-the-job exercises (e.g., challenging job or task-force assignments), participation in training or retraining programs, continuing education seminars or workshops, college or correspondence courses, and independent reading.

The amount of research concerned with the relation between age and career development activities is much less than that concerned with the relation between age and job performance. However, some evidence suggests that fewer training experiences may be available for older workers (e.g., Lee & Clemens, 1985), that older workers may be less likely to volunteer for retraining (e.g., N. Rosen, Williams, &

Foltman, 1965), and that a smaller proportion of older workers than younger workers are involved in on-the-job training or career counseling with a supervisor (e.g., Cleveland & Shore, 1992).

To the extent that age is related to involvement in career development activities, it is important to understand how and why that relation exists. The goal in this section, therefore, is to briefly examine several person and system factors that might function as potential mediators of relations between age and participation in career development activities.

## A. Person Factors

In the following discussion, three major types of person variables that are relevant to updating and employee development activity are discussed. All of these variables are taken from the *Other* category in Figure 1. Although KSAs are frequently discussed in the industrial psychology literature, and are known to have an impact on many aspects of work behavior, the variables described below have been somewhat neglected in discussions of career development and training processes (Noe, 1986) and may be related to age.

Three categories of relevant person variables are *outcome needs*, *process values*, and *expectations for success* in updating and development activities. Outcome needs affect the degree to which a person desires the results of participating in updating or employee development activity. Process values reflect the degree to which a person values various aspects (e.g., supervisor support and feedback) of an updating or employee development program. Expectations for success refer to self-efficacy beliefs, and particularly to beliefs that one's efforts will be successful. Each of these variables has been linked to employee career development activity (Dubin, 1990; Maurer & Tarulli, 1994; Noe & Wilk, 1993; Sterns & Patchett, 1984).

### 1. Outcome Needs

Both Porter (1963) and Hall and Mansfield (1975) found a positive relation between worker age and security needs. In addition, the latter researchers found that self-actualization needs were less important with increased age. A recent meta-analysis of 11 correlations also found a small negative relation between age and measures of the strength of growth needs (Engle, Miguel, Steelman, & McDaniel, 1994). Learning, growth, and challenge may therefore have less intrinsic importance to older workers, which could make the pursuit of participation in career development activity less attractive to the older employee.

It is unclear exactly why various needs might shift with increased age, although the concept of *possible selves* may be involved. Possible selves are self-schemas (Markus, 1983) that include knowledge of what one might be like in the future. These may be positive in valence and reflect goals, aspirations, and values (Cantor, Markus, Niedenthal, & Nurius, 1986), or they may be negative in valence and represent feared possible selves. To the extent that an employee perceives development activity to be an effective means of attaining or avoiding a possible self, he or she might be more oriented toward career development or skill updating (Maurer, 1994). Furthermore, Markus and Herzog (1991) have reviewed research that suggests that relative to younger adults older adults may have a greater interest in the prevention of feared outcomes (e.g., being physically dependent), and a lesser interest in occupational or career-oriented goals. One mechanism that might therefore contribute to a decrease in career development activities with increased age is a shift in self-perceptions and goals.

### 2. Process Values

Maurer and Tarulli (1994) found small but significant positive relations between employee age and the degree to which the employee valued co-worker and supervisor support for development activity. However, research discussed next suggests that older workers are sometimes *less* likely to find their peers and supervisors supportive of their participation in challenging developmental pursuits. It is therefore possible that a higher need for support, coupled with lower available support, may inhibit participation in career development activities on the part of older workers.

### 3. Expectations for Success

Because expectations for attaining relevant KSAOs in training are often lower with increased age (Fossum, Arvey, Paradise, & Robbins, 1986), and because older workers sometimes lack confidence (Knowles, 1973) or self-efficacy, older workers may not volunteer for training as a result of having low levels of confidence (N. Rosen et al., 1965). Stronger self-efficacy beliefs have been found to be positively related to involvement in employee development activity (Maurer & Tarulli, 1994; Noe & Wilk, 1993), perhaps because the more confidence one has in one's ability to engage successfully in a task or challenge, the more one is likely to participate in those activities.

The possibility that self-efficacy, outcome needs, process values, and other motivationally relevant variables may affect career development activity has received only limited attention in the research literature. Further research is therefore warranted to investigate the relations of these variables both to age and to career development participation and outcomes.

### B. System Factors

Social and organizational system variables may also underlie relations between age and updating or development activity. That is, participation in career development activity may be influenced by age norms and social phenomena such as treat- ment by other workers, supervisory behavior, and miscellaneous factors within the social and organizational context (Avolio, 1991). These variables and phenomena are contained within the *System Factors* construct in Figure 1.

### 1. Norms and Social Phenomena

Zenger and Lawrence (1989) found that, inside project groups, age similarity of members exerted an influence on the frequency of technical communication. Specifically, there was less communication among employees of different age groups than among members from the same age group. The authors suggested that the demographic composition of a group affects communication between specific members because people communicate most often with those who are similar to themselves. This phenomenon has implications for performance and development because communication is a source of support, as well as a means of acquiring job-relevant information and job knowledge. Because job knowledge may have a direct impact on performance (Hunter, 1986), any normative social phenomena that regulate the flow of job-relevant information may affect job performance.

Furthermore, technical communication and information can be a source of on-the-job development. Thus, if the age composition of a group is skewed or unbalanced, then updating or development that results from such communication may be impeded. The consequences of the restricted communication could impair the effectiveness of the group as a whole, or it might selectively affect those members most in need of new or changing information, who in some circumstances may disproportionately be older workers.

Cleveland and Shore (1992) also emphasized the need to consider the age context in which a person operates. They found that perceived relative age interacted with chronological age to predict job performance and career development activity. In particular, their results led to the suggestion that "chronological age appears to have the greatest predictive power when combined with perceptions of the ages of other employees in the work setting" (p. 481). To the degree that age context moderates the relation of age to variables such as career development and job performance, the neglect of this variable in prior research may account for some of the inconsistencies in studies involving the age variable.

One possible consequence of an older worker's being perceived or treated differently within a context of predominantly younger workers is self-limiting behavior (Ilgen & Youtz, 1986). For example, it is known that persuasion, modeling, and mastery experiences can all affect self-efficacy (Gist & Mitchell, 1992). To the extent that older workers receive subtle (or overt) messages that persuade them that they do not have relevant capabilities to perform or to learn, they may begin behaving in that fashion, and their level of self-esteem may deteriorate. In a similar manner, if the older employee lacks an observable "model" within the younger context, self-efficacy may be reduced, which may in turn lead to reduced participation in learning or training activities (N. Rosen et al., 1965).

The research just described suggests that system factors in the form of normative and socially or contextually generated age effects may have an impact on professional, interpersonal, and intrapersonal dynamics relevant to career development. Similar types of processes can also be seen in relation to job and training assignments, as discussed below.

## 2. Treatment in Developmental Job Assignments

Kozlowski and Farr (1988) reported that challenging work can facilitate technical updating. Furthermore, the nature of one's job assignments can be a very important means of employee development (J. Davies & Easterby-Smith, 1984; McCall, Lombardo, & Morrison, 1988). In particular, challenging jobs with developmental components (McCauley, Ruderman, Ohlott, & Morrow, 1994) may lead to greater career development by enhancing and maintaining relevant knowledge and skills. However, older workers sometimes receive more routine (as opposed to complex) job assignments than younger workers (Price, Thompson, & Dalton, 1975). At least some of the lower participation of older employees in career development activities may therefore be a consequence of the type of job assignments they receive.

## 3. Treatment with Respect to Training Resources

Similarly situated older and younger workers have been found to be treated differently with respect to access to retraining (Crew, 1984; Fossum et al., 1986; Lee & Clemens, 1985). Specifically, older workers are less likely to be selected for training or retraining than younger workers, perhaps because decision makers feel that the return on the investment is lower for an older worker, or that the potential for development is higher for a younger worker (B. Rosen & Jerdee, 1976).

# IV. Conclusion

The time may have arrived to confront the question of whether it is necessary, or desirable, to treat age as a primary variable in discussions of job performance, career development, and other aspects of work. A fundamental assumption of the perspective we have advocated is that all age relations are mediated through other variables —that is, KSAOs, and variables reflecting system factors. If one accepts the premise that these are the variables of greatest relevance instead of age, then the focus in future research should be on identifying and understanding these mediating variables, and the mechanisms by which age is related to these variables, rather than on examining relations between age and work behavior. In other words, if aging is really a continuum along which factors exert their influence, then although it is true that an individual at any age is a product of those influences, aging *per se* is not a direct cause of work behavior.

We therefore suggest that careful consideration is needed before concluding that any work-related issues are really age specific. Our argument can be illustrated with an anecdote attributed to Kleemeier by Griew (1959). An enthusiastic, well-meaning, geriatric specialist was speaking to an architect and emphasizing the need to build warm and resilient floors in designing houses for old people when the architect replied, "And for whom, Sir, should I build them cold and hard?" The point in this context is that the goal should not be to design for the elderly, but to design for people with selected characteristics, which in certain situations could include a sizable proportion of the population.

It is important to emphasize that we are not advocating the use of functional age as a replacement for chronological age. Instead, we are suggesting that age is not meaningful as a causal variable in either a chronological, or a functional, sense (Avolio et al., 1984; Salthouse, 1986).

It is true that reliance on relevant predictors (i.e., KSAOs) in organizational settings may have an adverse impact on older adults because of negative relations between age and some of those predictors. Age may therefore function as a risk factor for low job performance or reduced participation in career development activities, not because of advanced age itself, but because of characteristics that are associated with age. It is therefore appropriate and desirable that research be directed at understanding the factors responsible for relations between age and what we have termed KSAO variables. Furthermore, if the relevant characteristics can be identified, then a more focused target will be available for intervention. That is, critical aspects of the workplace might be modified, or attempts could be made to train employees in very specific skills. In contrast, and despite valiant attempts by seekers of the fountain of youth or an antiaging elixir, no intervention is ever likely to be successful in altering an individual's age.

## References

Avolio, B. J. (1991). A levels-of-analysis perspective of aging and work research. *Annual Review of Gerontology and Geriatrics, 11,* 239–260.

Avolio, B. J., Barrett, G. V., & Sterns, H. L. (1984). Alternatives to age for assessing occupational performance capacity. *Experimental Aging Research, 10,* 101–105.

Avolio, B. J., Waldman, D. A., & McDaniel, M. A. (1990). Age and work performance in nonmanagerial jobs: The effects of experience and occupational type. *Academy of Management Journal, 33,* 407–422.

Birren, J. E., & Renner, V. J. (1977). Research on the psychology of aging: Principles and experimentation. In J. E. Birren & K. W. Schaie (Eds.), *Handbook of the psychology of aging* (pp. 3–38). New York: Van Nostrand-Reinhold.

Cantor, N., Markus, H., Niedenthal, P. & Nurius, P. (1986). On motivation and the self-concept. In R. Sorrentino & E. Higgins (Eds.), *Handbook of motivation and cognition: Foundations of social behavior* (pp. 96–121). New York: Guilford.

Cleveland, J., & Shore, L. (1992). Self- and supervisory perspectives on age and work attitudes and performance. *Journal of Applied Psychology, 77,* 469–484.

Cohen, J. (1992). A power primer. *Psychological Bulletin, 112,* 155–159.

Crew, J. (1984). Age stereotypes as a function of race. *Academy of Management Journal, 27,* 431–435.

Davies, D. R., & Sparrow, P. R. (1985). Age and work behavior. In N. Charness (Ed.), *Aging and human performance* (pp. 293–332). Chichester, UK: Wiley.

Davies, J., & Easterby-Smith, M. (1984). Learning and developing from managerial work experience. *Journal of Management Studies, 21,* 169–183.

Dubin, S. (1990). Maintaining competence through updating. In S. Willis & S. Dubin (Eds.), *Maintaining professional competence* (pp. 9–43). San Francisco: Jossey-Bass.

Engle, E., Miguel, R., Steelman, L., & McDaniel, M. (1994, April). *An examination of the relationship between age and work values.* Paper presented at the annual Conference of the Society for Industrial and Organizational Psychology, Nashville, TN.

Fossum, J., Arvey, R., Paradise, C., & Robbins, N. (1986). Modeling the skills obsolescence process: A psychological/economic integration. *Academy of Management Review, 11,* 362–374.

Ghiselli, E. E. (1973). The validity of aptitude tests in personnel selection. *Personnel Psychology, 26,* 461–477.

Gist, M., & Mitchell, T. (1992). Self-efficacy: A theoretical analysis of its determinants and malleability. *Academy of Management Review, 17,* 183–211.

Griew, S. (1959). Methodological problems in industrial ageing. *Occupational Psychology, 33,* 36–46.

Hall, D., & Mansfield, R. (1975). Relationships of age and seniority with career variables of engineers and scientists. *Journal of Applied Psychology, 60,* 201–210.

Hunter, J. E. (1986). Cognitive ability, cognitive aptitude, job knowledge, and job performance. *Journal of Vocational Behavior, 29,* 340–362.

Hunter, J. E., & Hunter, R. F. (1984). Validity and utility of alternative predictors of job performance. *Psychological Bulletin, 96,* 72–98.

Ilgen, D., & Youtz, M. (1986). Factors affecting the evaluation and development of minorities in organizations. *Research in Personnel and Human Resources Management, 4,* 307–337.

Knowles, M. (1973). *The adult learner: A neglected species.* Houston: Gulf Publishing Co.

Kozlowski, S., & Farr, J. (1988). An integrative model of updating and performance. *Human Performance, 1,* 5–29.

Lee, J., & Clemens, T. (1985). Factors affecting employment decisions about older workers. *Journal of Applied Psychology, 70,* 785–788.

Markus, H. (1983). Self-knowledge: An expanded view. *Journal of Personality, 51,* 543–565.

Markus, H., & Herzog, R. (1991). The role of the self-concept in aging. *Annual Review of Gerontology and Geriatrics, 11,* 110–143.

Maurer, T. (1994, August). *Individual differences in employee learning and development orientation: Toward an integrative model.* Paper presented at the annual meeting of the Academy of Management, Dallas, TX.

Maurer, T., & Tarulli, B. (1994). Perceived environment, perceived outcome, and person variables in relationship to voluntary development activity by employees. *Journal of Applied Psychology, 79,* 3–14.

McCall, M., Lombardo, M., & Morrison, A. (1988). *The lessons of experience: How successful executives develop on the job.* Lexington, MA: Lexington Books.

McCauley, C., Ruderman, M., Ohlott, P., & Morrow, J. (1994). Assessing the developmental components of managerial jobs. *Journal of Applied Psychology, 79,* 544–560.

McEvoy, G. M., & Cascio, W. F. (1989). Cumulative evidence of the relationship between employee age and job performance. *Journal of Applied Psychology, 74,* 11–17.

Noe, R. (1986). Trainee's attributes and attitudes: Neglected influences on training effectiveness. *Academy of Management Review, 11,* 736–749.

Noe, R., & Wilk, S. (1993). Investigation of factors that influence employees' participation in development activities. *Journal of Applied Psychology, 78,* 291–302.

Porter, L. (1963). Job attitudes in management: Perceived importance of needs as a function of job level. *Journal of Applied Psychology, 47,* 141–148.

Price, R., Thompson, P., & Dalton, G. (1975, November). A longitudinal study of technological obsolescence. *Research Management,* pp. 22–28.

Rhodes, S. R. (1983). Age-related differences in work attitudes and behavior: A review and conceptual analysis. *Psychological Bulletin, 93,* 328–367.

Rosen, B., & Jerdee, T. (1976). The nature of

job-related age stereotypes. *Journal of Applied Psychology, 61,* 180–183.

Rosen, N., Williams, L., & Foltman, F. (1965). Motivational constraints in an industrial retraining program. *Personnel Psychology, 18,* 65–79.

Salthouse, T. A. (1984). Effects of age and skill in typing. *Journal of Experimental Psychology: General, 113,* 345–371.

Salthouse, T. A. (1986). Functional age: Examination of a concept. In J. E. Birren, P. K. Robinson, & J. E. Livingston (Eds.), *Age, health, and employment* (pp. 63–92). Englewood Cliffs, NJ: Prentice-Hall.

Salthouse, T. A. (1991). *Theoretical perspectives in cognitive aging.* Hillsdale, NJ: Erlbaum.

Salthouse, T. A. (1995). Refining the concept of psychological compensation. In R. A. Dixon & L. Bäckman (Eds.), *Psychological compensation: Managing losses and promoting gains.* Hillsdale, NJ: Erlbaum.

Schmidt, F. L., & Hunter, J. E. (1992). Development of a causal model of processes determining job performance. *Current Directions in Psychological Science, 1,* 89–92.

Schmidt, F. L., Hunter, J. E., & Outerbridge, A. N. (1986). The impact of job experience and ability on job knowledge, work sample performance, and supervisory ratings of job performance. *Journal of Applied Psychology, 71,* 432–439.

Schmidt, F. L., Hunter, J. E., Outerbridge, A. N., & Goff, S. (1988). Joint relation of experience and ability with job performance: Test of three hypotheses. *Journal of Applied Psychology, 73,* 46–57.

Sterns, H., & Patchett, M. (1984). Technology and the aging adult: Career development and training. In P. K. Robinson, J. Livingston, & J. E. Birren (Eds.), *Aging and technical advances* (pp. 261–278). New York: Plenum.

Waldman, D. A., & Avolio, B. J. (1986). A meta-analysis of age differences in job performance. *Journal of Applied Psychology, 71,* 33–38.

Warr, P. (1994). Age and employment. In M. Dunnette, L. Hough, & H. Triandis (Eds.), *Handbook of industrial and organizational psychology* (Vol. 4, pp. 487–550). Palo Alto, CA: Consulting Psychologists Press.

Zenger, T., & Lawrence, B. (1989). Organizational demography: The differential effects of age and tenure distributions on technical communication. *Academy of Management Journal, 32,* 353–376.

# Twenty-One

# Aging and Mental Disorders

Margaret Gatz, Julia E. Kasl-Godley, and Michele J. Karel

## I. Introduction

The focus of this chapter is the prevalence, diagnosis, and risk factors for psychopathology in older adults. We pose four questions: First, what are age differences in rates of disorder? Second, to what extent do cases first appear in later life as opposed to constituting lifelong conditions? Third, are the characteristics of psychopathological syndromes different in older adults compared to younger cases; in particular, do diagnostic systems need to be adjusted when considering older adults? Fourth, can age differences in vulnerabilities and stressors explain age differences in rates and features of various mental disorders?

For purposes of looking at how frequently older adults suffer from emotional or cognitive symptoms, the most significant database for estimating rates of disorder remains the Epidemiologic Catchment Area survey (ECA), first reported a decade ago (Regier et al., 1984). Adult and aged samples, including both community-residing and institutionalized persons, were interviewed using a structured format that permitted diagnosing disorders according to the *Diagnostic and Statistical Manual of Mental Disorders, Third*

*Edition* (*DSM-III*) (American Psychiatric Association, 1980). More recent databases, such as the Established Populations for Epidemiologic Studies of the Elderly (EPESE) (Cornoni-Huntley, Brock, Ostfeld, Taylor, & Wallace, 1986) will be mentioned as well.

Consideration of age differences in prevalence and features of disorders is complicated by historical and cross-national differences in nomenclature and diagnostic criteria, rendering comparisons imprecise. For example, since the ECA was undertaken, the *DSM* has been revised (*DSM-III-R*) (American Psychiatric Association, 1987) and a fourth edition issued (*DSM-IV*) (American Psychiatric Association, 1994). A further impediment is that most data come from cross-sectional studies that provide only a snapshot at some point in time of the number of people who meet the criteria for a disorder. Moreover, there is an absence of definitive information about cultural and racial differences in rates and presentation of disorder.

Nonetheless, taking into account the proportion of older adults living in the community and in institutions, and extrapolating from information concerning rates of mental disorders in the community and in institutions, respectively, we can infer that about 22% of adults aged 65 and older meet criteria for some mental disorder, including both emotional dysfunction and cognitive impairment (Gatz & Smyer, 1992). This estimated rate converges with National Advisory Mental Health Council (1993) projections that during any given year 22% of the adult population has any mental disorder, and with the inference from a variety of data that 17–22% of those under age 18 have a developmental, emotional, or behavioral problem (Kazdin & Kagan, 1994). Thus, evidence tends to suggest that the proportion of the population with a mental disorder does not change greatly with age, although certainly different disorders are predominant at different ages.

In Section II, we consider five different clusters of diagnoses: depression, anxiety disorders, schizophrenia and paranoid disorders, personality disorders, and dementia. Although not comprehensively covering the *DSM* categories, these represent the most common and most concerning psychopathologies.

In this chapter we propose and apply a life span developmental diathesis-stress perspective. Most contemporary scholars of child and adult psychopathology think in terms of diathesis-stress. Zubin and Spring (1977) introduced the notion of a vulnerability-stress model (shown in Figure 1) for discussing the etiology of schizophrenia. On one dimension is diathesis (i.e., the individual's level of vulnerability) influenced by genetic propensities, acquired biological vulnerabilities, and psychological factors, such as attributional styles that put one at greater risk of disorder. On the other dimension is stress (i.e., negative life events), such as loss of a parent; chronic stressful situations, such as unemployment; or environmental exposures, such as toxic substances. Diatheses and stressors both contribute to an overall liability for the disorder. With greater liability, individuals are closer to the threshold at which a clinical diagnosis would be made.

We suggest that, by considering age and cohort differences in diathesis and stress, one should be able to explain age differences in rates, etiology, and phenomenology of mental disorder. For example, aging is associated both with changes in neurotransmitter functioning that could be rele-

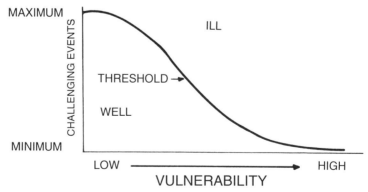

**Figure 1** Diathesis-stress model showing the relationship between vulnerability and life-event stressors. (From Zubin and Spring, 1977, Fig. 2, p. 110. Copyright 1977 by the American Psychological Association. Reproduced by permission.)

vant to cognitive and emotional symptoms and with changes in the likelihood of certain consensually stressful life events (e.g., bereavement). It is particularly important to note that genetic influences can change during development, with particular genes showing their effects at various ages. Thus, disorders thought to be heritable, entirely or in part, can appear in old age with no indication earlier in life (see Pedersen, Ch. 4, this volume). Relevant cohort-related differences encompass changes in educational and occupational opportunities for younger adults of today in comparison to younger adults of previous decades who now make up the older population.

Diathesis-stress models have not tended to take a developmental perspective. Recently, a few writers have begun to discuss models of developmental psychopathology, defined as the study of developmental pathways that lead to a disorder; however, their focus has been on children (e.g., Kazdin & Kagan, 1994). In this chapter, we extend this thinking to older adults.

Particularly in older adults, a critical developmental consideration is the distinction between mental disorder that occurs for the first time in old age and mental disorder that had its first onset in younger adulthood and has continued as a chronic or episodically recurring mental illness into old age (Kahn, 1977). This distinction can be expanded to encompass three sorts of older adults with mental disorders: (a) those who had the disorder earlier in life and are experiencing a continuation or recurrence; (b) those with a liability from earlier in life that is exacerbated in old age and only then results in mental disorder; and (c) those who experience a new disorder in later life. As well, there can be older adults who had a disorder earlier in life but do not show evidence of any disturbance in old age. These patterns may be interpreted in terms of the interaction of diatheses and stressors over time. For instance, stressors earlier in the individual's

development may alter biological or psychological vulnerability to other events later in life.

## II. Prevalence, Presentation, and Risk Factors for Selected Syndromes

### A. Depression

#### 1. What Are Age Differences in Rates of Depression?

Prevalence of depression can be assessed using either diagnostic criteria (which correspond to categorical models in which a person either has the disorder or does not) or symptom checklists (which provide scores along a continuum). Diagnostic criteria for major depressive disorder (American Psychiatric Association, 1994) require depressed mood or loss of interest in activities in combination with three or four additional symptoms (loss of appetite, sleep disturbance, fatigue, feelings of worthlessness, etc.). These symptoms cannot be physiologically caused by a general medical condition, and they must extend for a 2-week period. Diagnostic criteria for dysthymic disorder, a mood disorder that sometimes prefaces major depressive disorder, require fewer symptoms but an extended duration of being "down in the dumps" (American Psychiatric Association, 1994). Symptom checklists ask for presence, intensity, or frequency of a series of symptoms during the preceding 1 or 2 weeks. Thus, it is possible to score relatively high on a symptom checklist without meeting diagnostic criteria for depression.

Epidemiological studies show less major depressive disorder among older adults than among middle-aged adults, as exemplified in the ECA data in Table I, where 2.5% of older adults meet diagnostic criteria for either major depressive disorder or dysthymic disorder (Regier et al., 1988). In

**Table I**
Prevalence Rates for Mood and Anxiety Disorders
during the Preceding 1 Month
(Percentage in Each Age Group)[a]

| | Age | | |
| --- | --- | --- | --- |
| Disorder | 25–44 | 45–64 | 65 and older |
| Major depressive disorder | | | |
| Men | 2.2 | 1.2 | 0.4 |
| Women | 3.9 | 2.6 | 0.9 |
| Dysthymic disorder | | | |
| Men | 2.8 | 2.0 | 1.0 |
| Women | 5.1 | 5.4 | 2.3 |
| Anxiety disorders | | | |
| Men | 4.7 | 5.1 | 3.6 |
| Women | 11.7 | 8.0 | 6.8 |

[a]Data are from Regier et al. (1988), based on the Diagnostic Interview Schedule (DIS), with rates standardized according to age, gender, and race distributions of the U.S. population.

contrast, 27% of elderly ECA respondents had some depressive symptoms, without meeting criteria for depressive disorder (Koenig & Blazer, 1992).

On symptom checklists, data from the EPESE and other surveys converge in suggesting that there is a curvilinear relationship between age and depression scores over the entire adult life span, with the highest scores among younger adults and those over age 75 (Blazer, Burchett, Service, & George, 1991; Gatz & Hurwicz, 1990; Lewinsohn, Rohde, Fischer, & Seeley, 1991). Furthermore, the elevation in scores among the very old has generally *not* been found to be an artifact of greater endorsement of somatic symptoms (Gatz & Hurwicz, 1990; Kessler, Foster, Webster, & House, 1992).

Thus, clinical diagnostic and symptom checklist data concur in indicating that dysphoria and other subclinical symptoms increase across old age, whereas clinical depression by and large does not. Although women generally show higher rates of depression than men, several studies suggest that by age 80 women and men are equally elevated on depressive symptoms (e.g., Wallace & O'Hara, 1992).

Age differences in clinical depression cannot be accounted for by retrospective reporting errors or by differential mortality. However, data from the ECA (Klerman & Weissman, 1989), National Comorbidity Study (Kessler, McGonagle, Nelson et al., 1994), and other surveys (Lewinsohn, Rohde, Seeley, & Fischer, 1993) provide some indication of a cohort effect, with successively more recent adult cohorts showing higher rates of depressive disorder, earlier ages of initial onset, and higher rates of relapse, in contrast to those born earlier in the twentieth century. Increase in risk factors for depression in youth born since World War II (associated with urbanization and changes in family structure) have been mentioned as possible explanations. If the cohort interpretation is correct, then in the future older adults may have higher rates of depressive disorder compared to current cohorts of older adults.

### 2. To What Extent Does Depression in Older Adults Represent Early-Onset or Late-Onset Disorder?

Due to reliance on cross-sectional and retrospective data, insufficient attention has been paid to longitudinal patterns of onset and recurrence. It appears, however, that many older adults with major depressive disorder have a history of prior episodes (Koenig & Blazer, 1992). Using data from the ECA, Burke, Burke, Regier, and Rae (1990) found that median age of onset for depression was 25, although there was an elevated risk again after age 89. Thus, both incidence and prevalence of clinically diagnosed depression appear to be low in old age, with a possible upswing in very old age.

### 3. Is the Nature of Depression Different in Older Adults?

Depressed older adults characteristically indicate diminished interest in things around them, fatigue, difficulty with waking early in the morning and not being able to get back to sleep, complaints about their memory, thoughts about death, and general hopelessness (e.g., see Reifler, 1994). In turn, older adults have been shown to endorse dysphoria or depressed mood less often than would be expected according to their other symptoms (Gallo, Anthony, & Muthén, 1994), a finding that may help to account for the low prevalence of major depressive disorder or may indicate age-related differences in the nature of depression.

Newmann, Engel, and Jensen (1991) have promoted the term *depletion syndrome* to describe a form of depression commonly observed in older adults, primarily involving lack of interest and feeling that everything is an effort. Others have recommended a diagnostic category, tentatively called *minor depression*, to capture subclinical symptoms so often observed in older adults (Blazer, Burchett et al., 1991). In support of the notion that minor depression is clinically significant, Zonderman, Herbst, Schmidt, Costa, and McCrae (1993) demonstrated that depressive symptom scores, even below a clinical cutoff, predicted various psychiatric diagnoses 16 years later. At the same time, Coyne (1994) warned against confusing everyday sorts of distress and disappointments with diagnosable depression. Although his focus was college students, the concern deserves attention in relation to older adults as well.

Finally, an apparently distinguishing characteristic of depression in old age is its lethality. White males, particularly those with medical illness or living alone, show an increasing risk of suicide from age 60 to 85 (Conwell, 1994). A similar relationship between suicide and age is not found for women or for men from other ethnic subgroups. Conwell (1994) noted that two-thirds of elderly suicides had a depressive disorder, often their first episode (although Coyne, 1994, observed that for all ages, between one-half to two-thirds of suicides are related to depression).

### 4. Can Age Differences in Vulnerability and Stressors Explain Age Differences in Rates and Features of Depression?

The diathesis dimension includes genetic propensity, biological vulnerabilities, and psychological attributes. It is generally argued that genetic propensity is less important in late-onset than early-onset cases (Alexopoulos, Young, Abrams, Meyers, & Shamoian, 1989); however, genetic diathesis could conceivably play a role in predisposing an individual to acquired biological vulnerabilities.

Biological diathesis has received a great deal of attention with regard to depression in older adults. Age-related physiological and brain structure changes have been suggested as plausible risk factors for late-onset depression because of parallels between these changes and pathological changes observed in depression, such as dysregulation of the monoamine system, increased monoamine oxidase activity, deficits in norepinephrine functioning, down regulation of serotonin receptors, and deep white- and gray-matter disease (Alexopoulos et al., 1989; Leuchter, 1994).

Physical illness is consistently among the strongest risk factors for depression, and prevalence of major depressive disorder among older adults in medical settings has been estimated at approximately 15% (Reifler, 1994). One implication is that depression—or at least significant dysphoria—can occur as an outcome of certain somatic illnesses or medications, reflecting a biologically mediated process. Alternatively, physical illness can act as a stressor, and depression can be a reaction to being ill or disabled.

Whereas biological diathesis seems to increase with age, in terms of psychological diathesis, older adults may be *less* vulnerable than younger adults. Older individuals have had the opportunity to learn how to

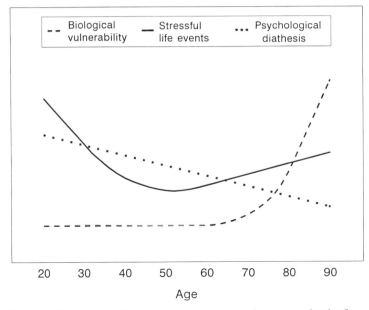

**Figure 2**   Depiction of developmental changes in the magnitude of influence on depressive symptomatology exerted by biological vulnerability
(dashed line), psychological diathesis (dotted line), and stressful life events
(solid line).

cope with stressors and how to adjust their
expectations so as to have fewer feelings of
failure (Nolen-Hoeksema, 1988).

   On the stress dimension, life events
have shown inconsistent relationships to
depression in old age. Bereavement, declining physical health status, existential
concerns, and other loss events are obvious examples of issues that might precipi-
tate depression in an older person because
of the greater frequency of these particular
events in older compared to younger persons. However, negative events are more
numerous in younger than in older adults,
and the relationship between life events or
chronic stress and depression may actually be less strong in older than in younger
adults (George, 1994).

   As shown in Figure 2, we can use the
existing literature to plot the relationship
between age and biological diathesis, psychological diathesis, and stressful life
events, respectively. The combined wax-
ing and waning of these influences corre-

sponds to the curvilinear relationship between age and depressive symptoms.[1] In
support of this interpretation, Blazer, Burchett et al. (1991) found that controlling
for factors that are correlated with age—
such as increased chronic illness and
physical disability, reduced income, and
loss of close relatives—resulted in a small
negative residual relationship between depressive symptoms and age. Thus, a developmental diathesis-stress approach provides a heuristic for understanding the
occurrence and correlates of depression in
older adults.

### B. Anxiety Disorders

In contrast to depression, there has been a
striking lack of attention to anxiety in old-

---

[1] The developmental diathesis-stress model with
respect to depression, especially as represented in
Figure 2, draws upon work in progress by Michele
Karel (1995).

er adults. Although anxiety disorders are less prevalent among older adults than any other age group, at the same time, anxiety disorders are more common in older adults than are depressive disorders (see data in Table I, from Regier et al., 1988). A variety of anxiety disorders are described in the *DSM-III-R* and *DSM-IV* (American Psychiatric Association, 1987, 1994), including (a) panic disorder, which refers to recurring sudden episodes of intense apprehension, palpitations, shortness of breath, and chest pain; (b) phobias, which are fears and avoidance out of proportion to the danger; and (c) generalized anxiety disorder, entailing chronic, persistent, and excessive anxiety and worry.

Anxiety disorders tend to begin early in life. Onset after age 65 is unusual, representing only 3% of older adult cases in the ECA data (Blazer, George, & Hughes, 1991), although the risk of new cases of phobia is equally distributed across age (Anthony & Aboraya, 1992).

Considering anxiety disorders from a diathesis-stress point of view, genetic propensity appears to play a minimal role. Panic disorder, which shows the most consistent evidence for heritability (Sheikh, 1992), has a lower prevalence in older adults compared with other age groups (Blazer, George, & Hughes, 1991).

Biological diathesis may become more important with age, insofar as changes in neurotransmitter systems associated with the aging brain could increase the predisposition toward anxiety in old age. Age-related decreases in noradrenergic function provide one plausible biological mechanism (Sunderland, Lawlor, Martinez, & Molchan, 1991). A number of physical disorders can produce anxiety-like symptoms (e.g., silent myocardial infarcts and pulmonary embolism), and anxiety can be a side effect of many medications (G. Cohen, 1991). In turn, anxiety can make people more vulnerable to physical disorder, an effect possibly mediated by autonomic arousal.

Psychological models of anxiety emphasize such mechanisms as learned avoidance, or oversensitivity to bodily reactions, which are interpreted catastrophically. There is no evidence from which to infer age differences in psychological diathesis, although in older adults there may be a basis in reality for many of their worries.

With regard to the stress dimension, anxiety—like depression—has been described as a response to negative life events. Comorbid anxiety and depression are not uncommon at any age (Kessler, McGonagle, Zhao et al., 1994), although Sheikh (1992) opined that differential diagnosis may be more difficult in older adults.

## C. Schizophrenia and Late Paraphrenia

Although late-onset schizophrenia is uncommon (Mulsant et al., 1993), consideration of schizophrenia and other psychotic disorders highlights fundamental issues in delineating psychopathology in later life. Schizophrenia is marked by peculiarities of thinking, behaving, and feeling. Bizarre thinking involves loose associations, hallucinations, or delusions. Peculiar behavior may include strange grimaces and unusual posture as well as poor social skills. Emotional symptoms generally comprise blunting of affect or inappropriate expressions of feeling. Symptoms have been classified as either positive (referring to the presence or excess of a characteristic, e.g., hallucinations) or negative (referring to the absence of a behavior, e.g., flat affect) (Andreasen, Flaum, Swayze, Tyrrell, & Arndt, 1990).

Lifetime prevalence for schizophrenia is slightly under 1% (Kessler, McGonagle, Zhao et al., 1994). Age of onset for schizophrenia is typically between late teenage and early thirties. The disorder tends to be chronic, with complete remission unusual, although the tendency is to stabilize by midlife (American Psychiatric Association, 1994). Thus, most elderly schizophrenic patients are chronic schizophrenics who have grown old. These patients tend to have a predominance of negative symptoms (Meeks & Walker, 1990), the features that are helped least by the neuroleptic drugs used to treat schizophrenia.

Most clinicians describe a small number of late-onset schizophrenics (e.g., Rabins, 1992). Some urge use of the term *paraphrenia* for these cases (e.g., Quintal, Day-Cody, & Levy, 1991). Paraphrenia is usually described as having an age of onset after 60 and entailing paranoid delusions with or without auditory hallucinations, less thought disorder, and less flattening of affect (Roth, 1955). The alternative argument holds that two diagnostic categories already available in the *DSM*—late-onset schizophrenia and delusional disorder— are sufficient to describe all cases that would fall under the heading of paraphrenia. Delusional disorder is characterized by an isolated delusion but no other symptoms, with the delusion not signaling neurological disorder (American Psychiatric Association, 1994).

As described by Post (1987), delusions in older patients characteristically take the form of "unshakable false beliefs" with remarkably "banal" content (pp. 44 and 50). Persecutory delusions are reported in over 90% of cases (Howard, Castle, O'Brien, Almeida, & Levy, 1991; Pearlson et al., 1989). The other distinctive symptom is a partition delusion, defined as "the belief that people, animals, materials, or radiation can pass through a structure that would normally constitute a barrier to such passage" (Howard et al., 1991, p. 720), such as a door or wall. Partition delusions are relatively rare in other diagnostic categories, including elderly early-onset schizophrenics.

The etiology of early-onset chronic schizophrenia served as the prototype for the diathesis-stress model. Twin and adoption studies have demonstrated that genetic propensity plays a role (e.g., risk to cotwins of monozygotic probands is near .50; Gottesman, 1981). Other biological risk factors probably represent intra-uterine complications resulting in neuro-logical abnormalities (e.g., see Cannon, Mednick, & Parnas, 1989). Excessive dopamine has been fingered as the relevant neurotransmitter pathway, and Finch and Morgan (1987) hypothesized that decrease with age in dopaminergic receptors may help to explain why chronic schizophrenics experience a diminution in symptoms with age. A disordered family situation, featuring parental overprotection and criticism, has been linked to relapse (Asarnow & Goldstein, 1986). Traumatizing events may have either a predisposing or a precipitating effect. Influences probably interact, such that, for example, a biologically at-risk individual would be more vulnerable to the effects of stress.

Risk factors for late-onset schizophrenia or paraphrenia present a slightly different pattern. It is generally accepted that there is somewhat less contribution of genetics to paraphrenia than to schizophrenia (Post, 1987). Biological diathesis may be of increased importance. Miller, Benson, Cummings, and Neshkes (1986) reported on five paraphrenics, all of whom were revealed by neuroimaging to have an organic condition. Naguid and Levy (1987) found that paraphrenics had ventricular enlargement compared with normal older adults, but this abnormality is also characteristic of younger schizophrenics (Andreasen, Swayze et al., 1990). Another difference in risk factors for different ages of onset is sex. Among younger cases of schizophrenia, there are more men than women, whereas there are more cases of paraphrenia among women than among men, beyond what can be explained by differences in life expectancy (Rabins, 1992). One reason may lie in relationships between reduced level of estrogen in older women and the dopaminergic system (Mayer, Kelterborn, & Naber, 1993).

Psychological diathesis for paraphrenia includes premorbid schizoid personality disorder (Pearlson et al., 1989). Traumas earlier in life, such as parental separation, being a refugee, and childlessness, may play a role in elevating vulnerability (Gurian, Wexler, & Baker, 1992; Holden, 1987), whereas recent stress may trigger the onset of disorder. Some researchers have reported that hearing loss is associated with late-onset schizophrenia or paraphrenia (Pearlson et al., 1989; Quintal et al., 1991). However, Gurian et al. (1992) found that hearing loss was most frequent among dementia patients with paranoid symptoms.

There are important issues of differential diagnosis as well. Although delusional disorders in older adults may sometimes represent disorders continuous with their early-onset counterparts, at other times the symptomatology reflects prethreshold organic brain change. For instance, paranoid delusions can occur either in connection with delirium or in the early phases of a dementia in order to fill in gaps created by impaired memory. Holden (1987) found that approximately a third of cases with paranoid delusions and no cognitive impairment at time of initial diagnosis later developed dementia.

## D. Personality Disorders

Personality disorders refer to individuals' characterological tendencies that are particularly enduring, pervasive, and inflexible, and consequently interfere with adaptive functioning or cause the individual to feel distress (American Psychiatric Association, 1994). Personality disorders tend to manifest themselves in distorted ways of perceiving oneself or other people, including obliviousness to one's effect on others; inappropriate emotional responses; or inconsistent control of impulsive behavior. In turn, individuals with these disorders behave in ways that help to create situations that confirm their biases.

Relatively little is known about personality disorders in older adults. Literature reviews relying mainly on clinical reports suggest that some personality disorders may become less prominent or less problematic in old age, for example, borderline, antisocial, and narcissistic, whereas others may persist or even become more intrusive, for example, paranoid, compulsive, and schizotypal (Rosowsky & Gurian, 1991; Sadavoy & Fogel, 1992). Rosowsky and Gurian (1991) conducted a small study to explore the question of whether diagnostic criteria for personality disorder should be age-specific. Among older patients deemed by their therapists to be borderlines, none met sufficient diagnostic criteria to qualify for a *DSM-III-R* diagnosis. Specifically, impulse control and identity disturbance were less likely, albeit the characteristic interpersonal difficulties (e.g., intensity, sense of entitlement, problems with boundaries) and affective instability (e.g., problems with controlling anger) were evident (Rosowsky & Gurian, 1991).

Although this finding lends support to use of age-specific criteria, a competing concern is overdiagnosis of personality disorders in old age. Sadavoy and Fogel (1992) cited an example of an 85-year-old who does not appear to desire close friends and who displays constricted affect, submitting that it would be inappropriate to apply a diagnosis of schizoid personality disorder.

Most personality disorders are presumed to be early-onset disorders. There is some evidence of a genetic diathesis for borderline personality disorder (see review by Carey & DiLalla, 1994), and early traumatic experiences have been related to borderline personality disorder (Nigg & Goldsmith, 1994). Although it is possible that some personality disorders arise in later life, Andrulonis, Glueck, Stroebel, and Vogel (1982) suggested that what may appear as late-onset borderline personality disorder—emotional overreactivity, impulsivity, and aggressive outbursts arising for the first time in later life—may represent an organic etiology. Indeed, this symptomatology would reflect early stages of dementia of the frontal-temporal type, in which personality and emotional changes—reflecting disinhibition due to frontal lobe pathology—typically precede cognitive changes (Gustafsson, 1987).

More often, personality disorders seemingly represent a vulnerable personality that becomes increasingly less adaptive with new stressful events in old age. For instance, severe life stress might propel long-standing personality patterns into personality disorder (Sadavoy & Fogel, 1992), or older adults with lifelong personality disorder may be more vulnerable to other late-onset disorders. For instance, Abrams, Alexopolous, and Young (1987) found that scores on a number of different personality disorders (compulsive, avoidant, dependent, masochistic, schizotypal, borderline, histrionic, and narcissistic) were all elevated in older adults with late-onset depression.

### E. Dementias

#### 1. What Is the Prevalence of Dementing Disorders?

Dementia is a mental disorder found almost entirely in old age. It is defined as an acquired impairment affecting multiple cognitive domains, especially memory, without disturbance of consciousness, and with the decrement sufficient to interfere with usual activities and social functioning (American Psychiatric Association, 1994). Alzheimer's disease, or dementia of the Alzheimer type (DAT), is customarily reported to be the most frequent type of dementia, followed by the vascular dementias (VaD), principally multi-infarct dementia. As indicated by the diagnostic criteria originating from the National Institute of Neurological and Communicative Disorders and Stroke and the Alzheimer's Disease and Related Disorders Association (NINCDS/ADRDA) (McKhann et al., 1984), Alzheimer's disease has an insidious onset and a progressive course, with the memory and intellectual problems eventually interfering with all self-care. It has primarily been a diagnosis of exclusion, assigned when other causes of dementia have been ruled out, substantiated by postmortem neuropathological examination.

VaD can be diagnosed using recent criteria from the National Institute of Neurological Disorders and Stroke and Association Internationale pour la Recherche et l'Enseignement en Neurosciences (NINDS-AIREN) (Roman et al., 1993). Characteristically, there has been occlusion of cerebral blood vessels leading to destruction of brain tissue. The remainder of dementias include Pick's disease, subcortical dementias such as dementia in Parkinson's disease, infectious dementias such as Jakob-Creutzfeldt disease, metabolic dementing disorders, and normal-pressure hydrocephalus (Cummings & Benson, 1992).

A variety of prevalence estimates for dementia are shown in Table II. The meta-analysis from Ritchie, Kildea, and Robine (1992) indicates that prevalence doubles every 5.7 years, although the exponential rate of increase does not continue after age 90. Also included in Table II are results from the ECA study for both "severe cognitive impairment" (Regier et al., 1988) and "mild cognitive impairment" (George, Blazer, Winfield-Laird, Leaf, & Fischbach, 1988). The latter corresponded to performance on a mental status screening test sufficient to warrant referral for a clinical examination for possible dementia.

Several prevalence estimates for Alzheimer's disease are shown in Table II as well. The data from EURODEM (the Commission of the European Community Concerted Action on the Epidemiology of Dementia) (Rocca et al., 1991a) represent a pooling of all recent prevalence studies in Europe. Evans et al. (1989), working with the EPESE sample in East Boston, estimated rates of Alzheimer's disease to be substantially higher than other scholars.

**Table II**
Rates of Dementia and Alzheimer's Disease (Percentage in Each Age Group)

| Author | Source | Age 60–64 | 65–69 | 70–74 | 75–79 | 80–84 | 85–89 | 90–94 |
|---|---|---|---|---|---|---|---|---|
| | | | | Rates of Dementia | | | | |
| Ritchie et al. (1992) | 13 studies | 0.8 | 1.4 | 2.6 | 4.7 | 8.7 | 15.8 | 29.0 |
| Regier et al. (1988) | ECA, severe impairment | | | 2.9[b] | | 6.8[c] | 15.8[d] | |
| George et al. (1988)[a] | ECA, mild impairment | | | 13.0[b] | | 19.5[c] | 24.0[d] | |
| Bachman et al. (1992) | Framingham Study | 0.4 | 0.9 | 1.8 | 3.6 | 10.5 | 23.8[d] | |
| | | | | Rates of Alzheimer's Disease | | | | |
| Ritchie et al. (1992) | 13 studies | 0.2 | 0.4 | 0.9 | 2.1 | 4.7 | 10.8 | 24.8 |
| Rocca et al. (1991a) | EURODEM | | 0.3[e] | | 3.2[f] | 10.8[g] | | |
| Evans et al. (1989) | EPESE | | | 3.0[b] | | 18.7[c] | 47.2[d] | |
| Bachman et al. (1992) | Framingham Study | | | 0.5[b] | | 4.1[c] | 13.1[d] | |

[a] Rates of mild cognitive impairment in ECA were extrapolated from data for separate sites provided in George, Blazer, Winfield-Laird, Leaf, and Fischbach (1988). [b] Rates for age 65–74. [c] Rates for age 75–84. [d] Rates for age 85+. [e] Rates for age 60–69. [f] Rates for age 70–79. [g] Rates for age 80–89.

There are two salient methodological explanations: First, in the East Boston Study, nearly a year and a half elapsed between memory screening and diagnostic assessment. Diagnostic outcomes within poor, intermediate, and good memory screening subgroups were used to estimate the number of cases within each respective subgroup. If some individuals with good memory became demented during the interval between screening and clinical assessment, the estimate for that group could be inflated in comparison with results that would have been obtained had memory level and diagnosis been determined contemporaneously (Johansson & Zarit, 1994). Second, in the East Boston Study, 84.1% of individuals with cognitive impairment were determined to have DAT. Usually not over 60% of cases are deemed to have DAT, especially when neuroimaging or other intensive assessment procedures are employed (Skoog, Nilsson, Palmertz, Andreasson, & Svanborg, 1993).

Gender differences in prevalence of DAT have been found in some studies, but not with a consistent direction. If an age category of 85+ is created, women aged 85+ almost invariably have a higher prevalence than men, due to their greater longevity (Bachman et al., 1992). At the same time, Bachman et al. (1993) found incidence of DAT to be the same for men and women. With respect to VaD, rates are quite diverse across gender and country, rendering any pooled estimate unreliable; however, prevalence typically has been greater for men than for women (Rocca et al., 1991b).

## 2. Can a Diathesis-Stress Model Be Applied to Explaining the Etiology of Dementia?

Application of a variation of the diathesis-stress model to dementia has been promulgated by several scholars (Gatz, Lowe, Berg, Mortimer, & Pedersen, 1994; Mortimer, 1994; Roth, 1986). The diathesis and stress dimensions have been construed as genetic propensity and environmental exposures. Supporting the importance of genetic diathesis for Alzheimer's disease, family history is the most noticeable risk factor after age (Breitner, Silverman, Mohs, & Davis, 1988). Genetic linkage techniques have been applied to families with large numbers of affected members, and two different chromosomes (21 and 14) have been associated with early-onset DAT. Work taking place to understand the underlying changes in brain chemistry—namely, beta amyloid deposits and decreases in choline acetyltransferase—is beginning to converge with the genetic linkage investigations. In particular, evidence has emerged that inheriting the $\epsilon$4 allelic variant of apolipoprotein E on chromosome 19 is related to susceptibility for DAT at older ages (Corder et al., 1993). These various genetic findings also point to the heterogeneity of DAT.

Although it is clear that genetic risk alone cannot offer a sufficient explanation for DAT, evidence for specific environmental exposures has been contradictory. Some exposures that have received empirical support include head trauma, hypothyroidism, aluminum (powdered or contained in antiperspirants), and significant alcohol consumption (Fratiglioni, Ahlbom, Viitanen, & Winblad, 1993; Graves & Kukull, 1994; van Duijn, Stijnen, & Hofman, 1991). Estrogen replacement therapy (Henderson, Paganini-Hill, Emanuel, Dunn, & Buckwalter, 1994) and nonsteroidal anti-inflammatories (Breitner et al., 1994) may have a protective effect.

Environmental risk factors for VaD include hypertension, heart disease, smoking, and diabetes (Cummings & Benson, 1992), thus aspirin is suggested as a protective factor (Skoog et al., 1993).

Placing these factors in a developmental context furnishes a model of how dementia may occur. The decline in cognitive reserve that takes place with normal aging would increase an individual's vulnerability. Thus, any environmental exposures that reduce cerebral capacity could bring a very old person more readily to a clinical threshold.

Evidence for a developmental process comes from findings that cognitive decline appears to precede clinically evident dementia. In a 20-year longitudinal study, LaRue and Jarvik (1987) have shown that there was detectably worse intelligence test performance in those who were destined to become demented compared to those who remained normal. In addition, depression—particularly depression that first appears in old age—may precede diagnosable dementia, probably representing an early manifestation of the underlying neuropathology. Among patients who complained about their memories but were diagnosed as depressed and not demented, within 3 or more years over half were found to have become demented (Kral & Emery, 1989; Reding, Haycox, & Blass, 1985).

Differential diagnosis is complicated by the fact that memory complaints often characterize elderly depressives, cognitive performance deficits may be present in patients with severe depression, and there is a substantial level of comorbidity of depression and dementia (Reifler, 1994). Changes in noradrenergic and serotonergic neurotransmitter systems that are related to the dementing process could explain depression that is comorbid with dementia (D. Cohen et al., 1993). Strauss (1995) further hypothesized that the neuropathological changes associated with DAT may release a latent vulnerability to depression.

## III. Conclusion

This chapter has provided an overview of the literature on rates and nature of mental disorders in older adults. We proposed a developmental diathesis-stress framework for examining the frequencies of various psychopathologies in later life, for discussing whether there is a need for different diagnostic categories or criteria to capture qualitative age differences, and for considering the etiology of disorders that appear for the first time in later life.

The literature suggests that there is not an increased risk of depression or anxiety associated with aging, except among the oldest-old or in connection with age-related events such as physical illness. There does appear to be reason to consider age differences in the presentation of depression, possibly due to age-related changes in diatheses and stressors. Personality disorders represent a way to operationalize the vulnerable personality and to hypothesize developmental pathways to some late-onset psychopathology. Schizophrenia is largely an early-onset disorder, but there is a late-onset variant, sometimes called paraphrenia, which shows conspicuous distinctions in its presentation. Prevalence of dementing disorders is unique in being highly associated with age.

Implications for research include a call for longitudinal investigations, separating mental disorder with initial onset in old age from conditions that had their first onset earlier in life, and taking into account different configurations of vulnerabilities and stressors that arise at different ages. These steps will begin to provide a clearer sense of the extent to which age is a risk factor for various diagnoses and whether there are systematic age differences in the types and nature of psychopathology. Elucidating these processes will offer a firmer empirical basis for intervention.

Although it has often been pointed out that aging is a biopsychosocial process and that physical and mental disorders are more complexly intertwined in old age, organizing these factors in a diathesis-stress model seemingly has been overlooked as a heuristic. Such a step offers the possibility of looking from a life span developmental point of view at risk factors in younger and older adults alike.

## Acknowledgments

Preparation of this chapter was facilitated by National Institute on Aging Grant No. R01 AG08724.

The authors are grateful to Gerald C. Davison, who had the patience to read and comment on several earlier drafts. His knowledge about adult psychopathology alerted us to important developments in the field.

## References

Abrams, R. C., Alexopoulos, G. S., & Young, R. C. (1987). Geriatric depression and DSM-III-R personality disorder criteria. *Journal of the American Geriatrics Society, 35,* 383–386.

Alexopoulos, G. S., Young, R. C., Abrams, R. C., Meyers, B., & Shamoian, C. A. (1989). Chronicity and relapse in geriatric depression. *Biological Psychiatry, 26,* 551–564.

American Psychiatric Association. (1980). *Diagnostic and statistical manual of mental disorders* (3rd ed.). Washington, DC: Author.

American Psychiatric Association. (1987). *Diagnostic and statistical manual of mental disorders* (3rd rev. ed.). Washington, DC: Author.

American Psychiatric Association. (1994). *Diagnostic and statistical manual of mental disorders* (4th ed.). Washington, DC: Author.

Andreasen, N. C., Flaum, M., Swayze, V. W., Tyrrell, G., & Arndt, S. (1990). Positive and negative symptoms in schizophrenia: A critical reappraisal. *Archives of General Psychiatry, 47,* 615–621.

Andreasen, N. C., Swayze, V. W., Flaum, M., Yates, W. R., Arndt, S., & McChesney, C. (1990). Ventricular enlargement in schizophrenia evaluated with computed tomographic scanning: Effects of gender, age, and stage of illness. *Archives of General Psychiatry, 47,* 1008–1015.

Andrulonis, P. A., Glueck, B. C., Stroebel, C. F., & Vogel, N. G. (1982). Borderline personality subcategories. *Journal of Nervous and Mental Disease, 170,* 670–679.

Anthony, J. C., & Aboraya, A. (1992). The epidemiology of selected mental disorders in later life. In J. E. Birren, R. B. Sloane, & G. D. Cohen (Eds.), *Handbook of mental health and aging* (2nd ed., pp. 27–73). San Diego, CA: Academic Press.

Asarnow, J. R., & Goldstein, M. J. (1986). Schizophrenia during adolescence and early adulthood: A developmental perspective on risk research. *Clinical Psychology Review, 6,* 211–235.

Bachman, D. L., Wolf, P. A., Linn, R., Knoefel, J. E., Cobb, J., Bélanger, A., D'Agostino, R. B., & White, L. R. (1992). Prevalence of dementia and probable senile dementia of the Alzheimer type in the Framingham Study. *Neurology, 42,* 115–119.

Bachman, D. L., Wolf, P. A., Linn, R., Knoefel, J. E., Cobb, J., Bélanger, A., White, L. R., & D'Agostino, R. B. (1993). Incidence of dementia and probable Alzheimer's disease in a general population: The Framingham Study. *Neurology, 43,* 515–519.

Blazer, D., Burchett, B., Service, C., & George, L. K. (1991). The association of age and depression among the elderly: An epidemiological exploration. *Journal of Gerontology: Medical Sciences, 46,* M210–M215.

Blazer, D., George, L. K., & Hughes, D. (1991). The epidemiology of anxiety disorder. In C. Salzman & B. D. Lebowitz (Eds.), *Anxiety in the elderly: Treatment and research* (pp. 17–30). New York: Springer.

Breitner, J. C. S., Gau, B. A., Welsh, K. A., Plassman, B. L., McDonald, W. M., Helms, M. J., & Anthony, J. C. (1994). Inverse association of anti-inflammatory treatments and Alzheimer's disease: Initial results of a co-twin control study. *Neurology, 44,* 227–232.

Breitner, J. C. S., Silverman, J. M., Mohs, R. C., & Davis, K. L. (1988). Familial aggregation in Alzheimer's disease: Comparison of risk among relatives of early- and late-onset cases, and among male and female relatives in successive generations. *Neurology, 38,* 207–212.

Burke, K. C., Burke, J. D., Regier, D. A., & Rae, D. S. (1990). Age at onset of selected mental disorders in five community populations. *Archives of General Psychiatry, 47,* 511–518.

Cannon, T. D., Mednick, S. A., & Parnas, J. (1989). Genetic and perinatal determinants of structural brain deficits in schizophrenia. *Archives of General Psychiatry, 46,* 883–889.

Carey, G., & DiLalla, D. L. (1994). Personality and psychopathology: Genetic perspectives. *Journal of Abnormal Psychology, 103,* 32–43.

Cohen, D., Eisdorfer, C., Gorelick, P., Paveza, G., Luchins, D. J., Freels, S., Ashford, J. W., Semla, T., Levy, P., & Hirschman, R. (1993). Psychopathology associated with Alzheimer's disease and related disorders. *Journal of Gerontology: Medical Sciences, 48,* M255–M260.

Cohen, G. (1991). Anxiety and general medical disorders. In C. Salzman & B. D. Lebowitz (Eds.), *Anxiety in the elderly: Treatment and research* (pp. 47–62). New York: Springer.

Conwell, Y. (1994). Suicide in elderly patients. In L. S. Schneider, C. F. Reynolds, III, B. D. Lebowitz, & A. J. Friedhoff (Eds.), *Diagnosis and treatment of depression in late life* (pp. 397–418). Washington, DC: American Psychiatric Press.

Corder, E. H., Saunders, A. M., Strittmatter, W. J., Schmechel, D. E., Gaskell, P. C., Small, G. W., Roses, A. D., Haines, J. L., & Pericak-Vance, M. A. (1993). Gene dose of apolipoprotein E type 4 allele and the risk of Alzheimer's disease in late onset families. *Science, 261,* 921–923.

Cornoni-Huntley, J., Brock, D. B., Ostfeld, A. M., Taylor, J. O., & Wallace, R. B. (Eds.). (1986). *Established populations for epidemiologic studies of the elderly resource data book.* Washington, DC: U.S. Government Printing Office.

Coyne, J. C. (1994). Self-reported distress: Analog or ersatz depression? *Psychological Bulletin, 116,* 29–45.

Cummings, J. L., & Benson, D. F. (1992). *Dementia: A clinical approach* (2nd ed.). Boston: Butterworth-Heinemann.

Evans, D. A., Funkenstein, H. H., Albert, M. S., Scherr, P. A., Cook, N. R., Chown, M. J., Hebert, L. E., Hennekens, C. H., & Taylor, J. O. (1989). Prevalence of Alzheimer's disease in a community population of older persons: Higher than previously reported. *JAMA, Journal of the American Medical Association, 262,* 2551–2556.

Finch, C. E., & Morgan, D. (1987). Aging and schizophrenia: A hypothesis relating asynchrony in neural aging processes to the manifestations of schizophrenia and other neurologic diseases with age. In N. E. Miller & G. D. Cohen (Eds.), *Schizophrenia and aging* (pp. 97–108). New York: Guilford.

Fratiglioni, L., Ahlbom, A., Viitanen, M., & Winblad, B. (1993). Risk factors for late onset Alzheimer's disease: A population-based case-control study. *Annals of Neurology, 33,* 258–266.

Gallo, J. J., Anthony, J. C., & Muthén, B. O. (1994). Age differences in the symptoms of depression: A latent trait analysis. *Journal of Gerontology: Psychological Sciences, 49,* P251–P264.

Gatz, M., & Hurwicz, M.-L. (1990). Are old people more depressed? Cross-sectional data on CES-D factors. *Psychology and Aging, 5,* 284–290.

Gatz, M., Lowe, B., Berg, S., Mortimer, J., & Pedersen, N. (1994). Dementia: Not just a search for the gene. *Gerontologist, 34,* 251–255.

Gatz, M., & Smyer, M. A. (1992). The mental health system and older adults in the 1990s. *American Psychologist, 47,* 741–751.

George, L. K. (1994). Social factors and depression in late life. In L. S. Schneider, C. F. Reynolds, III, B. D. Lebowitz, & A. J. Friedhoff (Eds.), *Diagnosis and treatment of depression in late life* (pp. 131–153). Washington, DC: American Psychiatric Press.

George, L. K., Blazer, D. F., Winfield-Laird, I., Leaf, P. J., & Fischbach, R. L. (1988). Psychiatric disorders and mental health service use in later life: Evidence from the Epidemiologic Catchment Area program. In J. Brody & G. Maddox (Eds.), *Epidemiology and aging* (pp. 189–219). New York: Springer.

Gottesman, I. I. (1981). *Schizophrenia genesis: The origins of madness.* New York: Freeman.

Graves, A. B., & Kukull, W. A. (1994). The epidemiology of dementia. In J. C. Morris (Ed.), *Handbook of dementing illnesses* (pp. 23–69). New York: Dekker.

Gurian, B. S., Wexler, D., & Baker, E. H. (1992). Late-life paranoia: Possible association with early trauma and infertility. *International Journal of Geriatric Psychiatry, 7,* 277–284.

Gustafsson, L. (1987). Frontal lobe degeneration of the non-Alzheimer type. II. Clinical picture and differential diagnosis. *Archives of Gerontology and Geriatrics, 6,* 209–233.

Henderson, V., Paganini-Hill, A., Emanuel, C., Dunn, M., & Buckwalter, J. (1994). Estrogen replacement therapy in older women: Comparisons between Alzheimer's disease cases and nondemented controls. *Archives of Neurology (Chicago), 51,* 896–900.

Holden, N. L. (1987). Late paraphrenia or the paraphrenias? A descriptive study with a 10-year follow-up. *British Journal of Psychiatry, 150,* 635–639.

Howard, R., Castle, D., O'Brien, J., Almeida, O., & Levy, R. (1991). Permeable walls, floors, ceilings and doors: Partition delusions in late paraphrenia. *International Journal of Geriatric Psychiatry, 7,* 719–724.

Johansson, B., & Zarit, S. H. (1994, May). *Incidence of dementia in the oldest old for a 6-year period.* Paper presented at the 12th Nordic Congress in Gerontology, Jönköping, Sweden.

Kahn, R. L. (1977). Perspectives in the evaluation of psychological mental health problems for the aged. In W. D. Gentry (Ed.), *Geropsychology: A model of training and clinical service* (pp. 9–19). Cambridge, MA: Ballinger.

Karel, M. (1995). *Aging and depression: A developmental diathesis-stress model.* Manuscript in preparation.

Kazdin, A. E., & Kagan, J. (1994). Models of dysfunction in developmental psychopathology. *Clinical Psychology: Science and Practice, 1,* 35–52.

Kessler, R. C., Foster, C., Webster, P. S., & House, J. S. (1992). The relationship between age and depressive symptoms in two national surveys. *Psychology and Aging, 7,* 119–126.

Kessler, R. C., McGonagle, K. A., Nelson, C. B., Hughes, M., Swartz, M., & Blazer, D. G. (1994). Sex and depression in the National Comorbidity Survey II: Cohort effects. *Journal of Affective Disorders, 30,* 15–26.

Kessler, R. C., McGonagle, K. A., Zhao, S., Nelson, C. B., Hughes, M., Eshleman, S., Wittchen, H.-U., & Kendler, K. S. (1994). Lifetime and 12-month prevalence of *DSM-III-R* psychiatric disorders in the United States: Results from the National Comorbidity Survey. *Archives of General Psychiatry, 51,* 8–19.

Klerman, G. L., & Weissman, M. M. (1989). Increasing rates of depression. *JAMA, Journal of the American Medical Association, 261,* 2229–2235.

Koenig, H. G., & Blazer D. G. (1992). Mood disorders and suicide. In J. E. Birren, R. B. Sloane, & G. D. Cohen (Eds.), *Handbook of mental health and aging* (2nd ed., pp. 379–407). San Diego, CA: Academic Press.

Kral, V. A., & Emery, O. B. (1989). Long-term follow-up of depressive pseudodementia of the aged. *Canadian Journal of Psychiatry, 34,* 445–446.

LaRue, A., & Jarvik, L. F. (1987). Cognitive function and prediction of dementia in old age. *International Journal of Aging and Human Development, 25,* 79–89.

Leuchter, A. F. (1994). Brain structural and functional correlates of late-life depression. In L. S. Schneider, C. F. Reynolds, III, B. D. Lebowitz, & A. J. Friedhoff (Eds.), *Diagnosis and treatment of depression in late life* (pp. 117–130). Washington, DC: American Psychiatric Press.

Lewinsohn, P. M., Rohde, P., Fischer, S. A., & Seeley, J. R. (1991). Age and depression: Unique and shared effects. *Psychology and Aging, 6,* 247–260.

Lewinsohn, P. M., Rohde, P., Seeley, J. R., & Fischer, S. A. (1993). Age-cohort changes in the lifetime occurrence of depression and other mental disorders. *Journal of Abnormal Psychology, 102,* 110–120.

Mayer, C., Kelterborn, G., & Naber, D. (1993). Age of onset in schizophrenia: Relations to psychopathology and gender. *British Journal of Psychiatry, 162,* 665–671.

McKhann, G., Drachman, D., Folstein, M., Katzman, R., Price, D., & Stadlan, E. M. (1984). Clinical diagnosis of Alzheimer's disease: Report of the NINCDS-ADRDA work group under the auspices of Department of Health and Human Services Task Force on Alzheimer's disease. *Neurology, 34,* 939–944.

Meeks, S., & Walker, J. A. (1990). Blunted affect, blunted lives? Negative symptoms, ADL functioning, and mental health among older adults. *International Journal of Geriatric Psychiatry, 5,* 233–238.

Miller, B. L., Benson, F., Cummings, J. L., & Neshkes, R. (1986). Late-life paraphrenia: An organic delusional syndrome. *Journal of Clinical Psychiatry, 47,* 204–207.

Mortimer, J. (1994). What are the risk factors for dementia? In F. Huppert, C. Brayne, & D. O'Connor (Eds.), *Dementia and normal aging* (pp. 208–229). Cambridge, England: Cambridge University Press.

Mulsant, B. H., Stergiou, A., Keshavan, M. S.,

Sweet, R. A., Rifai, A. H., Pasternak, R., & Zubenko, G. S. (1993). Schizophrenia in late life: Elderly patients admitted to an acute care psychiatric hospital. *Schizophrenia Bulletin, 19,* 709–721.

Naguid, M., & Levy, R. (1987). Late paraphrenia: Neuropsychological impairment and structural brain abnormalities on computed tomography. *International Journal of Geriatric Psychiatry, 2,* 83–90.

National Advisory Mental Health Council. (1993). Health care reform for Americans with severe mental illnesses: Report of the National Advisory Mental Health Council. *American Journal of Psychiatry, 150,* 1447–1465.

Newmann, J. P., Engel, R. J., & Jensen, J. E. (1991). Changes in depressive-symptom experiences among older women. *Psychology and Aging, 6,* 212–222.

Nigg, J. T., & Goldsmith, H. H. (1994). Genetics of personality disorders: Perspectives from personality and psychopathology research. *Psychological Bulletin, 115,* 346–380.

Nolen-Hoeksema, S. (1988). Life-span views on depression. In P. B. Baltes, D. L. Featherman, & R. M. Herner (Eds.), *Lifespan development and behavior* (Vol. 9, pp. 203–241). Hillsdale, NJ: Erlbaum.

Pearlson, G. D., Kreger, L., Rabins, P. V., Chase, G. A., Cohen, B., Wirth, J. B., Schlaepfer, T. B., & Tune, L. E. (1989). A chart review study of late-onset and early-onset schizophrenia. *American Journal of Psychiatry, 146,* 1568–1574.

Post, F. (1987). Paranoid and schizophrenic disorders among the aging. In L. L. Carstensen & B. A. Edelstein (Eds.), *Handbook of clinical gerontology* (pp. 43–56). New York: Pergamon.

Quintal, M., Day-Cody, D., & Levy, R. (1991). Late paraphrenia and ICD 10. *International Journal of Geriatric Psychiatry, 6,* 111–116.

Rabins, P. V. (1992). Schizophrenia and psychotic states. In J. E. Birren, R. B. Sloane, & G. D. Cohen (Eds.), *Handbook of mental health and aging* (2nd ed., pp. 463–475). San Diego, CA: Academic Press.

Reding, M., Haycox, J., & Blass, J. (1985). Depression in patients referred to a dementia clinic. *Archives of Neurology (Chicago), 42,* 894–896.

Regier, D. A., Boyd, J. H., Burke, J. D., Rae, D. S.,

Myers, J. K., Kramer, M., Robins, L. N., George, L. K., Karno, M., & Locke, B. Z. (1988). One-month prevalence of mental disorders in the United States. *Archives of General Psychiatry, 45,* 977–986.

Regier, D. A., Myers, J. K., Kramer, M., Robins, L. N., Blazer, D. G., Hough, R. L., Eaton, W. W., & Locke, B. Z. (1984). The NIMH Epidemiologic Catchment Area program: Historical context, major objectives, and study population characteristics. *Archives of General Psychiatry, 41,* 934–941.

Reifler, B. V. (1994). Depression: Diagnosis and comorbidity. In L. S. Schneider, C. F. Reynolds, III, B. D. Lebowitz, & A. J. Friedhoff (Eds.), *Diagnosis and treatment of depression in late life* (pp. 55–59). Washington, DC: American Psychiatric Press.

Ritchie, K., Kildea, D., & Robine, J.-M. (1992). The relationship between age and the prevalence of senile dementia: A meta-analysis of recent data. *International Journal of Epidemiology, 21,* 763–769.

Rocca, W. A., Hofman, A., Brayne, C., Breteler, M. M. B., Clarke, M., Copeland, J. R. M., Dartigues, J.-F., Engedal, K., Hagnell, O., Heeren, T. J., Jonker, C., Lindesay, J., Lobo, A., Mann, A. H., Mölsä, P. K., Morgan, K., O'Connor, D. W., da Silva Droux, A., Sulkava, R., Kay, D. W. D., & Amaducci, L. (1991a). Frequency and distribution of Alzheimer's disease in Europe: A collaborative study of 1980–1990 prevalence findings. *Annals of Neurology, 30,* 381–390.

Rocca, W. A., Hofman, A., Brayne, C., Breteler, M. M. B., Clarke, M., Copeland, J. R. M., Dartigues, J.-F., Engedal, K., Hagnell, O., Heeren, T. J., Jonker, C., Lindesay, J., Lobo, A., Mann, A. H., Mölsä, P. K., Morgan, K., O'Connor, D. W., da Silva Droux, A., Sulkava, R., Kay, D. W. D., & Amaducci, L. (1991b). The prevalence of vascular dementia in Europe: Facts and fragments from 1980–1990 studies. *Annals of Neurology, 30,* 817–824.

Roman, G. C., Tatemichi, T. K., Erkinjuntti, T., Cummings, J. L., Masdeu, J. C., Garcia, J. H., Amaducci, L., Orgogozo, J. M., Brun, A., Hofman, A., Moody, D. M., O'Brien, M. D., Yamaguchi, T., Grafman, J., Drayer, B. P., Bennett, D. A., Fisher, M., Ogaya, J., Kokmen, E., Bermejo, F., Wolf, P. A., Gorelick, P. B., Bick, K. L., Pajeau, A. K., Bell, M. A., Phil, D., DeCarli, C., Culebras, A., Korezyn,

A. D., Bogousslavsky, J., Hartmann, A., & Scheinberg, P. (1993). Vascular dementia: Diagnostic criteria for research studies. Report of the NINDS-AIREN international workshop. *Neurology, 43,* 256–260.

Rosowsky, E., & Gurian, B. (1991). Borderline personality disorder in late life. *International Psychogeriatrics, 3,* 39–52.

Roth, M. (1955). The natural history of mental disorder in old age. *Journal of Mental Science, 101,* 281–301.

Roth, M. (1986). The association of clinical and neurological findings and its bearing on the classification and aetiology of Alzheimer's disease. *British Medical Bulletin, 42,* 42–50.

Sadavoy, J., & Fogel, F. (1992). Personality disorders in old age. In J. E. Birren, R. B. Sloane, & G. D. Cohen (Eds.), *Handbook of mental health and aging* (2nd ed., pp. 433–462). San Diego, CA: Academic Press.

Sheikh, J. I. (1992). Anxiety and its disorders in old age. In J. E. Birren, R. B. Sloane, & G. D. Cohen (Eds.), *Handbook of mental health and aging* (2nd ed., pp. 409–432). San Diego, CA: Academic Press.

Skoog, I., Nilsson, L., Palmertz, B., Andreasson, L.-A., & Svanborg, A. (1993). A population-based study of dementia in 85-year-olds. *New England Journal of Medicine, 328,* 153–158.

Strauss, M. E. (1995). Ontogeny of depression in Alzheimer's disease. In M. Bergener, J. C. Brocklehurst & S. I. Finkel (Eds.), *Aging, health and healing* (pp. 441–456). New York: Springer.

Sunderland, T., Lawlor, B. A., Martinez, R. A., & Molchan, S. E. (1991). Anxiety in the elderly: Neurobiological and clinical interface. In C. Salzman & B. D. Lebowitz (Eds.), *Anxiety in the elderly: Treatment and research* (pp. 105–129). New York: Springer.

van Duijn, C., Stijnen, T., & Hofman, A. (1991). Risk factors for Alzheimer's disease: Overview of the EURODEM collaborative reanalysis of case-control studies. *International Journal of Epidemiology, 20*(Suppl. 2), S4–S12.

Wallace, J., & O'Hara, M. (1992). Increases in depressive symptomatology in the rural elderly: Results from a cross-sectional and longitudinal study. *Journal of Abnormal Psychology, 101,* 398–404.

Zonderman, A. B., Herbst, J. H., Schmidt, C.,

Jr., Costa, P. T., Jr., & McCrae, R. R. (1993). Depressive symptoms as nonspecific, graded risk for psychiatric illness. *Journal of Abnormal Psychology, 102,* 544–552.

Zubin, J., & Spring, B. (1977). Vulnerability: A new view of schizophrenia. *Journal of Abnormal Psychology, 86,* 103–126.

# Author Index

Numbers in italics refer to the pages on which the complete references are listed.

# Subject Index